The New York Public Library

American History Desk Reference

The New York Public Library

American History

Desk Reference

A Stonesong Press Book

Macmillan • USA

MACMILLAN
A Simon & Schuster Macmillan Company
1633 Broadway
New York, NY 10019

Back cover photo credits:

John F. Kennedy and Nikita Khrushchev courtesy of UPI/Corbis-Bettmann.
Clara Barton courtesy of The National Archives/Corbis.

Library of Congress Cataloging-in-Publication Data

The New York Public Library American history desk reference.

   p. cm.
   Includes index.
   ISBN 0-02-861322-8
   1. United States—History—Encyclopedias.   I. New York Public Library.
E174.N48   1996
973'.03—dc20   96-16054
                                         CIP

The New York Public Library
Project Sponsors

A Note from the Editors

Every attempt has been made to ensure that this publication is as accurate as possible and as comprehensive as space would allow. We are grateful to the many researchers, librarians, teachers, reference editors, and friends who contributed facts, figures, time, energy, ideas, and opinions. Our choice of what to include was aided by their advice and their voices of experience. The contents, however, remain subjective to some extent, because we could not possibly cover everything that one might look for in basic information. If errors or omissions are discovered, we would appreciate hearing from you, the user, as we prepare future editions. Please address suggestions and comments to The Stonesong Press, 11 East 47th Street, New York, NY 10017.

We hope you find our work useful.

Contents

3.   Territorial Expansion   61

4.   Immigration and
   Minorities   89

5.   Military History   129

6. Government, Politics, and Law 169

7. The Development of the American City 209

8. Foreign Affairs 243

9. Business, Labor, and Economics 273

10. Education 311

11. *Science and Medicine*   333

12. *Transportation and Communication*   363

14. American Culture   421

Introduction

The New York Public Library American History Desk Reference is a unique compilation of the most important events and people associated with our nation's past. It is not a narrative history, but a one-volume source containing information and answers on the most frequently asked questions about American history. It is not an in-depth encyclopedia, but a source of commonly needed information, facts, ideas, and figures on American history that often need to be verified, remembered, or used.

In compiling this book, the editors of The Stonesong Press and the staff of the Library used the same approach and methods developed for the original edition of *The New York Public Library Desk Reference*. Editors and librarians who were most familiar with the questions repeatedly asked by a wide range of readers about American history reviewed the subjects chosen for coverage. Historians, researchers, booksellers, and other experts in American history were also consulted. When there were differences of opinion about the facts regarding events or people, we relied on commonly accepted sources of information unless recent discoveries or unusually clear new interpretations persuaded us otherwise.

The editors had to be selective about which material was commonly needed, and our results are not intended to meet the needs of scholars of history. Most readers and reference users will find what they need in these pages. Readers seeking more information are referred to other sources in the selected bibliography that appears at the end of each chapter.

While history is, by definition, what happened in the past, it is also fluid, and every day we learn something new about previous times. Our interpretations and even our knowledge of the facts themselves are often subject to change as new generations of historians sift through the evidence of our past. *The New York Public Library American History Desk Reference* is based on a wide range of reliable sources. The editorial staff of The Stonesong Press, who prepared the material, and The New York Public Library hope that our efforts have made the book helpful, accurate, enjoyable, and accessible for you, its users.

The Editors

1

Indigenous Peoples

SIGNIFICANT EVENTS IN NATIVE AMERICAN LIFE

Native Americans—the indigenous peoples of the Americas—have a history and culture that stretches from the Paleolithic era to the present, encompassing literally thousands of tribes, or cultural groups, and more than 300 languages in North America alone. Although the dominant image of Indian life has been a composite picture, in fact Native Americans—even among the so-called Plains Indians—were and are remarkably diverse.

The Paleo-Indian Era

c. 40,000-10,000 B.C.	This is the last great Ice Age, when migration is possible from Siberia over the Bering Strait land bridge into North America.
c. 35,000-25,000 B.C.	This period has yielded the earliest archaeological evidence of life in North America in sites as diverse as Meadowcroft Rockshelter (Pennsylvania), Wilson Butte Cave (Idaho), and Folsom and Clovis (New Mexico).
c. 12,000 B.C.	Archaeological evidence indicates humans are living throughout North and South America.
c. 11,000-9000 B.C.	Ice recedes, and land immigration from Asia is no longer possible.
	Clovis technology in New Mexico offers the first indication of an advanced tool, the six-pointed spearhead.
	Old Cordilleran Culture exists in the Pacific Northwest.
	Desert Culture is established in the Great Basin.
c. 7000 B.C.	Cochise Culture descends from Desert Culture and is active in the Southwest.

The Pre-Columbian Era

c. 4000 B.C.	The first settled communities spring up along the Pacific coast.
	Old Copper Culture forms around the Great Lakes.
c. 3000-1000 B.C.	Aleuts and Inuits migrate by boat across the Bering Strait to settle in Alaska.
c. 3000-500 B.C.	Red Paint Culture is active in the Northeast.
c. 1500 B.C.	Mexican crops are introduced into the Southwest.
c. 1000 B.C.	The first pottery appears along the East Coast.
c. 500 B.C.-A.D. 400	Adena Culture flourishes in Ohio.
300 B.C.-A.D. 500	Hopewell Culture is predominant in the eastern United States, with its center in southern Ohio.
c. 300 B.C.-A.D. 1300	Mogollon Culture is active in the Southwest; by the end of the period it is absorbed into the Anasazi world.

c. 100 B.C.-A.D. 1500	Hohokam Culture is active in the Southwest.
c. 100 B.C.	Anasazi Culture takes shape and grows on the Colorado Plateau, where present-day Arizona, New Mexico, Utah, and Colorado meet.
c. A.D. 500-650	The bow and arrow, developed in the Plains, gain widespread use east of the Mississippi.
c. 700-900	The Mississippi Culture forms in the Mississippi River valley.
c. 1000	Tobacco is grown for ceremonial use.
1000-1300	This is the classic period of Mississippi and Anasazi Cultures.
1276-1299	Severe drought in the Southwest changes living patterns for many Indian peoples. Anasazis abandon villages and vanish as a culture.
1300s	Early northern migrants, the Athapaskans, arrive in the Southwest; Mandans migrate from the east-central region to the Missouri River region, reaching what is now North Dakota by the eighteenth century.
c. 1450	The Iroquois League, consisting of Cayugas, Mohawks, Oneidas, Onondagas, Senecas, and later the Tuscaroras, is founded in the Northeast.

NATIVE AMERICAN RIGHTS TODAY: WHO IS AN INDIAN?

Indian rights today consist of the civil rights Indians assert as individuals as well as the rights they are accorded by virtue of their status as members of a tribe.

- Individual Native Americans have the same rights and obligations as any U.S. citizen. Those who live on reservations are subject to tribal law, which the courts have recognized as being similar to states' powers; that is, reservations are for the most part self-governing, but Congress has the power to regulate them.

- As tribal members, Indians enjoy a special status and are subject to special regulations. Individuals can't, for example, sell tribal lands. They enjoy certain tax exemptions. Tribes have the authority to operate federally funded programs similar to the block grant system, but individual Indians do not automatically qualify for government subsidies.

- Tribal recognition is necessary to claim any subsidy but not to be counted as Indian in the census. Generally, an Indian is a person who is of some degree Indian blood and is recognized as an Indian by a tribe and/or the United States.

The Post-Columbian Era

1492	Christopher Columbus arrives in the Caribbean.
1516	The first major epidemic (smallpox) occurs in the New World.
1539	Spanish explorer Hernando De Soto lands in Florida and travels upward through the South, conquering many Indian communities along the way. In Alabama, ancestors of the modern Chickasaws hold him off but are weakened by the epidemic diseases his army introduces.

The 17th and 18th Centuries: Colonization

Claims and colonization by Europeans initiated three centuries of warfare. For a list of major Indian-white wars, see Chapter 5.

1607   Jamestown is founded in Virginia by the British. Its leader, John Smith, is captured by the Powhatan Confederacy and, supposedly, saved by Pocahontas.

1620   Pilgrims landing at Plymouth, Massachusetts, are helped by Wampanoag leader Massasoit and Squanto, a Patuxet.

Indian Peoples at the Time of Early European Settlement

1622   An uprising by the Powhatan Confederacy nearly wipes out the Jamestown settlement, killing some 350 settlers, and initiating a decade of hostilities. By 1645, Indian resistance ends.

1626   Peter Minuit buys Manhattan Island from the Canarsie Indians for 60 guilders (the proverbial $24); although that amount was then equal to several thousand dollars, the island was still dramatically underpriced.

1636-   The Pequots are wiped out in the Pequot War, a campaign deliberately waged by the
1637   Puritans.

1642- 1653	The Hurons and Iroquois clash over the fur trade in a war instigated—and supplied—by the Dutch and the French. The defeated Hurons withdraw west, to Michigan, Wisconsin, and western Ontario while the victorious Iroquois sign a peace treaty with the French.
1675- 1676	King Philip's War pits the New England colonists against the Wampanoags, Narragansetts, and Nipmucks; it is the last major Indian-white war in New England and drives the Indians out of the region, with the exception of Maine.
1676	In Bacon's Rebellion, Nathaniel Bacon and a band of vigilante followers eradicate the Pamunkey Indians.
Mid- to late 1600s	Intermittent warfare on the frontier continues between the Dutch and the Indians and the British and the Indians.
1680	Pueblos rebel against the Spanish in the Southwest and drive them out for twelve years. In 1692, the Spanish reconquest of New Mexico ends with reoccupation of Santa Fe.
1689- 1748	Native Americans play a key role in three wars involving France, Spain, and Britain: King William's War (1689–1697), Queen Anne's War (1702–1713), and King George's War (1744–1748). Various Indian nations ally with either the French or the English.

HORSES

Horses were native to North America but had disappeared by about 8000 B.C. and were unknown to the Indians when the Spanish arrived. The Indians of Mexico found them terrifying, and they no doubt contributed to the general impression that the Spanish were invincible. By 1700 horses were roaming wild in the Southwest, and they thrived on the grasslands of the plains. Indians quickly adopted the horse, which enabled Indians to hunt buffalo more efficiently. As Indian peoples were pushed onto the Plains by white settlements in the east they developed a distinctive nomadic culture. Meanwhile Spanish explorers and missionaries had introduced horses into Florida as well, and horseback riding spread among tribes north into Carolina.

c. 1700	The Mississippi Culture fades.
1700s	During the Golden Age of Mandan Culture, the five Mandan bands occupy nine villages and maintain a population of approximately 3,500 along the Missouri River in North Dakota.
1711- 1713	Following a massacre by Tuscaroras in Carolina, white settlers ally with other tribes. After a defeat in which more than 300 Tuscarora warriors are killed, the tribe's survivors flee north, where they join the Iroquois Confederation.
1712- 1737	The French and the Foxes in Wisconsin and Illinois fight repeatedly and the Foxes are almost annihilated. The remnant joins the Sacs, their traditional enemy.
1715- 1716	Enraged by the destruction of the Tuscaroras, Yamasees kill more than 200 settlers before the colonists, aided by the Cherokees, defeat them. The Yamasees retreat into Georgia and Florida, where they ally with the Spanish against the English.
1720- 1763	The French wage unrelenting war on the Chickasaws using French troops and the Choctaws; lack of coordination between the French and their Indian allies and vagaries of weather are exploited by the Chickasaws so that when the French leave the Mississippi valley at the end of the French and Indian War the Chickasaws remain unconquered.
1723	The first permanent school for Indians is built by colonists in Williamsburg, Virginia.
1729	The Natchez rebel against the French in the Southeast. At first the Natchez enjoy success but by 1731 they are almost decimated.

INDIAN WORDS INTO AMERICAN ENGLISH

Some Indian words that have entered the English language include *tepee, tobacco, toboggan, moccasin, papoose, hominy, wigwam,* and *succotash,* the latter being a vegetarian staple of frontier life.

The biggest single contribution of the Indian languages, though, is the names given to the thousands of lakes, rivers, towns, counties, and other geographic places in the United States. As early as 1916, one linguistics expert had located 196 Indian place names in California alone, and today there are more than 5,000 just in New England. More than half the states trace their names to Indian origins: Alabama, Alaska, Arizona, Arkansas, Connecticut, Idaho, Illinois, Indiana, Iowa, Kansas, Kentucky, Massachusetts, Michigan, Minnesota, Mississippi, Missouri, Nebraska, North Dakota, Ohio, Oklahoma, Oregon, South Dakota, Tennessee, Texas, Utah, Wisconsin, and Wyoming.

1754-1763	During the French and Indian War, several Indian nations ally with the French, who lose and then cede Canada and Indian lands around the Great Lakes to the British.
1759-1761	Cherokee War in southern Appalachian highlands results in Cherokee surrender of land in the Carolinas and Virginia.
1763	Under Pontiac, the Potawatomis and Ottawas organize a revolt over the seizure of Indian lands by the British in the aftermath of the French and Indian War.
	In response, the British issue the Proclamation of 1763, which forbids white settlement west of the Appalachians to reserve the area for Indian nations.
1768	The Iroquois relinquish their lands under the Treaty of Fort Stanwix, and under the Treaty of Hard Labor, the war-weary Cherokees do the same.
1774	Dunmore's War, led by Virginia governor John Murray, earl of Dunmore, forces the Shawnees to cede more of their land in the Ohio valley.
1776-1783	During the American Revolution, many Indians fight on the side of the British. When the war ends, the British abandon their Indian allies, allowing the colonists to claim victory over the Native American population as well as the British.
1777-1779	In the Midwest, General George Rogers Clark mounts a series of important campaigns in which he captures Vincennes, a strategic British fort in southern Indiana, then marches northwest to destroy the Shawnees and Delawares.
1790	Little Turtle's War, led by Miami chief Little Turtle, scuttles the forces of General Josiah Harmar along the Maumee River in Indiana.
1791	Little Turtle defeats Arthur St. Clair's forces along the Wabash River in Indiana.
1794	Anthony Wayne gets revenge for St. Clair's defeat at the Battle of Fallen Timbers, near the western shore of Lake Erie.
1795	In the Treaty of Greenville, Miamis cede most of Ohio (Old Northwest Territory).

The 19th Century: Indian Resistance and Displacement

1803	Shawnee chief Tecumseh forms a confederacy to defend Indian lands in the Old Northwest.
1809	In the Treaty of Fort Wayne, the Delawares and Potawatomis cede lands in Indiana.
1811	The Battle of Tippecanoe in northwestern Indiana dashes Tecumseh's hopes for a confederacy.

Corbis-Bettman

Pontiac, chief of the Potawatomis and Ottawas

1812-1814	During the War of 1812, between the British and the Americans, Indians side mostly with the British. Tecumseh dies at the Battle of the Thames (River), east of Detroit in Ontario, while providing cover for retreating British forces.
1814	Creek resistance in the South is crushed by Andrew Jackson at the Battle of Horseshoe Bend in Alabama.
1815	Indian Country is reestablished west of Missouri and Arkansas, on land regarded as unarable by whites. President James Madison proposes to relocate all the eastern tribes to the West.
1817-1818	In the First Seminole War, Andrew Jackson captures Pensacola but fails to subdue the Seminoles in Spanish Florida.
1820s	The government begins to move tribes into Indian Country, defined as the lands west of the Mississippi River.
1824	The Bureau of Indian Affairs is established in the War Department.
1830	The Indian Removal Act provides for moving all Indians to lands west of the Mississippi River.
1831, 1832	The Supreme Court rules that Cherokee Nation is subject to federal but not state law. Andrew Jackson ignores the ruling and orders the army to remove the Cherokees, Chickasaws, Choctaws, Creeks, and Seminoles. The Choctaws are the first to be moved west of the Mississippi River.

THE SLAUGHTER OF THE BUFFALO

With the introduction of the horse, some woodlands tribes moved to the Great Plains, where the buffalo became the mainstay of their new culture as well as their primary means of survival. Buffalo hides were used to make clothing, tepees, furniture, moccasins, religious regalia, and drums. Hoofs were used ceremonially and to make implements, utensils, and glue. The bladder served as a storage pouch. Meat was used for food and in ceremonies. Fat and marrow produced food, paint, and cosmetics. Fur was used ceremonially and to make rope. Buffalo dung provided fuel.

White settlers and adventurers were far less discriminate in their slaughter of the buffalo. While some was for profit (hides and tongue), often it was sheer fun. Where an estimated 70 million buffalo once roamed, by 1840 only 40 million remained. Between 1872 and 1874, 3.7 million buffalo were destroyed. By 1875, one million survived, and a mere decade later that population was reduced to 20,000. By 1895 there were fewer than 1,000 buffalo in North America.

In the late 1880s a few states passed laws to protect the buffalo, but a more typical attitude was that of General Philip Sheridan, who wrote: "Let them kill, skin, and sell until the buffalo is destroyed . . . it is the only way to bring lasting peace and allow civilization to advance." Not until the 1970s did pressure from environmentalists lead to serious protection of the animal, whose numbers today hover around 50,000.

1832	In Black Hawk's War, Sacs and Foxes are decimated defending the Mississippi River valley in present-day Illinois and Wisconsin.
1834	The federal government formally sets aside land, in present-day Oklahoma, Kansas, and Nebraska, as Indian Territory.
1835-1842	In the Second Seminole War, the United States begins moving Seminoles out of Florida to the West.
1836	Creeks are forcibly removed from their southeastern homeland to lands west of the Mississippi River; about 3,500 of the 15,000 tribal members perish.
1838	The Trail of Tears: 16,000 Cherokees are forcibly removed from their Georgia land of several centuries and escorted by 7,000 U.S. Army soldiers to a reservation in Oklahoma. En route, about one-quarter of the Cherokees die.
1847	At Taos, Pueblo people resist the American occupation of New Mexico during the Mexican War.
1851	The Sioux hand over large tracts of land on the Great Plains for resettlement by whites.
1854	The U.S. government abolishes about half of Indian Territory to accommodate the influx of white settlers to lands west of the Missouri River.
1855-1858	The Third Seminole War virtually destroys what remains of the tribe.
1855-1858	In the Pacific Coast wars (Rogue River War, 1855–1856; Yakima War, 1855–1856; and Spokane War, 1858), the U.S. Army devastates the Indian population in this region and forces the survivors onto reservations.
1861-1865	During the Civil War, the few Indians that do fight side with the Confederacy.
1862	The Homestead Act gives 160 acres of public domain land free to any settler who resides on it for five years. The act accelerates white settlement of the West.
1864	The Long Walk, which is actually several walks, takes place after Kit Carson employs a scorched-earth offensive against the Navajos to force them to move 300 miles across New Mexico. In all, between 5,000 and 8,000 Navajos are relocated.

1864　In the Sand Creek Massacre of Black Kettle's Cheyennes, volunteer forces kill 28 men and 102 women and children who have gathered near a white fort to sue for peace. Fewer men than women and children are killed because they are hunting at the time of attack.

1865-　Red Cloud's War (also called the Sioux War) forces the U.S. Army to abandon the
1868　Bozeman Trail in Montana, the Sioux's buffalo-hunting ground.

1867　The Treaty of Medicine Lodge compels more than 100,000 Apaches, Arapahos, Bannocks, Cheyennes, Kiowas, Navajos, Shoshones, and Sioux to accept reservation status in Indian Territory.

1868　The Fourteenth Amendment defines citizenship, stating that "Indians not taxed" are not to be included in population counts for purposes of representation.

1871　The Indian Appropriation Act decrees that Indian tribes no longer enjoy the status of separate nations. The federal government will no longer negotiate treaties with individual tribes.

1872　Apache chief Cochise, after 11 years' resistance, agrees to live on a reservation in Arizona that includes part of his tribe's ancestral land. After his death in 1874, his tribe is moved.

1872-　The Modocs, a northern California tribe, are forced onto land that is not part of their
1873　ancestral heritage.

1874　The Battle at Palo Duro Canyon is a U.S. Army victory over the Indians that includes the slaughter of 1,000 Indian ponies.

1874-　The Red River War is fought. Following a decade in which Arapahos, Cheyennes,
1875　Comanches, and Kiowas successfully wage guerrilla warfare against the U.S. Army, during a year of all-out warfare, and the tribes are conquered and forced onto reservations.

1876-　In the Sioux War a coalition of Plains Indians led by Crazy Horse and Sitting Bull fights
1881　the U.S. Army. An important early Indian victory is the defeat and annihilation of General George Armstrong Custer's forces at Little Bighorn, known as Custer's Last Stand. By 1877 the Plains Indians are driven into the Dakota Territory, and in 1881 the surrender of Sitting Bull ends the conflict.

1877　In the flight of the Nez Perce, Chief Joseph leads the U.S. Army on a 1,500-mile chase under war conditions through Idaho, Wyoming, and Montana to avoid being settled on a reservation. They are finally herded onto a desert reservation in Indian Territory.

1878-　In the Bannock-Pauite Uprising in Idaho, Bannocks, Pauites, Sheepeaters, and Utes
1879　resist—in vain—resettlement onto reservations.

1881-　Fought in New Mexico and Arizona, Geronimo's Resistance ends with the surrender of
1886　Apache leader Geronimo and effectively terminating Indian-white strife in the Southwest.

1887　The Dawes Severalty Act (General Allotment Act) imposes a system of individual—as opposed to tribal—land ownership on Indians, a serious blow to tribal sovereignty.

1890　In what is now South Dakota, the Battle of Wounded Knee is the last great act of Indian defeat, marking the end of centuries of Indian-white warfare over lands.

1891　By treaty, effective 1893, the rights of Indians in the Cherokee Outlet are terminated and the area is added to Oklahoma Territory.

1898　The Curtis Act overrides treaties promising southeastern tribes that their western lands will never be included in any state or territory without their approval.

The 20th Century: The Contemporary Era

1906　The federal government takes the Blue Lake region of New Mexico, an area sacred to Pueblos, to create a national forest.

Sitting Bull, the most famous of the great Sioux leaders

1907   Indian Territory is eliminated when Oklahoma achieves statehood.

1909   The Enlarged Homestead Act increases to 320 acres the size of a homestead in certain states, encouraging white landholding in areas that have been home to two-thirds of all Indians since 1865.

1913   The Indian Head nickel is produced in tribute to the "vanishing red man."

1917-
1918   During World War I, although not subject to the draft, many Indians volunteer.

1921   The Snyder Act makes the Department of the Interior responsible for Indian education, medical, and social services.

1924   The Citizenship Act makes all Indians citizens without impairing their status as tribal members. Nevertheless, few Indians are permitted to vote before the 1960s.

1930   The Northern Cheyenne Reservation becomes the last communally assigned tract of Indian land.

1933   John Collier becomes head of the Bureau of Indian Affairs and begins to clean up after years of corruption. He halts the sale of Indian lands, gets emergency work for 77,000 Indians under the Civilian Conservation Corps, and obtains millions of dollars to finance reservation schools.

THE WOUNDED KNEE MASSACRE: SITTING BULL AND THE GHOST DANCE

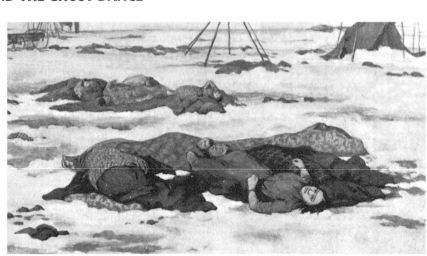

An early sketch of the massacre at Wounded Knee

A pan-Indian religious movement that swept the Great Plains in the 1880s and involved a ritual called the Ghost Dance may have started several decades earlier among the Nevada Paiutes. A shaman named Tavibo predicted the coming of a messianic prophet who would help the Indians regain their lost world and cause white people to vanish. Another version of the legend, related by the Pacific Northwest Indians, foretold a return to righteous ways—that is, a return to life as it was before the arrival of the whites. In 1889 the prophecies were tied to the dance when the Paiute prophet Wovoka, ill with scarlet fever, supposedly died and returned to life. He said the Creator had given him a ritual—the Ghost Dance—to perform with his people. Wovoka's prophecies and the Ghost Dance spread rapidly among the Arapahos, northern Cheyennes, and Sioux, indeed through most of the western tribes.

The white settlers on the Great Plains, who were themselves familiar with messianic visions after several decades of fierce Indian-white warfare, feared any teaching that forecast their demise. Their fears flourished in proportion to the Ghost Dance's growing popularity among the Indians. Armed conflicts often broke out between whites and Native Americans wherever the dance was to be performed, and these tensions culminated in the events at Wounded Knee in 1890.

The Miniconjous of the Lakota Sioux at Pine Ridge, South Dakota, led by Sitting Bull, were planning to perform the Ghost Dance. Federal agents, fearful of the Ghost Dance and of Sitting Bull and of what might happen should Sitting Bull openly endorse the Ghost Dance, went to his home at Standing Rock, North Dakota. They tried to arrest him, and in the argument that followed, two Indian policemen shot and killed Sitting Bull.

In a last sad chapter to the life of this great Indian leader, the Miniconjou people, fearing more armed conflict, fled. The army gave chase, and on December 28, 1890, the starving, horseless, and weaponless Indians were surrounded and taken to Wounded Knee, now in South Dakota. The next morning the troops began disarming the Indians. In the confusion, a gun fired, and the jittery troops fired on the Indian men, women, and children. Many were wearing white shirts that bore the symbols of their movement—an eagle, a buffalo, and the morning star—which they believed would protect them from the soldiers' bullets. More than 200 Indians died; perhaps as many as 300. Many wounded crawled away, hid in the snow, and died of their wounds in the bitter cold. Four men and 47 women and children were found alive or wounded after shooting stopped and were taken to Pine Ridge.

(continues)

THE WOUNDED KNEE MASSACRE: SITTING BULL AND THE GHOST DANCE (CONT.)

Sitting Bull's death and the massacre at Wounded Knee marked the end of the Sioux-white wars and the culture of the Plains Indians that Sitting Bull had hoped to preserve. The Ghost Dance was rarely performed after Wounded Knee, although some Plains Indians, notably the Pawnees, have incorporated parts of the dance, such as the hand game, into other dances, which survive today.

1934	The Indian Reorganization Act (Wheeler-Howard Act), pushed by John Collier, provides funds to help rebuild Indian culture and political life. Land is returned to tribal ownership.
1941-1945	During World War II Native Americans are allowed to register for the draft for the first time, and more than 25,000 enlist.
1946	The Indian Claims Commission is established to settle land disputes between the U.S. government and Indian nations.
1950	The Utes are compensated $31 million for tribal lands taken from them in Colorado and Utah between 1891 and 1938.
1953	House Concurrent Resolution No. 108 allows Congress to terminate by legislative fiat any tribe as a political unit.
1954-1962	Congress passes 12 termination bills, eliminating more than 60 tribes, all in the West.
1955	The Public Health Service takes over the administration of Indian health programs and subsequently establishes the Indian Health Service. Despite great improvements, Indians today have the highest mortality rates of any ethnic group.
1961	The republication of the 1932 book *Black Elk Speaks* sparks intense interest in Indian literature.
1964	The Civil Rights Act restores tribal law to reservations, and President Lyndon B. Johnson pledges to end paternalism.
	The first conference on Indian poverty is held in Washington, D.C.
	An "Indian desk" is established at the Office of Economic Opportunity.
1968	American Indian Movement (AIM) is founded in Minneapolis.
1969	Militants occupy the federal penitentiary on Alcatraz Island in San Francisco, demanding government funds for a cultural center and a university.
	Vine Deloria's book *Custer Died for Your Sins* rekindles interest in Indian history, told from the Indians' point of view.
1970	The federal government restores 48,000 acres of New Mexico's Blue Lake region to the Taos Pueblos.
	Dee Brown writes *Bury My Heart at Wounded Knee*, revealing that the historic battle was in fact an Indian massacre.
	The Native American Rights Fund (NARF) is established, eventually winning the return of lands for the Passamaquoddies and Penobscots of Maine, attempting to strengthen the regulations regarding remains and ceremonial objects, and offering assistance to unrecognized tribal entities.
1972	AIM and other Indian activists stage a sit-in at the Bureau of Indian Affairs in Washington, D.C., following a cross-country caravan called the Trail of Broken Treaties.

1973   AIM activists occupy Wounded Knee, South Dakota, demanding that the federal government honor treaties. The FBI, under the direction of J. Edgar Hoover, attacks, and two Indians and one federal marshal are killed.

1978   Passamaquoddy and Penobscot Indians become the first tribes to make a major land claim against the United States when they demand the return of two-thirds of the state of Maine. A tentative settlement is worked out in which they abandon their land claims in return for $27 million in a federal trust and $54.4 million in land-acquisitions funds.

1979   The Seminoles start bingo games, beginning the modern era of gambling on the reservations.

1982   President Ronald Reagan vetoes Congress's water-rights settlement of $112 million to the Papagos. The federal government eventually pays them $40 million.

1988   Congress passes the Indian Gaming Regulatory Act, ending the debate on the legality of gambling on the reservations. The law establishes the National Indian Gaming Commission with oversight responsibilities.

1992   *Time* magazine reveals that 140 tribes operate more than 150 casinos. Revenues in 1993 are in excess of $3.2 billion.

1994   President Bill Clinton, in recognition of Indians' newfound economic and political power, meets with representatives from 500 Indian tribes to pledge the federal government's support of their culture.

The first National Summit on Indian Health Care takes place.

ANCIENT INDIAN CULTURES

Because so much of what is known about them remains speculative, ancient Indian cultures are difficult to describe. Generally, these cultures are divided into three broad classifications: Paleo-Indian, Archaic, and Classic, alternately known as Formative.

Beyond this, there is little agreement regarding the specific time periods, or even the terms used to describe them. For example, Paleo-Indians are typically divided into three categories: Preprojectile, Paleo, and Protoarchaic. But sometimes Protoarchaic groups are classified with Archaic ones. The Classic Culture is often divided into two periods, the Formative and the Classic, the latter referring to a golden age that existed in several cultures toward the end of the period.

Finally, the cultures themselves refuse to fit neatly into niches. The Old Cordilleran Culture of the Pacific Northwest is an example of a culture that existed during the Paleo era that was nevertheless advanced enough to be classified as Archaic, while the Desert Culture of the Great Basin was still a foraging society well into the agriculturally oriented Archaic era.

Since no prehuman remains have been found thus far in the Americas, humans must have immigrated to them. Most archaeologists agree that the first humans came to North America from Asia by traveling across the Bering Strait land bridge that united Siberia and Alaska during the late Pleistocene era. The most recent evidence indicates that they could have come as early as 50,000 B.C., but more probably arrived somewhere between 35,000 or 25,000 B.C., or even as late as 15,000 B.C.

Paleo-Indian Culture

Dates: 50,000–30,000 B.C.

Mode of living: Nomadic forager-hunters hunt Pleistocene mammals, such as wooly mammoths, mastodons, lions, tigers, bighorn bison, and tapirs.

Technology: Bone and stone tools; ideas flow through the continent from north to south.
Social organization: Small bands of 30–40, probably organized around families with elders making decisions. Little or no trade. Fairly peaceable with loosely defined territories.
Housing: Lean-tos, cliff overhangs, caves.
Clothes: Animal furs and hides.

Divisions

Preprojectile: Tools and spears have no points. Sites: Old Crow Flats, Yukon Territory; Lewisville, Texas.
Projectile: Tools and spears have stone points, with shape determining names of dominant cultures. *Sites:* Clovis (or Llano) and Folsom, New Mexico, and spread to the Great Plains; Plano, throughout North America.

Archaic Culture

Dates: 8000 or 6000–1000 B.C.
Mode of living: Nomadic forager-hunters hunt bison, beaver, antelope, elk, and deer.
Technology: Projectile points used to make more specialized tools such as knives, drills, scrapers, and milling stones. Basket weaving and cloth weaving. First to build boats, also to domesticate dogs.
Social organization: Trade widespread, with evidence of gourds from Mesoamerica and copper from the West found in the East. Seminomadic when necessary, but communities becoming localized with a few permanent sites. Burial and occasionally cremation are now ceremonial. Corpses are buried in flexed position.
Housing: Earliest remains of constructed houses date to this period.
Clothes: Animal skins and vegetable materials. Ornaments beginning to appear.

Divisions

Eastern: Denser populations. *Sites:* Old Copper in Great Lakes region, unique for using copper.
Western: Also called Cochise Culture, less dense. *Sites:* New Mexico and Arizona.
Arctic and subarctic: Late Archaic (3000 to 1000 B.C.). Eskimos and Aleuts arrive in small boats, crossing the now-flooded Bering Straits.

Classic Culture

Dates: Generally 1000 B.C. to contact with whites at the end of the 15th century.
Mode of living: Sedentary farmers and hunters.
Technology: Agriculture develops. Techniques fairly primitive: slash-and-burn, no irrigation until the end of the period; digging stick and hoe are the only implements. Pottery begins and develops. Ideas now typically flow from south to north.
Social organization: Small villages, even city-states by end of period. Groups larger, up to 1,000. Greater differentiation among cultures.
Housing: Varied. *See* Divisions.
Clothes: Varied. *See* Divisions.

Divisions

Early Archaic: Adena (c. 500 B.C.–A.D. 400), located in the Ohio valley and spreading into Kentucky, West Virginia, Indiana, Pennsylvania, and New York; Hopewell (c. 300 B.C.–A.D. 500), located in the Ohio valley, spreading as far south as Alabama.

Adena Culture has some agriculture and grows tobacco for ceremonial use. Class divisions are more pronounced than in previous period. Circular wood-and-bark houses. Clothing consists of furs, hides, and woven garments; crafted goods becoming more sophisticated. Introduction of burial mounds in geometric shapes, the largest of which is the Great Serpent Mound in southern Ohio; grave objects rare. *Site:* Great Serpent Mound, Adams County, Ohio.

Hopewell Culture is a larger, more advanced version of Adena. Crafts very refined; clothes ornamental and sophisticated. Mounds are larger; elaborate grave objects now common. Housing consists of nearly rectangular-shaped buildings. Class divisions are still more pronounced, with priests at top, followed by merchants and warriors. *Site:* Enclosure, Newark, Ohio.

Late Archaic: Mississippi, Mogollon, Hohokam, Anasazi.

Mississippi Culture, prevalent A.D. 700–900, in the Mississippi River valley. Villages, the dominant form of community, now sometimes surrounded by stockades. Major sites often surrounded by smaller villages. Master mound builders; death-obsessed culture. Cemeteries now used for burial; large platform-shaped mud mounds used ceremonially. Rigid caste system. Crafts, especially pottery, very refined. Elaborate trade network. Influenced by Adena, Hopewell, and Mesoamerica. Modern-day descendants include (Mississippi) Creek, Natchez, Chickasaw, and (Plains) Hidatsa, Omaha, Mandan, Pawnee, Wichita. *Site:* Cahokia, Illinois, near Saint Louis.

Mogollon Culture (c. 300 B.C.–A.D. 1300) occupies mountains of southern Arizona and New Mexico. First in Southwest to adopt agriculture, make pottery, and build houses. Housing consists of subterranean pit houses, an excellent adaptation to the hot climate. Excellent weavers. Descended from Cochise Culture; absorbed into Anasazi. *Sites:* Chaco Canyon, New Mexico; Flagstaff, Arizona; Mesa Verde, Colorado.

Hohokam Culture (c. 100 B.C.–A.D. 1500) active in the desert in the Gila and Salt River valleys. Greatest achievement is complex system of irrigation and possible invention of etching (on shells). Descended from Cochise Culture, perhaps southern tradition; modern-day descendants include Hopi, Zuni, and Pueblo. *Sites:* Snaketown, Arizona; Point of Pines, Arizona.

Anasazi Culture (c. 100 B.C.–A.D. 1300) occupies the Four Corners country where Utah, Colorado, Arizona, and New Mexico now converge. The apex of southwestern cultures, it combines characteristics of Mogollon and Hohokam Cultures but is more extensive and more influential. Known to Navajos as the "ancient ones." Produce excellent refined crafts, both pottery and woven; colorful and often ceremonial clothes; many ceremonial objects. Anasazi originally live in pit houses but invent pueblos—mud-constructed, aboveground buildings that eventually evolve into interconnected, terraced villages. First in North America to do terraced farming and to cultivate maize. They abandon their sites, possibly due to drought or invasions from warring Plains Indians.

INDIAN POPULATION SINCE WHITE CONTACT

1492 Estimates of the Native American population of the Americas, all completely unscientific, range from 15 to 60 million. All scholars agree that the bulk of inhabitants reside in Mexico, Central America, and in the Andes. Areas north of Mexico may have contained 1 million persons.

1800 Native Americans estimated to be 600,000.

1824 When the Bureau of Indian Affairs is established, the population is estimated at 471,000.

1890 Population stands at 274,000. This is the first census to count all Indians. Previously Indians in Indian Territory and on reservations were not counted.

1900   Population reaches a low of 267,000.

1930   Population grows to 362,000.

1950   Population reaches 377,000.

1960   Population reaches 552,000.

1970   Indian population rises to 827,000, primarily because many persons who formerly did not identify themselves as Native Americans begin to do so.

1990   Indian population reaches 1.95 million, of whom 86,000 are Alaska natives. More than 739,000 live on reservations.

RESERVATIONS: WHAT THEY ARE AND HOW THEY WORK

Reservation lands set aside for the use of Native Americans at present occupy approximately 50 million acres and take several forms. The quality of the land dedicated to Indian use varies widely, but much of it is fairly remote and otherwise undesirable. Much of the reservation land in the West is nonarable, for example, a factor that has obviously contributed to the persistent poverty that has plagued reservation Indians for two centuries. Indians in the Southwest have been the most successful at continuing to live on land that they consider theirs. The Shinnecocks of Long Island, New York, who inhabit some of the country's richest real estate, are a notable exception.

Reservations, which were first established in the mid-17th century as whites began to take away Indian lands to use for their own purposes, have been created in three different categories: those established by an act of Congress or by treaty before 1871, those created after 1871, and those created by Executive Order. In the latter instance, for example, the Reno tribe of Nevada has purchased land for its own colony.

The date establishing a reservation usually refers to when the U.S. government recognized the land as dedicated to Indian use rather than when the Indians began to live on it. Although the U.S. government officially recognized the Pueblo reservation in New Mexico in 1864, for example, Pueblos have lived on this land for hundreds of years.

Initially, reservations were established to "missionize" Indians, that is, to convert them to Christianity and to get them to conform to European ideas of civilization. This was the purpose of the very first reservation, established by the Puritans in 1638 for the Quinnipiacs in New Haven, Connecticut. Since then, they have variously been used to segregate Indians, assimilate them, destroy their culture, preserve their culture, and since the 1970s, to accord tribal Indians a special status. In the 1980s a series of Supreme Court decisions greatly expanded the rights of reservation tribes by establishing their right to control gaming on Indian lands, an activity that is reducing poverty among many tribes and bringing them wealth. Today Indian tribes have jurisdiction on reservation lands and are not usually subject to state laws or taxes (although individual Indians may be).

The 1990 census shows that 739,000 Indians, or 37 percent of all Indians, live on reservations or other forms of tribally owned land.

MAJOR INDIAN EPIDEMICS

Inhabitants of the Western Hemisphere had no exposure to, and therefore no natural immunity to, the diseases Europeans brought with them. Measles and smallpox became plagues that wiped out entire peoples.

1516   The first major smallpox epidemic is introduced when a shipload of colonists carry it to Hispaniola with devastating results. From there it spreads throughout the Caribbean and travels up and down North and South America along trade routes. Pizarro writes that it kills half the Indians it touches.

1531	Measles sweeps through the Southwest.
1545	Bubonic plague surfaces in the Southwest.
1592	Smallpox is found throughout North America east of the Mississippi and in the Southwest.
1602	Smallpox strikes the Southwest.
1615-1660	Several outbreaks of smallpox devastate East Coast and Great Lakes tribes.
1637	Scarlet fever sweeps through Indian communities.
c. 1738	White slave traders spread smallpox to Cherokees in Georgia.
1782-1783	Smallpox introduced into the Northwest.
1837	Smallpox among the Mandans reduces a people who had numbered about 9,000 in 1750 to fewer than 200.
1837-1870	Four major smallpox epidemics devastate western Indian nations.
1847	An outbreak of measles, along with other factors, develops into Cause War of 1847–1850.
1902	The Eskimo population of Southhampton Island in the Hudson Bay is wiped out by typhus.

INDIAN CULTURE AREAS

Indian cultures have been divided into geographic regions, each exhibiting several common characteristics. Apart from geography, a culture often (but not always) shared tribes, languages, modes of living, and political organization.

The Northeast Culture Area

Area: Atlantic Ocean to the Mississippi River, uppermost region of the northeast United States south to the Tidewater region of Virginia and North Carolina.

Tribes: Descendants of mound builders. Iroquois-speaking: Cayuga, Huron, Mohawk, Oneida, Onondaga, Seneca, Tuscarora, Tobacco. Algonquian-speaking: Delaware, Fox, Illinois, Kickapoo, Mahican, Massachuset, Menominee, Miami, Mohegan, Ottawa, Pequot, Potawatomi, Sauk, Shawnee, Shinnecock, Wampanoag.

Languages: Iroquoian and Algonquian dialects.

Mode of living: Foraging and some horticulture. Small, semisedentary villages. Communal longhouses, gabled or vaulted log-frame structures are unique to the Iroquois. Algonquins live in wigwams; are among the first Indians to be destroyed after contact with the whites.

Political organization: Strong familial and tribal ties; chiefs are leaders. In the mid-15th century the Iroquois organize into a political, intertribal league, whose political symbol is the communal longhouse. Algonquins are less politically organized.

Unusual feature: The Iroquois League is believed by some historians to have been at least a partial model for the federalist form of government of the United States.

The Southeast Culture Group

Area: Tidewater region to the Gulf of Mexico; Atlantic Ocean to the Trinity River in Texas, extending into parts of Oklahoma, Arkansas, Missouri, Kentucky, Virginia, and North Carolina.

Tribes: Alabama, Atakapa, Biloxi, Caddo, Cherokee, Chickasaw, Chitimacha, Choctaw, Creek, Natchez, Quapaw, Seminole, Timucua, and Tunica.

Languages: Predominantly Muskogean, Sioux, Iroquoian, Algonquian, and Caddoan; also isolated languages such as Timucuan, Atakapan, Natchez, Chitimacha.

Mode of living: Farming, supplemented with hunting, gathering, and fishing. Wattle-and-daub housing; also chickees—raised, thatched-roof platform structures unique to the Seminoles.

Political organization: Chiefs and priests rule large groups and villages.

Unusual feature: Considered among the most advanced culturally of any Amerindian group outside Mesoamerica. Cherokees, Choctaws, Chickasaws, Creeks, and Seminoles were referred to as the Five Civilized Tribes because they readily adopted white culture, including farming of large plantations and slaveholding, and frequently intermarried with whites.

The Great Plains Culture Area

Area: Mississippi River valley to the Rocky Mountains; south from the northern U.S. border to southern Texas.

Tribes: Arapaho, Arikara, Blackfeet, Cheyenne, Crow, Hidatsa, Iowa, Kiowa-Apache, Mandan, Osage, Pawnee, Plains Cree, Sarci, Sioux, and Wichita.

Languages: Sioux and Caddoan.

Mode of living: Initially nomadic foraging; then forming seminomadic villages; some farming; mainly bison hunting. Tepee is the primary form of housing.

Political organization: Loosely organized initially; then form hunter-warrior societies.

Unusual feature: Plains Indians, a familiar image often depicted in Western literature, art, and movies, are in large part the result of the European presence in North America. In the 1600s the introduction of horses entirely changes their way of life, converting them from seminomadic gatherers to hunting societies. The need to defend their diminishing lands from whites leads a once-peaceable people to form warrior societies. Another important factor that shapes their cultural landscape is the migration, often forced, of many tribes to the Great Plains, which intermingles their cultures with that of those already living there. Not surprisingly, the Plains Culture Area is the seedbed for the revivalist movements, such as the Ghost Dance religion, that spring up in the mid-19th century.

The Southwest Culture Area

Area: Present-day Arizona, New Mexico, and parts of adjoining states.

Tribes: Apache, Havasupai, Seri, Walapai, Yavapai, all of whom are foragers. Acoma, Cocopa, Hopi, Laguna, Mojave, Navajo, Opata, Papago, Pima, Zuni, all of whom are horticultural.

Language: Athapaskan family.

Mode of living: Foraging, horticulture. Semisedentary village dwellers. Primary forms of housing are hogans, conical log-and-stick-framed, mud-covered structures, tepees, and pueblos, unique forms of architecture composed of multistoried, flat-roofed, terraced adobe or stone dwellings.

Political organization: Religious organizations dominate social life, which is organized around an active annual ceremonial cycle. Pueblos contain subterranean holy rooms or passageways called kivas, which may be routes to the spirit world. Later some warrior societies, largely defensive, form.

The Great Basin Culture Area

Area: Most of Utah and Nevada, parts of Oregon, Colorado, Wyoming, Idaho, and the eastern border of California.

Tribes: Comanche, Klamath, Paiute, Panamint, Shoshone, Ute, and Washo.

Languages: Uto-Aztecan family except for the Washo, who speak a Hokan dialect.

Mode of living: A harsh environment condemns these Native Americans to a life of gathering and foraging; they are sometimes called "diggers." Some hunting of small game. Wickiups, domed huts covered with reeds, grasses, or brush, are their homes.

Political organization: Typically one-family units. Leadership is minimal and informal, usually falling to the male elder. Territories are large—130 square kilometers or 50 square miles to the individual—so there is little warfare. Occasional cooperation for a group hunt.

The California Culture Area

Area: Present-day California, including Baja but exclusive of the state's eastern border region.

Tribes: Chumash, Costano, Maidu, Miwok, Modoc, Patwin, Pomo, Salinan, Wintun, Yana, Yokuts, and Yuki.

Languages: More than 200 independent dialects. Hokan dominates in the northern region, Penutium in the middle, and Shoshonean in the south.

Mode of living: Semisedentary, foraging and fishing. Housing is plankhouses, made of hand-split planks over a log frame, and wickiups, domed huts covered with reeds, grass, or brush.

Political organization: Single villages as large as 100 members or more, often composed of related families. Inherited chiefdoms are largely ceremonial.

Unusual feature: Some groups, such as one that becomes known as the Mission Indians, are forced to lead a serflike existence under the hierarchical rule of the Spanish missions between 1769 and the 1860s. Their culture is destroyed in the process.

The Plateau Culture Area

Area: Rocky Mountains to the Cascade Mountains on the west.

Tribes: Cayuse, Chinook, Coeur d'Alene, Flathead, Kutenai, Lillooet, Modoc, Nez Perce, Okanogan, Shuswap, Spokane, Thompson, Umatilla, and Yakima.

Languages: Mosan or Penutian dialects; also the isolated language Kitenai, spoken by the Kutenai; some Algonquian and Athapascan.

Mode of living: Foraging and fishing in river bank villages. Many of these groups move to the Great Plains after horses are reintroduced. Housing varies from wigwams in Baja to domed, thatched-roof houses in midregion, to plankhouses along the northern coast.

Political organization: Headsmen run the villages.

The Northwest Coast Culture Area

Area: Pacific coast in the Northwest; bordered by Columbia and Fraser rivers on the west.

Tribes: Haida, Hupa, Karok, Kwakiutl, Nootka, Salish, Tlingit, Tsimshian, Yurok.

Languages: Athapascan, Penutian, Mosan dialects.

Mode of living: Semisedentary, fishing and hunting of small game; live in plankhouses.

Political organization: Independent villages of 100 or more are headed by chiefs. Societies are highly hierarchical with persons ranked by kinship to chiefs. Well-organized, ancestral-based religion involving huge public dramas, spirit quests, and visionary encounters with ancestors.

Unusual feature: Noted for totem poles, symbolic representations of ancestors. Wealth is both individual and group and often is exhibited at ritualized gift-giving ceremonies called potlatches.

The Subarctic Culture Area

Area: From interior Alaska across and including most of Canada south of the Arctic coastal plain to Newfoundland.

Tribes: Chilcotin, Chipewyan, Eastern Algonquians, Kaska, Koyukon, Kutchin, Nabesna, Naskapi, Northern Ojibway, Swampy Cree, Tagish, Wood Cree, and Yellowknife.

Languages: Athapaskan, Algonquian, and Beothukan on Newfoundland.

Mode of living: Nomadic, following the seasonal migrations of caribou; lived primarily in log houses, wigwams, and tepees.

Political organization: Live in small bands bonded by blood and language.

Unusual feature: Very low population in a region marked by long, harsh winters and short, miserable summers with clouds of mosquitoes and black flies.

The Arctic Culture Area

Area: From coasts of Greenland along Arctic coasts of Canada and Alaska to extreme eastern Siberia.

Tribes: Inuit (Eskimo) and Aleut, who inhabit Aleutian Islands.

Languages: Eskimo-Aleut.

Mode of living: Fishing, hunting of sea mammals and large game such as moose, caribou, and bear. Eskimos live in igloos, conical ice-block dwellings; and Aleuts live in pithouses, subterranean log-frame and mud structures, both unique to the region.

Political organizations: Little political affiliation; a few families or sometimes even one live as a unit, with male elder head of family.

Unusual feature: Remarkably uniform culture.

ACTS OF CONGRESS AFFECTING NATIVE AMERICANS

The following are the most significant acts of Congress affecting American Indian life and culture.

1786   An ordinance aims to define the economic relationship between Indians and settlers so that interaction will be as harmonious as possible. Successive acts in 1790, 1793, 1796, 1799, and 1802 continue the authority of the federal government. Shifts in public opinion by 1834 result in a new law, replacing the 1802 act, that provides more protection for persons doing business with Indians than for the Indians or the tribes.

1787   Northwest Ordinance. This states that "the utmost good faith shall always be observed towards the Indians; their lands and property shall never be taken from them without their consent."

1790   Intercourse Act. This multipronged legislation regulates Indian-white trade via licensing arrangements, makes purchases of Indian lands invalid unless approved by the federal government, and punishes whites for crimes in Indian Country.

1802   Intercourse Act. As well as extending the first act, this also establishes Indian Territory and forms the basis for the federal government's "wardship" over Indians until 1834.

1824   The Bureau of Indian Affairs is established by act of Congress.

THE BUREAU OF INDIAN AFFAIRS

The federal government's policies toward Native Americans are one and the same with the policies of the Bureau of Indian Affairs (BIA), the agency that oversees relations between the government and Indians. However misguided they may be judged by today's standards, early administrators believed that their task was to teach Indians English and agriculture and hoped that they would become Christians. The reservation system would thus speed them on the way to becoming good citizens. The creation of reservations was largely achieved via a system of treaties negotiated by the government in which Indians often believed they were leasing their land or land rights rather than selling the land outright.

Initially the Bureau of Indian Affairs was located within the Department of War, but in 1849, it was transferred to the newly created Department of the Interior. The BIA was also charged with administering Indian lands, which it did for the most part erratically, restrictively, and in a manner most Indians found denigrating.

During the late-19th century a new policy of acculturation was instituted. Its underlying purpose was to reduce the federal government's responsibility for a people it had spent decades making dependent. Reservations were broken up and land allotments were turned over to individuals in the belief that land ownership was the basis for the democracy the United States strived to create. Many of the people active in this program were former abolitionists who had used much the same philosophy in that struggle.

With the passage of time the BIA became one of the more corrupt and graft-ridden agencies of the federal government. Indian agents, on-site representatives of the BIA who were stationed on or near reservations, cheated Indians in countless ways, large and small, including private sales of Indian lands designed primarily to line individual agents' pockets with cash.

The corruption was not checked until 1933, when John Collier became head of the BIA. For the first time in its history, the bureau was run by someone interested in helping Native Americans. By that time, however, Indians had lost two-thirds of their lands, but Collier set up reform commissions and undertook studies to find ways to improve Indians' lives. He sued to protect Indian lands and establish their rights. A Division of Indian Health was established at the BIA, and other social, educational, and medical services became available. The 1930s and 1940s were an era of tribal restoration. Reservation lands were returned, and tribal law was recognized for the first time. Most important, under Collier, Indians were hired for the first time at the BIA.

The 1950s saw some backsliding as the BIA resumed the tribal-termination policy and began encouraging Indians to relocate to cities. Urbanization was an attempt to end reservation poverty, which for obvious reasons had been growing since the reservation system was initiated, but while the policy left Indians free to rebuild their own nations and tribes, it did little to eradicate poverty. Instead, the BIA simply moved poverty off the reservation while eradicating the safety net it had provided.

By the late 1960s, the country was in the midst of a civil rights revolution whose impact was felt on reservations across the country. Indians were at last emboldened to demand control of the BIA, which they were granted after they staged a sit-in at the agency in November 1972.

Indians suffered, as did many other groups, from a reduction in government services under President Ronald Reagan in the 1980s, but this was balanced with a great advance in the early 1990s, when Indians won the right to control gaming on their own lands and were further found to be exempt from paying federal taxes on the profits. With gambling booming around the country, many Indian nations suddenly found themselves rich. Indian nations became self-sufficient in a way they had not been in many decades. The full results of turning to gambling are not yet in. At best gambling may be a mixed blessing, for on some reservations the advent of crime connected to gambling is a potent factor that is not fully understood.

1830   Indian Removal Act. This provides for the removal of Indians west of the Mississippi.

1834   Intercourse Act. An expansion of the 1802 act, this redefines the boundaries of Indian Territory and calls for the removal of still more southeastern tribes from their lands to Indian Territory. It also empowers the federal government to intervene in Indian wars.

1868   Fourteenth Amendment. This defines citizenship, stating that "Indians not taxed" are not to be included in population counts for purposes of representation.

1871   Indian Appropriations Act. This terminates the treaty process by forbidding recognition of tribes as nations or independent powers. The federal government will no longer negotiate with Indian tribes before taking over their lands.

1885   Major Crimes Act. Passed in reaction to the *Crow Dog* case, in which the Supreme Court ruled that federal law does not apply to Indian lands unless so specified by Congress, this act affirms that federal law supersedes tribal sovereignty in specific serious crimes.

1887   General Allotment Act (Dawes Severalty Act). This provides for the dissolution of tribes and changes the status of many Indians from tribal members to individuals by allotting them 160 acres, to be held in trust by the federal government for 25 years to prevent exploitation. Although land has been granted to individuals before the act and tribal lands will be allotted after its passage, the act symbolically undermines tribal rights.

1898   Curtis Act. This overrides treaties promising certain tribes that their land will never be included in any state or territory without their approval.

1924   Indian Citizenship Act. All Native Americans born in the United States are defined as U.S. citizens. Few Indians are allowed to vote, but this act is generally accepted as the source of Indian enfranchisement.

1934   Indian Reorganization Act, also known as the Wheeler-Howard Act. This reverses the assimilationist policy that prevailed from the 1880s onward, returns tribal lands, permits the establishment of tribal constitutions, and funds social and welfare programs for Indians.

1946   Indian Claims Commission Act. This authorizes Indians to press claims relating to laws, treaties, executive orders, and even "dealings that are not recognized by any existing rule of law or equity" that have harmed them.

1953   Public Law 280. This gives some states jurisdiction over offenses by or against Native Americans.

1954   Termination Resolution. This permits the ending of the tribal status of Indian tribes believed competent to survive without federal assistance. Between 1954 and 1962 Congress passes 12 termination bills affecting more than 60 tribes. Many tribes are left impoverished and have since sued the federal government on grounds that they did not understand what termination involved.

1968   Indian Civil Rights Act. This extends the protections of the Constitution and the Bill of Rights to all Native Americans, including those with tribal status.

1988   Indian Gaming Regulatory Act. With the idea of promoting economic self-sufficiency, gambling is allowed on Indian land, if not prohibited by federal law. The National Indian Gaming Commission is given the task of overseeing all such activities.

SUPREME COURT DECISIONS AFFECTING NATIVE AMERICANS

The following Supreme Court decisions have significantly affected the lives of Native Americans.

1823   *Johnson v. McIntosh*. The Court rejects the validity of land titles granted to individuals by Indians.

1831   *Cherokee Nation v. Georgia*. This decision establishes the Cherokee Nation as a "domestic dependent nation," not a foreign state.

1832   *Worcester v. Georgia.* The Court declares that within the Cherokee Nation "the laws of Georgia can have no force." But Georgia defies the Court, and President Andrew Jackson reportedly quips, "John Marshall has made his decision. Now let him enforce it." With no means to prevent the encroachment of white settlers and state law, the Cherokees, by 1835, are forced to surrender their lands east of the Mississippi and prepare for removal.

1870   *Boudinot v. U.S.* (Cherokee Tobacco case). The Court begins to establish the principle that acts of Congress supersede prior treaties by ruling that Cherokees can be taxed on tobacco profits even though a treaty had specifically exempted this product.

1883   *Ex parte Crow Dog.* The Court overturns a death sentence handed down by a federal court, stating that tribal law prevails except when the United States has specifically claimed jurisdiction in a treaty. The case arose when a Sioux chief named Crow Dog murdered a fellow tribe member who had seduced his wife. Despite having been punished by his tribe, the chief was retried in federal court and sentenced to death. See also *United States v. Kagama.*

1884   *Elk v. Wilkins.* In this post–Fourteenth Amendment decision, the Court finds Native American John Elk ineligible to vote.

1886   *United States v. Kagama.* In a case related to *Crow Dog,* the Court finds that federal courts have jurisdiction over certain crimes committed by Indians on reservations. It was able to reverse itself because, in outrage over the 1883 *Crow Dog* decision, Congress passed the Major Crimes Act, extending its legal authority over reservation Indians.

1895   *Talton v. Mayes.* The Court upholds a punishment meted out by the Cherokee Nation court and denies a convicted killer, who claims his due-process rights were violated, the right to appeal the decision in a U.S. court.

1903   *Lone Wolf v. Hitchcock.* The Court rejects a plea that tribal lands were taken without due process and also forecloses any avenue of appeal on grounds that Indians are wards of the federal government and thus cannot sue their own guardian.

1908   *Winters v. United States.* The Court declares that Indian control of water rights is implied in the treaties and agreements that established reservations.

1955   *Tee-Hit-Ton Indians v. United States.* The Court caps interest payments to tribes for the loss of their lands, thus rendering moot several cases that are pending.

1956   *Squire v. Capoeman.* The Court rules that Indians are not subject to capital gains tax accruing from the sale of resources on lands they have been granted by treaty. An apparent victory for Indians, the decision was based on the underlying principle that a ward could not be taxed to benefit the guardian, a view widely held to be denigrating to Indians.

1959   *Williams v. Lee.* The Court rules that state courts do not have jurisdiction over civil suits by non-Indians against reservation Indians.

1960   *Federal Power Commission v. Tuscarora Indian Nation.* The Court rules that the federal government can take reservation land—or any land—under the right of eminent domain.

1962   *Organized Village of Kake v. Egan.* The Court upholds Alaska's right to regulate fishing on nonreservation lands on grounds that tribal law does not apply.

1968   *Menominee Tribe v. United States.* The Court says that Wisconsin cannot make Native Americans subject to its conservation laws.

1973   *McClanahan v. State of Arizona Tax Commission.* The Court finds that Arizona cannot tax the income of reservation Indians whose entire earnings were derived from reservation resources.

1974   *Morton v. Mancari.* The Court rules that provisions of the Indian Reorganization Act of 1934 giving preference to Indians in employment in the Bureau of Indian Affairs are not repealed by the Equal Employment Opportunities Act of 1972 and do not constitute racial discrimination in violation of the due process clause of the Fifth Amendment.

1978   *Oliphant v. Suquamish Indian Tribe*. The Court denies reservation tribes the right to arrest and punish trespassers who violate their laws.

1978   *United States v. Wheeler*. The Court reiterates the supremacy of tribal law except where specifically limited by treaty or act of Congress. (While the decision appeared to be favorable to Native Americans, some experts interpreted it to mean that tribal sovereignty existed, as one legal expert wrote, "only at the sufferance of Congress.")

1978   *United States v. John*. The Court rules that tribes can be dissolved only by their own members, thus negating the policy of termination.

1978   *Santa Clara Pueblo v. Martinez*. The Court rules that an individual tribe may be governed by its traditional laws, even if they conflict with the civil rights of individuals. The writ of habeas corpus is the sole instrument that an individual may use against a tribe.

1980   *Washington v. Confederated Tribes of the Colville Indian Reservation*. The Court rules that reservation Indians are subject to state jurisdiction and state sales tax.

1983   *New Mexico v. Mescalero Apache Tribe*. The Court decides that tribes have regulatory jurisdiction over hunting and fishing rights on their lands.

1985   *County of Oneida, N.Y. v. Oneida Indian Nation of New York State*. The Court says tribes have a right to sue to enforce aboriginal land rights.

1986   *United States v. Dion*. The Court abrogates treaty rights entitling Indians to hunt American eagles at a time when eagles are threatened with extinction.

1987   *California v. Cabazon Band of Mission Indians*. The Court rules that a state cannot enforce its gaming laws on a reservation.

1989   *Mississippi Band of Choctaw Indians v. Holyfield*. The Court confirms tribes' right to regulate adoptions of Native American children.

INDIAN RELIGION

Indian religions usually can be traced to one of two traditions: the northern hunting, which dates back to the Paleo-Indian era, and the southern agrarian. As Native Americans moved around (or were moved around by whites), the two strains of religious beliefs became intermingled.

The northern hunting tradition relied on individual shamans and was based, as its name suggests, on a hunting-healing culture. A master of animals, frequently a bear, was a primary source of regeneration. Winter in such cultures was typically considered a sacred season.

The southern agrarian tradition was led by secret societies or priesthoods rather than individual shamans. It was based on crops and the growing cycle. Plants (corn, for example) were seen as the source of new life, and, as was the case in the northern hunting tradition, winter was viewed as a sacred season.

Worship took many different forms: dancing and singing, visions and dreams (often induced by ceremonially used drugs such as tobacco and peyote), self-deprivation, and medicinal or healing ceremonies. Rituals were associated with curing illness, birth, coming of age, marriage, death, prowess in war, and maintenance of the world (as in solar or lunar worship) to assure harmony.

After whites arrived in North America, many Indians fended off conversion to Christianity—and many succumbed. The establishment of missions in the New World was undertaken by the English, the Spanish, and the French and often was a major factor contributing to a tribe's loss of its religious identity. Some Indians, such as the Pueblos during the rebellion of 1680, resisted to the point of violence, while others' religions, such as that of the California Mission Indians, were subsumed by Christianity. For more than a hundred years this tribe lived a life of virtual serfdom under the Spanish mission system. Until the early part of this century, the reservation system also had a strong Christian emphasis.

At the turn of the century, a man named Quanah Parker began a pan-Indian church that blended Christian and Native American religious practices. Originating in the Southwest, the Native American Church, as it became known, spread to the Great Plains and the Great Lakes regions and won large numbers of converts among urban Indians. Its membership numbers are unknown. Determined to use peyote sacramentally, the church has been involved in several lawsuits regarding freedom of religion. To date, in each case, it has been denied the right to use it.

The most recent religious development among Native Americans is a resurgence, primarily since the 1970s, of publicly enacted religious ceremonies, some of which may be attended by those who are not members of the tribe.

NATIVE AMERICANS IN AMERICAN HISTORY

Black Elk (1863–1950).   This Oglala Lakota author worked to preserve the culture of his people, especially the games, many of which had started as amusement and then taken on a sacred nature. He was the subject of Joseph Epes Brown's classic study, *The Sacred Pipe: Black Elk's Account of the Seven Sacred Rites of the Oglala Sioux* (1953). Black Elk wrote *Black Elk Speaks* in 1932.

Black Hawk (1767–1838).   From 1831 to 1832 this Sac chief led the Sacs and Foxes in a resistance movement and outright fighting, known as Black Hawk's War, in Illinois and Wisconsin when the U.S. government sought their land under the term of an illegal 1804 treaty. Eventually the tribes were forced to cede 6 million acres, and Black Hawk was captured in 1833 by the army. Black Hawk expounded the Indian belief that land could not be sold in his 1833 dictated autobiography, *Life of Ma-ka-tai-me-she-kia-kiak*, or *Black Hawk*.

Black Kettle (?–1868).   Known as a peaceful leader, this Cheyenne chief led his people to Sand Creek to sue for peace in 1864. While he and his warriors were out hunting, those who remained in the camp—mostly women and children—were the victims of a vicious massacre by white volunteers. In November 1868 Black Kettle and hundreds of other Cheyennes were killed in their village by Lt. Col. George Custer.

Brant, Joseph (1742–1807).   A Mohawk chief whose tribal name was Thayendanegea, he fought on the British side in the French and Indian War and in Pontiac's Rebellion. He was befriended by Sir William Johnson, who sent him to the Anglican Mohawk Mission School in New England and later took him to England. During the American Revolution, Brant helped to draw most Iroquois to the British side and led raids in New York State and Pennsylvania. After the Revolution, Brant obtained lands and subsidies in Canada for his people.

Campbell, Ben Nighthorse (1933–).   Campbell, whose father was a Cheyenne, served in the Colorado state legislature before he was elected to the U.S. House of Representatives in 1986 from Colorado's third congressional district. In 1992 he was elected U.S. senator from Colorado.

Chief Joseph (c. 1840–1904).   In 1877, this Nez Perce chief led his people on a 1,500-mile escape under war conditions through Idaho, Wyoming, and Montana to avoid settlement on a reservation. They were finally herded onto a reservation in Indian Territory. Joseph died on the Colville Reservation in eastern Washington.

Cochise (c. 1815–1874).   A Chiricahua Apache chief, Cochise, after being falsely accused of kidnapping a child in 1861 and having six Apaches hanged in the standoff that followed, waged an 11-year campaign of guerrilla warfare against the U.S. Army in the Southwest.

Crazy Horse (c. 1842–1877).   Along with Sitting Bull and Red Cloud, he was a forceful Sioux leader in the post–Civil War era and was considered by the U.S. Army to be one of the most effective guerrilla fighters for over a decade as he resisted settlement on a reservation. Crazy Horse was victorious in three actions against U.S. troops in 1876: Powder River (March), Rosebud (June), and Little Bighorn (June). In an altercation at the Red Cloud Agency, he was stabbed.

Curtis, Charles (1860–1936).   Curtis was the first senator partly of Indian background and an early activist on behalf of Indian rights. Elected to the House of Representatives from Kansas, he served there from 1892 to 1906, then served as senator from 1907 to 1913 and from 1915 to 1929. From 1929 to 1933 he was vice president under Herbert Hoover. He sponsored the Curtis Act, 1898.

Deganawida (fl. 1560–1570).   This legendary Mohawk mystic and leader, along with Hiawatha (another mystic, not to be confused with Longfellow's literary character of the same name), is credited with founding the Iroquois League (c. 1450), a confederacy of five (later six) northeastern tribes that historians believe was one of the models for the U.S. federal government.

Deloria, Vine (1933–).   This Dakota author wrote *Custer Died for Your Sins* (1969), *God Is Red* (1973), and *Metaphysics for Modern Existence* (1979), books that helped to reawaken interest in Indian culture and history.

Geronimo (1829–1909).   Along with Vitorio and Cochise, this Chiricahua Apache leader was the last of the great warriors who fought off Mexican and white domination in the American Southwest. Geronimo repeatedly eluded the army's attempts to capture him, and when captured, he often escaped. In 1886 he was forced to surrender at Skelton Canyon, about 25 miles from Apache Pass, where the Apache wars had begun three and a half decades earlier. By then an American folk hero, Geronimo spent the last years of his life at Fort Sill, Oklahoma. He marched in Theodore Roosevelt's inaugural parade in 1905 and became a member of the Dutch Reformed Church.

Little Turtle (c. 1752–1812).   A Miami chief, he organized the Miami, Shawnee, and other tribes to resist white settlement.

Mankiller, Wilma (1945–).   In 1987 this Cherokee became the first woman ever elected to head a major Indian tribe. Her book, *Mankiller: A Chief & Her People*, was published in 1993.

Martinez, Maria (c. 1881–1980).   A San Ildefonso (New Mexico) potter, Martinez, a Pueblo, rediscovered the lost method of making black-on-black pottery. By sharing the formula, she helped to start an economic and artistic renaissance among her people. Martinez's work is displayed in many museums.

Metacom (1639?–1676).   Known to the British as King Philip, this Wampanoag chief was the son of Massasoit, who had helped the Pilgrims survive their first winter in America. Metacom organized the last great resistance (also called King Philip's War) against New England colonists, which resulted in the Indians' being driven from the region. The Indians devastated 12 towns, and the war ended with Metacom's capture and beheading.

Montezuma, Carlos (c. 1865–1923).   A Yavapai physician-activist, he was kidnapped as a child and sold to photographer Carlos Gentile, whose name he assumed. Montezuma reestablished ties

The great Apache leader Geronimo

with his people as an adult and practiced medicine among them. Convinced that reservations were little more than prisons, he became a national spokesperson on behalf of Indian rights.

Osceola (c. 1800–1838).   A Seminole leader, he led a resistance movement, raiding farms, towns, and militia posts and often destroying the army's transportation lines, in the early 1830s when the southeastern Indians were resisting removal and resettlement onto reservations. Seized under a flag of truce, he was imprisoned at Fort Moultrie, South Carolina, where he soon died.

Parker, Quanah (c. 1845–1911).   This Comanche chief was one of the great post–Civil War warriors who resisted resettlement. On the advice of a mystic, he organized a Sun Dance and used it to recruit a war party of 700. He suffered a serious setback at Palo Duro Canyon when the army killed more than 1,000 of his men's ponies. Parker never signed a treaty until his ultimate surrender in 1875, but then he settled into reservation life at Fort Sill, Oklahoma, where he worked to ensure fair land rights and leases for his people. Parker also organized a pan-Indian religious movement that became the Native American Church.

Pocahontas (c. 1595–1617).   Daughter of the powerful Algonquin leader Powhatan, Pocahontas is primarily remembered for having saved John Smith, the Jamestown colony's founder, from execution by her father, a story that may be apocryphal. The 12-year-old girl befriended the English at Jamestown, and when her father, dissatisfied with the settlers' intentions, made plans to starve them out, Pocahontas became an informer. Open warfare soon broke out. In 1613, in hopes of forcing a truce, the British lured Pocahontas to a ship and took her captive. During her captivity she wed colonist John Rolfe, an event that may have contributed to the ensuing truce, which lasted until 1622. In 1616, the Rolfes sailed to England, where Pocahontas was presented at court. In 1617, while en route home, she took ill and died suddenly.

Pocahontas in Elizabethan dress, from a period illustration

Pontiac (c. 1720–c. 1769).   When the French ceded Indian lands around the Great Lakes to the British in the aftermath of the French and Indian War, this Ottawa chief organized a confederacy to reclaim them. In response, the British issued the Proclamation of 1763, which decreed that land west of the Appalachians was Indian Country and would not be settled by whites.

Powhatan (c. 1547–1618?).   Known as Wahunsonacoch by his people, Powhatan strengthened the confederacy of Tidewater tribes established by his father. He was instrumental in maintaining peaceful relations with the Jamestown colonists in the early days of the settlement. His daughter Pocahontas married the Englishman John Rolfe.

INDIAN CONTRIBUTIONS TO AMERICAN CULTURE

Native Americans have rarely been given enough credit for their contributions to American culture. Their inventions and products have influenced what we eat, how we dress, the shapes of our buildings, and even, some historians believe, the federal form of the U.S. government. Among the Indians' most notable contributions are the following (some are from Central and South America):

- **Foods.** Native American staples now eaten around the world include the potato, sweet potato, corn (maize), manioc, tomatoes, beans, artichokes, squash, turkey, maple sugar, vanilla, and cacao, used to make chocolate. Tobacco, not a food, is a New World crop; cotton, so strongly associated with the American South, was also known in Africa and Asia.
- **Medicine.** Indian remedies served as the model for many drugs that are now laboratory made. Since its first publication in 1820, the official *United States Pharmacopeia* has listed more than 200 drugs used originally by Indians. Coca, for example, was used to make novocaine for pain relief during dental procedures, and quinine was until the 1940s the only treatment for malaria. For many years curare was used in surgery to stop breathing long enough to insert rubber tubing into the windpipe to prevent choking, and ipecac is still used as an emetic.
- **Housing and architecture.** Sibley tents, variations on Plains Indians' tepees, have been used by armies around the world. Arctic and Antarctic explorers relied on a unique form of Indian housing known as the igloo. The Pueblo influence on architecture also is seen in many domestic and public buildings in the Southwest. The University of New Mexico, for example, was patterned after Pueblo housing (known as pueblos), and I. M. Pei, the renowned Japanese-American architect, acknowledges using the 13th-century pueblos at Mesa Verde National Park as inspiration for the laboratories he designed at the National Center for Atmospheric Research in Boulder, Colorado.
- **Furniture.** The hammock, common in many different Indian cultures, found its way onto navy and merchant-marine ships as a space-saving bed—and into our backyards as well. Toboggans (not, strictly speaking, furniture), Indian inventions, have given pleasure to millions of children and adults.
- **Textiles and clothing.** Parkas, a perennial fashion staple, were first worn by Indians and originally taken up by whites as military garb. Ponchos saw new life during World War I as soldiers' rain gear and have enjoyed spurts of popularity ever since. Indian moccasins have been adapted as house slippers, and people living in snowy climes rely on Indian-originated snowshoes.
- **Federalism.** Some historians believe the United States' unique form of government, in which federal and state governments exist in a delicate balance of power, was inspired by the Iroquois League, an organization of six northeastern tribes.
- **Image.** Last, but hardly least, many of the qualities associated with being an "American"—being strong, action-oriented, and independent—are values held in high esteem among Native Americans.

The Prophet (also known as the Shawnee Prophet) (1775?–1837?). Tenskwatawa, the brother of Tecumseh, claimed to have had a divine revelation from the Native American master of life that urged him to denounce white culture and encourage a return to Native American ways. In 1808 he founded Tippecanoe (later called Prophetstown) where Indians of different tribes could live separate from white society. His influence is said to have helped precipitate the Creek resistance that ended at Horseshoe Bend in 1814.

Red Cloud (1822–1909). A Lakota Sioux chief, Red Cloud, along with Sitting Bull, was a leader in the Sioux War, also called Red Cloud's War, from 1865 to 1868, which reclaimed the

Bozeman Trail, the primary hunting ground of the Plains Indians. After the railroad was built, Red Cloud retired to a reservation, where he lived until his death.

Sacajawea (c. 1786–c. 1812).   Also known as Bird Woman, this Shoshone was the only woman and guide on the Lewis and Clark Expedition (1804–1806). Later, she served as an interpreter-liaison with several other tribes. Captured as a child by Mandans, she lived most of her life with them.

Sequoyah (1766–1843).   Sequoyah, a Cherokee also known as George Guess, developed a syllabary for the Cherokee language and taught thousands of Native Americans to read and write.

Sitting Bull (c. 1831–1890).   A holy man rather than a chief, this Lakota Sioux leader organized the Plains tribes to fight the Sioux War (also known as Red Cloud's War). The Indians routed the U.S. Army and successfully reclaimed their hunting ground, but in 1868, when the Lakota agreed to move to a reservation, Sitting Bull refused to go and organized a new resistance movement. Sitting Bull and his 2,000 resisters, the largest force of Indians ever gathered at that time, defeated and killed all the troops under Custer's immediate command (more than 260 men) on June 25–26, 1876. Fearing retribution, Sitting Bull and his warriors fled into Canada, but dwindling food supplies forced them to return to the United States, where Sitting Bull was immediately taken prisoner. On his release two years later, he moved to the Standing Rock reservation in North Dakota, where he hoped to influence his people not to sign away any more of their land. Sitting Bull's last political act was to become involved in the Ghost Dance movement. During a scuffle, when Indian police attempted to arrest Sitting Bull, he was shot and killed.

Tallchief, Maria (1925–).   An Osage, Tallchief became a classical ballerina who danced with George Balanchine's company (and who was also for a time his wife) and with the Paris Opera Ballet. Her most famous role was the title role in *The Firebird*, which Balanchine created for her.

Tecumseh (1768–1813).   The dream of this great Shawnee leader was to forge an Indian state out of the Old Northwest Territory around the Great Lakes. With his brother, known as the Prophet, he organized a confederacy of tribes in the region. At the Battle of Tippecanoe, in 1811, his forces (in his absence) were lured into battle by William Henry Harrison, and the power of the confederacy was broken.

Tekakwitha, Kateri (1656–1680).   Tekakwitha, a Mohawk, was the first American Indian ever proposed for Roman Catholic sainthood. Converted by Jesuits, she was known for her piousness and bravery in the face of suffering. Documentation to canonize her was introduced in 1932, and in 1980 Pope John Paul II beatified her.

Thorpe, Jim (1888–1953).   Sac athlete Jim Thorpe won parts of the pentathlon and the decathlon at the 1912 Olympic Games. He was later stripped of his medals for playing one season of semipro baseball, but his medals were restored in 1983.

Ward, Nancy (c. 1738–c. 1824).   This Cherokee leader was the daughter of a Delaware man and a Cherokee woman. Ward lived with her mother's people and married a fellow Cherokee, a warrior who later died in a skirmish between the Cherokees and the Creeks. Although it was virtually unheard of for a woman to be included in a war party, Ward donned men's clothing and took over her husband's role in battle. Her reward for helping to rout the enemy was a position on the Council of Chiefs, making her possibly the first Cherokee woman ever to wield such power. She was also awarded the title Beloved Woman, with the responsibility of deciding the fates of prisoners. She married a pro-Cherokee white man and spent her remaining years working for Indian-white peace.

ADDITIONAL SOURCES OF INFORMATION

Andrist, Ralph K. *The Long Death: The Last Days of the Plains Indian*. Macmillan, 1964.

Brown, Dee. *Bury My Heart at Wounded Knee*. Holt, 1970.

Dennis, Henry C. *The American Indian, 1492–1977*. Oceana Publications, 1977.

Fiedel, Stuart. *Prehistory of the Americas*. 2d ed. Cambridge University Press, 1992.

Josephy, Alvin M., Jr. *The Indian Heritage of America*. Knopf, 1968.

Kehoe, Alice B. *North American Indians: A Comprehensive Account*. Prentice Hall, 1981.

Markowitz, Harvey, et al., eds. *American Indians*. 3 vols. Salem Press, 1995.

Neihardt, John G. *Black Elk Speaks: Being the Life Story of a Holy Man of the Oglala Sioux*. University of Nebraska Press, 1961.

Prucha, Francis Paul. *The Great Father: The United States Government and the American Indians*. 2 vols. University of Nebraska Press, 1984.

Sale, Kirkpatrick. *The Conquest of Paradise: Christopher Columbus and the Columbian Legacy*. Knopf, 1990.

Spicer, Edward H. *Cycles of Conquest: The Impact of Spain, Mexico and the United States on Indians of the Southwest, 1533–1960*. University of Arizona Press, 1962.

Utley, Robert M. *The Indian Frontier of the American West, 1846–1890*. University of New Mexico, 1984.

Utley, Robert M., and Wilcomb Washburn. *The American Heritage History of the Indian Wars*. American Heritage, 1977.

Waldman, Carl. *Atlas of the North American Indian*. Facts on File, 1985.

White, Richard. *The Middle Ground: Indian Empires and Republics in the Great Lakes Region, 1650–1815*. Cambridge, 1991.

2

Exploration and Colonization

WHY WERE THE EUROPEANS ABLE TO EXPLORE AMERICA?

Although the Vikings were the first Europeans to colonize the New World, more than 500 years elapsed between their voyages and the earthshaking first voyage of Christopher Columbus in 1492. Among the developments that provided the impetus for the European rediscovery of America were the Protestant Reformation, the Catholic Counter-Reformation, and the Renaissance, each of which encouraged the individualism necessary for exploration. In addition, by 1492 Portugal, France, Spain, and England had grown from small territories of warring noble families into nation-states. Their rulers, supported by the powerful merchant class, eagerly sought to expand trade, especially with Asia and Africa, by financing overseas exploration and to claim new territories in the rapidly escalating drive for power and domination. The ability to find one's position at sea, already known on land, gave the sailors the confidence they needed to press forward into uncharted waters. These were people driven by ideas of adventure, by hopes of becoming fabulously wealthy, and by the inherent belief that it was their duty to spread Christianity.

SIGNIFICANT EVENTS IN THE EXPLORATION OF AMERICA

c. 982	Norseman Eric the Red discovers Greenland.
c. 986	Eric the Red leads an expedition to colonize Greenland and, with 500 settlers, establishes the first Viking settlement there.
1000	Leif Ericsson, son of Eric the Red, lands on the coast of what is now either Newfoundland or Nova Scotia, Canada, probably becoming the first European to discover America. Finding grapes (probably berries) there, the Vikings call the region Vinland (Wineland).
1492	On his first voyage, sponsored by Isabella of Castile and Ferdinand of Aragon, Italian navigator Christopher Columbus lands on the Bahaman island of Guanahani, which he names San Salvador. Columbus also sights Cuba and lands on Haiti.
1493	On his second voyage, Christopher Columbus comes upon Puerto Rico, Jamaica, and Dominica.
1497	John Cabot lands on the east coast of North America either at Newfoundland or Cape Breton Island and claims the region for England's King Henry VII.
1498	On his second voyage, John Cabot's fate is unknown, although some believe he may have reaced North America.
	On his third voyage, Columbus sails to Trinidad and the Orinoco River in South America.
1499	Italian explorer Amerigo Vespucci sails to the northern and eastern coasts of South America and arrives at the mouth of the Amazon River.
1502- 1503	On his fourth and last voyage, Columbus comes upon Saint Lucia, Honduras, Costa Rica, and Panama.
1507	Mapmaker Martin Waldseemüller shows the name America on the first map indicating the New World distinct from Asia.

Corbis-Bettmann

Italian navigator Christopher Columbus

1508?   Searching for a northwest passage (a short sea route around or through North America to east Asia), British explorer Sebastian Cabot may have reached Hudson Bay. His exploits are debated.

1513   Spaniard Juan Ponce de León, according to legend searching for the Fountain of Youth, reaches Florida.

Vasco Núñez de Balboa leads an expedition across the Isthmus of Panama and becomes the first European to sight the Pacific Ocean from the New World.

1519-
1521   Spanish explorer Hernando Cortés conquers Mexico, capturing the Aztec capital Tenochtitlán (now Mexico City) and imprisoning and eventually killing the Aztec emperor Montezuma.

Alvarez de Pineda explores the Gulf of Mexico from Florida to Veracruz.

1519-
1521   Ferdinand Magellan sails around the world. After his death in 1521 in the Philippines, the voyage is completed by Juan Sebastian del Cano, the commander of the *Vittoria,* the only remaining vessel of Magellan's five-ship fleet.

1524   Italian navigator Giovanni da Verrazzano sails along the Atlantic Coast from Cape Fear north into New York Bay.

1532-
1535   Spaniard Francisco Pizarro conquers Peru, seizing control of the rich Inca empire and founding Lima.

1534   On his first voyage to New World, Frenchman Jacques Cartier sights Labrador, Newfoundland, New Brunswick, and enters the mouth of the Saint Lawrence.

1535-   On his second voyage, Cartier sails up the Saint Lawrence River.
1536

1536   Álvar Núñez Cabeza de Vaca reaches the area of the Gulf of California after an eight-year overland journey from Texas through New Mexico, Arizona, and possibly California.

European Exploration in North America

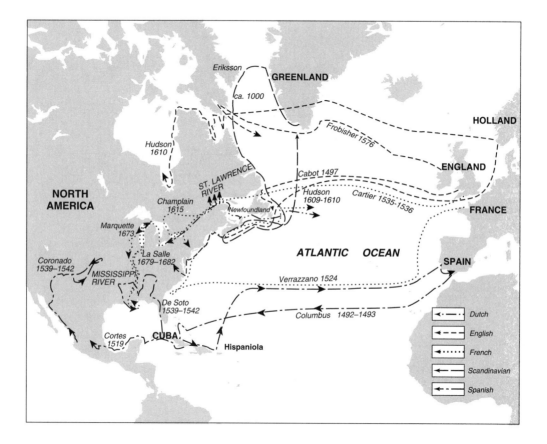

1539-   Spaniard Hernando de Soto leads an expedition from Florida and in 1541 crosses the
1542   Mississippi River.

1540-   Francisco Vásquez de Coronádo leads an army from Mexico through the American
1542   Southwest and reaches the Pueblo villages of New Mexico; his lieutenant, Garcia López de Cárdenas, sights the Grand Canyon.

1542   Juan Rodríguez Cabrillo explores the coast of California.

1562   Jean Ribault and 140 French Huguenots (Protestants) establish a colony on Parris Island, off the coast of South Carolina, calling it Charlesfort. While Ribault is in France obtaining supplies, the other colonists are rescued from starvation by an English ship and return to France.

1564   René de Laudonnière establishes Fort Caroline, a post near the mouth of the Saint Johns River, Florida.

1565   Spanish naval officer Pedro Menéndez de Avilés, ordered by King Philip II to found a Spanish colony in Florida, establishes the fort of Saint Augustine, which becomes the oldest permanent European city in North America.

         Jean Ribault sails with reinforcements for Fort Caroline, but the fleet is wrecked in a tropical storm, leaving the survivors stranded on the coast of Florida, south of Saint Augustine. The undefended colonists at Fort Caroline are massacred by Spanish forces under Pedro Menéndez de Avilés, who has been dispatched by King Philip II of Spain to crush the French Huguenots. The Spanish murder most of Ribault's men as they attempt to reach Fort Caroline by land.

1567   In revenge for the Spanish destruction of Fort Caroline, French soldier Dominique de Gourgues and his men decimate San Mateo, the colony the Spanish have set up on the same spot.

1576   Englishman Martin Frobisher discovers what will be called Frobisher Bay in Canada.

1579   Englishman Francis Drake reaches northern California on his voyage of circumnavigation, 1577–1580.

1585   Navigator and courtier Sir Walter Raleigh sends a group of British to found a colony on the mid-Atlantic coast of North America. They land on Roanoke Island, North Carolina, where they establish a settlement. A year later, Sir Francis Drake, returning to England from raiding Spanish treasure ships, rescues the surviving colonists and takes them back to England.

1587   A group of colonists, organized by Raleigh, establishes a second settlement on Roanoke Island. Virginia Dare, the first child of English parents to be born in America, is born here. Her fate is unknown.

1590   The first relief expedition reaching Roanoke Island finds no trace of the colony, hereafter referred to as the Lost Colony.

1596   Spanish merchant Sebastián Vizcaíno unsuccessfully attempts to colonize southern California.

1598   On his first expedition, Juan de Oñate takes possession of New Mexico for Spain.

1601   On his second expedition, Juan de Oñate explores what will become Oklahoma, crossing into Kansas.

1603   Frenchman Samuel de Champlain sails up the Saint Lawrence River to what is now Montreal. Over the next four years he explores the coasts of Maine, New Brunswick, and Nova Scotia.

1605   On his third expedition, Juan de Oñate reaches the Colorado River and descends it to the Gulf of California.

1606   England's King James I grants a charter to the Virginia Company of London, a joint stock company, to establish colonies in America.

1607   The Virginia Company sends more than 100 colonists to the Chesapeake Bay region, where they found Jamestown, Virginia, the first permanent English settlement in North America. Captain John Smith, Jamestown's military commander, is, according to legend, rescued from execution at the hands of the Indians by Chief Powhatan's daughter, Pocahontas. (Historians now believe that Smith misinterpreted a traditional Indian adoption ceremony.)

1608   Samuel de Champlain founds French colony of Quebec.

1609   In search of a northwest passage, Henry Hudson sails up the New York river that bears his name and gives the Dutch their claim to the region.

1609-
1610 Only a fraction of the Jamestown colonists survive the terrible winter. Preparing to abandon the colony and return to England, their numbers are bolstered by the arrival from England of a large additional force of men, women, and livestock.

c. 1612 Jamestown colonist John Rolfe begins the cultivation of West Indies tobacco, a less bitter variety than that grown by Virginia Indians. With some refinements the Orinoco leaf proves to be a valued cash crop.

1614 Pocahontas marries colonist John Rolfe; soon afterward Powhatan agrees to a truce with the Jamestown colony, which lasts until 1622.

1617 After boarding a ship for her return to Jamestown following a visit to England sponsored by the London Company to encourage new settlers, Pocahontas dies and is buried in England.

1619 The House of Burgesses, the first colonial legislature, meets in Jamestown, Virginia.

A Dutch ship transports 20 black African bound servants to Jamestown. They are probably the first African Americans in the English colonies of America.

Among the 1,200 colonists to arrive this year are a number of single women, recruited by the company to go to Virginia to become wives.

AFRICAN ROOTS

Most slaves were seized in the interior of Africa by European and African traders and then marched to the West African coast, where they were sold to ships bound for the colonies. Some were kidnapped by slavers, some captured during local wars, and some sold into slavery for transgressing tribal laws. Among the West African peoples enslaved were the Ashantis, Bakongas, Fantis, Hausas, Ibos, Mandingos, Sekes, Wolofs, and Yorubas. The majority of the enslaved were between the ages of 15 and 30, with men outnumbering women about two to one.

1620 After a two-month voyage on the *Mayflower*, 102 Pilgrims sponsored by the Virginia Company establish a colony at Plymouth on Cape Cod. Before landing, the Pilgrims sign the Mayflower Compact, an agreement establishing self-government.

1621 William Bradford is elected the second governor of the Plymouth Colony. He is to serve 31 terms between 1622 and 1656.

The Plymouth Colony negotiates a peace treaty with the Wampanoag Indians.

1623 English colonists found a settlement at Dover.

The Dutch West India Company is chartered in the Dutch Republic for trading and colonizing in the New World.

1626 The Dutch establish the colony of New Netherland, which would soon include the town of New Amsterdam (present-day New York City) at the lower tip of Manhattan, Fort Orange (present-day Albany), and Fort Nassau (present-day Gloucester, New Jersey).

Dutchman Peter Minuit gives local Indians about $25 worth of trinkets in exchange for the island of Manhattan.

Led by Roger Conant, a group of English Puritans arrive at Massachusetts Bay and attempt to create a settlement on Cape Ann. They leave and go to Naumkeag, which they rename Salem.

1630 John Winthrop and other members of the Massachusetts Bay Company found Boston, initiating what becomes known as the Great Migration to the Massachusetts Bay Colony; about 20,000 people will settle there in the next 15 years.

Pilgrims praying aboard the Mayflower

1633   The Dutch build a trading post near present-day Hartford.

The New Sweden Company (or New South Company) is organized. In 1637 it is granted a charter for settlement on the Delaware River.

1634   Frenchman Jean Nicolet explores Lake Michigan and present-day Wisconsin.

Under a grant to the Catholic Calvert family, the Lords Baltimore, colonists settle Saint Mary's, Maryland. Maryland becomes the only English colony in North America with a large Catholic minority.

John Oldham and Bay Colony settlers winter at Wethersfield.

1635   At the mouth of the Connecticut River, the English build Fort Saybrook.

1636   Dissenting minister Roger Williams, expelled the year before from Massachusetts, founds Providence, Rhode Island, on land he purchases from Indians.

Thomas Hooker, another dissenting minister, leads his followers from Cambridge, Massachusetts, to Connecticut, where they found Hartford.

1637   English settlers and Pequots clash in the Connecticut valley in a brief war that destroys the Pequot tribe.

1638   New Haven, Connecticut, is founded by Puritans.

Swedes build Fort Christina (now Wilmington, Delaware).

Dissenter Anne Hutchinson, expelled the previous year from Massachusetts, and her followers found present-day Portsmouth, Rhode Island.

1639   The Fundamental Orders, which Thomas Hooker helped write, is adopted by the Connecticut Colony. The orders constitute the basic law of the colony until 1662.

1642   The French found Montreal, Canada.

1647   Peter Stuyvesant arrives in New Amsterdam to assume his position as governor of New Netherlands.

1648   Landowner and lawyer Margaret Brent asks for a vote in the Maryland assembly, but her request is rejected.

1649   Maryland Act for Religious Toleration is passed.

1650   The English and the Dutch agree on the respective boundaries of their North American colonies.

1652   Massachusetts General Court decides that Maine belongs to the Massachusetts Bay Colony.

1655   Dutch forces, led by Peter Stuyvesant, take Swedish forts on the Delaware River.

1659-
1661   Pierre Radisson explores Lake Superior and the northern Mississippi regions.

1662   The New Haven Colony is united with Connecticut.

1663   Carolina is chartered.

1664   British forces annex New Netherland from Connecticut to Delaware. New Amsterdam is renamed New York, and Fort Orange becomes Albany.

       The New Jersey Colony is founded.

1666   Connecticut Puritans found Newark, New Jersey.

1668   The French establish a fur-trading post and a Jesuit mission at Sault Sainte Marie, on the waterway between Lakes Superior and Huron.

1672   Mail service begins between New York and Boston.

1673   Frenchmen Louis Jolliet and Jacques Marquette descend the Wisconsin River to the Mississippi. Paddling their canoes southward, they conclude that the Mississippi flows not into the Pacific but into the Gulf of Mexico.

       Dutch forces reoccupy New York.

1674   The English regain control of New York and, by treaty with the Netherlands, recognize it as British.

1675-
1676   King Philip's War in New England forces back the line of English settlement and wipes out the Wampanoag tribe.

1676   Bacon's Rebellion in Virginia, sparked by the colonial government's inability to protect settlements from Indian attack, collapses when leader Nathaniel Bacon dies.

1677   Massachusetts purchases part of Maine from heirs of Spanish explorer Sir Ferdinando Gorges.

1679   New Hampshire is established as a royal colony separate from Massachusetts.

1679-
1682   Frenchman René-Robert Cavelier de Sieur La Salle, with his lieutenant, Henri de Tonti, and Louis Hennepin explore the Great Lakes. La Salle and his party reach the mouth of the Mississippi River at the Gulf of Mexico in 1682 and claim the Mississippi Valley for Louis XIV.

       The French found the first white settlement in Arkansas.

1681   England's King Charles II grants a royal charter to English Quaker William Penn for the region that becomes Pennsylvania.

1683   German Mennonites found Germantown, Pennsylvania.

1684   England annuls the original charter of the Massachusetts Bay Company.

1686   In an effort to restructure England's North American colonies, James II forms the Dominion of New England. Composed of New Jersey, New York, Connecticut, Rhode Island, Massachusetts, New Hampshire, and the territory of Maine, the dominion is now governed by Sir Edmund Andros with Francis Nicholson as lieutenant governor.

1689   Armed conflict between England and France for control of eastern North America begins. Hostilities start with English and Iroquois attacking Montreal and violence between French and English traders on Hudson Bay. These conflicts are part of a bigger conflict between England and France, which is called the War of the League of Augsburg in Europe, and King William's War in North America. Warfare between the two nations will continue for nearly 75 years.

        In the wake of the Glorious Revolution, German-born merchant Jacob Leisler seizes New York in the name of William and Mary of England and appoints himself governor.

1690   French troops join with Algonquin warriors to attack and burn settlements in New York, New Hampshire, and Maine.

        A Massachusetts fleet captures the strategic French harbor at Port Royal, Nova Scotia. A year later, the French recapture it.

1691   English troops regain New York. Jacob Leisler, convicted of treason, is hanged.

        A new royal charter is issued to Massachusetts, incorporating Maine and Plymouth.

1692   Twenty-seven people are tried for witchcraft in Salem, Massachusetts, after being accused by a group of teenaged girls; 20 are executed.

1696   French forces successfully defend Quebec against English-Iroquois attacks.

1697   King William's War ends. The Treaty of Ryswick restores territories to prewar status.

1699   Pierre le Moyne, Sieur d'Iberville, founds Old Biloxi (now Ocean Springs, Mississippi), the first European settlement in French Louisiana, and explores the Mississippi Delta.

1701   Led by Antoine de la Mothe Cadillac, French colonists build a fort at Detroit. The French establish fur-trading posts and other forts in Michigan and Illinois.

1702   Queen Anne's War, the second North American colonial war between France and England, begins. The English burn Saint Augustine, Florida.

        This is the traditional date for the founding of Vincennes, the first permanent European colony in Indiana, established by French colonists at a site on the Wabash River long known to fur traders; the site is fortified in 1732.

1704   The *News-Letter*, the first newspaper in the colonies, begin publication in Boston.

        French and Indians raid Deerfield, Massachusetts, massacre 50 colonists, then take more than 100 others hostage.

        English colonial forces are unable to capture Port Royal, Nova Scotia.

1707   English forces again fail to seize Port Royal.

1710   English and colonial forces finally seize Port Royal, renaming it Annapolis Royal.

1711   British colonials fail to take Quebec.

1711-   In Carolina, Tuscarora Indians massacre more than 150 settlers. War ensues.
1713   Using a divide-and-conquer strategy, Carolina settlers ally with other tribes against the Tuscaroras. More than 300 Tuscarora warriors are killed near the Neuse River. The war ends disastrously for the tribe, whose survivors flee north, where they join the Iroquois Confederation.

        The Peace of Utrecht ends Queen Anne's War.

1715-   Enraged by the colonists' treatment of the Tuscaroras, the Yamasee Indians stage an
1716   uprising in South Carolina. More than 200 settlers are killed before the colonists, aided by the Cherokees, defeat the Yamasees, driving them into Georgia and Florida. There the Yamasees ally with the Spanish against the English.

1716   To defend themselves against a possible French threat from Louisiana, the Spanish begin to establish missions in Texas.

1717   In France, Scottish financier John Law, having gained a monopoly of trading rights in Louisiana, forms the Mississippi Company.

1718   French colonists found New Orleans.

San Antonio, Texas, is founded by Spanish Franciscans and is established as a Spanish military post and mission.

1720   Although John Law's Mississippi scheme collapses due to overspeculation, it has successfully encouraged French settlement in the southern Mississippi valley.

In an attempt to woo the Iroquois away from the French, William Burnet, governor of New York, expands trade with the Indians.

1724   Fort Drummer (near present-day Brattleboro), the first permanent European settlement in Vermont, is built to protect English settlers from nearby Indians.

1729   Carolina is split into two crown colonies, North Carolina and South Carolina.

Baltimore, Maryland, is founded, incorporated 1745.

1731-   Frenchman Pierre Gaultier de Varennes, Sieur de La Vérendrye, and his three sons explore
1743   the Northwest as far as Saskatchewan.

1732   By an act of the English Parliament, Georgia, the last of the original 13 colonies, is created. The colony's founder, James Oglethorpe, hopes to establish a buffer against the Spanish in Florida and the French in Lousiana and a refuge for the persecuted and the poor.

1734   John Peter Zenger, the founder of the *New York Weekly Journal,* is arrested and charged with seditious libel for his paper's attacks on William Crosby, the royal governor of New York. Tried in 1735, he is defended by Andrew Hamilton, who argues that his client had not libeled Crosby because the material printed in the paper was true. Zenger is acquitted, and his case becomes a milestone in the battle for a free press.

1737   English colonist William Byrd founds Richmond, Virginia.

1739   Angered by border problems, the English colonists and Georgia decide to go to war against the Spanish in Florida.

1740   James Oglethorpe tries and fails to capture Saint Augustine, Florida, from the Spanish.

1742   At the Battle of Bloody Marsh on Saint Simons Island, Georgia, colonists led by James Oglethorpe repulse a Spanish counterattack.

1743   Three years after his attempt to seize Saint Augustine, James Oglethorpe tries and fails again.

The American Philosophical Society is founded in Philadelphia.

1744   The French failure to take Annapolis Royal is the first military action of King George's War in America, the third of the French-English North American colonial wars.

1745   Saratoga, New York, is burned by French and Indian forces, who also raid forts and towns in Maine.

Colonial and British forces capture Louisbourg on Cape Breton Island, Canada.

1746   The British successfully defend Cape Breton Island from the French, and rivalry between the French and the English for the upper Ohio region intensifies.

1747   The Ohio Company is created by a group of Virginians to expand settlement westward from Virginia.

American Colonies in the Early 18th Century

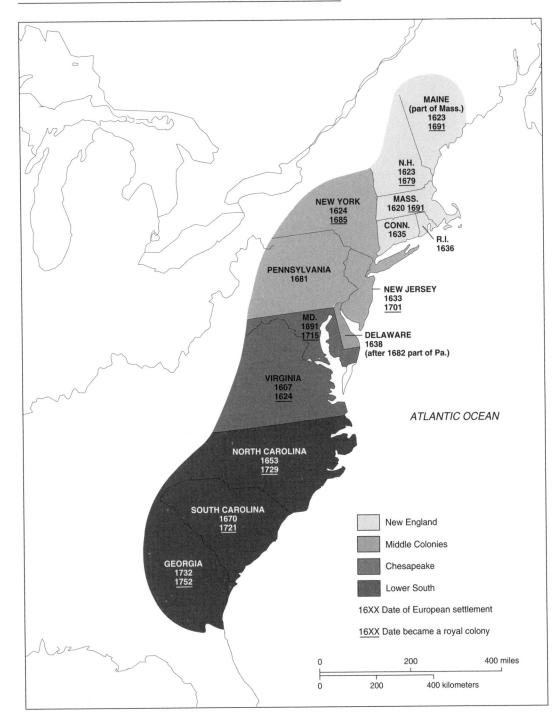

MAINE
(part of Mass.)
1623
_1691_

N.H.
1623
_1679_

NEW YORK
1624
_1685_

MASS.
1620 _1691_

CONN.
1635

R.I.
1636

PENNSYLVANIA
1681

NEW JERSEY
1633
_1701_

MD.
1691
_1715_

DELAWARE
1638
(after 1682 part of Pa.)

VIRGINIA
1607
_1624_

ATLANTIC OCEAN

NORTH CAROLINA
1653
_1729_

SOUTH CAROLINA
1670
_1721_

GEORGIA
1732
_1752_

New England

Middle Colonies

Chesapeake

Lower South

16XX Date of European settlement

_16XX_ Date became a royal colony

| 0 | | 200 | | 400 miles |

| 0 | 200 | | 400 kilometers |

1748   King George's War ends and the Treaty of Aix-la-Chapelle returns Louisbourg to France. But hostility between France and England continues.

1749   The Ohio Company receives a royal charter and an enormous land grant for the area along the forks of the Ohio River—the junction of the Monongahela and the Allegheny rivers (now Pittsburgh, Pennsylvania).

       Acting first, the French send a heavily armed force to the Ohio valley to warn off the British from the region.

1751   The Ohio Company begins colonization of the Ohio valley.

1752   To prevent the British from gaining control of the Ohio valley, the French begin constructing forts south of Lake Erie to the forks of the Ohio River.

       At the same time, the Iroquois and Delawares cede lands south of the Ohio to Virginia.

       Thomas Bond opens the first general hospital in the colonies, in Philadelphia.

1753   Young militia officer George Washington is dispatched by Virginia's governor to effect French withdrawal from the Ohio Territory.

       The Liberty Bell is hung in the newly built Pennsylvania State House, later called Independence Hall.

1754   The contest between the French and the Ohio Company for control of the Ohio valley heats up as the French build Fort Duquesne at the forks of the Ohio. George Washington is defeated by French forces near the headwaters of the Ohio River (Great Meadows).

       The Albany Congress, with representatives from seven colonies, concludes a treaty with the Iroquois and recommends Benjamin Franklin's Plan of Union.

1755   British regulars and colonial militia led by British general Edward Braddock are ambushed and destroyed by French and Indians on the upper Ohio. Braddock is killed during the battle, and Washington assumes command. Full-scale warfare erupts after this defeat.

1756   England formally declares war on France. The conflict in America is called the French and Indian War and in Europe the Seven Years' War.

1757   General Louis Joseph, Marquis de Montcalm, captures Fort Oswego, restoring control of Lake Ontario to France.

       Fort William Henry on Lake George, New York, falls to French forces under General Montcalm. Many British prisoners taken during the battle are killed by Indian allies of the French.

1758   General Montcalm repels an English attack on Fort Ticonderoga, New York. The British seize two Canadian forts in French hands—Louisbourg on Cape Breton Island and Fort Frontenac on Lake Ontario. After the French burn Duquesne, Pennsylvania, the British rebuild it, renaming it Fort Pitt.

1759   British forces take Fort Niagara, New York, and the French abandon Crown Point and Fort Ticonderoga. At the Plains of Abraham, above Quebec, the British General James Wolfe defeats General Montcalm. Both generals die in the epic battle, and Quebec falls to the British.

1760   After British troops seize Montreal, the French governor of Canada surrenders the province to the British. Although Canadian resistance continues for another year, the loss of Montreal signifies the end of the French empire in America. The French surrender Detroit to the British.

1762   To prevent the Louisiana Territory from falling into British hands, France secretly cedes it to Spain in the Treaty of Fontainebleau.

1763   In the Treaty of Paris, which ends the French and Indian War, France cedes to England all its territories east of the Mississippi River except for two small islands in the Saint Lawrence

George Washington as a soldier

River, which France retains, and New Orleans, which passes to Spain. In exchange for the return of Cuba and the Philippines, Spain cedes Florida to Britain. In sum, the imperial competition for eastern North America, begun in the 16th century, has ended in a total English victory. France has lost all its American possessions except for the two islands mentioned above and Martinique and Guadeloupe. However, for the next three years Native-American tribes wage war against the English in the Ohio–Great Lakes region, destroying all forts there, except for Forts Detroit and Pitt.

The Proclamation of 1763 forbids British settlement west of the Appalachian Mountains to reserve an Indian territory and defuse tension. It also creates three new provinces: Quebec, East Florida, and West Florida.

1767   The survey of the boundary between Maryland and Pennsylvania, and Maryland and Delaware, is completed, establishing the Mason-Dixon line.

1768   In the Treaty of Hard Labor, the Cherokees cede a huge tract of land around the upper Tennessee River to British settlers. Hoping to keep English settlements away from their home-land, the Iroquois, in the Treaty of Fort Stanwix, give up their claims to the Ohio valley.

1769   Francisco Junípero Serra begins establishing a string of forts and missions in California, from San Diego (1769) north to San Francisco (1776).

1773   The first publicly supported mental hospital opens in Williamsburg, Virginia.

1775   The Second Continental Congress establishes the postal system. Benjamin Franklin is post-master general.

SIGNIFICANT EVENTS LEADING TO THE REVOLUTION

1764   To raise money to help pay the British debt incurred in the French and Indian War, Parliament passes the Sugar Act, imposing duties on sugar, textiles, coffee, and other imports. The colonists protest this act through resolutions and boycotts.

Parliament passes the Currency Act, prohibiting the colonies from printing their own paper money.

1765   Parliament passes the Quartering Act, requiring that colonists provide food and shelter for British troops. The colonial assemblies protest the act.

Parliament passes the Stamp Act, requiring that printed documents such as newspapers, licenses, and legal documents be issued solely on special stamped paper bought from stamp collectors or distributors. Delegates sent by nine colonies to the Stamp Act Congress, in New York City, protest taxation without representation. Protest mobs riot in cities such as Boston. Stamp collectors publicly resign, making it impossible for the revenue stamps to be sold.

1766   Parliament repeals the Stamp Act but passes the Declaratory Act, asserting its right to make laws governing the colonies. The colonists, celebrating the repeal of the Stamp Act, ignore the new act.

1767   The New York Assembly is suspended for incompletely complying with the Quartering Act.

The Townshend Acts, imposing import duties on glass, lead, paints, and tea sent to the colonies, are passed by Parliament. Determined not to import or consume British goods, Boston and then other major ports set up nonimportation associations. The colonial assemblies protest the acts, as do colonial newspapers.

"The Repeal," a 1776 etching depicting the "funeral procession of Miss Americ-Stamp"

Patrick Henry

Wealthy lawyer John Dickinson, writing as "a Farmer in Pennsylvania," acknowledges Parliament's right to regulate trade but not to tax to raise revenue.

1769   Virginia's House of Burgesses is dissolved by the colony's governor after the assembly establishes the first provincial association, which then bans goods enumerated in the Townshend Acts. Its members then meet in private. In the next few months every colony except New Hampshire establishes these nonimportation associations.

1770   British soldiers kill five Boston colonists (including Crispus Attucks, whose mother was Indian and father African American) in what comes to be known as the Boston Massacre. The violence erupts when the troops fire on a rock-throwing mob—aroused by the quartering of 400 British troops around Boston—attacks the offices of the customs commissioners. Parliament repeals the Townshend Acts, except for the tax on tea. Colonists respond by ending their nonimportation policy.

1771   Backcountry North Carolina Regulators, protesting official corruption, lawlessness, and lack of representation in the assembly in the eastern part of the state, are defeated at Alamance Creek.

1772   The governor of Massachusetts announces that his salary and those of other royally appointed officials of the colony will be paid for by the Crown, making them financially independent of the colony. Leaders in Boston appoint a committee of correspondence to

A HEAVY PRICE TO PAY: THE BOSTON TEA PARTY (1773)

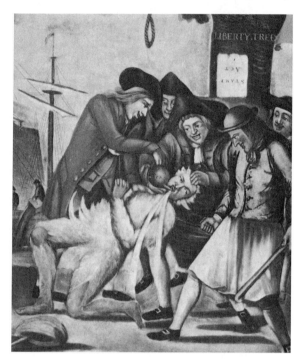

Period illustration of John Malcomb, commissioner of customs in Boston, tarred and feathered and forced to drink tea for collecting customs duties

The colonists loved tea, but English taxes on it caused them to sharply reduce consumption, pushing the East India Company, a major importer of colonial tea, toward bankruptcy. As the company was the main agent of British power in India, Parliament tried to shore it up financially by passing the Tea Act of May 10, 1773. The new law adjusted import taxes to enable the company to undersell—at prices alluring to even the most patriotic colonist—all competitors. Four months later, the company shipped 1,700 chests of tea to selected consignees in the major colonial ports—Boston, New York, Philadelphia, and Charleston. Patriot groups were outraged, arguing that Parliament was only trying to make it easy for colonists to swallow paying an unconstitutional tax. In addition, local merchants who had not been picked saw their exclusion as an attempt by England to subvert their prosperity and independence.

Organized by colonial committees of correspondence, opposition to the Tea Act mounted. Protests caused the consignees in every port but Boston to resign. The first tea shipped reached Boston Harbor in late November, and two others arrived shortly afterward. In mass meetings in Old South Church, colonists demanded that the tea be returned to England with the duties unpaid. On December 16 patriots meeting in the church heard that Governor Thomas Hutchinson refused their demand. At midnight a small group of patriots (perhaps including Sam Adams) disguised themselves as Indians and marched to the ships, boarded them, and dumped 45 tons of tea into Boston Harbor. Other colonial cities quickly followed Boston, either dumping tea or burning it. Such actions confirmed for the British that Massachussets was the bastion of resistance to their legitimate power over the colonies. In response, in 1774 an angry Parliament passed a series of acts, called the Coercive Acts (the colonists labeled them the Intolerable Acts), designed to punish the rebellious colony.

communicate with other towns about this challenge; Samuel Adams and other radicals assume control of the Boston committee.

Rhode Islanders burn the grounded English schooner *Gaspee*, a customs warship.

1773   In Virginia, the House of Burgesses appoints Patrick Henry, Richard Henry Lee, and Thomas Jefferson, among others, to the just-formed Committee for Intercolonial Correspondence. A year later all other colonies, except conservative Pennsylvania, have formed committees. These become the main channels for sharing information about British actions affecting the colonies, building intercolonial cooperation, and shaping public opinion.

To save the East India Company from bankruptcy, Parliament passes the Tea Act, which gives the company the right to sell tea directly to the colonies, bypassing an export tax but retaining an import tax on the colonies. The colonists protest the unconstitutional tax and the threat of a tea monopoly. In the most dramatic protest, the Boston Tea Party, colonists dressed as Indians dump British tea into Boston Harbor.

As punishment for the Boston Tea Party, Parliament passes the Coercive Acts, which close the city's port pending restitution for the destroyed tea; put the royal governor in charge of all civil officials, virtually annulling the Massachusetts Charter; permit an official who commits a capital offense in the performance of duties to be tried in Britain instead of the colonies; and authorize the quartering of British soldiers in private homes. Together with the Quebec Act, which enlarges the province and gives it a centralized government that preserves the privileges of the Catholic church, the colonists label these the Intolerable Acts.

1774   Delegates from all the colonies except Georgia meet in Philadelphia as the First Continental Congress, where they denounce the Coercive Acts, advise the people to arm, and propose to cut off trade with Britain.

1775   In a speech against British rule, Patrick Henry pronounces, "Give me liberty or give me death."

Paul Revere rides at night to tell colonists that British redcoats are marching to Concord, Massachusetts, to destroy colonial arms supplies. In the first clashes of the American Revolution, minutemen fight the British at Lexington and Concord.

1776   The Declaration of Independence, drafted by Thomas Jefferson, is adopted by Congress and signed by the delegates.

THE SIGNERS OF THE DECLARATION OF INDEPENDENCE

Signer	*Colony*	*Signer*	*Colony*
Adams, John	Massachusetts	Floyd, William	New York
Adams, Samuel	Massachusetts	Franklin, Benjamin	Pennsylvania
Bartlett, Josiah	New Hampshire	Gerry, Elbridge	Massachusetts
Braxton, Carter	Virginia	Gwinnett, Button	Georgia
Carroll, Charles	Maryland	Hall, Lyman	Georgia
Chase, Samuel	Maryland	Hancock, John	Massachusetts
Clark, Abraham	New Jersey	Harrison, Benjamin	Virginia
Clymer, George	Pennsylvania	Hart, John	New Jersey
Ellery, William	Rhode Island	Hewes, Joseph	North Carolina

(continues)

THE SIGNERS OF THE DECLARATION OF INDEPENDENCE (CONT.)

Signer	Colony	Signer	Colony
Heyward, Thomas, Jr.	South Carolina	Penn, John	North Carolina
Hooper, William	North Carolina	Read, George	Delaware
Hopkins, Stephen	Rhode Island	Rodney, Caesar	Delaware
Hopkinson, Francis	New Jersey	Ross, George	Pennsylvania
Huntington, Samuel	Connecticut	Rush, Benjamin	Pennsylvania
Jefferson, Thomas	Virginia	Rutledge, Edward	South Carolina
Lee, Francis Lightfoot	Virginia	Sherman, Roger	Connecticut
Lee, Richard Henry	Virginia	Smith, James	Pennsylvania
Lewis, Francis	New York	Stockton, Richard	New Jersey
Livingston, Philip	New York	Stone, Thomas	Maryland
Lynch, Thomas, Jr.	South Carolina	Taylor, George	Pennsylvania
McKean, Thomas	Delaware	Thornton, Matthew	New Hampshire
Middleton, Arthur	South Carolina	Walton, George	Georgia
Morris, Lewis	New York	Whipple, William	New Hampshire
Morris, Robert	Pennsylvania	Williams, William	Connecticut
Morton, John	Pennsylvania	Wilson, James	Pennsylvania
Nelson, Thomas, Jr.	Virginia	Witherspoon, John	New Jersey
Paca, William	Maryland	Wolcott, Oliver	Connecticut
Paine, Robert Treat	Massachesetts	Wythe, George	Virginia

SIGNIFICANT EVENTS IN THE INTRODUCTION OF SLAVERY INTO THE COLONIES

1441   African slaves are first transported to Portugal.

1518   Spain licenses Portuguese slavers.

1619   Twenty African bound servants disembark from a Dutch ship at Jamestown, Virginia. They probably are the first Africans in the English colonies of America.

1641   The Massachusetts Body of Liberties decrees that "no bond slavery" will exist in the colony, except for captives in a just war.

1661   Colonial statutes in Virginia first recognize the legal existence of slavery.

1662   In Virginia a new law makes slavery hereditary.

1663   In London, the Royal African Company, a slave-trading enterprise, is reincorporated.

1670   Virginia law assumes classifications defining slavery.

A Massachusetts law states that the offspring of slaves can be sold into slavery.

1681   Maryland's assembly decrees that the children of a white woman and black man inherit the status of the mother.

1684   New York laws recognize slavery as a legitimate institution.

1686   By this date South Carolina statutes define slavery in the fashion in which it will be known until 1865.

1688   Quakers in Germantown, Pennsylvania, issue a protest against slavery.

1698   England ends the monopoly of the Royal African Company, allowing independent merchants to engage in the slave trade.

1699   The Spanish open Florida as a refuge for runaway slaves.

TRIANGULAR TRADE

By the 18th century, the Atlantic was a busy place. Merchant ships transported raw materials and manufactured goods—and slaves—in a series of triangles that have come to be known as the Triangular Trade. Its base was West Indian sugar, a staple crop so seductive and labor-intensive that it transformed Europe's taste and economy and enslaved the people of Africa. New England merchants transported raw sugar and molasses up the Atlantic coast for manufacture into rum before transshipping it to Africa. Ships bound for Britain carried the raw materials (naval stores, lumber), agricultural products (tobacco, rice, indigo), and animal products (furs, fish, whale oil) that many British entrepreneurs and manufacturers assumed were the colonies' primary purpose. Manufactured goods went in British and colonial ships back to the colonies and the West Indies, and to Africa, where they were traded for human beings, who then endured the cruel Middle Passage to arrive in the West Indies as slaves.

1705   Virginia enacts a comprehensive slave code.

1708   Virginia counts 12,000 slaves in a total population of 30,000.

1712   Following a slave revolt in New York City, nine whites are dead and about 20 African Americans are executed.

1713   The Treaty of Utrecht ending the War of the Spanish Succession gives Great Britain the monopoly on the slave trade. New England shippers thrive on the insatiable demand for slaves in Spanish America, the Caribbean, and Brazil.

1715   Virginia counts 23,000 slaves in a total population of 95,500.

1730-   Pennsylvania declines to allow the importation of slaves.
1750

1731   New York restricts the number of slaves at a burial to 12 plus the grave digger and pallbearers.

1732   Georgia is founded with the specific proviso that "no Negro slaves" be allowed in the colony. The inhabitants petition the trustees for a reversal of this policy. Slavery is finally allowed in 1750, though slaves had been hired from South Carolina on 100-year leases since 1741.

1739   In South Carolina three slave revolts leave dozens of blacks and whites dead. In one of these revolts, a group of Angolans sack the armory at Stono, killing 30 whites.

1741   In New York City about 30 African Americans are executed for arson.

1756   Virginia has 120,156 slaves in a total population of 293,472.

1758   New Jersey Quakers oppose the importation and sale of slaves.

1767   Delaware requires that a £60 bond be posted for each manumitted slave.

1770   The population for the Thirteen Colonies is 1,688,254 whites and 459,822 blacks, almost all slaves.

1774   The Continental Congress asks that the slave trade be terminated, while Thomas Jefferson calls for the abolition of slavery in "A Summary of the Rights of British America."

1775   In Philadelphia the first antislavery organization, the Pennsylvania Society for the Abolition of Slavery, is formed.

1807   The international slave trade is terminated in the United States.

THE MIDDLE PASSAGE: CROSSING THE ATLANTIC TO SLAVERY

The Middle Passage—that leg of the Triangular Trade that took Africans to the West Indies as slaves—was a six- to eight-week voyage of terror. To pack as many human beings as possible into ships—called "slavers"—designed for this purpose, Africans were chained on shelves less than three feet apart. Sickness and insanity were rampant. So was death; at least one in every six Africans died. But, with an eye to potential profits, slave traders did exercise and feed their cargo. In the 18th century, some 600,000 Africans crossed the Atlantic this way.

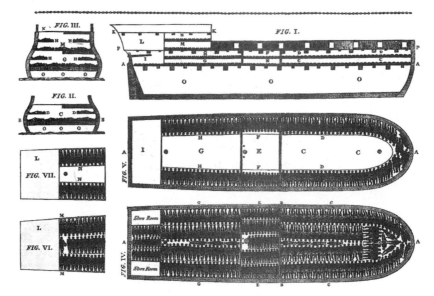

DESCRIPTION OF A SLAVE SHIP.

Drawing of slaveship interior depicting the packing of bodies

SIGNIFICANT PEOPLE IN EXPLORATION, COLONIZATION, AND THE COLONIES

Adams, John (1735–1826).   A Revolutionary leader and the second U.S. president, Adams, a lawyer, entered politics by opposing the Stamp Act. He served as a delegate to the Continental Congress and was a member of the committee that drafted the Declaration of Independence.

Adams, Samuel (1722–1803).   This Revolutionary leader wrote a protest to the Stamp Act, helped found the Non-Importation Association to repeal the Townshend Acts, and drafted the

Circular Letter to the other colonies, in which he argued that the acts constituted taxation without representation. He also formed the Boston Committee of Correspondence, organized the Boston Tea Party, served as a delegate to the First and the Second Continental Congress, and signed the Declaration of Independence.

Bacon, Nathaniel (1647–1676).   Disobeying the orders of Virginia governor William Berkeley, Bacon led expeditions against local Indians. After Berkeley declared him a rebel, in 1676 Bacon organized a popular revolt called Bacon's Rebellion during which Jamestown was captured and burned. In effective control of the colony, Bacon died suddenly, probably of dysentery, and the rebellion collapsed.

Balboa, Vasco Núñez de (c. 1475–1519).   While crossing the Isthmus of Panama, Balboa discovered the Pacific Ocean and claimed it and the lands it touched for Spain. He was unique among the conquistadors for gaining the friendship of the Indians by not displaying cruelty or greediness. Accused and found guilty in Spain of treason as he prepared for a voyage to Peru, Balboa was beheaded.

Boone, Daniel (1734–1820).   This frontiersman traveled through the Cumberland Gap (near where Virginia, Kentucky, and Tennessee meet) and in 1775 led settlers into Kentucky, where he built a fort at Boonesboro. Boone lived in Kentucky until 1799, when he moved into what is now Missouri. Many legends grew up around his exploits.

Cabeza de Vaca, Álvar Núñez (c. 1490–c. 1557).   After surviving a shipwreck off the Texas coast and subsequent slavery by Native Americans, this Spanish explorer and three companions trekked overland from Texas to Mexico. It is believed that they were the first Europeans to see buffalo. Their stories about the Pueblo villages may have been the source of the tales of the legendary Seven Cities of Cíbola, supposed lands rich with gold, silver, and jewels.

Cabot, John (fl. 1461–1498).   An Italian explorer in the service of England, Cabot discovered the North American coast on his first voyage. The fate of his second voyage is unknown. England based its claims to the New World on Cabot's discovery.

Cabot, Sebastian (b. 1483–1486?–d. 1557).   In the service of England, this Italian explorer searched for a northwest passage and in 1509 he may have reached as far north as the Hudson Bay and as far south as North Carolina. Between 1526 and 1530, in the service of Spain, Cabot explored the Rio de la Plata region of South America.

Cartier, Jacques (1491–1557).   A Frenchman, Cartier was the first explorer of the Gulf of Saint Lawrence and the discoverer of the Saint Lawrence River. The French based their claims to the Saint Lawrence valley on his discoveries.

Champlain, Samuel de (1567–1635).   This Frenchman explored the Saint Lawrence River, founded Quebec, and discovered Lake Champlain. He also sailed up the New England coast for three years (1605–1608), discovering Mount Desert Island and most of Maine's big rivers.

Columbus, Christopher (1451–1506).   In the service of Ferdinand and Isabella of Spain, Columbus, an Italian, made four voyages in search of a western route to Asia. Instead of finding this route he sailed to the Caribbean and the West Indies. Columbus is credited as the first European to discover the New World. He died in poverty in Valladolid, Spain.

Coronado, Francisco Vásquez de (c. 1510–1554).   Between 1540 and 1542, Coronado, a Spaniard, explored the American Southwest. He reached the fabled Cíbola, actually the Zuni lands of New Mexico, but found no cities of gold, although his lieutenant, Garcia Lopez de Cardenas, did discover the Grand Canyon. Coronado himself is credited with encountering the Pueblo Indians and opening the Southwest to exploration.

Cortés, Hernando (1485–1547).   Cortés is known as the conquerer of Mexico. He landed on the Mexican coast with 600 armed Spanish troops in 1519 and marched to the Aztec capital at Tenochtitlán (now Mexico City). After the emperor Montezuma welcomed him as a descendant of the god Queztalcoatl, Cortés seized the ruler and used him as a figurehead. The Aztecs rebelled in 1520; Montezuma was killed, but the Spanish had to retreat from Tenochtitlán. The following year Cortés regained the capital after a three-month siege that destroyed the Aztec empire. He conquered most of Mexico before returning to Spain. Cortés's triumph has been attributed to superior arms and horses (the Indians were terrifed of the latter, which they had never before seen), the slow response of the cumbersome Aztec bureaucracy to crisis, and his clever exploitation of the anger of native peoples who lived under Aztec domination.

Dare, Virginia (1587–?).   Dare was the first child born to English parents in America. Her grandfather was the founder of the Roanoke Island colony who left her nine days after her birth when he sailed to England for supplies. In 1591 aid for the colony finally arrived, but all traces of the settlement had disappeared.

De Soto, Hernando (c. 1500–1542).   On a quest for gold, silver, and jewels, De Soto, a Spaniard, explored the American Southeast and discovered the Mississippi River, on whose banks he died. To conceal his death from the Indians, whom he had treated cruelly, De Soto was buried in the Mississippi.

Dickinson, John (1732–1808).   A Philadelphia lawyer, Dickinson was a member of the Stamp Act Congress and the author of the famous *Letters from a Farmer in Pennsylvania to the Inhabitants of the British Colonies* (1767–1768). In 1776 he helped draft the Articles of Confederation but, still hoping for a peaceful solution with England, voted against the Declaration of Independence.

Drake, Sir Francis (1540?–1596).   The first Englishman to circumnavigate the world between 1577 and 1580, Drake sailed possibly as far north as what is now the state of Washington. Then, deciding to cross the Pacific, he repaired his ship north of present-day San Francisco, naming the region Nova Albion and claiming it for Queen Elizabeth I.

Eric the Red (fl. 10th century).   Seeking land west of Iceland, this Norse explorer discovered Greenland. About four years later he returned and with 500 settlers established a colony there. Although it gradually died out, other Viking settlements in Greenland survived.

Ericsson, Leif (fl. 1000).   Son of Norse explorer Eric the Red, Ericsson is probably the discoverer of America. According to a Norse saga, Ericsson sighted the unknown land he named Vinland when he was blown off course during a voyage from Norway to Greenland.

Franklin, Benjamin (1706–1790).   A Renaissance man, Franklin was a printer, writer, philosopher, scientist, and inventor as well as a Revolutionary leader and statesman. In 1727 he founded a discussion club called the Junto, which later became the American Philosophical Society. He also helped create a library for public use, which developed into the Philadelphia Library, contributed to making that city's streets better lit, and served jointly, with William Hunter, as postmaster general for the colonies, 1753–74. A member of the Continental Congress (1775), he served as the first postmaster general for the Congress. He also served on the committee that drafted the Declaration of Independence, which he also signed. In 1776 he was sent by Congress with two others to France to win French recognition of the new republic, which was accomplished in 1778. With John Jay and John Adams, he negotiated peace with England in the Treaty of Paris (1783).

Printer, writer, philosopher, scientist, inventor, statesman, and Revolutionary leader Benjamin Franklin

Frobisher, Sir Martin (1535?–1594).   Backed by merchants, Englishman Frobisher made three voyages along the North American coast in search of a northwest passage. During the first voyage, he entered what is now Frobisher Bay in Canada, returning with an Eskimo as "proof" that he had reached China.

Hancock, John (1737–1793).   The president of the Continental Congress from 1775 to 1777, Hancock, a Massachusetts businessman, was the first signer of the Declaration of Independence.

Hennepin, Louis (1640–1701?).   Hennepin was a Franciscan missionary among the Iroquois before accompanying the French explorer René-Robert Cavelier de Sieur La Salle in his expedition to the Mississippi River valley. Hennepin named the Falls of Saint Anthony, later the site of Minneapolis. His accounts of his explorations, published when he returned to France, are lively and contain the first description of Niagara Falls.

Henry, Patrick (1736–1799).   Henry's speeches in defense of individual liberty, which included the famous "If this be treason, make the most of it" and "Give me liberty or give me death," fueled colonial Revolutionary fire. With fellow Virginians Richard Henry Lee and Thomas Jefferson, Henry, a lawyer and a leader of the so-called radicals, formed the Committee for Intercolonial Correspondence. Elected to the First and Second Continental Congress (1774–1776), he later served as governor of Virginia.

Hooker, Thomas (1586–1647).   Discontent with the strictness of Massachussetts Puritanism, Hooker, a minister, led many of his Cambridge congregation to found Hartford, Connecticut, where he continued as pastor to his followers until his death.

Hudson, Henry (fl. 1607–1611).   Hoping to find a northwest passage for the Dutch East India Company, English navigator Hudson explored in 1609 the Chesapeake Bay, the Delaware Bay, the New York Bay, and the Hudson River, laying the base for Dutch claims to this region. A year later he reached the Hudson Strait and Hudson Bay, which lay between Labrador and Greenland. This exploration enabled England to claim the entire Hudson Bay region.

Hutchinson, Anne (1591–1643).   Hutchinson was convicted and exiled from the Massachusetts Bay Colony for preaching that salvation could be gained through faith rather than through obedience to the laws of church and state. Following her banishment, she and her followers moved first to Rhode Island and then to present-day Pelham Bay Park, New York, where Hutchinson and all but one of her family were killed by Indians.

Jefferson, Thomas (1743–1826).   Before becoming the third U.S. president, Jefferson served in Virginia's House of Burgesses between 1769 and 1775. After forming the Committee for Intercolonial Correspondence with fellow Virginians Richard Henry Lee and Patrick Henry, he wrote the first draft of the Declaration of Independence, presenting it on July 2, 1776, to the Continental Congress, of which he was a member. Jefferson was also one of the signers of the declaration.

Jolliet, Louis (1645–1700).   With French Jesuit priest Jacques Marquette, Frenchman Jolliet discovered the upper Mississippi River and proved that a water highway existed from the Saint Lawrence to the Gulf of Mexico. In 1673 the two descended the Mississippi and concluded that it emptied into the Gulf of Mexico. Ascending the Illinois River in the same year, they came upon the site of what is now Chicago.

La Salle, René-Robert Cavelier de Sieur (1643–1687).   With his lieutenant, Henri de Tonti, Frenchman La Salle explored the Great Lakes in 1679, sailed to Green Bay (in present Wisconsin), and continued on to the Illinois River. Two years later he descended the Mississippi to its mouth, claiming the river's valley, which he called Louisiana, for France. In 1683 he built Fort Saint Louis in Illinois. Four years later he was killed by his men in a mutiny while attempting to reach the mouth of the Mississippi overland from Texas.

Lee, Richard Henry (1732–1794).   As a member of Virginia's House of Burgesses from 1758 to 1775, this Revolutionary patriot defended colonial rights. With Thomas Jefferson and Patrick Henry, he formed the Committee for Intercolonial Correspondence in 1773. A delegate to the Continental Congress from 1774 through 1779, he presented a resolution that resulted in the Declaration of Independence, which he later signed.

Leisler, Jacob (1640–1691).   Leisler and his followers ousted England's New Amsterdam agent in 1689, proclaiming loyalty to England's William and Mary. Leisler ruled the colony until 1691, when he relinquished his power to an appointed governor. He was subsequently convicted of treason and hanged.

Magellan, Ferdinand (c. 1480–1521).   Looking for a route around South America to Asia, Magellan, a Portuguese, commanded the first globe-circling voyage, much of it over unknown parts of the world. After he was killed (1521) in a conflict between Philippine natives, his lieutenant, Juan Sebastian del Cano, completed the more than 50,000-mile voyage in 1522. Besides conclusively proving that the earth was round and the Americas were separate from Asia, the voyage changed views of the proportions of land to water.

Marquette, Jacques (1637–1675).   Marquette, a French explorer and Jesuit missionary, was appointed by Louis Frontenac, governor of New France, to accompany Louis Jolliet in his search for the Mississippi River. In 1673 they descended the Mississippi and concluded that it emptied into the Gulf of Mexico. Next they ascended the river's eastern bank, entered the Illinois River, and came upon the site of present-day Chicago. A journal of the voyage by Marquette was published in 1681.

Oñate, Juan de (fl. 1595–1614).   In three expeditions, Oñate, a Spaniard, explored the American Southwest from the Colorado River to Kansas. His first expedition was to New Mexico, which he claimed for Spain.

Penn, William (1644–1718).   An English religious reformer and colonist, Penn received a charter for Pennsylvania from Charles II in repayment of a debt owed to Penn's father. In 1682 Penn visited his colony, where he made peace with the local Indians and directed the laying out of the city of Philadelphia. Returning to Pennsylvania in 1699, he reestablished peace with the Indians and granted a liberal constitution, the Charter of Liberties, to the colony.

Pocahontas (c. 1595–1617).   Pocahontas was the favorite daughter of Algonquin chief Powhatan. Captain John Smith wrote that she had saved his life after he had been captured by Powhatan's warriors. Modern historians, believe, however, that Smith may have mistaken a religious rite for an execution. Pocahontas was seized by the English in 1613 as a way of making Powhatan cease hostilities against the colonists. Converted to Christianity during her captivity, she married colonist John Rolfe and accompanied him to England, where she was presented to the king and queen. Pocahontas died as she was returning to the New World.

Ponce de León, Juan (c. 1460–1521).   According to legend seeking the Fountain of Youth, Ponce de León, the Spanish governor of Puerto Rico, sailed to Florida. Landing near Saint Augustine, he named the land he had first sighted on Easter Sunday La Florida after the Spanish Easter feast Pascua Florida.

Radisson, Pierre Esprit (1632–1710).   A French explorer and fur trader, Radisson, with his brother-in-law, Medard Chouart, set off from Canada, entered Lake Superior, and went as far west as present-day Minnesota, becoming the first Europeans to venture there, before returning with a rich bounty of furs. Their explorations and the furs they brought back led to the establishment of the Hudson Bay Company.

Rolfe, John (1585–1622).   A Jamestown settler, Rolfe introduced the cultivation of West Indies, Orinoco, tobacco, which had a better taste than varieties native to Virginia. Such a valuable cash crop helped the colony to survive and became the basis for Virginia's prosperity during the colonial era. Rolfe married Pocahontas in 1614. He was probably killed by Indians.

Smith, John (c. 1580–1631).   Smith, an Englishman, helped establish Jamestown, Virginia, and served on the colony's governing council. Captured by the Algonquin Indians, Smith believed that he was about to be executed but was saved by Chief Powhatan's daughter Pocahontas. His version of this event, modern historians suggest, may have been incorrect in that he probably mistook a religious rite for an execution. Afterward Smith explored the areas around the Potomac and Rappahannock rivers and the Chesapeake Bay. He was the leader of Jamestown from 1608 to 1609 and is credited with helping it survive. Smith also explored the New England coast before finally returning to England, where he spent the rest of his life. He wrote several accounts of his experiences in the New World.

Tonti, Henri de (1650–1704).   Selected by René-Robert Cavelier de Sieur La Salle to be his lieutenant at Fort Niagara, Tonti built the first sailboat ever to be used on the Great Lakes. He then went ahead of La Salle to Detroit, where he established good relations with the Illinois Indians. The two men joined forces to travel down to the mouth of the Mississippi River, claiming the surrounding region for France.

Verrazzano, Giovanni da (c. 1480–1527?).   An Italian navigator in the service of France, Verrazzano voyaged west seeking Asia, and sailed into New York Bay in 1524.

Vespucci, Amerigo (1454–1512).   An Italian navigator, Vespucci helped outfit vessels for the third and the fourth voyages of Christopher Columbus. In 1507 German mapmaker Martin Waldseemüller named the New World America after Vespucci, in honor of his exploration of the mouths of the Amazon in 1499 and the Rio de la Plata in 1501, as well as his exploration of the northern and southern coasts of South America.

Williams, Roger (1603?–1683).   Williams, a pastor in Plymouth, Massachusetts, believed in religious toleration. He was the first to propose complete freedom of conscience. When the Massachusetts General Court banished him from the colony for his criticism of the local authorities, he and his followers founded Providence, the first Rhode Island settlement. There Williams formed good relations with the local Narragansett Indians. Williams served as president of the colony for three terms, 1654–1657.

Winthrop, John (1588–1649).   One of the original Salem, Massachusetts, colonists, Winthrop was elected the first governor of the Massachusetts Bay Colony. He served again in 1631, 1632, 1633, 1637–1640, 1642–1644, and 1646–1649. Winthrop presided over the trial of Anne Hutchinson, which resulted in her banishment from Massachusetts. In 1643 he helped establish the United Colonies of New England, serving as the confederation's first president. Three volumes of his journal, including *The History of New England from 1630 to 1649*, were published posthumously.

ADDITIONAL SOURCES OF INFORMATION

Bailyn, Bernard. *The Ideological Origins of the American Revolution*. Belknap Press, 1967.

Bannon, John Francis. *The Spanish Borderlands Frontier, 1513–1821*. University of New Mexico Press, 1970.

Boorstin, Daniel J. *The Americans: The Colonial Experience*. Random House, 1958.

Crane, Verner W. *The Southern Frontier, 1670–1732*. 1928; reprint, Norton, 1981.

Crosby, Alfred. *The Columbian Exchange: Biological and Cultural Consequences of 1492*. Greenwood, 1972.

Eccles, W. J. *The Canadian Frontier, 1534–1821*. Rev. ed. University of New Mexico Press, 1983.

———. *France in America*. Harper & Row, 1972.

Gibson, Charles. *Spain in America*. Harper & Row, 1966.

Goetzmann, William. *Exploration and Empire: The Explorer and the Scientist in the Winning of the American West*. Norton, 1966.

Goetzmann, W., and G. Williams. *The Atlas of North American Exploration*. Prentice Hall, 1992.

Hofstadter, Richard H. *America at 1750: A Social History*. Knopf, 1971.

Kammen, Michael. *Colonial New York: A History*. Scribner's, 1975.

Miller, Perry. *Errand into the Wilderness*. Belknap Press, 1956.

Morgan, Edmund S. *American Slavery, American Freedom: The Ordeal of Colonial Virginia*. Norton, 1975.

———. *The Birth of the Republic, 1763–1789*. Rev. ed. University of Chicago Press, 1977.

———. *The Puritan Dilemma: The Story of John Winthrop*. Little, Brown, 1958.

Morgan, Edmund S., and Helen M. Morgan. *The Stamp Act Crisis: Prologue to Revolution*. Macmillan, 1983.

Morison, Samuel Eliot. *The European Discovery of America: The Northern Voyages, A.D. 500–1600*. Oxford University Press, 1971.

Parry, John H. *The Spanish Seaborne Empire*. Knopf, 1966.

Peckham, Howard H. *The Colonial Wars, 1689–1762*. University of Chicago Press, 1964.

Quinn, David Beers. *Set Fair for Roanoke: Voyages and Colonies, 1584–1606*. University of North Carolina Press, 1985.

Tate, Thad W., and David L. Ammerman, eds. *The Chesapeake in the Seventeenth Century: Essays on Anglo-American Society and Politics*. University of North Carolina Press, 1979.

Weber, David J. *The Spanish Frontier in North America*. Yale University Press, 1992.

3

Territorial Expansion

SIGNIFICANT EVENTS IN WESTWARD AND TERRITORIAL EXPANSION

Westward expansion began with the very first movement of European settlers inland from the Atlantic Coast. As colonists from Plymouth and Massachusetts Bay moved west into what would be Connecticut and the leaders of Massachusetts Bay annexed towns in what would be New Hampshire and Maine, they were engaging in a territorial expansion that would be repeated in a multitude of ways and places over the next three centuries. From tiny coastal settlements a nation grew to encompass a continent and far-flung islands. Abundant resources and an advancing frontier marked the American character, unless the perspective is that of the indigenous peoples, who experienced only continuing encroachment and knew only broken promises.

1749   The Ohio Company receives a royal charter and an enormous land grant for the area along the forks of the Ohio River (where the Monongahela and Allegheny Rivers join, now Pittsburgh).

1754-   During the French and Indian War both France and Britain attempt to secure the west by
1763   building forts. Their forces clash repeatedly, while fierce Indian raids signify that no European claim to these lands can be secure.

1763   Britain wins the French and Indian War, and by the Treaty of Paris all French claims in North America except the two small islands of St. Pierre and Miquelon pass to Britain.

        The Proclamation of 1763 forbids British settlement west of the Appalachian Mountains to reserve an Indian territory and deflate tension.

1767   Daniel Boone makes his first trip to Kentucky.

1774   Parliament passes the Quebec Act, organizing land west of the Appalachians and south to the Ohio River into a new province of Quebec, thus violating colonial charters.

WESTERN LANDS

Most colonial charters granted rights to land "from sea to sea." Only Pennsylvania, New Jersey, Delaware, Maryland, New Hampshire, and Rhode Island had no western lands. Britain's disregard for colonial claims angered the colonists before the Revolution, and during the Revolution states with western lands promised land bounties to veterans. Fearing domination by the large states in the new confederation, Maryland announced in 1778 that it would not ratify the Articles of Confederation until all western lands were ceded to Congress. By 1781 all states had promised to comply, and Maryland signed the Articles, completing ratification. By 1802 all western land claims were finally settled and western lands had become the public domain.

1776-   On his third voyage to the Pacific, Englishman James Cook explores the northwest coast of
1779   North America and becomes the first white person to set foot on Hawaii.

1781   The Articles of Confederation are finally ratified only when states with claims to western lands agree to give them up.

1783   By the Treaty of Paris, ending the Revolutionary War, Britain cedes its empire in North America to the new United States, retaining only Canada (which the colonists had hoped would join them in rebellion). Indian lands are considered a prize of war.

1785   The Land Ordinance provides for the survey and sale of public lands.

1787   The Northwest Ordinance provides for the governance of public lands in the Old Northwest Territory, establishing the process by which U.S. territories will qualify for statehood.

Slavery is banned in the Old Northwest Territory, establishing another precedent.

1788   The Constitution of the United States, ratified by nine states, goes into effect. It gives Congress the power to make rules and regulations for the territories of the United States and to admit new states into the Union.

The first lands surveyed under the Land Ordinance Act are made available for sale. Federal troops are brought in to maintain order.

1793   Alexander Mackenzie completes the first overland trek across North America to the Pacific Ocean.

THE RECTANGULAR SURVEY

From the western slopes of the Appalachians to the Pacific coast, lines running due east and west and lines running due north and south intersect every six miles, marking off the United States into townships. Prior to the first surveys in 1785, mandated by the Land Ordinance of that year, property lines ran along waterways, ridgetops, or meandered along tree lines and corners were noted by distinctive trees, springs, or physical features. Over time trees died, decayed, and disappeared, streams shifted course or dried up, and boundaries became difficult to ascertain. Title to a piece of land could be hard to verify, because the same piece of land might be described two different ways; often land had been settled upon before it had been surveyed. Wanting to sell the vast public domain it had acquired when the states ceded their western lands, and recognizing that clear land titles were essential to stability, Congress ordered a rectangular survey of all land in the public domain and required that land be surveyed before it could be sold.

Beginning at the point where Ohio, Pennsylvania, and Virginia (today West Virginia) meet as the Ohio River leaves Pennsylvania, the land was surveyed and divided into townships, each six miles square and consisting of 36 sections, each containing 640 acres or one square mile. The proceeds from the sale of one section in each township went to support public education. Every so often on the way west a correction was made to take into account the curvature of the Earth. Each section of a township was numbered in precisely the same way once the details were worked out in Ohio, and the practice continued as the survey moved west. Each township had its own unique description that could never be confused with any other township. Anyone following the legal description could find the piece of land described; ambiguity was impossible. Following the surveyors, townships marched westward across the continent without respect to any physical feature, creating the pattern of straight roads and rectangular fields that remain a source of amazement as we fly over the vast land west of the Appalachians today.

1803   The Louisiana Purchase more than doubles the size of the country. At 827,192 square miles, this huge parcel of land includes most of today's Great Plains and is the largest single acquisition of land the United States will make.

1803-   In what will become the prototype for western exploratory expeditions, Meriwether Lewis
1806   and William Clark explore the Louisiana Purchase territory to find "the most direct and practical water communication across the continent for purposes of commerce." Jefferson's scientific curiosity makes certain that they will report on all aspects of the peoples they meet and the country through which they pass. Sacajawea, a Shoshone woman married to a French Canadian, is their guide and interpreter.

Bas-relief of the signing of the Louisiana Purchase

1805   Zebulon Pike leads an expedition to find the source of the Mississippi River. He does not find the source but explores the upper Mississippi valley.

1806- Zebulon Pike undertakes a major expedition through the Great Plains and the southern
1807   Rocky Mountains. He pronounces the high western plains he traverses on this trip "incapable of cultivation," a characterization that lasts most of the century.

1807- David Thompson, a Hudson's Bay Company fur trader, crosses the Canadian Rockies, dis-
1810   covers the source of the Columbia, and explores the area of present-day Washington, Idaho, and Montana.

1810   United States takes over West Florida.

1812   Louisiana is admitted to statehood.

       The Missouri Territory is established.

1814- After the Creek War large land concessions are forced on the Choctaws, the Chickasaws,
1820   and the Creeks, opening more new land to white settlement in the Old Southwest.

1815- Their attention no longer diverted by the War of 1812, Americans become even more
1820   interested in settling the western lands. In what is one of the most rapid migrations the nation will ever experience, large numbers of settlers move into the Old Southwest, which will become the states of Alabama and Mississippi. In one decade the population of Alabama grows 16 times and that of Mississippi doubles. Another wave of settlers sweeps into the Northwest Territory.

1817–
1818
While the federal government is negotiating with Spain to obtain parts of present-day Florida, General Andrew Jackson, while fighting the Seminoles, oversteps his order and invades the Florida Territory.

1818
The United States and Britain extend the boundary between the United States and British North America along the 49th parallel, from the Lake of the Woods to the crest of the Rocky Mountains. The Oregon Country, between 42° and 54°40', is occupied jointly.

1819
A national crisis and two years of public debate begin when Missouri applies to enter the Union as a slave state; abolitionists oppose this expansion of slavery.

Stephen Long departs on a two-year, army-supported expedition to explore and map the Great Plains. In part, the federal government plans these expeditions as a show of power to other nations occupying North American territories. He confirms Pike's assessment of the Great Plains.

By treaty with Spain, the United States acquires Florida.

1820
The Missouri Compromise attempts to settle the pressing question of whether slavery will be extended in the new states that will be created out of the Louisiana Purchase: Missouri is admitted as a slave state, and Maine as a free state to maintain the balance of free and slave states in the Senate. Slavery is banned in the Louisiana Territory north of a 36°30' boundary.

1821
Following Mexico's independence from Spain, the Santa Fe Trail is opened. From Independence, Missouri, to Santa Fe—over 800 miles of open desert and Indian Country—the trail makes a lucrative trade possible.

1823
The Monroe Doctrine warns European nations that the Americas are not open to any future colonization and that any such move will be considered as dangerous to the United States. In return, the United States promises to respect existing colonies and to stay out of the internal affairs of European nations.

1824
The fur trade in the West takes shape with the rendezvous system. Eventually the American Fur Company will succeed the Rocky Mountain Fur Company.

1824–
1826
Jedediah Strong Smith reaches South Pass through the Rocky Mountains into the Great Basin and then leads the first overland expedition to southern California.

1825
James Bridger comes upon Utah's Great Salt Lake.

1827
The first volume of *Birds of America* by John James Audubon is published.

1830
A removal policy with roots in the administrations of James Monroe and John Quincy Adams finds full articulation in the Indian Removal Act, which gives the president power to move all Indians west of the Mississippi.

1832–
1835
Benjamin L. E. de Bonneville takes an expedition through the Rocky Mountains to the Columbia River in the Oregon Territory.

1836
Texas declares its independence from Mexico. To put down this "rebellion," 3,000 Mexican troops massacre the 187 men defending the Alamo. Six weeks later Texans crying "Remember the Alamo" are victorious at the battle of San Jacinto.

1837
President Andrew Jackson recognizes the Republic of Texas on his last day in office.

John Deere invents a steel, one-piece plow and moldboard, a much-needed tool for working the heavy, rich sod cutting through the roots of prairie grass of the Midwest and the Great Plains.

Missionaries Marcus and Narcissa Whitman move to the Oregon Territory, where they establish a mission to convert the Cayuse Indians to Christianity and to adopt white ways. In a struggle that repeatedly will be played out in various parts of the West, the Whitmans are insensitive to the culture of the Native Americans, who in turn resist giving up their traditional ways.

1837   A serious economic panic becomes added impetus for westward migration.

1842   The first wagon train reaches the Oregon Country and brings about 120 settlers who establish themselves along the Pacific coast. They are led by Elijah White. The previous year a group led by John Bidwell abandoned its wagons at Fort Hall. In 1843 almost 1,000 persons make the journey.

1843-   John C. Frémont maps the Oregon and the California trails, which cross Indian lands.
1844   Thousands of settlers will follow the trails west before the land boom is over. Frémont's guide is Christopher "Kit" Carson.

1844   Democrat James K. Polk, who runs on a heated expansionist platform that asks for the "re-occupation of Oregon and the re-annexation of Texas," wins the presidency.

Increasingly chauvinistic Americans in Oregon desire American occupation of the entire Oregon Country. British wish to retain the Columbia River.

1845   Journalist John O'Sullivan coins the term *manifest destiny*, which provides a rationale for the taking of western lands by any means possible; overnight it gains popularity with both politicians and the public.

Texas is admitted to the Union.

President Polk asserts U.S. title to Oregon and proposes to divide the Oregon Country along the 49th parallel. The British minister to the United States rejects the offer, whereupon Polk asserts the U.S. claim to the entire Oregon Country using the Monroe Doctrine to strengthen his argument. Internal affairs in Britain require quieting external problems, and Britain agrees to a diplomatic solution.

John C. Frémont mounts his third major expedition, again guided by Kit Carson, this time to California. There he joins the Bear Flag Revolt, named for the logo on the flag.

MANIFEST DESTINY

In 1776 when Thomas Paine wrote, "We have it in our power to begin the world again," Americans were already trying to figure out their place in the world order and were increasingly convinced that theirs was a special destiny. But not until the mid-19th century did this thinking take action.

Not surprisingly, this special fate even got a name, when John L. O'Sullivan, an editor at *United States Magazine and Democratic Review*, wrote in 1845 that it was "the fulfillment of our manifest destiny to overspread the continent allotted by Providence for the free development of our yearly expanding millions." "Manifest destiny" started out as the campaign rhetoric of the Democratic party and ended up the rallying cry of a nation.

O'Sullivan was speaking of the annexation of Texas, but once expounded, the idea encompassed the continent. Americans quickly adapted to the idea that it was their natural right to annex the Oregon Country, California, Mexican lands in the Southwest, Alaska, Hawaii, and, over and over again, the lands of Native Americans. Manifest destiny was used to justify the proposed annexation of Cuba, and it played a role in the Mexican and the Spanish-American wars. Vestiges of this idea still influence American foreign policy.

In the late 19th century, Darwinist ideas were appropriated by expansionists, who gave manifest destiny a boost by suggesting that Americans were the fittest nation that had ever existed. Seen in this light, it seemed only right that the United States should set its sights on the Caribbean and the Pacific as well, and indeed once the continent was secured the nation imposed its presence south into Latin America and across into the Pacific.

Eventually, critics of manifest destiny saw the concept for what it was: a rationalization for colonization.

1846-
1848
The United States and Mexico fight the Mexican-American War, which is enormously popular with some Americans and criticized by others. When the U.S. Army reaches southern California, it discovers the region has already been claimed by the leader of the Bear Flag Revolt. When the war ends, Mexico cedes California and New Mexico, which includes present-day Arizona, Utah, and Nevada, to the United States. In return, the United States pays Mexico $15 million and assumes the claims of Texans against Mexico.

1846
Mormons begin leaving Nauvoo, Illinois, for the West. After wintering along the Missouri River they continue the journey, arriving in the valley of the Great Salt Lake in July 1847. Ultimately about 70,000 Mormons follow this overland trail on foot or in wagons, before the advent of the railroad in 1869.

Under President Polk, the United States signs an agreement with Great Britain to divide the Oregon Country south of the 49th parallel.

The acquisition of the new territory once again raises the question of whether slavery will be expanded. Representative David Wilmot attempts to attach a rider, known as the Wilmot Proviso, to an appropriations bill banning slavery in any territory acquired as a result of the Mexican War. The proviso never passes Congress, but its terms are adopted by the antislavery Free-Soil party, and its successor, the Republican party, to further stir up the issue.

The Donner party, a group of 87 people headed by George and Jacob Donner, sets out in 1846, mostly from Illinois and Iowa, along an untested route across the Sierras. Lost and snowbound, the party splits, with some heading off to look for rescuers. Before help can arrive, some of those who stay behind starve to death, and some of those who do not resort to cannibalism to stay alive. Less than half of the party remains alive by spring, when rescue parties reach them.

1847
When white settlers, ill with measles, stop to recover at the Whitmans' mission, the disease spreads among the Indians, with devastating results. The Cayuse kill Marcus and Narcissa Whitman. White settlers retaliate by waging a war of extermination against the remaining Cayuse.

Horticulturalist Henderson Luelling transports about 1,000 trees and shrubs—about half survive—from Iowa to the Oregon Country; fruit remains a major agricultural product to this day.

1848
In a presidential election in which a third party, the Free-Soilers, plays a major role, Whig candidate Zachary Taylor narrowly defeats Democratic candidate Lewis Cass. Free-Soil candidate Martin Van Buren, though winning no electoral votes, splits the Democratic vote to Taylor's advantage.

Gold is discovered at a mill being built by John Augustus Sutter, born in Baden and considered a Swiss citizen. In 1839 Sutter had arrived in San Francisco and gone on to the junction of the Sacramento and American rivers where he founded a colony, Nueva Helvetia, with the blessing of Mexican authorities.

Mormon farmers begin irrigation in Utah.

1849
San Francisco becomes the primary supply station for the gold rush and, as a result, its population grows from 1,000 to 35,000 in two years. The population of California expands from 93,000 to 380,000 from 1850 to 1860. During this peak year of the gold rush, 50,000 "forty-niners" will pass through Saint Joseph, Missouri, population 3,000.

The first of several cholera epidemics that will fell westbound settlers throughout the 1850s strikes along the Platte River.

Francis Parkman writes *The California and Oregon Trail.*

The Department of the Interior is established, incorporating the General Land Office.

Sutter's Mill, famed site of the discovery of gold in California, which brought on the gold rush of 1849

Secretaries of the Interior

Secretary	President	Year Appointed	Secretary	President	Year Appointed
Thomas Ewing	Taylor	1849	Walter L. Fisher	Taft	1911
Thomas M. T. McKennan	Fillmore	1850	Franklin K. Lane	Wilson	1913
			John B. Payne	Wilson	1920
Alex H. H. Stuart	Fillmore	1850	Albert B. Fall	Harding	1921
Robert McClelland	Pierce	1853	Hubert Work	Harding	1923
Jacob Thompson	Buchanan	1857		Coolidge	1923
Caleb B. Smith	Lincoln	1861	Roy O. West	Coolidge	1929
John P. Usher	Lincoln	1863	Ray Lyman Wilbur	Hoover	1929
	Johnson, A.	1865	Harold L. Ickes	Roosevelt, F. D.	1933
James Harlan	Johnson, A.	1865		Truman	1945
Orville H. Browning	Johnson, A.	1866	Julius A. Krug	Truman	1946
Jacob D. Cox	Grant	1869	Oscar L. Chapman	Truman	1949
Columbus Delano	Grant	1870	Douglas McKay	Eisenhower	1953
Zachariah Chandler	Grant	1875	Fred A. Seaton	Eisenhower	1956
Carl Schurz	Hayes	1877	Stewart L. Udall	Kennedy	1961
Samuel J. Kirkwood	Garfield	1881		Johnson, L. B.	1963
Henry M. Teller	Arthur	1882			
Lucius Q. C. Lamar	Cleveland	1885	Walter J. Hickel	Nixon	1969
William F. Vilas	Cleveland	1888	Rogers C. B. Morton	Nixon	1971
John W. Noble	B. Harrison	1889		Ford	1971
Hoke Smith	Cleveland	1893	Stanley K. Hathaway	Ford	1975
David R. Francis	Cleveland	1896	Thomas S. Kleppe	Ford	1975
Cornelius N. Bliss	McKinley	1897	Cecil D. Andrus	Carter	1977
Ethan A. Hitchcock	McKinley	1898	James G. Watt	Reagan	1981
	Roosevelt, T.	1901	William P. Clark	Reagan	1983
James R. Garfield	Roosevelt, T.	1907	Donald P. Hodel	Reagan	1985
Richard A. Ballinger	Taft	1909	Manuel Lujan	Bush	1989
			Bruce Babbitt	Clinton	1993

| 1850 | The Compromise of 1850, masterminded in large part by Illinois senator Stephen Douglas, but based on the work of John C. Calhoun, Henry Clay, and Daniel Webster, is another attempt to resolve North-South tensions over extending slavery. Under its terms, California is admitted as a free state, the borders of Texas are defined, the slave trade is ended in the District of Columbia, and the Fugitive Slave Act of 1850 is passed. Increasingly a line is drawn between the North and the South in an already sectionalized country. |

Mid-1850s   The gold rush is over, with the suppliers, for the most part, having gotten richer than the seekers. Its draw has turned the United States into a continental country.

1852   Wells, Fargo & Co., a name synonymous with the West, is founded in New York City to ship "Gold Dust, Bullion, Specie, Packages, Parcels and Freight all kinds" between the two coasts.

1853   The Gadsden Purchase adds 29,670 square miles to the western section of the country and costs the federal government $10 million, which is paid to Mexico. It comprises present-day southern Arizona and extreme southwestern New Mexico.

1854   Hoping to build a transcontinental railroad with its terminus in Chicago, the Illinois senator Stephen Douglas proposes to divide Indian Territory, opening all areas above Oklahoma to white settlement. Rather than extend the 36°30' boundary of the Missouri Compromise, Douglas promotes the idea of popular sovereignty as a means of determining whether slavery will be permitted in a state. The cost to the nation is enormous: Indians are robbed of their land; the Whig Party is destroyed in the ensuing national debate over slavery; northern Democrats lose two-thirds of their seats, giving control of their party to southerners; and Kansas, which Douglas himself did not believe would be a slave state, becomes a bloody battleground, suffering rioting, massacres, looting, and lynchings before the issue is settled.

Railroads now reach as far west as the Mississippi.

The city of Omaha is founded.

1855   In the struggle to control Kansas, actions so divide people that the state in effect ends up with two governments and two constitutions. The Free-Soilers, who oppose slavery, hold forth in Topeka, while the proslavery forces operate from Pawnee and Shawnee Mission.

1856   In one shocking week in May, proslavery guerrilla forces destroy Lawrence, Kansas, an abolitionist stronghold. Abolitionist John Brown and his followers retaliate along the Pottawatomie Creek, brutally killing five proslavery persons. Open warfare continues through the summer.

1857   The Supreme Court's *Dred Scott* decision establishes that Congress has no authority to restrict slavery in the territories.

1857-
1858   President James Buchanan proposes to admit Kansas with its Lecompton Constitution, a proslavery frame of government. Congressional opposition demands a statewide referendum in which the document is overwhelmingly defeated. Kansas does not achieve statehood until 1861.

1858   Denver is founded in the Kansas Territory, which will one day be the state of Colorado.

Another gold rush begins in Colorado. Miners pour into the state; their motto: "Pikes Peak or bust."

1859   Oregon becomes a state.

The first telegraph message is transmitted between Washington, D.C., and San Francisco, putting the Pony Express—founded a year earlier and operating between Saint Joseph, Missouri, and Sacramento, California—out of business.

1863   The Idaho Territory is formed out of parts of present-day Nebraska, Utah, and Washington.

A new gold rush occurs at Alder Gulch, Idaho.

1864   Montana Territory is formed out of Idaho Territory.

Abolitionist John Brown

1866   Cattle are driven along the Chisholm Trail for the first time. Before it is closed down in the late 1880s, millions of head of cattle will have made the "long drive" between San Antonio and the shipping center of Abilene, Kansas.

THE EXODUSTERS: AFRICAN AMERICANS IN KANSAS

In 1877 Reconstruction ended and conservative whites returned to power throughout the South. African Americans, fearing that their new freedoms might be in jeopardy, turned to the West as a haven from mounting social and political repression. Already in the years immediately after 1865 a few black colonies had been established in Kansas. Life, though hard, was an improvement over what the former slaves had known.

Railroad promoters and land speculators were ready to lure even more migrants. In 1879 alone more than 20,000 African Americans left the South for Kansas. These migrants, known as the Exodusters, created the first, but hardly the last, significant migration of the black population.

The huge numbers of new settlers pouring into Kansas strained charitable and government resources, but some Kansans—those with racist leanings—also were not happy with this influx of African Americans. By 1880 black migration to Kansas had slowed to a trickle once again as word of difficulties in Kansas became known in the South. During the exodus, several black communities were established and still exist today. Nicodemus was named a National Historic Site in 1996.

WAGONS WEST: SAILING ACROSS THE PRAIRIE

Settlers streamed west on steamboats, trains, horses, stagecoaches, and foot, but the most significant mode of transportation—the one that became the symbol of westward migration—was the prairie schooner. Named because their white-covered tops seemed to float like graceful sails through the tall prairie grass, these wagons were more properly called Conestogas, after the town in Pennsylvania where they were originally built. The Conestoga that transported people west, though, was a variation on the original wagon, with shallower sides and a flat floor.

Covered wagons preparing to head west

Although they were sturdy, there was nothing comfortable about prairie schooners. They offered no heat on chilly nights, no ventilation on warm ones, no windows, and no privacy, but their great advantage was that they were big enough to hold the essential tools and household items to start over in a new land and food to make the journey. What they lacked in comfort, they made up for in reliability. Their wide, flat wheels were ideal for cutting through the prairie, whether it was drenched with spring rains or dry and hard as rock.

Prairie schooners, which were pulled by horses or oxen, traveled in wagon trains that sometimes stretched out for four or five miles. The heyday of the wagon train was the 1840s, and during the gold rush more than 12,000 wagons were counted crossing the Mississippi at just one spot. By the 1870s railroads were commonplace, and wagon trains had disappeared from the western landscape.

1869   The building of the transcontinental railroad is completed. More than 300,000 people have traveled west via wagon train along the California and Oregon trails.

1870s   Good well-drilling machinery and windmills pull water up from aquifers on the high plains.

1874   The first barbed wire is sold. This cheap and practical fencing will put an end to cattle drives and the indiscriminate use of land.

1879   The United States Geological Survey is established to monitor the nation's water and mineral resources, to study and evaluate the surface of the land, to collect geologic and geographic information, and to prepare topographic maps.

1890   The Bureau of the Census announces the closing of the American frontier. The United States can no longer be divided into settled and unsettled lands.

Continental Expansion

Territory	Date	How Acquired	Amount of Land	Present Status
Original Territory	1783	Treaty with Great Britain	888,811 square miles	Maine, New Hampshire, Vermont, Massachusetts, Rhode Island, Connecticut, New York, New Jersey, Pennsylvania, Maryland, West Virginia, Virginia, North Carolina, Georgia, Tennessee, Kentucky, Ohio, Michigan, Wisconsin, Illinois, Indiana, and part of Minnesota, Alabama, and Mississippi
Louisiana Purchase	1803	Purchase from France for $15 million	827,192 square miles	Louisiana, Arkansas, Missouri, Nebraska, Iowa, South Dakota, North Dakota, and part of Minnesota, Montana, Colorado, Kansas, Wyoming, and Oklahoma
Florida	1819	Treaty with Spain	71,993 square miles	Florida and part of Alabama and Mississippi
Texas	1845	Annexation; Texas Republic had won independence from Mexico in 1836	390,144 square miles	Texas and part of New Mexico, Oklahoma, Colorado, and Wyoming
Oregon Cession	1846	Treaty with Great Britain	285,580 square miles	Washington, Oregon, Idaho, and part of Montana and Wyoming
Mexican Cession	1848	Treaty with Mexico following victory in Mexican War and payment of $15 million	529,017 square miles	California, Nevada, Utah, and part of Wyoming, Colorado, New Mexico, and Arizona
Gadsden Purchase	1853	Purchase from Mexico for $15 million (later reduced to $10 million)	29,640 square miles	Part of New Mexico and Arizona

Overseas Expansion

Territory	Date	How Acquired	Amount of Land	Present Status
Alaska	1867	Purchase from Russia for $7.2 million	589,757 square miles	State since 1959
Midway Islands	1867	Annexation	2 square miles	Territory
Wake Island	1898	Annexation	3 square miles	Territory
Palmyra	1898	Annexation	4 square miles	Territory
Hawaii	1898	Annexation of independent kingdom	6,423 square miles	State since 1959
Philippine Islands	1898	Treaty with Spain, following U.S. victory in Spanish-American War and payment of $20 million	115,600 square miles	Independent since 1946
Puerto Rico	1898	Treaty with Spain, following U.S. victory in Spanish-American War	3,435 square miles	Self-governing commonwealth

Territory	Date	How Acquired	Amount of Land	Present Status
Guam	1898	Treaty with Spain following U.S. victory in Spanish-American War	206 square miles	Territory
American Samoa	1900	Treaty with Germany and Great Britain, which with the United States had administered Samoa as a protectorate after 1889, and by treaty with Samoan chiefs, with whom treaties had been negotiated for the use of harbors since 1872	76 square miles	Territory
Canal Zone	1904	Treaty with Panama (which had just broken away from Colombia and declared its independence, recognized by the United States three days later), the United States agreeing to pay $10 million and a $250,000 annual fee	553 square miles	Full sovereignty to be restored to Panama by 2000
U.S. Virgin Islands	1917	Purchase from Denmark for $25 million	133 square miles	Territory
Pacific Island Trust Territories (Mariannas, Carolines, Marshall Islands)	1947	Trusteeship agreement with the United Nations (former Japanese mandates)	716 square miles	Administering authority of United Nations' trusteeship

Empire-Building, 1865–1940

1866   In the aftermath of the Civil War, the export market booms, more than tripling between 1866 and 1900.

1867   When Alaska is purchased from Russia for $7.2 million, it is jokingly referred to as Seward's Icebox or Seward's Folly, after Secretary of State William Henry Seward, who promoted the purchase.

The United States annexes Midway, a central Pacific island.

1875   The United States expands its commercial interests, especially sugar, in Hawaii.

1881   Secretary of State James Blaine issues invitations to a hemispheric conference. Blaine's successor, Frederick Frelinghuysen, withdraws the invitations, 1882.

1884   Secretary of State Frederick Frelinghuysen in defiance of the Clayton-Bulwer Treaty (the United States and Great Britain had promised to cooperate on any isthmian canal, 1850) negotiates a treaty of alliance and of possible construction of a canal. Incoming President Grover Cleveland withdraws it from the Senate.

1890   Alfred Thayer Mahan publishes *The Influence of Sea Power upon History, 1660–1783*. His belief that controlling the seas enables a state to conduct an effective foreign policy influences Theodore Roosevelt, who is assistant secretary of the navy, 1897–1898.

1893   In an attempt to outmaneuver the domineering U.S. government, Hawaiian queen Liliuokalani writes a new constitution, granting herself and subsequent Hawaiian rulers additional powers. At the urging of pineapple magnate Sanford B. Dole, marines from a U.S. warship are brought on shore as a show of power. Liliuokalani is deposed, and the United States installs a protectorate government without Hawaii's consent. President Grover Cleveland is urged to annex Hawaii but resists.

1895- A boundary dispute between Venezuela and British Guiana finds the United States
1897   attempting to give an extreme interpretation of the Monroe Doctrine when Secretary of
       State Richard Olney declares that the Doctrine allows the United States to enter into any
       western hemisphere dispute. In time passions cool when the British agree to arbitration.

1896   Congress passes a resolution in favor of Cuban rebels fighting against Spanish rule.

1898   In the first action of the Spanish-American War (war declared by Spain April 24, by the
       United States April 25 but retroactive to April 21), the U.S. fleet sails into Manila Bay
       and defeats the Spanish fleet in a few hours. By mid-August Spanish forces throughout the
       Philippines surrender. In Cuba the war lasts ten weeks. On August 12 an armistice goes
       into effect and the Treaty of Paris is signed December 10.

       Spain grants independence to Cuba and cedes Guam and Puerto Rico to the United States.
       The United States pays Spain $20 million for the Philippines. What little organized oppo-
       sition there is to U.S. colonialism takes shape in the form of the Anti-Imperialist League
       with roots in Chicago and Boston.

       After 50 years of increasing economic involvement, Hawaii is annexed by joint resolution.
       Japan, with 25,000 nationals living there and its own ambitions for empire, had hoped to
       derail American plans.

1899- The Anti-Imperialist League, with many respected figures among its membership, has little
1901   influence over U.S. expansionist policies.

1900   The United States annexes Samoa in the south-central Pacific Ocean.

Construction of the Panama Canal

1901　The Platt Amendment further undermines Cuba's autonomy by insisting that it provide land for U.S. bases, sign no treaty that is against U.S. interests, and permit the United States to intervene any time it becomes necessary to protect U.S. interests.

1903-　The United States expedites the building of the Panama Canal with what comes to be
1904　called "gunboat diplomacy." Under the Hay-Bunau-Varilla Treaty, the United States agrees to lease a six-mile strip on either side of the canal in exchange for $10 million plus annual payments of $250,000.

1917　Because they are strategically located near the Panama Canal, the United States buys the Danish West Indies, which include Saint John, Saint Thomas, Saint Croix, and about 50 smaller islands, for $25 million.

1947　The United States begins administering the Trust Territory of the Pacific Islands (the Marianas, the Carolines, and the Marshall Islands) in the west-central Pacific, thus completing the chain of way stations to Asia that it began to acquire in 1867.

SUPREME COURT DECISIONS AFFECTING WESTWARD EXPANSION

1823　*Johnson v. McIntosh.* In a decision that will aid white settlement of western lands, the Supreme Court rejects the validity of land titles granted to individuals by Indians.

1857　*Dred Scott v. Sandford.* In one of its most controversial decisions, the Court asserts that Dred Scott, a slave who has sued for his freedom because his owner had taken him to a free state, is not a citizen and therefore has no standing to sue in the federal courts. Moreover, slaves are classified as property, and the federal government cannot interfere with the rights of private property. Thus the federal government cannot prohibit slavery in the territories, and the Missouri Compromise is overturned as unconstitutional.

1901　*Insular Cases.* The Court rules that Puerto Rico, recently annexed by the United States, is neither a foreign country nor a state with constitutional protection. Congress must decide whether the Constitution should apply to particular territories.

1903　*Lone Wolf v. Hitchcock.* The Court rejects a plea that tribal lands were taken without due process, thus putting its seal of approval on white ownership of western lands.

ACTS OF CONGRESS AFFECTING WESTWARD EXPANSION

1785　Land Ordinance. This plan for developing the western lands, one of the major achievements of the Confederation government, is created in part by Thomas Jefferson. The territories will be surveyed, subdivided into 36-square-mile townships, then sold.

1787　Northwest Ordinance. This act imposes federal authority in the Northwest Territory and sets forth the protocol for creating states. Initially, a governor, secretary, and three judges are appointed by Congress to govern. When the free adult male population reaches 5,000, an elected territorial legislature is formed and the territory can send a nonvoting delegate to Congress. When the adult male population reaches 60,000, a territory is eligible to apply for statehood. No fewer than three and no more than five states are to be carved out of the territory.

States Admitted to the Union

State	Date	State	Date
1. Delaware	Dec. 7, 1787	26. Michigan	Jan. 26, 1837
2. Pennsylvania	Dec. 12, 1787	27. Florida	Mar. 3, 1845
3. New Jersey	Dec. 18, 1787	28. Texas	Dec. 29, 1845
4. Georgia	Jan. 2, 1788	29. Iowa	Dec. 28, 1846
5. Connecticut	Jan. 9, 1788	30. Wisconsin	May 29, 1848
6. Massachusetts	Feb. 6, 1788	31. California	Sept. 9, 1850
7. Maryland	April 28, 1788	32. Minnesota	May 11, 1858
8. South Carolina	May 23, 1788	33. Oregon	Feb. 14, 1859
9. New Hampshire	June 21, 1788	34. Kansas	Jan. 29, 1861
10. Virginia	June 26, 1788	35. West Virginia	June 19, 1863
11. New York	July 26, 1788	36. Nevada	Oct. 31, 1864
12. North Carolina	Nov. 21, 1788	37. Nebraska	Mar. 1, 1867
13. Rhode Island	May 29, 1790	38. Colorado	Aug. 1, 1876
14. Vermont	Mar. 4, 1791	39. North Dakota	Nov. 2, 1889
15. Kentucky	June 1, 1792	40. South Dakota	Nov. 2, 1889
16. Tennessee	June 1, 1796	41. Montana	Nov. 8, 1889
17. Ohio	Feb. 19, 1803	42. Washington	Nov. 11, 1889
18. Louisiana	Apr. 30, 1812	43. Idaho	July 3, 1890
19. Indiana	Dec. 11, 1816	44. Wyoming	July 10, 1890
20. Mississippi	Dec. 10, 1817	45. Utah	Jan. 4, 1896
21. Illinois	Dec. 3, 1818	46. Oklahoma	Nov. 16, 1907
22. Alabama	Dec. 14, 1819	47. New Mexico	Jan. 6, 1912
23. Maine	Mar. 15, 1820	48. Arizona	Feb. 14, 1912
24. Missouri	Aug. 10, 1821	49. Alaska	Jan. 3, 1959
25. Arkansas	June 15, 1836	50. Hawaii	Aug. 21, 1959

1790   Southwest Ordinance. This act organizes the Southwest Territory on similar principles but permits slavery.

1820   Missouri Compromise. Temporarily and awkwardly solving the problem of free versus slave states in the territories, the Compromise permits Maine to enter the Union as a free state and Missouri to enter as a slave state and forbids slavery in the Louisiana Purchase north of 36°30' latitude.

1830   Indian Removal Act. This creates an Indian Country (later known as Indian Territory) west of Missouri and Arkansas, and appropriates funds for the resettlement there of southeastern Indian tribes (Cherokees, Chickasaws, Choctaws, Creeks, and Seminoles).

1850   Compromise of 1850. This is another attempt to resolve North-South tensions over the extension of slavery. California is admitted as a free state; territorial governments for Utah and New Mexico are organized without mention of slavery; Texas borders are settled and the federal government assumes Texan debts incurred before statehood; the slave trade is forbidden in the District of Columbia; and a more stringent fugitive slave law is enacted.

1854   Kansas-Nebraska Act. This act, proposed by Stephen A. Douglas, opens Kansas, in Indian Territory, to white settlement and applies Douglas's principle of popular sovereignty by permitting territorial voters to decide whether to permit slavery. Although ostensibly leaving the question open, Douglas did not believe Kansas would choose slavery—and could not have foreseen the guerrilla warfare that would break out after the act was passed.

1862   Homestead Act. This act offered any head of household (including widows and single men) 160 acres of the public domain by registering the claim, making some improvement on the land within six months, and living on it for five years.

The Morrill Act authorizes grants of land to support state schools teaching agriculture or the mechanical arts.

1871 The Indian Appropriations Act. Bolstering white settlement on Indian lands, this act terminates the treaty process between Native Americans and the federal government over land rights and provides that tribal affairs can be managed by the federal government without tribal consent.

1873 Timber Culture Act. Designed to encourage the planting of trees and thereby improve the climate and soil on the prairie and plains, this act grants homesteaders an additional 160 acres of land for every 40 acres of trees they plant. Because settlers are not required to reside on this land, land speculators use this act (as well as the Homestead Act) to their advantage, often buying up the best land and then reselling it to settlers. Trees do not solve the dry conditions of the high plains, and the act is repealed in 1891.

1877 Desert Land Act. This permits homesteaders to buy 640 acres at $1.25 per acre, with the obligation that they would irrigate the land within three years.

TEXAS: THE STRUGGLE FOR INDEPENDENCE AND STATEHOOD

Texas is the only state to have been an independent republic, then annexed by the United States.

pre-1682 Apaches, Comanches, and other Indian tribes live in present-day Texas.

1682 The Spanish arrive, claiming Texas as part of Mexico. The first settlement is at Yselta, near present-day El Paso.

1718 The Spanish begin establishing missions, including San Antonio.

1744 A fort-cum-chapel named the Alamo, which means "cottonwood," is built at San Antonio.

1821 The first Anglo settlers arrive in Texas, led by Stephen F. Austin, a Missourian.

1820s Austin's settlements prosper, and by 1830 Americans in Texas outnumber Mexicans two to one.

1826-
1827 In the Fredonia Rebellion, two American settlers attempt to break away from Mexico and establish "Fredonia," but, lacking Austin's support, the effort collapses at the approach of Mexican troops. The incident draws attention to the conflict of cultures in Texas and raises American interest in the area.

1829 Newly elected Mexican president Vicente Guerrero abolishes slavery in Mexico, including the province of Texas, and levies new taxes.

1830 Texans seek to exempt Texas from the antislavery decree. Mexico responds by banning any further colonization by Americans and any additional importation of slaves, and by sending troops.

1833 Stephen Austin travels to Mexico City to present American grievances and ask that Texas be a separate state. He is imprisoned.

1835 Fighting breaks out between Americans and Texans in Gonzales.

1836 On March 2, Texas declares its independence. But Mexican troops are already besieging the Alamo, and on March 6 the fort is overrun. Davy Crockett, Jim Bowie, and William Travis are among the 187 defenders who are killed, inspiring the battle cry, "Remember the Alamo!"

Sam Houston retaliates and, at the decisive battle of San Jacinto on April 21, overcomes a larger Mexican force. Mexican president Antonio López de Santa Anna is taken prisoner, and the Mexican army is routed. The Lone Star flag is raised as Texas declares itself a republic. Sam Houston becomes its first president (and serves again from 1841 to 1844).

1837   On his last day in office, President Andrew Jackson formally recognizes the Republic of Texas.

Texas petitions for annexation to the United States, but the opposition of antislavery forces embroils Texas in the slavery issue, and the Republic of Texas sets an independent course.

1842   The Mexicans invade Texas, hoping to regain the territory. A truce is negotiated the next year, as the question of the United States' annexation of Texas is reopened.

1845   Over the protests of Mexico, Texas is annexed by the United States, becoming the 28th state and the 15th slave state.

THE LONG RIDE: ALONG THE CHISHOLM TRAIL

Much emphasis is placed on the routes settlers took west, but traffic soon developed in the other direction as well—and it usually meant business for the expanding West. One of the most lucrative western enterprises was supplying the East Coast with beefsteak, but for many years this was also a challenging prospect since the only way to transport the cattle was to drive them along the legendary Chisholm Trail.

1866   A trapper named Jesse Chisholm cuts a permanent trail between San Antonio, Texas, and Abilene, Kansas, when he takes a load of buffalo skins west. Later the same year cattle are driven from Texas to the railhead—a feat that is possible in part because there are not any fences yet.

1867   Entrepreneur Joseph McCoy buys 450 acres in Abilene, a "small, dead place" by one description, and immediately sets to work building pens and loading chutes out of raw lumber. Ranchers hire drovers and begin sending cattle from San Antonio, where the long drive originated, to Abilene, the major shipping point.

In early fall the first shipment of 20 cars of cattle departs for the East. By year's end, more than 350,000 head of cattle have been shipped east out of Abilene.

1871   Congress charters the Texas Pacific Railroad to build into the heart of Texas cattle country.

1879   By this date more than 4 million cattle have traveled the Chisholm Trail.

1880s   When the trunk rail lines are extended south into Texas, trail driving comes to an end. Cow country and the Chisholm Trail become relics. Today, it is mostly grown over, although its tracks can still be seen in a few places.

CONSERVATION

Conservation was not an idea that occurred to the first Europeans who came to North America. Here was good land and plenty of it, free for the taking. If land gave out—as it did when intensively farmed for tobacco—more land farther west could be cleared and the old fields abandoned. Little matter, too, that the land already had inhabitants; they were unschooled, uncivilized heathens who could be pushed aside if they did not relinquish their titles—a concept unknown to Native Americans—in a manner that was acceptable to the new inhabitants. Forests, which were unlike those people had known in Europe, seemed inexhaustible; new growth would replace anything that was cut. Not until late in the 19th century did a few writers begin to raise disturbing questions about how the land was used and about how the original inhabitants had been treated. Though lands had been withdrawn from the public domain to preserve thermal springs in Hot Springs, Arkansas, to preserve Yosemite Valley in California, and to create the first national park at Yellowstone in Wyoming, the land's intrinsic value was not the reason. They were simply seen as having no commercial or mineral value, and the whims of those who advocated preservation could be indulged.

Gradually, however, attitudes began to change as Americans came to realize that some agricultural practices caused more abuse to the land than others; that the mighty forests were indeed finite; that stripping the lands of the virgin stands of trees had adverse effects on water quality and caused erosion; and that the demands of a rapidly growing population sometimes outran water supplies, especially in the West. A few farsighted individuals began stressing forest management rather than harvesting, and others called for preservation of the battlegrounds of the Civil War and historic places from the early days of the republic. Advocates of crop rotation and contour plowing promised better yields, cleaner water, and less erosion. At the end of the 20th century, we now know that population growth and pesticides can destroy the land, water, and air that the people of 1790 took for granted. Attempting to manage land in the public interest while respecting the rights of individual property owners is proving a critical test of democratic government.

1832	Four sections of land are withdrawn from the public domain to protect the hot springs of Arkansas "for the future disposal of the United States."
	The artist George Catlin, traveling up the Missouri River, keeps a journal in which he proposes the large stretches of the Great Plains be turned into "a nation's Park" to preserve the buffalo, the Plains Indians, and the landscape. His writings are later published as *Letters and Notes on the Manners, Customs, and Conditions of the North American Indians* (1841).
1849-1862	In his writings, published in these years, Henry David Thoreau provides the intellectual foundation of the environmental movement.
1856	Frederick Law Olmsted begins the work of developing and planning New York City's Central Park, a determined effort to provide and preserve parklands for the use of city dwellers.
1858	The Mount Vernon Ladies' Association of the Union purchases the home of George Washington to protect it from falling into decay.
1864	The federal government transfers Yosemite Valley and the Mariposa Big Tree Grove to the state of California on the condition that these lands remain "inalienable for all time."
	George Perkins Marsh publishes *Man and Nature; or, Physical Geography as Modified by Human Action*. His ringing indictment of the effect of deforestation on water quality is the beginning of the conservation movement.
1869	One-armed John Wesley Powell leads an expedition down the Colorado River. His party is the first to pass through the Grand Canyon. His studies and observations are published in 1878 as the *Report of the Lands of the Arid Region of the United States*. In 1881 Powell becomes director of the Geological Survey.
1872	The world's first national park, Yellowstone, is created by act of Congress.
1877-1881	Carl Schurz serves as secretary of the interior and advocates a responsible policy of forest management and replanting.
1885	New York State establishes the Adirondack Forest Preserve, later renamed Adirondack State Park.
1891	The Forest Reserve Act authorizes the president to proclaim forest reserves out of the public domain; in 1907 these reserves are renamed national forests.
1892	John Muir founds the Sierra Club, one of today's premier conservation organizations.
1893	Gifford Pinchot is named chief of the Division of Forestry, later to become the United States Forest Service, in the Department of Agriculture.

1902   The Newlands Reclamation Act devises a scheme whereby public lands in arid portions of the country could be made available for sale if they were "reclaimed" by irrigation. The Bureau of Reclamation is also established.

1903   President Theodore Roosevelt signs legislation creating the National Wildlife Refuge System. Initially the system was established to protect birds whose plumage was in great demand for women's hats. Today the Fish and Wildlife Service manages more than 500 areas throughout the country where habitats for birds, marine animals, fish, and land mammals are protected.

1905   William Dutcher incorporates several state organizations into the National Audubon Society.

1906   The Antiquities Act authorizes the president to proclaim as national monuments "historic landmarks, historic and prehistoric structures, and other objects of historic or scientific interest." The first national monument is Wyoming's Devils Tower, prominently featured in the movie *Close Encounters of the Third Kind*. In 1978 President Jimmy Carter uses this authority to proclaim 15 new and two expanded national monuments in Alaska that total more than 30 million acres.

1908   President Theodore Roosevelt invites a distinguished gathering of national leaders and the state governors to the White House to discuss the various conservation issues confronting the country.

1913   Hetch Hetchy Valley within Yosemite National Park is dammed to provide drinking water for San Francisco. The dispute over this use pits a specific local need against a greater national need.

1916   The National Park Service is established, with Stephen T. Mather as its first director.

1920   Visitors to 43 units of the National Park System, consisting of 8,560,760 acres, total 1,058,455.

1921   Benton MacKaye proposes in an article that an Appalachian trail be laid out along the mountain crests from Maine to Georgia. MacKaye later becomes one of the founders of the Wilderness Society.

1926   The restoration of Colonial Williamsburg begins, financed by John D. Rockefeller, Jr., at the urging of the rector of Bruton Parish Church in Williamsburg. This is the laboratory where the work of historic preservation comes of age. Wallace Nutting's work on historic architecture and household furnishings also contributes to this movement.

Shenandoah (Virginia) and Great Smoky Mountains (Tennessee and North Carolina) national parks are created. With Acadia National Park (Maine), created seven years earlier, these are the first national parks east of the Mississippi, created to make the park system truly national.

1930   Visitors to 55 units of the National Park System, consisting of 10,339,507 acres, total 3,246,656.

1933   The Civilian Conservation Corps is one of many New Deal programs to give jobs to out-of-work Americans. This small army of young men builds roads, bridges, culverts, trails, cabins, and entrance stations and lays water and sewage lines. At its peak there are 118 CCC camps in national parks and 482 camps in state parks. All told, more than 120,000 young men participate in the program.

Congress creates the Tennessee Valley Authority (TVA), an ambitious regional planning effort. Basically, the TVA is responsible for flood control, navigation on the Tennessee River and its tributaries, and the production of electricity. But it has become a model for dealing with an entire river basin in ways that go far beyond its basic environmental concerns.

1934-
1937 Drought strikes the high plains of Texas, Oklahoma, Kansas, and Colorado, creating a "dust bowl" in this semi-arid region in the midst of the Great Depression.

1935 The Wilderness Society is organized, with Benton MacKaye and Robert Marshall among its founders. Marshall, an independently wealthy Forest Service employee, argues for the protection of wilderness.

1940 Visitors to the 161 units of the National Park System, consisting of 21,550,783 acres, total 16,755,251.

1949 Aldo Leopold's *Sand County Almanac* is published posthumously. Leopold is one of the first modern writers to go beyond an appreciation of nature and consider human beings and all the plants and animals as part of one great whole. He attracts interest with his advocacy of wildlife management.

1950 Visitors to the 182 units of the National Park System, consisting of 24,597,613 acres, total 33,252,589.

1956 Plans for the Echo Park Dam on the Green River inside Dinosaur National Monument in northeastern Utah are permanently scrapped, ensuring that a Hetch Hetchy situation will not be repeated.

1960 Visitors to the 187 units of the National Park System, totaling 26,193,774 acres, total 80,039,100.

1962 Rachel Carson publishes *Silent Spring*.

1963 The Clean Air Act becomes law with the assignment of monitoring smog, acid rain, automobile emissions, and toxic aid pollutants. Initially it is administered by the Public Health Service and later by the Environmental Protection Agency.

1964 The Wilderness Act, authored by Howard Zahniser, executive secretary of the Wilderness Society, is enacted into law. It proposes to preserve into perpetuity, with the approval of Congress, those pieces of land of at least 5,000 acres in extent that are "untrammeled by man, where man himself is a visitor who does not remain."

1970 The Environmental Protection Agency is created and begins work to monitor the nation's environmental health.

Visitors to the 281 units of the National Park System, consisting of 29,620,444 acres, total 172,004,600.

1978 The New York State Commissioner of Health decrees the Love Canal area outside Niagara Falls to be a "threat to human health and the environment." From 1942 to 1953 Hooker Chemical disposes of more than 44 million pounds of toxic wastes (sludges, solvents, ash, pesticide residue) in this area. In 1954 an elementary school is built on the site; a playground operates here until 1978. The outcry over conditions at Love Canal leads to the establishment of the EPA's Superfund to clean up toxic waste dumps.

1979 A near meltdown in a nuclear reactor at Three Mile Island near Harrisburg, Pennsylvania, gives new fuel to those wishing to severely limit the construction of nuclear power plants.

1980 Visitors to the 333 units of the National Park System, consisting of 77,440,418 acres, total 190,185,155.

1989 The Exxon *Valdez* founders and spills 11.2 million gallons of crude oil into Prince William Sound in Alaska. One of the largest oil spills in North America, it damages more than 730 miles of coastline.

1990 Visitors to the 357 units of the National Park System, consisting of 80,155,984 acres, total 258,682,828.

SIGNIFICANT PEOPLE IN THE WESTWARD EXPANSION

Audubon, John James (1785–1851).   Born in Santo Domingo, Audubon began observing and studying birds on his family's estate near Philadelphia. His famous *Birds of America*, published from 1827 to 1838, reflected his studies and travels from 1810 to 1824 in the Ohio and Mississippi valleys, where he made sketches and took specimens. His drawings, still impressive today, exemplify the scientific interest some Americans took in the country's expanding territories.

Austin, Stephen Fuller (1793–1836).   Called the Father of Texas, Austin took over his father's plans to establish the first Anglo settlement in Texas. Named San Felipe de Austin, the community soon drew 8,000 white settlers. Austin was active in the Texas Revolution and later served as secretary of state in the Texas Republic.

Benton, Thomas Hart (1782–1858).   As an influential Democratic politician who represented Missouri in both the House and the Senate, he worked hard to settle the West and keep the territories free of slavery.

Blaine, James Gillespie (1830–1893).   As secretary of state (1881; 1889–1892), this Maine Republican was actively involved in developing U.S. interests in Latin America, including building a canal on the isthmus between Central and South America. He also worked on Alaskan, Canadian, and Hawaiian relations and called the first Pan-American conference. Although the best-known political figure of his time—having served in both the House and the Senate—he lost in his bid for the presidency in 1884.

Boone, Daniel (1734–1820).   Legendary in his own time, this frontiersman mounted several expeditions into the unsettled Kentucky Territory and blazed the Wilderness Trail, which homesteaders later used to move into this region. In the 1760s, when his land titles in Kentucky proved to be invalid, he migrated to Missouri.

Bowie, James (c. 1795–1836).   Inventor of the Bowie knife, which was widely used on the frontier, Bowie was one of the commanders of the Alamo and died in the battle that led to the liberation of Texas.

Bridger, James (1804–1881).   A fur trader, Bridger accompanied Jedediah Smith on many of his treks and is credited with discovering the Great Salt Lake.

Brown, John (1800–1859).   An abolitionist most remembered for his 1859 raid on a government arsenal at Harpers Ferry, Brown was deeply involved in the territorial struggle in Kansas, which centered around the issue of slavery. By 1855 he controlled the Free-Soil militia in the territory, and in retaliation for the Lawrence Massacre in 1856, he and his sons are believed to have brutally murdered five settlers along the Pottawatomie Creek.

Bryan, William Jennings (1860–1925).   This three-time Democratic presidential candidate was known in part for his anti-imperialist efforts and for his insistence on the free coinage of silver.

Carson, Christopher "Kit" (1809–1868).   Born in Kentucky and reared in Missouri, Carson traveled as a youth to the far western frontier and made it his home. He served as guide on the expeditions of John C. Frémont and distinguished himself as a Union general during the Civil War.

Carson, Rachel (1907–1964).   A writer and marine biologist, Carson is best known for her book *Silent Spring* (1962), which demonstrated the devastating effect of agricultural chemicals and insecticides on wildlife. Eggshells full of DDT residue are incapable of supporting the weight of the mother bird during incubation and of protecting the chick until ready for birth. With declining songbirds—only one of many manifestations—some future springtime will be silent. Her book raised a storm of protest, especially from chemical companies and agricultural interests. But independent tests confirmed her work, and many insecticides have since been banned.

Catlin, George (1796–1872). Catlin is known for his moving and dignified portraits of American Indians. He lived among the Indians in the Southeast, Old Northwest, and Great Plains. His work was published in books, the best known of which is *Letters and Notes on the Manners, Customs, and Conditions of the North American Indians* (1841).

Clark, William (1770–1838). An army officer, Clark was selected by his friend Meriwether Lewis to lead an expedition exploring the Louisiana Purchase. His observations of nature contributed to the expedition's success, and his records of the journey rendered in his maps and journals proved invaluable. His oldest brother was George Rogers Clark, a Revolutionary War hero.

Clay, Henry (1777–1852). Serving in both the House and the Senate, Clay, known as the Great Compromiser, presided over the Missouri Compromise and the Compromise of 1850, both of which, while failing to outlaw slavery in the territories, at least served to stave off the Civil War. Clay was one of the founders of the Whig party, and also served as John Quincy Adams's secretary of state.

Crockett, Davy (1786–1836). Crockett, a frontiersman who served in the Tennessee legislature and the U.S. House of Representatives, then went to Texas to fight in the Revolution and died at the Alamo. He was also known for his folksy humor, and several books were written under his name, although historians are not convinced of his authorship.

Douglas, Stephen (1813–1861). Although best remembered for debating Abraham Lincoln, as a Democrat Douglas played a significant role during the westward expansion in the controversy over slavery in the territories. He sponsored the Kansas-Nebraska Act, which replaced the Missouri Compromise, and promoted the idea of popular sovereignty, in which territorial settlers would decide for themselves whether to permit slavery once they joined the Union. Douglas did not foresee the bloody guerrilla war that would break out as a result of the Kansas-Nebraska Act, ruining his political future. In 1860 he and two other candidates were defeated by Abraham Lincoln in a bid for the presidency.

Frémont, John Charles (1813–1890). An American explorer and general, Frémont mapped the overland trails to Oregon and California (1843 and 1844). The first presidential candidate of the newly formed Republican party, Frémont was defeated in 1856 by the Democratic candidate, James Buchanan.

Houston, Sam (1793–1863). A popular fighter in Andrew Jackson's Indian campaigns, Houston was sent to the House of Representatives by his home state of Tennessee. He was elected governor in 1827 but resigned when his very short-lived first marriage dissolved. He moved to Indian Territory and lived among the Cherokees, whom he knew and revered from his childhood in Tennessee. He adopted Cherokee citizenship. Houston headed the Revolutionary Army during the Texas Revolution and became the first president of the Republic of Texas, later serving in the post a second time. He was also senator and governor, but he lost favor (and the governorship) when he opposed secession at the time of the Civil War.

Jackson, Andrew (1767–1845). Old Hickory, as this president (1829–1837) was affectionately known, was, among many other things, a great promoter of western settlement. He fought ruthlessly against Native Americans and favored their relocation, which partly explained his popularity among the Anglo settlers.

James, Jesse (1847–1882).   In a land famous for its lawlessness, James might best be described as the prototypical desperado. A Confederate sympathizer during the Civil War, he joined the proslavery guerrillas led by William Quantrill but reserved most of his energy for robbing banks, trains, and stagecoaches. He and his brother Frank formed their own gang, and Jesse was killed by one of its members for the reward.

Jefferson, Thomas (1743–1826).   As president, Jefferson brought about the Louisiana Purchase in 1803. During his administration both the Lewis and Clark expedition and the exploration of Zebulon Pike took place.

Lewis, Meriwether (1774–1809).   This former army officer led an expedition, with William Clark, to explore the Louisiana Purchase. Lewis was President Thomas Jefferson's secretary when Jefferson chose him to explore a land route to the Pacific. In 1807 he was appointed governor of the Louisiana Territory. As inept a politician as he was a brilliant explorer, he began to fall into ever deeper depressions. In 1809 he died under mysterious circumstances, now judged to have been a suicide.

Long, Stephen Harriman (1784–1864).   An army engineer, he was best known for his expeditions to the upper Mississippi and, in 1820, the Rocky Mountains. Long's Peak is named after him. Later, as a surveyor for the Baltimore and Ohio railroad route, he compiled an authoritative topographical manual.

Mackenzie, Alexander (c. 1763–1820).   Scottish-born Mackenzie went to Canada as a fur trader. Eventually he became a partner in the North West Company. In 1789 he led an expedition to the Arctic Ocean, and in 1793 he guided a party across northern Canada to the Pacific, completing the first transcontinental journey north of Mexico.

Muir, John (1838–1914).   Born in Scotland, Muir immigrated to the United States in 1849 and eventually settled in California. A naturalist, he traveled throughout the country, often on foot, arguing that scenic beauty was a value in itself and advocating conservation measures and the establishment of national parks.

Oakley, Annie (1860–1926).   Although countless anonymous women helped to settle and build the West, figures like Oakley, whose forte was her ability to shoot a playing card in half from 90 feet, loom larger in the American imagination. Oakley, whose life was immortalized in the Broadway musical *Annie Get Your Gun*, traveled for nearly two decades with Buffalo Bill's Wild West Show.

THE WOMEN OF THE WEST

Although most women who migrated west with their husbands have remained anonymous figures, virtually all played an important role in building their families' new lives. To be successful a farmer or rancher needed a wife. Western women, in turn, often used this power to make their marriages more egalitarian than those of their counterparts back East. Pioneer women had many activities that went far beyond simply supporting their men.

A woman's first big task was to turn whatever awaited her arrival into a home. This was no small achievement in living quarters that ranged from the dirty, leaky, mud-brick "soddy" cabins to cavelike dugouts built into the sides of hills to, at their most sophisticated, one-room, dirt-floor log cabins. Rugs were made from buffalo or cow hides, and flour sacks or greased paper were put up in windows until glass could be ordered. Trunks were converted into tables, and chairs were carved out of barrels.

Unlike the East, where there were many social constraints on women, the West offered women the opportunity to participate as much as they liked, and many women went to work alongside their husbands, plowing, planting, and harvesting.

In addition there were the jobs considered "women's work." Around the farm or ranchwomen were often in charge of rearing the heifers, lambs, and other livestock, managing a flock of chickens, milking the family cow, and tending the vegetable garden and fruit trees.

Women were responsible for the family's food. They rose early to bake biscuits and churn butter, two staples of the western diet, and they learned to make do with less when the wheat crop failed and there was no flour. They did the skinning and the butchering, the salting, curing, and sausage-making. They brought in the daily supply of water, which often meant a walk of a mile or two to the nearest creek before a well could be dug. Many women supplied the family's fuel, no easy task on the treeless prairie. They collected twigs, hay, cornstalks, corncobs, and buffalo chips for this purpose.

Women were also in charge of providing the family's clothing, and when they weren't consumed with other chores, they made and remade, mended, knitted, and embroidered. Where cloth was unavailable, they sheared and spun and wove as well. Without benefit of sewing machines, animal skins were turned into leather coats, hats, and shoes.

Long before women were admitted to medical schools, pioneer women were nurses, midwives, and doctors. Sometimes they even had to doctor themselves. One Kansas woman had to deliver her own baby when she was left alone, except for an infant and a four-year-old, for the day. When she realized she was in labor, she calmly drew fresh water, made sandwiches to sustain herself, put out milk for her two children, and set out clothes for the baby. At noon she gave birth to a baby, whom she cared for alone until her husband returned at sunset.

Women not only worked hard, but they worked in isolation. It was not only at such important times as childbirth that women lacked the comfort and companionship of other women, but all the time, since farms and ranches were far apart.

Parkman, Francis (1823–1893).   The eminent historian of his era, Parkman wrote vividly about the opening of the West in his book *The California and Oregon Trail* (1849), about his experiences living with the Sioux in *History of the Conspiracy of Pontiac* (1851), and about the struggle between the French and the British for North America in his masterful *France and England in North America* (1865–1892).

Pike, Zebulon (1779–1813)   Supported by the army, Pike explored the Rocky Mountains and Spanish New Mexico in a major expedition mounted in 1806–1807. In 1810 he published *An Account of Expeditions to the Sources of the Mississippi and through the Western Parts of Louisiana.*

Pinchot, Gifford (1865–1946).   Pinchot, chief of the Division of Forestry in the Department of Agriculture, was the first American to have chosen forestry as a career. After schooling in France and work on George Vanderbilt's estate in North Carolina, Pinchot promoted his belief that forests, if managed wisely, could be as profitable and enduring as any cash crop.

Polk, James (1795–1849).   The first "dark horse" ever to win the presidency (1845), Polk campaigned on a prowestern platform. He advocated annexation of Oregon and statehood for California. Polk resolved the dispute over Oregon amicably and led the United States into the Mexican War, which resulted in the annexation of large parts of the Southwest and California.

Powell, John Wesley (1834–1902).   Under the auspices of the Smithsonian Institution and the U.S. Congress, geologist-ethnologist Powell explored the West, specifically the Green and Colorado rivers, and studied and classified many Indian languages. Powell did a great deal of work for the U.S. Bureau of Ethnology; he served as the second director of the U.S. Geological Survey.

Sacajawea (c. 1784–c. 1812).   This Shoshone woman, who was wed to a French Canadian, acted as Lewis and Clark's guide and interpreter on their major 1804–1806 expedition and was the sole woman on the trip.

Smith, Jedediah Strong (1799–1831).   Smith's explorations opened trails and territory for westward-bound pioneers as well as fur trappers and land traders. In 1824 Smith traveled into Montana and north to the Canadian boundary before returning to Great Salt Lake. A year later, in his most famous trek, he journeyed into California to what is now San Diego, crossing the Colorado River and the Mojave Desert along the way. Smith was murdered by Comanches soon after setting out from Saint Louis on the Santa Fe Trail.

Starr, Belle (1848–1889).   Along with Jesse James, Belle Starr, who was born Myra Belle Shirley, was a notorious western outlaw. She also belonged to William Quantrill's gang and during the Civil War supplied information to Confederate guerrilla forces regarding the location of Union troops. She died of gunshot wounds.

Taylor, Zachary (1784–1850).   A popular general during the Mexican War, he was president only 15 months (1849–1850) before succumbing to cholera. Taylor worked to ban slavery in the western territories and for rapid admission of California and New Mexico to statehood.

Travis, William (1809–1836).   As co-commander of the Alamo, he died there during the Texas Revolution. Travis also fought in the Battle of San Antonio.

Turner, Frederick Jackson (1861–1932).   Turner, a historian, originated the highly influential "frontier thesis," also called the "Turner thesis," which held that the development of the West strengthened American democracy and nationalism as well as forging character traits that distinguished Americans from Europeans.

THE TURNER THESIS

Historian Frederick Jackson Turner (1861–1932) believed that the opening of the West was the seminal event in American history and that it, more than any other single factor, shaped the national character and institutions. It was, in fact, responsible for the much-touted image of Americans as individualistic, adventurous, gregarious, and democratic.

Raised on the frontier and educated at the University of Wisconsin and Johns Hopkins, where he obtained his Ph.D., Turner initially studied the then-popular view, known as the "germ thesis," which held that American customs and character were rooted in German tribalism. Eventually he rejected this idea to develop his own theory. In his charismatic speaking manner, he presented his theory in a paper entitled "The Significance of the Frontier in American History," which he read in 1893 at an American Historical Association meeting. Within ten years Turner's view was taught in every U.S. history course and abroad as well. If it had served no other purpose, it would at least have been important for inspiring Americans to look within themselves rather than to Europe for their roots.

American historians have long debated the Turner Thesis. It has come under recent attack for its bias in describing the experience of white Americans and overlooking Native Americans and Hispanics. Still, it has had a pervasive influence in defining the American spirit.

Vérendrye, Pierre Gaultier de Varennes, Sieur de la (1685–1749).   A French Canadian, Vérendrye began to explore the American West in 1731. He sent two of his sons to explore the lands beyond the Missouri River, which led them to the Dakotas, western Minnesota, and possibly part of Montana.

Whitman, Marcus (1802–1847).   Accompanied by his wife, Narcissa Prentiss Whitman, Whitman went west to convert and teach the Indians in his Christian mission. The Whitmans were also energetic recruiters of other settlers. Their missionizing effort failed when, seeking revenge for the epidemic of diseases spread by white settlers, the Cayuse killed the Whitmans.

ADDITIONAL SOURCES OF INFORMATION

Billington, Ray A. *The Frontier Thesis.* Krieger, 1977.

———. *Westward to the Pacific: An Overview of America's Westward Expansion.* University of Washington Press, 1979.

Cronon, William, George Miles, and Jay Gitlin, eds. *Under an Open Sky: Rethinking America's Western Past.* Norton, 1992.

Faragher, John Mack. *Women and Men on the Overland Trail.* Yale University Press, 1979.

Goetzmann, William H. *The West of the Imagination.* Norton, 1986.

Horsman, Reginald. *The Frontier in the Formative Years, 1783–1815.* Holt, Reinhart and Winston, 1970.

Jeffrey, Julie Roy. *Frontier Women: The Trans-Mississippi West, 1840–1880.* Hill & Wang, 1979.

LaFeber, Walter. *The New Empire: An Interpretation of American Expansion, 1860–1898.* Cornell University Press, 1963.

Lamar, Howard R., ed. *The Reader's Encyclopedia of the American West.* Norton, 1987.

Limerick, Patricia N. *The Legacy of Conquest: The Unbroken Past of the American West.* Norton, 1987.

Nash, Roderick. *Wilderness and the American Mind.* 3rd rev. ed. Yale University Press, 1982.

Philbrick, Francis S. *The Rise of the West, 1754–1830.* Harper & Row, 1965.

Smith, Henry Nash. *Virgin Land: The American West as Symbol and Myth.* Harvard University Press, 1950.

Starr, Kevin. *Americans and the California Dream, 1850–1915.* Oxford University Press, 1973.

Stratton, Joanna L. *Pioneer Women: Voices from the Kansas Frontier.* Simon & Schuster, 1981.

Turner, Frederick Jackson. *The Frontier in American History.* University of Arizona Press, 1920; repr. 1985.

White, Richard. *It's Your Misfortune and None of My Own: A History of the American West.* University of Oklahoma Press, 1991.

4

Immigration and Minorities

Since its beginnings, America has been a nation of immigrants. For nearly 100 years after the Revolution, immigration was virtually unrestricted. However, not all immigration was the result of choice. By 1820, the first census in which reliable figures are available, approximately 17 percent of the 9.6 million Americans were slaves.

Although each wave of immigrants renewed American society, making it culturally diverse and vital, immigration has also been a source of controversy, mainly because of concerns about whether great numbers of newcomers could fit into the society without in some way tearing it apart. One prevailing fear has been that the newcomers would take away jobs from other Americans. To this day, even though many Americans are aware of their own immigrant roots and know the benefits of a culture made up of many minorities, the struggle over immigration continues.

SIGNIFICANT EVENTS IN IMMIGRATION AND MINORITY LIFE

1564 French Huguenots establish Fort Caroline on the Saint Johns River in Florida.

1565 Spanish soldiers build a fort at Saint Augustine and defeat the French at Fort Caroline.

1607 English settlers found Jamestown.

1609 The Spanish establish Santa Fe.

1619 A Dutch ship transports 20 black African bound servants to Jamestown; they are probably the first African Americans in the English colonies.

Two forms of immigration, voluntary and forced: the Mayflower *(reproduction, left) and a slave ship (right)*

1620 Plymouth Colony on Cape Cod, Massachusetts, is founded by 102 English Pilgrims.

1624 The Dutch establish New Netherland, which will soon include New Amsterdam (present-day New York City).

1628 English Puritans settle at Naumkeag, which they rename Salem, on Massachusetts Bay.

1630 John Winthrop and other members of the Massachusetts Bay Company found Boston, initiating the "Great Migration" of English Puritans to Massachusetts and Connecticut. About 20,000 English men and women will settle in New England in the next 15 years.

1633   The Dutch build a trading post near present-day Hartford.

1634   Under a grant from Charles I to the Calvert family, the Lords Baltimore, English men and women settle Saint Mary's, which will become the colony of Maryland. The Calverts will encourage both Roman Catholic and Protestant settlement, making Maryland the only English colony in North America with a large Catholic minority.

1636   Banished from Salem, dissenting minister Roger Williams founds Providence, Rhode Island.

            Puritan minister Thomas Hooker, escaping the strict religious rule of Massachusetts, founds Hartford, Connecticut.

1638   Swedish and Finnish settlers establish Fort Christina (present-day Wilmington), Delaware.

            Banished from Massachusetts for her religious beliefs, Anne Hutchinson, with her followers, founds present-day Portsmouth, Rhode Island.

            Puritans found New Haven.

1641   The Massachusetts Body of Liberties decrees that "no bond slavery" will exist in the colony.

1649   Maryland passes an Act for Religious Toleration.

1650   Scottish royalists, taken as prisoners of war by Oliver Cromwell, are shipped to Boston.

1654   Jewish immigrants from Brazil arrive in New Amsterdam. They are not allowed to worship in public or have a synagogue.

1658   Jews arrive in Rhode Island, attracted by the colony's religious freedom.

1661   Colonial statutes in Virginia first recognize the legal existence of slavery.

1662   In Virginia a new slave law makes slavery hereditary.

1664   It is reported that 18 different languages are spoken in New Amsterdam, where the population includes not only Dutch but Walloons, Swedes, English people, French people, and Germans. In this year, British forces annex New Amsterdam and rename it New York.

1668   The French establish a fur-trading post and a Jesuit mission at Sault Sainte Marie, on the waterway between Lakes Superior and Huron.

1670   Virginia law assumes classifications defining slavery.

            English settlers found Charles Town (later Charleston) in the Carolinas.

            A Massachusetts law states that the offspring of slaves can be sold into slavery.

1677   French Huguenots settle New Paltz, New York.

1680   French Huguenots settle near Charles Town and give the English settlement there momentum.

1681   England's Charles II grants Quaker William Penn an immense tract of land that becomes Pennsylvania. Penn and other Quakers purchase East Jersey.

            Maryland's assembly decrees that the children of a white woman and a black man inherit the status of the mother.

1682   The French establish the first white settlement in Arkansas.

            Early settlers in Pennsylvania include groups of Welsh and Irish, as well as Quakers from England, the Rhineland, and the lower Palatinate.

1683   German Mennonites found Germantown, Pennsylvania.

1684   New York laws recognize slavery as a legitimate institution.

1686   Following the repeal of the Edict of Nantes in 1685, French Huguenots settle in Rhode Island, Massachusetts, Maine, New York, Pennsylvania, Virginia, and South Carolina.

1688   German Quakers in Germantown declare that slavery is contrary to Christian principles.

1689   An unfavorable religious and political climate in Britain prompts increasing numbers of Scots and Scots-Irish to leave Scotland and Ireland for America.

1699   Old Biloxi (today Ocean Springs, Mississippi) is the first permanent settlement in French Louisiana.

The Spanish open Florida as a refuge for runaway slaves.

1700   English and Welsh settlers make up 80 percent of the population in the British colonies, Africans 11 percent, the Dutch 4 percent, Scots 3 percent, and other ethnic groups 2 percent. Of the African population, some 27,817 are slaves, with about 22,600 of them in the southern colonies.

French colonists build a fort at Detroit.

1705   Virginia enacts a comprehensive slave code.

1708   Virginia counts 12,000 slaves in a total population of 30,000.

1710   Germans, many from the Palatinate, begin to immigrate in large numbers, settling in North Carolina and along the Hudson River in New York.

1712   In New York City a slave revolt ends in the execution of about 20 blacks.

1714–1720   A mass exodus of Scots and Scots-Irish begins, following failed revolts in Scotland and increased rents in Ireland. Many settle in the back country from Pennsylvania south to Georgia.

1715   Virginia counts 23,000 slaves in a total population of 95,500.

1716   To defend themselves from a possible French threat in Louisiana, the Spanish begin to establish missions in Texas.

1718   French settlers found New Orleans, Louisiana.

San Antonio is founded by Spanish Franciscans.

1730–1750   Pennsylvania declines to allow the importation of slaves.

1730   In New York, Jews establish Congregation Shearith Israel and open a synagogue.

1731   New York restricts the number of slaves at a burial to 12 plus the grave digger and pallbearers.

1732   French families incorporate Vincennes on Indiana's Wabash River at a site known to fur traders and a post since 1702.

Georgia is founded with the specific proviso that "no Negro slaves" be allowed in the colony. The white inhabitants petition the trustees for a reversal of this policy. Slavery is finally allowed in 1750, though slaves have been hired from South Carolina on 100-year leases since 1741.

1739   In South Carolina a group of Angolans sack the armory at Stono, killing 30 whites. Two other slave revolts erupt in the colony and are quashed.

1741   In New York City about 30 African Americans are executed for arson.

1753   Moravians settle Wachovia, North Carolina, today part of the city of Winston-Salem.

1756   Virginia has 120,156 slaves in a population of 293,472.

1758   New Jersey Quakers oppose the importation and sale of slaves.

1763   Touro Synagogue in Newport, Rhode Island—the second synagogue in the colonies—is dedicated.

1767   Delaware requires that a £60 bond be posted for each manumitted slave.

1768   Immigrants from Minorca, Leghorn, and Greece settle New Smyrna, East Florida.

1769   Spanish Franciscans found San Diego. In the next ten years the Spanish establish a string of missions up the California coast.

1770   The population of the Thirteen Colonies is 1,688,254 whites and 459,822 blacks, almost all slaves.

      British troops kill five colonists in the Boston Massacre; one of the victims is Crispus Attucks, whose mother was Indian and whose father was African American.

1774   The Continental Congress calls for the end of the slave trade, while Thomas Jefferson urges the abolition of slavery in "A Summary of the Rights of British America."

1775   In Philadelphia the first antislavery society is formed.

1776   Thomas Jefferson's proposed abolition of slavery is not included in the Declaration of Independence.

      English Shakers found a colony at Watervliet, New York.

      Spanish Franciscans establish San Francisco.

1778   Rhode Island passes an act guaranteeing freedom after the war to any slave who enlists.

1780   Pennsylvania passes a law providing for the gradual emancipation of slaves.

1781   Spanish settlers found Los Angeles.

1783   Virginia legislature says that slave veterans who fought against the British in the Revolutionary War cannot be returned to the condition of slavery.

1784   Rhode Island and Connecticut follow Pennsylvania and pass gradual abolition acts.

1785   The New York Society for Promoting Manumission is founded.

1787   The Constitutional Convention agrees to the three-fifths compromise, whereby for purposes of representation and taxation five slaves are counted as the equivalent of three whites.

      The Northwest Ordinance prohibits slavery in the Northwest Territories.

1788   The Constitution is ratified. One provision guarantees that the importation of slaves cannot be banned for 20 years. Another establishes that slaves escaping to nonslave areas will not be free but must be returned.

      In Philadelphia, Richard Allen and other African Americans establish the Free African Society, withdrawing from the Methodist church.

1790   The first United States Census reveals that less than half the population is English, nearly 20 percent is African, 15 percent is Irish or Scottish, 7 percent German, with the remaining composed of other ethnic groups. Of the 757,208 African Americans, 697,681 are slaves.

      Exiled by the French Revolution, French royalists settle on the Ohio River at Gallipolis.

      Quakers submit the first petition to Congress for the emancipation of slaves.

      Revolution and war in Europe suppress immigration. Fewer than 300,000 newcomers arrive between 1790 and 1820.

1791   African-American astronomer and mathematician Benjamin Banneker helps survey the site of the District of Columbia.

1793   Congress passes the first of several Fugitive Slave Acts, making it illegal to aid runaway slaves or interfere with their arrest.

1795   In Louisiana, 23 slaves are executed after a failed slave revolt.

1798   Congress passes the Alien and Sedition Acts, which extend the residency requirements for citizenship, authorize the president to deport aliens dangerous to the public safety, and in wartime authorize the government to arrest, jail, and remove aliens.

1800   In Virginia, after a plan for a slave revolt led by slave Gabriel Prosser is revealed, Prosser and at least 25 followers are hanged.

      According to the second census, there are 1,002,037 African Americans in the United States, 893,602 of whom are slaves.

1803   With the Louisiana Purchase, the United States gains 43,000 people, primarily French. Only 6,000 describe themselves as Americans.

1807   Congress prohibits importation of African slaves as of January 1, 1808. This is the earliest date the Constitution will allow.

1810   The third U.S. Census counts more than 7.2 million Americans, including 1,377,808 African Americans; 1,191,362 are slaves.

1811   Near New Orleans, U.S. army troops and state militia put down a rebellion by several hundred slaves.

1817   The American Colonization Society is founded; its goal is to resettle freed blacks in Africa. By 1860 it will have resettled about 12,000 blacks, mostly in Liberia.

1819   Congress passes the first immigration law, ordering ship captains to prepare passenger lists in an effort to improve conditions on the Atlantic crossing and decrease mortality.

Some 3,000 Irish contract laborers arrive to help build the Erie Canal.

1820s   Following the conclusion of the Napoleonic Wars in Europe, immigration begins to rise. During the decade 150,000 immigrants enter the United States, mostly from Ireland, Germany, England, and Scandinavia. Many are escaping starvation in their native lands; others are attracted by the possibility of religious and political freedom or greater economic opportunity.

1820   In the Missouri Compromise, Congress admits Missouri to the Union as a slave state but declares all parts of the Louisiana Purchase territory north of 36°30' latitude, Missouri's southern boundary, forever free.

1821   In West Africa, the American Colonization Society establishes Liberia as a refuge for ex-slaves.

Benjamin Lundy founds *The Genius of Universal Emancipation*, one of the first abolitionist journals.

1822   In Charleston, South Carolina, former black slave Denmark Vesey plans a slave rebellion; the conspiracy is discovered, and Vesey and 34 others are hanged.

1825   A small group of Scandinavians settle in western New York. Later, hundreds of thousands will come to America, many settling in the Midwest and northern plains.

1826   In Tennessee, the Nashoba community is established to train blacks for resettlement outside the United States.

Pennsylvania passes a personal liberty law, prohibiting forceful seizure and removal of fugitive slaves.

1827   In New York City, John Russwurm and Samuel Cornish begin publishing *Freedom's Journal*, the first newspaper owned by African Americans.

1829   African American David Walker publishes *Appeal to the Colored Citizens of the World*, calling for a slave insurrection; the pamphlet is banned in the South.

1830s   Six hundred thousand Europeans immigrate to the United States.

1830   The fifth United States Census counts 12.9 million Americans. The first count in Florida following its acquisition from Spain in 1819 reports 18,000 whites and 16,000 blacks, almost all slaves.

A failed revolution in Germany results in an influx of German immigrants into the United States.

1831   In Virginia, black slave and preacher Nat Turner leads slaves in a revolt that kills more than 50 whites; Turner is hanged for his role.

The New England Anti-Slavery Society is founded.

William Lloyd Garrison begins publication of his antislavery newspaper *The Liberator*.

The Missouri Compromise, 1820–1821

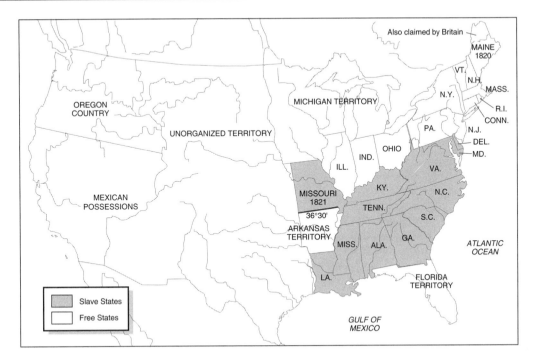

1833   The American Anti-Slavery Society is founded by New York and New England abolitionists.

In Philadelphia, Lucretia Mott helps found the Female Anti-Slavery Society.

1834   In a New York City riot, free black churches and homes are damaged and abolitionist Arthur Toppan's home and store sacked. A riot in Philadelphia also destroys churches and homes and results in the death of one African American.

1836   Congress passes the gag rule, preventing abolitionist petitions from being introduced, read, or discussed in Congress.

Lorenzo de Zavala, with other Texans, signs Texas's declaration of independence from Mexico. He will be the new republic's vice president.

1837   In Alton, Illinois, mobs murder abolitionist editor Elijah Lovejoy and destroy his printing press.

Sisters Angelina and Sarah Grimké begin addressing small groups of women on the subject of abolition for the American Anti-Slavery Society.

The Native American Association is formed in Washington, D.C. Anti-Irish, anti-Catholic, and anti-immigrant, it testifies to a growing nativism.

1838   Frederick Bailey escapes from slavery, changing his name to Frederick Douglass. He will be a leading writer and lecturer for the abolitionist cause.

1839   Led by Cinque, African slaves on the Spanish slave ship *L'Amistad* mutiny and sail the ship to Long Island. In 1841 the Supreme Court orders the slaves freed and returned to Africa. John Quincy Adams represents the Africans before the Supreme Court.

NATIVISM

It may seem strange that nativism should develop in a nation of immigrants, in a country in which all but Indian peoples (and actually even they) have roots elsewhere. Yet almost from the very beginning some early arrivals have sought to preserve their priority by excluding or limiting newcomers, especially those who seemed less like themselves.

In the 1830s and 1840s, as waves of German and Irish immigrants increased, nativists complained that the newcomers drank too much, that the Catholicism some of them practiced was opposed to American democratic principles, and that their willingness to work for the lowest wages was threatening the jobs and livelihoods of American workers. Immigrants were blamed for their poverty, for their lack of education, for urban crime, and for the political corruption that their presence seemed to encourage. Nativism turned political, and the American ("Know-Nothing") party formed in upstate New York became a national party. In the 1854 midterm election the Know-Nothings made strong showings in Massachusetts and Pennsylvania, but by 1856, the next presidential election year, the party had split over the dominating slavery issue and was swallowed up in the vortex of civil war.

After the war nativism reemerged, this time buttressed with "scientific" evidence about racial and ethnic classifications that, for nativists, seemed to confirm the superiority of white, Anglo-Saxon, Protestant culture. This culture seemed more threatened than ever by the "new immigrants"—darker-skinned people from southern and eastern Europe and Russia, some of them Jews, who came in ever greater numbers as the century drew to a close. These newcomers, like their predecessors, crowded in city tenements, worked for low wages, and spoke languages not heard before in the United States. Again they were blamed for their poverty and ignorance but now also for a lack of "cleanliness." They were also accused of fomenting labor unrest and of holding Socialist views that were contrary to American economics and politics.

Some old Know-Nothing proposals, such as immigration restriction, began to be passed into law. Chinese laborers, convicts, paupers, "lunatics" and "idiots," and those who might become public charges were excluded first. Later, as immigration from northern and western Europe paled beside the masses of "new immigrants," immigration laws sought to shift the balance back to the "Nordic races" through a quota system that assigned immigration slots based on the population profile of 1910, then back to 1890, before the great surge of southern and eastern Europeans peaked.

In these same years, the nativism that in northern cities targeted foreigners found its expression in the South against black people, who were systematically disenfranchised and segregated. When the Ku Klux Klan revived during the 1920s, its targets encompassed all those who seemed to be threats: blacks and foreigners, Catholics and Jews.

After midcentury, with the example of Nazi Germany's pushing nativism to its logical extreme, the legal structures supporting a nativist outlook in the United States were dismantled. Within a year of each other, segregation and the quota system were ended by acts of Congress, and the nation embarked on an effort to make equal protection, equal opportunity, and equal access realities. It hasn't proved easy, however, and as the century ends, debates over new waves of immigration from Asia and Latin America, over welfare rights and public education for illegal aliens, and over English as the proposed official language are threaded again with nativist concerns, now modernized but not completely unlike those heard more than a century and a half ago.

1840   In London, American abolitionists attend the World's Anti-Slavery Convention. Lucretia Mott and Elizabeth Cady Stanton are barred because they are women.

The Liberty party, founded by abolitionists, nominates James G. Birney for president. It pushes for an end to slavery in the District of Columbia, the abolition of the interstate slave trade, and a ban on the admission of slave states to the Union.

British immigrants numbering 2,613 enter the United States, as do 39,430 Irish immigrants.

1841 Slaves being transported from Virginia to New Orleans aboard the ship *Creole* revolt and sail to the Bahamas, where they are given asylum.

1842 The Supreme Court strikes down a Pennsylvania law prohibiting fugitive slaves from being seized in that state.

In Boston, abolitionists buy captured fugitive slave George Latimore from his owner; it is the first of many such acts.

In Philadelphia, a riot by Irish Catholics targets African Americans.

Immigration from Scandanavia reaches its pre–Civil War peak at 1,777.

1843 Massachusetts passes a new personal liberty law that forbids state officials from catching fugitive slaves, forcing federal officials to act.

To provide services to Jews and others, American Jews found the organization B'nai B'rith.

Isabella, daughter of James and Betsy, slaves in Ulster County, New York, adopts the name Sojourner Truth and starts giving eloquent speeches around the country against slavery and for women's rights.

1844 In Philadelphia clashes erupt between native-born Americans and Irish Catholic immigrants; 20 are killed.

1845 Irish potato famines spark the beginning of large-scale Irish immigration. Throughout the next decade about 1.5 million Irish will immigrate to the United States.

Unable to agree on the issue of slavery, the Baptist Convention breaks into northern and southern conventions and the Southern Baptist Convention is established.

1846 The Wilmot Proviso, which would ban slavery in territory captured from Mexico, is passed by the House but repeatedly defeated in the Senate.

1847 Former slave Frederick Douglass begins publishing the *North Star*; it will become the most influential antislavery newspaper.

1848 The Free-Soil party, which opposes slavery with the slogan "Free soil, free speech, free labor, and free men," nominates Martin Van Buren for president.

Another failed revolution in Germany, followed by a series of crop failures, sparks a great exodus to the United States. More than 1 million Germans, including future senator Carl Schurz, will immigrate over the next decade. Many prosperous Germans settle in the Midwest and the Mississippi valley.

1849 California, now a U.S. possession following the Mexican War and with an influx of more than 100,000 following the gold rush, writes a constitution prohibiting slavery and requests statehood. More than 10,000 of the new Californians are from Mexico and Latin America, and 7,000 are from Europe and Asia.

The Supreme Court declares in the *Passenger Cases* that New York and Massachusetts cannot impose a tax on each alien who enters the United States.

1850 The U.S. population is 23.2 million, including about 3.2 million slaves and 2.2 million immigrants.

The Compromise of 1850 admits California as a free state and permits residents of New Mexico and Utah Territories to decide whether they will be a slave or free state. It ends the slave trade in the District of Columbia, but it also enacts a new Fugitive Slave Law compelling citizens in free states to turn in runaway slaves.

Escaped slave Harriet Tubman returns south to lead her family to freedom. As a famed "conductor" on the Underground Railroad, she will rescue an estimated 300 slaves before the Civil War.

African-American abolitionist Frederick Douglass

UNDERGROUND RAILROAD

The Underground Railroad was not a railroad; nor was it underground. It was rather an informal system for helping fugitive slaves flee to the North or Canada. It is estimated that perhaps as many as 100,000 escaped between 1800 and 1861. Quakers, one of the first groups to question slavery, often gave assistance and shelter to the runaways. Free blacks and other slaves played equally important roles in helping many individuals reach safety. The courage and ingenuity of the runaways also played a large part in the success of the enterprise. Both North and South saw the Railroad's propaganda advantages: The North, especially the abolitionists, used it to publicize the horrors of slavery, whereas the South used it to prove that the North was undermining Fugitive Slave Laws, Southern institutions, and a distinctive way of life.

1851   Irish immigration peaks at 221,253. Most Irish settle in the seaport cities of the East.

1852   Harriet Beecher Stowe's antislavery novel *Uncle Tom's Cabin* is published in book form; a runaway best-seller, it increases northern antislavery sentiment.

1854   The Kansas-Nebraska Act repeals the Missouri Compromise and establishes the territories of Kansas and Nebraska according to the principles of popular sovereignty; the residents themselves will decide whether to permit slavery.

Founded in reaction to the Kansas-Nebraska Act, the Republican party calls for the abolition of slavery.

The Massachusetts Emigrant Aid Society is established in New England to promote antislavery immigration to Kansas.

Thirteen thousand Chinese immigrate to the United States, marking the start of a mass influx (the highest number for a previous year was 42). Attracted by the gold rush, many stay to help build the transcontinental railroad.

Appealing to anti-immigrant and anti-Catholic sentiment among "native" Protestants, the new American, or Know-Nothing, party wins many local races in Massachusetts, New York, and Pennsylvania.

Castle Garden, a former theater in Manhattan's Battery, is selected to become an immigrant receiving station.

1855   In Kansas, a bloody war breaks out between pro- and antislavery forces for control of the government.

German immigration reaches its pre–Civil War peak, at 215,009.

1856   Proslavery groups sack Lawrence, Kansas. In response, abolitionist John Brown, his four sons, and three others murder five proslavery colonists at Pottawatomie Creek. Warfare continues between pro- and antislavery forces until federal troops restore order.

In Congress, Senator Charles Sumner makes a strong antislavery speech, criticizing, among others, Senator Andrew Butler. Representative Preston Brooks, Butler's nephew, attacks and nearly kills Sumner with a cane in the Senate.

1857   In the *Dred Scott* decision the Supreme Court holds that African Americans are not citizens, that a slave who lives in free territory is still a slave, and that slavery cannot be prohibited from the territories.

Kansas elects an antislavery legislature, but proslavery delegates meet at Lecompton and draft a constitution that permits slavery in the territory. President James Buchanan splits the Democratic Party by accepting the Lecompton constitution.

1858   In the Lincoln-Douglas debates, Abraham Lincoln and Illinois senator Stephen Douglas argue the slavery issue during the campaign for the U.S. Senate. Douglas is reelected, but the debates make Lincoln a national figure.

Kansans reject the Lecompton constitution, and Kansas enters the Union as a free state in 1861.

1859   Led by John Brown, 22 men, including five African Americans, seize the federal arsenal at Harpers Ferry, Virginia, hoping to ignite a slave rebellion. Brown is hanged for murder, treason, and insurrection; the North sees him as a martyr, the South as a traitor.

In Vicksburg, Mississippi, the Southern Commercial Convention urges repeal of state and federal laws prohibiting the importation of slaves.

In Texas, Juan Cortina leads a raid on Anglo-controlled settlements in retaliation for Anglo abuses of Mexican Americans.

1860   Republican Abraham Lincoln is elected president without a single electoral vote from a slave state.

On December 20 South Carolina becomes the first southern state to secede from the Union; in the following weeks six other southern states—Florida, Alabama, Georgia, Mississippi, Louisiana, and Texas—follow suit.

1861   The Confederate States of America is established, and the Civil War begins.

1862   Congress approves the recruitment of African Americans to serve in the Union forces during the Civil War. Ultimately about 179,000 serve. More than 2,700 die on the battlefield and almost 30,000 die of wounds and disease.

1863   President Lincoln issues the Emancipation Proclamation, freeing all slaves in rebelling states.

In New York City about 40 people die in draft riots. The rioters, largely Irish workers too poor to hire a substitute or pay a draft commutation fee of $300, turn against African Americans. The riots are as much about economic inequity as they are about the draft. Racism and unsolved urban problems are also factors.

A period print showing Lincoln delivering the Emancipation Proclamation

1865   The North wins the Civil War. Reconstruction of Confederate states, begun under President Lincoln, is taken over in December by Congress.

To provide former slaves with fuel, food, clothing, provisions, and medical and economic help, the Freedmen's Bureau is established as part of the War Department. In 1866 its scope is enlarged.

The Thirteenth Amendment, abolishing slavery, is ratified.

1855- New southern governments pass Black Codes, harsh vagrancy, apprenticeship, and civil
1866   rights laws that severely limit former slaves' freedom.

1866   The Ku Klux Klan, founded as a social club in Pulaski, Tennessee, spreads quickly and begins intimidating and terrorizing southern blacks.

Congress passes the first Civil Rights Act, giving African Americans full citizenship and equal rights under the law, thereby overturning the *Dred Scott* decision and the Black Codes.

The Freedmen's Bureau is given the power to establish courts to prosecute violators of African-American civil rights.

Fearing that the Supreme Court might declare the Civil Rights Act unconstitutional, Congress passes the Fourteenth Amendment, making African Americans citizens and guaranteeing all citizens "the equal protection of the laws." The amendment will be ratified in 1868.

1869   Congress passes the Fifteenth Amendment, stating that the right of citizens to vote "shall not be denied or abridged . . . on account of race, color, or previous condition of servitude." The amendment will be ratified in 1870.

1870   Hiram Revels of Mississippi becomes the first African American elected to the U.S. Senate.

        British immigration (excluding Irish) peaks at 103,677.

1870-   Congress makes the violent abuse of civil and political rights a federal crime and authorizes
1871   the use of the armed forces to subdue Klan violence. Hundreds are arrested and imprisoned or fined, causing Klan activity to decline.

1873   Slavery is ended in Puerto Rico.

1875   Congress passes a Civil Rights Act that prohibits discrimination in public places such as inns, conveyances, and amusements.

1877   Federal soldiers are withdrawn from the South, ending Reconstruction.

        Following Reconstruction, thousands of African Americans begin to migrate from the rural South to Kansas and Oklahoma.

        Anti-Chinese riots break out in San Francisco.

        Jewish population numbers 299,087 persons, about half of one percent of the total U.S. population.

LYNCHINGS

The withdrawal of federal troops from the South in 1877 effectively ended Reconstruction and protections for African Americans. New laws and penal systems enforced many restrictions, and vigilantes often took the law into their own hands. Between 1882 and 1900 there were at least 100 lynchings a year. By 1968 more than 3,500 African Americans would be lynched, mostly in the South. The record year was 1892, when 161 African Americans were lynched.

In the 1890s African-American journalist Ida Wells Barnett initiated a campaign to make people aware of the lynching and prevent it. She headed the Anti-Lynching Bureau of the National Afro-American Council, which proved that most lynchings were not the outcome of rape or attempted rape. Instead the victims were lynched for outspokenness, and lynching was a device used to frighten and intimidate African Americans both politically and socially.

1878   In the El Paso "Salt War," Mexican Americans and Mexicans in Texas revolt against Anglo politicians and profiteers, accusing them of trying to seize communal salt mines. Numerous deaths and destruction of property result.

1879   President Rutherford B. Hayes vetoes a bill limiting Chinese immigration.

        California's new constitution prohibits employing Chinese workers.

1880s   Southern states pass "Jim Crow" laws, consigning black passengers to segregated seating in railway cars and ultimately enforcing a barrier between blacks and whites in all aspects of public life.

1880   The United States signs an agreement with China giving the United States the right to regulate but not exclude laborers from China.

        There are 250,000 Jews in the United States. Before 1924, some 2.5 million more will arrive from Eastern Europe and Russia. Many settle in Eastern cities, especially New York.

Immigration Before and After the Civil War

Immigration, 1820–1860

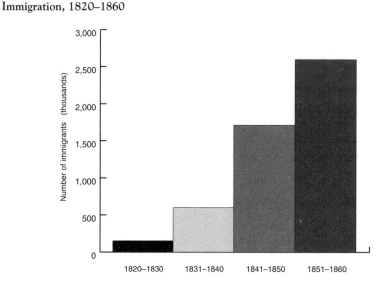

Immigration, 1860–1920

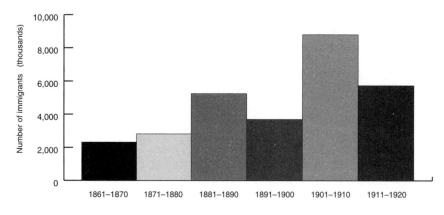

1882   Chinese immigration peaks at 39,579.

Congress passes, and President Chester A. Arthur signs, the Chinese Exclusion Act, which bars Chinese laborers from immigrating to the United States for ten years. The ban is subsequently extended.

Scandinavian immigration peaks at 105,326. Many, taking advantage of the Homestead Act, settle in the northern Great Plains.

German immigration reaches its post-Civil War peak, at 250,630.

An Immigration Act bars entry to criminals, paupers, the insane, and other undesirables.

In this year, 87 percent of immigrants are from northern and western Europe.

Immigrants are pouring into the United States number 789,000; more than 350,000 come from Germany and England, 32,000 from Italy, and 17,000 from Russia.

Immigrants to the United States, 1820–1975

Country of origin	Numbers in approximate millions
Germany	6.9
Italy	5.2
Ireland	4.7
Austria-Hungary	4.3
Canada	4.0
Soviet Union/Russia	3.3
Great Britain	3.1
Mexico	1.9
West Indies	1.4
Sweden	1.2

Immigrants to the United States, 1976–1986

Country of origin	Approximate numbers
Mexico	720,000
Vietnam	425,000
Philippines	379,000
Korea	363,000
China/Taiwan	331,000
Cuba	258,000
Dominican Republic	211,000
Jamaica	200,000
United Kingdom	150,000
Canada	129,000

SOURCE: Foner, Eric, and John A. Garraty, eds. *The Reader's Companion to American History* (Boston: Houghton Mifflin, 1991), 534, 538.

1883	Touro Synagogue in Newport, Rhode Island, closed in the 1790s, is reopened to serve the many Jews now arriving from central and eastern Europe.
	The Supreme Court rules the Civil Rights Act of 1875 unconstitutional, as the rights enumerated are social rather than civil and government has no jurisdiction in such matters. The provision prohibiting the exclusion of blacks from jury duty is valid.
1885	The importation of contract laborers is prohibited.
1886	In Chicago, police try to break up a meeting of anarchists; a bomb explodes, and in the ensuing riot seven policemen are killed and many others injured. The Haymarket bombing fans nativist rage at foreign-born extremists, especially Catholics and other minority groups.
1887	The American Protective Association, an anti-immigrant, anti-Catholic organization, is founded. Its membership peaks at 2.5 million in 1846.
1889	In Chicago, Jane Addams opens Hull-House, the most famous of the settlement houses that will help immigrants adjust to life in America (see Chapter 7).
1890	Substantial Japanese migration begins. During the next decade at least 25,000 Japanese will enter the United States. Most are young men who work as laborers on the West Coast.

1890   Jacob Riis publishes *How the Other Half Lives*, exposing the living conditions of New York's slum dwellings and immigrant neighborhoods.

1891   After three of them are acquitted, 11 Italians indicted for the murder of the New Orleans police chief are lynched by a mob.

1892   African-American journalist Ida B. Wells begins an antilynching crusade in a Memphis newspaper of which she is part owner.

New York Harbor's Ellis Island opens as an immigration depot; more than 12 million immigrants will pass through it by 1924.

ELLIS ISLAND

For years New York City, as the nation's largest port, served also the unofficial port of entry for immigrants. By the 1840s, as German and Irish newcomers pointed out the benefits of having an official receiving station to assist immigrants, New York State set up a Board of Commissioners of Emigration. In 1855 it opened Castle Garden, at the tip of Manhattan Island, where officials helped immigrants change money, buy railroad tickets, and find a place to stay. Critics complained, however, that the depot ruined property values and that the immigrants caused "pestilential odors." When a larger facility was sought, the U.S. government built a depot on an island in New York Harbor.

The new immigration station at Ellis Island opened on January 1, 1892. Eventually it consisted of more than 35 buildings on 27 acres. Here newcomers underwent a medical examination and an interview with questions about their work, their destination, the amount of money they had with them, and whether they had been in prison. Later a literacy test was added. Those who could not quality for admittance were liable to be deported.

Immigrants being processed on Ellis Island

At its peak, more than 5,000 people a day were processed at Ellis Island. More than a million entered in 1907 alone, and on its busiest day officials recorded 11,745 arrivals. In all, more than 12 million newcomers passed through Ellis Island before 1924, when new immigration restrictions were passed.

In 1954 Ellis Island was declared "surplus property," and in 1965 President Lyndon Johnson made it a national monument. After an eight-year restoration project, in 1990 the Ellis Island Immigration Museum opened, displaying artifacts, photographs, and documents recording the experience of arriving in America as an immigrant.

One aspect of that experience, for many, remains the same—a welcome from the Statue of Liberty. This huge statue, a gift from the people of France as a symbol of French-American friendship, was erected in 1886 on Bedloe's Island, commanding a view of New York Harbor right beside Ellis Island. At its base is inscribed a poem written by Emma Lazarus, a young Jewish-American poet who, outraged by pogroms against Jews in Russia, sought to make known the hope America embodied:

> *. . . Give me your tired, your poor,*
> *Your huddled masses yearning to breathe free,*
> *The wretched refuse of your teeming shore.*
> *Send these, the homeless, tempest-tossed to me,*
> *I lift my lamp beside the golden door!*

1893 The Supreme Court upholds the constitutionality of the Chinese Exclusion Act.

An agreement between the United States and Canada provides for surveillance of illegal immigrants entering into the United States through Canada's western ports.

1894 In Boston the Immigration Restriction League is founded; it suggests literacy tests be given to immigrants to keep out "undesirables."

1895 In Atlanta, at the Cotton States Exposition, Booker T. Washington delivers his famous "Atlanta Compromise" speech, asking African Americans to give up the struggle for civil rights and submit to segregation. Social and political equality will come from self-reliance and economic advancement, he argues.

1896 In *Plessy v. Ferguson*, the Supreme Court rules that "separate but equal" facilities for blacks and whites are constitutional. The ruling legalizes segregation.

1897 President Grover Cleveland vetoes a bill requiring that immigrants take literacy tests.

1898 With the annexation of Hawaii comes a population of 154,000: 29,000 are whites, and 125,000 are classified as "other," including native Hawaiians and Chinese and 25,000 Japanese nationals. The Chinese Exclusion Act is extended to this territory.

1900 The U.S. population is 75.9 million, including 3.6 million immigrants who have entered since 1890.

Over the next decade almost 9 million immigrants will pour into the United States from Italy, Russia, and central Europe.

1905 In Ontario, Canada the Niagara Movement organizes at a conference of African-American leaders called to protest the denial of civil rights and to oppose the conciliatory views of Booker T. Washington.

In Chicago Robert Abbott begins publishing the *Chicago Defender*; the paper will mount a militant attack against racism.

In San Francisco the Asiatic Exclusion League is established.

1906 The San Francisco school board orders that Chinese, Japanese, and Korean children attend a separate school. Whites talk of a "yellow peril."

1907 In this year, 81 percent of immigrants are from southern and eastern Europe—Poles, Russian Jews, Ukrainians, Slovaks, Hungarians, Romanians, Italians, and Greeks. For the first time, these peoples are becoming important elements in the U.S. population. The new immigrants, mostly poor and uneducated, almost always settle in cities.

Black conciliator Booker T. Washington

1907   Theodore Roosevelt intervenes in the San Francisco School Board decision, concluding a "gentleman's agreement" that reverses the segregation decision, with Japan agreeing to stop the emigration of laborers. Japanese immigration peaks this year at 30,226.

1908   African-American boxer Jack Johnson wins the world heavyweight title; his reign inspires a search for a "white hope" to depose him.

1909   The National Association for the Advancement of Colored People (NAACP) is founded to advance the rights of African Americans.

At the North Pole African-American explorer Matthew Henson, a member of Admiral Robert Perry's expedition, raises the American flag.

1910   The U.S. population is 91.9 million; 8.8 million immigrants have entered since 1900, and 14.7 percent of the population is foreign-born.

The Mexican Revolution begins; in the next decade the fighting will drive hundreds of thousands of Mexicans over the easily crossed border, with many settling in cities such as Tucson, El Paso, San Antonio, Laredo, and San Diego. Mexican refugees help spur the economic growth of the Southwest, particularly in agriculture, ranching, and mining.

The NAACP publishes the first issue of its journal, the *Crisis*, edited by W.E.B. Du Bois.

The National Urban League is founded by African Americans to help end racial segregation and provide community services in housing, employment, education, and social welfare.

1913   In California the Alien Land Law prevents Japanese from owning land in the state.

1914   Immigration reaches its all-time high, reduced in the following years by war in Europe. This year, 1,218,480 persons enter the United States. Nearly three-quarters are from southern and eastern Europe, including 278,152 from central Europe and 283,738 from Italy (both peaks), and 255,660 from Russia and the Baltic States, a flow that peaked the previous year at 291,040.

The Great Migration of blacks out of the rural South to cities in the North begins. Between 1914 and 1920 500,000 or more blacks go north for jobs in industry and better opportunities.

1915   In Fulton County, Georgia, the Ku Klux Klan is revived.

African-American scholar Carter Woodson establishes the Association for the Study of Negro Life and History.

1916   Black nationalist Marcus Garvey establishes the Universal Negro Improvement Association and launches the Back to Africa Movement.

1917   Despite President Woodrow Wilson's two vetoes, an immigration act is passed by Congress requiring immigrants to pass a literacy test. The act keeps out immigrants from an Asiatic barred zone but exempts refugees from religious persecution.

Puerto Ricans are granted U.S. citizenship.

In East Saint Louis, Illinois, at least 200 African Americans die in a race riot and hundreds are injured.

1919   At least 25 serious race riots break out in cities across the nation, including Charleston, Knoxville, Omaha, and Washington, D.C.

In Paris, W.E.B. Du Bois organizes the first Pan-African Congress, whose goals are to promote self-determination for colonized peoples and to abolish Western imperialism.

Attempts by a handful of terrorists to murder prominent Americans result in a public outcry against foreign-born radicals, especially Italian, Jewish, or Slav immigrant industrial workers. In the ensuing "Red Scare," thousands of political and labor agitators are arrested, and hundreds of aliens, including anarchists Emma Goldman and Alexander Berkman, are deported.

1920s   Throughout the decade the revived Ku Klux Klan expands to the North and Midwest. Besides African Americans, its new targets are immigrants, Catholics, and Jews. At its peak in the mid-1920s, it attracts 4 to 5 million members.

1920   A new California law prohibits Japanese from leasing farmland in California.

There are 3.5 million Jews in the United States. Jews constitute a quarter of New York City's population.

In many industrial cities, immigrants and their children constitute more than half the population.

1921   Congress passes the Emergency Quota Act (Dillingham Bill), which establishes a quota system as the basis of immigration policy. Only 3 percent of the people of any nationality (Mexicans and other Latin Americans exempted) who lived in the United States in 1910 may enter each year. The total maximum is 375,000. Immigration from eastern and southern Europe now slows to a trickle. Some maintain that the act is designed to keep out Jews.

1921   After a widely reported trial, two Italian immigrants, Nicola Sacco and Bartolomeo Vanzetti, are convicted of murder during a Massachusetts shoe-factory robbery and sentenced to death. Many believe they are innocent, and protests delay their execution until 1927.

1924   Congress passes the Johnson-Reed Immigration Act, halving the maximum and limiting the annual quota from a country to 2 percent of U.S. residents of that nationality in 1890, thereby reducing further the proportion of eastern and southern Europeans admitted. Asians are also severely restricted by quotas, and the Japanese are completely excluded. The act does not limit immigration from Canada or Latin America. Family exemptions pertain only to wives and minor children of American citizens.

The Jewish population is now 4.2 million, but because of the restrictive quotas of 1924 and the Depression beginning in 1929, Jewish immigration falls sharply. Between 1933 and 1934 up to 25,000 intellectual refugees from Nazism, many of them Jews, find a haven in the United States (see Chapter 11).

1925   Internal scandals cause the Ku Klux Klan to lose much of its power.

African American A. Philip Randolph organizes the Brotherhood of Sleeping Car Porters and is elected its president.

1927   The Supreme Court strikes down as unconstitutional a Texas law prohibiting African Americans from voting in the state's Democratic primary.

The Jewish population numbers 4,228,029, or 3.6 percent of all Americans.

1928   In New Mexico, Octaviano Larrazolo becomes the first Hispanic elected to the United States Senate. He had been elected governor of New Mexico in 1918.

1929   The national-origins quota for immigration goes into full effect. The yearly maximum is 150,000, and from 1931 until after World War II the annual number of immigrants never exceeds 100,000.

In Texas, the League of United Latin American Citizens (LULAC) is formed.

1931   In Detroit, Elijah Poole, later Elijah Muhammad, joins the Temple of Islam, a black separatist sect founded by Wali Farad (W. D. Fard). In 1934 he will take over the leadership of the Black Muslims.

In Scottsboro, Alabama, nine young African Americans are charged with raping two white women. The convictions of the "Scottsboro boys" are reversed by the Supreme Court on procedural grounds. Following retrials, charges against five are dropped. There is widespread belief that the charges are unfounded and the boys the victims of prejudice.

1933   Nearly 16,000 Mexicans are deported, having entered the United States illegally. The campaign to deport illegal aliens, intensified by competition for jobs during the Great Depression, reduces the Mexican population in the United States by one-third during the 1930s.

Albert Einstein accepts a post at Princeton's Institute for Advanced Study. He is only the most famous of refugees from Hitler (see Chapter 11). Between 1935 and 1941, about 150,000 Jewish refugees are accepted by the United States.

1935   African-American educator Mary McLeod Bethune founds the National Council of Negro Women.

1937   African American Joe Louis becomes world heavyweight boxing champion. Called the "Brown Bomber," Louis, who will retire undefeated in 1949, becomes a symbol of black achievement.

1938   Elected to the Pennsylvania House of Representatives, Crystal Bird Fauset becomes the first African-American female to serve in a state legislature.

1939   After the Daughters of the American Revolution (DAR) bars her from performing in Washington, D.C.'s Constitution Hall, African-American contralto Marian Anderson sings before 75,000 at the Lincoln Memorial.

The United States does not allow entry to 937 Jewish refugees aboard the SS *St. Louis* from Germany, bound for Cuba. The refugees have to return to Germany.

1940   In the South, 5 percent of blacks eligible to vote are registered.

Congress passes the Alien Registration Act, also called the Smith Act, requiring all aliens to be registered and fingerprinted. The act also provides for their deportation and makes it illegal to advocate the forceful overthrow of the American government.

1941   A. Philip Randolph threatens a march on Washington to demand equal employment for blacks. President Franklin Roosevelt responds by issuing an executive order banning discrimination in government and defense industries. Randolph calls off the strike.

1942   President Franklin Roosevelt issues an executive order to intern more than 110,000 Japanese Americans living on the West Coast, two-thirds of whom are American citizens. They are sent to camps in remote regions of Arkansas, Arizona, California, Colorado, Utah, Idaho, and Wyoming, where they are guarded by military police. Those interned lose about $400 million in property (see Chapter 5).

In Chicago, the Congress of Racial Equality (CORE) is founded by James Farmer and others who seek to end racial discrimination and segregation through the use of nonviolence. In May it conducts the first sit-in, ever, at the Jack Spratt restaurant.

The *bracero* program negotiated by Mexico and the United States offers short-term employment to Mexicans. It is extended through 1964.

1943   Chinese Exclusion Acts are repealed, and annual Chinese immigration has a quota of 105.

Close to 275 race riots break out in some 50 cities, including Detroit and New York City's Harlem.

In Los Angeles a five-day riot targets Mexican Americans in "zoot suits."

1944   Gunnar Myrdal, a Swedish sociologist, publishes *An American Dilemma*, an examination of a racial caste system in a democracy.

Harlem voters elect civil rights activist and minister Adam Clayton Powell to the U.S. House of Representatives, where he serves for nearly a quarter century.

1945-   Emergency measures allow the United States to permit entry to "displaced persons." Ulti-
1951   mately about 400,000 Europeans are admitted.

1947   When he is brought up from a farm club, where he has won the batting crown, to the Brooklyn Dodgers, Jackie Robinson becomes the first African-American major-league baseball player.

The first issue of *Ebony* magazine is published.

1948   President Harry Truman signs executive orders ending segregation in the military and banning discrimination in the civil service.

In *Shelley v. Kraemer*, the Supreme Court declares that deed covenants preventing sales of houses to certain racial groups are not enforceable by law.

1949   William Hastie becomes the first African-American federal judge.

1952   The Immigration and Nationality Act, also called the McCarran-Walter Act, is passed by Congress over the veto of President Harry Truman, who objects to the continuation of the quota system. The act removes the ban on Asian and Pacific immigration to the United

States and allows spouses and minor children to enter as nonquota immigrants, but it preserves the national-origins quota system. African and Asian nations have annual quotas of 100 each. The act bans "subversives" and permits the deportation of Communist immigrants.

In the South, 28 percent of blacks eligible to vote are registered.

1953   A Refugee Relief Act permits emergency entry into the United States, outside immigration quotas, of refugees from Communist persecution. Between 1954 and 1959 more than 200,000 refugees are admitted.

1954   In a unanimous decision, the Supreme Court rules that segregated schools are unconstitutional and in a related ruling the next year orders that desegregation must proceed with "all deliberate speed" (see Chapter 10).

1955   In Mississippi 14-year-old African American Emmett Till, visiting from Chicago, is murdered because he allegedly made suggestive remarks to a white woman. The case gets nationwide attention, especially when the two defendants receive verdicts of not guilty from an all-white jury.

In Montgomery, Alabama, Rosa Parks is arrested for refusing to give up her bus seat to a white. Her arrest sparks Reverend Martin Luther King, Jr., and others to organize a bus boycott, which ends a year later when the Supreme Court declares bus segregation illegal.

1956   Led by Martin Luther King, Jr., a Prayer Pilgrimage draws 25,000 to the Lincoln Memorial.

Rosa Parks in Montgomery, Alabama

The nearly 6,000 Japanese Americans who renounced their citizenship when interned in concentration camps have their citizenship fully reinstated.

1957 To join together nonviolent civil rights groups, the Southern Christian Leadership Conference (SCLC) is cofounded by Martin Luther King, Jr., and Ralph Abernathy.

Central High School in Little Rock, Arkansas, is integrated, but only after President Dwight Eisenhower dispatches federal troops to Little Rock to protect the nine black students and ensure order.

Congress passes the first civil rights bill since Reconstruction; it establishes federal safeguards for voting rights and sets up a Civil Rights Commission.

1958 In Oklahoma City, sit-ins to desegregate lunch counters are begun by the NAACP Youth Council.

1959 After Fidel Castro comes to power, about 20,000 Cubans leave for the United States. These and later waves of Cubans settle in Florida.

1960 In Greensboro, North Carolina, African-American college students stage a sit-in at an F. W. Woolworth lunch counter, leading the city to desegregate eating places a few months later. Within a year sit-ins are organized in more than 100 cities in the South and border states.

Massachusetts senator John F. Kennedy is elected president; he will be the first Catholic to hold this office.

Congress passes a Civil Rights Act authorizing federal referees to assist blacks attempting to register and vote.

The Student Nonviolent Coordinating Committee (SNCC) is formed to fight segregation through direct confrontation.

1961 The biracial Congress of Racial Equality (CORE) sends several busloads of "freedom riders" through the South to test compliance with federal laws integrating bus stations; the riders are attacked by white mobs, with order restored only after Attorney General Robert Kennedy sends in federal marshals.

The Twenty-third Amendment is ratified, permitting residents of the District of Columbia, which has a black majority, to vote in presidential elections.

1962 Attempting to organize migrant farmworkers into unions, César Chávez founds the National Farm Workers Association, mainly made up of Mexicans and Mexican-American grape pickers in California. In 1966 it merges with an AFL-CIO affiliate to form the United Farm Workers.

James Meredith, trying to register as the first black student at the University of Mississippi, is refused entrance. A riot ensues, and federal troops are called in to restore order. Protected by federal marshals, Meredith graduates the next summer.

An executive order signed by President John Kennedy places a partial ban on racial discrimination in federal housing programs.

1963 After television viewers see Birmingham, Alabama, police use water hoses and police dogs against peaceful demonstrators led by Martin Luther King, Jr., there is a large public outcry against the police tactics.

In Mississippi, civil rights leader Medgar Evers is murdered.

Addressing some 250,000 participants in the March on Washington, Martin Luther King, Jr. delivers his "I Have a Dream" speech.

"I HAVE A DREAM"

Perhaps even as he delivered his famous speech from the Lincoln Memorial that August afternoon in 1963, Dr. Martin Luther King, Jr., knew that this was the high tide of the civil rights movement. The fire hoses and bombings of Birmingham, the killing of civil rights leader Medgar Evers, were recent, painful memories, but he couldn't have known, then, of the bombings and killings to come: four little girls in a Birmingham Sunday school, three civil rights workers in Mississippi, marchers in Selma, and then there were the riots—the burning cities in the long, hot summers of the mid-1960s, and the worst of all in the wake of his own assassination.

But on that August afternoon, after years of struggle, it must have seemed like everything was coming together instead of poised to fall apart. The march had been organized by all the great leaders: James Farmer of CORE, John Lewis of SNCC, Roy Wilkins of the NAACP, Whitney Young of the National Urban League, A. Philip Randolph, who had planned a march like this almost a quarter century ago, and King himself, head of SCLC. President John Kennedy had stated his support and had already submitted a civil rights bill to Congress.

And so many were there. As Joan Baez led the crowd in singing "We Shall Overcome," the people who joined her were famous: Nobel Peace Prize winner Ralph Bunche, author James Baldwin, baseball star Jackie Robinson, singers and entertainers Ruby Dee, Mahalia Jackson, Odetta, Lena Horne, Marian Anderson, Harry Belafonte, Sidney Poitier, Dick Gregory, and Sammy Davis, Jr. Some 75 members of Congress sat in a special section down front. And there were 250,000 more black and white Americans, who had driven and ridden and flown and walked to be there. It was an incredible gathering, and for those who were there, it bespoke an incredible sense of identity and power.

When King rose to speak, he galvanized the crowd, and ultimately the nation. Long after the riots and the killings, long after the legislation and the litigation, his words are still fresh in their challenge:

I have a dream that one day this nation will rise up and live out the true meaning of its creed: "We hold these truths to be self-evident; that all men area created equal."

I have a dream that one day on the red hills of Georgia the sons of former slaves and the sons of former slave owners will be able to sit down together at the table of brotherhood.

I have a dream that one day even the state of Mississippi, a desert state sweltering with the heat of injustice and oppression, will be transformed into an oasis of freedom and justice.

I have a dream that my four little children will one day live in a nation where they will be judged not by the color of their skin but by the content of their character.

I have a dream that one day every valley shall be exalted, every hill and mountain shall be made low, the rough places will be made plains, and the crooked places will be made straight, and the glory of the Lord shall be revealed, and all flesh shall see it together.

I have a dream today. . . .

When we let freedom ring, when we let it ring from every village and hamlet, from every state and every city, we will be able to speed up that day when all of God's children, black men and white men, Jews and Gentiles, Protestants and Catholics, will be able to join hands and sing in the words of that old Negro spiritual: "Free at last! Free at last! Thank God Almighty, we're free at last!"

1964   Congress passes a Civil Rights Act, banning discrimination in education, employment, and public accommodations.

A project to register Mississippi blacks to vote becomes Freedom Summer, with schools and community centers offering legal and medical assistance. But the murder, in June, of three civil rights workers creates an atmosphere of tension and fear.

The Mississippi Freedom Democratic party is not recognized at the Democratic National Convention.

The Reverend Martin Luther King, Jr., addressing crowds in Washington, D.C.

Martin Luther King, Jr., wins the Nobel Peace Prize.

The Twenty-fourth Amendment, outlawing the poll tax, is ratified.

Cassius Clay wins the heavyweight boxing title; later in the year he will convert to Islam, renaming himself Muhammad Ali.

1965   A Voting Rights Act sends federal agents to register African-American voters in states and districts where there was evidence that voting rights had been denied.

In February in Harlem, militant civil rights leader Malcolm X is shot dead as he is about to make a speech. The following year three men, possibly members of a rival Black Muslim sect, will be convicted of the shooting.

In Selma, Alabama, Martin Luther King, Jr., starts a campaign to register black voters. After a violent confrontation King and other civil rights leaders and 4,000 peaceful demonstrators march from Selma to the state capital, Montgomery. During the campaign, three participants are killed.

In the Watts section of Los Angeles, one of the worst race riots in U.S. history leaves 34 dead and up to $200 million in property damage.

The establishment of Medicare begins to draw foreign-born physicians. More than 75,000 will enter the country by 1974.

A new immigration act ends the national-origins quota system. The act sets a limit of 120,000 visas a year for Western Hemisphere countries and 170,000 per year for all other nations. Relatives of U.S. citizens and those with special education and skills have preferences.

1966   Edward Brooke of Massachusetts is elected to the U.S. Senate as the first African-American senator to serve since Reconstruction.

Robert Weaver becomes the first African-American cabinet member, heading the new Department of Housing and Urban Development.

Malcolm X

1966   Race riots erupt in a number of cities, including Chicago and New York.

The new leader of the Student Nonviolent Coordinating Committee (SNCC), Stokely Carmichael, advocates black power, a more militant approach to civil rights.

Huey Newton and Bobby Seale found the militant Black Panthers.

To celebrate African-American culture, the holiday of Kwanzaa is created, based on ancient African festivals surrounding the gathering of crops that will feed the community. It runs seven days, from December 26 through January 1.

Chicano rights activist Rudolfo Gonzalez founds the Crusade for Justice to pursue social and political equality for Mexican Americans.

1967   During the "long, hot summer" race riots erupt in more than 100 American cities. The worst riots are in Detroit and Newark.

President Lyndon Johnson names Thurgood Marshall, the NAACP attorney who argued the landmark *Brown v. Board of Education*, to be the first African-American Supreme Court justice.

1968   The National Advisory Committee on Civil Disorders (the Kerner Commission), established by President Johnson following the race riots of 1967, issues a report stating that America is "moving toward two societies, one black, one white, separate and unequal."

On April 4 in Memphis, Tennessee, Martin Luther King, Jr., is shot to death on the balcony of his motel room. White former convict James Earl Ray is arrested for the murder. Ray pleads guilty and is sentenced to 99 years in prison. After the shooting, riots break out in 125 cities across the country, with 46 deaths resulting.

Participating in the Poor People's Campaign planned by Martin Luther King, Jr., before his death, African Americans led by Ralph Abernathy, head of the Southern Christian Leadership Conference, demonstrate in Washington, D.C., to protest racial discrimination.

Brooklyn's Shirley Chisholm becomes the first African-American woman elected to the House of Representatives.

1970s   More than 4.5 million immigrants enter the United States; 1.6 million come from Asia, and 1.3 million come from Latin America and Asia. From Mexico, 60,000 come each year.

1970   The percentage of foreign-born persons in the United States hits its century low, at 4.8 percent.

1971   The Supreme Court declares that "objective" criteria unrelated to job skills for hiring employees are discriminatory if they put minorities at a relative disadvantage.

In a separate decision the Court upholds busing of schoolchildren where segregation had been official supported policy and no acceptable alternative has been suggested by local authorities.

More than 1,000 black and Latino prisoners, angered over prison conditions and a lack of educational opportunities, riot at the Attica Correctional Facility in New York; 42 people are killed.

To fight racism, Reverend Jesse Jackson organizes People United to Save Humanity (PUSH).

1972   The Supreme Court declares that people living in segregated housing developments may sue to have them integrated.

In California, black militant Angela Davis is found not guilty of murder, kidnapping, and conspiracy during a courtroom shooting in 1970.

African-American congresswoman Shirley Chisholm, a Democrat, fails in her campaign for U.S. president.

1973   Cuban-born Mercedes Cubria retires as a lieutenant colonel in the U.S. Army; the recipient of the Bronze Star and the Legion of Merit, she has had one of the most distinguished military careers of any American woman.

1975   Federal judge Arthur Garrity rules that the Boston School Committee has deliberately segregated schools by race; he suggests a plan for exchanging students in black Roxbury and white Boston, but white mob-incited violence erupts, and extra police are called to the scene to restore order.

Congress broadens the protections of the Voting Rights Act of 1965 to include Spanish-speaking Americans and other "language minorities."

After the fall of Saigon, the United States accepts 130,000 Vietnamese.

1976   The Supreme Court decides that it is constitutional to order mainly white suburbs to provide low-cost public housing to minorities, even if the suburbs do not deliberately practice housing discrimination.

Louis Farrakhan splits the Black Muslims by founding a more militant organization.

1977   The attorney general authorizes 15,000 Indochinese refugees to enter the United States on an emergency basis.

Korean immigration is significant. By this date more than 4,500 Korean Americans operate small businesses in southern California.

1977 More than 130 million viewers watch the TV miniseries *Roots*, based on Alex Haley's book about the African-American experience; the last episode has the largest television audience to date.

1978 The Supreme Court rules that a special admissions program in a medical college favoring minority students is unconstitutional.

The federal government estimates that there are 8.2 million illegal aliens in the United States, 90 percent of Hispanic origin.

1979 The Supreme Court rules that unions may create programs designed to help African Americans be hired and gain promotions where "manifest racial imbalance" exists.

Membership in the Ku Klux Klan is once again on the rise, from 8,000 to 10,000 during the past two years.

Immigration from the Philippines is up, at 41,300 this year.

1980 In Miami 14 people are dead as a result of riots following the acquittal of four white ex-policemen charged with beating black motorcyclist Arthur McDuffie to death.

The Supreme Court declares that Congress can impose quotas in awarding federal contracts as a way of redressing past racial discrimination.

The United States permits more immigrants to enter from Cuba; more than 125,000 Cubans leave the country before Fidel Castro closes the port of Mariel.

The population of the United States is 228 million, including 26.5 million African Americans and 14.6 million Hispanics. In the 1980s, about 1 million illegal aliens are sent back to Mexico each year.

1983 The Supreme Court rules that private schools practicing discrimination are ineligible for tax exemptions.

Lieutenant Colonel Guion Bluford is the first African American in space.

Jesse Jackson begins his campaign to win the Democratic nomination for president; despite winning several primaries, he will fail in his bid.

1986 The United States receives 601,516 immigrants; most of them come from Asia and Latin America.

Martin Luther King Day is a national holiday, celebrated the third Monday in January.

Congress passes the Immigration Control and Reform Act (Simpson-Mazzoli Act), which allows illegal aliens who can prove they have resided continuously in the country since 1982 to remain in the country legally. The act also imposes sanctions on employers who hire undocumented workers. The act responds to concerns over illegal aliens. Thousands, mainly from Latin America, also enter the United States illegally by crossing the Mexican border; some are refugees escaping from repressive regimes in Cuba, Central America, and Haiti. Other illegals come from Asian countries like Vietnam.

1987 Mae Carol Jemison is the first African-American female selected to become an astronaut in training.

1988 In his campaign to be the Democratic party's presidential nominee, Jesse Jackson wins millions of primary votes, but Michael Dukakis gains the nomination.

Congress enacts legislation giving Japanese Americans interned during World War II $20,000 each.

Asian Americans are estimated to number 6.5 million.

1989 In Virginia, Lawrence Douglas Wilder is elected governor; taking office in 1990, he becomes the first elected African-American governor since Reconstruction.

New York City elects David Dinkins as its first black mayor.

The Supreme Court invalidates a Richmond, Virginia, set-aside program requiring that 30 percent of the city's public works funds be set aside for minority-owned construction companies.

1990   The proportion of foreign-born persons in the U.S. population is on the rise, at 7.9 percent. About 14 percent of Americans speak a language other than English at home; for more than half of these people, the language is Spanish.

1991   Unarmed black motorist Rodney King is severely beaten by Los Angeles police. An amateur videotape of the incident is shown on national television, and the officers are indicted. Their acquittal the following year sparks the worst urban violence in the nation's history, with more than 50 dead and 2,000 injured in south-central Los Angeles.

Clarence Thomas becomes the second African-American Supreme Court judge.

1991-   Thousands of Haitian refugees, mainly fleeing political oppression, try to enter America by
1992   boat, but the U.S. Coast Guard starts intercepting them and returning them to Haiti.

1993   President Bill Clinton, vowing to select a cabinet that "looks like America," appoints a record number of women and minorities to cabinet posts and other top-level positions.

1995   Former football star O. J. Simpson is acquitted in the murder of his wife and an acquaintance after a trial in which race plays a major role. Most blacks applaud the verdict, while most whites disagree.

In Washington, D.C., Nation of Islam leader Louis Farrakhan leads the Million-Man March to encourage black men to take responsibility for their own lives.

ACTS OF CONGRESS AFFECTING IMMIGRATION AND MINORITIES

1787   Northwest Ordinance. This act, passed by the Confederate Congress, bans slavery in the Northwest Territories.

1793   Fugitive Slave Act. This act makes it illegal to aid runaway slaves or to interfere with their arrest.

1795   Naturalization Act. Under this act, a five-year residency is required for U.S. citizenship. Allegiance to foreign sovereigns and the titles of nobility must be renounced.

1798   Alien and Sedition Acts. The Naturalization Act raises the residency requirements for citizenship from 5 to 14 years. The Alien Act gives the president the power to deport any dangerous or treasonable alien during peacetime. The Alien Enemy Act empowers the government to arrest, imprison, and banish aliens in the employ of an enemy nation during times of war. The Sedition Act, providing penalties for obstructing the government or publishing slanderous writing against it, does not apply directly to aliens.

1807   Act to Prohibit the Importation of Slaves. This act, authorized by the Constitution, prohibits the importation of African slaves as of January 1, 1808.

1820   Missouri Compromise. In this series of acts Missouri is admitted to the Union as a free state, Maine as a slave state, and slavery is forbidden in the rest of the Louisiana Purchase north of 36°30' latitude.

1850   Compromise of 1850. In this series of acts the slave trade is prohibited in the District of Columbia, but the Fugitive Slave Law of 1793 is amended to require citizens in free states to assist in the capture of runaway slaves and makes those who aid them liable to fines and imprisonment. The territories of New Mexico and Utah are established and allowed to decide for themselves the slavery issue.

1854   Kansas-Nebraska Act. This act establishes the territories of Kansas and Nebraska and repeals the Missouri Compromise by allowing the residents of these territories to decide whether to permit slavery.

1866   Freedmen's Bureau Act. This act Expands the Bureau's power to include establishing courts to prosecute violations of African-American civil liberties. The Bureau is also empowered to construct schools and pay teachers.

Civil Rights Act. In this landmark act, passed over President Andrew Johnson's veto, Congress confers full citizenship on "all persons born in the United States . . . excluding Indians not taxed." These citizens, "without regard to any previous condition of slavery or involuntary servitude," are guaranteed the same rights to "security of person and property" as "white citizens."

1870-   Ku Klux Klan Acts. These acts grant the president the power to suspend habeas corpus,
1871   declare martial law, and dispatch troops to combat Klan violence and maintain order. The act also gives federal courts jurisdiction over cases involving terrorism against freed slaves.

1875   Civil Rights Act. The second Civil Rights Act recognizes that all people are equal before the law and establishes penalties for interfering with any citizen's "full and equal enjoyment" of inns, theaters, "public conveyances," and "other places of public amusement." It is declared unconstitutional in 1883.

1882   Chinese Exclusion Act. The act bars Chinese laborers from immigrating to the United States for ten years. It will be extended until it is repealed in 1943.

Immigration Act. This act bars entry to criminals, the insane, paupers, and persons likely to become a public charge.

1917   Immigration Act. This act establishes literacy as a requirement for entry and sets up an Asiatic barred zone but exempts refugees from religious persecution.

1918, 1920   Alien Acts. The acts exclude anarchists and others advocating the overthrow of government. They authorize the government to deport any aliens who are members of revolutionary organizations.

1921   Emergency Quota Act. This act establishes a national-origins quota system. Only 3 percent of the people of any nationality who lived in the United States in 1910 may enter from a country each year. The total maximum is 375,000. Mexicans and other Latin Americans are exempted.

1924   Johnson-Reed Immigration Act. This act halves the maximum and sets the annual quota of immigrants entering the United States from a country at 2 percent of U.S. residents of that nationality in 1890. Immigrants from Canada and Latin America are exempted.

1940   Alien Registration (Smith) Act. This act requires that all aliens be registered and fingerprinted and provides for their deportation.

1943   Chinese Act. This act repeals the Chinese Exclusion Acts, makes Chinese residents eligible for naturalization, and sets an annual Chinese immigration quota of 105.

1952   Immigration and Nationality (McCarran-Walter) Act. Spouses and minor children become nonquota immigrants under this act, but the national-origins quota system is preserved for European countries. The ban against Asian and Pacific immigration is lifted, and African and Asian nations have annual immigration quotas of 100 each. "Subversives" are barred, and the deportation of Communist immigrants is permitted.

1957   Civil Rights Act. This act protects the right to vote and establishes a Civil Rights Commission.

1964   Civil Rights Act. This prohibits discrimination in education, employment, and public accommodations on the basis of "race, color, religion, or national origin."

1965   Voting Rights Act. By this act, federal agents are empowered to register black voters in states and districts where there is evidence that voting rights have been denied. The act is expanded in 1975 to include Spanish-speaking Americans and other "language minorities" and to mandate bilingual elections in some circumstances.

Immigration and Nationality Act. This act ends the national-origins quota system. A limit of 120,000 visas a year for Western Hemisphere countries and 170,000 a year for all other nations is set. Relatives of U.S. citizens and those with special education and skills have preferences.

1968   Fair Housing Act. This act forbids discrimination in the sale or rental of housing.

1980   Refugee Act. The act raises the annual number of refugees admitted to 320,000 and provides a new definition of *refugee*, no longer limited to those fleeing Communist persecution.

1986   Immigration Reform and Control (Simpson-Mazzoli) Act. This act allows illegal aliens who can prove they have resided continuously in the country since 1982 to stay in the country legally, but criminal sanctions will be imposed on employers using undocumented workers.

1990   Immigration Act. By this law, the first three years following passage, 700,000 immigrants (excluding refugees) will be granted visas annually. Afterward, the yearly limit will be 675,000, of which 140,000 visas will be given to immigrants sponsored by employers with specified jobs for them to fill. In addition, 55,000 nationals of countries restricted by previous immigration acts will receive "diversity" visas.

SUPREME COURT DECISIONS AFFECTING IMMIGRATION AND MINORITIES

1837   *New York v. Miln.* The Court declares that state statutes requiring ship captains to supply descriptions of passengers entering the country are constitutional, a legitimate exercise of police power to promote public welfare and not a violation of the commerce clause.

1842   *Prigg v. Commonwealth of Pennsylvania.* The Court declares unconstitutional a Pennsylvania law that prohibits the seizure of fugitive slaves.

1857   *Dred Scott v. Sandford.* The Court holds that African Americans are not citizens, Congress cannot prohibit slavery in the territories, and residence in a free state does not confer freedom on African Americans. The decision hastens the start of the Civil War by sweeping aside legal barriers to the expansion of slavery and inciting the anger of Northerners.

1883   *Civil Rights Cases.* The Court strikes down the Civil Rights Act of 1875, saying that "social" rights are beyond federal control, but blacks cannot be excluded from juries.

1890   *Louisville, New Orleans, and Texas Railroad v. Mississippi.* The Court upholds the constitutionality of states' attempts to segregate railway cars.

1896   *Plessy v. Ferguson.* The Court decides that if segregated railroad cars offer equal accommodations, then such segregation is not discriminatory against blacks and does not deprive them of their Fourteenth Amendment rights to equal protection under the law. The "separate but equal" doctrine is not struck down until 1954 in *Brown v. Board of Education of Topeka.*

1898   *Williams v. State of Mississippi.* The Court rules that the state has a right to require voters to pass a literacy test.

1915   *Guinn v. United States.* The Court rules that the "grandfather clause," which disenfranchised most African Americans, is unconstitutional. The clause, adopted by Oklahoma and Maryland, exempted citizens from certain voter qualifications if their grandfathers had voted; obviously, this could not apply to blacks whose grandparents lived before the ratification of the Fifteenth Amendment.

1917   *Buchanan v. Warley.* The Court strikes down as unconstitutional a law that prohibits members of one race to buy, reside in, or sell property on streets where a majority of residents are of another race.

1927   *Nixon v. Herndon.* State laws prohibiting blacks from voting in primaries are held to be in violation of the Fourteenth Amendment.

1940   *Hansberry v. Lee.* The Court rules that African Americans cannot be prevented from buying homes in white neighborhoods.

1944   *Korematsu v. United States.* The Court upholds as "military necessity" the relocation of Japanese Americans from the West Coast to inland detention camps.

    Smith v. Allwright. The Court rules that excluding blacks from a political party on the basis of race violates the Fifteenth Amendment.

1946   *Morgan v. Commonwealth of Virginia.* The Court rules that segregation on interstate buses is unconstitutional.

1948   *Shelley v. Kraemer.* The Court rules that racially restrictive covenants in housing contracts are not enforceable.

1954   *Brown v. Board of Education of Topeka.* The Court unanimously overrules *Plessy v. Ferguson* and declares that segregated public schools violate the equal protection clause of the Fourteenth Amendment.

1960   *Gomillion v. Lightfoot.* The Supreme Court rules that the drawing of election districts so that blacks constitute a minority in all districts is a violation of the Fifteenth Amendment.

1964   *Heart of Atlanta Motel, Inc. v. United States.* The Court declares constitutional Title II of the Civil Rights Act of 1964, which outlaws private discrimination in public accommodations. Congress has the power to bar racial discrimination in facilities that serve interstate travelers.

1966   *South Carolina v. Katzenbach.* The Court upholds the right of the federal government to intervene to protect voting rights.

1971   *Griggs v. Duke Power Co.* The Court makes its first ruling on the job-bias provisions of the Civil Rights Act of 1964, declaring that "objective" criteria, unrelated to job skills, for hiring workers are discriminatory if they result in minorities' being relatively disadvantaged.

    Swann v. Charlotte-Mecklenburg Board of Education. The Court unanimously upholds school busing for the purpose of racial balance in situations where segregation has been official policy and the school authorities have not come up with a viable alternative to busing.

1977   *United Jewish Organization of Williamsburgh, N.Y., v. Carey.* The Court upholds the use of racial quotas in reapportioning legislative districts to comply with the Voting Rights Act of 1965.

1978   *University of California Regents v. Bakke.* The Court requires that the University of California Medical School at Davis admit white applicant Allan Bakke, who had argued that the school's minority admissions program made him a victim of "reverse discrimination."

1979   *Weber v. Kaiser Aluminum and Chemical Corporation.* The Court upholds affirmative-action programs, declaring that a job-training program that gives preference to African Americans in situations with a "manifest racial imbalance" is constitutional.

1989   *City of Richmond v. J. A. Croson.* The Court declares illegal a Richmond, Virginia, set-aside program mandating that 30 percent of the city's public works funds go to minority-owned construction firms. Such programs are only legal if they redress "identified discrimination."

SIGNIFICANT PEOPLE IN THE HISTORY OF MINORITIES

Abernathy, Ralph (1926–1990).   A clergyman, Abernathy helped Martin Luther King, Jr., organize and lead the civil rights movement in the 1950s and 1960s. In 1957 he and King founded the Southern Christian Leadership Conference (SCLC) to coordinate activities of civil rights groups. On King's death in 1968 he became its president and the same year led the Poor People's Campaign, a protest against racial discrimination held in Washington, D.C.

Ali, Muhammad, formerly **Cassius Clay** (1942–).   After first winning the title of world heavyweight champion in 1964, Clay joined the Black Muslims and changed his name to Muhammad Ali. He then refused to serve in the military, citing religious objections; he also opposed the Vietnam War. He was stripped of his title and convicted of draft evasion, but in 1970 the Supreme Court reversed the lower-court decision and upheld his draft appeal on religious grounds. His title was restored and he went on to win the world heavyweight title again in 1974.

Anderson, Marian (1902–1993).   Because of discrimination against African Americans in the United States, Anderson, a contralto, had to win fame mainly by performing in Europe during the 1930s. In 1939 she was prevented from singing in Washington, D.C.'s Constitution Hall by the Daughters of the American Revolution (DAR). The incident caused a large public outcry against the DAR, and Anderson sang instead before 75,000 people at the Lincoln Memorial. In 1955 she became the first black to perform at New York City's Metropolitan Opera. She was named alternate delegate to the United Nations in 1958 and in 1963 was awarded the President's Medal of Freedom.

Antin, Mary (1881–1949).   A Russian Jew who immigrated with her family in the 1890s, Antin published a series of letters she had written to her uncle about the immigrant experience, *From Plotzk to Boston* (1899). She went on to write *The Promised Land* (1912) and *They Who Knock at Our Gates* (1914), an argument against the growing movement for the restriction of immigration.

Attucks, Crispus (1723?–1770).   Attucks, born to an Indian mother and African-American father, is remembered as one of five colonists killed by British soldiers in the Boston Massacre in the 1770s, an event leading to the American Revolution.

Baker, Ella (1903–1986).   A civil rights activist, in 1938 Baker became a field secretary in the South for the National Association for the Advancement of Colored People (NAACP). She later worked in the South with the Southern Christian Leadership Conference (SCLC), where she helped students create the Student Nonviolent Coordinating Committee (SNCC). After leaving SCLC for SNCC, she remained at the center of the struggle for black voting rights in the South.

Banneker, Benjamin (1731–1806).   An astronomer and mathematician, Banneker helped to survey Washington, D.C., in 1791 and defended the equality of fellow African Americans in his correspondence with Thomas Jefferson.

Bethune, Mary McLeod (1875–1955).   An educator, Bethune founded the Daytona Normal and Industrial Institute for Negro Girls (today Bethune-Cookman College) in 1904. During the presidency of Franklin Roosevelt, Bethune was director of Negro Affairs for the National Youth Administration from 1936 to 1944. She also founded the National Council of Negro Women, serving as its first president from 1935 to 1949.

Brooke, Edward (1919–).   Brooke, a Republican, was elected attorney general of Massachusetts in 1962. Four years later, he was elected to Congress, becoming the first African-American senator since Reconstruction.

Brown, John (1800–1859).   A militant abolitionist, Brown and his five sons moved in 1855 to Kansas, where he and a small group of supporters murdered five supposed proslavery settlers along Pottawattamie Creek. In 1859 he led an attack on the federal arsenal at Harpers Ferry, Virginia. In the ensuing battle with the militia, Brown was wounded and captured; later he was hanged. The raid was widely popular in the North, where some considered Brown a martyr, but enraged and terrified the South.

Bunche, Ralph (1904–1971).   The grandson of a slave, Bunche drafted the sections of the UN charter on trusteeship territories. In 1948 as chief UN mediator in Palestine he arranged for a cease-fire between the Arabs and the Jews, for which he was awarded the 1950 Nobel Peace Prize. From 1967 he was undersecretary-general of the UN, the highest rank held so far by an American.

Carmichael, Stokely, now **Kwame Toure** (1942–).   Elected chairman of the Student Nonviolent Coordinating Committee (SNCC) in 1966, Carmichael championed militant civil rights activism by African Americans, coining the term *black power*. His position split the SNCC, and he eventually joined the Black Panthers. Later he preached Pan-Africanism.

Carver, George Washington (1864?–1943).   The son of slaves, Carver, a botanist, directed the Tuskegee Institute's department of agriculture and agricultural research from 1896 to 1915. He urged southern farmers to diversify their crops by using such soil-enriching crops as peanuts, sweet potatoes, and soybeans, and developed a multitude of products and uses for these crops. In 1943 the George Washington Carver National Monument in Missouri became the first national park area honoring an African American.

Chávez, César (1927–1993).   The son of Mexican-American migrant farmworkers, Chávez founded the National Farm Workers Association in 1962. His United Farm Workers (UFW) union became part of the AFL-CIO in 1972. Chávez used nonviolent tactics such as boycotts against California's vineyard owners to gain better working conditions for migrant workers.

Chavez, Dennis (1888–1962).   Chavez was the first American-born Hispanic to be elected United States senator. A Democrat, he was appointed in 1935 to fill the seat made vacant by the death of New Mexico's Bronson Cutting. A year later Chavez was elected to that seat, which he held until his death.

Chisholm, Shirley (1924–).   In 1968 Chisholm, a Brooklyn Democrat, was elected to Congress, becoming the first black woman in the House of Representatives. In 1972 she made an unsuccessful bid for president.

Clark, Kenneth (1914–).   This psychologist's research on the negative effects of segregation on African-American children influenced the 1954 landmark case *Brown v. Board of Education of Topeka,* in which the Supreme Court ruled that segregation in public schools was unconstitutional.

Delaney, Martin (1812–1885).   An early black nationalist and proponent of black emigration to Africa, Delaney served as co-editor of the *North Star* with Frederick Douglass. Briefly a medical student at Harvard, he organized the National Emigration Conventions and went to Liberia to investigate sites for colonization. Later he served in the Civil War and the Freedmen's Bureau.

Douglass, Frederick, originally **Frederick Bailey** (1817?–1895).   Douglass was born a slave but escaped in 1838, settling in Massachusetts and renaming himself Frederick Douglass. In 1841 he spoke at the antislavery convention and became an agent of the Massachusetts Anti-Slavery Society. After buying his freedom with money from lecturing, Douglass settled in Rochester, New York, where in 1847 he founded and co-edited the *North Star*, an abolitionist paper. During the Civil War he helped recruit black soldiers. In 1845 he published his autobiography, *Narrative of the Life of Frederick Douglass*.

Du Bois, William Edward Burghardt (W.E.B.) (1868–1963).   An educator, editor, writer, and civil rights activist, Du Bois in 1905 was one of the founders of the Niagara Movement, which led, four years later, to the establishment of the NAACP, which he also helped create. From 1910 to 1934, as editor of the NAACP magazine, the *Crisis*, he argued for a more militant approach to civil rights. From 1934 to 1944 Du Bois, the first black to receive a Ph.D. from Harvard, was professor of sociology at Atlanta University. Du Bois also pioneered the concept of Pan-Africanism. Among his influential writings are *The Souls of Black Folk* (1903) and *Black Reconstruction in America* (1935).

Farmer, James (1920–).   Farmer helped found the Congress of Racial Equality (CORE) in 1942 and served as its national director from 1961 to 1966, when he organized the first "freedom rides" through the South. During the Nixon administration he was briefly assistant secretary for the Department of Health, Education, and Welfare. He later returned to teaching and lecturing and in 1985 published his autobiography *Lay Bare the Heart*.

Farrakhan, Louis (1933–).   Born Louis Walcott, Farrakhan joined the Nation of Islam in his twenties, becoming the organization's national representative after Malcolm X's death, and then the leader of one faction of the movement. In 1995 Farrakhan organized the Million-Man March in Washington, D.C., to encourage African-American males to assume greater personal responsibility for their own lives, those of their families, and the community.

Garrison, William Lloyd (1805–1879).   From 1831 to 1865 Garrison, a radical abolitionist, published *The Liberator*, one of the most influential antislavery journals. In 1833 he founded the American Anti-Slavery Society, serving as its president from 1843 to 1865. Before the Civil War, Garrison advocated Northern secession from the Union. He was an early supporter of women's rights.

Garvey, Marcus (1887–1940).   Jamaican-born Garvey arrived in the United States in 1916 and, urging blacks to be proud of their race and to become economically self-sufficient, initiated the Back to Africa Movement to establish a black-run nation there. Within the year, branches of his Universal Negro Improvement Association had sprung up in the United States. In 1925 he was convicted of mail fraud; two years later President Calvin Coolidge commuted his five-year sentence, and Garvey was deported to Jamaica.

Gutierrez, José (1944–).   Gutierrez founded the Mexican American Youth Organization (MAYO) and La Raza Unida (United Race) party, which attracted Mexican Americans in the Southwest.

Harris, Patricia (1924–).   In 1965 President Lyndon Johnson appointed Harris ambassador to Luxembourg, making her the first African-American woman to achieve the rank of ambassador. Eleven years later, president-elect Jimmy Carter named Harris secretary of the Department of Housing and Urban Development, making her the first African-American female cabinet member.

Huerta, Dolores Fernandez (1930–).   Huerta helped César Chávez to found the Farm Workers Association (later the United Farm Workers), organizing strikes and boycotts that bettered the lives of migrant farmworkers.

Jackson, Jesse (1941–).   An associate of Martin Luther King, Jr., Jackson, a clergyman, was executive director from 1966 to 1971 of Operation Breadbasket, a Southern Christian Leadership Conference program to assist blacks in northern cities. In 1971 he founded Operation PUSH (People United to Save Humanity) to fight racism. Since 1981 he has headed the National Rainbow Coalition, an organization linking racial minorities, peace activists, the poor, and environmentalists. In 1984 and 1988 Jackson sought the Democratic nomination for president, the first serious presidential bids by an African American.

Johnson, James Weldon (1871–1938).   As NAACP field secretary from 1916 to 1920 and then its executive secretary from 1920 to 1930, Johnson, a writer and civil rights leader, helped make the organization into the nation's dominant civil rights unit. While in office, he mounted a legal assault on lynching and segregation, deftly using publicity and lobbying to achieve his ends. During the 1920s Johnson was also a key member of the Harlem Renaissance, writing songs, poems, and novels. He is known for the anonymously published *Autobiography of an Ex-Colored Man* and for "Lift Every Voice and Sing," the Negro National Anthem.

King, Coretta Scott (1927–).   The widow of Martin Luther King, Jr., Coretta Scott King in 1970 helped found the Martin Luther King, Jr., Center for Nonviolent Social Change, which she later headed, in Atlanta. She also established the Martin Luther King, Jr., Library, a collection of materials on the civil rights movement.

King, Martin Luther, Jr. (1929–1968).   The pastor of a Montgomery, Alabama, Baptist church, King became nationally known in 1956 after he helped organize a Montgomery bus boycott, which led to integrated busing in that city and to a Supreme Court decision declaring segregated seating unconstitutional. A believer in nonviolence, King founded the Southern Christian Leadership Conference (SCLC) in 1957 to coordinate activities of civil rights groups. In 1963 he led the great civil rights March on Washington, delivering there his famous "I Have a Dream" speech. King received the 1964 Nobel Peace Prize. In 1968 he initiated the Poor People's Campaign to fight for economic rights not obtained by civil rights gains. The campaign was cut short later that year, on April 4, when he was assassinated by white ex-convict James Earl Ray as he stood on the balcony of a Memphis, Tennessee, motel. The third Monday of January is celebrated as Martin Luther King Day in the United States.

Larrazolo, Octaviano (1859–1930).   An important figure in New Mexico politics, Larrazolo was elected governor in 1918 and to the U.S. Senate in 1928. Throughout his life he fought for bilingual education and the rights of Hispanics.

Lincoln, Abraham (1809–1865).   During his campaign for senator from Illinois, Lincoln debated slavery and unionism with his Democratic opponent, the incumbent Stephen Douglas. Elected president in 1860, Lincoln issued the Emancipation Proclamation three year later, declaring free all slaves in states fighting against the North. Reelected in 1864, he was assassinated while watching a play at Washington's Ford Theatre on April 14, 1865, by actor and Confederate sympathizer John Wilkes Booth.

Louis, Joe (1914–1981).   In 1937 boxer Louis, nicknamed the "Brown Bomber," defeated James Braddock to win the world heavyweight championship, a title he held for a record 12 years, until his retirement in 1949. Throughout his career many African Americans looked with pride to Louis, who in their eyes symbolized black achievement.

Malcolm X, Muslim name **el-Hajj Malik el-Shabazz**, originally **Malcolm Little** (1925–1965).   Imprisoned for robbery from 1946 to 1952, he became a Black Muslim, changing his name to Malcolm X. In 1963 Malcolm X became the organization's first national minister, preaching black separatism, racial pride, and racial achievements. In 1964, after splitting from the Muslims, he formed the Muslim Mosque, Inc. The same year he created the Organization of Afro-American Unity and converted to orthodox Islam. Before he was assassinated in Harlem, possibly by Black Muslims, he had begun to back away from his separatist views. His book, *The Autobiography of Malcolm X*, was published in 1964 and is widely read today.

Marshall, Thurgood (1908–1993).   Before becoming the first African-American Supreme Court justice in 1967, Marshall helped establish the NAACP's Legal Defense and Education Fund to legally challenge racial segregation. He himself argued more than 30 cases before the Supreme Court, including *Brown v. Board of Education of Topeka*, in which the Court declared unconstitutional racially segregated public schools. While a Court Justice he supported individual rights, affirmative action, and First Amendment freedoms.

Muhammad, Elijah, originally **Elijah Poole** (1897–1975).   After assisting Wali Farad (W. D. Fard), who founded the Nation of Islam for blacks, in Detroit, Muhammad became the movement's leader. He called for the formation of an independent, all-black nation within the United States.

Muñoz Marín, Luis (1898–1980).   Having spent most of his youth in the United States, Puerto Rican–born Muñoz Marín, the son of Luis Muñoz Rivera, returned to Puerto Rico in 1926 to edit the family newspaper, *La Democracía*. In 1938 he founded the Popular Democratic party and ten years later became Puerto Rico's first elected governor, serving until 1964. In 1952 he secured commonwealth status for Puerto Rico.

Muñoz Rivera, Luis (1859–1916).   In 1889 Muñoz Rivera founded the Puerto Rican newspaper *La Democracía*, which he used to fight for greater Puerto Rican autonomy and the end of military governorship. A key figure in gaining a Spanish charter for home rule in 1897, he served for the next two years as the president of the autonomist cabinet during the U.S. occupation. Between 1910 and 1916 he served in Washington, D.C., as resident commissioner of Puerto Rico, lobbying for U.S. citizenship for Puerto Ricans, a goal achieved in 1917.

Owens, Jesse (1913–1980).   In the 1936 Olympic Games held in Berlin, Owens won four gold medals in track events. His achievements refuted the Nazi myth of Aryan superiority and enraged German chancellor Adolf Hitler.

Parks, Rosa (1913–).   Parks's refusal to give up her seat to a white person on a segregated bus in Montgomery, Alabama, in December 1955, sparked the bus boycott led by Martin Luther King, Jr., which began the civil rights movement.

Powell, Adam Clayton (1908–1972).   A Harlem clergyman, Powell was from 1945 to 1955 the only black congressman besides Chicago's William Dawson. In Congress, Powell was a strong voice against discrimination and segregation. In 1967, the House denied his seat in Congress on grounds of misuse of public funds. But in 1968 Powell was reelected, returning to Congress in 1969. That year the Supreme Court declared Congress had acted unconstitutionally in excluding Powell in 1967.

Randolph, Asa Philip (1889–1979).   In 1925 Randolph organized the Brotherhood of Sleeping Car Porters, serving as its first president until 1968. He ensured that railway porters and maids, most of whom were African Americans, were included under the protections of the 1934 Federal Railway Labor Act, and he successfully campaigned for President Roosevelt in 1941 to sign the executive order banning discrimination in defense industries and federal bureaus. He led the 1963 March on Washington for Jobs and Freedom.

Riis, Jacob (1849–1914).   This Danish-born journalist and social reformer documented life in the city slums. His powerful photographs in *How the Other Half Lives* (1890) exposed the wretched conditions of the urban immigrant.

Robeson, Paul (1898–1976).   The son of a former slave, Robeson had an outstanding career as a college athlete and graduated from law school before beginning a career as an actor and concert singer. He became identified with the title role in Eugene O'Neill's play, *The Emperor Jones* (1925; film, 1933). Touring the world from 1928 to 1939, Robeson returned to America convinced that the Soviet Union was a society without racial prejudice. He helped found the Progressive Party, campaigned for civil rights, and spoke up against discrimination against blacks. In 1950 the government revoked his passport, charging that he would not sign an anti-Communist oath; the passport was restored in 1958.

Rølvaag, Ole Edvart (1876–1931).   A Norwegian-American novelist and teacher, Rølvaag is most famous for his *Giants in the Earth* (1927), the first of a trilogy that hauntingly depicts the exhilaration and despair of making a life in a new land and becoming American.

Schurz, Carl (1826–1906).   One of the nation's most famous immigrants, Schurz was born in Germany but left after the collapse of the 1848 revolutions. A supporter of Lincoln, he was named minister to Spain in 1861 but resigned to fight in the Civil War, rising to the rank of major general. He served in the U.S. Senate from 1869 to 1875, then was named secretary of the interior by President Rutherford B. Hayes. His wife is credited with introducing German kindergartens to the United States, the first at Watertown, Wisconsin, in 1855.

Seale, Bobby (1936–).   In 1966 Seale co-founded the militant Black Panthers with Huey Newton. In 1968 he was arrested for inciting a riot during the 1968 Democratic National Convention but was tried separately from the Chicago Seven. In 1974 he resigned from the Black Panthers and has attempted to work within the political system, encouraging black youth to enroll in doctoral programs.

Stowe, Harriet Beecher (1811–1896).   Stowe became famous for her antislavery novel *Uncle Tom's Cabin; or Life Among the Lowly*, first serialized between 1851 and 1852 in the newspaper *The National Era* and then published in book form in 1852. A runaway best-seller (300,000 copies sold in America in a year), Stowe's sympathetic depiction of slave life strengthened antislavery sentiment in the North, thereby helping to bring about the Civil War.

Tijerina, Reies Lopez (1926–).   During the 1960s this controversial Chicano leader sought to improve the lives of poor Mexican Americans in the Southwest, organizing protests and La Alianza, an organization that aimed at restoring lands to Mexican Americans that Tijerina believed were wrongfully taken in 1848.

Truth, Sojourner (c. 1797–1883).   Born a slave with the name Isabella, Truth gained freedom in 1827. In 1843 she changed her name to Sojourner Truth and became a religious missionary, nationally famous for preaching against slavery and for women's suffrage.

Tubman, Harriet, originally **Araminta** (c. 1820–1913).   An escaped slave, Tubman made 19 trips into the South, leading more than 300 slaves to freedom in the North on the Underground Railroad. During the Civil War she acted as a spy for federal forces in the South.

Turner, Nat (1800–1831).   A charismatic slave preacher, in 1831 Turner led an uprising of about 75 slaves in Southampton County, Virginia, in which about 50 whites were killed. He was hanged for his role in the revolt.

Washington, Booker T. (1856–1915).　Born a slave, Washington was educated at the Hampton Institute. In 1881 he organized Alabama's Tuskegee Institute, founded to train African Americans for trades and professions. Washington's conservative, accomodationist views aroused the ire of civil rights activists like W.E.B. Du Bois.

Wells Barnett, Ida (1862–1931).　A journalist and newspaper owner in Memphis, Wells launched a crusade against lynching. Barnett helped found the National Association for the Advancement of Colored People (NAACP) and the National Association of Colored Woman. She also headed the Anti-Lynching Bureau of the National Afro-American Council.

ADDITIONAL SOURCES OF INFORMATION

Acuna, Rodolfo. *Occupied America: A History of Chicanos.* 3rd. ed. HarperCollins, 1987.

Archdeacon, Thomas J. *Becoming American: An Ethnic History.* Free Press, 1983.

Billington, Ray Allen. *The Origins of Nativism in the United States, 1800–1844.* Ayer, 1974.

Bodnar, John. *The Transplanted: A History of Immigrants in Urban America.* Indiana University Press, 1985.

Branch, Taylor. *Parting the Waters: America in the King Years, 1954–1963.* Simon & Schuster, 1988.

Chamlers, David. *Hooded Americanism: The History of the Ku Klux Klan.* 3rd ed. Duke University Press, 1987.

Curtin, Philip D. *The Atlantic Slave Trade: A Census.* University of Wisconsin Press, 1969.

Daniels, Roger. *Coming to America: A History of Immigration and Ethnicity in American Life.* HarperCollins, 1991.

De Leon, Arnoldo. *The Tejano Community, 1836–1900.* University of New Mexico Press, 1982.

Friedman, Lawrence J. *Gregarious Saints: Self and Community in American Abolitionism.* Cambridge University Press, 1982.

Garrow, David J. *Bearing the Cross: Martin Luther King, Jr., and the Southern Christian Leadership Conference.* Morrow, 1986.

Genovese, Eugene D. *Roll, Jordan, Roll: The World the Slaves Made.* Random House, 1974.

Glazer, Nathan, ed. *Clamor at the Gates: The New American Immigration.* ICS Press, 1985.

Glenn, Susan A. *Daughters of the Shtetl: Life and Labor in the Immigrant Generation.* Cornell University Press, 1990.

Handlin, Oscar. *Boston's Immigrants: A Study in Acculturation.* Rev. ed. Belknap Press, 1959.

———, ed. *Harvard Encyclopedia of American Ethnic Groups.* Harvard University Press, 1980.

Harding, Vincent. *There Is a River: The Black Struggle for Freedom in America.* Harcourt Brace Jovanovich, 1981.

Higham, John. *Send These to Me: Immigrants in Urban America.* Johns Hopkins University Press, 1975.

Jones, Jacqueline. *Labor of Love, Labor of Sorrow: Black Women, Work, and the Family from Slavery to the Present.* Basic Books, 1985.

Jordan, Winthrop D. *White Over Black: American Attitudes Toward the Negro, 1550–1812*. Norton, 1968.

Kluger, Richard. *Simple Justice: The History of Brown v. Board of Education and Black America's Struggle for Equality*. Knopf, 1976.

Litwak, Leon. *North of Slavery: The Negro in the Free States, 1790–1860*. University of Chicago Press, 1961.

McPherson, James M. *Struggle for Equality: Abolitionists and the Negro in the Civil War and Reconstruction*. Princeton University Press, 1964.

Reimers, David M. *Still the Golden Door: The Third World Comes to America*. Columbia University Press, 1985.

Stampp, Kenneth M. *The Era of Reconstruction, 1865–1877*. Random House, 1965.

Weisbrot, Robert. *Freedom Bound: A History of America's Civil Rights Movement*. Norton, 1990.

Woodward, C. Vann. *The Strange Career of Jim Crow*. 3rd rev. ed. Oxford University Press, 1974.

5

Military History

SIGNIFICANT EVENTS IN AMERICAN MILITARY HISTORY

From ragtag militias fighting for independence from Britain to the most powerful military establishment in the world, the United States has protected and advanced its interests through force, when necessary.

The Revolutionary War

1763-
1775
Growing unease over America's colonial status is punctuated by heavier taxes, which colonists argue were passed without representation; the Boston Massacre, in which five colonial protesters are killed by British soldiers; and finally the Boston Tea Party, in which colonists dressed as Indians dump tea in Boston Harbor (see Chapter 2).

1775
War erupts April 19 after British troops based in Boston head to Concord to destroy colonists' munitions there. Paul Revere and William Dawes embark on a late-night ride to alert the minutemen, and at dawn fighting breaks out at Lexington, later at Concord. Americans quickly lay siege to Boston, headquarters for the British army.

On May 10 Ethan Allen and Benedict Arnold capture Fort Ticonderoga. The Continental Army is organized, and on June 15 George Washington is appointed its head. On June 17 the British suffer heavy losses at the Battle of Bunker Hill, actually fought on Breed's Hill.

With the British reconnoitering in Canada and the Americans afraid that they will use it as a staging ground, Continental Army Brigadier General Richard Montgomery stages a Canadian invasion. Americans fight all the way to the city of Quebec, which they surround and blockade.

Battle of Bunker Hill

American Wars: When and Why

War	Dates	Causes	Enemies and Allies
American Revolution	1775–1783	Economic (British tax colonists too heavily) and political (liberty was in the air) issues. Rising up against its mother country, the United States became the first new nation of the modern era.	Enemies: Britain Allies: France (formal alliance); Spain (declares war on Britain but does recognizes U.S. independence), and Holland
War of 1812	1812–1815	Trade, border, and maritime issues	Enemy: Britain
Mexican War	1846–1848	Land acquisition	Enemy: Mexico
Civil War	1861–1865	Slavery and states' rights	Union vs. Confederacy: nation divided against itself
Spanish-American War	1898	Imperial ambitions	Enemy: Spain
World War I (also called the Great War)	1914–1918; U.S. participation, 1917–1918	Nationalism, imperialism, anticolonial unrest, hostile alliance systems, militarism, and an arms race	Allies: France, Russia, Britain, Italy Enemies (Central Powers): Germany, Austria-Hungary, Ottoman Empire
World War II	1939–1945; U.S. participation, 1941–1945	Fascism, militarism, imperialism	Allies: Great Britain, France, USSR Enemies (Axis Powers): Germany, Italy, Japan
Korean War	1950–1953	First limited war of the cold war era, played out as Korean civil war	Allies: South Korea, UN Enemies: North Korea, China, support from USSR by Soviets
Vietnam War	1964–1975	Second limited war of the cold war era, played out as Vietnamese civil war	Ally: South Vietnam Enemy: North Vietnam, supported by the USSR

1776   Nearly 5,000 free African Americans, many from Massachusetts and Rhode Island, fight in the Continental Army, but in the South the British promise of freedom lures slaves to escape and join British ranks. The Cherokees and most Iroquois also fight for Britain. France and ultimately Spain help the colonists.

In March, British soldiers escape from the colonists surrounding Boston and head to Halifax, Nova Scotia, to regroup.

With the Canadian threat much diminished, the blockade of Quebec ends in May.

1776   In June, Americans successfully hold off General Henry Clinton's forces along the East Coast, and the focus of the war shifts to New York, where the British hope to capture New York City and its strategic harbor.

The Continental Congress signs the Declaration of Independence on July 4.

In August, Washington loses the Battle of Long Island. The British occupy New York City, defeat Washington again at White Plains in October, and pursue his army into New Jersey but give up the chase when Washington's troops escape across the Delaware River into Pennsylvania. The Americans recross the Delaware in December and rout the British and their Hessian mercenaries at Trenton and Princeton.

George Washington and troops at Valley Forge

The British execute Nathan Hale as a spy.

The first year of fighting ends in a draw. Neither army has the upper hand, but both are inclined to continue fighting.

1777   The British strategy to seize control of the Hudson Valley and separate New England from the rest of the colonies is thwarted at Saratoga, where John Burgoyne's army surrenders. The American victory encourages French support, realized in an alliance the next year.

In Pennsylvania, Washington falls back at Brandywine Creek, and British troops under Sir William Howe occupy Philadelphia. Washington establishes his winter camp 20 miles away at Valley Forge.

1778   In February, after two years of secretly sending aid to the Americans, the French, who now believe the Americans can win the war, formally recognize the new nation and conclude an alliance.

Sir Henry Clinton, who replaced Howe, sets out for New York but is pursued by Washington's army, which in June overtakes the British at Monmouth Court House. The British press on to New York, and Washington camps above the city.

On the frontier, George Rogers Clark seizes British outposts in Illinois country while Daniel Boone does the same in Kentucky. The British turn their attention to a southern campaign. By December they hold most of Georgia.

1779   Fighting continues to be focused in the South, but repeated skirmishes along the Georgia–South Carolina border do not produce a clear victor.

Spain declares war on Britain.

In a war in which a single naval battle is a major victory, Americans are thrilled when the *Bon Homme Richard,* captained by John Paul Jones, triumphs over the HMS *Serapis* in the North Sea, in the most famous sea battle of the war.

1780   Early in the year General Sir Henry Clinton lays siege to Charleston. In the spring the Americans under the command of Major General Benjamin Lincoln surrender to Clinton, who then heads north to deal with a French sea blockade.

In August, in the war's concluding campaign, General Charles Cornwallis's forces crush an American army commanded by General Horatio Gates at Camden, South Carolina. Guerrilla fighters Francis Marion and Thomas Sumter continue to plague Cornwallis. Major General Nathanael Greene replaces Gates and cleverly employs such tactics as rapid troop movement, division of his forces (an especially brave move with his lesser might), and guerrilla warfare.

1781   In January the Americans beat the British at Cowpens, South Carolina. When Cornwallis chases one division though North Carolina, another one moves in behind him. After Cornwallis retreats, Greene systematically knocks off every southern British outpost.

On October 19, while waiting for reinforcements from General Henry Clinton, a weary Cornwallis surrenders to combined French and American forces at Yorktown, Virginia.

1783   The Treaty of Paris is signed on September 3; John Adams, Benjamin Franklin, and John Jay represent the United States.

The War of 1812

1812   War erupts between the United States and Great Britain over trade and border disputes, the rights of neutrals, and freedom of the seas, including maritime practices. New Englanders generally oppose the war, and westerners support it.

Early land campaigns in Canada bring defeat to U.S. forces, who surrender Detroit and Fort Dearborn (Chicago).

A series of early sea victories creates optimism and make heroes at home, but ultimately the British slowly strangle the East Coast with a naval blockade. Among notable U.S. sea victories are: USS *Essex* captures *Alert,* USS *Constitution* destroys *Guerrière,* USS *Wasp* seizes *Frolic,* USS *United States* defeats *Macedonia* off the Madeira Islands, USS *Constitution* beats *Java.*

1813   The United States claims victory at the Battle of Lake Erie. When the fleet of Oliver Hazard Perry destroys the British fleet there, the British are forced out of the Great Lakes region, including Detroit. In retreat, the British are overtaken and further destroyed at the Battle of the Thames. Indians fight alongside the British, and the great Shawnee leader Tecumseh dies in this battle.

1814   Despite these victories, the United States is nearly bankrupt and near defeat at the start of the new year, and the British, having just defeated Napoleon, can now turn their full attention toward this war. They plan a three-pronged attack that they believe will bring the Americans to their knees.

One campaign is directed at the Chesapeake Bay. The British win at the Battle of Bladensburg on August 18, and then they march on the nation's capital, burning much of it and forcing President James Madison to flee.

In the second campaign, just as 10,000 British troops are preparing to march southward from Canada and take New York City, in September the American fleet decisively wins the Battle of Lake Champlain, destroying the British fleet.

Days later, back in the Chesapeake, the Battle of Fort McHenry in Baltimore provides another pivotal American victory, inspiring Francis Scott Key to write "The Star-Spangled Banner."

The Battle of Fort McHenry, inspiration for Francis Scott Key's "The Star-Spangled Banner"

Even the duke of Wellington can promise little success without control of the Great Lakes, and when British negotiators learn of the Battle of Lake Champlain, they decide not to request the territorial concessions they had hoped for, and return to the bargaining table at Ghent.

The Treaty of Ghent is signed on December 24: no land has changed hands, and neither side has gained anything from the war.

1815   The third British campaign was to have attacked New Orleans, but the battle here—an American victory—does not take place until two weeks after the treaty is signed.

The Mexican War

1845   The United States annexes Texas, a move that Mexico has warned will be tantamount to an act of war because Mexico has never recognized Texas's independence. President James K. Polk sends troops, led by General Zachary Taylor, to the Nueces River in Texas.

1846   Polk orders Taylor to advance south to the Rio Grande, which the United States claims is the southern border of Texas. Mexico maintains the Nueces is the border, and when Mexican troops attack a reconnoitering party of Americans, Polk claims that Mexico has invaded the United States and "shed American blood upon American soil." Congress declares war.

The United States attacks in three campaigns: a campaign in northern Mexico, spearheaded by Taylor; a campaign along the Santa Fe Trail, led by Brigadier General Stephen Kearny and set to culminate in California; and a push into Mexico City, headed by General Winfield Scott.

In June, even before hearing that war has broken out, Anglo settlers under Mexican rule in southern California stage the Bear Flag Revolt and declare themselves an independent republic.

Kearny heads down the Santa Fe Trail in July. In August his troops occupy Santa Fe.

By sea, Commodore John Drake Sloat lands at Monterey, California. He takes San Francisco.

Kearny heads for San Diego, which he reaches in December to complete the occupation of California.

Taylor advances on Monterrey, Mexico, which he captures in September.

1847   Antonio López de Santa Anna counterattacks at Buena Vista in February and is beaten. Taylor remains in command of a small occupying force for nine months.

Scott's army lands at Veracruz in March. At Cerro Gordo, Santa Anna is routed. The Americans advance toward Mexico City.

In September, Scott's men surround Mexico City. The final battle takes place on Chapultepec Hill, stormed in a savage American assault.

1848   The Treaty of Guadelupe Hidalgo, agreed to on February 2, ends the Mexican War. Ulysses S. Grant, William T. Sherman, George B. McClellan, George G. Meade, Robert E. Lee, Thomas J. Jackson, Albert Sidney Johnson, James Longstreet, and many more officers who will later be enemies are colleagues in arms.

The Civil War

1860   With the nation deeply divided over the issue of slavery, Abraham Lincoln's election to the presidency by winning only in the free states brings the situation to the boiling point. South Carolina secedes from the Union.

1861   By February 1, six other southern states—Mississippi, Florida, Alabama, Georgia, Louisiana, and Texas—secede.

The Confederacy government forms in February. Its first capital is in Montgomery, Alabama; after Virginia secedes Richmond becomes its capital. The Confederacy easily raises an army of more than 100,000 men.

Although the Confederates fire the first shots of the war at Fort Sumter in Charleston Harbor on April 12, antagonism has built steadily on both sides, and Abraham Lincoln may have baited the South into making the first move. Four other states—Arkansas, Tennessee, North Carolina, and Virginia—secede. The remaining slave states—Missouri, Kentucky, Maryland, and Delaware—stay with the Union despite obviously divided loyalties. The western counties of Virginia secede from Virginia and enter the Union as West Virginia in 1863.

In the First Battle of Bull Run (Manassas Junction, Virginia) in July, outnumbered Confederate forces under General P.G.T. Beauregard beat back Union forces under General Irvin McDowell. Union troops retreat to Washington, and Confederate commander Thomas J. Jackson earns his nickname, "Stonewall."

Abraham Lincoln

1862   The Union naval blockade of the South is in place, but few ships are stopped in the first year.

In February, Ulysses S. Grant, newly promoted to brigadier general, successfully takes Forts Henry and Donelson in Tennessee, forcing a Confederate retreat toward Mississippi.

The great naval battle of the Civil War is fought in March between two ironclad ships, the Confederate *Merrimac* and the Union *Monitor.* Although the battle is a draw, it is the first time that ironclad ships have met in battle.

At the Battle of Glorieta Pass, Colorado volunteers keep the Confederate troops out of the rest of the West.

At the Battle of Shiloh in April, Grant, Union commanders William T. Sherman, Don Carlos Buell, and John Pope meet the forces of Confederates Albert Sidney Johnston and Beauregard. The Confederates first rout Union troops, but the next day Grant routs the Confederates, who fall back exhausted. Grant, however, shaken by his losses, does not pursue the enemy. Casualties are extraordinarily high on both sides. The Union Navy, headed by Admiral David Farragut, takes New Orleans and begins to move up the Mississippi River, cutting off Arkansas, Louisiana, and Texas from the rest of the South.

After months of preparation, General George B. McClellan, a reluctant soldier at best, begins the Peninsular Campaign. But when Robert E. Lee, new commander of the Army of Northern Virginia, mounts a strong counterattack, McClellan is caught off guard during the Seven Days' Battles in late June. Lee wins, but both armies suffer heavy losses.

Opposing Civil War commanders Ulysses S. Grant (left) and Robert E. Lee (right)

U.S. Congress passes legislation allowing blacks to serve in the U.S. Army.

In late August, in the Second Battle of Bull Run (Manassas Junction, Virginia), the Confederates, led by generals Lee, Jackson, and James Longstreet, force Union General John Pope to retreat to Washington.

In September, at the Battle of Antietam (near Sharpsburg, Maryland), McClellan and Lee duel to a draw in the bloodiest one-day battle of the war. Although Lee's position is highly vulnerable, McClellan does nothing and the Confederates are able to cross the Potomac into Virginia.

At the December Battle of Fredericksburg, Virginia, the Confederates manage another victory.

1863   After the Emancipation Proclamation effective January 1, state governments begin enrolling African Americans in the Union army; ultimately about 179,000 serve in the federal forces. More than 2,700 die on the battlefield and almost 30,000 die of wounds and disease.

In June, Lee heads to Maryland and Pennsylvania. In early July, he is stopped at Gettysburg. The next day Grant takes Vicksburg, Mississippi, which has been under siege for seven weeks.

Grant and General William Tecumseh Sherman seize Chattanooga in November, opening the way to Atlanta and ultimately for Sherman's infamous march through the South.

1864   By this time, the Union sea blockade is increasingly effective, halting about one-third of the ships trying to enter or exit the South.

In March, Grant becomes supreme commander of all the Union armies. Leaving General Sherman in Chattanooga, he moves into northern Virginia and begins to attack civilian supply lines.

In September, General Sherman marches into Atlanta.

In November, Sherman begins his march to the sea. Taking Savannah in December, he gives it to Lincoln as a Christmas present. The march is deliberately destructive in an attempt to demoralize both the military and civilian population.

AFRICAN AMERICANS SERVE THEIR COUNTRY

Even when they were forced to serve in segregated units under white commanders, African-Americans have always responded to the country's need for soldiers and have enlisted in numbers greater than their population warrants.

Segregation was in effect throughout both world wars. Blacks and whites ate in separate messes and slept in separate barracks. Worst of all from many blacks' point of view, blacks were not permitted to serve in certain units. African-American women who tried to enlist in the WAVES, for example, were turned away on the grounds that there were no black fliers for them to support. During World War II the lines began to break down gradually (the WAVES opened to black women in 1944), and in 1948 President Harry Truman ordered complete integration of the armed forces. Here are the numbers of African-Americans who served in major U.S. wars:

Revolutionary War	5,000
Civil War	200,000
World War I	367,000
World War II	1,000,000
Vietnam War	275,000
Persian Gulf War	104,000

1864   Grant continues to hammer Lee's troops at the Battles of the Wilderness, Spotsylvania, and Cold Harbor. Lee fights well, but his troops are weary, and the hard fact is that the more populous North can continue to send reinforcements while the South cannot.

Grant surrounds Lee at Petersburg and besieges the city.

General McClellan runs for president against Lincoln, who is reelected.

1865   In April, Lee retreats. The Confederates burn Richmond behind them.

On April 9, Lee surrenders at Appomattox Court House, Virginia. Grant is remembered for his compassion at the surrender. He immediately orders that "each officer and man will be allowed to return to his home, not to be disturbed by United States authorities." Grant also provides Lee's starving army 25,000 rations.

The Spanish-American War

1895-   The drift toward war begins when Cuba revolts against Spain's dictatorial colonial policy
1898   and the United States once again casts a longing gaze (see Chapter 8) on the "Pearl of Antillies." U.S. tabloids, especially those of William Randolph Hearst, inflame public opinion by describing the unsanitary Cuban concentration camps, in which about 100,000 Cubans die. Some Americans want to "rescue" Cuba.

1898   On February 9, Hearst publishes an inflammatory private letter in which Dupuyde Lôme, Spanish minister to Washington, refers to President William McKinley as "weak" and a "would-be politician."

On February 15 the U.S. battleship *Maine* explodes in Havana harbor, killing 260 Americans. Although a mine is blamed, the *Maine* actually suffered an internal explosion. "Remember the *Maine* and to hell with Spain" becomes the slogan of the hour.

In April, McKinley asks for war, and Congress complies, although the Teller Amendment asserts that the United States does not seek to annex Cuba.

In the Pacific, the U.S. fleet of modern, steel battleships, under Commodore George Dewey, destroys the outdated Spanish fleet in the Manila harbor in the Philippines in May. In Cuba the Spanish fleet is blockaded in the Santiago harbor.

The Rough Riders, led by Theodore Roosevelt and Leonard Wood, are victorious at San Juan Hill on July 1. Black troops make a significant contribution.

On July 3, in a battle at Santiago Bay, the Spanish fleet is destroyed.

U.S. troops seize Spanish Guam and unclaimed Wake Island, thus achieving a much desired foothold in the Pacific that will facilitate commercial expansion after the war.

Commodore Dewey's forces in the Philippines take the city of Manila on August 13.

The Treaty of Paris is signed on September 10. Cuba is independent. Spain cedes Puerto Rico, Guam, and the Philippines to the United States.

World War I

1914-1918   World War I erupts when Archduke Franz Ferdinand, heir to the throne of Austria-Hungary, is assassinated by Gavrilo Princip, a Serbian, in Sarajevo. Austria-Hungary declares war against Serbia, and due to a set of alliances among the European nations, Russia mobilizes against Austria, Germany declares war against Russia, and France mobilizes to help Russia. The war, though centered in Europe, will gradually expand to include most of the world's nations. It will consume at least 10 million lives, 116,516 of them American. At the onset, the United States claims strict neutrality, although France has been a longtime friend. ("Forget us God, if we forget the sacred sword of Lafayette.") President Woodrow Wilson hopes to negotiate a peace.

1915   On May 7 a German submarine sinks the British ship *Lusitania*, and 128 Americans are killed. The ship was carrying war matériel, and passengers were warned it might be attacked, but the unfairness of submarine warfare turns American public opinion against Germany.

1916   In March a German submarine in the English Channel torpedos the unarmed leisure vessel *Sussex*, injuring a few Americans. Public outrage forces Germany to promise to halt unrestricted submarine warfare.

1917   In February, hoping to bring Britain and France to their knees, before the United States can enter the war, Germany unexpectedly resumes unlimited submarine warfare against all shipping headed for Britain.

In March the United States intercepts a note proposing a Mexican-German alliance. Germany promises Mexico the return of territory taken by the United States in the Mexican War. When Congress still proves lukewarm about entering the war, Wilson responds by arming merchant marine ships.

With Wilson insisting that the "world must be made safe for democracy," on April 6 the United States declares war on Germany. Wilson calls for volunteers. Quickly, however, he and his military advisors realize that much greater numbers will be needed, and Congress passes the Selective Service Act, which requires all males between the ages of 21 and 35 to register for the draft. Ultimately the draft enables the 200,000-man army to grow to one of almost 5 million.

The first American troops arrive in France in July following General John J. Pershing, who arrives in June. Eventually 2 million Americans serve in France. The navy convoys ships and engages in antisubmarine activity by helping to lay 56,000 to 70,000 mines in the North Sea. Five U.S. battleships work with the British Grand Fleet.

In France the United States does not formally join the Allies, being an Associated Power and naming its army the American Expeditionary Force. Initially American troops are assigned to the sector around Verdun.

In December, Congress declares war on Austria-Hungary.

1918   Once Russia makes peace with Germany, March 1918, great numbers of German soldiers are moved west, and Pershing comes under increasing pressure to amalgamate American forces in British and French units.

U.S. infantry with little or no battle experience help stem German advances at Castigny in May and Chateau-Thierry and Belleau Wood in June.

German losses in July and August convince German military leaders that the war cannot be won, though they are not certain it is lost. They urge civilian leaders to consider entering into peace negotiations. A major consideration for the Germans is the apparently inexhaustible American resources.

Still an independent fighting force, on September 12 U.S. troops under Pershing move to reduce the salient at Saint-Mihiel. With Allied air support—about 1,500 planes (609 American) under the command of U.S. Colonel Billy Mitchell—the U.S. forces are successful. Under cover of darkness, Pershing now begins moving the troops engaged at Saint-Mihiel along with fresh units to a new front: the Argonne Forest along the Meuse.

In late September inexperience, difficult terrain, and strong German positions slow American advances.

In October, Pershing renews his offensive, clearing the Argonne Forest of German forces.

On October 30 the U.S. Army pushes through the last German line, clearing the way for a major French offensive.

Germany formally surrenders, and an armistice is signed, with the cease-fire going into effect at 11:00 A.M. on November 11. The United States has enabled its allies to wage war more effectively by bringing them much needed replacements. Germany cedes Alsace-Lorraine and is effectively disarmed by the Treaty of Versailles.

World War II

1931-1935   The specter of a major war once again hangs over the world when Japan, seeking its own empire in Asia, invades Manchuria (September 1931), Hitler assumes power in Germany (January 1933), and fascism is on the rise elsewhere in Europe. Italy, led by Benito Mussolini since 1922, invades Ethiopia and declares it a colony. A plebiscite in the Saar (January 1935) results in the area's returning to Germany. Germany advances into the Rhineland (March 1936), a region demilitarized by several international agreements at the end of World War I.

1935   The Nazi government passes the Nuremberg Laws, which deprive all Jews (anyone with at least one Jewish grandparent) of citizenship and forbid marriage with Gentiles. Gradually all civil rights for Jews are rescinded.

1935-1937   Strongly isolationist, the United States passes the Neutrality Acts, which forbid U.S. companies to sell raw materials, fuel, and matériel to warring nations and tells its citizens that they travel in war zones at their own risk.

1936-1937   Germany and Italy form the Berlin-Rome Axis in October, and one month later Germany and Japan conclude a pact that is the basis for future cooperation. One year later, in November 1937, Japan and Italy sign a pact.

1936-1939   Fascist forces led by Francisco Franco wage a civil war to overthrow Spain's center-left elected government. Germany and Italy supply Franco throughout the struggle.

1937   Japan invades China. It also sinks the *Panay*, a U.S. patrol boat in Chinese waters, but apologizes, wishing to avoid a confrontation.

In March, Germany annexes Austria.

Adolf Hitler addressing the crowd at the 1936 Olympics, Berlin, Germany

1938   Britain and France meet with Germany in Munich in September and agree to let Hitler take over a part of Czechoslovakia called the Sudetenland, German-speaking territories bordering Germany and Austria.

Ostensibly in retaliation for the murder of a German diplomat in Paris by a Polish Jew, Jewish shops, homes, and synagogues throughout Germany are pillaged, burned, and destroyed. A fine of 1 billion marks is levied against the Jewish community.

1939   Germany annexes the rest of Czechoslovakia and sets up the puppet state of Slovakia. Western nations are stunned when Germany and the USSR sign a nonaggression pact on August 23. When Germany invades Poland September 1, hostilities break out. France declares war on Germany. President Franklin Roosevelt issues a proclamation of neutrality on September 5.

In late November, Russia invades Finland.

The Declaration of Panama warns belligerents away from Western Hemisphere seas south of Canada.

1940   Germany goes on the march in northern Europe, invading Denmark and Norway in April and Holland, Belgium, Luxembourg, and France in May. British, French, and Belgian forces are surrounded at Dunkirk in northeastern France. The Nazi war machine inexplicably comes to a halt, and more than 330,000 Allied troops escape to Britain.

The Selective Service and Training Act begins to increase military ranks.

In June, France signs an armistice with Germany.

During the Battle of Britain, Germany relentlessly pounds England by air from mid-August to the end of October, but Britain does not succumb.

Germany, Italy, and Japan sign a ten-year treaty in which they pledge murtual assistance in case of attack.

In an executive order Roosevelt gives Great Britain 50 World War I–vintage destroyers in return for eight sites for U.S. naval bases on British territory.

The New York Times *headlines announcing the attack on Pearl Harbor*

1941 In March the United States institutes Lend-Lease, a program designed to aid any country whose continued existence is deemed in the vital interests of the United States. The hope is that the aid will enable these nations to successfully prosecute the war and the United States will not need to fight.

The United States agrees to defend Greenland. U.S. troops land in Iceland to take over the defense of the North Atlantic nation.

In August, Roosevelt and British prime minister Winston Churchill meet in the North Atlantic to formulate broad postwar aims—the Atlantic Charter (see Chapter 8).

Despite its nonaggression pact, Germany marches against Russia on June 22.

Roosevelt decrees an embargo on all iron and steel exports except to Western Hemisphere nations in September, having frozen all Japanese exports in July.

Roosevelt extends Lend-Lease aid to the Soviet Union

Eager to disable the United States in the Pacific, on December 7 Japan launches a surprise attack on Pearl Harbor and destroys much of the Pacific Fleet. Casualties total 2,280 killed and 1,109 wounded. Sixty-eight civilians lose their lives. At the same time, though it is December 8 west of the Date Line, Japanese forces attack the Philippines, Guam, Midway, Hong Kong, and the Malay Peninsula.

On December 8 Congress declares war on Japan. On December 11 Germany and Italy declare war on the United States.

Russia, helped by an especially harsh winter and overextended German supply lines, rallies against the Germans just in time to stop them from entering Moscow.

1942 In the Pacific, the Japanese win the battles of Manila, Luzon, and the Java Sea in January and February.

In the United States, Japanese Americans are forced into internment camps.

In May the Battle of the Coral Sea, an air struggle over the east coast of Australia, provides a much-needed Allied victory in the Pacific theater.

JAPANESE AMERICANS DURING WORLD WAR II

The Japanese immigrants who began arriving in significant numbers on the West Coast of the United States after 1890 confronted a wall of hostility that had already led to a law specifically prohibiting Chinese immigration. The Japanese were excluded from many occupations, and when in 1906 the San Francisco school board sought to segregate Japanese students, President Theodore Roosevelt intervened to negotiate a "gentleman's agreement" whereby the children would not be segregated but Japan would agree not to permit any more laborers to emigrate to the United States. California soon passed laws prohibiting Japanese from owning or leasing farm land, and in 1924 the federal new immigration law specifically excluded Japanese as "aliens ineligible for citizenship."

Following the surprise attack on Pearl Harbor, the long-standing prejudice against people of Japanese descent reached a fever pitch. And, as the great majority were concentrated on the West Coast, where a Japanese air attack or actual invasion seemed most likely, fears of sabotage seemed to justify racial animosity. Although there were no instances of disloyalty, in February 1942 President Franklin Roosevelt authorized the creation of military areas from which suspect persons could be excluded. A month later, more than 110,000 persons of Japanese descent (41,000 *issei*, or first-generation aliens, and 72,000 *nisei*, or second-generation U.S. citizens) were removed from the strategic military areas in California, Oregon, and Washington and into detention centers in the interior.

The camps themselves were miserable—inadequate in size, sanitation, food rations, and even protection from the elements. The assets of the issei had been frozen, and the property the evacuees had to leave behind was sold at prices far below market value to opportunists, or vandalized. Its total loss is estimated to be more than $400 million. In *Korematsu v. United States* (1944), the Supreme Court upheld the relocation on the grounds of national security.

Even as the evacuees lived behind barbed wire, the 442d Combat Team, an all–Japanese-American unit fighting in Italy and France, established a military record: more casualties and more decorations than for any other unit of its size in American history. More than 25,000 Japanese Americans served in the armed forces during the war.

While German and Italian noncitizens were also designated as enemy aliens during the war, no group suffered the humiliation, loss of wages and property, and loss of civil rights that Japanese Americans endured. In 1988 the U.S. government issued a formal apology and granted each of the 60,000 surviving Japanese Americans who had been interred $20,000 in restitution.

A month later, the Allies are again victorious at Midway, in a three-day naval battle. Four Japanese aircraft carriers are sunk; the United States loses the *Yorktown*. The victory is assured in part by Operation Magic, in which the Allies crack the Japanese secret code and learn Japan's battle plans in advance. This victory renders Hawaii safe from Japanese attack.

The top-secret Manhattan Project is assigned the task of trying to build an atomic bomb.

The United States and Australia mount a counteroffensive in the Solomon Islands and Papua New Guinea. In a protracted, six-month battle, lasting until January 1943, the U.S. marines win Guadalcanal in the Solomon Islands, gaining a strategic airstrip.

In November, during Operation Torch, General Dwight David Eisenhower coordinates amphibious landings with the British at Casablanca, Oran, and Algiers to follow up on the earlier British army victory over Erwin Rommel's forces at El Alamein. By mid-May 1943 all Axis forces in North Africa have surrendered.

At Stalingrad, Soviet forces rally again and besiege German forces there.

1943   Churchill and Roosevelt meet at Casablanca. They agree to unconditional surrender of the enemy and to launch an invasion of Italy. Eisenhower is named supreme commander in North Africa.

1943   German troops at Stalingrad surrender.

Allied air strikes target civilian populations in Germany to weaken morale. As in Britain in 1940, the population becomes more unified, and war production is not stopped. The only lasting result is that many cultural monuments are destroyed.

In July the Allies invade Sicily. Their victory results in the downfall of Italian dictator Benito Mussolini. The Italian mainland is invaded in September, and American and British troops begin the slow and methodical advance northward.

1944   In the Pacific theater, the Battle of the Marshall Islands from November through February 1944 provides another Allied victory.

Under Eisenhower's command, Operation Overlord begins on June 6 with the invasion of France, the largest air and sea invasion ever mounted. Initially 176,000 soldiers and 20,000 vehicles hit the beaches of Normandy. Within a month more than 1 million troops, almost 600,000 tons of supplies, and about 200,000 vehicles are in Normandy. By late July the Germans realize the Battle of Normandy is lost and begin withdrawing east across the Seine. Paris is liberated August 25.

In the Pacific in July, the United States wins the Mariana Islands with the Battle of the Philippine Sea consolidating those wins. Airfields are constructed on Guam and Saipan to begin the bombing of Japan.

In September victories at Palau and Yap open the way for the invasion of the Philippines.

The Battle of Leyte Gulf in late October destroys Japanese naval support for their armed forces in the Philippines. The land battle rages from October to late February 1945.

1945   In February, Roosevelt, Churchill, and Stalin meet at Yalta to begin to plan the postwar peace. They agree to organize the United Nations.

President Franklin Roosevelt dies April 12. Harry Truman becomes president.

Germany surrenders unconditionally, May 7. The war in Europe is over.

The last major land battles of the Pacific are won at Iwo Jima (March) and Okinawa (June).

In July the Big Three—the United States, Britain, and the USSR—meet at Potsdam to hammer out details of the peace.

In August the United States drops leaflets warning the civilian population of Hiroshima that it will obliterate the city if Japan does not surrender immediately. On August 6 the United States drops an atomic bomb on Hiroshima. Three days later a second atomic bomb is dropped on Nagasaki. Two hundred thousand people eventually lose their lives; 100,000 die immediately. On August 14 Japan surrenders, and World War II ends.

The Korean War

1945   After the Axis defeat, the Soviets occupy Korea (previously a Japanese colony) north of the 38th parallel and the Americans occupy the area south of that line. These arrangements had been made at the last minute and were considered temporary. In North Korea, the USSR supports Kim Il Sung, while in South Korea, the United States supports Syngman Rhee.

1950   President Harry Truman interrupts a long weekend in Independence, Missouri, to return to the capital when North Korea invades South Korea on June 25.

On June 27 President Truman orders American forces to give South Korea air and sea support. This same day the UN Security Council unanimously calls on member states to support South Korea (the USSR is boycotting meetings to protest the continued presence of the Nationalist Chinese and is unable to veto the resolution).

A 20-kiloton atomic bomb like the one dropped on Hiroshima

On June 30 President Truman authorizes General Douglas MacArthur to lead American ground forces into Korea.

By September 14 North Korea controls all but the southeastern corner of the peninsula.

President Truman meets with General MacArthur in October at Wake Island. MacArthur assures Truman the Chinese won't get into the war.

By mid-November UN forces under MacArthur's command stage a successful counter-attack that pushes the North Koreans back behind the 38th parallel, almost to the Chinese border. China issues a warning that it will fight if UN forces move any closer, but the U.S. public, buoyed by this victory and egged on by MacArthur himself, demands total victory.

In late November the Chinese enter the war and mount a counteroffensive into South Korea.

1951   In the beginning of the year the UN forces stage their final counterattack and drive the Chinese and North Koreans back to the 38th parallel.

On April 12 President Truman removes General MacArthur from command. MacArthur had tried to continue to widen the war, while Truman sought to initiate peace talks.

Fighting continues throughout the summer, but the warring parties have reached a stalemate.

1953   Negotiations, which have been under way since June 1951, finally produce a settlement in the summer. The fighting stops where it began, along the 38th parallel. Little territory has changed hands, and little has been accomplished by this first war of containment.

The Vietnam War

1950-   Eager to maintain an anti-Communist regime in Asia, the United States supports the French
1956   colonial effort in Indochina. It gives France $2.6 billion in aid, almost as much as the French themselves pour into the region. When the French are finally forced out, Vietnam is divided along the 17th parallel, with the north being supported by the USSR and the south by the United States. Vietnam is supposed to be unified two years later, but South Vietnamese ruler Ngo Dinh Diem, with U.S. assent, refuses to hold elections because he

fears the Communists will win. The Diem regime is harsh, and as a result, guerrilla forces form in North and South Vietnam. Civil war—and another "hot war" of the cold war—looms.

1962   United States troops on a training mission in Vietnam are told to fire back if fired upon. A military assistance command is set up in South Vietnam.

1963   Ngo Dinh Diem is overthrown.

1964   Alleged attacks on U.S. destroyers prompt President Lyndon Johnson to ask Congress "to join in affirming . . . that the United States will continue in its basic policy of assisting the free nations of the area to defend their freedom." Congress responds with the Gulf of Tonkin Resolution, which provides the legal basis for the escalation of the war.

1965   In February, South Vietnamese Communist rebels attack the U.S. military compound at Pleiku and kill eight Americans. President Johnson responds with Operation Rolling Thunder—air raids over North Vietnam.

The first war protests take place at home.

At year's end 184,000 troops are in Vietnam.

1966   The buildup of U.S. troops continues—385,000 soldiers are now in Vietnam—as does the bombing. Hanoi and Haiphong, major cities in North Vietnam, are heavily bombed, and for the first time the United States bombs Communist strongholds in Cambodia.

1967   The war is stalemated. Heavy and continuous warfare is waged. In a pattern that will be repeated regularly, President Johnson restricts (but does not halt) the bombing so that peace talks can take place, then escalates the bombing when the talks break down.

War protesters march against the Pentagon.

1968   The war reaches a turning point with the massive North Vietnamese attack known as the Tet Offensive. In three weeks of intense fighting, the United States holds its own militarily but sustains severe psychological losses. American public opinion is making it difficult to conduct the war, and the North Vietnamese have proven to be a far more determined enemy than the United States ever imagined. With 536,000 troops in Vietnam, U.S. manpower reaches its highest level.

The My Lai massacre takes place when U.S. troops on a search-and-destroy mission kill almost 500 South Vietnamese civilians—men, women, children, and babies—in one village. First reported on in the press in 1969, the troops involved are later charged with war crimes and tried for murder; one man is convicted of murder.

1969   With the United States still employing a strategy of "talk and fight," peace talks begin again. When they fail, President Richard Nixon secretly orders B-52s to bomb Communist strongholds in Cambodia.

1970   After the invasion of Cambodia, public pressure escalates to a fever pitch in the United States when Ohio National Guardsmen kill four students during a protest at Kent State University and two at Jackson State.

American troop strength is reduced to 334,600 by year's end as a policy of Vietnamization is introduced: The war will be gradually turned over to the South Vietnamese people. U.S. troops continue to fight, and the United States continues to bomb Cambodia. President Richard Nixon defends the bombing and invasion in a speech, but his power to wage war is undermined by his failure to be frank and honest with members of Congress and by their relentless questioning when military realities differ from Nixon's and Kissinger's public and private statements.

Congress repeals the Gulf of Tonkin Resolution, December 31. Nixon believes this action is irrelevant.

Soldiers in trenches at Tet Offensive

1971   The Pentagon Papers, which reveal deeper U.S. involvement in the war than the executive branch has ever acknowledged, are published, further undermining what little congressional support is left for the war.

      The United States continues to bomb North Vietnam, hoping to cut off matériel from China and the USSR. U.S. troop strength is down to 156,800. Morale for the troops that remain is low.

1972   Following North Vietnam's Easter Offensive, B-52 bombers again bomb Hanoi and Haiphong. Initially the North Vietnamese are successful, and Quang Tri in South Vietnam falls under their control. President Nixon retaliates with bombing and mining of North Vietnamese harbors. Finally the invasion is brought to a halt and Quang Tri is recaptured.

      After Nixon is reelected, he escalates the bombing on a massive scale. At year's end 24,000 U.S. troops are in Vietnam.

1973   U.S. involvement in Vietnam ends with a whimper when peace accords are signed on January 27 by the United States, North Vietnam, South Vietnam, and the Provisional Revolutionary Government (the Vietcong). U.S. military at year's end number 50. This same day Nixon also announces an end to the draft.

1975   The North Vietnamese seize Saigon in April, as U.S. helicopters rescue about 1,100 Americans and 5,500 South Vietnamese. North Vietnam has won.

WOMEN WARRIORS: BREAKING DOWN THE BARRIERS OF PREJUDICE

In most wars, some women have passed as men and fought alongside them. Beginning with the Civil War, women served informally as nurses, moving alongside divisions of fighting men, but they were not formally enlisted in the armed forces until World War I, when 11,000 women served as nurses and in certain circumstances as naval yeomen.

World War II saw the creation of female auxiliary units: the Women's Auxiliary Army Corps, or WAACS (later WACS), and a naval corps called Women Accepted for Volunteer Emergency Service, or WAVES. There were also auxiliary services for the air force, marine corps, and coast guard. Although 350,000 women joined them, women still could not serve in combat positions or on active duty, nor could they attend military academies. Yet they served in war zones, enduring the same dangerous and physical hardships as combat troops. One thousand women flew planes in World War II, although not in combat. In the Korean War they were regularly stationed in combat zones.

Although women had been generals since 1970, not until 1973 did the Department of Defense undertake a formal program to expand women's roles in the military. One big step came in 1976 when women were admitted into military professional schools. Another came in 1993, when women were allowed to serve aboard warships and fly combat missions. During the Persian Gulf War, 11 U.S. women were killed in combat and 4 in noncombat situations.

As women's numbers in the military expand, so will their roles. In 1996 women were 13.8 percent of the army, 12.6 percent of the navy, 4.9 percent of the marines, and almost 16.3 percent of the air force.

A barrier of another sort was broken in 1993 when the nurses who served in Vietnam were finally honored with a special memorial in the nation's capital.

The Persian Gulf War

1990   Iraq invades Kuwait in August, and President George Bush immediately sends troops and air support to the Persian Gulf region. The UN imposes economic sanctions, but Iraq continues to amass huge forces along Kuwait's border.

1991   After warning Iraq's Saddam Hussein to stand down, the United States initiates massive bombing on January 16. On February 24, U.S. armed forces invade Kuwait and in little more than four days clear Kuwait of Iraqi forces.

America's Costly Wars*

War	Length of Time	Number Serving	Battle Deaths	Other Deaths	Direct Cost	Veterans Payments	Interest	Total
American Revolution	8 years	180– 250,000	4,435	—	$100– $140 mil.	$80 mil.	$20 mil.	$220 mil.
War of 1812	2 years	286,700	2,260	—	$89 mil.	$49 mil.	$14 mil.	$152 mil.
Mexican War	3 years	79,000	1,733	11,500	$82 mil.	$64 mil.	$10 mil.	$156 mil.
Civil War	4 years	600,000– 1,500,000						
Confederacy		1,500,000	74,524	59,297	$1 bil.	—	—	—
Union		2,213,363	140,414	224,097	$2.3 bil.	$8,574 mil.	$1,200 mil.	$12,074 mil.

War	Length of Time	Number Serving	Battle Deaths	Other Deaths	Direct Cost	Veterans Payments	Interest	Total
Spanish-American War	5 months	306,760	385	2,061	$270 mil.	$5,964 mil.	$60 mil.	$6,294 mil.
World War I	2 years	4,743,826	53,513	63,195	$32.7 bil.	$81,000 mil.	$11,000 mil.	$124,000 mil.
World War II	4 years	16,353,659	242,131	115,185	$360 bil.	$301,000 mil.	—	—
Korean War	3 years	5,764,143	33,651	—	$50 bil.	$72,000 mil.	—	—
Vietnam War	11 years	8,744,000	47,369	10,799	$140.6 bil.	136,000 mil.	—	—

*Total cost through 1993 where available

MAJOR INDIAN-WHITE WARS

Conflict between Native Americans and whites began with the first contact in the 16th and 17th centuries and ended tragically in 1890 at the Battle of Wounded Knee. This last conflict was a massacre of a band of Indians who believed they would prevail, if not in this life then in an afterlife, against the onslaught of white culture. In between were more than three centuries of warfare, including border disputes, raids, skirmishes, guerrilla warfare, and massacres on both sides—all for possession of the North American continent (see also Chapter 1).

1636-1937 The Pequots are wiped out in the Pequot War, a campaign deliberately waged by the Puritans.

1675-1676 Metacom's Rebellion, also called King Philip's War. In this last major New England war, which effectively drives the Indians out of southern New England, Narragansetts, Wampanoags, and Nipmucks fight the Puritans in a battle that devastates 12 towns. The Indian effort is led by Metacom, a chief whom the English call "King Philip." The war ends when he is captured and beheaded.

1680 Pueblo Revolt. Pueblos rebel against the Spanish in the Southwest and drive them out for 12 years.

1711-1713 Tuscarora War. Following a massacre by Tuscaroras in Carolina, white settlers ally with other tribes. After a defeat in which more than 200 Tuscarora warriors are killed, the tribe's survivors flee north, where they join the Iroquois Confederation.

1715-1716 Yamasee War. Enraged by the destruction of the Tuscaroras, Yamasees kill more than 200 settlers before the colonists, aided by the Cherokees, defeat them. The Yamasees retreat into Georgia and Florida, where they ally with the Spanish against the English.

1763 Pontiac's Rebellion. Seeking to break the British claim on Indian lands around the Great Lakes, Ottawa chief Pontiac organizes a confederacy of Indian forces in a series of campaigns. In response, the British issue the Proclamation of 1763, which forbids white settlement west of the Appalachians.

1774 Lord Dunmore's War. Forces led by Virginia governor John Murray, earl of Dunmore, compel the Shawnees to cede more of their land in the Ohio valley.

1790-1794 Little Turtle's War. Miami chief Little Turtle organizes Miamis, Shawnees, and other tribes and scuttles the forces of Josiah Harmar along the Maumee River, then defeats Arthur St. Clair along the Wabash River. But his forces are defeated at the Battle of Fallen Timbers.

1811   Battle of Tippecanoe. This Indian defeat dashes Shawnee chief Tecumseh's hopes for an Indian confederacy of Old Northwest tribes.

1814   Battle of Horseshoe Bend. Creek resistance in the South is crushed by Andrew Jackson.

1817-   First Seminole War. Forces led by Andrew Jackson capture Pensacola but fail to subdue the
1818   Seminoles in Spanish Florida.

1832   Black Hawk's War. Sacs and Foxes are crushed while defending the Mississippi River valley in present-day Illinois and Wisconsin.

1835-   Second Seminole War. The United States begins moving the Seminoles out of the region
1842   to land west of the Mississippi. A war of resistance follows, known for its guerrilla-style fighting.

1855-   Third Seminole War. Remaining members of the tribe are crushed.
1858
        Pacific Coast Wars: the Rogue River War, 1855–1856; the Yakima War, 1855–1856; and the Spokane War, 1858. These wars devastate the Native American population in the Northwest, forcing the remaining Indians onto reservations.

1865-   Red Cloud's War, also called the Sioux War. In this campaign, Sioux, Northern Chey-
1867   ennes, and Arapahos force the U.S. Army to abandon the Bozeman Trail in Montana, the Sioux's primary buffalo range.

1874-   Red River War. The Kiowas, Comanches, Cheyennes, and Arapahos mount several suc-
1875   cessful campaigns against the U.S. Army, but in a year of all-out war the Indians are finally defeated and forced onto reservations.

1874   Battle at Palo Duro Canyon. Whites are victorious over the southwestern Indians in a battle noted for the slaughter of more than 1,000 Indian ponies.

1876-   Sioux War. The U.S. Army fights a Plains Indian coalition composed chiefly of Sioux,
1881   Cheyennes, and Arapahos and led by Crazy Horse and Sitting Bull. In a major battle, General George Armstrong Custer is defeated at Little Bighorn—Custer's Last Stand—in 1876 when an estimated 2,000 Indian warriors, one of the largest contingents ever gathered, fells Custer's troops, numbering about 260. The army continues to harass the Indians, however, throughout 1877 until the Indians, driven back into the Dakota Territory, sue for peace. The surrender of Sitting Bull in 1881 officially ends the conflict, although resistance movements persist for years.

1881-   Geronimo's Resistance. Apache leader Geronimo engages in a guerrilla war against white
1886   settlers in Arizona and New Mexico.

1890   Battle of Wounded Knee. Hardly a battle, the tragic events at Wounded Knee unfold as the Ghost Dance sweeps the northern Plains, holding out for Indians the promise that performance of the dance can make whites disappear. Jittery troopers open fire when officials try to intervene and soon more than 200 Sioux men, women, and children are dead.

NATIVE-AMERICAN SERVICE IN U.S. WARS

War	Dates	Numbers Served
World War I	1917–1918	12,000 volunteers
World War II	1941–1945	24,000
Vietnam War	1965–1975	42,500
Persian Gulf War	1991	3,000

OTHER MILITARY ACTIONS

1893   Hawaii. U.S. sailors land to protect American property, and the U.S. minister proclaims Hawaii an American protectorate.

1898   Cuba. Following the U.S. victory in the Spanish-American War, U.S. military occupation of Cuba continues until 1902.

1899   Samoa. Native conflict over royal succession triggers action by the British-German-U.S. protectorate, and U.S. and British sailors land to restore order. In a new protectorate agreement, Germany and the United States divide the island group.

   The Philippines. A year after the Spanish-American War, during which the United States seized the Philippines, Filipino nationalist forces, led by Emilio Aguinaldo, fight a three-and-a-half-year war of liberation but are unable to rout the United States. The Philippines remain a U.S. territory until 1946.

1900   China: The United States sends troops to help put down the Boxer Rebellion and maintain the Open Door policy (see Chapter 8).

1903   Panama. President Roosevelt sends warships to Panama even before the province declares its independence from Colombia. Three days later the United States recognizes the Republic of Panama and begins to negotiate a treaty establishing a canal zone.

1906   Cuba. The military occupation of Cuba is reinstalled, until 1909.

1911   Nicaragua. The United States takes over the supervision of Nicaragua's finances until 1924. Marines are not finally withdrawn until 1933.

1912   Cuba. U.S. troops intervene to put down internal unrest.

1914   Mexico. When Mexico stands on the brink of a civil war that could endanger U.S. business interests, President Wilson sends a naval force to bombard and occupy Veracruz.

1915   Haiti. U.S. troops invade Haiti, making it a U.S. protectorate, which it will remain until 1934. U.S. fiscal control continues until 1947.

1916   Mexico. A border raid by Pancho Villa in New Mexico launches a punitive expedition under General John J. Pershing that fails to capture Villa but succeeds in creating considerable ill will.

   Santo Domingo. Military occupation by U.S. marines is proclaimed as necessary to stabilize the country's finances, under American protection since 1907. U.S. financial management continues until 1924.

1918   Russia. The United States sends 15,000 troops into Russia to support anti-Bolshevik forces and to counter Japanese influence in Siberia.

1954   Guatemala. When the elected progressive president of Guatemala proposes land reforms and trade unionism, changes that would threaten the considerable U.S. commercial interests there, the CIA supports the opposition and installs a military leader sympathetic to U.S. interests.

1958   Lebanon. U.S. forces land to put down rioting and rebellion.

1961   Cuba. At the Bay of Pigs, the United States backs 1,500 CIA-trained and -armed Cuban expatriates in an attempted invasion of Cuba that is intended to overthrow Fidel Castro. Most of the invaders are taken prisoner.

1965   Dominican Republic. President Lyndon Johnson sends troops to end a civil war and impose a truce.

1983   Grenada. Following a military coup, U.S. troops invade to protect and evacuate American citizens and to see that the hard-line Marxist regime is deposed.

1989   Panama. The United States invades Panama in an attempt to capture Manuel Noriega, a former U.S. ally and head of state whom the United States now holds responsible for much of the drug traffic. The UN denounces the U.S. invasion as a "flagrant violation of international law." Noriega eludes capture and finally turns himself in.

1993   Somalia. U.S. and UN forces attack rebel factions and administer humanitarian aid.

1995   Bosnia. NATO, U.S., and UN forces attempt to secure a cease-fire in an ethnic war.

See also entries on the Korean War, the Vietnam War, and the Persian Gulf War—all undeclared.

BUILDING THE ARMED FORCES

Having themselves been subjects of British colonial rule, the framers of the U.S. Constitution sought to disperse military power, giving Congress the power to declare war and making the president the commander-in-chief of the armed forces. As a result, two forces have continuously shaped U.S. military establishment: the need to build and maintain a professional army countered by an equally strong push to keep the military under civilian control.

1774   The First Continental Congress urges the people to arm and form their own militias.

1775   The Second Continental Congress resolves to raise six companies of riflemen, appoints a committee to establish rules for the army, and elects George Washington to be commander in chief.

1783   The Confederation Congress discharges the troops in the Continental Army, and George Washington resigns his commission.

1784   The Confederation Congress authorizes a small force that is the nucleus of the institution maintained by government under the Constitution (1789).

1789   Congress's power to "raise and support armies" is established in the Constitution.

        The War Department is established, with Henry Knox named its first secretary.

1791   The Second Amendment accepts the idea of compulsory military service that is the legacy of the individual colonial militias.

1791-   Even though a small standing army of "regulars" is maintained, the United States primarily
1898   draws on volunteers and state militias throughout this period. Volunteer militias provide the primary source of manpower in the Indian wars, the Mexican War, and the Spanish-American War. They are the basis of both the Union and the Confederate armies.

1798   The Navy Department is established, with Benjamin Stoddert named its first secretary.

        The U.S. Marine Corps is established under control of the secretary of the navy. Marines have participated in all U.S. wars, and their specialized training has made them experts not only in amphibious landings but in counterinsurgency and guerrilla warfare. Today they are self-sufficient units, with their own tanks, armor, artillery, and air forces.

Secretaries of War

Secretary	President	Year Appointed	Secretary	President	Year Appointed
Henry Knox	Washington	1789	John A. Rawlins	Grant	1869
Timothy Pickering	Washington	1795	William T. Sherman	Grant	1869
James McHenry	Washington	1796	William W. Belknap	Grant	1869
	Adams, J.	1797	Alphonso Taft	Grant	1876
Samuel Dexter	Adams, J.	1800	James D. Cameron	Grant	1876
Henry Dearborn	Jefferson	1801	George W. McCrary	Hayes	1877
William Eustis	Madison	1809	Alexander Ramsey	Hayes	1879
John Armstrong	Madison	1813	Robert T. Lincoln	Garfield	1881
James Monroe	Madison	1814		Arthur	1881
William H. Crawford	Madison	1815	William C. Endicott	Cleveland	1885
John C. Calhoun	Monroe	1817	Redfield Proctor	Harrison, B.	1889
James Barbour	Adams, J. Q.	1825	Stephen B. Elkins	Harrison, B.	1891
Peter B. Porter	Adams, J. Q.	1828	Daniel S. Lamont	Cleveland	1893
John H. Eaton	Jackson	1829	Russel A. Alger	McKinley	1897
Lewis Cass	Jackson	1831	Elihu Root	McKinley	1899
Benjamin F. Butler	Jackson	1837		Roosevelt, T.	1901
Joel R. Poinsett	Van Buren	1837	William H. Taft	Roosevelt, T.	1904
John Bell	Harrison, W. H.	1841	Luke E. Wright	Roosevelt, T.	1908
	Tyler	1841	Jacob M. Dickinson	Taft	1909
John C. Spencer	Tyler	1841	Henry L. Stimson	Taft	1911
James M. Porter	Tyler	1843	Lindley M. Garrison	Wilson	1913
William Wilkins	Tyler	1844	Newton D. Baker	Wilson	1916
William L. Marcy	Polk	1845	John W. Weeks	Harding	1921
George W. Crawford	Taylor	1849		Coolidge	1923
Charles M. Conrad	Fillmore	1850	Dwight F. Davis	Coolidge	1925
Jefferson Davis	Pierce	1853	James W. Good	Hoover	1929
John B. Floyd	Buchanan	1857	Patrick J. Hurley	Hoover	1929
Joseph Holt	Buchanan	1861	George H. Dern	Roosevelt, F. D.	1933
Simon Cameron	Lincoln	1861	Harry H. Woodring	Roosevelt, F. D.	1937
Edwin M. Stanton	Lincoln	1862	Henry L. Stimson	Roosevelt, F. D.	1940
	Johnson, A.	1865	Robert P. Patterson	Truman	1945
John M. Schofield	Johnson, A.	1868	Kenneth C. Royall	Truman	1947

Secretaries of the Navy

Secretary	President	Year Appointed	Secretary	President	Year Appointed
Benjamin Stoddert	Adams, J.	1798	Smith Thompson	Monroe	1818
	Jefferson	1801	Samuel L. Southard	Monroe	1823
Robert Smith	Jefferson	1801		Adams, J. Q.	1825
Paul Hamilton	Madison	1809	John Branch	Jackson	1829
William Jones	Madison	1813	Levi Woodbury	Jackson	1831
Benjamin Crowninshield	Madison	1814	Mahlon Dickerson	Jackson	1834
	Monroe	1817		Van Buren	1837
			James K. Paulding	Van Buren	1838

(continues)

Secretaries of the Navy (cont.)

Secretary	President	Year Appointed	Secretary	President	Year Appointed
George E. Badger	Harrison, W. H.	1841	William C. Whitney	Cleveland	1885
	Tyler	1841	Benjamin F. Tracey	Harrison, B.	1889
Abel P. Upshur	Tyler	1841	Hilary A. Herbert	Cleveland	1893
David Henshaw	Tyler	1843	John D. Long	McKinley	1897
Thomas W. Gilmer	Tyler	1844		Roosevelt, T.	1901
John Y. Mason	Tyler	1844	William H. Moody	Roosevelt, T.	1902
George Bancroft	Polk	1845	Paul Morton	Roosevelt, T.	1904
John Y. Mason	Polk	1846	Charles J. Bonaparte	Roosevelt, T.	1905
William B. Preston	Taylor	1849	Victor H. Metcalf	Roosevelt, T.	1906
William A. Graham	Fillmore	1850	Truman H. Newberry	Roosevelt, T.	1908
John P. Kennedy	Fillmore	1852	George von L. Meyer	Taft	1909
James C. Dobbin	Pierce	1853	Josephus Daniels	Wilson	1913
Isaac Toucey	Buchanan	1857	Edwin Denby	Harding	1921
Gideon Welles	Lincoln	1861		Coolidge	1923
	Johnson, A.	1865	Curtis D. Wilbur	Coolidge	1924
Adolph E. Borie	Grant	1869	Charles Francis Adams	Hoover	1929
George M. Robeson	Grant	1869	Claude A. Swanson	Roosevelt, F. D.	1933
Richard W. Thompson	Hayes	1877	Charles Edison	Roosevelt, F. D.	1940
Nathan Goff, Jr.	Hayes	1881	Frank Knox	Roosevelt, F. D.	1940
William H. Hunt	Garfield	1881	James V. Forrestal	Roosevelt, F. D.	1944
William E. Chandler	Arthur	1882		Truman	1945

1802   The United States Military Academy at West Point, New York, is founded to train professional army officers.

1845   The United States Naval Academy is founded at Annapolis, Maryland, to train professional naval officers.

THE HOME FRONT

No war is fought without support at home, and in a democracy like the United States, rounding up support on the home front can be a challenge. Much of the so-called war effort is a combination of law and voluntary means with a good bit of cajoling thrown in. And where capitalism prevails, there must be profits, even in wartime. It becomes necessary, then, to generate volunteerism, both individual and industrial, and to provide profits while preventing profiteering. Americans made sacrifices during most of their wars, but in the two world wars the efforts were organized and government-sponsored.

Even before the United States entered World War II, the federal government was calling for "meatless Mondays" and "wheatless Wednesdays" as a means of stockpiling food. Americans were encouraged to grow their own vegetables.

Huge rallies were held to encourage people to buy war bonds, which in turn reduced the amount of money in circulation and increased the amount available in loans for the government to use in fighting the war. Buying war bonds also gave each individual a financial stake in the war effort.

The biggest mobilization in U.S. history occurred during World War II. In February 1942, two months after the United States entered the war, the last new car rolled off the Detroit assembly lines, which were then turned over to the production of jeeps and tanks. Steel pennies replaced copper ones. Virtually all heavy industry was co-opted into the war-manufacturing effort. Gasoline was rationed, not only to save fuel but also to preserve rubber, effectively banning pleasure driving, and the speed limit, even for truckers, was reduced to 35 mph.

Food was also rationed. Coupons were issued for reduced amounts of coffee, flour, sugar, and milk, and people stood in line for hours to buy what little was available. People were encouraged to grow "victory gardens," and 20 million sprung up across America—only to fade just as quickly when the war ended. Metals were recycled.

Shoes were rationed to save leather. Wool was in short supply, as the soldiers needed wool socks and pants. Silk stockings became scarce when all the silk was used to make parachutes. Shorter skirts saved cloth and manufacturing time and let industry get on with the real business of making uniforms.

Americans at home learned to make do with far less and to spend more for it. The sacrifices, however, often produced a sense of community and uplifted spirits among civilians who believed their savings—large and small—helped the fighting men.

1862	During the Civil War, the Confederacy imposes a national draft, conscripting men aged 17 to 50. But only 21 percent of the soldiers are draftees; most volunteer.
1863	The Union institutes a national draft, enlisting men aged 20 to 45 years, but draftees are permitted to buy a replacement or pay a commutation fee (eliminated 1864) of $300. Draftees constitute 2 percent of the army, and 6 percent of those fighting are substitutes.
	When draft riots occur in several cities (the worst is in New York City), the federal government rescinds the right to commute army service.
1876	The U.S. Coast Guard Academy is founded in New London, Connecticut.
1884	The Naval War College is established at Newport, Rhode Island.
1900	With its new steel navy, built in the course of nearly two decades, the United States ranks third among world naval powers.
1901	The Army War College opens, designed to improve officer training as part of a general army reorganization.
1907	The Division of the Army Signal Corps is established and is variously renamed until in 1949 amendments to the National Security Act make the air force a military department within the new Department of Defense.
1915	The U.S. Coast Guard is established, combining the Revenue Cutter Service and the Life Saving Service.
1917	Upon entering World War I, the United States initiates its first wide-scale draft; 72 percent of the army is conscripted.
1940	World War II in Europe prompts the first peacetime draft in U.S. history. Men 21 to 35 are conscripted for one year of service, to be served within the Western Hemisphere.
1941	In the summer, the term of service for the draftees is extended. After the United States enters World War II, all men between the ages of 18 and 38 and at one time up to age 45 are conscripted for the duration of the war.
1943	The U.S. Merchant Marine Academy is founded in Kings Point, New York.
1945	The draft remains in existence after peace is established.
1947	The Joint Chiefs of Staff is organized to provide military advisors to the secretary of defense and the president. It consists of the chief of staff of the army and of the air force, the chief of naval operations, the commandant of the marines, and the chairman, whose job is to represent the other committee members' opinions.

1947   The National Security Act coordinates the army, navy, and air force into a new Department of Defense, with James V. Forrestal named its first secretary. The act also creates the National Security Council and Central Intelligence Agency.

1948   The draft, ended in 1947, is reinstituted.

1954   The U.S. Air Force Academy is founded at Colorado Springs, Colorado.

1965   Draft quotas rise automatically during the escalation of the Vietnam War, soaring from 100,000 men in 1964 to 400,000 men in 1966. Draftees make up 16 percent of the army but are 88 percent of the troops in Vietnam.

1969   Under growing public pressure to end the draft, a lottery is instituted for all 18-year-olds.

1970   A government report on the military recommends an all-volunteer army, with a standby draft for emergencies.

1971   After the invasion of Cambodia the draft is extended for two more years only after long debate, and student deferments are eliminated. In preparation for an all-volunteer armed force, the military pay scale is increased substantially.

1973   On January 27, the day a cease-fire is reached in Vietnam, the draft ends, although 18-year-old men are still required to register for the draft.

1975   President Gerald Ford halts compulsory draft registration.

1976   The National Defense University is established combining the Industrial College of the Armed Forces and the National War College.

1980   President Jimmy Carter reinstitutes compulsory draft registration when the Soviets invade Afghanistan.

1986   The Joint Chiefs of Staff is reorganized to strengthen the role of its chairman, who is now the president's chief military advisor.

1988   The Department of Veterans Affairs is established, with Edward J. Derwinski named its first secretary.

Secretaries of Defense

Secretary	President	Year Appointed	Secretary	President	Year Appointed
James V. Forrestal	Truman	1947	Elliot L. Richardson	Nixon	1973
Louis A. Johnson	Truman	1949	James R. Schlesinger	Nixon	1973
George C. Marshall	Truman	1950		Ford	1974
Robert A. Lovett	Truman	1951	Donald H. Rumsfeld	Ford	1975
Charles E. Wilson	Eisenhower	1953	Harold Brown	Carter	1977
Neil H. McElroy	Eisenhower	1957	Caspar W. Weinberger	Reagan	1981
Thomas S. Gates, Jr.	Eisenhower	1959	Frank C. Carlucci	Reagan	1981
Robert S. McNamara	Kennedy	1961	Richard B. Cheney	Bush	1989
	Johnson, L. B.	1963	Les Aspin	Clinton	1993
Clark M. Clifford	Johnson, L. B.	1968	William J. Perry	Clinton	1994
Melvin R. Laird	Nixon	1969	William S. Cohen	Clinton	1997

Chairmen of the Joint Chiefs of Staff

Chairman	Branch	Year Appointed
General of the Army Omar Bradley	Army	1949
Admiral Arthur Radford	Navy	1953
General Nathan Twining	Air Force	1957
General Lyman Lemnitzer	Army	1960
General Maxwell Taylor	Army	1962
General Earle Wheeler	Army	1964
Admiral Thomas H. Moorer	Navy	1970
General George Brown	Air Force	1974
General David C. Jones	Air Force	1978
General John Vessey, Jr.	Army	1982
Admiral William Crowe, Jr.	Navy	1985
General Colin Powell	Army	1989
General John Shalikashvili	Army	1993

Secretaries of Veterans Affairs

Secretary	President	Year Appointed
Edward J. Derwinski	Bush	1989
Jesse Brown	Clinton	1993

HISTORY OF PROTEST: PACIFISM AND ANTIWAR ACTIVISM

Pacifism and war protest are intertwined in U.S. history, and considering that the nation was founded by religious and political dissidents, it is hardly surprising that the federal government has repeatedly had to contend with these two forces. Conscientious objectors, who oppose war on religious, moral, and philosophical grounds, have sought to avoid military service or to serve only under conditions acceptable to their beliefs. War protesters have sought to halt wars whenever possible. The nation's response to conscientious objectors and war protesters has, predictably, been mixed.

Mid-1600s   Setting a precedent that will prevail after the United States becomes a nation, some colonies exempt conscientious objectors—Quakers, Mennonites, Moravians, Schwenkfelders, and other pacifistic religious communities—from service in state militias.

1798   The Kentucky (written by Thomas Jefferson) and Virginia (written by James Madison) Resolutions argue that the Alien and Sedition Acts are unconstitutional because the federal government is exercising powers not delegated to it.

1799   John Fries, a Pennsylvanian, leads an armed tax revolt in opposition to the expenditure of tax money on a war with France. Although he is more opposed to taxes than to war, his action demonstrates the willingness of citizens to challenge decisions of the federal government.

1815   In general disgruntled by the disruption to commerce during the long prelude to the War of 1812, and opposing the war itself, delegates from New England meet in Hartford to attest to the power of states to protect their citizens against the federal government, including protection from conscriptions not authorized by the Constitution. The convention also calls for the use of federal revenues for defense and an interstate defense unit for repelling invasions.

1846-
1848 Peace groups and some pacifist churches oppose the Mexican War. Writer Henry David Thoreau is jailed for one night for refusing to pay a tax to support the war effort. In "Civil Disobedience" he defends his actions by declaring that unjust laws should be resisted: "The only obligation which I have a right to assume is to do at any time what I think right."

1863 During the Civil War draft riots break out in northern cities, and in New York, about 110 people are killed. The new draft law allows draftees to buy their way out of serving by paying $300, a sum only the wealthy can afford. Scholars now believe that the riots were as much about this economic inequity as about the draft. Racism and unsolved urban problems were also factors.

1864 Quakers, the country's leading religious pacifists, sponsor a successful campaign for legislation that allows alternate service. The Confederate draft originally exempts conscientious objectors on religious grounds. As the need for men grows, the exemption is repealed.

1898 The Teller Amendment to the declaration of war against Spain disavows any claims on Cuba's sovereignty.

The Anti-Imperialist League is organized in Boston to protest military action, especially in the Philippines, and by 1899 it has a half-million members.

1915 As Europeans are destroying each other in battlefields in France and Russia, Americans organize for peace. Jane Addams help found the Woman's Peace Party and attends the International Women's Conference at The Hague.

1917 Once the United States enters the war, Americans stand behind the effort, and conscientious objectors, exempt on religious grounds only, encounter considerable prejudice. Five hundred conscientious objectors are court-martialed for their beliefs, 17 are sentenced to death (none are carried out), and 142 receive life sentences.

1918 Under the Alien Act, foreign-born conscientious objectors are deported without a trial. One famous conscientious objector, Alvin York, who is drafted despite his beliefs, fights heroically and is awarded both the Medal of Honor and the French Médaille Militaire and the Croix de Guerre.

Eugene V. Debs, a Socialist labor leader, is sentenced to jail for ten years for violating provisions of the Espionage Act. While in prison he receives 920,000 votes for president in the election of 1920. President Warren G. Harding releases him from prison in 1921.

1919 The Women's International League for Peace and Freedom is founded, and Jane Addams is elected its president.

1940 With World War II raging in Europe, U.S. conservatives (again called isolationists) eager to stay out of the war form an America First Committee. The most famous World War II isolationist is Charles Lindbergh. Conscientious objectors are exempted from service only on religious grounds, and alternate service is mandatory. Many are imprisoned for seeking conscientious objector status. More than 400 blacks are conscientious objectors: Some belong to the Nation of Islam, while others object to serving in a segregated army.

1941 A. Philip Randolph, head of the Brotherhood of Sleeping Car Porters, threatens to stage a march on Washington to demand jobs for blacks in defense industries. President Franklin Roosevelt issues Executive Order 8802 outlawing discrimination in the defense industries.

1961 In his Farewell Address, President (and former general) Dwight D. Eisenhower warns of the "unwarranted influence" of the "military-industrial complex." "The potential for the disastrous rise of misplaced power exists and will persist."

1964-
1975 The Vietnam War is the nation's most unpopular war. Joining in protests and antiwar agitation are pacifists, clergy, students, Old Leftists, liberals, intellectuals, civil rights leaders,

feminists, and eventually even soldiers and members of Congress. There are demonstrations, protest marches, draft-card burnings, "teach-ins," and violence, including break-ins at draft boards, destruction of records, and bombings. Hundreds of cities and campuses experience unrest.

More than 50,000 conscientious objectors are believed to have left the country; 250,000 to have never registered for the draft; and 110,000 to have burned their draft cards to protest the war. The Supreme Court rules that exemptions for CO status can be based on moral and ethical grounds as well as religious grounds.

1967   Influential persons speak out against the war. The Reverend Martin Luther King, Jr., describes the United States as the "greatest purveyor of violence in the world today." In the Senate, J. William Fulbright (Ark.), Eugene McCarthy (Minn.), Robert Kennedy (N.Y.), George McGovern (S.D.), George Aiken (Vt.), Edward Kennedy (Mass.), Frank Church (Idaho), and Mark Hatfield (Ore.) are critics of the war. So are scientist Linus Pauling, historian Arthur Schlesinger, economist John Kenneth Galbraith, and boxing champion Muhammad Ali, who is stripped of his crown for refusing induction. Pediatrician-author Benjamin Spock, Beat poet Allen Ginsberg, and folksinger Joan Baez show up regularly at protests.

In response to this escalation of antiwar activism, the CIA launches Operation Chaos, a massive, overreaching effort to catalog antiwar protesters and interfere with their activities. More than 1,000 organizations and 200,000 individuals are logged in files, and CIA informants penetrate most antiwar groups.

Fifty thousand protest at the Pentagon.

1968   Between January and June, the National Student Association reports 221 demonstrations at 101 colleges and universities involving 40,000 students.

Nine Jesuit priests, including brothers Daniel and Philip Berrigan, enter a Selective Service office in Catonsville, Maryland, burn draft records, and then wait outside to be arrested.

In August, outside the Democratic National Convention in Chicago, 5,000 activists stage five days of protest and at least 1,000 are clubbed by Chicago police in what some term a "police riot."

1969   Between January and June, 232 campus protests are reported.

In November, on Moratorium Day, up to 750,000 protesters in Boston, New York, Washington, and other cities stage peaceful candlelight vigils.

By year's end, draft board offices and Army Reserve installations are subject to repeated break-ins and vandalism.

1970   Campuses erupt in protest of the U.S. invasion of Cambodia. On May 4 at Kent State University National Guardsmen open fire on a crowd of protesters, killing four and wounding nine. A few days later Mississippi policemen kill two and wound 11 students at Jackson State. Construction workers on Wall Street force City Hall officials to raise the flag to full staff after it is lowered in honor of the Kent State students. On May 9, at the largest antiwar rally in U.S. history, several hundred thousand protesters march on Washington, D.C. At the University of Wisconsin an antiwar activist blows up a laboratory to protest the university's involvement in war research. The explosion kills one person and injures four. Two million students protest at 350 campuses. Many colleges close early to avoid student unrest over the war.

1971   Former Defense Department employee Daniel Ellsberg arranges for the publication of a classified analysis of U.S. involvement in Vietnam. The government sues to stop publication of the papers but loses. The *Pentagon Papers* are published in *The New York Times*.

1971   In May, antiwar protesters attempt to disrupt the federal government, and more than 10,000 are arrested in dragnet operations carried out by the Washington, D.C., police.

1974   The Boland Amendment prohibits sending military aid to the rebels (contras) fighting against the Marxist-leaning government in Nicaragua.

1977   President Jimmy Carter grants a blanket pardon to draft evaders, who can now return to the United States without fear of arrest.

SIGNIFICANT LEGISLATIVE ACTS AND SUPREME COURT CASES AFFECTING THE MILITARY

According to the Constitution, Congress has the power "to raise and support armies," "to provide and maintain a navy," and "to make rules . . . for the regulation of land and naval forces." (See "Building the Armed Forces" earlier in this chapter.) Most actions concerning the armed forces listed there came by acts of Congress. A few are highlighted below.

1798   Alien and Sedition Acts. This series of four acts, passed when war against France seemed imminent, extends the period of residence required for citizenship, authorizes the president to imprison or deport enemy aliens during wartime, and provides for penalties for "writing, printing, uttering or publishing any false, scandalous, and malicious writing or writings" against the government of the United States, the Congress, or the president.

1863   Conscription Act. This draft is actually the second in U.S. history, as the Confederacy had enacted a draft a year before. It makes all men between 20 and 45 liable for military service but provides that service can be avoided by a payment of $300 or by hiring a substitute.

1917   Selective Service Act. This draft, passed the month after the United States entered World War I, makes all men between the ages of 21 and 30 liable for military service. An amendment the following year requires registration of all men between the ages of 18 and 45.

Espionage Act. This act seeks to prevent treasonable and disloyal activities by providing penalties for aiding the enemy, obstructing recruitment of armed forces, or uttering, printing, writing, or publishing "any disloyal, profane, scurrilous, or abusive language about the form of government of the United States, or the Constitution of the United States, or the military or naval forces of the United States."

1918   Sedition Act. This amendment to the Espionage Act provides further penalties for disloyalty. Both acts are rigidly enforced, and freedom of speech and of the press virtually disappear.

Selective Draft Law Cases. In a landmark ruling, the Court rules that the draft is constitutional.

1919   *Schenck v. United States.* The Supreme Court upholds the Espionage Act (1917), which provided penalties for acts of disloyalty, including writing or speaking out against the draft. Justice Oliver Wendell Holmes introduces the "clear and present danger test" for limiting free speech.

Abrams v. United States. The Supreme Court upholds the Sedition Act (1918), an amendment to the Espionage Act that specified additional acts of disloyalty.

1940   Alien Registration Act (Smith Act). Passed before the United States becomes involved in World War II, this act requires the registration and fingerprinting of aliens and provides for their deportation and prohibits certain subversive activities, including advocating the overthrow of the U.S. government.

Selective Service and Training Act. This first peacetime draft in U.S. history requires the registration of all men between ages 21 and 35. After the United States enters World War II, the draft age is lowered to 18 and raised to 38.

1944   *Korematsu v. United States.* The Supreme Court upholds the relocation of Japanese Americans from the West Coast on the grounds of national security.

1947   The National Security Act coordinates the army, navy, and air force into a new Department of Defense and creates the National Security Council and Central Intelligence Agency.

1948   Selective Service Act. This peacetime draft, requiring registration of all males between the ages of 18 and 26, continues throughout the cold war and the Vietnam War. In 1973, on the day the cease-fire is announced, President Richard Nixon suspends the draft.

1964   Gulf of Tonkin Resolution. Passed with only two dissenting votes in the Senate, this resolution affirms that Congress "approves and supports the determination of the President, as Commander in Chief, to take all necessary measures to repel any armed attack against the forces of the United States and to prevent further aggression." Giving the president almost a free hand, the resolution furnished the legal basis for the escalation of the Vietnam War.

1971   *New York Times v. United States (Pentagon Papers Case).* The Supreme Court rules that the government has not demonstrated sufficient cause for an injunction against publication of the *Pentagon Papers,* a Defense Department analysis of involvement in Vietnam.

1973   War Powers Resolution. Passed over President Richard Nixon's veto, this resolution limits presidential war-making power by establishing guidelines for military emergencies. The president must consult Congress before sending troops into hostilities "in every possible instance," must report to Congress during the hostilities, and, unless Congress acts to declare war, must withdraw troops within 60 days.

SIGNIFICANT PEOPLE IN MILITARY HISTORY

Abrams, Creighton (1914–1974).   After fighting in World War II and in Korea, General Abrams became commander of the U.S. forces in Vietnam in mid-1968. He later served as army chief of staff.

Addams, Jane (1860–1935).   Known primarily as a social worker and the founder of Hull-House in Chicago, Addams was also an ardent pacifist, helping to found the Woman's Peace Party in 1915 and attending the International Women's Conference at The Hague, where she was appointed head of a commission to seek an end to World War I. At the Second Women's Peace Conference in 1919, she was elected the first president of the new Women's International League for Peace and Freedom, a post she held for the rest of her life. Her account of women's work for peace, *Peace and Bread in Time of War,* was published in 1922, and in 1931 she was a co-recipient of the Nobel Peace Prize.

Allen, Ethan (1738–1789).   During the Revolutionary War, Allen headed the Green Mountain Boys, a Vermont independent force that captured Fort Ticonderoga and fought in the Battle of Bennington. Allen was an important figure in Vermont's struggle to remain free of New York.

Arnold, Benedict (1741–1801).   Remembered mostly as the most notable traitor in the Revolutionary War, Arnold fought bravely with the colonists during the American Revolution before becoming involved in a plot to turn over West Point to the British. He died in Britain.

Arnold, Henry (1886–1950).   Head of the air force during World War II and one of five men after World War II who was awarded the rank of five-star general, Arnold worked to turn the air force, which was initially part of the army, into the world's best.

Barry, John (1745–1803).   During the Revolution, Barry served in the Continental Army and fought in several major naval battles. He commanded the brig *Lexington,* which took the first

British ship, the tender *Edward,* captured during the war. He went on to command several more ships and to capture two more British ships.

Beauregard, Pierre G. T. (1818–1893). As commander of the Confederate forces at the start of the Civil War, General Beauregard issued the order to fire on Fort Sumter, which began the war. He was second in command at First Manassas.

Bradley, Omar (1893–1981). Recognized by his superiors for his planning abilities, Bradley played a key role in North Africa and later in Sicily, and still later in the Normandy invasion. He became the first chairman of the Joint Chiefs of Staff in 1948. He supported President Harry Truman in his clash with General Douglas MacArthur.

Chennault, Claire (1890–1958). A flyer in both world wars, General Chennault organized the Flying Tigers, an elite group of volunteer American fighter pilots in China, in 1941.

Clark, Mark (1896–1984). Clark commanded the Fifth Army in North Africa and Italy during World War II and was supreme commander of the UN forces in Korea from May 1952 to October 1953.

Clay, Lucius (1897–1978). Clay directed the Berlin Airlift in 1948–1949. He was later President John Kennedy's representative in Berlin.

Decatur, Stephen (1779–1820). A naval officer, Decatur was noted for his daring exploits in the Barbary wars and was engaged in some of the most important sea battles during the War of 1812. He was forced to surrender once while trying to fight four British ships with his one.

Dewey, George (1837–1917). Dewey commanded the naval forces that destroyed the Spanish fleet at Manila during the Spanish-American War. In 1899 he became admiral of the Navy.

Early, Jubal (1816–1894). Early fought with the Confederate Army in most of the major Civil War battles along the East Coast. He led a raid on Washington in July 1864 that was more dramatic than effective. After his forces were defeated by Philip Sheridan in the Shenandoah Valley, Early was relieved of his command.

Eisenhower, Dwight David (1890–1969). Head of the Allied forces in North Africa and later supreme allied commander in Europe, Eisenhower oversaw the Normandy invasion and accepted the Germans' surrender (though he did not sign the official document). After the war, he served as chief of staff and headed NATO forces in Europe in 1950. Eisenhower later became the 34th president of the United States.

Farragut, David (1801–1870). During the Civil War this Southerner became one of the Union's most admired naval officers and was responsible for the capture of two strategic posts, New Orleans and Mobile Bay.

Forrest, Nathan Bedford (1821–1877). A Confederate cavalry commander during the Civil War, Forrest carried out strategic raids that played havoc with the Union Army's supply lines.

Gates, Horatio (1728–1806). This Revolutionary War general headed the army at the Battle of Saratoga, which was the turning point in the Revolutionary War, for it ensured French support.

Grant, Ulysses (1822–1885). After fighting in most of the major battles of the Civil War in the west, Grant was appointed to head the Union Army. He accepted Robert E. Lee's surrender at Appomattox Court House. Grant later became the 18th president of the United States.

Gravely, Samuel (1922–). Gravely was the first African American to achieve the rank of admiral, in 1971. He served in the U.S. Navy during World War II, Korea, and Vietnam and was commander of the Third Fleet, 1976–1978.

Greene, Nathanael (1742–1786). During the American Revolution, General Greene, a superb strategist, planned the defense of New York City, stood with Washington at the Battle of Trenton, and though frequently defeated, weakened the British during the southern campaign that led to their defeat at Yorktown.

Hale, Nathan (1755–1776). Sent to Long Island to gather intelligence during the Revolution, Hale was captured by the British and hung without a trial. On the gallows, he allegedly declared: "I only regret that I have but one life to lose for my country."

Halsey, William (1882–1959). A naval commander, Halsey led forces in many of the major battles in the Pacific theater during World War II and was responsible for the 1944 defeat of the Japanese fleet at Leyte Gulf.

Hull, Isaac (1773–1843). In the War of 1812, Hull commanded the USS *Constitution*, also known as Old Ironsides, which defeated the British frigate *Guerrière*.

Jackson, Andrew (1767–1845). This president of the United States had a long military career that began when he was a teenager, fighting against the British in the Revolution. During the War of 1812 he defeated Creek warriors at the Battle of Horseshoe Bend and the British in the Battle of New Orleans. His reputation as an Indian fighter increased with his incursions into Spanish Florida against the Seminoles.

Jackson, Thomas (Stonewall) (1824–1863). A Civil War general, Jackson headed the Confederate forces in the Shenandoah Valley. Jackson was mistakenly shot by his own men and died a few days later.

Johnson, Henry (1897–1929). Private Henry Johnson, an African American, was one of the first Americans to receive the Croix de Guerre, awarded for his valor during World War I.

Jones, John Paul (1747–1792). This professional naval officer was known for his daring ingenuity during the Revolution. He commanded the *Bon Homme Richard* in a major battle against the British ship *Serapis*. When his smaller vessel appeared to be defeated, he rallied with the cry "I have not yet begun to fight"; several hours later the *Serapis* was forced to surrender.

Kearny, Stephen (1794–1848). During the Mexican War, Kearny headed the Army of the West. As military governor of New Mexico he established the civil government. He also was active in California. He was briefly civil governor of Veracruz and Mexico City as well.

Kosciuszko, Thaddeus (1746–1817). An ardent believer in the ideas of the American Revolution, this native Pole, as a general, fought valiantly alongside Americans during the Revolution. His skill with positioning artillery contributed to the victory at Saratoga.

Lafayette, Marie Joseph Paul Yves Roch Gilbert du Motier, Marquis de (1757–1834). A native Frenchman, Lafayette came to the colonies and offered his services in the American Revolution. He became a close friend of George Washington and fought at Brandywine, Valley Forge, and in the Yorktown campaign. His grave in France is covered with earth from Bunker Hill.

Lee, Henry (Lighthorse Harry) (1756–1818). Lee, who was the father of Confederate general Robert E. Lee, was an army officer who fought daringly in the Revolution.

Lee, Robert E. (1807–1870). Head of the Army of Northern Virginia during the Civil War, Lee surrendered to General Ulysses Grant at Appomattox Court House in 1865.

Lincoln, Abraham (1809–1865). As president from 1861 to 1865, Lincoln was closely involved in directing the course of the Civil War, always with the goal of preserving the Union.

MacArthur, Douglas (1880–1964).   One of the most controversial and brilliant officers in military history, MacArthur led a brigade during World War I, served as superintendent of West Point, 1919–1922, headed U.S. forces in the southwest Pacific theater during World War II, and the occupation forces after the war in Japan, and was UN commander during the Korean War. When he made public his dispute with President Harry Truman over the conduct of the war, Truman removed him from command.

Mahan, Alfred Thayer (1840–1914).   This West Point graduate, naval officer, and historian is best known for his writings on the importance of sea power, which convinced Theodore Roosevelt to expand the navy and embark on overseas expansion.

Marion, Francis (c. 1732–1795).   A Revolutionary War hero, Marion led guerrilla battles in South Carolina.

Marshall, George (1880–1959).   A staff army officer during World War I, when he served under General Pershing, Marshall later rose to the rank of five-star general in World War II. Marshall was an important strategist. As President Harry Truman's secretary of state, he organized the European Recovery Program, better known as the Marshall Plan, and also served briefly as secretary of defense.

McClellan, George (1826–1885).   A Union general, McClellan commanded the Army of the Potomac during the early days of the Civil War. He was responsible for the Union victory at Antietam. In 1864 he opposed Lincoln in the general election.

Meade, George (1815–1872).   During the Civil War Meade led the victorious Union forces at Gettysburg.

Mitchell, Billy (1879–1936).   Having played the lead role in developing aviation in World War I, Mitchell was one of the first to recognize the value of air power in fighting wars. After the war he pioneered tests that showed that planes were capable of sinking ships. His determination to promote air power brought him into conflict with conservative members of the military establishment. His public statements, critical of the leadership in the departments of War and Navy, led to his subsequent court-martial. He was found guilty and suspended from duty for five years. He resigned. Many of his ideas were later put into effect.

Montgomery, Richard (1738–1775).   A Continental Army general during the Revolution, Montgomery fought in several major battles and died during an unsuccessful attempt to take Quebec.

Morgan, Daniel (1736–1802).   Commanding several companies of Virginia sharpshooters during the Revolution, Morgan fought at Saratoga and Cowpens.

Murphy, Audie (1924–1971).   Murphy was the most decorated American soldier in World War II. He was granted the Medal of Honor for single-handedly holding off and killing or wounding more than 50 Germans.

Nimitz, Chester (1885–1966).   During World War II Nimitz was the chief strategist of the naval war against the Japanese in the Pacific. He commanded the Pacific fleet and was present at the surrender. Nimitz became a five-star admiral.

Patton, George (1885–1945).   During World War II General Patton played a role in the invasion of North Africa, headed the Third Army forces during the invasion of Normandy, and helped to stop the Germans at the Battle of the Bulge.

Perry, Oliver (1785–1819).   A naval officer who fought victoriously at the Battle of Lake Erie during the War of 1812, Perry's report of his victory, "We have met the enemy, and they are ours," is now famous.

Pershing, John (1860–1948).   Pershing commanded forces during the Spanish-American War and in the Philippines from 1906 to 1913. During World War I he headed the American Expeditionary Force and was known to be expert at shaping unskilled soldiers into skilled fighters.

Pickett, George (1825–1875).   A Confederate general who led an assault, known as Pickett's Charge, at the Battle of Gettysburg during the Civil War.

Powell, Colin (1937–).   Powell was the first African American to serve as national security advisor and chairman of the Joint Chiefs of Staff. His term coincided with the Persian Gulf War.

Quantrill, William (1837–1865).   During the Civil War, Quantrill's proslavery raiders burned, looted, and murdered their way through Union camps and communities in Kansas and Missouri, thus causing thousands of Union troops to be diverted to these trouble spots from the more pressing war theater in the South. In 1863 he raided Lawrence, Kansas, killing more than 140 civilians and burning more than 200 buildings.

Rankin, Jeannette (1880–1973).   A social worker who had campaigned for woman suffrage, Rankin was twice elected to the U.S. House of Representatives and has the unusual distinction of being the only member of Congress to vote against the declaration of war against Germany in both World War I and World War II.

Rickover, Hyman (1900–1986).   Admiral Rickover pioneered in the development of the nuclear navy, directing the construction of the world's first nuclear-powered submarine, the USS *Nautilus*, launched in 1954.

Roosevelt, Franklin Delano (1882–1945).   As president during World War II, Roosevelt, who had served as assistant secretary of the navy, was intimately involved in the direction of the war, especially working wth the various military leaders.

Roosevelt, Theodore (1858–1919).   During the Spanish-American War, Roosevelt resigned his position as secretary of the navy, rounded up his East and West coast friends to form the First Regiment, better known as the Rough Riders, and fought valiantly and victoriously at San Juan Hill in Cuba. Roosevelt went on to serve as the 26th president of the United States.

Scott, Winfield (1786–1866).   Made a brigadier general during the War of 1812, Scott went on to serve in Seminole and Creek campaigns and as supreme commander of the U.S. Army during the Mexican War, capturing Mexico City. He was still supreme commander when the Civil War began but retired in November 1861.

Sheridan, Philip (1831–1888).   An outstanding cavalry commander, Sheridan led the Union Army of the Shenandoah during the Civil War.

Sherman, William (1820–1891).   During the Civil War, General Sherman marched the Union army through Atlanta and then to the sea, destroying everything in his path.

Spaatz, Carl (1891–1974).   Spaatz commanded the strategic air bombing of Germany and Japan during World War II.

Steuben, Baron von Friedrich (1730–1794).   A Prussian army officer who became a general for the Americans during the Revolutionary War, Steuben was invaluable in building the Continental Army into a tough fighting force.

Stilwell, Joseph (1883–1946).   As commander of U.S. troops in the China-Burma-India theater during World War II, Stilwell also served as chief of staff to China's Generalissimo Chiang Kai-shek.

Taylor, Zachary (1784–1850).   Taylor fought in the War of 1812, against the Seminoles, and in Black Hawk's War. President Polk dispatched him to the Texas-Mexico border, where a skirmish initiated the Mexican War. A popular hero, especially after his victory at Buena Vista, he was elected president in 1848.

Thomas, George (1816–1870).   A Civil War general, Thomas is credited with saving the Union Army during the Chattanooga campaign and winning the Battle of Nashville. He headed the Army of the Cumberland.

Truman, Harry (1884–1972).   Inheriting the presidency from Franklin Roosevelt, Truman oversaw the end of World War II, made the decision to drop the world's first two atomic bombs on Japan, and negotiated the peace.

Washington, George (1732–1799).   In addition to being the first president of the United States, Washington headed the Continental Army during the Revolution.

Wayne, Anthony (1745–1796).   Wayne fought in the Revolution, capturing the British outpost at Stony Point, N.Y. Later, he decisively defeated the Ohio Indians at the Battle of Fallen Timbers.

Wilson, Woodrow (1856–1924).   As president from 1912 to 1919, Wilson claimed to be a great foe of imperialism, but no president meddled more in Latin America. Although much more interested in establishing a lasting peace, Wilson led the United States during World War I.

ADDITIONAL SOURCES OF INFORMATION

Adamthwaite, Anthony P. *The Making of the Second World War.* 2d ed. Unwin Hyman, 1977.

Calvocoressi, Peter, Guy Wint, and John Pritchard. *Total War: Causes and Courses of the Second World War.* 2d rev. ed. Pantheon, 1989.

Catton, Bruce. *The Centennial History of the Civil War.* 3 vols. Doubleday, 1961–65.

Coffman, Edward M. *The War to End All Wars: The American Military Experience in World War I.* University of Wisconsin Press, 1968.

Cummings, Bruce. *The Origins of the Korean War.* Princeton University Press, 1981.

Daniels, Roger. *Concentration Camps: North American Japanese in the United States and Canada During World War II.* Krieger, 1981.

Eisenhower, Dwight D. *Crusade in Europe.* Doubleday, 1948, repr. 1990.

Foote, Shelby. *The Civil War: A Narrative.* 3 vols. Random House, 1974.

Freeman, Douglas S. *Lee's Lieutenants.* 3 vols. Scribner's, 1986.

Fussell, Paul. *The Great War and Modern Memory.* Oxford University Press, 1975.

Gluck, Sherna Berger. *Rosie the Riveter Revisited: Women, the War, and Social Change.* Macmillan, 1987.

Grant, Ulysses S. *Personal Memoirs.* Da Capo, repr. 1982.

Herring, George C. *America's Longest War: The United States and Vietnam, 1950–1975.* Random House, 1979.

Hickey, Donald. *The War of 1812: A Forgotten Conflict.* University of Illinois Press, 1989.

Iriye, Akira. *Power and Culture: The Japanese-American War, 1941–1945*. Harvard University Press, 1981.

Isaacs, Arnold R. *Without Honor: Defeat in Vietnam and Cambodia*. Johns Hopkins University Press, 1983.

Johannsen, Robert W. *To the Halls of the Montezumas: The Mexican War in the American Imagination*. Oxford University Press, 1985.

Keegan, John. *The Second World War*. Viking, 1989.

Kennedy, David. *Over Here: The First World War and American Society*. Oxford University Press, 1988.

McPherson, James M. *Battle Cry of Freedom: The Era of the Civil War*. Oxford University Press, 1988.

Marshall, A.L. *The American Heritage History of World War I*. Random House, 1964, repr. 1988.

Middlekauff, Robert. *The Glorious Cause: The American Revolution, 1763–1789*. Oxford University Press, 1985.

Sifry, Micah L., and Christopher Cerf, eds. *The Gulf War Reader*. Random House, 1991.

Whelan, Richard. *Drawing the Line: The Korean War, 1950–1953*. Little, Brown, 1990.

Wood, Gordon. *The Creation of the American Republic, 1776–1787*. University of North Carolina, 1969.

6

Government, Politics, and Law

SIGNIFICANT EVENTS IN AMERICAN LAW AND POLITICS

The early years of the nation were devoted to devising the best form of government. Once that was established, attention was turned to forging and protecting individual and collective rights.

The Colonial Era

1619   The first colonial legislature, the House of Burgesses, meets at Jamestown, Virginia. This house, and its present-day successor, the Virginia General Assembly, is the oldest representative government in the Western Hemisphere.

1620   The Mayflower Compact, establishing self-government for the Plymouth Colony, is signed aboard the *Mayflower*.

1639   The first American constitution, the Fundamental Order of Connecticut, is written.

1641   In an early gesture of colonial independence, the Massachusetts Bay Colony establishes its own legal code, the Body of Liberties.

1647   Rhode Island's code of laws guarantees freedom of conscience: "Otherwise than . . . what is herein forbidden, all men may walk as their consciences persuade them, everyone in the name of his God."

1774   With a war for independence now on the horizon, the First Continental Congress meets in Philadelphia and draws up a list of grievances to give to the king of England.

1775   The Revolutionary War begins.

1776   Thomas Jefferson drafts the Declaration of Independence, which asserts the colonies' independence from England and defines the natural rights of Americans. The Continental Congress adopts it.

The Early Republic

1776   States begin writing state constitutions.

Virginia adopts a Declaration of Rights, asserting that "all men are by nature free and independent" and outlining rights and freedoms, such as the free exercise of religion, that will eventually be written into the U.S. Constitution and the Bill of Rights.

1777   The Continental Congress adopts the Articles of Confederation, which provide for a loose union of states and a weak central government with virtually no power to tax. It goes into effect in 1781.

The Continental Congress drafts the Articles of Confederation.

1786   Virginia adopts a statute of religious freedom, written by Thomas Jefferson.

1786-
1787   Shays's Rebellion, a tax protest, is the first internal challenge to the new nation's power.

1787   Beset by financial and diplomatic crises, Congress endorses a plan for a convention to revise the Articles of Confederation. Delegates write a new Constitution instead, one that significantly strengthens the central government. Federalists support this Constitution, while Anti-Federalists oppose it.

Written by James Madison, Alexander Hamilton, and John Jay, *The Federalist Papers* present a masterly interpretation and analysis of the Constitution, and argue for its ratification.

1788   The new Constitution takes effect when nine states ratify it.

1789   George Washington becomes the first president, and John Adams the first vice president.

Congress adopts the Bill of Rights, ratified as the first ten amendments to the Constitution in 1791.

A federal judiciary is organized.

Three federal departments—State, War, and Treasury—are formed, and the office of the attorney general is established. A postmaster general is also named, under the secretary of the treasury. When Washington consults with these heads, he sets a precedent for cabinet meetings, well established by the time he leaves office.

EXECUTIVE BRANCH DEPARTMENTS

The creation of departments—the responsibility of Congress—reflects the changing nature and concerns of the Union. The First Congress created only the State Department, the War Department, and the Treasury Department. The attorney general was a cabinet member, but the Justice Department that he heads today wasn't officially created until 1871. A postmaster general was also named, at this time under the secretary of the treasury. The following table lists the executive departments in order of their creation. Secretaries are listed in the chapter specified. A table of attorneys general follows.

Department	Year	Chapter
State	1789	Chapter 8
War	1789	Chapter 5
Treasury	1789	Chapter 9
Navy	1798 (consolidated with Defense in 1947)	Chapter 5
Interior	1849	Chapter 3
Agriculture	1862 (raised to cabinet status in 1889)	Chapter 7
Justice	1871 (with attorney general as head)	Chapter 6
Commerce	1913 (originally Commerce and Labor, 1903)	Chapter 9
Labor	1913 (originally Commerce and Labor, 1903)	Chapter 9
Defense	1947 (consolidates War, Navy, and other military units)	Chapter 5
Housing and Urban Development	1965	Chapter 7
Transportation	1966	Chapter 12
Energy	1977	Chapter 9
Health and Human Services	1979 (originally Health, Education, and Welfare, 1953)	Chapter 11
Education (originally Health, Education, and Welfare, 1953)	1979	Chapter 10
Veterans Affairs	1988	Chapter 5

Attorneys General

Attorney General	President	Year Appointed	Attorney General	President	Year Appointed
Edmund Randolph	Washington	1789	William H. H. Miller	Harrison, B.	1889
William Bradford	Washington	1794	Richard Olney	Cleveland	1893
Charles Lee	Washington	1795	Judson Harmon	Cleveland	1895
	Adams, J.	1797	Joseph McKenna	McKinley	1897
Levi Lincoln	Jefferson	1801	John W. Griggs	McKinley	1898
John Breckinridge	Jefferson	1805	Philander C. Knox	McKinley	1901
Caesar A. Rodney	Jefferson	1809		Roosevelt, T.	1901
	Madison	1797	William H. Moody	Roosevelt, T.	1904
William Pinkney	Madison	1811	Charles J. Bonaparte	Roosevelt, T.	1906
Richard Rush	Madison	1814	George W. Wickersham	Taft	1909
	Monroe	1817	J. C. McReynolds	Wilson	1913
William Wirt	Monroe	1817	Thomas W. Gregory	Wilson	1914
	Adams, J. Q.	1825	A. Mitchell Palmer	Wilson	1919
John M. Berrien	Jackson	1829	Harry M. Daugherty	Harding	1921
Roger B. Taney	Jackson	1831		Coolidge	1923
Benjamin F. Butler	Jackson	1833	Harlan F. Stone	Coolidge	1924
	Van Buren	1837	John G. Sargent	Coolidge	1925
Felix Grundy	Van Buren	1838	William D. Mitchell	Hoover	1929
Henry D. Gilpin	Van Buren	1840	Homer S. Cummings	Roosevelt, F. D.	1933
John J. Crittendon	Harrison, W. H.	1841	Frank Murphy	Roosevelt, F. D.	1939
	Tyler	1841	Robert H. Jackson	Roosevelt, F. D.	1940
Hugh S. Legare	Tyler	1841	Francis Biddle	Roosevelt, F. D.	1941
John Nelson	Tyler	1843	Thomas C. Clark	Truman	1945
John Y. Mason	Polk	1845	J. Howard McGrath	Truman	1949
Nathan Clifford	Polk	1846	J. P. McGranery	Truman	1952
Isaac Toucey	Polk	1848	Herbert Brownell, Jr.	Eisenhower	1953
Reverdy Johnson	Taylor	1849	William P. Rogers	Eisenhower	1957
John J. Crittendon	Filmore	1850	Robert F. Kennedy	Kennedy	1961
Caleb Cushing	Pierce	1853		Johnson, L. B.	1963
Jeremiah S. Black	Buchanan	1857	Nicholas Katzenbach	Johnson, L. B.	1964
Edwin M. Stanton	Buchanan	1860	Ramsey Clark	Johnson, L. B.	1967
Edward Bates	Lincoln	1861	John N. Mitchell	Nixon	1969
James Speed	Lincoln	1864	Richard G. Kleindienst	Nixon	1972
	Johnson, A.	1865	Elliot L. Richardson	Nixon	1973
Henry Stanbery	Johnson, A.	1866	William B. Saxbe	Nixon	1974
William M. Evarts	Johnson, A.	1868		Ford	1974
Ebenezer R. Hoar	Grant	1869	Edward H. Levi	Ford	1975
Amos T. Akerman	Grant	1870	Griffin B. Bell	Carter	1977
George H. Williams	Grant	1871	Benjamin R. Civiletti	Carter	1979
Edwards Pierrepont	Grant	1875	William French Smith	Reagan	1981
Alphonso Taft	Grant	1876	Edwin Meese 3d	Reagan	1985
Charles Devens	Hayes	1877	Richard Thornburgh	Reagan	1988
Wayne MacVeaugh	Garfield	1881		Bush	1989
Benjamin H. Brewster	Arthur	1881	William P. Barr	Bush	1991
Augustus Garland	Cleveland	1885	Janet Reno	Clinton	1993

1790   Congress meets in Philadelphia and votes to establish a new capital on the Potomac.

1791   Although there is not a national currency, Congress charters a national bank. It is responsible in part for regulating state banks.

The Bill of Rights becomes the first ten amendments to the Constitution.

THE BILL OF RIGHTS

When the Constitution was ratified, many objected that it contained no specific guarantees of rights or liberties. So in the First Congress, James Madison proposed a series of amendments; by 1791 ten had been added to the Constitution as the Bill of Rights. They are:

First: Freedom of speech, press, assembly, and religion.

Second: The right to bear arms.

Third: No requirement to quarter troops in peacetime.

Fourth: No unreasonable searches and seizures.

Fifth: No arrest without a grand jury indictment; no double jeopardy; no taking of life, liberty, or property without due process of law or of private property for public use without just compensation.

Sixth: Right to a public and speedy trial; right to counsel.

Seventh: Right to a trial by jury.

Eighth: No excessive bail or fines or cruel or unusual punishment.

Ninth: The rights of the people are not to be understood as limited to those enumerated.

Tenth: All powers not delegated to the federal government are reserved to the states, or to the people.

For additional amendments, see pages 183–184.

1792   The Democratic-Republican party, led by Thomas Jefferson, takes shape in opposition to the Federalists. It advocates strong states' rights.

Kentucky is admitted to the Union with universal manhood suffrage. Other states drop property qualifications in the following decades.

Thomas Jefferson

1793   Regional issues arise early; one such issue is solved by passage of the first Fugitive Slave Act, which makes it illegal to aid runaway slaves or to interfere with their arrest.

1794   The federal government uses force to quell the Whiskey Rebellion by frontier farmers who refuse to pay an excise tax on their whiskey.

1796   John Adams, a Federalist, is elected president, and Thomas Jefferson, a Democratic-Republican, is elected vice president.

Presidents and Vice Presidents of the United States

President	Term	Birth and Death	Party	Vice President
1. George Washington	1789–1793	1732–1799	F	John Adams
	1793–1797			
2. John Adams	1797–1801	1735–1826	F	Thomas Jefferson
3. Thomas Jefferson	1801–1805	1743–1826	D-R	Aaron Burr
	1805–1809			George Clinton
4. James Madison	1809–1813	1751–1836	D-R	George Clinton
	1813–1817			Elbridge Gerry
5. James Monroe	1817–1821	1758–1831	D-R	Daniel D. Tompkins
	1821–1825			
6. John Quincy Adams	1825–1829	1767–1848	D-R	John C. Calhoun
7. Andrew Jackson	1829–1833	1767–1845	D-R	John C. Calhoun
	1833–1837			Martin Van Buren
8. Martin Van Buren	1837–1841	1782–1862	D	Richard M. Johnson
9. William Henry Harrison	3/4–4/4 1841	1773–1841	W	John Tyler
10. John Tyler	1841–1845	1790–1862	W	—
11. James K. Polk	1845–1849	1795–1864	D	George M. Dallas
12. Zachary Taylor	1849–1850	1784–1850	W	Millard Fillmore
13. Millard Fillmore	1850–1853	1800–1874	W	—
14. Franklin Pierce	1853–1857	1804–1869	D	William R. King
15. James Buchanan	1857–1861	1791–1868	D	John C. Breckinridge
16. Abraham Lincoln	1861–1865	1809–1865	R	Hannibal Hamlin
	3/4–4/15 1865			Andrew Johnson
17. Andrew Johnson	1865–1869	1808–1875	NU	—
18. Ulysses S. Grant	1869–1873	1822–1885	R	Schuyler Colfax
	1873–1877			Henry Wilson
19. Rutherford B. Hayes	1877–1881	1822–1893	R	William A. Wheeler
20. James Garfield	3/4–9/19 1881	1831–1881	R	Chester A. Arthur
21. Chester A. Arthur	1881–1885	1829–1886	R	—
22. Grover Cleveland	1885–1889	1837–1908	D	Thomas A. Hendricks
23. Benjamin Harrison	1889–1893	1833–1901	R	Levi P. Morton
24. Grover Cleveland	1893–1897	1837–1908	D	Adlai E. Stevenson
25. William McKinley	1897–1901	1843–1901	R	Garret A. Hobart
	3/4–9/14 1901			Theodore Roosevelt
26. Theodore Roosevelt	1901–1905	1858–1919	R	—
	1905–1909			Charles W. Fairbanks
27. William H. Taft	1909–1913	1857–1930	R	James S. Sherman
28. Woodrow Wilson	1913–1917	1856–1924	D	Thomas R. Marshall
	1917–1921			
29. Warren G. Harding	1921–1923	1865–1923	R	Calvin Coolidge
30. Calvin Coolidge	1923–1925	1872–1933	R	—
	1925–1929			Charles G. Dawes
31. Herbert C. Hoover	1929–1933	1874–1964	R	Charles Curtis

President	Term	Birth and Death	Party	Vice President
32. Franklin D. Roosevelt	1933–1936	1882–1945	D	John N. Garner
	1936–1941			
	1941–1945			Henry A. Wallace
	1/20–4/12 1945			Harry S. Truman
33. Harry S. Truman	1945–1949	1884–1972	D	—
	1949–1953			Alben W. Barkley
34. Dwight D. Eisenhower	1953–1961	1890–1969	R	Richard M. Nixon
35. John F. Kennedy	1961–1963	1917–1963	D	Lyndon B. Johnson
36. Lyndon B. Johnson	1963–1965	1908–1973	D	—
	1965–1969			Hubert H. Humphrey
37. Richard M. Nixon	1969–1973	1913–1994	R	Spiro T. Agnew
	1973–1974			Gerald R. Ford
38. Gerald R. Ford	1974–1977	1913–	R	Nelson A. Rockefeller
39. James (Jimmy) Earl Carter, Jr.	1977–1981	1924–	D	Walter F. Mondale
40. Ronald Reagan	1981–1985	1911–	R	George Bush
	1985–1989			
41. George Bush	1989–1993	1924–	R	J. Danforth Quayle
42. William (Bill) Clinton	1993–1997	1946–	D	Al Gore
	1997–			

F = Federalist; D-R = Democratic-Republican; D = Democrat; W = Whig; R = Republican; NU = National Union party, a coalition of Republicans and War Democrats (Andrew Johnson was a Democrat)

1798   The Eleventh Amendment is ratified, in effect stating that a state cannot be sued by a citizen of another state.

With war against France seeming imminent, Congress passes the Alien and Sedition Acts, which extend the residency requirements for citizenship, authorize the president to deport aliens dangerous to the public peace or safety, and make it a crime to obstruct the execution of the national laws or to publish "any false, scandalous, or malicious writing" against the U.S. government, Congress, or the president. Targeted were newspaper editors aligned with Jefferson's Democratic-Republicans and supporting Revolutionary France.

The Kentucky (written by Thomas Jefferson) and Virginia (written by James Madison) Resolutions argue that the Alien and Sedition Acts are unconstitutional because the federal government was exercising powers not delegated to it. A second set of Kentucky Resolutions outlines the doctrine of nullification—that states can nullify actions of the U.S. Congress.

The Department of the Navy is established. In 1947 it will be consolidated with other military units in the Department of Defense.

The Rise of Sectionalism and States' Rights

1800   The seat of the federal government moves from Philadelphia to Washington, D.C.

The first election involving political parties is held, with Democratic-Republican Thomas Jefferson running against Federalist John Adams. Jefferson beats Adams, but thanks to party discipline, Jefferson receives the same number of votes as the vice presidential candidate Aaron Burr.

1801   The election is forced into the House of Representatives, where 36 ballots are required to elect Jefferson.

THE ELECTORAL COLLEGE

When the framers of the Constitution established the office of president, they hesitated to allow this powerful individual to be elected directly by the people. Instead they devised a system, known as the electoral college, whereby the president is actually elected by electors, who in turn are elected by the people. Each state has as many electors as its Senate and House members combined, and the electors usually vote as a block for the candidate who has received the greatest number of votes in the state.

This system has produced some erratic results. In 1800, Thomas Jefferson and Aaron Burr were tied for the electoral vote. As a consequence, the House of Representatives made the final decision, and passage of the Twelfth Amendment made sure this kind of tie would not occur again.

But there have been other problems. For example, a president with a larger popular vote majority can lose in the electoral college, as happened to Grover Cleveland in 1888. When there is no majority in the electoral college, the House of Representatives decides the outcome, each state's delegation voting as a block. Following the election of 1824 the House awarded the presidency to John Quincy Adams, even though he had received more than 38,000 *fewer* votes than contender Andrew Jackson. And following the election of 1876, with disputed returns in four states, the House appointed a commission that put Rutherford B. Hayes in office, even though Samuel J. Tilden had an edge, in the popular vote, of more than 264,000 votes.

Reformers say that the system is flawed and the electoral college should be abolished. But most of the time it has worked remarkably well to reflect the choice of the people and today is more of a tradition than the buffer against the people that the framers envisioned.

1803	In *Marbury v. Madison*, the Supreme Court establishes its right to review the constitutionality of acts of Congress.
1804	The Twelfth Amendment, which remedies the problem of the 1800 election by providing for the separate election of president and vice president, is ratified.
	Thomas Jefferson is reelected president. His presidency is increasingly preoccupied with neutral rights, an embargo that hurts U.S. commerce, and increasing tensions with Britain.
1807	Aaron Burr becomes the first major public official to be tried for treason. Charged with trying to establish an independent country in the Southwest, he is acquitted.
1808	James Madison is elected president on the Democratic-Republican ticket.
	Congress halts the slave trade but not slavery.
1812	James Madison is reelected president as the country is already at war against Britain.
	The Second Bank of the United States is granted a charter.
1816	James Monroe is elected president on the Republican ticket. The Federalist party, in disarray, does not nominate a candidate. Monroe's election (he receives all electoral votes but one) ushers in the Era of Good Feeling, a period when the country is expanding its territory and settling its boundary disputes.

POLITICAL PARTIES

Political parties aren't written into the Constitution, and indeed some of the framers, especially James Madison, feared factionalism and parties. But Madison also recognized that "the causes of faction are . . . sown in the nature of man," and inevitably, even in George Washington's first term, political factions began to align around the differing positions of Thomas Jefferson and Alexander Hamilton. At issue was nothing less that the nature of the Union: Hamilton hoped for a stronger,

James Madison

more centralized federal government than Jefferson could tolerate. Jefferson's followers became known as the Republicans, or Democratic-Republicans, and Hamilton's as the Federalists.

By the time of the War of 1812 the Federalists were torn by internal strife and conservative Federalists in New England were so highly critical of the war that when it was successfully concluded the party practically self-destructed. James Monroe, a Democratic-Republican from Virginia, had no real opposition in the elections of 1816 and 1820: hence the Era of Good Feeling.

In 1824 there were five candidates for president, all Republicans. But that contest proved decisively divisive. Andrew Jackson won the popular vote but failed to get a majority of the electoral vote. Consequently the election was decided by the House of Representatives, which awarded the presidency to John Quincy Adams. Claiming that Adams had entered into a "corrupt bargain" to secure the presidency, Jackson's followers vowed revenge, and in 1828 Jackson—this time running as a Democrat—beat National Republican Adams in both the popular and electoral vote. There hasn't been an uncontested presidential election since.

Adams's National Republicans gave way to the Whigs by 1840, when William Henry Harrison was elected, and in 1856 the new Republican party, fusing various antislavery factions, set the stage for the familiar two-party races that have been an American political tradition since the Civil War.

Occasionally a third party has mounted a serious challenge. For a survey of third parties, see pages 186–187.

Supreme Court Justices of the United States

Justice	Term	Justice	Term
John Jay*	1789–1795	Melville W. Fuller*	1888–1910
John Blair	1789–1796	Lucius Q. C. Lamar	1888–1893
William Cushing	1789–1810	David J. Brewer	1890–1910
Robert H. Harrison	1789–1790	Henry B. Brown	1891–1906
John Rutledge	1789–1791	George Shiras, Jr.	1892–1903
James Wilson	1789–1798	Howell E. Jackson	1893–1895
James Iredell	1790–1799	Edward D. White	1894–1910
Thomas Johnson	1791–1793	Rufus W. Peckham	1896–1909
William Paterson	1793–1806	Joseph McKenna	1898–1925
John Rutledge*	1795 (Congress	Oliver W. Holmes	1902–1932
	rejected his	William R. Day	1903–1922
	appointment as	William H. Moody	1906–1910
	Chief Justice)	Edward D. White*	1910–1921
Oliver Ellsworth*	1796–1799	Charles E. Hughes	1910–1916
Samuel Chase	1796–1811	Horace H. Lurton	1910–1914
Bushrod Washington	1798–1829	Joseph R. Lamar	1911–1916
Alfred Moore	1799–1804	Willis Van Devanter	1911–1937
John Marshall*	1801–1835	Mahlon Pitney	1912–1922
William Johnson	1804–1834	James C. McReynolds	1914–1941
Henry Livingston	1806–1823	Louis D. Brandeis	1916–1939
Thomas Todd	1807–1826	John H. Clarke	1916–1922
Joseph Story	1811–1845	William H. Taft*	1921–1930
Gabriel Duval	1812–1835	Pierce Butler	1922–1939
Smith Thompson	1823–1843	George Sutherland	1922–1938
Robert Trimble	1826–1828	Edward T. Sanford	1923–1930
John McLean	1829–1861	Harlan F. Stone	1925–1941
Henry Baldwin	1830–1844	Charles E. Hughes*	1930–1941
James M. Wayne	1835–1867	Owen J. Roberts	1930–1945
Roger B. Taney*	1836–1864	Benjamin N. Cardozo	1932–1938
Philip P. Barbour	1836–1841	Hugo L. Black	1937–1971
John Catron	1837–1865	Stanley F. Reed	1938–1957
John McKinley	1837–1852	William O. Douglas	1939–1975
Peter V. Daniel	1841–1860	Felix Frankfurter	1939–1962
Samuel Nelson	1845–1872	Frank Murphy	1940–1949
Levi Woodbury	1845–1851	Harlan F. Stone*	1941–1946
Robert C. Grier	1846–1870	James F. Byrnes	1941–1942
Benjamin R. Curtis	1851–1857	Robert H. Jackson	1941–1954
John A. Campbell	1853–1861	Wiley B. Rutledge	1943–1949
Nathan Clifford	1858–1881	Harold H. Burton	1945–1958
David Davis	1862–1877	Fred M. Vinson*	1946–1953
Samuel F. Miller	1862–1890	Tom C. Clark	1949–1967
Noah H. Swayne	1862–1881	Sherman Minton	1949–1956
Stephen J. Field	1863–1897	Earl Warren*	1953–1969
Salmon P. Chase*	1864–1873	John Marshall Harlan	1955–1971
Joseph P. Bradley	1870–1892	William J. Brennan, Jr.	1956–1990
William Strong	1870–1880	Charles E. Whittaker	1957–1962
Ward Hunt	1873–1882	Potter Stewart	1958–1981
Morrison R. Waite*	1874–1888	Arthur J. Goldberg	1962–1965
John M. Harlan	1877–1911	Byron R. White	1962–1993
Stanley Matthews	1881–1889	Abe Fortas	1965–1969
William B. Woods	1881–1887	Thurgood Marshall	1967–1991
Samuel Blatchford	1882–1893	Warren E. Burger*	1969–1986
Horace Gray	1881–1902	Harry A. Blackmun	1970–1994

Justice	Term	Justice	Term
Lewis F. Powell, Jr.	1971–1987	Anthony Kennedy	1988–
William H. Rehnquist*	1971–	David H. Souter	1990–
John Paul Stevens, III	1975–	Clarence Thomas	1991–
Sandra Day O'Connor	1981–	Ruth Bader Ginsburg	1993–
Antonin Scalia	1986–	Stephen G. Breyer	1994–

Chief Justice

1818	Connecticut abolishes ownership of property as a voter qualification.
1820	Henry Clay engineers the Missouri Compromise, which admits Maine to the Union as a free state, Missouri as a slave state, and forbids slavery in the Louisiana Territory north of 36°30' (the southern boundary of Missouri).
	President Monroe is reelected.
1824	Neither the populist war hero Andrew Jackson nor National Republican John Quincy Adams garners a majority in the electoral college, although John Calhoun is elected vice president.
1825	The presidential election is forced into the House of Representatives, and John Adams wins with the support of Henry Clay. Jackson supporters vow revenge.
1828	Andrew Jackson runs again, this time as a disaffected Democrat, as the Democratic-Republicans now call themselves. As the "new" party's first nominee, he is elected.
1829	Overturning the Jeffersonian precedent, Jackson introduces a spoils system to the federal bureaucracy, in which winners of elections reward their friends and party members with government jobs. The "kitchen cabinet," an informal group of advisors, are among the most powerful men in Washington.
1830	With South Carolina angered over high tariffs and promoting the doctrine of nullification, whereby a state may choose to nullify a federal law within its borders, South Carolina senator Robert Y. Hayne and Massachusetts senator Daniel Webster debate the power of the Union. Hayne takes the states' rights position, while Webster, an eloquent orator, defends the Union: "Liberty and Union, now and forever, one and inseparable."
	Former president John Quincy Adams is elected to Congress.

AFTER THE PRESIDENCY

What else is there after you've been president? Many former presidents have simply retired, but a few have gone on to have surprising careers. John Quincy Adams, disappointed in losing his bid for reelection in 1828, was approached by a Massachusetts delegation who asked him to run for Congress. He agreed, and in 1830 was elected to the House of Representatives, where he served until the end of his life. In 1836 he opposed the "gag rule," which suppressed all petitions for the abolition of slavery, and in 1844 finally succeeded in getting it rescinded. He also defended the slave mutineers of the *Amistad* before the Supreme Court. On February 21, 1848, Adams suffered a stroke and collapsed in the House of Representatives. He was carried from his seat to the Speaker's Room, where he lay until he died two days later.

Andrew Johnson was the only other president to serve in Congress after his term of office. He ran for the House of Representatives in 1872, but lost. In 1875 he was elected to the Senate, perhaps relishing a return to the very institution that had given him so much trouble when he was president.

(continues)

AFTER THE PRESIDENCY (CONT.)

Theodore Roosevelt had picked William Howard Taft to be his successor, but once Taft was in office, Roosevelt could hardly stand not to be there himself. He ran against Taft in 1912, splitting the Republican party and spoiling his former friend's chances for reelection. Former presidents Martin Van Buren and Millard Fillmore had also accepted third-party nominations for president, but ran with less success.

Herbert Hoover was another president who would have liked to continue. Hardly retired after 1933, he took up again the relief work that had first made him famous. After World War II he conducted a study of food and economic conditions in defeated Germany for President Truman and chaired a commission to study reorganization of the executive branch. President Eisenhower asked him to direct a similar effort. Hoover may have lost the presidency but certainly not the respect of those who held it.

More recently Jimmy Carter has pursued, out of office, the themes of his presidency: international peace through missions to Panama, North Korea, and Haiti, and social justice through Habitat for Humanity.

1832   A state convention in South Carolina passes an Ordinance of Nullification, nullifying the tariff acts of 1828 and 1832.

The "Bank War" erupts when Andrew Jackson attempts to disband the Second National Bank by refusing to renew its charter, due to expire in 1836. Merchants and businessmen, who want state banks to maintain hard currency reserves, favor a national bank, while western farmers, land speculators, and urban workers, who like the easy money policies of state banks, support the state banks.

Andrew Jackson is reelected president.

1833   Congress responds to South Carolina's Ordinance of Nullification by passing the federal government's first Force Bill, which specifies the federal government's ability to use armed force to enforce federal laws in the states. The crisis is averted when the tariff bill is rewritten to make it more acceptable to the South.

Jackson escalates the Bank War by pulling $10 million in government funds out of the national bank and putting it in favored state banks. The head of the national bank responds by calling in commercial loans, thus causing a panic, which soon turns to recession.

1835   Recession turns to boom as state banks proliferate, the price of cotton soars, and western land speculation reaches new highs.

1836   President Andrew Jackson, concerned about widespread use of paper money, issues the Specie Circular, declaring that the federal government will henceforth require hard currency to buy western public lands.

English banks raise interest rates and reduce credit, sending shock waves in the cotton market that initiate a six-year depression.

Martin Van Buren, a Democrat, succeeds Andrew Jackson as president.

1839   The Liberty party forms, organized in opposition to slavery.

1840   William Henry Harrison is elected president.

1841   When Harrison dies one month after taking office, Vice President John Tyler succeeds him (the first vice president to do so). Tyler vetoes several Whig measures, and becomes increasingly isolated from the party.

THE VICE PRESIDENCY

When John Tyler took the oath of office on April 6, 1841, no one knew quite what would happen. President William Henry Harrison, dead exactly a month after his inauguration, was the first president to die in office. Would the vice president be the president, or just the acting president?

Tyler set the precedent by being the president, and since his term eight vice presidents presidents have similarly moved up. They are:

President	Year	Reason
Millard Fillmore	1850	Death of Zachary Taylor
Andrew Johnson	1865	Assassination of Abraham Lincoln
Chester A. Arthur	1881	Assassination of James A. Garfield
Theodore Roosevelt	1901	Assassination of William McKinley
Calvin Coolidge	1923	Death of Warren G. Harding
Harry S. Truman	1945	Death of Franklin D. Roosevelt
Lyndon Johnson	1963	Assassination of John F. Kennedy
Gerald R. Ford	1974	Resignation of Richard M. Nixon, whose vice president, Spiro T. Agnew, had also resigned

Other vice presidents have been elected president in their own right. Aside from those who succeeded to the presidency and were then reelected (Theodore Roosevelt, Calvin Coolidge, Harry Truman, and Lyndon Johnson), a few vice presidents have managed to use their office as the road to the White House.

Vice President	Under President	Became President
John Adams	George Washington	1797
Thomas Jefferson	John Adams	1801
Martin Van Buren	Andrew Jackson	1837
Richard M. Nixon	Dwight Eisenhower	1969
George Bush	Ronald Reagan	1989

1842 Dorr's Rebellion in Rhode Island leads to a liberalization of the voting laws in that state by 1848.

1844 James K. Polk, a Democrat, becomes the first dark-horse candidate ever to win the presidency. He settles the Oregon question and fights the Mexican War, encouraging expansionism.

1846 David Wilmot of Pennsylvania proposes that no territory acquired from Mexico as a result of war shall be open to slavery. Passed by the House but defeated by the Senate, the proviso exacerbates the growing bitterness between the North and South.

1846- The Free-Soil party forms, an alliance of antislavery northern Democrats, so-called Con-
1847 science Whigs, and old Liberty party members. In 1848 the Free-Soilers run Martin Van Buren for president.

1848 Zachary Taylor, a Whig, is elected president. A national hero from the Mexican War, he supports the expansion of the nation and the admission of California as a free state.

1849 The Department of the Interior is created to act as custodian of the nation's natural resources and manage land sale and Indian affairs (see Chapter 3).

1850   When President Zachary Taylor dies, Vice President Millard Fillmore becomes president.

Congress engages in acrimonious debate over slavery and finally passes the Compromise of 1850, in which California is admitted as a free state and Utah and New Mexico residents are permitted to decide the slavery issue in their territories. The slave trade is abolished in the District of Columbia; a more stringent Fugitive Slave Law is enacted; and questions concerning the Texas boundary and debt are resolved. In this debate three men who have dominated U.S. politics for decades are heard for the last time: John C. Calhoun, Henry Clay, and Daniel Webster.

1852   Franklin Pierce, a compromise candidate in the deeply divided Democratic party, defeats the Whig candidate but does not fare well as president. His one accomplishment is to sign the Gadsden Purchase, but he also signs the Kansas-Nebraska Act, which leaves the issue of slavery up to settlers of various territories. This angers Northerners and leads to a bloody civil war in Kansas. Although opposed to slavery, Pierce also opposes the civil war in Kansas. His party denies him the nomination a second time.

1854   The Republican party, with a staunch antislavery platform, is founded in opposition to the Kansas-Nebraska Act.

1856   James Buchanan, a Democrat, is elected president. His administration reels from bad to worse, lacking the strength or wisdom to avert civil war.

1857   In the *Dred Scott* decision, the Supreme Court holds that blacks are not citizens and overrules the Missouri Compromise on grounds that Congress has no right to make any laws prohibiting slavery in the territories.

1858   The seven Lincoln-Douglas debates focus still more attention on the issue of slavery. Stephen Douglas, a brilliant debater, supports popular sovereignty. Lincoln takes the position that slavery is morally wrong and that the federal government should decide the slavery question in the territories. Douglas wins reelection to the U.S. Senate (elected, as are all senators at the time, by the state legislature, in this case Illinois).

1859   Abolitionist John Brown captures the federal arsenal at Harpers Ferry, intending to incite a slave revolt. Although Brown is hanged for treason, he is venerated as a religious martyr by many in the North.

1860   In a vote that severely divides the nation into pro- and antislavery camps, Abraham Lincoln, a Republican, is elected president. The Civil War follows. A major achievement of his administrations is the emancipation of the slaves.

1861   The Civil War begins when South Carolina forces fire on Union-held Fort Sumter in Charleston Harbor.

The Civil War and Reconstruction

1862   Slavery is abolished in the nation's capital.

1863   The Emancipation Proclamation is issued, freeing slaves in areas in rebellion.

Lincoln delivers the Gettysburg Address.

1864   Lincoln wins reelection, largely because after four years of fighting, the tide has begun to turn in favor of the North.

1865   President Lincoln is assassinated at Ford's Theatre, and Andrew Johnson becomes president. His presidency is largely occupied with the Reconstruction, which wins him many enemies in Congress.

The Thirteenth Amendment, abolishing slavery, is ratified.

The firing on Fort Sumter

CONSTITUTIONAL AMENDMENTS

Amendments are serious business. While many have been proposed, few have actually been passed by Congress (it takes a two-thirds vote of each house), and even fewer ratified by the states (three-quarters of the states must ratify before an amendment goes into effect).

Following the Civil War, several constitutional amendments were necessary to establish the status of the newly freed slaves. These are detailed below, together with the additional amendments that in the course of the nation's 200 years have been considered serious and important enough to be added to the Constitution.

1798   Eleventh: Forbids suits against a state by citizens of another state or nation.

1804   Twelfth: Provides for separate ballots for the president and vice president.

1865   Thirteenth: Abolishes slavery.

1868   Fourteenth: Defines citizenship; guarantees to all persons the equal protection of the laws.

1870   Fifteenth: Guarantees that the right to vote cannot be abridged on account of race, color, or previous condition of servitude.

1913   Sixteenth: Permits an income tax.

1913   Seventeenth: Provides for the direct election of senators (previously senators had been elected by state legislatures).

1919   Eighteenth: Prohibits the manufacture, sale, or transportation of intoxicating liquors.

1920   Nineteenth: Guarantees that the right to vote cannot be denied or abridged on account of sex.

(continues)

CONSTITUTIONAL AMENDMENTS (CONT.)

1933 Twentieth: Sets date for beginning of Congress (January 3) and presidential terms (January 20); provides for presidential succession.

1933 Twenty-first: Repeals the Eighteenth Amendment (Prohibition).

1951 Twenty-second: Limits the president to two terms.

1961 Twenty-third: Permits citizens residing in the District of Columbia to vote in presidential elections.

1964 Twenty-fourth: Prohibits poll taxes.

1967 Twenty-fifth: Provides for presidential disability.

1971 Twenty-sixth: Gives 18-year-olds the right to vote.

1992 Twenty-seventh: Prohibits Congress raising its own pay within a session.

1866 In an attempt to put some backbone into the Thirteenth Amendment, Congress passes the first Civil Rights Act, which decrees that all persons born in the United States (except Native Americans who are not taxed) are citizens. When President Andrew Johnson vetoes the bill, Congress overrides the veto. Congress also passes the Fourteenth Amendment.

1867 Congress passes a series of Reconstruction Acts initiating military rule of the former Confederate States, except Tennessee. When President Johnson realizes that his secretary of war, Edwin Stanton, is feeding information to the opposition, Johnson fires him—in violation of the newly passed Tenure of Office Act, which prohibits the president from firing high-ranking officials without Senate approval.

1868 The House of Representatives impeaches President Andrew Johnson for defying the Tenure of Office Act. He is tried in the Senate; he is acquitted by only one vote.

The Fourteenth Amendment, granting citizenship to former slaves, is ratified.

Ulysses S. Grant, a Republican, is elected president. A major achievement of his administration is civil-service reform.

1869 The temperance movement goes political when the Prohibition party is founded in Chicago.

1870 The Fifteenth Amendment, guaranteeing that the right to vote cannot be denied on account of race, color, or previous condition of servitude, is ratified.

The Ku Klux Klan Acts (1870, 1871) place congressional elections under federal control, and the militia is used to enforce the voting rights of blacks.

1871 President Ulysses S. Grant, in an attempt to clean up the spoils system, institutes civil service reforms.

The Department of Justice is established, with the attorney general named its head.

1872 President Grant ushers an amnesty bill for Southerners through Congress.

Women's rights activist Victoria Woodhull is the first woman presidential candidate, running on the People's Party ticket with Frederick Douglass as her running mate.

President Grant is reelected.

1873 In the *Slaughterhouse Cases*, the Supreme Court rules that the Fourteenth Amendment only protects the national rights of citizens, not the rights conferred—or withheld—by the states.

1875 A second major Civil Rights Act gives equal rights to African Americans in public accommodations and on jury duty. It is ruled unconstitutional in 1883.

1876   A crisis is precipitated when Samuel J. Tilden, a Democrat, wins the popular vote but not the electoral vote, as the returns in four states are disputed.

1877   An electoral commission gives Rutherford B. Hayes the electoral college majority by assigning all the disputed votes to him.

President Hayes orders federal troops withdrawn from the South.

Industrialism and Imperialism

1878   The American Bar Association is established.

1880   James Garfield, a Republican, is elected president.

1881   President James Garfield is assassinated in a railroad station in Washington, D.C, and Vice President Chester A. Arthur succeeds him. Arthur's administration is marked by civil service reform and agrarian discontent.

1883   The Supreme Court finds most of the Civil Rights Act of 1875 to be unconstitutional; only the provision that black men may serve on juries survives. In reality, African Americans and other minorities and women neither serve on juries nor vote.

Congress passes the Pendleton Act, which establishes a Civil Service Commission to administer a merit-based civil service.

1884   Grover Cleveland, a Democrat, is elected president with a mandate to clean up machine politics.

1886   A Presidential Succession Act is passed, stipulating that cabinet members, in the order of the creation of their offices, will succeed to the presidency if both the president and vice president die or are removed or unable to serve.

1887   The Electoral Count Act authorizes states to certify their own electoral votes, thus avoiding the possibility of another disputed national election like the Tilden-Hayes contest.

1888   Benjamin Harrison, a Republican, is elected president with fewer popular votes but more electoral votes than Democrat Grover Cleveland.

The Bureau of Labor is made the Department of Labor but in 1903 it is reorganized as the Department of Commerce and Labor.

1891   Congress passes the Circuit Courts of Appeals Act, giving the Supreme Court the right to review all cases.

1892   President Grover Cleveland is reelected. His second administration is plagued by a money crisis and a deepening depression.

1893   Colorado becomes the first state to enact women's suffrage, but Wyoming Territory has permitted women to vote since 1869 and Utah Territory since 1870.

1894   Congress passes the first graduated federal income tax.

1895   The Supreme Court, in *Pollock v. Farmers' Loan and Trust Company*, finds the federal income tax unconstitutional.

1896   The Supreme Court in *Plessy v. Ferguson* rules that separate-but-equal facilities in railway facilities, and by implication in education and all public accommodations, are acceptable for blacks, thus legitimating segregation.

William McKinley, a Republican, is elected president. His administration reluctantly goes ahead with the short-lived Spanish-American War, passes the highest tariff in U.S. history, and initiates the Open Door policy with China.

1898   Labor leader Eugene V. Debs helps to organize the Social Democratic party, later renamed the Socialist party.

An Emerging World Power

1901   President William McKinley is shot by anarchist Leon Czolgosz on September 6. Eight days later McKinley dies, and Vice President Theodore Roosevelt becomes president. An energetic Progressive, he initiates 44 lawsuits to break up trusts and champions such social reforms as the Food and Drug Act. Through the force of his personality and his seemingly inexhaustible energy, Roosevelt expands the powers of the presidency. Through a series of forays into the foreign arena, he establishes the United States as a world power.

1903   The Department of Commerce and Labor is established.

1904   President Theodore Roosevelt is overwhelmingly reelected. In a statement that he will come to regret he promises not to run again.

1908   William Howard Taft, a Republican, is elected president. Groomed by Roosevelt to be his successor, Taft begins 90 antitrust actions and continues to press for the dissolution of the Standard Oil Trust. Nevertheless he alienates Progressives by supporting high tariffs and by becoming embroiled in a public lands controversy that pits him against Forest Service chief Gifford Pinchot.

   The Bureau of Investigation is established. J. Edgar Hoover becomes director in 1924 and over time, with the cooperation of Congress, greatly expands the bureau's duties and jurisdiction. It is renamed the Federal Bureau of Investigation in 1935.

1911   Wisconsin senator Robert La Follette helps found the National Progressive Republican League, which seeks to deprive President William Howard Taft of the Republican nomination in 1912.

   Congress submits an amendment providing for direct election of senators to the states. The House had passed such legislation in 1893, 1894, 1898, 1900, and 1902. The Senate had either not acted or defeated the legislation

1912   Angry at Taft, Theodore Roosevelt organizes the Bull Moose party and runs against his protégé but succeeds only in splitting the vote. Woodrow Wilson, a Democrat, wins the presidency. Wilson initially works to keep the United States out of World War I but then enters the war in 1917. Throughout the war he works to establish the League of Nations, a forerunner to the United Nations.

THIRD PARTIES

Third parties in the American political system are possible but not likely. The high point may have been in 1912, when Theodore Roosevelt, disgusted with the conservatism of his hand-picked successor, William Howard Taft, bolted from the Republican party to form his own Progressive party, better known as the Bull Moose. He attracted 27 percent of the popular vote and 88 electoral votes, spoiling Taft's chances for a second term and putting Democrat Woodrow Wilson in the White House.

Before the Civil War the most significant third parties were the Free-Soil party, which in 1848 nominated ex-president Martin Van Buren and got 10 percent of the vote; and the American (or Know-Nothing) party, which in 1856 ran ex-president Millard Fillmore and got 22 percent. On the brink of war there were four serious contenders. In addition to Abraham Lincoln, the Republican, and Stephen A. Douglas, the Democrat, there was John C. Breckinridge, a southern Democrat, and John Bell of the Constitutional Union party, which attempted to unite the remnants of the Whig and American parties. But the nation seemed beyond a political solution, and when Abraham Lincoln won the presidency without a single electoral vote from a southern state, secession and civil war were inevitable.

Late in the 19th century, James B. Weaver's People's (or Populist) party made a strong showing in 1892, attracting 9 percent of the popular vote, but in 1896 the Democrats co-opted the Populists' message and candidate, William Jennings Bryan.

In the 1912 election, beside Roosevelt's spectacular showing with the Bull Moose party, Eugene V. Debs, running on the Socialist party ticket, got 6 percent of the vote. In 1924 Robert M. La Follette, running as a Progressive party candidate (not the same party as Roosevelt's) got 17 percent. In 1948 Strom Thurmond, leading a group of southern Democrats who found Harry Truman too strong on civil rights, got 2 percent of the vote with his States' Rights party, or Dixiecrats. Henry A. Wallace, running on yet another Progressive party ticket, also got 2 percent. In 1968, George C. Wallace, another southerner who balked at his party's civil rights stand, ran as an American Independent and picked up 14 percent of the vote. John Anderson, in 1980, ran as an independent and got 7 percent. Finally, in one of the strongest showings ever, Ross Perot, running for an organization called United We Stand, America, that he said was not a political party, garnered 19 percent of the vote. In 1996 he formed the Reform party but got less than 10 percent.

Third parties do not do very well in national elections. Their chief successes are in pushing issues onto the national agenda and getting major parties to adopt them as their own. The major parties, ever jealous of their priority, know that's one sure way to make a third party go away.

1913   The Sixteenth Amendment, giving Congress the power to impose federal income taxes, is ratified.

The Seventeenth Amendment, providing for the direct election of senators, is ratified.

The Department of Commerce and Labor is split into two departments.

1915   The House of Representatives restricts its membership to 435 to keep it from getting even more unwieldy.

1916   President Woodrow Wilson is reelected.

1917   The United States enters World War I.

Women picket in front of the White House for the right to vote.

Even though women cannot yet vote, Montana's Jeannette Rankin takes her seat in the House of Representatives to which she was elected the previous fall.

1918   For his opposition to the government's prosecution of citizens charged with sedition, Socialist party leader Eugene V. Debs is sentenced to ten years in prison under the Espionage Act. He will eventually receive a presidential pardon in 1921. While in prison Debs is the Socialist party candidate for U.S. president. He receives almost 1 million votes.

World War I ends.

1919   The Eighteenth Amendment, enacting Prohibition, is ratified.

The Supreme Court holds that in wartime rights and privileges that would have been considered normal may be curtailed when a "clear and present danger" exists.

The Communist party of America is founded, but it never becomes an important force in American politics.

Using the authority of the 1918 Alien Act, which permits the government to deport any alien who is, or has been, a member of a revolutionary organization, the Justice Department deports hundreds of aliens, among them anarchists Emma Goldman and Alexander Berkman.

1920   The Nineteenth Amendment is ratified, giving women the right to vote.

Republican Warren Harding is elected president. He pledges to return the nation to "normalcy" after the chaos of the war.

Women's suffrage march

1920   The American Civil Liberties Union (ACLU) is founded by Jane Addams, Felix Frankfurter, Helen Keller, Judah Magnus, and Norman Thomas.

1921   Former President Taft becomes chief justice of the Supreme Court, the only person ever to hold both positions.

THANKS, WINNIE

In 1921 Winifred Huck dared to propose that she might fill out the unexpired congressional term of her father. When she was refused this honor, she ran and won the seat on her own in 1922. But she still deserves the credit for establishing this precedent, which was for many decades the only way a woman could make it to the House or Senate. As a result of Huck's suggestion, many of the women who came to Congress in the next years were filling the unexpired terms of fathers and husbands.

1923   President Warren Harding dies unexpectedly just as the Teapot Dome Scandal is about to break. Calvin Coolidge assumes the presidency.

1924   The Progressive party runs Senator Bob La Follette for president. President Coolidge is elected. Coolidge, who is laissez-faire about the government's role in regulating business, presides over an economic boom, although the speculation that occurs during this administration leads to the Great Depression.

1926   The Supreme Court in *Myers v. United States* supports the president's right to fire executive-branch employees, voiding the Tenure of Office Act of 1867 that was used to impeach Andrew Johnson.

1928   The Socialist party runs Norman Thomas for president. Herbert Hoover, a Republican, is elected.

1929　The stock market crashes, plunging the nation into the Great Depression.

Convinced of the fundamental strength of the economy and that the deepening depression will run its course, Hoover keeps government intervention to a minimum. In foreign relations, he arranges for a one-year moratorium on the nation's World War I loans.

1932　Franklin Roosevelt, a Democrat, is elected president.

Hattie Caraway of Arkansas is the first woman elected to the Senate.

1933　In the first few months of his term Roosevelt introduces a package of economic and social legislation designed to end the Great Depression; it becomes known as the New Deal.

The Twentieth Amendment, changing terms of office for Congress, president, and vice president to prevent lame ducks, is ratified. As a result, Congress will now convene on January 3 and new presidents will be inaugurated on January 20.

The Twenty-first Amendment, repealing Prohibition, is ratified.

Roosevelt appoints Frances Perkins, the first woman to sit in a president's cabinet, to the post of secretary of labor.

Depression-era businessman forced to sell apples for a living

1936   Franklin Roosevelt is reelected.

1938   The House of Representatives establishes a committee to investigate "un-American activities." In 1945 it is renamed the House Committee on Un-American Activities. Its task is to investigate Socialists, Communists, and other individuals and organizations deemed un-American.

1940   The Alien Registration Act, also known as the Smith Act, requires all aliens to register with the government and be fingerprinted and makes it illegal to advocate the overthrow of the federal government.

With the nation on the verge of entering World War II, Franklin Roosevelt wins an unprecedented third term.

1941   After African Americans press the issue, President Roosevelt issues an executive order creating the Fair Employment Practices Committee and barring war manufacturers from racial discrimination in hiring workers.

The United States enters World War II.

1944   President Franklin Roosevelt is reelected for a fourth term.

Congress passes the first GI Bill of Rights, which provides benefits for veterans.

1945   Franklin Roosevelt dies and Harry Truman becomes president. His administration will oversee the conclusion of the war, the development of the Marshall Plan, and the establishment of NATO.

1946   The Atomic Energy Commission is formed to monitor and control all research on atomic energy.

1947   The Presidential Succession Act establishes the Speaker of the House as next in line for the presidency following the vice president, followed by the president *pro tempore* of the Senate and then the cabinet members according to the date on which each cabinet department was established.

1948   President Harry Truman, a Democrat, is reelected president.

1950   Senator Joseph McCarthy accuses State Department employees and many members of the American literary, film, and theatrical communities of being members of the Communist party. His accusations cast a shadow no one wishes to stand in.

1951   The Twenty-second Amendment is ratified, limiting the president's service to two terms.

In New York, a federal judge finds husband and wife Julius and Ethel Rosenberg and their friend Morton Sobell guilty of selling atomic secrets to the Soviet Union; the couple is executed in 1953. Sobell is sentenced to 30 years in prison.

1952   Dwight David Eisenhower, a World War II leader, president of Columbia University, and Republican, is elected president. A dedicated moderate, Eisenhower takes a laissez-faire approach to the economy, and only when pressed, sends the military to enforce civil rights for blacks in the South.

1954   Congress censures Senator Joseph McCarthy for behavior during hearings conducted by his subcommittee on Investigations of the Senate Committee on Governmental Operations.

1956   Eisenhower is reelected president.

1957   Under the Civil Rights Act, the first legislation on the rights of minorities to be passed since the Reconstruction, the Civil Rights Commission is set up and in the Justice Department the Civil Rights Division is established to investigate cases in which people are prevented from voting.

1960   John F. Kennedy, a Democrat, is elected president. Although he is most interested in domestic affairs, Kennedy is forced to attend to foreign policy for much of his presidency.

He initiates the space exploration program, establishes the Peace Corps, stands up to the Soviets in Berlin, and organizes the Alliance for Progress to provide aid to Latin America. He is a strong voice for civil rights just as civic unrest is growing over this issue. His most notable foreign-affairs disaster is the Bay of Pigs invasion of Cuba. At the same time one of his greatest successes also involves Cuba: the Cuban missile crisis, in which he forces the Soviets to remove their missiles from the island nation.

1961   The Twenty-third Amendment, granting voting rights in presidential elections to citizens residing in the District of Columbia, is ratified.

The Peace Corps is established.

1963   President Kennedy is assassinated, and Lyndon Johnson becomes president. The Warren Commission finds that there was no conspiracy to assassinate Kennedy and that Lee Harvey Oswald was the sole assassin. The report is greeted skeptically by many.

Congress passes the first Clean Air Act.

1964   Lyndon Johnson, a southern Democrat, is elected president. Vowing to win the "war on poverty," Johnson works with Congress to develop a network of social programs more expansive than any since Franklin Roosevelt's New Deal. Johnson also works to guarantee civil rights for minorities. Despite his unprecedented efforts at home, his administration is weakened by his inability to extricate the United States from the increasingly unpopular Vietnam War, and Johnson does not run for a second term.

Congress passes a powerful Civil Rights Act.

The Twenty-fourth Amendment prohibits poll taxes.

The Wilderness Act becomes law.

1965   The Voting Rights Act, a major piece of civil rights legislation, makes the federal government responsible for ensuring that all citizens are able to vote.

The Department of Housing and Urban Development is created.

Medicare, which pays the health-care expenses of senior citizens, is enacted.

1966   The National Organization for Women (NOW) is formed to push for greater political power and civil rights for women.

The Department of Transportation is established.

1967   Thurgood Marshall becomes the first black Supreme Court justice.

Edward Brooke of Massachusetts becomes the first black senator since Reconstruction.

In re Gault is handed down by the Supreme Court. In this landmark ruling for youth, the Court finds that juveniles have the same constitutional rights as adults in legal proceedings.

The Twenty-fifth Amendment is ratified, providing for presidential disability.

1968   In a campaign marked by violence and unrest, Senator Robert Kennedy, a presidential candidate and the brother of President John Kennedy, is assassinated hours after a California-primary victory.

Even after protesters disrupt the televised Democratic National Convention, revealing the deep divisions with the Democratic party, Richard Nixon, a Republican, has a difficult time getting elected. Alabama governor George Wallace mounts a creditable third-party effort. Hubert Humphrey does much better than anyone expects; less than 1 percentage point divides the two when all votes are counted. Nixon, like Johnson, will spend much of his term in office mired in the Vietnam War. His accomplishments are in foreign affairs; he establishes relations with China and detente with the Soviet Union. Domestically, he creates the Office of Management and Budget, an oversight agency for the federal budget.

Shirley Chisholm is the first black woman elected to Congress.

1968   The Kerner Commission cites widespread racial discrimination as the cause for racial unrest and riots of the 1960s.

1969   The Chicago Seven trial takes place as the leaders of the protest at the Democratic National Convention are tried on charges of conspiracy to riot. They will be found not guilty, although five are convicted of lesser charges.

1970   The Environmental Protection Agency is established.

Congress passes the Occupational Safety and Health Act (OSHA).

1971   The Twenty-sixth Amendment lowers the voting age to 18.

1972   President Richard Nixon is reelected, but a burglary at Democratic National Headquarters, staged by persons representing the Republican party, ultimately mars his victory; this affair and its subsequent cover-up, known as the Watergate scandal, eventually bring down his presidency.

The Supreme Court declares capital punishment unconstitutional.

The Equal Rights Amendment, banning discrimination on the basis of gender, is submitted to the states.

TEN SCANDALS IN AMERICAN POLITICS

Political corruption is nothing new, predating the country itself. Colonial governors were involved in land, customs, and military scams. In contemporary times, only the administrations of Franklin Roosevelt, John Kennedy, and Lyndon Johnson have been, relatively speaking, among the most scandal-free.

1797–1798   XYZ affair. The new nation encountered a foreign affairs scandal when President John Adams sent three prominent envoys to France, with a mandate to establish trade and amity between the two nations. The envoys were told by French agents (later designated in documents X, Y, and Z) that they would need to pay bribes to achieve their ends. The American envoys refused. When word of the requested bribe became public knowledge in the United States, Americans were scandalized and the trade talks collapsed. "Millions for defense, not one cent for tribute!" was the slogan that helped galvanize anti-French feeling.

1807   Aaron Burr's trial. Burr, brilliant but bristly, seemed to annoy everyone. His career in politics appeared over after he killed political foe Alexander Hamilton in a duel, but when Burr became involved in a scheme to carve an independent nation out of the American Southwest, President Thomas Jefferson, another political foe, ordered him arrested for treason. Burr's trial was a highly partisan event, although Burr was eventually acquitted.

1871   Tammany Hall. The quintessential political machine, Tammany Hall won elections for New York City Democrats by paying voters and then rewarding them with jobs. Boss William Marcy Tweed was arrested in 1871 and eventually imprisoned for graft. Although the Tweed Ring was gone, Tammany survived until the 1940s when Mayor Fiorello La Guardia's attack finally ended its power.

1872–1873   Crédit Mobilier scandal. Ulysses Grant's administration was wracked with major and minor corruption scandals. The worst revolved around an attempt to divert funds for building the Union Pacific Railroad into public officials' hands. A dummy company called Crédit Mobilier was created to hold the funds, in the form of stocks, for high-level Republicans and other government officials. The scandal ended the political career of Vice President Schuyler Colfax and led to the reprimand of two congressmen.

1923-1924 Teapot Dome affair. Warren G. Harding's presidency was also plagued by scandal and corruption, the worst being the last. Secretary of the Interior Albert Fall accepted a $100,000 interest-free loan and additional "loans" for oil-leasing rights to a site called Teapot Dome. Convicted of bribery, Fall paid a fine and spent a year in jail. Harding died unexpectedly just as the scandal was breaking.

1972-1974 Watergate scandal. The granddaddy of all political scandals, this affair toppled the presidency of Richard Nixon, who was the only U.S. president ever to resign. It began when some low-level political operatives in the employ of the Committee to Re-elect the President (CREEP) burglarized the Democratic National Committee's headquarters. What started as an attempt to sabotage the Democratic challengers soon led to an illegal cover-up. Nixon resigned the presidency the day after the House Judiciary Committee voted three articles of impeachment.

1980 Abscam scandal. Under Jimmy Carter's presidency, members of Congress were caught in a "sting" operation. FBI agents posing as sheiks offered bribes in exchange for introducing legislation. Six representatives and one senator were found guilty of bribery.

1986-1988 Iran-Contra affair. President Ronald Reagan's National Security Council undertook a series of covert operations in which they traded arms for American hostages with Iran, and then diverted the profits, in defiance of Congress, to contra forces in Nicaraugua, seeking to topple a Marxist government.

1991 Keating Five. Charles H. Keating, a wealthy banker, had asked five senators, all of whom had received large campaign contributions from him, to convince federal regulators not to examine his savings and loan, which eventually failed. The affair highlighted the connection between money and influence in Congress.

1995 Robert Packwood became the first senator since the Civil War to resign his office. His resignation was prompted by numerous charges of sexual harassment, coupled with tampering with files subpoenaed by the Senate Ethics Committee. Had he not resigned, he would have been expelled.

1973 President Nixon signs the Endangered Species Act, more wide-ranging than its 1966 predecessor.

Passed over President Richard Nixon's veto, the War Powers Resolution limits presidential war-making power by establishing guidelines for military emergencies.

Charged with tax evasion, Vice President Spiro Agnew resigns and is replaced by Gerald Ford, the first person ever to hold his office without being elected.

The Supreme Court rules that women have a legal right to obtain abortions.

The Watergate hearings begin.

1974 The Budget and Impoundment Control Act strengthens the role of Congress in budget making.

When asked to turn over tape recordings that could implicate him in the Watergate crime, President Nixon claims executive immunity, but the Supreme Court finds that his privilege is not unlimited, as he claims. The House Judiciary Committee institutes impeachment proceedings against President Nixon, who then becomes the first person to resign the presidency. Gerald Ford, a Republican, assumes the office. One of his first acts is to pardon Nixon. Ford is mostly a caretaker president, although he vetoes 66 bills in fewer than two years in office. Twelve of the vetoes are overridden.

1975   Several top advisors to former President Richard Nixon are found guilty in the Watergate trial.

Two unsuccessful attempts are made to assassinate President Gerald Ford.

1976   Jimmy Carter, a Democrat, is elected president. He makes human rights part of American foreign policy and pardons approximately 10,000 draft evaders from the Vietnam War. Although Carter negotiates the first important breakthrough in Middle East peace, this one-term president's administration is plagued by foreign policy problems and a troubled economy.

The Supreme Court reverses itself and rules that the death penalty is legal.

1977   The Department of Energy, a cabinet-level post, is created, partly in response to concerns over fuel resources.

1978   The Supreme Court decides that reverse discrimination is illegal.

1979   The Department of Education is established.

Iranian Islamic militants seize the U.S. embassy in Tehran and hold 52 embassy employees hostage for 444 days. The humiliation contributes to Carter's defeat in the 1980 election.

1980   Republican Ronald Reagan is elected president. At 69, he is the oldest president when elected. Reagan presides over some of the largest tax cuts in U.S. history as well as the biggest buildup of the deficit, but neither this nor a scandal in which some of his top aides are found guilty of trading arms for hostages tarnishes the personal popularity of this president. Reagan wins passage of a major tax-reform bill. He survives an assassination attempt, though seriously wounded.

1981   Sandra Day O'Connor becomes the first woman Supreme Court justice.

President Ronald Reagan appoints conservatives who oppose quotas to the Civil Rights Commission and stirs up a controversy that nearly leads to the commission's demise. Congress renews its mandate in 1983, with the added provision that members have fixed terms.

1982   Three-fourths of the states having failed to ratify it even with an extended deadline, the proposed Equal Rights Amendment dies.

1984   Ronald Reagan is reelected.

1988   George Bush, a Republican, is elected president. His administration is beset by an ailing economy after the boom of the early 1980s comes to an abrupt end. Unable to jump-start the economy, Bush is also seen by many Americans as uncaring on domestic issues. Despite this, his popularity does not plummet—largely due to the apparent success of the war against Iraq—until the very end of his presidency.

1992   Bill Clinton, a Democrat, is elected president, defeating incumbent George Bush. A notable feature of the campaign is the candidacy of Ross Perot, who wins 19 percent of the popular vote but no electoral votes. This is an achievement second only to Theodore Roosevelt's in 1912. Plagued by an uncooperative Congress, Clinton manages to bring down the deficit a small amount each year, largely by increasing taxes and cutting spending. He begins a national service program.

The Twenty-seventh Amendment, prohibiting Congress from raising its own pay within a session, is ratified—after 203 years! It was first proposed in 1789 as part of a package that became the Bill of Rights, ratified by only 6 of the 13 original states, then practically forgotten until revived in 1982 by a student at the University of Texas.

1994   Newt Gingrich becomes an unusually powerful Speaker of the House following a Republican landslide in the congressional elections.

1995-
1996   The White House and the Republican-dominated Congress reach an impasse over the fiscal year 1996 budget. President Clinton refuses to agree to the cuts the Republicans want and takes his case to the country. The Republican leadership also refuses to negotiate, and the government shuts down for three weeks. Clinton's stand boosts his approval rating at the Republicans' expense.

1996   President Clinton is reelected.

1997   Speaker Newt Gingrich's financial arrangements are questioned, and he is fined.

In *Clinton v. Jones* the Supreme Court rules that a sitting president is not immune from prosecution.

A CHRONOLOGY OF PROTEST

Not surprisingly for a nation born out of revolution, Americans have resorted to organized civil disobedience—and rebellion—when they have felt abused by the government. In the early days of the nation, the reason was usually taxes, but since the turn of the century most protest has centered around the struggle for individual rights.

1712   Slave Uprising. About two dozen armed slaves march through lower Manhattan, killing at least nine whites, mostly women and children, before they are apprehended. About 20 of the rebels are sentenced to die and indeed are tortured to death, thus setting a precedent for punishment of slave revolts.

1786-   Shays's Rebellion. Led by Revolutionary War veteran Daniel Shays, farmers in Massachu-
1787   setts protest high taxes and strict foreclosure laws. The rebellion triggers protests by farmers in other states and fuels public sentiment that a stronger central government is needed, which in turn leads to the convening of the Constitutional Convention in 1787.

1794   The Whiskey Rebellion. In the first test of the new government's power, Pennsylvania farmers are subdued with armed power when they protest a liquor tax.

1799   Fries's Rebellion. Among the militia who put down the Whiskey Rebellion is John Fries, who now finds himself on the other side when he leads Pennsylvania farmers in revolt against tax assessors. Later found guilty of treason and sentenced to die, his sentence is pardoned by the president.

1800   Gabriel's Rebellion. In one of several planned slave uprisings that don't happen but nevertheless have great psychological impact on slaveowners and slaves, Gabriel Prosser, an abolitionist preacher, makes plans to march on Richmond, Virginia. A storm on the night of the gathering washes out the roads and scatters his armed cohorts, but slaveowners who hear of the plan punish and restrict their slaves anyway.

1831   Nat Turner's Rebellion. Of the hundreds of slave rebellions, this is the one that most frightens whites and constricts the lives of slaves. In a region of small farms in southeastern Virginia, a band of five slaves, which soon expands to 80, is led by Nat Turner in a march through the countryside, killing 60 whites before they are finally stopped by the militia. To the utter terror of slaveowners, Turner himself remains at large for several weeks, but eventually he and about 20 of his followers are caught and executed. Most slave uprisings, like this one, take place not on plantations, where slaves are strictly guarded, but in towns and on small farms, where slaves are less constrained physically.

1859   Harpers Ferry. John Brown, a white abolitionist active in the Kansas border wars who is determined to keep slavery out of the state, gathers followers and moves to Harpers Ferry, Virginia, where his band seizes a government arsenal. His intention is to incite a slave rebellion and establish a slave sanctuary and stronghold that will end slavery in the South, but local militia and federal troops stop him. In a nation increasingly divided over slavery, Brown's rebellion is a pivotal event. He is a martyred hero to abolitionists.

1863   Civil War draft riots. The worst of these take place in New York City, where Irish and other new immigrants protest the fact that draftees can buy their way out of military service. Their rage is misdirected at blacks, and at least 40 people, mostly African Americans, die in the riot.

1955- Montgomery Boycott. Following Rosa Parks's arrest for refusing to give up her seat to a
1956 white person on a city bus, the blacks of Montgomery, Alabama, boycott city buses for more than a year. The boycott produces a Supreme Court ruling outlawing segregation on buses and catapults Reverend Martin Luther King, Jr., into the leadership of the emerging civil rights movement.

1961 Freedom Riders Protest. An interracial group of protesters organized by the Congress of Racial Equality (CORE) rides buses throughout the South attempting to test the desegregation of bus station restrooms, waiting rooms, and restaurants. A mob attacks the buses in Alabama. The first bus is set on fire, and those who flee it are beaten—all in full view of television cameras covering the story.

1963 Birmingham Protest. Martin Luther King, Jr., and the Southern Christian Leadership Conference plan to desegregate Birmingham, Alabama, department stores. Violence erupts as the number of protesters swells. Bombs are set off at SCLC headquarters and in a black church, where four little girls die. Thousands are arrested, including King, who writes his eloquent Letter from Birmingham Jail outlining the justification for direct action.

1964 Freedom Summer. White college students converge on Mississippi to work with local blacks to mount a voter registration drive. Two white students, Michael Schwerner and Andrew Goodman, and one local black youth, James Chaney, are beaten to death. Their bodies are not found for six weeks.

1965 Selma Protests. Selma, Alabama, is targeted by Martin Luther King, Jr.'s organization for voter registration. Protesters and police clash, and the ensuing publicity draws attention to the need for a national voting rights act, which is soon passed.

1968 Chicago police riot. Thousands of youthful antiwar activists converge on the Democratic National Convention in Chicago, chanting, "The whole world is watching"—and indeed it is, for the first time, thanks to satellite television. Mayor Richard Daley orders 22,000 armed police officers, National Guard, and federal troops to deal with the protesters, and at least 1,000 are clubbed in what is termed a police riot. Seven antiwar leaders, known as the Chicago Seven, are tried on conspiracy and other charges, and five are found guilty of lesser charges. Black Panther Bobby Seale is tried separately.

1969 The Stonewall Riot. Protesting police raids and harassment, gay people take to the streets in anger in Greenwich Village, New York, and the gay rights movement is born.

THE ROAD TO CIVIL RIGHTS

Since the Civil War era the Supreme Court, Congress, and the presidency have variously led and impeded the process of ensuring and protecting equal rights and opportunities for all Americans. In addition to the entries listed here, see the following section on women's rights and the summary of amendments to the Constitution.

1866 Civil Rights Act grants citizenship to former slaves (but not Native Americans), but President Andrew Johnson vetoes it. Congress passes the bill over his veto.

1868 The Fourteenth Amendment confers citizenship on former slaves and guarantees all citizens "the equal protection of the laws."

1870 The Fifteenth Amendment makes it illegal to deprive any citizen of the right to vote on account of "race, color, or previous condition of servitude." In the following decades, states impose many restrictions, such as poll taxes and literacy requirements, that keep African-American men from voting.

1875   A Civil Rights Act guarantees equality in public places, especially places of public accommodation such as in hotels, on trains, and in public parks.

1883   The Supreme Court rules the Civil Rights Act of 1875 unconstitutional.

1896   In *Plessy v. Ferguson*, the Supreme Court endorses segregation when it finds "separate but equal" public facilities acceptable.

1940   The Supreme Court in *Hansberry v. Lee* outlaws discrimination in housing.

1954   The Supreme Court ruling *Brown v. Board of Education* overturns the "separate but equal doctrine," stating "separate educational facilities" are inherently unequal.

1957   A Civil Rights Act protects the right to vote and establishes the Civil Rights Commission.

1957-   The civil rights movement brings great pressure to bear on the federal government to
1965   pursue equality for all citizens (see Chapter 4).

1964   Congress passes its most important civil rights legislation. The Civil Rights Act bans discrimination in employment, public accommodations, and federally funded programs and establishes the Equal Employment Opportunity Commission (EEOC), which will become a powerful tool in stamping out job discrimination. Literacy tests of voters are banned.

      The Twenty-fourth Amendment bans the poll tax, which has been used to prohibit many blacks from voting.

1965   Voting Rights Act greatly strengthens federal enforcement of the rights of blacks and other minorities to vote.

1968   Legislation bans discrimination in housing and real estate.

1970   African-American legislators form the Congressional Black Caucus, which will work to advance the political interests of blacks and other minorities.

1991   The Americans with Disabilities Act prohibits discrimination based on disability.

      A new Civil Rights Acts counters Supreme Court limitations on civil rights interpretations and enforcement.

THE ROAD TO THE HOUSE (AND SENATE): WOMEN AND POLITICS

1776   Abigail Adams appeals to her husband, John Adams, and his colleagues in the Continental Congress to "Remember the Ladies" and consider granting women some rights in the new code of laws.

      The New Jersey Constitution grants the right to vote to "all free inhabitants," thus enfranchising women until 1807, when a new state constitution restricts suffrage to males.

1848   The Women's Rights Convention, the first public meeting to advocate for women's rights, is held in Seneca Falls, New York. Led by Elizabeth Cady Stanton and Lucretia Mott, participants issue a "Declaration of Sentiments" denouncing tyranny of men and demanding equal rights for women under the law and in public and private life. A series of similar meetings follow.

1864   Anna Elizabeth Dickinson, who addresses the House of Representatives on abolition and women's rights, is considered the first woman to speak before Congress.

1869   Susan B. Anthony and Elizabeth Cady Stanton found the National Woman Suffrage Association, whose goal is to obtain the vote for women.

The Wyoming Territory grants women the right to vote.

1872   Victoria Woodhull is the first woman to run for president.

1878   A Constitutional amendment to grant women the right to vote is introduced in Congress.

1890   Two rival suffrage organizations, the National Woman Suffrage Association and the American Woman Suffrage Association, unite to form the National American Woman Suffrage Association.

1912   When she is appointed director of the Children's Bureau, Julia Clifford Lathrop becomes the first woman to head a federal agency.

1916   The National Woman's Party is founded with the purpose of obtaining the vote for women.

1917   Jeannette Rankin becomes the first woman elected to the House of Representatives.

1920   The Nineteenth Amendment passes, granting women the right to vote.

The League of Women Voters is organized to educate women about politics and promote the status and rights of women.

1923   An Equal Rights Amendment is first introduced in Congress.

1924   Nellie Ross is elected governor of Wyoming, and Miriam ("Ma") Ferguson is elected in Texas, the first women to serve as state chief executives.

1929   Genevieve Cline is the first woman appointed to serve as a federal judge.

1932   Hattie Wyatt Caraway is the first woman elected to the Senate.

1933   Secretary of Labor Frances Perkins becomes the first woman appointed to a cabinet position.

1940   Elected to serve out her husband's term, Margaret Chase Smith serves in and is reelected to the House and is elected to the Senate in 1948, the first woman to serve in both chambers.

1945   Eleanor Roosevelt becomes the first former first lady to be appointed to a public position when she assumes the post of UN delegate.

1966   The National Organization for Women, the first powerful women's group to advocate for women's legal rights since the 19th century, is organized. Betty Friedan, author of *The Feminine Mystique* (1963), a book that changed women's consciousness about their personal and political status, is a founder and the first president.

1972   The Equal Rights Amendment is approved by Congress, although it must still be ratified by the states. The women's movement, headed by such figures as Betty Friedan and Gloria Steinem, have worked hard for equality on other fronts as well.

1979   Patricia Roberts Harris becomes the first woman ever to hold two cabinet posts. She is appointed to Housing and Urban Development in 1977 and in 1979 heads Health, Education, and Welfare.

1981   Sandra Day O'Connor is the first woman Supreme Court justice.

1982   The Equal Rights Amendment fails to achieve ratification.

1984   Democrat Geraldine Ferraro is the first woman ever nominated by a major political party to run for vice president.

1993   Newly inaugurated president Bill Clinton appoints his wife, lawyer Hillary Rodham Clinton, to head his task force on national health care.

THE WELFARE OF CHILDREN

During the colonial era and for many years afterward, as in most parts of the world children were permitted to work, if not on the family farm or in the shop, then as apprentices. Gradually, however, the United States joined other progressive nations in outlawing child labor and even eventually turned its attention to child welfare. The United States still lags behind the other Western nations in providing child care and universal medical coverage. For an account of education, see Chapter 10.

1886   The Knights of Labor, at the height of its membership and power, advocates the abolition of child labor.

1904   The National Child Labor Committee is organized to eliminate child labor.

1912   The Children's Bureau is established in the Labor Department to monitor and enforce child labor laws, issue reports, and promote the protection of children.

1916   Congress passes the Child Labor Act, also known as the Keating-Owen Act, which bars any company involved in interstate commerce from employing a child under age 14.

1918   In *Hammer v. Dagenhart*, the Supreme Court rules that the Keating-Owen Act is unconstitutional.

1924   Congress passes a constitutional amendment making child labor illegal, but it fails to be ratified by the states.

1935   Title V of the Social Security Act provides the nation's first maternal and child health services, including Aid to Families with Dependent Children.

1938   The Fair Labor Standards Act prohibits manufacturing and mining businesses involved in interstate commerce from employing anyone under age 16.

1941   The Supreme Court upholds the constitutionality of the Fair Labor Standards Act.

1949   The Fair Labor Standards Act is amended to cover more industries.

1950   With only 26 states having ratified the 1924 constitutional amendment to outlaw child labor (36 are needed), the bill is dropped.

1964   Head Start, primarily an educational program for disadvantaged preschool children, provides some emergency health and social services.

1965   The Elementary and Secondary School Act provides aid to schools based on the number of poor children.

The Medicaid program, enacted under a new extensive federal welfare law, provides medical services to indigent children and is later expanded to include preventive health services.

1972   The Special Supplemental Food Program for Women, Infants, and Children (WIC) is the first major support for mothers and children. It grows out of nutrition programs and does not exist initially as a separate program.

1990s   Because of mounting budget deficits, Congress debates cuts in programs that may affect women and children.

ACTS OF CONGRESS AFFECTING INDIVIDUAL AND COLLECTIVE RIGHTS

1866   Civil Rights Act. This initial civil rights act grants the rights of citizenship to all persons born in the United States, and is specifically intended to cover former slaves. Native Americans are excluded.

1875   Civil Rights Act. This is the first act to address the issue of equality on a broader scale, by ordering that public places and accommodations be open to all. In 1883 the Supreme Court rules this legislation unconstitutional.

1957   Civil Rights Act. This first important piece of civil rights legislation since Reconstruction signals renewed government interest in protecting the rights of minorities. The most important element of the act is the establishment of the Civil Rights Commission. Although intended to be temporary, the commission has survived to the present day.

1964   Civil Rights Act. The most comprehensive piece of legislation on civil rights, this act prohibits discrimination in public places, in public spending or government contracts, and in employment. The latter clause is enforced by the Equal Employment Opportunity Commission (EEOC), which is also created by the act.

1965   Voting Rights Act. The right to vote is enforced by the federal government, which is also given the right to review state voting laws. Literacy tests as a requisite to voting are banned.

1967   Age Discrimination in Employment Act. This act prohibits job discrimination against employees aged 40 to 65. An amendment in 1986 eliminates mandatory retirement.

1968   Fair Housing Act. The act prohibits discrimination in sales and rentals on the basis of race, color, religion, or national origin.

1988   Civil Rights Restoration Act. This act counters a Supreme Court decision by affirming that antibias provisions apply to an entire institution even if only one department in it is receiving federal funds.

1991   Americans with Disabilities Act. This act prohibits discrimination based on disability in employment, public accommodation, and public services and requires that facilities be made accessible to people with disabilities.

Civil Rights Act. This act strengthens civil rights enforcement by countering the specifics of nine Supreme Court decisions.

SUPREME COURT DECISIONS AFFECTING LAW AND POLITICS

1803   *Marbury v. Madison.* The Supreme Court establishes the right to review the constitutionality of acts of Congress.

1810   *Fletcher v. Peck.* The Court, for the first time, overturns a state law violating the Constitution. In this case an act of the Georgia legislature is held to impair "the obligation of contracts."

1816   *Martin v. Hunter's Lessee.* The Supreme Court establishes the right of the federal judiciary to review state court decisions involving constitutional issues.

1819   *McCulloch v. Maryland.* The Supreme Court, in deciding that the federal government has a right to charter a national bank, establishes that the federal government has implied powers beyond those expressly stated in the Constitution. The case greatly enhances the power of the federal government to do what is "necessary and proper" to run the country.

Dartmouth College v. Woodward. The Court rules that a charter issued to a private corporation is a contract protected by the Constitution.

1842   *Prigg v. Pennsylvania.* The Court rules that state laws obstructing the capture and return of slaves are unconstitutional.

1857   *Dred Scott v. Sandford.* The Court declares that Congress cannot prohibit slavery in the territories and that African Americans are not citizens and have no legal standing. The Court also rules that the federal government cannot deprive a person of his property, including slaves.

1883   *Civil Rights Cases.* The Court strikes down the Civil Rights Act of 1875, saying that "social rights" are beyond federal control but blacks cannot be excluded from juries.

1896   *Plessy v. Ferguson.* The Supreme Court accepts the principle of "separate but equal" facilities for blacks and whites public transportation and by implication other public facilities and education, thus instituting an era of legal segregation that will last until 1954.

1919   *Schenck v. United States.* In its first major First Amendment decision, the Court sustains the Espionage Act and finds that free speech can be constrained if the words used "present a clear and present danger."

1925   *Gitlow v. New York.* The Court decides that states cannot interfere with free speech any more than the federal government can. This decision also establishes that the Fourteenth Amendment, guaranteeing all citizens the right of due process, extends to state as well as federal actions.

1951   *Dennis et al. v. United States.* The Supreme Court upholds the Smith Act of 1940, which made it a crime to advocate the overthrow of the government by force.

1957   *Yates v. United States.* The Court modifies its earlier ruling in *Dennis et al. v. United States* to protect free speech advocating the overthrow of the government in the abstract so long as it is not connected to any actions.

1961   *Mapp v. Ohio.* In the first of several decisions extending the rights of those accused of crimes, the Court finds that evidence obtained through illegal search and seizure is inadmissible in court.

1962   *Baker v. Carr.* The Court rules that arbitrarily drawn federal districts violate constitutional rights and voters have the right to challenge reapportionment. This overturns an earlier decision that found such issues to be political rather than constitutional.

1963   *Gideon v. Wainwright.* The Supreme Court decides that free legal counseling must be provided to indigent persons accused of felonies.

1964   *Griswold v. Connecticut.* The Court rules that a ban on the use of contraceptives and on medical advice concerning them is unconstitutional and reinforces the notion of privacy as a constitutional right.

1966   *Miranda v. Arizona.* The Court decides that before those accused of a crime can be interviewed by the police, they must be informed of their rights, which include the right to remain silent, the fact that anything they say can be used against them, and the right to counsel.

1973   *Roe v. Wade.* The Court rules that the right to privacy protects a woman's decision whether to bear a child. State laws that make abortion a crime are overturned.

1975   *Goss v. Lopez.* The Court finds that suspended students are entitled to notice and a hearing before any disciplinary action can be taken against them.

1978   *University of California Regents v. Bakke.* The Court declares that affirmative-action programs with required racial quotas are unconstitutional, thus undermining one of the major
strategies that has been used for several decades to equalize opportunity.

1986   *Bowers v. Hardwick.* In upholding a Georgia law prohibiting sodomy that was enforced only
against same-sex couples, the Court declines to extend to same-sex couples the same rights
of privacy extended to heterosexual couples.

1992   *R.A.V. v. St. Paul.* The Court upholds the right to "symbolic speech," including burning crosses.

SIGNIFICANT PEOPLE IN AMERICAN LAW AND POLITICS

Adams, Abigail (1744–1818).   The wife of the second U.S. president, John Adams, Adams is
best remembered for admonishing her husband and his fellow delegates at the Constitutional
Congress in 1776 to "Remember the Ladies" and "Do not put such unlimited power into the
hands of the Husbands" when they wrote laws for the new nation.

Adams, John (1735–1826).   The second U.S. president and a signer of the Declaration of
Independence, Adams also helped negotiate the peace with Britain and served as a minister to
that country. His son, John Quincy Adams, was the sixth president.

Anthony, Susan B. (1820–1906).   A feminist reformer, Anthony co-founded, along with
Elizabeth Cady Stanton, the National Woman Suffrage Association, the first major organization
to work in behalf of women's right to vote. She is also the first woman to be depicted on a U.S.
coin, the Susan B. Anthony silver dollar.

Black, Hugo (1886–1971).   As a Supreme Court justice Black was a strong advocate of unfet-
tered civil liberties, free speech, and the Fourteenth Amendment, which guarantees all due
process to all persons.

Brandeis, Louis (1856–1941).   A Supreme Court justice, Brandeis was the first person to use
statistics, demographics, and other sociological factors, in addition to the traditional legal analysis, to shape legal arguments, and his strategy became the model for what is known as the Brandeis
brief. He showed a remarkable understanding of industrialization and its effects on the law and
helped to shape business law. He was an advocate of judicial liberalism and social reform.

Bryan, William Jennings (1860–1925).   This Democratic party leader and three-time presidential candidate is best remembered for his "Cross of Gold" speech in favor of free silver. He
served as secretary of state under Woodrow Wilson and resigned rather than abandon his isolationist policy in the face of World War I. Bryan supported women's suffrage and women's rights
but, as a religious fundamentalist, increasingly opposed the evolution theory, eventually serving
on the prosecution team in the Scopes Monkey trial.

Burr, Aaron (1756–1836).   One of the more irascible persons ever to cross the American political landscape, Burr was a New York attorney general, a senator, and vice president under Thomas
Jefferson. An ongoing political feud with Alexander Hamilton led to a duel and Hamilton's death.
The incident ended his political career. When he became involved in a scheme to carve a new
nation out of the American Southwest, he was arrested for treason, but acquitted in 1807.

Calhoun, John C. (1782–1850).   With Henry Clay, Daniel Webster, and Andrew Jackson,
Calhoun was one of the powerful political figures of his time. A secretary of war, vice president,
senator from South Carolina, secretary of state, and political theorist, he defended the institution

of slavery, promoted nullification, and predicted the demise of the Union if the slave states were not permanently protected.

Cardozo, Benjamin (1870–1938).   Known as a lawyer's lawyer, Cardozo worked in contract and commercial law before becoming a judge. He sat on the supreme court of New York, the court of appeals in New York, which he single-handedly turned into one of the great courts of its era, and finally on the U.S. Supreme Court. His most famous opinions emanated from the court of appeals, since he only served on the Supreme Court six years before he died. He was an advocate of sociological jurisprudence.

Catt, Carrie Chapman (1859–1947).   As president of the National American Woman Suffrage Association (NAWSA) from 1900 to 1904 and then from 1915 to 1920, Catt, a superb strategist and organizer, helped gain the vote for women in 1920. She also helped organize the League of Women Voters.

Chisholm, Shirley (1924–).   The first black woman elected to Congress (in 1968), Chisholm was an advocate for minority and women's rights and the urban poor. She retired from Congress in 1982, and in 1984 organized the National Political Congress of Black Women.

Clay, Henry (1777–1852).   For more than 40 years, Clay, a Kentuckian and the leader of the Whig party, was a dominant force in American politics. He served as secretary of state, was Speaker of the House of Representatives, and then became the most powerful member of the Senate during his time. A nationalist, Clay was called "the Great Compromiser" for his role in bringing about the Missouri Compromise of 1820, the Tariff Compromise of 1833, and the Compromise of 1850. Clay is also identified with the American System, a program of economic development.

Darrow, Clarence (1857–1938).   One of the greatest lawyers of his time, Darrow achieved notoriety in a series of sensational first-degree murder trials. He is most famous for his defense of schoolteacher John Scopes, who was charged with violating a Tennessee state law against teaching evolution in public schools. The so-called Monkey trial in 1925 pitted Darrow against William Jennings Bryan, who had joined the prosecution. His withering examination of Bryan was intended to show how literal interpretation of the Bible revealed scientific ignorance.

Douglas, William O. (1898–1980).   As a Supreme Court justice from 1939 to 1975, Douglas had the longest tenure of the any Supreme Court justice and also wrote more opinions—and dissents—than any other justice in history. Douglas's judicial philosophy was to keep government "off the backs of the people," and to achieve this he wrote many opinions defending free speech, especially during the protest era of the late 1960s and early 1970s. He defended civil liberties, civil rights, and conservation.

Ferraro, Geraldine (1935–).   A New York Democratic congresswoman, in 1984 she was the first woman ever nominated by a major political party to run as vice president.

Frankfurter, Felix (1882–1965).   This law professor and Supreme Court justice was appointed by Franklin Roosevelt and was one of the great legal defenders of the New Deal legislation and civil liberties. Born in Austria, he was also the only naturalized citizen ever to sit on the Supreme Court. He helped found the American Civil Liberties Union (ACLU).

Hamilton, Alexander (1755–1804).   An aide to George Washington during the Revolution, Hamilton was a delegate to the Constitutional Convention and a strong advocate of the new Constitution, defending it in *The Federalist Papers*. As the first secretary of the treasury, he advocated a strong central government and decisively shaped economic policy. Hamilton was killed by Aaron Burr in a duel.

Harris, Patricia Roberts (1924–).   After an early career devoted to civil rights activism, in 1965 Harris became the first African-American woman appointed to the rank of ambassador, when President Lyndon Johnson sent her to Luxembourg. In 1976 President Jimmy Carter named her the first female African-American Secretary of Housing and Urban Development.

Holmes, Oliver Wendell (1841–1935).   A legal scholar, Civil War veteran, and Massachusetts judge before sitting on the Supreme Court, Holmes was most influential in shaping what is known as a "loose" interpretation of the Constitution. He believed the law should keep pace with social change and toward that end was reluctant to dismantle what he considered to be good social legislation, especially minimum wage and maximum hours laws. He enunciated the "clear and present danger doctrine" for interpreting free speech.

Hughes, Charles Evans (1862–1948).   This former governor of New York was also chief justice of the Supreme Court, secretary of state, a Republican presidential candidate who nearly won the election of 1916, and a World Court judge. Hughes wrote several landmark opinions involving the free press and free speech. He presided over the Court during the transitional New Deal era.

Jackson, Andrew (1767–1845).   A military hero before he ran for president, Jackson had a popular appeal among Westerners, farmers, working men, and artisans. He attacked privilege, especially the U.S. Bank, introduced the spoils system to the federal bureaucracy, and preferred his "Kitchen Cabinet," an informal group of friends and advisors, to the official elite.

Jay, John (1745–1829).   With Hamilton and Madison, Jay wrote *The Federalist Papers* (see **Madison**). This delegate to the first Continental Congress really made his mark negotiating the truce after the end of the Revolutionary War and was, throughout his career, an effective diplomat. George Washington persuaded him to become the first chief justice of the Supreme Court, a post he later resigned because he thought it would be an ineffective vehicle of government.

Jefferson, Thomas (1743–1826).   Jefferson was the author of the Declaration of Independence, minister to France, secretary of state under Washington, vice president under Adams, and the third president of the United States. Opposed to Hamilton in the first administration, he advocated a limited federal government. Jefferson was a scientist, an architect, the author of Virginia's statute of religious freedom, and founder of the University of Virginia.

Johnson, Lyndon Baines (1908–1973).   A powerful leader in the Senate, Johnson was John F. Kennedy's vice president, becoming president following Kennedy's assassination, and then elected in 1964. Although the war in Vietnam overshadowed his accomplishments, this Democratic president pushed hard to forge a federal program of economic and social welfare, collectively known as the Great Society, that would end poverty. A southerner, he was also a strong supporter of civil rights, pushing the Civil Rights Act of 1964 and the Voting Rights Act of 1965 through Congress.

Jordan, Barbara (1936–1995).   Best known for her eloquent speeches, this stateswoman was the first black law student at Boston University, the first and only black legislator in the Texas senate, and served in Congress for six years. A defender of the poor, Jordan was often consulted by presidents on civil rights issues. She is the only black and the only woman to have given the keynote speech at the Democratic National Convention.

Kennedy, John F. (1917–1963).   A charismatic Democrat, whose presidency ended prematurely with his assassination in 1963, Kennedy is best remembered for his contribution to civil rights, for starting the Peace Corps, and for facing down the Soviets, who had moved missiles into the Western Hemisphere, during the Cuban Missile Crisis.

Lincoln, Abraham (1809–1865).   The 16th president of the United States, Lincoln was elected president on the Republican ticket, then led the nation through the Civil War. He is known as the Great Emancipator, for signing the Emancipation Proclamation that freed the slaves. A fine writer and rhetorician, he is also remembered for his speeches, especially the Gettysburg Address and the Second Inaugural Address.

Madison, James (1751–1836).   Known as the Father of the Constitution, Madison brought a scholarly voice to the Constitutional Convention of 1787. With Alexander Hamilton and John Jay, he co-authored *The Federalist Papers*, a brilliant series of essays defending the Constitution. He also worked to add the Bill of Rights to the Constitution. As the fourth president, he oversaw the War of 1812.

Marshall, John (1755–1835).   The second chief justice of the United States, Marshall took over a foundering Court and turned it into a respected institution. His court laid the groundwork for federalism. In his most famous ruling, *Marbury v. Madison*, he invoked the right of the Court to review state and federal laws. He also instituted joint opinions. In addition, he served as a diplomat, congressman, and secretary of state.

Marshall, Thurgood (1908–1993).   A Supreme Court justice and a prominent civil rights lawyer, Marshall helped to lay out the strategy for *Brown v. Board of Education*, the Supreme Court decision that desegregated schools. The first black Supreme Court justice, he was one of the most egalitarian persons ever to sit on the Court.

Mason, George (1725–1792).   A political theorist, he wrote the Virginia Declaration of Rights, a brilliant document that helped to establish individual rights. It formed the basis of many state constitutions and, as the Bill of Rights, was later incorporated into the U.S. Constitution.

Monroe, James (1758–1831).   The fifth U.S. president, he was also governor of Virginia, secretary of state, and secretary of war. He issued the Monroe Doctrine, a cornerstone of U.S. foreign policy that warned European nations not to interfere in political affairs in the Western Hemisphere.

Nixon, Richard (1913–1994).   A congressman, senator, and vice president, Nixon was also the only president ever to resign, facing certain impeachment for obstructing justice and abusing presidential authority. His administration's successes included opening diplomatic relations with China and extricating the nation from Vietnam.

O'Connor, Sandra Day (1930–).   As the first woman ever to sit on the Supreme Court, O'Connor has been considered a swing vote in cases involving gender discrimination and sexual harassment. She is considered a centrist.

Perkins, Frances (1882–1965).   The first woman to serve in a president's cabinet, Perkins was secretary of labor under Franklin Roosevelt. She fought for many lasting pieces of legislation, such as unemployment insurance, child labor laws, and public works.

Rangel, Charles (1930–).   Rangel has served the Harlem and upper Manhattan community in the House of Representatives since 1971 and is the first black person to hold the chairmanship of the powerful House Ways and Means Committee.

Rankin, Jeannette (1880–1973).   The first woman ever elected to Congress (1917), Rankin was a dedicated pacifist and cast one of 50 votes against entry into World War I. She was returned to Congress in 1941, where she cast the only vote against entry into World War II. An advocate of women's rights, Rankin's last official antiwar gesture was to lead the Jeannette Rankin Brigade in the 1968 march on Washington to oppose the Vietnam War.

Rehnquist, William (1924–).   Present chief justice of the United States, Rhenquist was named to the Court by President Nixon. A strong advocate of law and order, he has guided the Court toward a more conservative orientation.

Roosevelt, Franklin D. (1882–1945).   As 32nd president of the United States, Roosevelt, a Democrat, guided the country through the Great Depression. His primary vehicle was the New Deal, a package of social and political programs that restored economic health to the nation. He also served as president during World War II and was the only president ever elected to four terms.

Roosevelt, Theodore (1858–1919).   When he took over the presidency after McKinley's assassination in 1901, Roosevelt was at 43 the youngest person ever to hold the office. An active reformer, he was known as a trust-buster and a proponent of conservation. Dissatisfied with the conservatism of his successor William Howard Taft, Roosevelt formed the Progressive (Bull Moose) party in 1912, splitting the vote of his party and ensuring the election of Woodrow Wilson.

Roosevelt, Eleanor (1884–1962).   One of most influential first ladies in history, Eleanor Roosevelt served as FDR's "ears and eyes" as she traveled around the country. She was a strong supporter of civil rights, women's issues, and programs for the poor. After Roosevelt's death, she was delegate to the United Nations.

Stanton, Elizabeth Cady (1815–1902).   Along with Lucretia Mott, Stanton was one of the organizers of the 1848 Seneca Falls Women's Rights Convention, the first public meeting ever held to advocate women's rights. A leader in the women's suffrage movement, she co-founded, with Susan B. Anthony, the National Woman Suffrage Association, serving as its president and later also as president of the National American Woman Suffrage Association. As a lecturer, she spoke around the country, advocating not only voting rights for women but full legal and social equality.

Truman, Harry (1884–1972).   This Democratic president (1945–1953) is remembered for authorizing the use of the atomic bomb on Japan in order to end World War II, instituting the Marshall Plan to rebuild Europe, and at home sponsoring the Fair Deal and civil rights legislation.

Warren, Earl (1891–1974).   Like John Marshall, Warren was one of two or three Supreme Court justices whose name personifies an era. The Warren Court will be remembered for such decisions as *Brown v. Board* of Education, which reversed the "separate but equal doctrine" and ordered that public schools be desegregated; *Gideon v. Wainwright*, which established that poor persons were entitled to free legal counsel; and *Miranda v. Arizona*, which expanded and protected the rights of crime suspects. During the late 1950s and early 1960s, under the guidance of this chief justice, the Court became known for its liberal interpretation of the Constitution and for taking on social and racial issues.

Washington, George (1732–1799).   Commander of the Continental Army and the first president of the United States, Washington was elected to a second term as president but refused a third. He was one of the architects of the present federal system of government and set precedents for the presidency that have lasted to this day.

Webster, Daniel (1782–1852).   The highest-paid lawyer of his time, Webster, also known for his skill as an orator and his defense of the Constitution, won several significant, precedent-setting cases before the Marshall Court. Originally a supporter of states' rights, he later became a unionist. As a secretary of state and senator, he was a leading political figure of his time.

Willard, Frances (1839–1898).   One of the most famous women of the 19th century, Willard is best remembered for her work in temperance. She organized the Women's Christian Temperance Union and worked with women's suffrage activists to combine the two causes.

Wilson, Woodrow (1856–1924).   As president during World War I, Wilson was an advocate for world peace and a supporter of the League of Nations, the forerunner to the present-day United Nations.

ADDITIONAL SOURCES OF INFORMATION

Abraham, Henry J. *Freedom and the Court*. 5th ed. Oxford University Press, 1988.

———. *Justices and Presidents*. 2d ed. Oxford University Press, 1985.

Adams, Henry. *The History of the United States During the Administrations of Jefferson and Madison*. Abr. ed. University of Chicago Press, 1979.

Cardozo, Benjamin. *The Nature of the Judicial Process*. Yale University Press, 1921.

Corwin, Edward Samuel. *Edward S. Corwin's the Constitution and What It Means Today*. 14th ed. Princeton University Press, 1978.

Cox, Archibald. *The Court and the Constitution*. Houghton Mifflin, 1987.

de Tocqueville, Alexis. *Democracy in America*. HarperCollins, 1988.

Foner, Eric. *Politics and Ideology in the Age of the Civil War*. Oxford University Press, 1992.

Hall, Kermit. *The Oxford Companion to the Supreme Court of the United States*. Oxford University Press, 1992.

Hofstadter, Richard. *The American Political Tradition*. Random House, 1989.

Kammen, Michael. *A Machine That Would Go of Itself: The Constitution in American Culture*. Knopf, 1986.

Kluger, Richard. *Simple Justice: The History of Brown v. Board of Education*. Random House, 1977.

Lewis, Anthony. *Gideon's Trumpet*. Vintage, 1966.

Madison, James, Alexander Hamilton, and John Hay. *The Federalist Papers*. Viking Penguin, 1987.

Myrdal, Gunnar. *An American Dilemma*. Harper & Row, 1962.

Neustadt, Richard. *Presidential Power: The Politics of Leadership from FDR to Carter*. Macmillan, 1980.

Reedy, George. *Twilight of the American Presidency: From Johnson to Reagan*. Rev. ed. New American Library-Dutton, 1971.

Streamer, Robert J. and Richard J. Maiman. *American Constitutional Law: Cases and Commentary*. McGraw-Hill, 1992.

Weisbrot, Robert. *Freedom Bound: A History of America's Civil Rights Movement*. Norton, 1989.

Wills, Gary. *Inventing America: Jefferson's Declaration of Independence*. Random House, 1979.

Wood, Gordon S. *The Creation of the American Republic, 1776–1787*. University of North Carolina Press, 1969.

7

The Development
of the American City

SIGNIFICANT EVENTS IN THE DEVELOPMENT OF THE AMERICAN CITY

The United States evolved from a nation of farms at the beginning of the 19th century to a nation of cities by the beginning of the 20th. In 1820 a mere 7 percent of the population were city dwellers. By 1860 nearly 20 percent of Americans were urban. By 1920 the balance had shifted: 51 percent of Americans lived in urban areas. This shift from rural to urban was essentially finished by the 1970s, and more recent population shifts reflect migration inside the urban system itself: from one city to another, from city to suburb, or from suburb to city.

Many processes contributed to the urbanization of America. The number of cities increased as the new country expanded westward. Cash crops spurred the growth of market towns and port cities. Advances in transportation sped movement of goods. Industrialization drew rural youth into manufacturing towns. City populations grew dramatically with the influx of immigrants from abroad.

During and after World War I, the migration of mainly rural, southern blacks to the industrial North also caused a major population shift, institutionalizing the urban ghetto and the idea of the inner city. An industry pulled out of the Northeast, older cities decayed and population shifted toward the Sunbelt. And with the rise of the suburb, then the "exurb," and the concept of the megalopolis, the American city with a distinctive boundary and identity may be disappearing, giving way to the sprawling metropolitan areas that now define the contemporary American landscape.

1524   Italian navigator Giovanni da Verrazzano sails into New York Harbor. A rugged forested island in the harbor will later be called Manhattan.

1564   French Huguenots build Fort Caroline near the mouth of the Saint Johns River.

1565   Saint Augustine, Florida, is founded by Spanish conquistador Pedro Menéndez de Avilés. It is the first American city. Menéndez de Avilés routs the French Huguenot Fort Caroline, slaughtering the entire male population.

1607   The Virginia Company sends more than 100 colonists to Virginia, where they found Jamestown.

1609   Henry Hudson sails up the river in New York that eventually will bear his name.

Sante Fe is founded by the Spanish, on the site of ancient ruins.

1614   The coast of Manhattan is mapped by Dutch navigator Adriaen Block.

1620   The Pilgrims establish Plymouth.

1626   Peter Minuit buys Manhattan Island from chiefs of the Canarsie tribe for 60 guilders (the proverbial $24) worth of gadgets and trinkets. Dutch settlers build thirty houses and call their settlement New Amsterdam.

1628   English Puritans settle at Naumkeag, which they rename Salem, on Massachusetts Bay.

1630   A thatched cottage with a wooden chimney burns down in Boston. Authorities require that thatched houses not have wooden chimneys in what may be the first "building code" in the New World.

Under their leader, John Winthrop, members of the Massachusetts Bay Company establish "a city on a hill," named Boston in 1633 after a town in Lincolnshire, England.

"A CITY ON A HILL"

In 1630, somewhere in the middle of the Atlantic Ocean, John Winthrop delivered a sermon, "A Model of Christian Charity," to the Puritans aboard the *Arabella* who had selected him as governor of their enterprise. He exhorted his shipmates, who would soon establish a new community in a new land, to put their ideals of harmony and Christian charity into practice. We must enter into a covenant, he explained, "to do justly, to love mercy, to walk humbly with our God. For this end, we must be knit together in this work as one man. We must entertain each other in brotherly affection, we must be willing to abridge ourselves of our superfluities, for the supply of others' necessities. We must uphold a familiar commerce together in all meekness, gentleness, patience and liberality. We must delight in each other, make others' conditions our own, rejoice together, mourn together, labour and suffer together, always having before our eyes our commission and community in the work, our community as members of the same body. So shall we keep the unity of the spirit in the bond of peace." If we do these things, Winthrop promised, then God will be among us. "He shall make us a praise and glory that men shall say of succeeding plantations, 'the lord make it like that of New England.' For we must consider that we shall be as a city upon a hill. The eyes of all people are upon us. . . . We shall be made a story and a by-word through the world."

While Winthrop's "city on a hill"—soon to be named Boston—did not turn out the way he had hoped, his vision would be repeated again and again in the New World, in hundreds of new communities founded by groups of like-minded people who sought to carve from wilderness a community that would realize an ideal. For more on those societies that hoped to be utopias, see "The Land of Utopia" in Chapter 13.

1631	One year after its founding, Boston begins its long association with the sea and shipbuilding when *Blessing of the Bay* is launched.
1634	Under a grant to the Catholic Calvert family, the Lords Baltimore settle Saint Mary's, Maryland, on the Chesapeake Bay.
1635	English settlers build Fort Saybrook at the mouth of the Connecticut River.
1636	Providence, Rhode Island, is founded by dissenting minister Roger Williams, who has been banished from Massachusetts.
	Thomas Hooker, another dissenting minister, founds Hartford, Connecticut.
1638	Puritans establish New Haven, Connecticut.
	Swedish colonists establish Fort Christina, now Wilmington, Delaware.
	John Wheelwright, a Puritan clergyman who publicly defends the views of his sister-in-law Anne Hutchinson, is banished from Massachusetts Bay and establishes Exeter, in what will eventually be New Hampshire. When Massachusetts claims authority over Exeter and nearby towns, he moves to Wells, Maine.
1640	Dutch colonists in New Amsterdam settle Hoboken, across the Hudson River, in what is now New Jersey.
1653	Fearing hostile Indian attacks as well as assaults by the British, New Amsterdam colonists construct a defensive wall across lower Manhattan. Extending from the North Hudson River to the East River, it gives Wall Street its name.
1658	Dutch settlers in New Amsterdam move north on Manhattan Island to found Nieuw Haarlem, today Harlem.
1664	New Amsterdam becomes New York as the English take the town and rename it after the king's brother, the duke of York.
1666	Connecticut Puritans found Newark, New Jersey.

1668	The French establish a fur-trading post and Jesuit mission at Sault Sainte Marie, on the waterway between Lakes Superior and Huron.
1670	British settlers found Charles Town (later Charleston) in the Carolinas.
1679	Most of Boston is destroyed in a fire; its wooden buildings are densely packed.
1682	William Penn founds Philadelphia. The city is designed by Thomas Holme and other members of the Society of Friends (Quakers) with a grid pattern in a successful effort at town planning.
	Norfolk, in Virginia, is established. Its excellent natural harbor will be an important port and eventually a naval headquarters.
	Members of La Salle's expedition establish Arkansas Post.
1683	German Mennonites found Germantown, Pennsylvania.
1694	The capital of Maryland is moved from Saint Mary's to Annapolis.
1699	Pierre le Moyne, sieur d'Iberville, founds Old Biloxi (now Ocean Springs, Mississippi), the first European settlement in French Louisiana.
	Middle Plantation, on the peninsula between the James and York Rivers in Virginia, is laid out and named Williamsburg, the new capital of the colony.
1701	The French establish a fort on the Detroit River that will become the city of Detroit.
1710	Swiss and German immigrants settle New Bern, North Carolina. It will later be an early colonial capital.
1713	Boston begins grading streets so that water drains to the side.
1718	New Orleans is founded by the sieur de Bienville. Near the mouth of the Mississippi, it will become one of the most important port cities in the country.
1729	Baltimore is founded, and its excellent harbor soon makes it an important shipping center.
1733	Savannah, founded by James Oglethorpe, is laid out on a grid pattern with wide streets and many parks.
1751	Philadelphia becomes the first city to have a police force.
1754	Pittsburgh has its roots in the establishment of Fort Duquesne. The French erect the fort where the Allegheny River meets the Monongahela, forming the Ohio River. Four years later the British capture the fort and rename it Fort Pitt. A village surrounding the fort is settled in 1760.
	Philadelphia's Christ Church is completed, and its 200-foot steeple makes it the tallest structure in North America.
1763	Pierre LaClede selects the site of Saint Louis, near the junction of the Mississippi and Missouri Rivers, for a fur-trading post.
1765	Philadelphia's population reaches 25,000. New York's is 12,500, up from 5,000 in 1700.
1766	Irish soldiers in the British army stage New York City's first Saint Patrick's Day parade.
1776	San Francisco begins with the settlement of Yerba Buena as a Spanish mission.
1781	Spanish settlers found Los Angeles, which they call El Pueblo de Nuestra Señora la Reina de los Angeles de Porciuncula (The Town of Our Lady the Queen of the Angels of Porciuncula).
1788	Cincinnati is founded, named in 1790. This Ohio River city will be an important shipping and trade center.
	The Ohio Company founds Marietta, on the Ohio River.
1789	New York City is the capital of the United States when George Washington is inaugurated as the first president on April 30 at Federal Hall.

A customs house is opened in New York, which soon becomes the new nation's major port of entry.

1790   The first ten-year census of the United States is taken; there are only 24 urban places—areas with 2,500 people or more. Philadelphia is the largest city, with New York second. Ten years later New York moves into first place, a position it has not relinquished.

The site for the new national capital is selected on the banks of the Potomac River. Maryland and Virginia each cede sections to establish a federal district of 100 square miles. In 1847 the underutilized portion south of the Potomac is retroceded to Virginia.

THE FIRST URBAN PLANNING

Those who settled America had an unusual opportunity—to plan, from scratch, the towns they would settle. Colonists from Spain, France, the Netherlands, and England arrived in the New World with many kinds of ideas of what their new communities should look like.

The Spanish built missions—adobe and stone churches surrounded by fields, vineyards, and orchards that the Indians would farm, converted to the Christian, peaceful, and servile life that the Spanish envisioned for them. The French built fur-trading posts and small farming towns—with a manor house for the lord and a church, surrounded by fields that the *habitants* would farm—resembling those of northern France. The Dutch built a farming village, with narrow, crooked streets, on the tip of Manhattan Island. The Bowery (in Dutch, *bouwerie*, meaning "farm"), the street that gave the area its name, once went to the farm of Governor Peter Stuyvesant. The English in Virginia built forts. It was in New England that urban planning, in this country, first began.

In New England, individuals owned houses on individual lots that were clustered around a public common, owned by the whole community. On the main street around the common stood the church, and probably the minister's house and a school. The community was actually a corporation, organized through the church, in which all families held shares. Each individual holder had a house, kitchen garden, barn, orchard, and a strip of land on the outskirts for cultivation. Additional jointly owned land was used for pasturage and as a woodlot.

When the new nation sited a new capital on the banks of the Potomac, planners had an opportunity to plan a new city on a grand scale. George Washington selected Major Pierre Charles L'Enfant—artist, draftsman, and Revolutionary War soldier—to create the design. Thomas Jefferson sent him plans of a dozen European cities, and L'Enfant himself studied the plans of Annapolis, Savannah, Williamsburg, Philadelphia, and New York.

L'Enfant's final plan seemed to combine them all: a geometric grid with diagonal avenues that were to allow for wide vistas and create rectangles, squares, triangles, and even circles for public purposes, parks and gardens, statues and fountains. While today trees and traffic sometimes obscure the "reciprocity of sight" L'Enfant so desired, Washington remains a beautiful city, with a low profile and a green complexion that is unlike any capital city in the world.

1793   A yellow fever epidemic in Philadelphia causes the city to be evacuated and 4,000 deaths. Many cities suffer from epidemics caused by poor sanitary conditions: no municipal water supplies, outdoor privies, and no organized public garbage removal.

1798   Benjamin Latrobe designs a public water supply system for Philadelphia, the first in the United States. It is hoped that a plentiful, dependable supply of clean water will help combat disease.

1800   Washington, D.C., becomes the U.S. capital; the city has 3,210 residents, of whom 623 are slaves.

1801   Boston's board of health begins to improve the city's hygiene, ordering vaccinations against smallpox; it also regulates burials and imposes quarantines.

Philadelphia completes a city water system, but customers have to pay for the service, so it only benefits the richest citizens.

New York's Common Council creates a commissioner of police who coordinates the work of city marshals and the city watch.

1803   Fort Dearborn is built by U.S. troops on Lake Michigan; it will later become Chicago.

1810   New Orleans has a population of 17,242; Pittsburgh has 4,768; Cincinnati has 2,540; Louisville 1,357; Savannah 5,215; and Richmond 9,735.

1811   New York institutes a grid pattern to mark off future streets and avenues.

1814   During the War of 1812, the British occupy Washington, D.C., and burn its public buildings.

1818   Boston establishes public elementary schools.

1820   Only 6 percent of Americans live in cities.

New York City's population is now almost 152,056. Pittsburgh has a population of 7,248.

1822   The Boston Associates begin to build a factory at the junction of the Concord and Merrimack rivers, renaming the settlement Lowell in memory of Francis Cabot Lowell, who had improved on British models for a spinning machine and a power loom. When the factory opens the next year, it employs young girls from New England farm families, who live in dormitories provided by the company. Lowell is the first designed manufacturing city.

1825   The Erie Canal opens, bolstering the economy of New York City; commerce is facilitated between the rapidly developing interior of the country and the city's flourishing financial center. The port of New York, already the busiest on the eastern seaboard, becomes the Atlantic port for the Midwest. The opening of the canal also sparks the economies of Buffalo, Rochester, Cleveland, Columbus, Detroit, Chicago, and Syracuse.

Erie Canal

1827 The Baltimore and Ohio Railroad is chartered on February 28 to connect Baltimore to the West and thus position Baltimore in direct competition with New York (and the Erie Canal) for trade with the Midwest.

1829 New York City's first public transportation is provided by a horse-drawn bus, or omnibus. Philadelphia and Boston follow suit in the 1830s.

Boston opens the first modern hotel, Tremont House. A prototype of modern hostelries, it sets new standards. Unlike earlier inns, where strangers were forced to share rooms and even beds, each guest has a private room. The basement held eight waterclosets for the 170 rooms.

1820s- The earlier notion of the city as a harmonious community breaks down. Rapid growth,
1830s immigration, and industrialization create pressures that eventually explode in a series of riots, often against the two poorest urban groups: Catholics (mainly Irish) and free blacks.

Cities become divided along class lines. The rich and poor segregate in separate neighborhoods. Some areas become slums, marked by poverty and foreign-born residents.

New York City responds to the worries of prosperous citizens by expanding on the old colonial system of city watchmen, adding to the informal force of constables and marshals. The militia is called out to handle riots.

More than half of city dwellers live in four cities: New York, Baltimore, Philadelphia, and Boston.

THE TEN LARGEST CITIES, 1790–1990

1790

1. Philadelphia, Pa.
2. New York, N.Y.
3. Boston, Mass.
4. Baltimore, Md.
5. Providence, R.I.
6. New Haven, Conn.
7. Richmond, Va.
8. Albany, N.Y.
9. Norfolk, Va.
10. Alexandria, Va.

1810

1. New York, N.Y.
2. Philadelphia, Pa.
3. Baltimore, Md.
4. Boston, Mass.
5. New Orleans, La.
6. Albany, N.Y.
7. Providence, R.I.
8. Richmond, Va.
9. Norfolk, Va.
10. Alexandria, Va.

1830

1. New York, N.Y.
2. Baltimore, Md.
3. Philadelphia, Pa.
4. Boston, Mass.
5. New Orleans, La.
6. Cincinnati, Ohio
7. Albany, N.Y.
8. Washington, D.C.
9. Richmond, Va.
10. Providence, R.I.

1850

1. New York, N.Y.
2. Baltimore, Md.
3. Boston, Mass.
4. Philadelphia, Pa.
5. New Orleans, La.
6. Cincinnati, Ohio
7. Saint Louis, Mo.
8. Albany, N.Y.
9. Pittsburgh, Pa.
10. Buffalo, N.Y.

1870

1. New York, N.Y.
2. Philadelphia, Pa.
3. Saint Louis, Mo.
4. Chicago, Ill.
5. Baltimore, Md.
6. Boston, Mass.
7. Cincinnati, Ohio
8. New Orleans, La.
9. San Francisco, Calif.
10. Buffalo, N.Y.

1890

1. New York, N.Y.
2. Chicago, Ill.
3. Philadelphia, Pa.
4. Saint Louis, Mo.
5. Boston, Mass.
6. Baltimore, Md.
7. San Francisco, Calif.
8. Cincinnati, Ohio
9. New Orleans, La.
10. Pittsburgh, Pa.

(continues)

THE TEN LARGEST CITIES, 1790–1990 (CONT.)

1910

1. New York, N.Y.
2. Chicago, Ill.
3. Philadelphia, Pa.
4. Saint Louis, Mo.
5. Boston, Mass.
6. Cleveland, Ohio
7. Baltimore, Md.
8. Detroit, Mich.
9. Cincinnati, Ohio
10. Los Angeles, Calif.

1930

1. New York, N.Y.
2. Chicago, Ill.
3. Philadelphia, Pa.
4. Detroit, Mich.
5. Los Angeles, Calif.
6. Cleveland, Ohio
7. Saint Louis, Mo.
8. Baltimore, Md.
9. Boston, Mass.
10. San Francisco, Calif.

1950

1. New York, N.Y.
2. Chicago, Ill.
3. Philadelphia, Pa.
4. Los Angeles, Calif.
5. Detroit, Mich.
6. Baltimore, Md.
7. Cleveland, Ohio
8. Saint Louis, Mo.
9. Washington, D.C.
10. Boston, Mass.

1970

1. New York, N.Y.
2. Chicago, Ill.
3. Los Angeles, Calif.
4. Philadelphia, Pa.
5. Detroit, Mich.
6. Houston, Tex.
7. Baltimore, Md.
8. Dallas, Tex.
9. Washington, D.C.
10. Cleveland, Ohio

1990

1. New York, N.Y.
2. Los Angeles, Calif.
3. Chicago, Ill.
4. Houston, Tex.
5. Philadelphia, Pa.
6. San Diego, Calif.
7. Detroit, Mich.
8. Dallas, Tex.
9. Phoenix, Ariz.
10. San Antonio, Tex.

1831 New York's Gramercy Farm is transformed into Gramercy Park, the first of New York's planned neighborhoods. Only the wealthy people who purchase surrounding lots have keys to the park, where they can enjoy walkways and carriageways.

1832 New York City's first horse-drawn streetcar is put into service. Streetcars make trips cheaper, easier, and safer.

1833 In Boston, the top 4 percent enjoy 59 percent of the city's wealth. In most cities, the rich and poor lead mainly separate lives, with the rich joining elite churches and voluntary associations with restricted membership.

1835 A major fire destroys about 700 buildings in New York near Hanover Square and Pearl Street.

Omnibuses, horse-drawn coaches operating on fixed routes, operate in Boston, Brooklyn, New Orleans, New York, Philadelphia, and Washington. Fares range from six to twelve cents, relatively expensive.

1837 Buildings and paved streets occupy only one-sixth of Manhattan; the rest of the land is still farmed.

A depression hits the cities hard. In New York, unemployment leaves most laborers without work.

Atlanta is founded as Terminus, the end of the rail line. It will become a major rail junction and shipping center.

1840 The Mississippi steamboat trade makes New Orleans prosper; by the 1850s its port will overtake New York in volume of shipping as half the country's exports move through it.

The population of New York City is now 391,114, but the U.S. population is still 90 percent rural.

1842   New York City pipes water from the Croton watershed to a reservoir on Fifth Avenue at the current site of the New York Public Library. Voters approve the scheme in 1837.

1845   New York City has a permanent, professional police force. In 1853 those members of the police force who had objected to uniforms as "undemocratic" agree to wear them.

Lemuel Shattuck and John H. Griscom report on urban conditions in *Sanitary Conditions of the Laboring Population of New York*. This report and others like it prompt social reformers to become involved in urban planning and in public works, including sewage treatment and disposal, adequate clean water supplies, public safety, and recreational areas.

1846   William Gregg re-creates a New England mill village in Graniteville, South Carolina, with homes for 300 employees in his cotton mill.

1847   Salt Lake City is founded by Mormon leader Brigham Young.

1850   The first prefabricated cast-iron-and-glass buildings are constructed in Manhattan. Designed by James Bogardus, these "curtain wall" buildings will soon be erected in other U.S. cities including Philadelphia and Saint Louis.

The population of New York exceeds 700,000. About 140,000 New Yorkers are foreign-born, mostly Irish. Irish immigrants coming at midcentury settle in eastern cities; German immigrants settle in the Midwest (see Chapter 4).

One in seven Americans is a city dweller. Ten U.S. cities have populations of more than 50,000.

1852   Elisha Otis invents the safety elevator, which will eventually permit construction of the high-rise buildings that will transform American cities.

1853   The Children's Aid Society raises consciousness about the plight of homeless urban children.

1855   Philadelphia's Fairmont Park, the largest park within a city in the country, is established.

More than three-quarters of New York City's workforce is foreign-born (Irish and German)

1856   The value of real estate in Chicago's central business district has increased 6,000 percent over its value in 1846.

The first Boston street railway begins with a single horsecar between Cambridge and Boston. Street railways differ from omnibuses in that they operate over rails laid in the street. Omnibuses differ little from coaches.

The land for New York City's Central Park is acquired. Designed by Frederick Law Olmsted and Calvert Vaux, the park will take 20 years to complete.

1857   Virginia City, Nevada, becomes a boom town when the Comstock Lode is discovered nearby. Within a few years it has a population of 6,000. By 1880, 11,000 people live here. In 1990 the county in which Virginia City is located contains 2,705 people.

The world's first passenger elevator begins operating in a New York City building.

1858   Denver is incorporated. The city lies at the junction of the South Platte River and Cherry Creek.

New York City's Central Park, 840 acres of reclaimed urban space, opens to the public. Although intended for the working classes, it is too far north—and too far from public transportation—to be used by anyone but the rich. It will become the model for future urban and suburban parks.

R. H. Macy Company opens in New York City.

1860   One in ten southerners lives in a city, one in three northeasterners, and one in seven midwesterners. Slavery, however, remains a rural institution with less than 10 percent of the population of the ten largest southern cities being slaves.

1860-
1900   The expansion of the nation's railroads as well as the improvements in seagoing vessels will not only accelerate the export of agricultural produce but will also cause major population expansion and shifts as immigrants populate U.S. cities, the interior, and the plains. Some cities are founded as railroad junctions and centers (see Chapter 12).

An early steam locomotive

1860s   William Marcy Tweed, whose name becomes synonymous with political corruption, dominates New York City politics.

URBAN BOSSES AND MACHINE POLITICS: THE TWEED RING

The urban boss—a powerful political figure in 19th- and 20th-century city politics—helped city dwellers handle the huge changes wrought by urbanization. So goes one interpretation of the role of the boss and the political machine.

Growing numbers of immigrants—mainly German and Irish at the period when the urban political machines gained ascendance—strained the cities' infrastructure almost to the breaking point. Housing, transportation, jobs, and general crowding made city life miserable for the poor and new arrivals. New York, Chicago, and Boston bore the brunt of the influx, but even smaller cities like Cincinnati were stressed. Water supplies kept running out, and inadequate sewer systems created serious health hazards. Outside of church groups and private philanthropy, social welfare organizations barely existed during that era.

Thus the political bosses and their machines sprang up, in part to fill a niche in urban society. Operating outside the constraints of formal government, ward workers could address problems of individual families or workers for whom the official city government had no time.

Always alert to the opportunity to line their own pockets, machine politicians pursued excessive spending plans to modernize American cities. More buildings, paved roads, and lighting meant more jobs for their constituents, which eventually meant more votes, more power, and eventually more opportunities for graft. Meanwhile, the cities evolved slowly into more modern, better-serviced places to live—with the taxpayers and honest citizens bilked out of millions of dollars along the way. Graft and corruption became synonymous with urban politics and were often accepted as just the way things had to be done. The consequence was the inevitable rise of reform candidates and movements, for voters' tolerance of graft had definite limits.

A particularly notorious example of the political boss and his machine was Tammany Hall's Boss Tweed. Tweed and his cronies came to be known as the Tweed Ring.

Tammany Hall was formed in 1789 as a benevolent group to help mayoral campaigns in New York City. It became a controlling factor in that city's Democratic party. William Marcy Tweed, who had served in the state legislature, eventually became a supervisor of municipal elections. His political circle included the city comptroller, city chamberlain, and the mayor, Abraham Hall. Tweed and his circle continued to sponsor urban improvement projects, and money paid for city projects eventually found its way into Tweed's pockets. The exorbitant costs—almost double the Alaska purchase price—of building an opulent courthouse aroused suspicions in the community, and the building that became known as the Tweed Courthouse led to Tweed's eventual downfall. Cartoonist and political reformer Thomas Nast brutally caricatured Tweed in *Harper's Weekly*, and a series in *The New York Times* exposed him.

Tweed was finally arrested in 1871 and prosecuted for not auditing contractors' bills. Though the Tweed Ring was essentially broken, Tammany Hall continued to be an active force in New York politics into the 1940s, when Mayor Fiorello La Guardia set out with the help of President Franklin D. Roosevelt to reform New York's Democratic party.

Other urban bosses in charge of powerful political machines over the years include Mayor Richard J. Daley of Chicago, C. A. Buckley of San Francisco, David L. Lawrence of Pittsburgh, Thomas Pendergast in Kansas City, and Daniel P. O'Connell in Albany.

1860	Twenty percent of the country's population lives in cities, which are defined as having 2,500 or more inhabitants. New York is the largest city, with 1,174,779 residents, 20 percent of them Irish-born immigrants.
	One-fourth of all cities use private water companies. Service is worse in poor neighborhoods.
	In Milwaukee, the great majority of the German population lives in German neighborhoods.
	Some 330,000 free blacks live in the North; most of them are in cities. There, they compete with native-born poor whites and immigrants for work as domestic servants and laborers. Philadelphia has the largest African-American population of 22,000.
1861-1865	The Civil War causes northern industry to boom. In the South, Richmond, Atlanta, and Columbia, South Carolina, are destroyed (see Chapter 5). But after the war, southern cities grow faster than those in any other part of the country.
1864	A gold rush leads to the founding of Butte, Montana. The city is platted in 1867 and incorporated in 1879. When copper is discovered about 1880, the Anaconda Copper Mining Company and Butte flourish together.
1868	In an Iowa case, the Dillon Rule—the principle that local governments are the creations of state governments, with their powers and responsibilities defined by the state—is formulated.
1869	Abilene, Kansas, the railhead and shipping point for cattle driven up from Texas along the Chisholm Trail, is incorporated. The two Kansas Cities (in Kansas and Missouri) also boom as markets, shipping points, and processing and packaging centers for newly opening cattle and agricultural frontiers (see Chapter 3).
	A. T. Stewart, owner of New York's largest department store, starts a planned middle-income community in Garden City, Long Island.
	New York City's first apartment house, the Rutherford-Stuyvesant on East 18th Street, is built.

1870   The first U.S. elevated railroad opens in New York City; a section for demonstration purposes had opened two years earlier.

The population of Kansas City has climbed from 4,418 to more than 32,000 in just ten years.

Chicago also experiences a major growth spurt. Its population, 29,963 in the late 1850s, has soared to 298,977.

1871   Rumored to have been started by Mrs. O'Leary's cow kicking over a lantern in a barn, the Chicago fire burns out of control for almost three days, beginning October 8, destroying four square miles of the city. At least 250 people are believed to have died in Chicago. Ironically, a greater loss of human life occurs simultaneously in forest fires in Wisconsin.

Birmingham, incorporated this year, is soon on its way to being an iron and steel center, the "Pittsburgh of the South."

Illustration depicting Mrs. O'Leary's cow, rumored cause of the 1871 Chicago fire

1872   Dallas, a small Texas town, is linked by rail to eastern markets. By 1880 its population has more than tripled.

Boston now extends outward from its civic center for a distance of 2.5 miles—a direct result of the new horsecar transportation, which allows people to live farther than walking distance from their places of work. However, an explosion results in a fire that destroys the most prosperous part of the city.

1873   San Francisco's cable cars begin to run; the underground cable system is the world's first.

1874   Boston annexes Charlestown, home of the Boston naval shipyard.

1875   Frederick Law Olmsted begins working on the foundations of the Boston public park system.

1876   The Southern Pacific Railroad arrives in Los Angeles, and the Santa Fe arrives in 1885.

The nation marks its first 100 years with the Centennial Exposition in Philadelphia.

1877   In New York City, the Museum of Natural History opens at the edge of Central Park.

Gastonia, North Carolina, one of the new textile towns in the South, is incorporated. During the next two decades, cotton mills in the Piedmont of the Carolinas and Georgia, close to cotton, energy, and cheap labor, surpass New England. Greenville, Spartanburg, Macon, and Columbus are only the biggest. Small company towns spring up throughout rural areas.

1879   Cleveland begins to use carbon-arc street lamps.

1880   New York City lights a strip of Broadway—14th to 26th Streets—with arc lamps.

San Francisco's population reaches 233,959.

Los Angeles's population grows from about 11,000 to more than 50,000 by the end of the decade.

On the Lower East Side of New York, housing conditions are among the worst in the world.

1880-   During this period even stable older cities such as Boston experience tremendous popula-
1890   tion flux. Boston's population swells to more than 448,000 from just under 363,000. In the same decade New York and Chicago each grow by 600,000.

1882   Parts of New York City are lit by electricity; soon Manhattan will be entirely supplied with electric power. An 1884 law requires that wire be placed underground, a job not completed until 1905.

1882   Cable cars begin operating in Chicago.

1883   The Brooklyn Bridge opens. Designed by J. A. Roebling, who dies before it is completed, the span links Manhattan and Brooklyn. It is completed by his son, W. A. Roebling.

William Le Baron Jenney designs the first true skyscraper, the Home Insurance Building in Chicago. Its steel framework means that buildings no longer have to rely on heavy, thick, solid masonry.

1886   The Statue of Liberty, a gift to the United States from France, is dedicated in New York Harbor.

A sand garden for children, an import from Berlin, Germany, is established in Boston.

An electric street railway begins operating in Baltimore over a three-mile line. It draws its power from an electrified third rail.

1888   The first electric trolley starts running in the city of Richmond, Virginia. The system covers more than 12 miles. Electric trolleys will be operating in 200 other American cities by around 1889.

New York City's first skyscraper, the Tower Building, is constructed at 50 Broadway.

1889   Boston, with one of the largest horse-drawn street railways, begins electrifying its system. Within six years almost the entire system is electric.

The world's first electric elevators are installed in a New York office building by Otis Brothers.

Jane Addams opens Hull-House, the most famous settlement house in the country, in Chicago.

THE SETTLEMENT HOUSE MOVEMENT

When Jane Addams and her college classmate Ellen Gates Starr opened the doors at Hull-House, on Chicago's West Side, in 1889, they were not initiating an original institution. The idea of the settlement—a house in a slum where university-trained people would "settle" to help relieve poverty—had originated in London. The first settlement house in the United States was established by Stanton Coit on New York's Lower East Side in 1886. But Addams's Hull-House would become the most famous.

(continues)

THE SETTLEMENT HOUSE MOVEMENT (CONT.)

Hull-House, modeled on London's Toynbee Hall, which Addams had visited in 1887–1888, quickly became a center of community life. Here the impoverished working people of the Halsted Street neighborhood, many of them immigrants, could find help and friendship. The women of Hull-House helped secure support for deserted wives and insurance for bewildered widows. They served as an information and interpretation bureau between individuals who needed help and city bureaucracies. At Hull-House there was a working girls' home, a day nursery, a labor museum, a boys' club, a social science club, a little theater, and reading parties. In addition to tutorials, there were classes in sewing, mending, and embroidering, in Shakespeare, mathematics, physics, and electricity.

The Henry Street settlement house in New York City grew out of Lillian Wald's visiting nursing service, which provided nursing care of the sick in their homes—mostly tenements in New York's immigrant neighborhoods. Combating ignorance and poverty daily, both Hull-House and Henry Street moved into the forefront of social reform, then political reform movements. Settlement house women did statistical studies, wrote reports, and campaigned for housing reform and child labor laws. Lillian Wald lobbied for the U.S. Children's Bureau, established in 1912. Jane Addams founded the Woman's Peace Party in 1915 and the Women's International League for Peace and Freedom in 1919. Settlement house women went on to careers in government, industry, and academic life. They were the first social workers, and their impact on the profession continues to be felt today.

Settlement houses, too, are still alive in the shelters for abused women and the homeless, in the free medical clinics and community centers that even today seek to ease the immigrant's transition to American life and to alleviate the problems of urban poverty with soup, services, and kindness.

1890   *How the Other Half Lives* by Jacob Riis is published. This book exposes the living conditions in the slums of New York and gives impetus to urban reform movements.

The population of Los Angeles is now 50,395. New York counts 2,507,414. More than 700 people per acre are packed into Lower East Side tenements measuring 25 by 100 feet and five stories high.

SKYSCRAPERS

Towering structures of metal, stone, and glass, skyscrapers define the 20th-century urban skyline. Depending on one's viewpoint, the tall buildings transform cities into sparkling places of light and architectural marvels or into canyons of gloom.

Before the 1870s the urban cityscape lay low-slung against the horizon. Young cities were mainly conglomerations of row houses, warehouses, and shops, over which lived merchant owners or craftspeople. The tallest buildings were generally just six stories high; with plenty of land to spare there was no need to economize on lot size or to pack more tenants into a particular square footage. And the technology just didn't exist to create taller, habitable structures.

Soon, however, population growth led to overcrowding. Real estate in downtown areas became a more valuable commodity in the nation's boomtowns. By the 1870s the stage was thus set for the rise of the skyscraper. The event that triggered the building revolution was the 1871 Great Chicago fire, which gutted the city's downtown. Plans to rebuild were thwarted by the existing grid pattern of the city, which was now also the hub of the nation's railroads: tracks crisscrossed sections of town.

Spurred on by developers seeking to make the most use of limited and expensive downtown lots, architects set out to find ways to build the tallest buildings possible. The first ten-story building erected in the Windy City was the Montauk Building designed by Daniel Burnham and John Wellborn Root. It was built using a cast-iron cage or frame, which supported the weight of the building.

Despite the unprecedented height of the building, as much significance could be attached to its foundation, for it "floated" on the sand and clay soil of Chicago. Both the engineering developments permitted the construction of even taller buildings.

The Auditorium, by Louis Sullivan and Dankmar Adler, completed in 1889

Chicago, in the aftermath of the fire, which had consumed the entire central business district, was a stimulus to architects, who competed to create modern, tall, fireproof buildings. With steel structural framework and sturdier foundations, non–load-bearing building walls were free to be lighter. More windows allowed light into the hitherto heavy stone buildings and made outside surfaces more reflective. Technological breakthroughs, such as the invention of electricity by Edison and Otis's elevator, helped fuel the skyscraper revolution. Tall buildings were a new feature on the architectural horizon. Their design and construction freed architects to pursue new ideas regarding style, function, and form.

One of the great architects of the era, Louis Sullivan, in "The Tall Office Building Artistically Considered," welcomed the opportunity to build unhampered by the need to follow historical conventions and old styles.

1891   The Bronx becomes home to the New York Botanical Garden.

1893   The World's Columbian Exposition is celebrated in Chicago.

Frederick Law Olmsted and Daniel Burnham's "White City," a model of urban planning, demonstrates everything that city planners have worked toward over the years.

Louisville, Kentucky, builds fieldhouses where city children can play in bad weather.

1894   Manhattan's tenement district has 986.4 people per square acre, the highest population density in the world.

1898   The first U.S. subway begins operation in Boston.

1900   Street railways total more than 20,000 miles.

The turn of the century still finds a majority of Americans—60 percent—living in rural areas.

The effects of immigration and urbanization are evident. In the Northeast, two-thirds of the population is urban, and 23 percent is foreign-born. An additional 28 percent has at least one foreign-born parent. In New York City in 1910, 40 percent of the 4.8 million residents are foreign-born. An additional 38 percent have at least one foreign-born parent.

The population of New York City is 43 times greater than in the year 1800.

Electric trolleys have transformed Boston into a metropolis, encompassing 31 towns in a ten-mile radius, and more than 1 million residents.

Work begins on the construction of the New York subway.

A hurricane and tidal wave destroy Galveston, Texas. When the mayor and alderman prove unable to cope with the emergency, businessmen propose a new form of city government by a board of commissioners.

One in six southerners lives in an urban place.

1901   In Washington, D.C., the McMillan Commission plan to update L'Enfant's vision for the city receives federal government approval.

Streetcars and elevators in New York City are now run by electricity, though horsecars still travel Fifth Avenue.

1902   The Flatiron Building is finished in New York City. At 20 stories high, the steel-frame structure is a wonder of urban architecture and quickly becomes a tourist mecca.

Lincoln Steffens's series *The Shame of the Cities* exposes corruption in urban politics. It is published in book form in 1904.

1904   The first New York City subway opens on October 27, and passengers pay a nickel. Eventually the New York subway system will become the largest in the United States.

Fire guts downtown Baltimore.

1905   Cleveland developers Oris and Mantis Van Sweringen purchase land, which had belonged to a Shaker congregation, to build a model suburban complex. After completion of a rail line, subsidized in part by the Sweringens, from Cleveland to the new community, Shaker Heights blossoms into one of America's premier upper-middle-class suburbs.

1906   A devastating earthquake strikes San Francisco on April 18. Severed and broken gas lines spark a fire that destroys two-thirds of the city and results in a property loss of more than $400 million. At least 2,300 people are killed as the fire blazes out of control for three days; there is little water to fight the fire, since the city's water mains have cracked in the quake. It is the worst earthquake ever to hit a U.S. city.

1907   New York City replaces its Fifth Avenue horsecars, the last in use in the city, with motorbuses.

1908   Union Station, a Beaux Arts masterpiece designed by Daniel H. Burnham, consolidates rail lines at the foot of Capitol Hill in Washington, D.C.

1909   Chicago architect Daniel Burnham writes *Plan of Chicago,* which will spearhead a movement in Chicago and other American cities to adopt master plans for future growth. Burnham's plan is far-reaching and ambitious. The forest preserves to the west and the lakefront parks and beaches are his legacy. "Make no little plans. They have no magic to stir men's blood," Burnham writes.

1910   Congress legislates against construction by any private builder of any edifice in Washington, D.C., higher than the Capitol.

San Francisco after the 1906 earthquake

About 1 million blacks live in northern cities. By 1940 this number has grown to 2.8 million. More than half the increase is due to migration from the South, where more than three-quarters of black Americans live.

The National Urban League is founded by African Americans to help end racial segregation and provide community services in housing, employment, education, and social welfare.

1911   The Triangle Shirtwaist Factory fire in New York City kills 146 women. The tragedy underscores the terrible working conditions of urban sweatshops and prompts both unionization and reform.

1913   The 792-story Woolworth Building becomes the world's tallest and largest office building when it opens.

Los Angeles becomes a boomtown at last when it is assured an adequate water supply by the opening of the Los Angeles Owens River Aqueduct. The project of superintendent and chief engineer of the Los Angeles waterworks William Mulholland, the pipeline can carry 26 million gallons of water a day from the Sierra Nevada.

Congress approves the building of a reservoir in Yosemite that will supply the city of San Francisco with water.

1914   The Great Migration of blacks out of the rural South to the cities of the North begins, Between 1914 and 1920 some 500,000 or more blacks go north for jobs in industry and better opportunities. During the 1920s 1.5 million more go north and the black populations of New York, Chicago, and Detroit double.

1915   New York City's Jewish population is 1.4 million, almost 30 percent of inhabitants.

Joseph Lee publishes *Play in Education*. Arguing for the constructive use of leisure, he promotes playgrounds in congested city neighborhoods.

1916   New York City passes the first U.S. urban zoning law; in ten years, almost 600 cities will have zoning codes.

Congress passes a Federal Roads Aid Act providing for matching federal aid to states for road improvement. U.S. involvement in World War I prevents any notable activity.

1917   A new aqueduct linking the upstate Catskill Mountain watershed to New York City provides the country's largest metropolis with 250 million gallons a day of pure water.

1920s   Al Capone becomes the boss of the Chicago bootleggers. Capone, who will come to dominate gambling, prostitution, and the underworld, becomes synonymous in the American mind with the bloody era of the Chicago gangster—an image of a violent urban landscape that will continue to plague the American imagination for decades to come.

The Harlem Renaissance is under way. For the next decade, Harlem is the "Negro Capital of the World." W.E.B. Du Bois and Marcus Garvey stimulate intellectual debate and book publishing; Ethel Waters and Duke Ellington introduce jazz; Zora Neale Hurston writes novels; and Langston Hughes writes poetry. Dance and jazz clubs make Harlem the place to be, even for wealthy whites from uptown.

1920   The U.S. population is now 106.5 million. For the first time urban residents (51.2 percent) outnumber rural (48.8 percent). Nevertheless, one-third of all Americans still live on farms. By 1970 only 1 in every 20 people will be farm dwellers.

1921   Congress passes a Federal Highway Act that creates the Bureau of Public Roads and proposes a system of highways that will connect all cities of more than 50,000 inhabitants.

1922   The Country Club Plaza in Kansas City is the country's first shopping center.

1924   Robert Moses, who serves the New York State council of parks, as New York City park commissioner, and head of the New York City tunnel authority, begins building a succession of urban and suburban bridges and parkways around the New York metropolitan area. His numerous projects include the Bronx-Whitestone, Henry Hudson, Throgs Neck, Triborough, and Verrazzano bridges, as well as the Bruckner, Brooklyn-Queens, Long Island, Major Deegan, and West Side highways.

The first "new town" is designed by Clarence Stein and Henry Wright. Their community, Radburn, New Jersey, is planned to protect its population from urban stresses such as air and noise pollution. Though the building of Radburn will be put off, Stein eventually designs other "planned communities" such as Chatham Village on the outskirts of Pittsburgh.

1927   The Holland Tunnel opens, linking Canal Street in Manhattan with Jersey City. Until now ferryboats have been the sole means of surface transport across the Hudson River.

1929   Chicago's gang warfare erupts in the brutal Saint Valentine's Day Massacre as mobsters "rub each other out" in a massive effort to control the illegal sale of liquor during Prohibition.

Sociologists Robert and Helen Lynd publish *Middletown: A Study in Contemporary American Society*; the book, which uses anthropological field methods to examine the lives of ordinary Americans in a midwestern city (Muncie, Indiana), influences a whole generation of sociologists.

On Wall Street in New York City, the stock market crashes, and the effects are felt in every small town across America.

A breadline during the Great Depression

1930   More than 23 million automobiles are registered in a population of 123 million people. By 1970 the number of automobiles has almost quadrupled—89 million—while the population has increased to 203 million.

1931   The George Washington Bridge is completed and spans the Hudson River between New York City and New Jersey. At 3,500 feet it is, at present, the world's longest suspension bridge.

    When the Empire State Building opens April 30, the 102-story skyscraper, designed by the firm of Shreve, Lamb, and Harmon, is the world's tallest building.

1933-   New Deal legislation and policies enhance urban life through the development of federally
1945   funded public-housing programs and the use of WPA workers to build and improve schools, hospitals, parks, and other civic structures, institutions, and services.

1933   New York's Tammany Hall, long a symbol of urban political graft and corruption, is finally quashed when Fiorello La Guardia is elected mayor of the city on a reform ticket. He will be mayor for 12 years.

    The federal Home Owners Loan Corporation is established to rescue homeowners from mortgage foreclosures. Ultimately it covers 1 million mortgages.

1934   The Federal Housing Administration insures home mortgages. This demonstration of support by the federal government results in lending institutions typically requiring only 10 percent of the purchase price as a down payment. Previously half the cost had been a usual payment.

1937   Greenbelt, Maryland, is incorporated. Planned and built by the federal government as a model community for families with modest incomes, it is a garden city, surrounded by a "belt" of parkland.

    The Golden Gate Bridge connecting San Francisco and Marin County is completed; until 1964, its 4,200 feet make it the world's longest suspension bridge.

1938   Chicago begins construction of a subway in the Loop.

1940   New York's Puerto Rican population is 61,000; by 1960 it will have increased to 613,000.

1942   As a wartime measure, Congress passes the Emergency Price Control Act. Its provisions allow for rent control in certain areas. The next year the act is extended to cover the entire country.

1944   The GI Bill of Rights (officially the Servicemen's Readjustment Act) helps provide cheap home mortgages to veterans, thus promoting the postwar housing boom and the growth of the suburbs.

1945   The end of World War II and the boom that follows sparks the move to the suburbs. The GI Bill and the Federal Housing Administration make buying a home more affordable for the middle- and working-class populations. Flight from the crowded urban centers begins. Later it will be described as white flight.

1947   Using mass production technology, William Levitt completes the first Levittown, in Hempstead, New York. Consisting of 17,000 landscaped homes for 80,000 people, Levittown offers young American families affordable housing. Levitt builds other Levittowns during the 1950s and 1960s. His methods will be copied by builders across the country.

1949   Congress states the need to fund slum clearance and affordable housing through an alliance of private initiative and public money in the Federal Housing Act.

1950s   Suburban land values skyrocket as middle-class white Americans leave deteriorating inner cities.

SUBURBS AND THE AMERICAN DREAM

Just as 19th-century advances in transportation had a profound impact on urban growth, the 20th-century advent of the "Automobile Age" has fueled the rise of the American suburb.

As early as the mid-19th century, more prosperous city dwellers built homes in outlying districts. The usual pattern saw the immigrant or working-class family advance up the socioeconomic ladder and abandon the old overcrowded neighborhoods.

At first families moved to more upscale areas of town, then to closer outlying districts still within the reach of public transportation, the "streetcar suburbs." But as train service improved and the automobile ceased to be a luxury item, the American dream of owning a house and having a better life fell within the reach of the middle class. Suburban growth accelerated in the 1920s, although it was slowed by the Great Depression. However, once World War II ended, several factors besides transportation led to suburban flight: the GI Bill for returning war veterans, which provided easy mortgage terms for buying houses; new generous credit and mortgage policies of the Federal Housing Administration; the development of prefabricated building techniques that made housing affordable for a greater number of people; federal and local tax breaks for homeowners and mortgage holders; and finally, a pattern of federal funding for national highway transportation that facilitated travel from suburb to city.

Planned suburban communities such as Shaker Heights outside of Cleveland—one of the more prosperous upper-middle-class suburbs—or the various Levittown developments sprang up from coast to coast. Levittown—the first preplanned "cookie-cutter community"—took full advantage of pre-fab housing and mass production techniques, enabling families with incomes only marginally over $5,000 to purchase a house with a down payment of only $100. The inexpensive houses were in pleasant, landscaped surroundings and fully equipped with the latest modern appliances.

Downtown became a place of work—a nine-to-five world. At five the commuter retreated back home to the suburbs, which became known as bedroom communities. For the most part the only people who stayed in the cities were those too poor to leave.

Criticism leveled at suburbia targets the isolation, homogeneity, and sterility. Yet until the 1980s suburbs remained the image of American prosperity, and realization of the American dream was to own one's own house. In that decade, social ills seen hitherto as city problems—drugs, rising crime rates, pollution, and violence—began to be suburban problems as well. Suburbanites were forced to reevaluate the notion that suburbs provided safe haven from late-20th-century ills.

Suburban communities also remain controversial in the national picture as having detached themselves from the urban areas that support them financially. Generally commuters pay little or no taxes to the cities where they work. The cities are faced with dwindling revenues to support increasing social, structural, and cultural services.

Suburbs are probably a permanent fixture in the American landscape, though their nature and role will probably change over the next few decades. Today most suburban families contain two working adults who usually both commute. The lack of neighborhoods and nearby family-support systems make issues of child care no longer a problem for just the poor of America. On the other hand, the advent of the computer age may put the problems of commuting to rest. The information superhighway and telecommuting might make trips downtown unnecessary. Then the suburbs may become self-contained communities that lack any ties to the cities that spawned them.

1955   A bus boycott by the black community of Montgomery, Alabama, draws nationwide attention to the indignities and loss of civil rights endured by African Americans in the South. In subsequent years Americans will hear much about Little Rock, Greensboro, Birmingham, Selma, and Philadelphia, Mississippi (see Chapter 4).

1956   The Interstate Highway Act funds an interstate highway system of more than 40,000 miles to connect major cities; inadvertently the law also spurs the growth of suburbs. Railroads and public transportation systems remain unsubsidized.

1959   In an attempt to halt the deterioration of the inner cities, Congress provides $650 million for slum clearance and rehabilitation.

URBAN RENEWAL

After World War II, patterns of urban growth slowed and shifted. Old industries moved out, choosing to locate new plants where labor and land were cheaper. The middle classes moved out, too, attracted by suburban land and lifestyles. The central cities were left with vacant factories and slum housing. Inner city residents as a whole were poorer, more likely to be minorities or recent immigrants, and less powerful than they had been before the war. The race riots of the 1960s only hastened all these processes. With declining tax bases, the cities were in trouble. By the 1970s, New York and Cleveland were bankrupt.

One solution was urban renewal, a program of federal money for slum clearance. But the program was fraught with mixed consequences. When decayed inner-city housing was bulldozed, the business community erected gleaming new office towers, but the poor and the powerless who had been displaced found themselves with even fewer options than before. Homelessness became a nationwide problem.

Another solution came from the private sector. Planners such as James L. Rouse and Robert Davis turned vacant factories into new marketplaces, with gourmet restaurants, specialty stores, and museums that attracted the middle classes back to the city—if not to live, at least to spend leisure time and money. Baltimore's Harborplace and New York City's South Street Seaport were, and are, great successes. So is Boston's Faneuil Hall, and at Museum Wharf the Children's Museum and Museum of Transportation transformed a run-down brick wharf warehouse in an industrial, largely unoccupied section of South Boston into a lively public space.

(continues)

URBAN RENEWAL (CONT.)

There was federal money to support these large ventures, which came to be known as adaptive use or reuse, and on a personal scale young men and women with college degrees and mortgage money began to renovate city brownstones that had been multifamily apartments back into the luxury homes they once were. Sections of major cities were gentrified, but again displacing the poor and the powerless.

Yet another solution came in the form of new towns, planned communities with their own industries, recreational centers, and community services. Reston, Virginia, and Columbia, Maryland, established in the 1960s, are both "exurbs" of Washington, D.C., and self-sufficient communities. Yet despite the innovations there seemed to be a sameness about all these "makeovers"—the same curving streets mimicking country lanes, the same fast-food franchises on the corners, the same retailers in enclosed malls that by this time had put most independent "downtown" shops out of business everywhere.

The story of American cities isn't over, but cities won't be what they were. In the 1990s, some sections of the old cities look pretty good, and they remain centers for business, shopping, and tourism. But as social critic Jane Jacobs has pointed out, the cities have lost their souls, and those who fled them sense an emptiness, too. Suburbanites long for the neighborliness, the sense of community, that was once part of the urban scene. The grandiose front porches of "tract mansions" built in former cow pastures are almost always vacant, and children don't play outside much anymore. As political scientist Robert D. Putnam has observed, more Americans are "bowling alone," a fact and a metaphor for the psychic isolation and decline of civic culture that have accompanied the decline of the city and city life.

1961   Social critic Jane Jacobs publishes *The Death and Life of American Cities*. She theorizes that cities were more livable when they were smaller and consisted of neighborhoods and that many sanitized efforts at urban renewal destroy the very soul the reforms wish to save.

Bay area voters approve a new regional transit system that will link communities on both sides of San Francisco Bay.

Hawaii institutes a comprehensive plan acknowledging that certain areas are reserved for agriculture and conservation as well as for urban development.

1963   At its completion, New York's Pan Am Building over Grand Central Terminal is the world's largest office building.

1964   President Johnson declares the "War on Poverty" in the United States. He names R. Sargent Shriver head of the Office of Economic Opportunity. Shriver directs programs like the Job Corps, Head Start, the Neighborhood Youth Corps, and other community-action programs, many of which are aimed at benefiting residents of the inner city.

The Verrazzano-Narrows Bridge is completed linking Staten Island with Brooklyn. At 4,260 feet it is the longest suspension bridge in the United States.

1965   A massive power failure on November 9 causes a blackout in seven states on the Eastern Seaboard. Parts of New York City, including Manhattan, do not have power until the next morning. All electric transit systems, suburban trains, streetlights, and elevators are shut down.

A race riot erupts in the Watts section of Los Angeles. During the "long hot summers" that follow, Detroit, Newark, and other cities succumb to racial violence that destroys lives and property (see Chapter 4).

The Department of Housing the Urban Development is established to administer programs providing assistance for housing and the development of the nation's communities. Robert Weaver, the first African American to serve in the cabinet, is named secretary.

Secretaries of Housing and Urban Development

Secretary	President	Year Appointed	Secretary	President	Year Appointed
Robert C. Weaver	Johnson, L. B.	1966	Patricia Roberts Harris	Carter	1977
Robert C. Wood	Johnson, L. B.	1969	Moon Landrieu	Carter	1979
George W. Romney	Nixon	1969	Samuel R. Pierce, Jr.	Reagan	1981
James T. Lynn	Nixon	1973	Jack F. Kemp	Bush	1989
	Ford	1974	Henry G. Cisneros	Clinton	1993
Carla Anderson Hills	Ford	1975	Andrew Cuomo	Clinton	1997

1966   A model cities program, passed by Congress, encourages rehabilitation of slums and promotes metropolitan planning in "model" or demonstration cities.

1967   Carl Stokes in Cleveland and Richard Hatcher in Indianapolis are the first blacks elected mayor of major cities.

1970   There are 2.3 million blacks and Puerto Ricans in New York City.

1972   Congress earmarks $18 billion in assistance grants to municipalities to build sewage treatment plants.

1975   New York City teeters on the brink of bankruptcy until it receives a bailout loan from the federal government. The city's financial woes stem partially from a shrinking tax base as white suburban flight continues, coupled with a loss of manufacturing jobs and light industry.

Mid-1970s   Increasing numbers of homeless people, often carrying all their possessions in bundles or shopping carts, begin to be noticeable in public urban places; by the mid-1980s the problem will reach crisis proportions.

1976   With the reopening of Boston's Quincy Market, urban developer James Rouse brings the idea of the urban mall to the downtowns of various cities. He designs malls for downtown Richmond, Baltimore's Harborplace, and New York City's South Street Seaport. The urban malls revitalize areas that had deteriorated because of shifts in demographics and business locations.

The D.C. Metro opens; it is the largest urban public works project ever undertaken as a single unified design. Costing more than $8 billion when it opens, with extensions to come, it has an 80 percent federal subsidy. In its first five years it will generate more than $1 billion in private real estate development around Metro stations, changing the pattern of urban growth.

1977   President Jimmy Carter visits the impoverished South Bronx in New York City and leaves promising aid for urban renewal. A $500 million program is enacted but takes years to be put into effect.

1980   Data from the U.S. Census shows that for the first time in the 20th century the rural population growth almost matches that of urban areas. Rural population, however, includes outer suburban areas and small towns on the distant periphery of sprawling metropolitan areas.

New York City experiences an 11-day transit strike. New Yorkers end up walking, biking, or sharing cabs to get to work.

Wisconsin senator Gaylord Nelson reports that between 1945 and 1980, 75 percent of government funding for transportation went to highways, while just 1 percent was put aside for public transportation. Thus urban development is sacrificed for the "American dream" of life in the suburbs.

1985   It is estimated by the federal government that between 250,000 to 300,000 people are homeless, most of them in cities.

1988   The federal government estimates that 60,000 family members are using emergency shelters for the urban homeless.

1989   California's strict air-pollution standards, a consequence of notorious, unfit-to-breathe air, are adopted by a number of other states. The laws will eventually improve urban air quality in areas affected.

The U.S. Department of Education estimates that 273,000 children are homeless. The General Accounting Office puts the number at 310,000.

The worst earthquake since 1906 strikes San Francisco on October 17 in the middle of the World Series. Bridges buckle, fires blaze, and 90 people die.

As the decade ends, Miami has a Hispanic majority.

1990   New York City subways have undergone a facelift. Though fares rise once again, the trains are more efficient and without graffiti, and most of the cars are air-conditioned.

During the 1990 census, workers survey more than 39,000 locations where they know homeless persons can be found. The count turns up almost 460,000 people. The accuracy of these figures is open to debate.

The 900,000 Puerto Ricans in New York City constitute about 11 percent of the population.

Los Angeles is the city with the largest Mexican population outside of Mexico City.

1992   Islamic terrorists successfully detonate a bomb at the World Trade Center in New York on February 26. Six people die and hundreds are injured in the blast; the terrorist group is quickly apprehended, but tensions of living and working in the crowded metropolis increase.

When an all-white jury acquits the four white policemen accused of beating Rodney King, a black man, Los Angeles erupts in a race riot that leaves 52 dead and up to $1 billion in destroyed property. Americans despair that so little progress has been made since the Watts riots of 1965.

1995   The Alfred P. Murrah Building in Oklahoma City is destroyed in a bomb blast shortly after 9:00 A.M. on April 19. The explosion kills at least 167 people, including many of the children in a day-care center housed in the federal office building. Timothy McVeigh, a disgruntled ex-marine sympathetic with right-wing militia groups that advocate few governmental controls, is tried and convicted of planting the car bomb.

SIGNIFICANT EVENTS IN THE RISE AND FALL OF RURAL AMERICA

Thomas Jefferson's vision of the new nation as a land of independent, yeoman farmers was reality in his day, and even as late as the end of the 19th century, most Americans made their livelihood in agriculture. Advances in transportation and technology in the 19th and 20th centuries enabled farmers to cultivate large quantities of land with enormous productivity. Cycles of national economic boom and depression coupled with America's dependence on international markets for its massive agricultural output have affected the nature as well as the growth of agriculture. Although a very small percentage of Americans farm today, agriculture remains an important and vital part of the national economy.

c. 1612   John Rolfe introduces the cultivation of tobacco at Jamestown, and by 1615 it is the cash crop of the Virginia colony.

1615   The Virginia Company, which owns all the land, allows settlers to become tenants on company property.

1621   Squanto, a Patuxet Indian who had been kidnapped and lived in England for a few years, gives the Pilgrims seed corn and teaches them native planting practices. Corn, or maize, becomes a principal grain in New England; wheat and rye are also successful.

1690s   German immigrant farmers settle in Pennsylvania because of the colony's promise of religious tolerance. While the English settlers girdle trees to kill them, then farm among the stumps, the Germans, with their superior farming technology—including heavy draft horses that can pull plows and weighty loads—clear their land completely and plow the soil deeply. They choose to plant wheat, and they house their livestock in barns, which they construct even before they build their own houses. The English, on the other hand, let their stock forage. The Germans prove to be highly successful farmers and eventually bring their superior agricultural practices to Maryland, western Virginia, and other colonies.

1693   Rice cultivation is introduced in South Carolina. It is well suited to the colony's freshwater swamps and sluggish rivers near the sea, and it quickly becomes a staple crop. By 1730 South Carolina rice is called the best in the world.

1745   Indigo cultivation, introduced to South Carolina a few years earlier by Elizabeth (Eliza) Lucas Pickney, reaches a stage of profitable production, stimulating a dye-stuffs industry. Indigo becomes one of the colony's major export crops, long before cotton, which is difficult to harvest and process until the invention of the cotton gin.

1785   The Land Ordinance provides for the survey and sale of public lands at auction in lots of 640 acres at a cash price of at least $1 per acre. Few would-be settlers have the money to take advantage of this early land act.

1786-   In Shays's Rebellion, Massachusetts farmers led by Revolutionary War veteran Daniel Shays
1787   protest farm and home foreclosures during the post–Revolutionary War depression.

1790   Almost all Americans live in rural areas. Some are subsistence farmers and some are engaged in food production.

1793   Eli Whitney invents the cotton gin, and cotton production soon soars. U.S. cotton production rises from 4,000 bales in 1791 to 73,000 bales in 1800. A bale weighs about 500 pounds. Cotton's success also dooms the slavery system to success.

1794   In the Whiskey Rebellion, frontier farmers protest an excise tax on whiskey, which is a medium of exchange in western Pennsylvania—grain is easier to transport in liquid form.

1796   Congress passes a Public Land Act authorizing the sale of U.S. government lands in minimum lots of 640 acres for $2 per acre.

1800   The Land Ordinance of 1785 is amended by a new congressional bill that permits the sale of 320-acre plots at $2 per acre with a down payment of one-fourth and the balance to be paid in three annual installments. Finally land sales pick up.

1820   Congress passes another land act providing for the sale of 80-acre plots of public land at $1.25 an acre in cash. Farmers who have bought land under other acts are enraged, especially those in debt from earlier purchases at higher rates.

1831   Cyrus McCormick demonstrates his reaper, and the invention is patented in 1834. The reaper harvests four times faster than a man with a scythe, and wheat production expands rapidly.

1833   Edmund Ruffin founds the *Farmers' Register*. In other publications he promotes the application of marl, deeper plowing, and animal husbandry.

1837   John Deere invents a steel, one-piece plow and moldboard, which is capable of cutting through the roots of prairie grass in the Midwest and Great Plains and reduces the labor of plowing by half. Again acreage in production is expanded,

1847 Mormons begin farming in Utah, eventually creating communal farmlands with satellite villages and introducing dams and irrigation techniques to make crops grow in desert soil.

1860 The nation now has 2,044,000 farms. A farmer's work can support himself and three other people. In 1970 a farmer can support himself and 47 others.

1862 The Homestead Act offers 160 acres of public domain lands to any head of household who registers the claim, makes some improvement on the land within six months, and lives on it for five years. Unfortunately, much of the West is so arid that often 160 acres is not enough land for viable agriculture. Much of the land falls into the hands of speculators.

The Morrill Act authorizes grants of land to support state schools teaching agriculture or the mechanical arts.

The Department of Agriculture is established. Its head becomes a cabinet member in 1889.

Secretaries of Agriculture

Secretary	President	Year Appointed	Secretary	President	Year Appointed
Norman J. Coleman	Cleveland	1889	Charles F. Brannon	Truman	1948
Jeremiah M. Rusk	Harrison, B.	1889	Ezra Taft Benson	Eisenhower	1953
J. Sterling Morton	Cleveland	1893	Orville L. Freeman	Kennedy	1961
James Wilson	McKinley	1897		Johnson, L. B.	1961
	Roosevelt, T.	1901	Clifford M. Hardin	Nixon	1969
	Taft	1909	Earl L. Butz	Nixon	1971
David F. Houston	Wilson	1913		Ford	1974
Edwin T. Meredith	Wilson	1920	John A. Knebel	Ford	1976
Henry C. Wallace	Harding	1921	Bob Bergland	Carter	1977
	Coolidge	1923	John R. Block	Reagan	1981
Howard M. Gore	Coolidge	1924	Richard E. Lyng	Reagan	1986
William M. Jardine	Coolidge	1925	Clayton K. Yeutter	Bush	1989
Henry A. Wallace	Roosevelt, F. D.	1933	Edward Madigan	Bush	1991
Claude R. Wickard	Roosevelt, F. D.	1940	Mike Espy	Clinton	1993
Clinton P. Anderson	Truman	1945	Dan Glickman	Clinton	1995

1867 The percentage of Americans working on farms has risen to more than 50 percent.

Oliver H. Kelley founds the National Grange of the Patrons of Husbandry (*grange* is an outdated name for a barn). At first apolitical, the Grange's mission is educational and social, but after the Panic of 1873 local granges become political forums. Eventually the Grange will become a force in agricultural politics, centering around issues involving equitable freight rates and taxation. The Grange also sets up cooperative stores, grain elevators, and mills.

1873 The depression that follows the panic this year forces many southern farmers, black and white, into sharecropping.

Springfield, Illinois, is the site of a farmers' convention that attacks the power of monopolies, in particular railroads, as "detrimental to the public prosperity, corrupting in their management, and dangerous to republican institutions."

1874 Several states pass so-called Granger Laws, establishing maximum shipping rates railroads can change. Railroads have long charged high and discriminatory rates, charging farmers more to ship crops a short distance than for the long hauls industrial shippers required.

1876 The Grange lobbies for protection from the railroads, for better schools, and for regulation of grain elevators.

1880   About 80 percent of the land in black belt states—Mississippi, Georgia, and Alabama—has been divided into family farms, and almost 75 percent of black southerners are sharecroppers.

1887   The Hatch Act provides federal funds for state agricultural experimental stations.

1889   A cycle of poverty locked in by the crop-lien system continues to spark agrarian protest as several regional Farmers' Alliances unite to form the National Farmers' Alliance and Industrial Union. A parallel organization is the National Colored Farmers' Alliance and Cooperative Union. Like the Grange, the Alliance protests large combinations of industry and banks that have the power to dictate prices and interest rates. It also establishes cooperative cotton gins, flour mills, and grain elevators.

1890   Two-thirds of all Americans still live in rural communities; just 50 years earlier 90 percent of the population were farm dwellers.

Nearly one-half of southern farmers are sharecroppers.

"Pitchfork Ben" Tillman, supported by the Farmers' Alliance, is elected governor of South Carolina. He promotes agricultural education and railroad regulation. In 1894, he is elected to the U.S. Senate, where he continues to champion the interest of the farmer.

1891   Tom Watson is elected to the U.S. House of Representatives, where he promotes populism and rural free delivery.

1892   The Populist party unites farmer and labor organizations, calling for the free coinage of silver, the abolition of national banks, government ownership of railroads, a maximum workday, and immigration restriction. Its presidential candidate, James B. Weaver, polls more than 1 million votes. The party collapses after the 1896 election, in which the Democrats also nominate the Populist candidate, William Jennings Bryan, and steal many Populist issues.

The boll weevil appears in Texas. It annually destroys about 8 percent of the total cotton crop resulting in a $200–300 million loss.

The first gasoline engine tractor makes its appearance in South Dakota. It weighs more than 9,000 pounds.

1901   About 25–35 percent of U.S. agricultural produce is exported. These figures fall with rapid population growth and increasing urbanization.

1909   The Enlarged Homestead Act increases maximum permissible homesteads to 320 acres in cattle-raising areas of the West. The maximum is increased again in 1916 to 640 acres for grazing and forage land not suitable for crops unless irrigated.

1914   The Smith-Lever Act provides for agricultural extension services.

1916   Congress passes the Federal Farm Loan Act, which permits the establishment of farm loan banks as well as a Federal Farm Loan Board. This legislation eases the way for farmers to obtain credit to improve their farms with machinery and make additional land purchases.

1920-   Farm acreage at the beginning of this period equals 959 million acres. In 1969 farmland
1969   accounts for 1,063 million acres. From 1915 to 1945 almost 38 million acres of public and private lands are withdrawn from potential agricultural use and set aside as national forests, national parks, roadways, and urban areas.

1920s   Chemical pesticides are introduced to American agriculture.

1930   Thirty million Americans, about one-quarter of the population, still live and work on farms. In 1890 25 million, 40 percent of the population, made farms their homes and workplaces.

1932   Farm prices this year are only 40 percent of what they were in 1929. Wheat sells for less than 38 cents per bushel; oats 16 cents per bushel; cotton a mere 6.5 cents a pound; and wool goes for 8.6 cents a pound.

1933   The Tennessee Valley Authority is established. By controlling floods in the region and harnessing electric power, as well as through programs reclaiming land and preventing erosion, it will improve the area's agriculture.

1933   Congress passes the Agricultural Adjustment Act, establishing an Agricultural Adjustment Administration (AAA) as part of the Department of Agriculture. The idea is to decrease the amount of land under cultivation.

The Commodity Credit Corporation is created by Congress within the Department of Agriculture to buy farm surpluses and to process subsidies due farmers for withholding acreage from production.

The Farm Credit Administration is created to consolidate farm-credit agencies. Nevertheless the year sees 1 million farm families receive direct government aid.

1934   Congress legislates the Farm Mortgage Financing Act, establishing the Federal Farm Mortgage Corporation to assist farmers in refinancing their mortgages and avoid foreclosures.

A Crop Loan Act sanctions loans to farmers to assist them in production and harvesting.

Mid-1930s   Dust storms ravage the western states. A direct result of farming methods that stripped the land of vegetation, overproduction, especially during the First World War, and several seasons of severe drought, these storms, with clouds of dust so thick day turns into night, trigger the great trek of migrants from the Dust Bowl. Already poverty-stricken by the Great Depression, 350,000 farmers, behind in their mortgages and with their farms near foreclosure, pick up stakes and move west by the end of the decade.

1935   Only 12.6 percent of rural America has electric service. President Franklin Roosevelt establishes the Rural Electrification Administration by executive order. The REA will underwrite and extend loans to rural electric cooperatives for the express purpose of bringing electrical power to rural America.

The number of farms reaches 6.812 million and the farm population is 32,161 million. This is the high point of farming; after this year numbers of farms and farmers decline steadily.

Direct payments of $573 million are made by the federal government to farmers who are participating in various farm programs.

1940s   DDT becomes available in the United States. It is hailed as a godsend for its spectacular success in controlling insects. Only after the research of Rachel Carson and the publication of her book *The Silent Spring*, in 1962, are the perils of DDT recognized.

1945   More than 24 million people depend on the land for their livelihood.

1950   Seventy-seven percent of families living in rural America now have electricity. Six years later this figure jumps to 96 percent.

1950-
1970   Millions of bushels of grain are stockpiled and politicians question both the costs of storage and continued support payments to farmers. The Food for Peace program, passed in 1961, helps reduce stockpiles and storage costs. Rising demands for exports helps hold support payments down.

1954   The Watershed and Flood Protection Act is passed to protect U.S. farmers from the effects of soil erosion.

1955   The National Farmer's Organization (NFO) is established by disgruntled farmers from Iowa and Missouri. They hope to initiate bargaining to support the prices of stock, grain, and milk.

1956   At the instigation of President Dwight Eisenhower and Secretary of Agriculture Ezra Taft Benson, Congress authorizes a new soil-bank program, encouraging farmers to refrain from planting their land to conserve the land itself and to decrease production.

1960   Only 8 percent of U.S. workers are farm laborers, down from 12 percent in 1950.

1962   César Chávez organizes the National Farm Workers Association, to represent and help the impoverished migrant farmworkers.

1964   U.S. farmers now number only 12.9 million.

1965 President Johnson's plans to end poverty in the United States lead to a $1.4 billion program of federal and state aid to help Appalachia, one of the poorest rural regions of the country.

1968 Only 5 percent of the workforce are farm laborers.

1969 U.S. farms now number just 2.73 million, with a population of 10.3 million.

1970 Farm labor drops to just 5 percent of the workforce or almost 10 million people. One U.S. farm laborer can produce enough food for 47 people.

1985 An $87 billion farm bill, in the midst of an agricultural depression, brings temporary stability to beleaguered farmers.

1986 Many midwestern farms suffer foreclosure in an extended agricultural depression following inflated land values and extensive borrowing.

1990 Crop support payments are frozen in an attempt to get control of the federal budget deficit.

1995 Agricultural funding is reduced by $5.8 billion from the previous fiscal year.

1996 A revolutionary farm bill aims at weaning farmers from federal subsidies and giving them opportunities for expansion. Supports are scheduled for elimination by 2002.

MAJOR LEGISLATIVE ACTS AFFECTING CITIES

1921 Federal Highway Act. This coordinates state highway systems in an effort to create a national system. The act creates the Bureau of Public Roads. This is the first of several highway acts that will indirectly lead to the proliferation of suburbs, the decline of cities, and major population shifts among various metropolitan areas nationwide.

1933–1940 New Deal legislation. A series of laws, including creation of the Civil Works Administration (CWA) in 1933 and the Works Progress Administration (WPA) in 1935, will enhance urban life through the development of federally funded public works programs that benefit urban areas through housing construction, street paving, school improvement, and the construction of hospitals and other civic structures, institutions, and services. The Federal Housing Administration (FHA) in 1934 insures loans for construction and improvements.

1942 Emergency Price Control Act. Enacted by the federal government to control wartime inflation, this has a twofold effect on cities. Middle-class housing remains affordable, but low rents are detrimental to new rental-housing starts.

1944 Federal Highway Act lays the foundation for the Interstate Highway System. Enacted to strengthen America's infrastructure and provide fast movement of goods and possibly troops during wartime, this legislation authorizes funding for the creation of the interstate highway system that will be a potent force in postwar suburbanization. Full-scale funding, and therefore no construction, does not occur until 1956.

GI Bill of Rights (Servicemen's Readjustment Act). By making homes more affordable to war veterans, this legislation indirectly contributes to postwar flight to the suburbs.

1949 Federal Housing Act. Sponsored by Republican senator Robert Taft of Ohio, this provides funding for urban renewal through slum cleanup and the building of low-cost public housing.

1956 Interstate Highway Act. This funds a 42,500-mile system of limited access highways linking all major cities. Rail and public transportation systems remain unsubsidized.

1959 Housing Act. Congress legislates that $650 million out of this $1 billion housing bill should be spent for urban housing renewal and rehabilitation.

SUPREME COURT DECISIONS AFFECTING CITIES AND FARM AREAS

1877   *Munn v. Illinois.* The Court upholds an Illinois law establishing maximum rates for storing grains, one of the so-called Granger Laws enacted by state legislatures in the Midwest at the insistence of the Grange. The decision establishes the constitutional principle of public regulation of private business involved in serving the public interest.

1911   *United States v. Grimaud.* This states that Congress has the right to confer administrative power on the secretary of agriculture to establish rules and regulations on the use of federal lands.

1926   *Village of Euclid v. Ambler Realty Company.* The Court upholds municipal zoning ordinances and the right of communities to designate land for business, industrial, and residential purposes.

1934   *Nebbia v. New York.* The Court justifies state law in setting minimum prices in the dairy industry.

1942   *Wickard v. Filburn.* The Court upholds the Second Agricultural Adjustment Act of 1938. A farmer claimed that wheat grown but not brought to market was not subject to a penalty for overproduction since it was never sold. The Court rules against the farmer and for the New Deal legislation setting planting limits.

1944   *Bowles v. Willingham.* The Court upholds the right of the OPA (Office of Price Administration) to impose rent controls.

1962   *Baker v. Carr.* The Court rules that arbitrarily drawn electoral districts violate constitutional rights and voters have the right to challenge.

1964   *Wesberry v. Sanders.* The Court rules that Congressional districts must adhere to the "one person, one vote" test laid down in *Gray v. Sanders.* The cycle is completed four months later in *Reynolds v. Sims* when the Court rules that both houses of state legislatures must be based on population.

Reynolds v. Sims. In a ruling that will eclipse the disproportionate power of rural areas, long overrepresented in legislative districts, the Court invokes the "one person, one vote" principle to support its decision that both houses of a state legislature must be apportioned on the basis of population. As a consequence of massive redistricting throughout the 50 states, urban districts, long underrepresented, become more powerful.

1980   *City of Mobile v. Bolden.* The Court rules that election of city council members by voters at large does not violate the Fourteenth and Fifteenth amendments.

1981   *Poletown Neighborhood Council v. Detroit.* The Court expands the power of eminent domain—the authority of government to appropriate private property for public purposes.

1984   *Hawaii Housing Authority v. Midkiff.* The Court upholds Hawaii's right to take private property for private use. The ruling gives great latitude to the condemnation power of the state.

SIGNIFICANT PEOPLE IN THE DEVELOPMENT OF AMERICAN CITIES AND AGRICULTURE

Addams, Jane (1860–1935).   A social reformer, Addams was born into comfortable circumstances and became distressed over the plight of the urban poor. Inspired by a visit to Toynbee Hall, a London settlement house, in 1889 she founded Hull-House in Chicago with the help of

Ellen Gates Starr. Hull-House became a mecca for immigrants. There Addams instituted a series of community services, running the gamut from language courses to craft training to child care. She fought for fair labor practices and for general social-welfare programs.

Astor, John Jacob (1763–1848). Astor invested money made in the fur trade in real estate, much of it in Manhattan. At his death he was the wealthiest man in America, and one of his most important contributions to New York City was the $350,000 bequest that helped establish the famous New York Public Library (originally the Astor Library).

Burnham, Daniel H. (1846–1912). Architect Burnham was one of the founders of the Chicago School and pioneered new skyscraper designs, including New York's Flatiron Building. He was a staunch advocate of urban planning and a founder of the "City Beautiful" movement.

Capone, Alfonse ("Al") (1899–1947). This Italian-American gangster flourished in Chicago during the bootleg years of the 1920s.

Cooper, Peter (1791–1883). Born in New York City, Cooper was a typical self-made man of his era, who prospered financially through hard work in various trades and through farseeing investments in new technology—such as the laying of the first transatlantic cable. He was active in civic matters, and always keeping in mind his own lack of formal education, he founded New York's Cooper Union in 1859 to provide the opportunity for adult education in art and technical subjects.

Daley, Richard J. (1902–1976). The Chicago-born politician was chairman of the Cook County Democratic party, a powerful political machine. As Chicago's mayor for 20 years, he forged alliances with industry and unions that enabled Chicago to have an urban renaissance while many other northern industrial cities were declining. The violent confrontations between Chicago police and anti–Vietnam War demonstrators at the 1968 Democratic National Convention hurt Daley's reputation nationally. Daley's son, also Richard Daley, served as mayor of Chicago in the 1990s.

Edison, Thomas Alva (1847–1931). Edison invented and patented many devices, but it was his invention of the electric lightbulb in 1879 that revolutionized city life. Not only could dim interiors be lit without dangerous, fuel-burning candles, oil lamps, or gaslights, but the city streets, once problems with mass generation of electrical energy were solved, became bright and safer at night, and urban life was able to continue full-swing 24 hours a day.

Feinstein, Dianne (1933–). Active in Democratic politics from an early age, Feinstein served as a city and county supervisor in San Francisco from 1970 to 1978. When the mayor and supervisor were shot, Feinstein was selected by the remaining supervisors to fill out the term as mayor, and she was subsequently elected in her own right, serving for 10 years. In 1993 she was elected U.S. senator from California.

Franklin, Benjamin (1706–1790). A printer, writer, scientist, and statesman, Franklin was born in Boston and moved to Philadelphia seeking his fortune as a printer and publisher of newspapers. His many projects included plans to pave, clean, light, and police the streets of colonial Philadelphia. He was instrumental in supporting the volunteer fire companies that protected American cities until well into the 19th century.

La Guardia, Fiorello (1882–1947). One of New York City's best-loved mayors, La Guardia served three terms (1934–1945) and was instrumental in instituting not only political reform—he was one of the forces in the final downfall of New York's corrupt Democratic political machine, Tammany Hall—but also housing and welfare reform.

Lease, Mary Elizabeth (1853–1933).   A teacher who moved to Kansas after the Civil War, Lease became an agrarian activist and leader of the grass-roots Populist movement. She gained fame as a flamboyant orator and is best known for urging farmers to "raise less corn and more hell."

Levitt, William J. (1907–1994).   A New York–born builder and developer, Levitt gained experience with mass-produced residences during World War II when his family firm, Levitt and Sons, built housing for the U.S. Navy. He adapted his construction know-how to civilian life after the war when he developed and built his first Levittown in Long Island, 30 miles east of New York City.

Minuit, Peter (1580?–1638).   Minuet was the first leader of New Amsterdam, later to become New York. He purchased Manhattan from the Canarsie Indians in 1626.

Moses, Robert (1889–1981).   As New York City Parks commissioner (1934–1960) as well as the head of the city's Triborough Bridge and Tunnel authorities, Moses single-handedly and irrevocably altered the metropolitan area by supervising the building of most of its major highways, constructing parks and playgrounds, and erecting many bridges. He favored private over public transportation and was criticized for paving over neighborhoods with miles of highway.

Mulholland, William (1855–1935).   Irish-born Mulholland was a hydraulic engineer who became the superintendent and chief engineer of the Los Angeles waterworks in 1886. He devised the plans for and oversaw the construction of the Los Angeles aqueduct that brought the city a water supply from the Sierra Nevada, 250 miles away.

Nast, Thomas (1840–1902).   A German American who migrated to New York with his family at age five, Nast pioneered the political cartoon. In 1861 he began working for *Harper's Weekly*. His caricatures attacking New York's Tweed Ring were instrumental in unseating "Boss Tweed" and shaking down Tammany Hall.

Olmsted, Frederick Law (1822–1903).   A landscape architect, Olmsted, with Calvert Vaux, won a competition for the design of Central Park in New York City. They fashioned a pastoral rambling park out of what was then wilderness inhabited by squatters. He envisioned preserving natural habitats within urban areas, and after completing work on Central Park he went on to design major parks in Boston, Chicago, and Montreal.

Otis, Elisha Graves (1811–1861).   A native Vermonter, Otis was employed as a master mechanic for a firm in Yonkers, New York, when he developed the first elevator: a way of hauling supplies and workmen from one floor of a building to another. He eventually went on to patent his steam elevator. His sons continued his business after his death.

Pendergast, Thomas J. (1872–1945).   Pendergast created a powerful political machine in Missouri after he became head of the Kansas City Democrats in 1916. In control for 25 years, he gave Harry Truman his start in politics. He was indicted by the U.S. government for tax evasion and went to prison in 1939.

Riis, Jacob (1849–1914).   As a police reporter for the *New York Evening Sun*, this Danish-American photojournalist and social reformer documented life in the city slums. His powerful photographs exposed the wretched conditions of the urban immigrant, and his book *How the Other Half Lives* (1890) spurred then–New York police commissioner Theodore Roosevelt to support the tenement-reform movement.

Roebling, John Augustus (1806–1869).   Considered the greatest American bridge builder of the 19th century, Roebling emigrated from his native Germany when he was 25 years old and settled in Pittsburgh. He constructed canals and aqueducts, and his innovative use of wire rope facilitated all his engineering endeavors. After earlier successful bridge-building ventures, he was appointed chief engineer to oversee construction of New York's Brooklyn Bridge. He died of tetanus after being injured while working on the project, and his son, Washington Augustus Roebling, completed the bridge.

Rouse, James L. (1914–1996).   Rouse developed planned cities, urban marketplaces, and shopping centers. In 1960 he began building Columbia, Maryland; the city had a population of 56,000 by 1981. In the 1970s he designed the first of his "festival marketplaces" in Boston. He also helped found the Enterprise Foundation, which encouraged the building of affordable urban housing.

Stuyvesant, Peter (?1610–1672).   Stuyvesant became governor of the Dutch colony of New Netherland in 1647. He was a stern leader and had a contentious relationship with colonists living in New Amsterdam. Eventually the burghers of New Amsterdam won the right to self-municipal government, and Stuyvesant had to bargain with the young city on matters of taxes and defense.

Sullivan, Louis H. (1856–1924).   Boston-born Sullivan was the leading exponent of the Chicago School of architecture. The main tenet of his design philosophy was "Form follows function." One of the fathers of the contemporary skyscraper, Sullivan designed and realized more than 100 buildings over the course of his career. Among his most famous are the Chicago Stock Exchange (1886–1889) and the Wainwright Building in Saint Louis (1890–1891). His most famous student was Frank Lloyd Wright.

Tillman, Benjamin (1847–1918).   In South Carolina, Tillman became the political leader of backcountry whites. As governor of the state (1890–1894), he promoted agricultural education and regulation of railroads. While serving as a Democratic senator (1895–1918), he allied himself with Populists and strongly opposed President Grover Cleveland. He earned the name "Pitchfork Ben" because he once threatened to stick a pitchfork into the president.

Tweed, William Marcy ("Boss") (1823–1878).   Tweed was a major power in New York City's Tammany Hall Democratic organization. His corruption was eventually exposed through the efforts of reformer-cartoonist Thomas Nast. Tweed was arrested and convicted of graft and corruption. He skipped bail and fled to Spain, where he was finally extradited back to the United States. He died in prison.

Wright, Frank Lloyd (1869–1959).   Wright studied civil engineering but began his career by working for the eminent Chicago architect Louis Sullivan. After parting from Sullivan, he gained notice for his "prairie houses" with low, horizontal lines and projecting eaves. An innovative and influential designer, Wright advocated open planning in buildings and was a pioneer in textile-block slab construction.

ADDITIONAL SOURCES OF INFORMATION

Barton, Josef J. *Peasants and Strangers: Italians, Rumanians, and Slovaks in an American City, 1890–1950.* Harvard University Press, 1975.

Blumin, Stuart. *The Emergence of the Middle Class: Social Experience in the American City, 1760–1900.* Cambridge University Press, 1989.

Bremner, Robert H. *From the Depths: The Discovery of Poverty in the United States.* New York University Press, 1956.

Bridges, Amy. *A City in the Republic: Antebellum New York and the Origins of Machine Politics.* Cambridge University Press, 1984.

Gans, Herbert. *The Levittowners: Ways of Life and Politics in a New York Suburban Community.* Columbia University Press, 1967.

Jackson, Kenneth. *Crabgrass Frontier.* Oxford University Press, 1985.

Lynd, Robert, and Helen Lynd. *Middletown: A Study in American Culture.* Harcourt, Brace & World, 1929.

Osofsky, Gilbert. *Harlem: The Making of a Ghetto, 1890–1930.* Harper & Row, 1966.

Schiesl, Martin J. *The Politics of Efficiency: Municipal Administration and Reform in America, 1880–1920.* University of California Press, 1977.

Warner, Sam B., Jr. *Streetcar Suburb: The Process of Growth in Boston, 1870–1900.* Harvard University Press, 1962.

Warner, Sam B., Jr. *The Urban Wilderness: A History of the American City.* Harper & Row, 1972.

Wilentz, Sean. *Chants Democratic: New York City and the Rise of the American Working Class, 1788–1850.* Oxford University Press, 1983.

8

Foreign Affairs

SIGNIFICANT EVENTS IN FOREIGN AFFAIRS

According to our Constitution, foreign affairs are the joint responsibility of the president and Congress. Congress has the power to collect taxes and appropriate funds for defense, to raise and support an army and navy, to provide for the militia, to regulate commerce with foreign nations and Indian tribes, and to declare war. But the president is commander in chief. He also negotiates treaties (which the Senate must confirm), appoints ambassadors (which again the Senate must confirm), and receives ambassadors, so having the power to recognize or refuse to recognize other governments. The courts have the power to interpret treaties, but do not usually do so. In essence, the president is the leader in foreign affairs, and the State Department is expected to carry out policies established in the Oval Office.

Some presidents, such as Theodore Roosevelt and Woodrow Wilson, have been foreign policy activists. Others have had foreign involvement thrust upon them, such as John Adams and William McKinley. And some presidents, including Wilson and both Roosevelts as well as John Kennedy, have emerged as world leaders.

The Federalist Era: Asserting Independence

1783   The Treaty of Paris, which formally ends the Revolutionary War, is signed by Great Britain, France, and the United States. It recognizes the independence of the United States and settles issues relating to boundaries, debts, confiscated property, and fishing rights.

   While the United States is primarily preoccupied with nation-building, it establishes relations with France, Britain, Spain, the Netherlands, and Russia, the dominant and most important trading nations in Europe.

1789   President George Washington's first appointment is Thomas Jefferson, who becomes the new nation's first secretary of state and the highest ranking cabinet member.

1793   The French Revolution takes a violent turn and divided American opinion offers President Washington his administration's first serious foreign policy challenge. Washington issues a proclamation of neutrality, but Citizen Genêt (Edmond Charles), minister of the French Republic, tours the United States to organize American expeditions against Spain and Britain. Exasperated, Washington demands Genêt's recall, but by then the French Revolution has taken yet another turn and new French ministers arrive to arrest Genêt. Washington refuses to extradite Genêt (knowing he will be guillotined). Genêt becomes an American citizen and marries the daughter of New York governor George Clinton.

1794   Jay's Treaty, negotiated by Chief Justice John Jay, is signed; the British agree to withdraw troops from the Northwest Territory in return for a renewed commitment by the United States that debts incurred before the Revolution will be paid.

1795   Pinckney's Treaty with Spain accepts the 31st parallel as the northern boundary of Spanish Florida and grants Americans free navigation of the Mississippi and the right of deposit at New Orleans.

1796   In his farewell address, President Washington argues for isolationism when he warns: "It is our true policy to steer clear of permanent alliances with any portion of the foreign world."

1798   Revelation of the XYZ Affair, a diplomatic scandal in which the French attempt to bribe American commissioners, angers Americans.

1798-1800 Tensions with France increase to the point that the period is described as an undeclared war. The Federalists impose severe restrictions on French sympathizers in the Alien and Sedition Acts. In 1800 a Convention formally releases the United States from its defensive alliance with France and tensions subside.

1803 When President Thomas Jefferson learns that Napoleon has secretly bought the Louisiana Territory from Spain, he sends Secretary of State James Monroe to France to buy as much of the land around New Orleans as he can. Surprisingly, Napoleon is in the mood to sell the entire territory. Monroe seizes the opportunity, thereby scoring the new nation's first major diplomatic coup: The size of the United States is doubled without going to war.

1807 A foreign crisis looms as warring France and England challenge U.S. neutrality and desire to trade with both nations. Both interfere with free trade, and President Thomas Jefferson signs the Embargo Act, which forbids all imports and exports. Designed to hurt the British, it hurts U.S. commerce far more.

1809 The destructive Embargo Act, which has brought U.S. trade to a standstill, is rescinded, although both Britain and France remain hostile toward the United States.

1812 The United States and Great Britain fight the War of 1812 over disputed boundaries, neutral rights, trade relations (see Chapter 5).

1814 The Treaty of Ghent settles the War of 1812. No land has changed hands, and neither side has gained anything from the war, but it is the last that the United States and England will fight.

SECRETARIES OF STATE

The Department of State was the first executive department created under the Constitution of 1787, and secretaries of state have usually enjoyed great prestige. Today, the secretary of state is the fourth in line in succession to the presidency. In the 18th and 19th centuries many ambitious politicians saw the position as a stepping-stone to the presidency, though only Thomas Jefferson, James Madison, James Monroe, John Quincy Adams, and James Buchanan saw these ambitions realized.

Secretaries of State

Secretary	President	Year Appointed	Secretary	President	Year Appointed
Thomas Jefferson	Washington	1789	Louis McLane	Jackson	1833
Edmund Randolph	Washington	1794	John Forsyth	Jackson	1834
Timothy Pickering	Washington	1795		Van Buren	1837
	Adams, J.	1797	Daniel Webster	Harrison, W. H.	1841
John Marshall	Adams, J.	1800		Tyler	1841
James Madison	Jefferson	1801	Abel P. Upshur	Tyler	1843
Robert Smith	Madison	1809	John C. Calhoun	Tyler	1844
James Monroe	Madison	1811		Polk	1845
John Quincy Adams	Monroe	1817	James Buchanan	Polk	1845
Henry Clay	Adams, J. Q.	1825		Taylor	1849
Martin Van Buren	Jackson	1829	John M. Clayton	Taylor	1849
Edward Livingston	Jackson	1831		Fillmore	1850

(continues)

Secretaries of State (cont.)

Secretary	President	Year Appointed	Secretary	President	Year Appointed
Daniel Webster	Fillmore	1850	Philander C. Knox	Taft	1909
Edward Everett	Fillmore	1852		Wilson	1913
William L. Marcy	Pierce	1853	William J. Bryan	Wilson	1913
	Buchanan	1857	Robert Lansing	Wilson	1915
Lewis Cass	Buchanan	1857	Bainbridge Colby	Wilson	1920
Jeremiah S. Black	Buchanan	1860	Charles E. Hughes	Harding	1921
	Lincoln	1861		Coolidge	1923
William H. Seward	Lincoln	1861	Frank B. Kellogg	Coolidge	1925
	Johnson, A.	1865		Hoover	1929
Elihu B. Washburne	Grant	1869	Henry L. Stimson	Hoover	1929
Hamilton Fish	Grant	1869	Cordell Hull	Roosevelt, F. D.	1933
	Hayes	1877	E. R. Stettinius, Jr.	Roosevelt, F. D.	1944
William M. Evarts	Hayes	1877		Truman	1945
	Garfield	1881	James F. Byrnes	Truman	1945
James G. Blaine	Garfield	1881	George C. Marshall	Truman	1947
	Arthur	1881	Dean G. Acheson	Truman	1949
F. T. Frelinghuysen	Arthur	1881	John Foster Dulles	Eisenhower	1953
	Cleveland	1885	Christian A. Herter	Eisenhower	1959
Thomas F. Bayard	Cleveland	1885	Dean Rusk	Kennedy	1961
	Harrison, B.	1889		Johnson, L. B.	1963
James G. Blaine	Harrison, B.	1889	William P. Rogers	Nixon	1969
John W. Foster	Harrison, B.	1892	Henry A Kissinger	Nixon	1973
Walter Q. Gresham	Cleveland	1893		Ford	1974
Richard Olney	Cleveland	1895	Cyrus R. Vance	Carter	1977
	McKinley	1897	Edmund S. Muskie	Carter	1980
John Sherman	McKinley	1897	Alexander M. Haig, Jr.	Reagan	1981
William R. Day	McKinley	1898	George P. Shultz	Reagan	1982
John Hay	McKinley	1898	James A. Baker 3d	Bush	1989
	Roosevelt, T.	1901	Lawrence S. Eagleburger	Bush	1992
Elihu Root	Roosevelt, T.	1905	Warren M. Christopher	Clinton	1993
Robert Bacon	Roosevelt, T.	1909	Madeleine Albright	Clinton	1997
	Taft	1909			

1817 President James Monroe's secretary of state, John Quincy Adams, arranges for the United States and Great Britain to sign the Rush-Bagot Treaty, which demilitarizes the Great Lakes, setting a precedent for the demilitarization of the U.S.-Canadian border.

1818 The Convention of 1818, signed by the United States and Great Britain, sets the northern U.S. border from the Lake of the Woods to the Rocky Mountains at the 49th parallel and establishes joint custody of the Oregon Country, which both nations claim.

1819 The Adams-Onís Treaty cedes Spanish Florida to the United States. Spain cedes more readily, no doubt, when General Andrew Jackson exceeds his orders to put down an Indian dispute while the treaty is being negotiated and invades Florida. The treaty also defines the border between the Louisiana Purchase and Spanish Mexico

1821-
1822 Modeling their revolutions after the United States', Spain's colonies in Latin America declare their independence. The new nations quickly win recognition from the United States, which much prefers to share the Western Hemisphere with independent nations than with colonies.

1823   When Britain proposes joint action to prevent European intervention in Latin America, President James Monroe responds with the Monroe Doctrine, which declares an end to New World colonization by Europe and warns foreign powers that any intervention in the Western Hemisphere will be considered a threat to the United States.

James Monroe

1842   The Webster-Ashburton Treaty, whose terms are developed by Secretary of State Daniel Webster and Lord Ashburton, resolves several disputes over borders with Canada in Maine and upper Midwest, following the precedent for peaceful relations along this border.

Expansion and Imperialism: The United States Grows

1845   Mexico breaks diplomatic relations with the United States when Texas, a republic since 1836, becomes a state. In an attempt to find a peaceful solution, President Polk sends John Slidell to Mexico to buy California and New Mexico, but the mission fails.

1846   The Oregon Treaty, signed by the United States and Great Britain, resolves the disposition of the Oregon Country by extending the 49th parallel line to the Pacific.

A border skirmish persuades the United States to go to war against Mexico (see Chapter 5).

1848   The Treaty of Guadelupe Hidalgo ends the Mexican War. Mexico recognizes the independence of Texas and cedes all of present-day California, Nevada, Utah, and portions of Wyoming, Colorado, New Mexico, and Arizona.

1853-   Matthew Perry opens Japan to U.S. trade with two expeditions and a treaty of peace, friend-
1854   ship, and commerce.

1854-
1855   The Ostend Manifesto, prepared by the American ministers to France, Great Britain, and Spain, declares that Cuba ought to belong to the United States and should be taken by force if Spain refuses to sell. Made public in 1855, the manifesto angers Spain and inflames northern antislavery sentiment, as Cuba would be a slave state.

1855   William Walker leads an expedition to Nicaragua, where he sets himself up as dictator. President Pierce recognizes Walker's government, but it is overthrown in 1857. Walker tries to conquer Central America again that same year. After landing in Honduras in 1860, he is executed by a Honduran firing squad.

1858   Suspicious of European motives because of British and French demands on China, Japan signs additional trade agreements with the United States and the two nations exchange diplomatic representatives.

1861-
1865   During the Civil War, Secretary of State William Seward, ably assisted by Charles Francis Adams, the U.S. minister in London, works to make sure that neither Britain nor France recognizes the South. Despite strong antislavery leanings, both France and Britain need Southern cotton.

1863   When the Confederacy orders two ironclad ships (the Laird Rams) from Britain, the Union applies diplomatic pressure to halt the sale. Ultimately the British government buys them for the Royal Navy. The Confederacy is optimistic in the war's early stages that it will win support from the powerful European nations, but the loss at Antietam proves crucial (see Chapter 5).

Napoleon III takes advantage of the war to install Austrian archduke Maximilian on the throne in Mexico. The United States protests and refuses to recognize the new government but does not push the Monroe Doctrine out of fear that France will help the South.

1865-
1867   The United States uses increasing diplomatic pressure to persuade Napoleon III to end his support of Maximilian and to withdraw French troops from Mexico.

1871   The Treaty of Washington settles fishing rights claims for both American and British subjects, resolves claims stemming from Confederate raiders, and refers the San Juan Islands boundary dispute to the German emperor for arbitration.

1881   Secretary of State James Blaine calls for the first hemispheric conference in a year when he meddles uninvited in three separate Latin America border disputes: Mexico and Guatemala, Costa Rica and Colombia, and Peru and Chile.

1889   Blaine's plan for a Pan-American conference is finally realized as 17 nations meet in Washington and establish the Commercial Bureau of the American Republics, renamed the Pan-American Union in 1910 and eventually succeeded by the Organization of American States.

1893   The United States displays its new nationalistic pride by hosting other nations at the world's Colombian Exposition in Chicago.

Sugar magnates, fearing loss of power when Queen Liliuokalani ascends the throne, force her to yield. The U.S. minister to Hawaii proclaims the kingdom an American protectorate.

1895   When Britain and Venezuela cannot agree on the boundary between Venezuela and British Guiana, the United States offers to arbitrate the dispute, claiming the Monroe Doctrine makes this dispute of interest to the United States. At first Britain will have nothing to do with this idea. Eventually both Britain and the United States see the benefits of cooperating, and the foundation for future work together is laid.

1898   Long a champion of independence for Cuba, the United States goes to war against Spain when the USS *Maine* blows up under mysterious circumstances in Havana harbor (see Chapter 5). The Spanish-American War comes to an end after only four months.

1899   When Spain and the United States sign the Treaty of Paris, Cuba gains its independence and the Philippines, Puerto Rico, and Guam are ceded to the United States. Filipinos, who had been expecting independence, mount a guerrilla war in protest. Armed resistance ends in mid-1902 with sporadic incidents until 1906.

1899   Seeking some advantage in Asia, which the European nations have already carved into colonies, or spheres of influence, the United States proposes an Open Door policy popularly believed to give all nations equal trading rights with China. In reality little is accomplished. One year later, during the Boxer Rebellion, the United States makes an important addition to this doctrine proclaiming that it supports the territorial integrity of China.

1901   Again Europe is warned away from the Western Hemisphere when Vice-President Theodore Roosevelt says: "There is a homely adage which runs, 'Speak softly and carry a big stick; you will go far.' If the American nation will speak softly and yet build and keep at a pitch of the highest training a thoroughly efficient navy, the Monroe Doctrine will go far." Theodore Roosevelt's approach to foreign affairs becomes informally known as the Big Stick policy.

1903   The Hay–Bunau-Varilla Treaty with Panama grants the United States the right to build and operate a canal across the Isthmus of Panama.

GUNBOAT DIPLOMACY AND THE BUILDING OF THE PANAMA CANAL

Few events in U.S. history illustrate more fully the meddling paternalism of U.S. foreign policy toward its neighbors in Latin America than the United States handling of the Panama Canal. The world's nations had long been interested in finding a shorter route from the Atlantic Ocean to the Pacific, and one obvious solution was to build a canal across Central America. As the United States gained power, it became determined to control this project, which would reap enormous commercial benefits to the canal's owner.

To this end the United States and Great Britain signed the Clayton-Bulwer Treaty in 1850, with both nations agreeing not to independently seek rights to such a canal. Fifty years later, in a major diplomatic coup, Secretary of State John Hay got the British to renounce their rights to the canal in the Hay-Pauncefote Treaty of 1901.

In 1891 the French had actually started a canal, but this and other attempts were thwarted by inferior equipment and disease—two challenges the United States would later conquer. Another problem was where to build the canal. In 1901 a U.S. commission had recommended Nicaragua over Panama, but American business interests that had taken over the French effort lobbied for Panama. Initially they wanted $109 million to build the canal, and not until they reduced the sum to $40 million did Roosevelt agree to the deal. In 1902 the commission issued a revised report, favoring the Isthmus of Panama as the site of the canal.

The next step was to obtain the land—or the rights to it—from Colombia. When Colombia's senate rejected the U.S. offer on grounds that it was insubstantial, Roosevelt resorted to gunboat diplomacy. The United States fomented insurrection in Colombia and let it be known that U.S. warships were steaming toward the region. Just as the USS *Nashville* arrived on November 3, 1903, the United States extended recognition to Panama. The new nation of Panama declared its independence from Colombia on November 6, 1903.

The Hay–Bunau-Varilla Treaty was signed November 18,1903, Philippe Bunau-Varilla being one of the instigators of the revolt and an engineer working for the Panama Canal Company. As minister of the newly formed nation, Bunau-Varilla agreed to rent to the United States in perpetuity a ten-mile strip of land on the isthmus for the sum of $10 million and an annual payment of $250,000.

In 1906 work on the 40-mile lock canal began, and in 1914 it was completed at a cost of $300 million and the lives of hundreds of people who supplied cheap local labor. In 1927 Colombia formally recognized Panama in exchange for a payment of $25 million.

(continues)

GUNBOAT DIPLOMACY AND THE BUILDING
OF THE PANAMA CANAL (CONT.)

In the 1960s and 1970s, riots in the canal zone against U.S. control and a changed foreign policy in the United States led to a renegotiation of the agreement. The Panama Canal was an issue in the 1976 presidential election, and the newly elected Jimmy Carter agreed to an increased payment and home rule by 2000.

1904 President Theodore Roosevelt issues what comes to be known as the Roosevelt Corollary to the Monroe Doctrine, which insists that the United States has a right to intervene, "however reluctantly," in Latin American internal affairs when these nations experience political or fiscal instability or flagrant wrongdoing or impotence.

1908 Secretary of State Elihu Root reaches an agreement with Japanese ambassador Kogoro Takahira that the two nations will respect each other's possessions in the Pacific and uphold the Open Door policy in China.

1911 Despite a vow to substitute "dollars for bullets," President William Howard Taft moves a warship off Nicaragua and lands troops to collect customs so the country's debts can be paid. Most troops leave the next year, but a remnant force stays until 1925. Taft's goal of enforcing stability to protect the approaches to the canal is achieved at the expense of goodwill.

The Open Door policy is compromised when President Taft and his secretary of state, Philander Knox, insist on a U.S. role in building railroads in Manchuria, and thus alienate the Japanese. Japan and Russia, recently at war, now begin to see their common interests, and U.S.-Japanese relations begin a slow decline that will reach its nadir during World War II.

1913 President Woodrow Wilson repudiates what he views as his predecessors' imperialistic foreign policy in Latin America, though the Republican-controlled Senate frustrates a number of his attempts.

1914 When war breaks out in Europe, President Woodrow Wilson keeps the United States out of it.

The Panama Canal is completed.

Despite his vow not to interfere in other nations' domestic affairs, Wilson intervenes in Mexico, Haiti, and the Dominican Republic when their domestic problems jeopardize U.S. business interests.

1916 Under the Jones Act, the Philippines obtain home rule and a promise of future independence.

The Modern Era: Onto the World Arena

1917 The United States purchases the Danish Virgin Islands for $25 million.

When Germany takes aggressive action against the United States, President Wilson asks Congress to declare war against Germany, which it does, with the overwhelming support of the nation. The United States provides much-needed reinforcements to a beleaguered England and France (see Chapter 5).

A second Jones Act grants political autonomy to Puerto Rico and grants Puerto Ricans U.S. citizenship.

1918 The arrival of U.S. troops at the front toward the end of 1917 helps to bring the war to a victorious close for the Allies. Russia, which had overthrown the czar the previous year and made a separate peace with Germany, is in the midst of the Bolshevik Revolution.

1919 President Woodrow Wilson, a heroic figure throughout Europe, personally leads the U.S. delegation to the Paris peace talks, which will result in the Treaty of Versailles. Wilson presses the Fourteen Points, which include a covenant for the League of Nations, but is otherwise unable to forge a satisfactory peace. Germany is made to pay huge war reparations. On his return home, Wilson mounts a national speaking tour trying in vain to sell the American people on the League of Nations. When he has a stroke in September, support for the organization fades. The Senate refuses to ratify the Treaty of Versailles.

1921   Perhaps feeling a bit guilty for not joining the League of Nations, the United States invites Great Britain, Japan, France, Italy, Belgium, China, Portugal, and the Netherlands to a naval disarmament conference in Washington. A series of treaties follow, limiting navies by ratios and outlawing poison gas. The territorial integrity of China is guaranteed.

WOODROW WILSON AND WORLD PEACE

In 1990 when Iraq invaded Kuwait, the world's nations were unanimous in their condemnation of Iraq's actions. But the idea that war is an unacceptable solution to national conflict has taken a long time to develop, and its roots can be traced to President Woodrow Wilson and the Fourteen Points. When hostilities broke out in Europe in 1914, President Wilson initially sought a negotiated settlement, even going so far as to send advisors to Europe who would try not only to forestall war but also plant the seeds for an organization of nations that would work to maintain world peace.

When it became necessary, Wilson led the United States into World War I in 1917, but still he divided his energies between waging war and working on the peace that would follow. In 1918 he presented Congress and the world with the Fourteen Points, a program for a fair postwar settlement. Wilson and other progressives hoped it would form the basis for an entirely new kind of diplomacy.

The Fourteen Points announced "the principle of justice to all peoples and nationalities, and their right to live on equal terms of liberty and safety with one another whether they be weak or strong." To this end, the program sought to avoid the pitfalls—annexations of disputed lands, secret covenants, disputes over the high seas, colonial claims—that had precipitated the war.

Specific points called for open treaties among the world's nations, recognition of the rights of neutrals, freedom of the high seas, free trade among all nations, reduced armaments, self-determination for all nations, and mediation of colonial claims. The resolution of territorial disputes was outlined, and Point 14 called for the establishment of an organization of nations that would work together to ensure fairness in international relations and world peace. The Fourteen Points bolstered the Allied forces and encouraged forces within Germany that wished to rid themselves of the Kaiser before seeking an armistice.

At the Paris Peace Conference that followed World War I, several of the points were rejected or rewritten, and the peace with Germany was harsher than Wilson had hoped for, but less harsh than it might have been had he not personally negotiated many of the terms. Most important, from Wilson's point of view, Point 14 was accepted, and a covenant for the League of Nations became part of the Treaty of Versailles.

The League of Nations was established in 1920. Although the United States had played a pivotal role in its establishment, hard-line Senate Republicans, led by Henry Cabot Lodge, opposed U.S. membership, and even though Wilson appealed directly to the American public, the United States never joined. The League effectively settled several disputes during the decade that followed, but it was unable to resolve the larger issues of the 1930s, which included the worldwide depression, Japanese aggression in Asia, and the rise of Hitler in Germany. These events made World War II inevitable—ironically after World War I had reputedly been fought "to make the world safe for democracy;" the League of Nations was established to ensure world peace; and the Kellogg-Briand Pact had outlawed war.

But the League of Nations had set a precedent; it had shown the world that cooperation on a large scale was possible. Even before the end of World War II, delegates from Allied nations met to organize a second league—the United Nations.

1923-1924 When France and Belgium seize Germany's industrial Ruhr district in exchange for unpaid war reparations, the United States resolves the crisis by presenting the Dawes Plan (named after Vice President Charles Dawes), a renegotiation of Germany's war debt.

1928 In the Kellogg-Briand Pact, named for Secretary of State Frank B. Kellogg and French foreign minister Aristide Briand, the idea is advanced that war be outlawed. The idea is promoted by Professor James Shotwell in conversations with French foreign minister Aristide Briand, who seizes upon the concept and advances it in a direct appeal to the American people. Briand's goal is an alliance between France and the United States should war break out again in Europe. Angered at Briand's political maneuver and the obligations of a bilateral pact, Kellogg counters with a proposal for a multinational pact, which he knows will be unenforceable. Eventually 62 nations sign it.

Shortly after winning the election, President-elect Herbert Hoover sets out on a goodwill tour of Latin America. Throughout his term as president Hoover slowly but steadily shows that the United States has embarked on a new course and is trying to be a "good neighbor," a term he coins. The Good Neighbor policy is continued by his successor, Franklin D. Roosevelt, and is promoted actively by FDR's secretary of state, Cordell Hull.

1931-1932 When Japan seizes Manchuria, setting up the puppet state of Manchukuo, Secretary of State Henry Stimson warns Japan that the United States condemns aggression. The Japanese ignore Stimson's statement and launch an attack in Shanghai, forcing Chinese troops out of the city. World opinion compels the Japanese to withdraw but not to abandon their designs on Asia.

1933 In reference to Latin America, Secretary of State Cordell Hull at the Seventh International Conference of American States in Montevideo, Uruguay, agrees to a pact stating "that no state has the right to intervene in the internal or external affairs of another." This pledge to respect these nations' rights and to honor obligations toward them is a major new development in the Good Neighbor policy.

President Franklin Roosevelt extends diplomatic recognition to the USSR.

1934 The Tydings-McDuffie Act promises the Philippines complete independence at the end of a ten-year move to self-government.

1938 When Hitler annexes Austria, many worry that a world war is inevitable. France and Great Britain agree to the dismemberment of Czechoslovakia later the same year.

1939 Germany marches into Poland, prompting France and Great Britain to declare war. Many Americans believe it is only a matter of time before the United States will join the fighting.

1940 As the war expands, President Franklin Roosevelt keeps the United States out but takes steps to arm and otherwise aid the Allies against the Axis powers. Preparing Americans for their inevitable entry into the war, he says he is building an "arsenal of democracy."

1941 In the kind of personal diplomacy that will be a trademark of U.S.-British relations, President Franklin Roosevelt and Prime Minister Winston Churchill meet at sea to discuss common concerns. They put forth their ideas in the Atlantic Charter. Churchill tries to persuade Roosevelt to enter the war, still to no avail, but Roosevelt pledges additional support.

Tensions grow between the United States and Japan as Japan moves into China. Worried about where Japan will stop, President Franklin Roosevelt bans the export of petroleum, petroleum products, and metals in the summer and in the fall freezes Japanese assets in the United States, making war between the two nations inevitable.

When the Japanese bomb Pearl Harbor, home of the Pacific fleet, the United States declares war on Japan, and within days Germany has declared war on the United States (see Chapter 5).

THE ATLANTIC CHARTER

Like Woodrow Wilson before him, whose Fourteen Points had outlined peace (rather than war) aims, Franklin D. Roosevelt set forth a series of lofty goals for peace even before the United States entered World War II. In a secret meeting in August 1941 with British Prime Minister Winston Churchill, on a ship in the North Atlantic, the Atlantic Charter was written. Its principles renounced territorial aggrandizement by the Allies and any changes in territories not in accord with the wishes of the people concerned. The charter also affirmed the right of all people to choose their own form of government, the right of all nations to equal access to trade and raw materials, the importance of collaborative efforts to secure economic advancement and social security, and the right of all people "to live out their lives in freedom from fear and want." Finally, the charter called for freedom of the seas (a principle of American foreign policy since France and Britain first threatened American shipping in the 1790s), the disarmament of aggressors, and "the establishment of a wider and permanent system of general security."

1943   At the Casablanca Conference, Winston Churchill and Franklin Roosevelt discuss Germany's surrender and decide that it must be unconditional.

1944   The June 6 invasion of Normandy by Allied forces presages Germany's total defeat.

Preparing for peace while war still rages, 44 nations gather at the Bretton Woods Conference in New Hampshire to discuss financial issues. The International Monetary Fund and the International Bank for Reconstruction and Development are created; both are powerful forces in the postwar world.

1945   With the end of World War II in sight, the Big Three—Great Britain, the USSR, and the United States—meet at Yalta in the Crimea. President Roosevelt is tired and ill (he will die two months later). Critics charge that he gave away too much to Josef Stalin. Under secret agreements, the Allies and France arrange to occupy Germany and to oversee free elections in all liberated nations. Some specific boundaries and territories are discussed, and the USSR agree to enter the war against Japan.

The United States joins 50 other nations in chartering the United Nations at a conference in San Francisco.

The United States drops two atomic bombs on Japan, and Japan surrenders, concluding the most devastating conflict the world has ever known.

World War II in Europe formally ends a few weeks after the death of President Franklin Roosevelt in April. The peace settlement is hammered out by President Harry Truman, Joseph Stalin, and Winston Churchill (replaced halfway through by Clement Attlee, the new Labour prime minister) at Potsdam. Unconditional surrender is demanded of Japan.

THE UNITED NATIONS

The need for an international organization to replace the League of Nations became increasingly clear as the Second World War drew to a close, and in spring of 1945 delegates from Allied nations, who had been fighting as the United Nations, met in San Francisco to draft a charter. Initially the organization was conceived as a forum through which peace-loving nations could work together to prevent aggression and promote humanitarian purposes. But shortly two former Allies—the United States and the Soviet Union—became major rivals, and many attempts to handle crises crumbled for lack of unanimity among the five permanent members of the Security Council. Meanwhile, in

(continues)

THE UNITED NATIONS (CONT.)

the General Assembly, the United States often found itself attacked by member nations, many of which were aligned with the Soviet bloc or aggressively independent.

Since the end of the cold war, however, the United Nations has moved with greater unity toward a more prominent peacekeeping role, and its blue-helmeted peacekeeping forces have been deployed in trouble spots such as the Persian Gulf, Cambodia, Somalia, and Bosnia. The United States funds more than a quarter of the organization's budget and supplies a substantial proportion of its troops.

In nonmilitary matters, the organization's record is impressive. Its related agencies have coordinated humanitarian aid, improved disease control, helped refugees, and set standards for human rights. Although agencies are located throughout the world and 185 nations are currently members, the United States continues to play a lead role. The organization's headquarters are in New York City, on a tract of land along the East River donated by John D. Rockefeller, Jr.

1946	Winston Churchill issues a prophetic warning to the world in a speech at Westminster College in Fulton, Missouri, using the term "iron curtain" as a metaphor for the intensifying schism between Western Europe and Soviet-dominated Eastern Europe.
	The Philippines are granted independence.
1946-1960	In the wake of World War II, the United States enjoys a remarkable and a rare era of bipartisan foreign policy in which both the president and Congress stand united against the Communists. The growing threat posed by the Soviet Union and communism gives birth to the cold war, a fierce ideological and economic struggle between the United States and the USSR, marked primarily by huge arms buildups on both sides.
1947	The Truman Doctrine signals the United States' intention to offer military and economic aid to nations that resist Communist aggression
	George Kennan, a policy director in the State Department, gives the name *containment* to the U.S. policy of fighting communism around the world. He first describes the idea in an article, signed "X," in *Foreign Affairs*. Kennan's concept will guide U.S. foreign policy throughout the cold war.
	Under the Marshall Plan, first proposed by Secretary of State George Marshall, the United States declares the program is not aimed "against any country or doctrine but against hunger, poverty, desperation, and chaos." At a meeting of foreign ministers in Paris to work out the details, the Soviets walk out stating that this is a thinly disguised plan to take over Europe. An initial amount of $540 million is authorized for France, Italy, and Austria, with a portion for China. During the next three years Congress will authorize another $12.5 billion. This is the first time the United States has given significant amounts of foreign aid, and it will soon become an important foreign-relations tool.
	The National Security Council is created to coordinate military and foreign policy. The council, which is be brought into the Executive Office and thus strengthens the president's role as foreign-policy maker, will play a significant role in shaping U.S. foreign policy throughout the cold war. The CIA is created to handle foreign intelligence activities.

THE NATIONAL SECURITY COUNCIL

Although President Franklin Roosevelt relied heavily on his own counsel during World War II, after that war it was formally recognized that planning and coordinating the nation's foreign policy had become a more complex task than any one person could reasonably be expected to handle. As a result, the National Security Council was formed in 1947.

The council's job is to advise the president on affairs of national security, taking into account the military, domestic, and foreign resources for carrying out policy. The NSC, as it is familiarly known, is part of the executive branch of government. Its members are the president, the vice president, and the secretaries of state and defense, backed up, of course, by an ever-enlarging staff of policy experts. Advisors to the NSC include the attorney general, the Joint Chiefs of Staff, and the head of the Central Intelligence Agency. The position of national security adviser is powerful and has been filled by such prestigious figures as McGeorge Bundy, Henry Kissinger, Zbigniew Brzezinski, and Colin Powell.

1948	The Organization of American States, succeeding the Pan-American Union, is established to work with the United Nations in promoting peace, justice, hemispheric solidarity, and economic development.
	In a series of meetings designed to consolidate the occupation zones of Germany, the USSR opposes unification. When Soviet forces begin a blockade that cuts off Berlin from Allied-controlled West Germany, the United States and Britain respond with an airlift of food and supplies to the 2.5 million citizens of West Berlin and the British, French, and American garrisons. At the height of the airlift, up to 8,000 tons of supplies—food and fuel mostly—are flown in daily. The blockade lasts little less than a year though the airlift itself continues a few more months to build up supplies.
	Political theorist Hans J. Morgenthau publishes *Politics Among Nations*, a seminal work that seeks to redefine the concept of national interest.
194⁹	Immersed in the cold war, the nations of Western Europe and the United States create the North Atlantic Treaty Organization (NATO) to provide a unified defense system in Western Europe in the face of growing Soviet power in Eastern Europe.
	China institutes a Communist regime, and China-U.S. relations cool swiftly.
1950	The Korean War begins when Soviet-controlled North Korea invades U.S.-controlled South Korea along the 38th parallel, the dividing line between the two nations (see Chapter 5).
1951-1953	Truce negotiations begin in Korea, marked by lengthy delays and bad faith on both sides. When a settlement is reached, it is unsatisfactory to everyone. No borders are changed; the peninsula remains divided roughly along the 38th parallel. The war has mainly served to expand the foreign policy of containment far beyond Europe at the same time that it has made containment look like a losing proposition. It has also resulted in about 2 million casualties.
1952	Japan regains its sovereignty when a peace treaty with the United States is ratified by the Senate.
	The United States successfully detonates a hydrogen bomb.
1953	The USSR explodes a hydrogen bomb.
1954	The Soviet Union again rejects German unification, thus heightening cold war tensions. The CIA supports rebels who wish to overthrow Guatemala's liberal leader, Jacobo Arbenz Guzmán, an advocate of land reform and trade unionism. A military leader is installed.
	In response to worries about communism in Southeast Asia, the United States creates the Southeast Asian Treaty Organization (SEATO), an attempt at duplicating NATO. But this organization is much weaker and does not include India or Indonesia among its members.
1956	During President Eisenhower's second term, Secretary of State John Foster Dulles takes a new hard line toward the USSR. Bolstered by the United States' successful test of a new hydrogen bomb and equally worried about the USSR's subsequent successful test, Dulles employs an aggressively anti-Communist foreign policy. The policy of ensuring massive

retaliation to a first strike requires an unprecedented peacetime buildup of arms. Despite the tough posturing, the United States does nothing to support rebels in Hungary in 1956. The short-lived rebellion is brutally suppressed by the USSR.

When Israel, France, and Britain attack Egypt, which has recently nationalized the Suez Canal and flirted with China and the USSR, Eisenhower is furious. Hopes for bringing the Arabs and Israelis to some sort of modus vivendi are dashed, and Eisenhower and Dulles believe a major war is narrowly averted.

1959   In Cuba, Fidel Castro stages a successful coup against the right-wing government of Fulgencio Batista. The new government accepts aid from the USSR. At the same time Castro announces that he will export his revolution throughout Central America.

1960   Summit diplomacy, promoted by Soviet leader Nikita Khrushchev, collapses when the USSR shoots down an American U-2 spy plane. The United States at first denies that these are spy planes, claiming instead that this is a weather plane gone off course. But the USSR has the pilot, who bailed out. A few days later, at the long-planned summit meeting in Paris, Khrushchev demands that Eisenhower stop the spy flights, apologize, and punish those behind the idea. Eisenhower refuses, and Khrushchev stalks out.

1961   The USSR closes the border between East and West Berlin and builds the Berlin Wall to halt the exodus from East Germany.

In his farewell address, President Eisenhower, who has developed reservations about the arms buildup he presided over, warns against the overwhelming power of the military-industrial complex.

Seeking nonmilitary means to forge relations with Latin America, newly elected president John Kennedy creates the Alliance for Progress, an aid program for the economic development of Latin American nations. His good intentions are undermined when the CIA-sponsored Bay of Pigs invasion of Cuba is made public. Under President John Kennedy and his defense secretary, Robert McNamara, a policy of flexible response replaces the concept of brinkmanship.

1962   The Cuban Missile Crisis occurs when the Soviet Union secretly begins building missile-launching sites in Cuba. President Kennedy demands removal of the missile and imposes a naval blockade of Cuba. Since a blockade in international law is an act of war, the administration calls it a quarantine. At the last moment Soviet freighters turn back from delivering supplies to Cuba and Khrushchev promises to remove the missiles. The United States offers to remove obsolete missiles in Turkey. Cuba releases the prisoners from the Bay of Pigs invasion in exchange for $53 million in medicine and food, which is raised via private U.S. investors.

1963   The United States, the USSR, and Great Britain sign a Limited Nuclear Test-Ban Treaty, barring all above-ground tests of nuclear weapons. The modest defense buildup instituted by President Eisenhower increases slightly under President Kennedy.

1964   In a cold war attempt to contain Soviet communism, the United States enters a decade of escalating involvement in Vietnam, in what will be the nation's longest war and one of its most costly in terms of human life and military spending. The first American casualties have occurred in the late 1950s (see Chapter 5).

Congress sanctions the war by passing the Gulf of Tonkin Resolution, which gives the president broad power to commit troops to Vietnam. Later, when it is revealed that Congress was given false information about the war, a so-called credibility gap develops in American foreign policy, in which neither Congress nor the public is particularly inclined to believe (or believe in) the president. Presidents Lyndon Johnson and Richard Nixon suffer from a credibility gap, which in turn spurs on the already considerable opposition to the Vietnam War.

John F. Kennedy and Nikita Khrushchev

Late 1960s   Opposition to U.S. involvement in Vietnam increases as various members of Congress of both parties announce their opposition to the war. Senator William Fulbright, chairman of the Senate Foreign Relations Committee, describes U.S. foreign policy during this era as an "arrogance of power." He becomes a harsh critic of the war.

1968   The Nuclear Non-Proliferation Treaty is signed by 115 nations, including the United States. The nuclear nations agree not to transfer nuclear power, and nonnuclear signers agree not to build or develop it. Eventually 140 nations sign the treaty.

1969   The Nixon Doctrine signals a new direction in American foreign policy when President Richard Nixon states that the United States will consider its vital interests first rather than trying to solve the problems of other nations.

Strategic Arms Limitation Talks (SALT) begin between the United States and the USSR.

1970s   A period of detente, marked by an easing of military and diplomatic strain, dominates U.S. relations with the Soviet Union. It is initiated in 1956 when the new Soviet leader, Nikita

Khrushchev, at the Twentieth Party Congress severely criticizes the tactics and crimes of Joseph Stalin, who died in 1953. Though it is a secret speech to party leaders only, details slowly leak out. Nevertheless, Soviet meddling in Berlin, Czechoslovakia in 1968, Latin America, and the Middle East continues to challenge the United States.

President Richard Nixon's foreign policy, marked by many successes, also exhibits paranoid tendencies. Many of Nixon's and Secretary of State Henry Kissinger's dealings with other governments are conducted in great secrecy, away from the gaze of government officials or members of Congress whom they distrust. Nixon and Kissinger support autocrats such as the shah of Iran, Ferdinand Marcos in the Philippines, and the South African regime, merely because they are anti-Communist and loyal to U.S. business interests.

1971   "Ping-Pong diplomacy" begins when the Chinese warm to a U.S. table-tennis team and signal a willingness to thaw out Sino-U.S. relations. Henry Kissinger travels secretly to China to pave the way for a state visit by President Richard Nixon.

The Pentagon Papers affair erupts when former Defense Department aide Daniel Ellsberg leaks incriminating materials regarding the federal government's involvement in Vietnam to *The New York Times*. The Nixon administration takes its case to the Supreme Court, where it loses.

1972   President Richard Nixon travels to China in what is widely considered to be the foreign-relations coup of his presidency. It is a breakthrough in Chinese-American relations, and good foreign relations as well, serving to separate the world's two Communist powers from one another. When the USSR expresses anxiety over the new alliance, President Nixon agrees to sell the Soviets $1 billion in U.S. wheat.

The Senate approves the SALT I Treaty.

1973   In the wake of the Yom Kippur War, Arab leaders are frustrated by Israel's success. Believing that success is largely due to U.S. aid, the Arab nations declare an embargo on shipments of oil to the United States and other Western nations and Japan. The embargo lasts from October until March.

In a CIA covert operation, the United States abets a Chilean coup in order to get rid of the duly elected Socialist government of Salvador Allende. Allende is subsequently murdered by the junta that replaces him. The United States welcomes the dictatorship of General Augusto Pinochet.

The direct involvement of U.S. ground forces throughout Indochina ends.

1975   Saigon falls to North Vietnamese forces.

1976   Under President Jimmy Carter, the United States weighs humanitarian concerns in executing its foreign policy. Repressive nations are pressured to grant their citizens freedom or risk losing U.S. support.

1977   The Panama Canal Treaty transfers ownership of the canal back to Panama by the year 2000.

1978   The Nuclear Non-Proliferation Act sets controls on the export of nuclear technology to other nations.

1979   America and Iran become at odds when religious conservatives oust the shah, a longtime U.S. friend. In the aftermath of the revolution, Iran takes 53 American diplomats hostage and holds them for 444 days.

In an initial overture toward Middle Eastern peace, Egypt and Israel sign the Camp David Peace Accords, which are named for the Maryland presidential retreat. Though the treaty proves to be largely symbolic, it does mark the beginning of serious discussions between Israel and its neighbors.

1980   In what will prove to be a major blow to the Carter administration, a mission to rescue the Iranian hostages fails.

President Carter requests that ratification of SALT II Treaty be delayed after the Soviet Union invades Afghanistan.

1982 When its debt soars to $81 billion, Mexico twice devalues the peso, then negotiates with the International Monetary fund for a rescheduling of payments. Other Latin American nations also have difficulty repaying U.S. loans, thus shifting the focus of foreign policy from arms to fiscal matters.

Signaling Congress's concern about human rights in Latin American internal affairs, Edward Boland, chairman of the House Intelligence Committee, introduces an amendment bearing his name that prohibits any U. S. funding of contra forces who are waging a guerrilla war against the elected leftist Sandinistas.

Mikhail Gorbachev comes to power in the USSR. He introduces the concept of *glasnost*, openness, and meets Reagan in Geneva. Tensions between the superpowers begin to relax.

1986 The Iran-Contra scandal erupts, followed by the Tower Commission investigation. During President Ronald Reagan's first administration, the National Security Council in defiance of the Boland Amendment mounts a covert operation to provide aid to contra forces fighting in Nicaragua. To fund the aid, the United States secretly sells arms to Iran with the hope that hostages in Lebanon will be freed. Profits from the arms sales go directly to the contras. The Tower Commission that subsequently investigates the Iran-Contra affair finds the president "disengaged" from foreign policy.

President Ronald Reagan disregards the SALT II Treaty when the limit on nuclear weapons is exceeded. Reagan states that the treaty was not ratified and that the Soviets also had not observed its limits.

In Reykjavík, Iceland, Gorbachev proposes a 50 percent reduction in all strategic nuclear weapons to Reagan. The two leaders cannot resolve differences over the Strategic Defense Initiative (SDI). Nevertheless, great strides are made.

1987 Gorbachev and Reagan meet in Washington and sign an agreement limiting medium-range nuclear arms.

Ronald Reagan and Mikhail Gorbachev

1989   In June Poland holds elections in which the Communist party loses power. In August Hungary dismantles its border with Austria, and allows thousands of East Germans to go west. In November East German officials, pressured by hundreds of thousands of protesters in Leipzig and Berlin, open the wall. In December the Velvet Revolution takes place in Czechoslovakia, and playwright Vaclav Havel, a political prisoner, finds himself elected president. In Romania and Bulgaria, new governments replace Communist regimes. The cold war is coming to an end.

The United States invades Panama to oust President Manuel Noriega, previously a U.S. friend and now viewed as too permissive about drug traffic.

KEY PLAYERS IN FOREIGN POLICY TODAY

President

Secretary of State

Department of State, including its Foreign Service

Executive Departments, including State, Defense, Treasury, Agriculture, Commerce, Labor, and Energy

Central Intelligence Agency

National Security Council

Office of the U.S. Trade Representative

1990   Germany is reunited after 45 years.

The Persian Gulf War breaks out when Iraq invades Kuwait. Within days the United States has organized a multinational force to compel Iraq to withdraw.

1991   President George Bush and Mikhail Gorbachev sign the Strategic Arms Reduction Treaty.

Despite tremendous international pressure on the Iraqis to withdraw from Kuwait, they refuse to do so. On February 23 allied forces attack; on February 27 President Bush orders a cease-fire.

1993   Congress ratifies the North Atlantic Free Trade Agreement (NAFTA) with Mexico and Canada. It is an attempt to form a free-trade zone similar to those formed by other groups of nations around the world.

1994   In one of the most important spy cases in U.S. history, authorities arrest CIA agent Aldrich Ames on charges of supplying the Soviets with information for more than a decade. The case seriously compromises the credibility of U.S. intelligence.

In what will prove to be indicative of the kind of foreign-policy problem it will encounter in the post–cold war era, the United States uses the military to provide economic aid, in the form of a food-and-medicine airlift, to Rwanda, which is mired in a civil war. Troops are also dispatched to Haiti, under UN auspices, to oust a repressive military regime.

1995   Mexico devalues the peso, seriously undermining U.S. investments there.

A major foreign-policy dilemma of Bill Clinton's presidency is continued fighting in the Balkans as Bosnian Serbs wage a war of "ethnic cleansing" to rid what they hope will be a new nation of Muslims and Croats.

MAJOR U.S. TREATIES

Treaties—formal agreements between nations—are negotiated by the president and his representatives in the Department of State and, to be implemented, must be ratified by a two-thirds majority in the Senate.

Year	Treaty	Signatories	Result
1783	Paris	Britain, France, United States	Formally ends the Revolutionary War
1794	Jay's	Britain, United States	Settles lingering issues related to the Revolution
1795	Pinckney's	Spain, United States	Sets border of Spanish Florida and opens Mississippi River to U.S. trade
1814	Ghent	Britain, United States	Ends the War of 1812
1817	Rush-Bagot	Britain, United States	Disarms the U.S.-Canadian border
1818	Convention	Britain, United States	Settles U.S.-Canadian border to the Pacific and agrees to joint occupation of Oregon Country
1819	Adams-Onís	Spain, United States	Spain cedes Florida
1842	Webster-Ashburton	Britain, United States	Settles U.S.-Canadian border in Maine and upper Midwest
1846	Oregon	Britain, United States	Divides Oregon Country between Canada and the United States
1848	Guadelupe Hidalgo	Mexico, United States	Ends the Mexican War
1871	Washington	Britain, United States	Resolves several issues
1899	Paris	Spain, United States	Ends the Spanish-American War
1903	Hay-Bunau-Varilla	Panama, United States	Grants the United States the right to lease the land it needs to build the Panama Canal
1919	Versailles	Allies, Germany; the United States never ratifies	Ends World War I; includes of the League of Nations
1922–1930	Naval Disarmament Treaties	Allies	Set limits on navies
1928	Kellogg-Briand	15 nations at first; ultimately 62	Bans war
1949	North Atlantic Treaty Organization (NATO)	Belgium, Britain, Canada, Denmark, France, Iceland, Italy, Luxembourg, the Netherlands, Norway, Portugal, United States, and later Greece, Turkey, and West Germany	Mutual defense pact
1954	South East Asian Treaty Organization (SEATO)	Australia, Britain, France, New Zealand, Pakistan, the Philippines, Thailand, United States	Mutual defense pact
1977	Panama Canal		United States agrees to transfer ownership of the Panama Canal Zone back to Panama

For disarmament treaties during the cold war, see pages 264–265.

DOCTRINES IN U.S. FOREIGN POLICY

1823   The Monroe Doctrine. Articulated by President James Monroe in his Annual Message to Congress, this is the United States' first comprehensive foreign-policy statement. It asserts that the Western Hemisphere is closed to European colonization and that the United States will regard any attempt by a European power to extend its system to the Western Hemisphere as "the manifestation of an unfriendly disposition toward the United States." In return, the United States vows not to interfere in the European affairs. The doctrine dominates U.S. foreign policy until the United States enters World War I in 1917, and still guides the U.S. role in this hemisphere.

1905   The Roosevelt Corollary. Widely viewed as an amendment to the Monroe Doctrine, this foreign-policy statement by President Theodore Roosevelt asserts the right of the United States to intervene in affairs of Latin American nations whenever they are politically, financially, or economically so unstable as to threaten U.S. interests. Although Woodrow Wilson repudiates this doctrine in 1913 upon taking office, he does not stay out of Latin American affairs, nor have most succeeding presidents done so.

1920s   Isolationism. This approach to foreign policy, dominant throughout the 19th century, enjoys a vigorous resurgence in reaction to U.S. participation in World War I. Following from President Washington's warning against entangling alliances in his farewell address, this approach seeks to avoid involvement in Europe's alliance systems and wars and often imposes high tariffs. Protected by two oceans, the United States can make isolationism a reality until the 20th century, when new technologies in transportation and communication begin to negate the protection offered by distance alone.

1947   The Truman Doctrine. In a message to Congress, President Harry Truman announces his intention to provide military and economic aid to free, democratic nations threatened by totalitarian regimes. The doctrine, initially advanced to build support for an aid bill for Greece and Turkey, is also useful in building support for NATO and the response to a variety of small and large crises all over the world that arise during the cold war.

   Containment. This foreign policy principle is aimed at containing communism and halting the influence of the USSR. Introduced in 1947, it is the dominant foreign and national security policy until the end of the cold war in 1991.

1969   The Nixon Doctrine. President Richard Nixon attempts to reduce the United States' role as the world's policeman when he states: "America cannot—and will not—conceive all the plans, design all the programs, execute all the decisions, and undertake all the defense of nations of the world. We will help where it makes a difference in our national interest and is considered in our interest."

1979   The Carter Doctrine. In the face of USSR encroachments in Afghanistan and the Middle East, Carter states that the United States will actively protect its interests in the Middle East.

1980   The Reagan Doctrine. President Ronald Reagan declares that the United States has a right—indeed an obligation—to intervene anywhere in the world where there is political insurrection, and thus combat the "evil empire" of the USSR. In many ways this doctrine is a return to the early days of the cold war.

THE COLD WAR

1947   The expression *cold war* is used for the first time in a speech written by journalist Herbert Bayard Swope for financier Bernard Baruch. Baruch testifies before Congress: "Let us not be deceived: Today we are in the midst of a cold war." Competition for "client" states begins when the USSR pressures Turkey and Greece, and President Harry Truman responds with an offer of aid. Secretary of State George Marshall announces a plan to help rebuild war-torn Europe, occupied by the Allies. The Kremlin protests the Marshall Plan.

POWER UNBOUND: THE CIA

The Central Intelligence Agency, an outgrowth of the Office of Strategic Services created in World War II, was established in 1947 under the same act that created the National Security Council. Its purpose is to gather, coordinate, and analyze the information necessary to conduct foreign policy and protect U.S. interests abroad. Its director often confers with the cabinet and the National Security Council.

While the cold war seemed tailor-made for the CIA's services, it also provided an atmosphere in which the agency often undertook controversial covert activities so that the U.S. government could deny any official involvement.

In the 1950s the CIA, headed by director Allen Dulles, brother of Secretary of State John Foster Dulles, expanded its operations enormously. Agents all over the world cast a wide net, infiltrating cultural institutions, undermining organizations, spying on writers and other intellectuals as well as students at American universities and church leaders. The CIA maintained its own radio stations and news-service organizations and financed several journals. It mounted covert military operations in Asia, Africa, and Latin America. It worked with France to maintain the colonial regime in Indochina. In 1953, when the premier of Iran was on the verge of nationalizing the oil industry, it deposed him and put the U.S.-friendly but at times despotic Muhammad Reza Shah Pahlavi on the throne.

The most notorious CIA intervention occurred in Guatemala, which since 1944 had struggled to become a democracy. In 1951 the liberal-spirited new president Jacobo Arbenz Guzmán encouraged trade unions and pursued land reform, appropriating uncultivated land owned by the United Fruit Company. The company complained to the State Department, charging that Arbenz was a Communist.

In 1954 the CIA secretly effected a coup by a right-wing military leader who initiated a crackdown that led to years of guerrilla warfare.

Fear that the CIA had exceeded its mandate became a campaign issue in the mid-1970s, and investigations by Congress and a presidential commission revealed that the CIA had attempted to assassinate several foreign leaders, including Fidel Castro of Cuba, been engaged in a secret war in Laos, supported antigovernment forces in Chile, and conducted extensive surveillance of U.S. citizens. The Senate established a permanent committee to oversee CIA activities, but in the late 1980s new congressional investigations uncovered CIA involvement in the Iran-Contra affair. The agency was further undermined in 1994 when a career officer, Aldrich Ames, was found to have been spying for the USSR for nearly a decade. The agency's primary task in the future will be to define a role for itself in a world where spies may no longer be needed. In 1996 a bipartisan commission recommended that the CIA focus its efforts on terrorism, narcotics trafficking, weapons proliferation, and organized crime.

1948   Czechoslovakia, a democracy, falls victim to a Soviet-sponsored coup.

When the USSR blockades Berlin, the United States responds with an airlift of supplies and food that breaks Soviet resolve.

1949   The nations of Western Europe, the United States, and Canada form the North Atlantic Treaty Organization (NATO) to provide an adequate military defense against the USSR. Communist forces, with USSR support, take over China, leaving the nationalists only the island of Taiwan.

1950   The first "hot" war of the cold war begins when USSR-supported North Korea invades U.S.-supported South Korea.

1961	The Bay of Pigs fiasco occurs when the United States, in an attempt to overthrow Fidel Castro, invades Cuba, sending in 1,500 CIA-trained and -armed Cuban expatriates.
1962	A crisis erupts when the USSR secretly builds a missile-launching site in Cuba. President Kennedy demands its removal, and the world spends an anxious few days before the USSR backs down. In exchange for the removal of Soviet missiles from Cuba, the United States agrees to remove obsolete missiles from Turkey.
1964-	In Vietnam, the United States and North Vietnam fight the second "hot" war of the cold war.
1974	By the end of the Vietnam War, the United States and USSR is moving toward detente, with a series of calculated and carefully calibrated friendly gestures toward each other. Detente is aided in part by a softening on the part of the United States toward Communist China under President Richard Nixon, and by a series of nuclear disarmament treaties.
1977	U.S.-Soviet relations become strained again under President Jimmy Carter, who interjects the issue of human rights into foreign affairs.
1979	When the USSR invades Afghanistan, President Carter withdraws his support of SALT II, and Congress refuses to ratify the treaty.
1980- 1985	With the cold war fully revived, President Ronald Reagan declares war on the "evil empire." Reagan permits covert operations in Latin America in an effort to undermine perceived Soviet interests there. He announces the development of the antinuclear Strategic Defense Initiative and also promotes a huge buildup of arms.
1991	The cold war dies a natural death when the USSR comes to an end.
	With the end of the cold war, U.S. foreign policy faces new challenges, particularly instability and ethnic strife in nations of the former Soviet Union and Soviet bloc as well as continuing tensions in the Middle East. Also of concern are the control of nuclear arms as well as chemical and biological weapons, foreign aid and intervention under the auspices of the United Nations, the role of NATO and the U.S. military, issues in trade equity and the relation of trade status to human rights violations, rapid population growth in the face of poverty and a growing gap between wealthy and poor nations, drug traffic, and the degradation of the global environment. In some ways, with the end of the cold war, the world is a more rather than a less dangerous place.

NO MORE NUKES: THE ROAD TO NUCLEAR DISARMAMENT

1945	The United States drops two atomic bombs on Japan, one at Hiroshima and another at Nagasaki.
1946	In its first session, the United Nations General Assembly establishes a commission to study international control of atomic energy. The Soviet-U.S. split in the Security Council make progress impossible.
1952	The United States explodes a hydrogen bomb.
1953	The Soviet Union explodes a hydrogen bomb.
	Disarmament talks are revived under the auspices of the United Nations. The United States and its allies propose on-site inspections of nuclear installations, while the USSR calls for a total ban of nuclear weapons, with specific controls to be settled at later talks.
1958	The United States, Great Britain, and the USSR institute talks on a nuclear-test ban.

1963   The Limited Nuclear Test Ban Treaty is signed by 99 nations, banning nuclear weapons tests in the atmosphere, underwater, and outer space; only underground testing is permitted.

1967   The United States, the USSR, and 57 other nations sign a treaty banning the use of nuclear weapons in outer space and establishing principles for the peaceful exploration of space.

1968   The Nuclear Non-Proliferation Treaty ultimately signed by 140 nations, among them the United States, the USSR, and Great Britain, aims to prevent the further spread of nuclear weapons, to foster peaceful uses of atomic energy, and to encourage negotiations to end the nuclear arms race.

1969   Strategic Arms Limitation Talks (SALT) between the United States and the USSR begin.

1972   The United States and the USSR sign the SALT I Treaty, which limits antiballistic weapons and offensive nuclear weapons and imposes a five-year freeze on the building of new nuclear weapons.

1974   The United States and the USSR sign a Threshold Test Ban Treaty, which limits the size of underground testing to weapons no larger than 150 kilotons.

1977   Although SALT I has expired, the United States and the USSR agree to abide by its terms. Strategic Arms Limitations Talks II are under way.

1979   SALT II is signed in Vienna by the United States and the USSR in June. It sets specific limits on long-range bombers and the number of nuclear weapons each nation can develop. Congress never ratifies SALT II, but both countries say they would abide by it.

1982   The United States and the USSR begin the Strategic Arms Reduction Talks (START).

1987   President Ronald Reagan and Soviet leader Mikhail Gorbachev sign the Intermediate-Range Nuclear Forces (INF) Treaty, which limits intermediate-range nuclear forces.

1991   The START Treaty, which further reduces nuclear arsenals, is signed by President George Bush and Mikhail Gorbachev. With the Soviet Union crumbling as a world power in the aftermath of liberalization and internal turmoil, President Bush announces the elimination of the majority of U.S. tactical nuclear arms and orders the U.S. military off alert status for the first time in decades. Bush calls for continued reduction in ballistic missiles. Soviet nuclear weapons fall into the hands of four of the newly formed republics. All but Ukraine pledge to abide by existing treaties.

1993   The United States and Russia sign a START II Treaty calling for a two-thirds reduction of nuclear weapons. North Korea withdraws from the Nuclear Non-Proliferation Treaty.

1994   Under START I Treaty modifications, the schedule for eliminating nuclear weapons is accelerated. Ukraine, which has held out on signing the 1993 treaty, signs.

SIGNIFICANT SUPREME COURT DECISIONS AND LEGISLATIVE ACTS AFFECTING FOREIGN AFFAIRS

1807   Embargo Act. The first important act of U.S. foreign policy, this legislation forbids trade with foreign nations. Designed to force Britain and France to recognize the rights of neutral traders, it ends up hurting American business far more. It is rescinded in 1809.

1924   Rogers Act. This combines the diplomatic service and consular service into the Foreign Service, a professional diplomatic corps in which promotion is based on merit. At the highest diplomatic levels appointments are still political.

1935- Neutrality Acts. This series of acts, which prohibits U.S. shipments of arms to belligerents
1937 and U.S. citizens from traveling on hostile ships, is an attempt to keep the United States out of conflicts in Europe that presage World War II.

1936 *United States v. Curtiss-Wright Export Corporation.* This decision affirms the president's "exclusive power . . . in the field of international relations." When Congress issues a joint resolution permitting the president to forbid the sale of arms to other nations, Curtiss-Wright sues on grounds of constraint of trade. The Supreme Court upholds the resolution, thus confirming that Congress may delegate foreign policy matters to the president.

1939 Neutrality Act. A new Neutrality Act, following the outbreak of war in Europe, authorizes the shipment of arms to belligerents.

1941 Lend-Lease Act. This enables the United States to furnish war supplies to Britain and other allies whose defense is defined as vital to U.S. interests.

1947 National Security Act. In addition to combining the armed forces into one organization, this act authorizes the establishment of the Central Intelligence Agency, which will coordinate the nation's intelligence-gathering activities. It also creates the National Security Council, which will become a major force in shaping U.S. foreign policy.

1962 *Baker v. Carr.* Although addressing legislative reapportionment, majority and dissenting opinions debated the role of the Court in foreign policy issues.

1971 *The New York Times v. United States.* The Supreme Court overrules the injunction of a lower court and permits the publication of *The Pentagon Papers*, a classified study of U.S. involvement in Vietnam that had been leaked to the *Times* by former Defense Department aide Daniel Ellsberg.

SIGNIFICANT PEOPLE IN AMERICAN FOREIGN POLICY

Abbott, Grace (1878–1939).   Nebraska native, resident of Chicago's Hull-House, and friend of Jane Addams and Florence Kelley, Abbott served in an unofficial capacity as the U.S. representative to the League of Nations Advisory Committee on Traffic in Women and Children. She was one of the planners of the Social Security Act. She wrote *The Immigrant and the Community*.

Acheson, Dean (1893–1971).   As secretary of state under Truman and advisor to Presidents Kennedy, Johnson, and Nixon, Acheson was a shaper of post–World War II foreign policy. He worked on the Marshall Plan, fought for giving aid to Greece and Turkey, played a role in the establishment of NATO, and also secured UN support for U.S. intervention in Korea. Critics charged that his policies led to the Communist takeover of China and the start of the Korean War. A staunch supporter of containment and early supporter of the war in Vietnam, he nevertheless advised President Johnson in 1968 that he should find a way to end U.S. involvement in Vietnam.

Adams, John Quincy (1767–1848).   The sixth U.S. president, he was the son of President John Quincy Adams and Abigail Adams. He helped to write the treaty that ended the War of 1812, as well as the Monroe Doctrine, the latter accomplished while serving as secretary of state under President James Monroe. He negotiated the cession of Florida from Spain.

Albright, Madeleine (1937–).   A naturalized American citizen born in Czechoslovakia, Albright was named the U.S. permanent representative to the United Nations by President Bill Clinton in 1993. In 1997 President Clinton appointed her as secretary of state; she was the first woman to hold this prestigious position.

Anderson, Eugenie Moore (1909–) President Harry Truman appointed Anderson ambassador to Denmark in 1953. She was the first woman to hold the rank of ambassador. President John F. Kennedy appointed her envoy to Bulgaria. She also served in an appointive post at the United Nations.

Baker, James (1930–). As secretary of state under President Bush, Baker rallied support for U.S. military action in the Persian Gulf War, presided over a major Middle East peace conference, and helped to negotiate several arms-reduction treaties with the USSR.

Blaine, James Gillespie (1830–1893). Blaine served as secretary of state under three presidents: Garfield, Arthur, and Benjamin Harrison. He helped to improve U.S.–Latin American relations by convening the Pan-American Congress and working for reciprocal trade agreements; he also advocated the annexation of Hawaii.

Bunche, Ralph Johnson (1904–1971). Bunche was the first African American to rise to a high position in the State Department. Bunche's major contribution was at the United Nations, where his work on the UN Special Commission on Palestine earned him a Nobel Peace Prize in 1950.

Carter, Jimmy (1924–). Carter's one-term presidency (1977–1981) was as marred by his foreign-policy problems as it was brightened by his considerable achievements in this area. His personal diplomacy led to the signing of the Camp David Peace Accords in 1979 between Anwar Sadat of Egypt and Menachem Begin of Israel. He signed the SALT II Treaty, although it was never ratified by the Senate. He was able to get ratification of the Panama Canal treaty. His administration was also plagued by fallout from the Iranian Revolution, which unsettled the Middle East, and the subsequent seizure of the U.S. embassy. Fifty-two U.S. diplomats were held hostage 444 days; they were released a few hours after Carter left office.

Dulles, John Foster (1888–1959). Dulles was a leader in the bipartisan foreign policy that emerged after World War II. He was also an internationalist who worked hard to establish the United Nations and served as U.S. representative. During the 1952 presidential campaign, however, he turned against his earlier ideas and became a staunch supporter of containment. He never hesitated to use strong language or to give the impression that the United States might use force.

Eisenhower, Dwight David (1890–1969). As president from 1953 to 1961, Eisenhower fulfilled his campaign promise to end the Korean War. He worked to advance the policy of containment of the USSR, which had been started under Truman, at the same time that he sought to assuage cold war tensions. A former general and hero of World War II, Eisenhower believed that a strong military was vital to peace. At the same time, he warned Americans in his farewell address to beware the power of the military-industrial complex, which could endanger liberties and democratic processes.

Fish, Hamilton (1808–1893). As President Grant's secretary of state, Fish negotiated the Treaty of Washington in 1871, which ended disputes with Great Britain over the Confederate raiders. He also negotiated a commercial treaty with Hawaii and settled American claims in Cuba with Spain.

Fulbright, William (1905–1995). As chairman of the Senate Foreign Relations Committee from 1959 until 1974, Fulbright was a strong voice in American foreign policy and an outspoken critic of foreign intervention, especially in Vietnam. His Fulbright Act (1946) continues to sponsor exchanges of students and teachers between the United States and foreign countries.

Gallatin, Albert (1761–1849). Swiss-born Gallatin helped negotiate the Treaty of Ghent and served as minister to France and Great Britain. While at the Court of Saint James's, he negotiated joint occupation of the Oregon Country.

Harriman, Averell (1891–1986).   In addition to serving under presidents Franklin D. Roosevelt, Truman, Kennedy, Johnson, and Carter in positions ranging from ambassador to the USSR and Great Britain, Lend-Lease coordinator, secretary of commerce, assistant secretary of state, undersecretary of state, and chief negotiator for the Nuclear Test Ban Treaty, Harriman was a negotiator at the Vietnam peace talks. He was also governor of New York from 1955 to 1959.

Harris, Patricia Roberts (1924–1985).   In addition to being the first African-American woman to hold a cabinet post (Housing and Urban Development, 1977), Harris also became one of the first black diplomats when she was appointed ambassador to Luxembourg.

Hay, John Milton (1838–1905).   In addition to being President Lincoln's private secretary, Hay served as secretary of state under Presidents McKinley and Theodore Roosevelt. He originated the Open Door policy in China and negotiated the Hay-Pauncefote Treaty, in which Great Britain renounced its interest in building the Panama Canal.

Hoover, Herbert (1874–1964).   A mining engineer by profession, Hoover chaired a commission that supplied food and clothing to civilians in war-torn areas of Belgium and France between 1915 and 1919. Following World War I he was made chairman of the European Relief and Reconstruction Commission, coordinating relief operations through Europe. He also directed an organization that fed millions in Revolutionary Russia during the famine of 1921–1923. His reputation for support of humanitarian aid and his excellent skills in organization were part of his appeal as a presidential candidate. His inaction in the face of the stock market crash and Great Depression, however, prevented his reelection, and he retired from public life. But following World War II he again coordinated relief efforts in Europe.

House, Edward (1858–1938).   An important and close advisor to President Wilson, he sought to prevent war in Europe and negotiate peace after World War I broke out. Accompanying Wilson to Paris after the war, House helped to draft the Versailles Peace Treaty and the Covenant of the League of Nations.

Hull, Cordell (1871–1955).   As FDR's secretary of state, Hull was a true internationalist. He supported U.S. membership in the League of Nations and played a dominant role in the establishment of the United Nations, work that led to his being awarded the Nobel Peace Prize in 1945. Ironically, Hull was shuffled aside during World War II, since Roosevelt preferred to direct his own war policy, but he continued his work in the international arena by continuing the Good Neighbor policy with Latin America.

Jay, John (1745–1829).   As a member of the U.S. delegation, Jay helped negotiate the Treaty of Paris, which ended the Revolutionary War. Sent to Britain in 1794, he also negotiated Jay's Treaty, which resolved issues derived from the Revolution. He also served as chief justice of the Supreme Court and governor of New York.

Kellogg, Frank (1856–1937).   A Republican senator and Calvin Coolidge's secretary of state, Kellogg is best known for the Kellogg-Briand Pact, in which 62 nations renounced war. He also worked on improved relations with Latin America. He won the 1929 Nobel Peace Prize.

Kennan, George (1904–).   A diplomat and historian, Kennan set out the principles of containment policy that dominated U.S.-Soviet foreign policy in the post–World War II era and throughout the cold war. He was a Foreign Service officer in Europe's hot spots before and during World War II and was ambassador to the USSR until the Soviets demanded his removal. He wrote, among other books, *American Diplomacy 1900–1950* (1951), his memoirs, and a study of Soviet-U.S. relations that won a Pulitzer Prize.

Kennedy, John F. (1917–1963). As president, from 1961 to 1963, Kennedy presided over several foreign-affairs crises, most notably the failed Bay of Pigs invasion and the Cuban Missile Crisis. He escalated the Vietnam War, established the Peace Corps, and developed the Alliance for Progress, which gave economic aid to Latin America.

Kissinger, Henry (1923–). This German-born statesman-scholar served Presidents Nixon and Ford during a tumultuous era in international relations. As secretary of state, he played a major role in formulating foreign policy, negotiating the end of the Vietnam War, a cease-fire in the 1973 Arab-Israeli war, and the reestablishment of relations, after a break of several decades, with China. A recipient of the Nobel Peace Prize, he is the author of several books on foreign policy.

Lodge, Henry Cabot (1850–1924). A powerful senator, as chairman of the Senate Foreign Relations Committee he opposed U.S. membership in the League of Nations and defeated the Treaty of Versailles.

Lodge, Henry Cabot, Jr. (1902–1985). Grandson of Henry Cabot Lodge, and like his grandfather a senator from Massachusetts, he became ambassador to the United Nations as well as to South Vietnam and West Germany. It was as a chief negotiator in the Vietnam peace talks that he put his stamp on American foreign policy.

Marshall, George (1880–1959). After building a stellar military career that spanned both world wars, Marshall served as Truman's secretary of state. His greatest achievement was organizing the program of postwar aid to European allies that bears his name and led to his being awarded the Nobel Peace Prize.

McGillivray, Alexander (1759–1793). This half-Scot, half-Creek statesman worked on behalf of his Indian nation, serving as a British agent during the Revolution and later signing a treaty with Spain to supply him with arms, which he then used to fight the new U.S. government. In 1790, he negotiated a treaty in which the Creeks acknowledged U.S. sovereignty over some Creek lands and agreed to keep the peace.

McKinley, William (1843–1901). McKinley's presidency (1897–1901) was dominated by foreign affairs: the Spanish-American War, the annexation of Hawaii and the Philippines, and the Open Door policy for China, which advanced American interests and commerce by promoting unrestricted trade.

Monroe, James (1758–1831). Monroe was the fifth U.S. president. After the Revolution, he undertook important diplomatic missions to establish the new nation's ties to France, England, and Spain. As envoy to France under Jefferson, he negotiated the Louisiana Purchase. Later, as Madison's secretary of state, he negotiated boundary settlements with Canada and, as president, oversaw the acquisition of Florida from Spain. He is best remembered for the 1823 Monroe Doctrine, the nation's first major foreign-policy statement, which warned European nations away from involvement in the Western Hemisphere.

Morgenthau, Hans J. (1904–1980). This German-American political scientist wrote a seminal work on foreign policy, entitled *Politics Among Nations: The Struggle for Power and Peace* (1948), which redefined the 19th-century concept of national interest by asserting that nations should act only where there is a realistic national interest, not merely out of ideological motivation.

Nixon, Richard (1913–1994). From 1969 to 1974, Nixon was an active foreign-policy president who promulgated the Nixon Doctrine, which rewrote the role of America in world affairs by stating that the United States would no longer be the world's policeman. He also opened relations with China and presided over detente, a relaxing of tensions with the USSR.

Perry, Matthew (1794–1858).   A U.S. naval officer, Perry undertook two important missions to Japan in 1853 and 1854 that opened Japan to trade.

Pinckney, Thomas (1750–1828).   Pinckney negotiated the Treaty of San Lorenzo, better known by his name, which established commercial relations with Spain and opened the Mississippi River to navigation.

Polk, James K. (1795–1849).   Elected to the presidency on an expansionist platform, Polk resolved the Oregon Question with Britain and went to war against Mexico, thus securing for the United States much of the West.

Reagan, Ronald (1911–).   Foreign policy during his presidency (1981–1989) involved taking a tough stand against Communist expansion, especially in Central America, which he backed with the largest peacetime defense buildup in U.S. history. Reagan, cajoled and led by Mikhail Gorbachev, also presided over negotiations to reduce arms that produced a major arms-reduction treaty with the USSR.

Rohde, Ruth Bryan Owen (1885–1954).   The daughter of William Jennings Bryan, Owens was named ambassador to Denmark in 1933, making her the first woman ever appointed to represent the United States in a foreign country.

Roosevelt, Eleanor (1884–1962).   As diplomat and first lady, Roosevelt traveled widely throughout the country and the world during the presidency of her husband, Franklin Roosevelt. After his death, President Truman appointed her delegate to the United Nations, where she became chairman of the Human Rights Commission.

Roosevelt, Franklin Delano (1882–1945).   As president from 1933 to 1945, in addition to leading the nation out of the Great Depression, Roosevelt also mobilized and led the United States during World War II. He gradually moved the nation toward war through the Lend-Lease program, which aided European allies by providing them with arms to fight Germany. Roosevelt had hoped to play a role in shaping the postwar peace, but he died shortly after the Yalta Conference in 1945. He coined the name United Nations and actively supported its establishment.

Roosevelt, Theodore (1858–1919).   A transitional president who served to move the United States onto a larger world stage, Roosevelt conducted foreign policy with a bold hand. He signed the treaties granting the United States the right to build the Panama Canal and also set forth the Roosevelt Corollary to the Monroe Doctrine, which justified U.S. intervention in Latin America. He helped to bring about an end to the Russo-Japanese War, for which he won the Nobel Peace Prize.

Root, Elihu (1845–1937).   As secretary of state under Theodore Roosevelt, Root was an internationalist who worked to improve U.S.–Latin American relations, and concluded an agreement with Japan in support of the Open Door Policy for China. He negotiated a series of treaties with European nations that encouraged arbitration, for which he was awarded the Nobel Peace Prize in 1912. Later he supported U.S. entry into the League of Nations and helped establish the World Court at The Hague.

Rusk, Dean (1909–).   As secretary of state under Presidents Kennedy and Johnson, he was a vehement defender of the Vietnam War and a strong advocate of containment.

Seward, William Henry (1801–1872).   As Lincoln's secretary of state, he helped keep Britain and France from recognizing the Confederacy, and continuing in the position, under Johnson negotiated the purchase of Alaska, known at the time as "Seward's Folly" and since considered an important acquisition.

Stettinius, Edward (1900–1949).   As secretary of state under Franklin Roosevelt, he helped to establish the United Nations and served as its first U.S. delegate.

Stimson, Henry (1867–1950).   Serving as President Hoover's secretary of state, Stimson led delegations to disarmament conferences. His Stimson Doctrine asserted that the acquisition of territories by force would not be recognized. An internationalist, Stimson also served as secretary of war under Taft, FDR, and Truman; he was the first American to serve in the cabinets of four presidents.

Taft, William Howard (1857–1930).   As president expanding upon the foreign policy of his predecessor, Theodore Roosevelt, Taft refocused its emphasis to "dollar diplomacy"—promoting business investment and increased trade as a means of gaining political influence.

Truman, Harry (1884–1972).   As president, Truman undertook the country's most massive foreign-aid bill, the Marshall Plan, which helped to rebuild a war-torn Western Europe in the face of Soviet aggression. He also worked to establish NATO, which rearmed Europe and provided for its joint defense. He made the decision to use the atomic bomb against Japan during World War II.

Tyler, John (1790–1862).   In 1841 Tyler became the first vice president to step into the presidency. He presided over the signing of the Webster-Ashburton Treaty, which settled a land dispute between the United States and Canada, as well as the annexation of Texas.

Vandenberg, Arthur (1884–1951).   As a senator, Vandenberg was a staunch isolationist until the attack on Pearl Harbor, after which he became a major figure in the war effort and, in its aftermath, a staunch supporter of the United Nations and NATO.

Webster, Daniel (1782–1852).   As congressman, senator, and secretary of state, Webster, who was also a great orator, was an important force in the pre–Civil War years. He presided over the Webster-Ashburton Treaty in 1842, which settled boundaries between the United States and Canada.

Wilson, Woodrow (1856–1924).   One of the few presidents to have an academic background, Wilson was a major force in U.S. foreign policy. An internationalist and idealist, he refuted the foreign policies of his predecessors and supported the Mexicans during their 1910 revolution. Yet his moralist's view gave his policies rigidity, and he eventually intervened, like his predecessors, to protect U.S. interests in Mexico. Attributing the outbreak of war in Europe in 1914 to imperialism, he tried unsuccessfully to mediate a settlement before leading the United States into the war against Germany in 1917. At the war's end, Wilson led the U.S. peace delegation in Paris, where he included in the treaty a covenant establishing the League of Nations. One of his greatest disappointments was his inability, due partly to his ill health, and partly to a popular disenchantment with Europe and its wars, to persuade Americans to join the world peace organization.

ADDITIONAL SOURCES OF INFORMATION

Barry, James P. *The Louisiana Purchase, April 30, 1803.* Watts, 1973.

Cohen, Warren I. *The Cambridge History of American Foreign Relations.* 4 vols. Cambridge University Press, 1993.

Dougherty, J. E. and Pfaltzgraff, R. L., Jr. *Contending Theories of International Relations.* 3rd ed. Harper College, 1990.

Garst, Rachel, and Tom Barry. *Feeding the Crisis: U.S. Food Aid and Farm Policy in Central America.* University of Nebraska Press, 1990.

Hendry, James M. *Treaties and Federal Constitutions.* Greenwood, 1955, repr. 1975.

Kolko, Joyce, and Gabriel Kolko. *The Limits of Power: The World and United States Foreign Policy, 1945–1954.* Harper & Row, 1972.

LaFeber, Walter. *Inevitable Revolutions: The United States in Central America.* 2d rev. ed. Norton, 1993.

Langley, Lester D. *The Cuban Policy of the United States: A Brief History.* Wiley, 1968.

———. *The United States and the Caribbean in the Twentieth Century.* 4th ed. University of Georgia, 1989.

Pastor, Robert, and Jorge Casteneda. *Limits to Friendship: The U.S. and Mexico.* Random House, 1989.

Smith, Robert Freeman. *The Caribbean and the United States.* Macmillan, 1994.

Welch, Richard E., Jr. *Response to Revolution: The U.S. and the Cuban Revolution, 1959–1961.* University of North Carolina Press, 1985.

9

Business, Labor, and Economics

SIGNIFICANT EVENTS IN AMERICAN BUSINESS

Some of the original 13 colonies were founded as business ventures, and from its beginnings as a nation, the United States has encouraged and protected commerce. Gradually its role in the world marketplace expanded, fueled by ample resources and an entrepreneurial spirit. Inventions and the hard work of the laboring class spurred the Industrial Revolution, and since the beginning of the 20th century the country has been one of the world's industrial giants.

The Colonial Era

1500s	Fishing fleets from England, France, Spain, and Portugal fish the waters of the Great Banks.
1607	The British settlement at Jamestown is sponsored by a group of London investors.
1608	Manufacturing begins at Jamestown, where a glass factory is set up a year after the settlement is established.
	Quebec is founded by Samuel de Champlain as a fur-trading center. Fish and fur drive French exploration and settlement in North America. They are less significant factors in British America, but still provide occupations for many and fortunes for a few.
c. 1612	John Rolfe introduces the cultivation of tobacco at Jamestown, and by 1615 it is the cash crop of the Virginia colony, bringing profits to the London investors who sponsored Jamestown.
1621	Squanto, a Patuxet Indian who had been kidnapped and lived in England for a few years, gives the Pilgrims seed corn and teaches them native planting practices. Corn, or maize, becomes a principal grain in New England; wheat and rye are also successful.
1643	The first ironworks in the colonies opens in Lynn, Massachusetts, northeast of Boston. In 1654, the colonies' first fire engine is made here. Lynn will continue to be an important manufacturing center for more than two centuries.
1651	Parliament passes the first of the Navigation Acts. It requires that all colonial products bound for England be carried in English-owned ships.

MERCANTILISM

If colonial industry and commerce did not always thrive, there was a reason: England did not want them to. According to the theory of mercantilism, colonies existed for the benefit of the mother country and were primarily intended to supply raw materials, not compete in their manufacture. Seeking to increase its own exports, Britain enacted a series of Navigation Laws starting in 1651 that eventually destroyed the commerce of Holland, its chief rival. First all raw materials bound for England had to be carried in English-owned ships. Later certain "enumerated articles"—including colonial sugar, tobacco, cotton, and indigo—could be shipped only to England, where they were reexported at great profits to English merchants.

The effect of these regulations not only devastated Holland and other colonial powers; it also limited American trade and enterprise. Through a series of additional acts Parliament further suppressed colonial industries that might unfavorably compete with industries at home. The Hat Act of 1732, for example, sought to enhance the prosperity of London felt makers by prohibiting Americans from exporting hats from one colony to another and placing various limitations on apprenticeships in the hat trades.

Still, until political tensions between Britain and the colonies in North America intensified, many restrictions were only loosely enforced. Despite the Molasses Act of 1733, New England imported great quantities of West Indian sugar for manufacture into rum. But when, after the French and Indian War, the colonists were taxed to support both British troops and British enterprise, they claimed that their rights as Englishmen were being violated. The tax on tea was only the last in a series of laws designed to manipulate American products and markets in favor of Britain, but it proved to be the last straw. Rather than pay reduced prices, even with a tax, to support a British monopoly, colonists in Boston and elsewhere dumped the tea they loved into harbors and burned tea ships in ports, setting in motion a drive toward independence that was every bit as much economic as political (see Chapter 2).

1693	Rice cultivation is introduced in South Carolina. It is well suited to the colony's freshwater swamps and sluggish rivers near the sea, and it quickly becomes a staple crop. By 1730 South Carolina rice is called the best in the world.
1705	Copper ore is discovered near Simsbury, Connecticut, and a small enterprise develops around the deposits. English law discourages this development, and most ore is shipped to England for smelting.
1712	Nantucket fishermen capture a sperm whale, and the superiority of its oil sparks the whaling industry.
1721	The Board of Trade reports that commerce with the colonies totals almost £2.4 million (£1.5 million in colonial products and £.9 million in English products).
1733	Now England's iron industry has 6 furnaces and 19 forges.
1740	Caspar Wistar's glass manufactory in Salem County, West Jersey, begins operations.
1742	Benjamin Franklin invents the Franklin stove, an improvement in efficiency and safety over fireplaces.
1745	Indigo cultivation, introduced to South Carolina a few years earlier by Elizabeth (Eliza) Lucas Pinckney, reaches a stage of profitable production, stimulating a dye-stuffs industry. Indigo becomes one of the colony's major export crops, long before cotton, which is difficult to process until the invention of the cotton gin.
1750s	The colonial shipbuilding industry thrives; by 1760 one-third of Britain's ships are built in the colonies.
	Worldwide increases in wheat prices encourage farmers in Virginia to turn away from tobacco, and wheat becomes the most dynamic element in the Virginia economy, especially in the Northern Neck and Great Valley.
1750	Parliament passes the Iron Act, which prohibits colonists from manufacturing iron products and restricts them to supplying raw iron to England, where manufacturing can be done. Many colonial finishing companies are thus forced out of business.
1755	The first whaler is outfitted at New Bedford, Massachusetts. For the next century New Bedford will be the greatest whaling port in the world.
1760	Jared Eliot publishes *Essay upon Field Husbandry in New England*, the first major treatise that describes modified farming techniques for the colonies.
	Lynn merchants are organizing the shoe industry that will make this industrial center famous.
1763	Henry William Stiegel, a German immigrant, brings glassworkers from England to his factory in Manheim, Pennsylvania.

1764   Rhode Island imports 14,000 barrels of molasses, which will be made into rum and shipped to Africa, where it will be exchanged for Africans, who will be taken to the West Indies and sold as slaves. (For more on the Triangular Trade, see Chapter 2.)

1765   The first chocolate factory opens at Milton Lower Mills, near Dorchester, Massachusetts. Chocolate is one of the colonies' most popular beverages.

The New England fishing industry, with 665 ships and 10,000 men, harvests a "crop" worth nearly £2 million.

1768   The New York City Chamber of Commerce is organized.

1769   Silversmith Abel Buell casts the first American type fonts.

1770   Three thousand tons of masts are shipped from the colonies to England.

1772   Philadelphia leads Boston, New York, and Charleston in overseas trade.

1775   The colonies supply close to 15 percent of the world's iron.

The Federal Era

1781   Robert Morris is appointed superintendent of finance. He is largely responsible for stabilizing the new nation's finances by chartering the Bank of North America, obtaining loans from Holland and France to back a new paper currency, and meeting interest payments on the war debt.

1784-   Wartime inflation, a flood of British goods following the Treaty of Paris, war debts, and a
1786   shortage of gold and silver coin send the new nation into its first depression.

c. 1784   Oliver Evans installs an automatic flour mill in Wilmington, with a number of grain-handling machines he has patented.

1785   Based on a decimal plan formulated by Thomas Jefferson, Congress makes the dollar the official currency.

1787   Robert Gray sails to Oregon and eventually, in 1790, to Canton, where he exchanges sea otter skins for Chinese goods, thus opening the lucrative China trade.

The new U.S. Constitution authorizes Congress to lay and collect taxes, to borrow money, to regulate interstate commerce, to coin money, to establish post offices and post roads, and to enact patent legislation. Clearly the new, stronger federal government will play a significant role in promoting and protecting commerce and industry.

1790   Slater's mill, built by Samuel Slater in Pawtucket, Rhode Island, begins spinning cotton. Slater, who arrived from England in 1789 having memorized textile machinery that the British hoped to keep secret, makes improvements that will successfully mechanize cotton carding and spinning—creating a textile industry for New England and a new market for the cotton South.

1791   Supported by Federalists and opposed by Jeffersonians, the first Bank of the United States is chartered by the federal government.

An excise tax is imposed on distilled liquor.

Alexander Hamilton, secretary of the treasury, issues his Report on Manufactures, outlining a program of tariffs to encourage domestic industry.

1792   The Mint of the United States in Philadelphia begins coining silver and gold.

1793   Eli Whitney invents the cotton gin, which makes cotton a cash crop, initiates a vast expansion of the textile industry, and entrenches the slave system.

Cotton gin

1794   Cordwainers in Philadelphia organize an early labor union.

1798   A direct federal property tax is levied in anticipation of war with France.

       Eli Whitney gets a federal contract and sets up a factory near New Haven, Connecticut, to build rifles with interchangeable parts, anticipating the assembly line production of the next century.

1802   The first brass-rolling mill, Abel Porter and Company, opens in Waterbury, Connecticut.

       Two shipments of Spanish merino sheep set a "merino mania" in motion that greatly stimulates the wool industry, especially during the Embargo of 1807 and the War of 1812 that follows.

       Gideon Putnam begins to build a hotel and village at Saratoga Springs, New York, which will in later years be a popular spa.

1807   Attempting to force warring Britain and France to stop interfering in neutral trade and shipping, Congress passes the Embargo Act, forbidding almost all foreign commerce. The embargo is repealed in 1809 but trade with Britain remains banned.

       Robert Fulton launches the *Clermont* on the Hudson River, the first commercially successful steamboat.

       Eli Terry and Seth Thomas begin their Connecticut clockworks concern, the first to mass-produce clocks with interchangeable parts.

       Cotton is the number one export. With the exception of 1809, 1815, and the four Civil War years, cotton continues as the leading U.S. export into the 1890s.

1811   The charter of the first Bank of the United States is allowed to expire, as it is opposed by entrepreneurs and agrarian interests.

1812   The first drug mill is established in Philadelphia by C. V. Hagner.

William Monroe begins to manufacture lead pencils.

1814   In Waltham, Massachusetts, the Boston Associates open the first mechanized factory for producing cotton fabric, combining spinning and weaving. New England mill production quickly rises and the region will be the leading center for cotton-textile manufacturing for the next 30 years.

1816   The Second Bank of the United States is chartered for 20 years, this time with the support of the Jeffersonians, thus establishing a central banking system that will regulate state banking and help to stabilize the economy.

The first protective tariff is passed.

1817   The New York stock exchange is established.

1818   Duties on iron products, cotton, and woolens are raised.

1819   A bank panic occurs following inflation, speculation in western lands, and contraction of credit, and a six-year depression sets in.

1820s   With the success of Erie Canal bonds, New York surpasses Philadelphia as a commercial center.

1822   The Boston Associates begin to build a factory at the junction of the Concord and Merrimack rivers, renaming the settlement Lowell in memory of Francis Cabot Lowell, who had improved on British models for a spinning machine and power loom. When the factory opens the next year, it employs young girls from New England farm families, who live in dormitories provided by the company. Lowell is the first designed manufacturing city.

1824   The Franklin Institute opens in Philadelphia, "for the promotion of the mechanic arts."

The tariff is raised again.

1825   The first patent for canning is issued.

1828   In the Tariff of Abominations, duties are raised to their highest levels yet. Southerners protest, and John C. Calhoun writes a treatise justifying the doctrine of nullification. The divergent economic interests of the nation are becoming increasingly clear.

1830   President Andrew Jackson vetoes the Maysville Road Bill, saying that the federal government ought not to support an internal improvement entirely within one state.

Peter Cooper operates *Tom Thumb*, the first commercially viable steam locomotive.

1832   South Carolina refuses to collect high federal tariffs and nullifies the tariffs of 1828 and 1832.

President Andrew Jackson creates a banking crisis by refusing to renew the charter of the Second National Bank and then transferring government funds from it to state banks. The head of the National Bank responds by calling in commercial loans, causing a panic that precipitates a recession.

1833   President Jackson threatens to use federal forces to collect the tariff but also proposes a reduced tariff bill that pacifies the South.

TARIFFS AND TRADE

Because all tariffs—duties on imported goods—benefit some and penalize others, the tariff has always been a hot political issue and a significant influence on the American economy. Alexander Hamilton was only the first to argue that high tariffs would benefit American industry—providing jobs for workers and profits for entrepreneurs.

Hamilton's program was gradually enacted in the early years of the republic, as the first tariff passed by the First Congress, designed primarily to raise revenue, was replaced following the War of 1812 by protectionist tariffs, designed to protect native industries. The tariffs of 1816, 1818, and 1824 steadily increased duties on wool and cotton cloth in support of the new textile industries of New England. They also taxed iron manufactures, lead, glass, and hemp. Eventually New England commercial and shipping interests objected, but the most vocal protests came from the South following the tariff of 1828—the Tariff of Abominations—which set the highest rates yet, approaching half the value on some items. A new tariff in 1832, followed by the Compromise Tariff of 1833, expanded the list of duty-free items and provided for a gradual reduction of duties, thus pacifying the South Carolinians who had threatened to refuse to collect these duties and asserted that a state had the right to nullify an unacceptable federal law.

The crisis was averted, but the tariff issue had clarified the divergent economies of North and South that would eventually lead to civil war. In 1861, facing a wartime economy and in the absence of any representation from the South, Congress enacted the Morrill Tariff, which raised duties, and the trend continued during the period of Republican domination after the war. The Dingley Tariff, passed in 1897, raised duties to the all-time high of 57 percent.

By this time American industries hardly needed protection, and the Payne-Aldrich Tariff (1909) and Underwood Tariff (1913) lowered duties. At the same time, the new income tax was about the replace import duties as the chief revenue source for the federal government. Although post–World War I tariffs were high, reflecting the isolationism that dominated the American outlook, the general trend throughout the 20th century has been toward free trade. As early as 1934 the Trade Agreements Act authorized the president, without congressional action, to enter into agreements with other nations for specific reductions, and following World War II the General Agreement on Tariffs and Trade (GATT) granted concessions among the 28 participating nations.

Formerly a political football in contests between states and sections, the tariff became primarily a foreign policy issue, with boycotts and most-favored nation status used as leverage to compel, for example, the Union of South Africa and the People's Republic of China to end human rights violations, the Union of Soviet Socialist Republics to permit the emigration of Soviet Jews, and Japan to open its markets to U.S. exports. Most recently, however, the North American Free Trade Agreement (1993), whereby the United States, Canada, and Mexico eliminated most tariffs on goods imported from each other, again raised regional and economic sector animosities. Organized labor feared that U.S. jobs would be eliminated as companies "moved south" to take advantage of cheaper labor in Mexico. Environmentalists argued that increased commerce would not only increase environmental degradation but that Mexico's laxer environmental protection laws would undermine U.S. standards. Even within Texas, where the administration of Governor Ann Richards strongly supported the agreement, the effects were recognized as uneven, with the manufacturing centers of Dallas, Fort Worth, and Houston anticipating an increase in jobs and border counties anticipating an increase in illegal immigration.

Today, in a world where the economy is increasingly global, where multinational corporations compete in international markets, tariff issues are likely to be increasingly complex and less capable of being directed by domestic or foreign policy goals.

1836   President Jackson, concerned about widespread use of paper money, issues the Specie Circular, declaring that the federal government will henceforce require hard currency for the purchase of western public lands. When, the next year, British banks call in their American loans, a six-year depression sets in.

The U.S. Patent Office is established.

1837   John Deere invents the steel plow, capable of breaking prairie sod.

1839   Inventor Charles Goodyear discovers vulcanized rubber.

1840 Samuel Cunard, a Canadian, begins the first steamship line between Britain and the United States.

1843 Congress authorizes $30,000 to build a 40-mile telegraph line between Baltimore and Washington, D.C.

The word *millionaire*, used, some say for the first time, in the obituary of Pierre Lorillard, tobacco grower and banker, has actually been around for decades.

1844 Samuel Morse sends the first long-distance telegraph message ("What hath God wrought!") from Washington, D.C., to Baltimore.

1846 The Walker Tariff Act, a moderate protective tariff, lowers import duties and expands the list of duty-free goods.

Elias Howe patents the lock-stitch sewing machine.

1847 Cyrus McCormick opens his reaper factory in Chicago.

1848 The first chewing gum is manufactured in Bangor, Maine.

1849 The Pacific Railroad Company becomes the first chartered railroad to operate west of the Mississippi.

Building the railroad

1851 Isaac Singer patents an improved sewing machine and organizes I. M. Singer and Company. He continues to patent improvements, and his company soon leads the industry.

The Industrial Era

1851 Western Union Company, an amalgamation of small telegraph firms, is founded.

1852 Elisha Otis invents a safety device to prevent the fall of the elevator should the hoisting mechanism fail. The first passenger elevator is installed in 1857.

1853	The New York Central Railroad is created when ten smaller railroads consolidate.
	The Baltimore & Ohio opens its rail line connecting the East Coast to Chicago.
1857	A short but sharp depression grips the nation as the financial markets experience their first wave of panic selling.
1858	The first message is conveyed by transatlantic cable. When it ceases working Cyrus Field funds a new project, successful in 1866.
1859	The first oil well is drilled at Titusville, Pennsylvania.
	The Great Atlantic and Pacific Tea Company is founded; it will later become the A&P, one of the first great chain stores.
1860	Macy's department store, destined to become one of the world's largest retail stores, opens in New York City.
1861	There are some 30,000 miles of railroad track in the country, almost three-quarters in the North.
	The first oil refinery is set up in Pittsburgh.
	The first transcontinental telegraph message is sent between San Francisco and Washington, D.C.
	The first federal income tax—3 percent—is enacted, but only on the rich.
1861-1865	The North and the South struggle to fund the Civil War; inflation soars.
1862	The Morrill Land-Grant College Act funds the establishment of colleges that will promote agricultural and industrial development.
	The Legal Tender Act empowers the federal government to print paper money, called "greenbacks."
	The first Pacific Railway Act authorizes the building of the first transcontinental railway, the Union Pacific. A second act, in 1864, authorizes the Central Pacific.
	The Internal Revenue Service is established.
1863	Ebenezer Butterick manufactures the first commercially produced paper dress patterns.
	The National Bank Act prohibits state banks from printing paper money.
1864	The Pennsylvania Railroad begins using steel for its rails.
	George Pullman invents the railway sleeping car that will carry his name.
	The Bessemer process of steel manufacturing is introduced in Troy, New York.
	"In God We Trust" appears on U.S. coins for the first time.
1865	About $450 million in greenbacks are in circulation.
	The Chicago Stockyards, which will become the world's largest meat-processing facility, opens in Chicago.
1866	Coinage of the first five-cent piece made from nickel is authorized. Ten years earlier a one-cent piece made with nickel has been introduced.
1867	Farmers organize the Grange movement, which supports farms in many cooperative endeavors.
	George Pullman organizes the Pullman Palace Car Company.
Late 1860s	A huge economic boom is fueled by the end of the Civil War in 1865. Manufacturing soars, with the expansion of railroads leading the way.
1868	Congress enacts an eight-hour day for laborers and mechanics employed on federal projects.

1869   The world's first transcontinental railroad is completed when the last spike is hammered into place at Promontory Point in Utah Territory, joining the Union Pacific and the Central Pacific.

Wall Street experiences its first Black Friday when financier Jay Gould and others try to corner the market on gold and fail.

John D. Rockefeller combines several smaller oil companies to found Standard Oil Company of Ohio.

1871   Luther Burbank experiments with plant hybrids; his Burbank potato achieves immediate success.

1872   Montgomery Ward, the first mail-order company, begins operations in Chicago.

1873   The Coinage Act puts the United States on the gold standard. Silverites call it the "Crime of '73."

Iron ore shipments from the Lake Superior region exceed 1 million tons, most bound for Pittsburgh, where Bethlehem Steel opens in this boom year.

The failure of the banking house of Jay Cooke and company sends the nation into a five-year depression.

I. M. Singer and Company, now selling 230,000 sewing machines a year, begins making machines with fully interchangeable parts.

Andrew Carnegie begins concentrating on steel manufacturing, acquiring firms that will be consolidated into the Carnegie Steel Company and turning Pittsburgh into a major center for steel production. Carnegie will reap enormous profits and give most of it ($350 million) away.

MILLIONAIRES: AN ALL-AMERICAN ACHIEVEMENT

Only in America is it acceptable to wear a T-shirt that announces: "The one who has the most when he dies wins." Americans' fascination with wealth, spurred on by the optimistic belief that anyone with enough energy can amass a lot of money, has led to a perverse head count involving the number of millionaires the nation can claim—only these days we are more likely to count billionaires instead. There was a time, though, when the number of millionaires felt like a measure of the nation's progress.

Consider, for example, that in 1840 the still relatively new nation boasted 40 millionaires. By 1880 the number had more than doubled to 100. Only 12 years later it had increased tenfold, to produce an amazing 4,000 millionaires, and in another 15 years it had increased tenfold a second time, for a count of 40,000—at which point millionaires became too commonplace to bother with.

1874   Several states pass so-called Granger laws, establishing maximum shipping rates railroads can charge. Railroads are charging farmers high rates for short-distance shipments but lower rates for long-haul industrial shippers.

1876   Alexander Graham Bell demonstrates the telephone.

1877   The Bell Telephone Company is organized.

The Socialist Labor party is founded in New York City, largely by German immigrants influenced by Karl Marx.

1878   The first U.S. copper refinery to use gaseous fuel operates in Ansonia, Connecticut.

1879   Frank W. Woolworth opens the first successful "five and dime" store in Lancaster, Pennsylvania. All goods sell for a fixed price—a nickel or a dime.

       Thomas Edison invents the lightbulb.

1880   George Pullman builds his railway car factory outside Chicago, eventually establishing a model industrial community with homes for workers and supervisors.

       U.S. copper production amounts to 30,000 tons. The industry is centered in Michigan's Upper Peninsula.

1882   John D. Rockefeller founds the Standard Oil Trust, the first megacorporation organized as a trust.

1883   Thomas Edison discovers that an incandescent lamp can be used as a valve to admit negative but not positive electricity—the so-called Edison effect. He sees no practical application, but it is later the basis of the vacuum tube in radio-telephony (for more on Edison, see Chapter 11).

1884   Inventor Nikola Tesla arrives in the United States from Budapest. In the next years he will work in Edison and Westinghouse labs, in applications for the principle of the rotating electromagnet field, with contributions to lighting, transmission, telephony, and telegraphy.

1885   American Telephone & Telegraph (AT&T) is formed.

1886   Police fire into a crowd of striking workers at the McCormick factory in Chicago, killing four. When anarchists organize a protest rally in Haymarket Square, a bomb explodes, killing seven policemen, and more workers are killed in the confusion that follows. Eight anarchists are tried for conspiracy. The episode discredits labor and heightens nativist fears of immigrants and radicals. Although not directly involved, the Knights of Labor rapidly loses members.

       The Westinghouse Electric Company is incorporated.

1887   A whiskey trust and a sugar trust are formed.

       The Interstate Commerce Commission is established to regulate interstate transportation, especially the railroads. It is a prototype for independent regulatory commissions.

1889   I. M. Singer and Company manufactures the first electric sewing machine.

       Otis Brothers installs an electric elevator in a New York City office building.

       Several regional Farmers' Alliances unite to form the National Farmers' Alliance and Industrial Union. A parallel organization is the National Colored Farmers' Alliance and Cooperative Union.

1890   A tobacco trust—the American Tobacco Company—is formed.

       The Silver Purchase Act has the effect of increasing the currency in operation and weakening the federal gold reserves. It is repealed following the panic of 1893.

       The Sherman Anti-Trust Act is the federal government's first attempt to break up the monopolies that now control American business, commerce, and industry.

THE TRUSTS

The merger mania of the 1980s was nothing compared to the first burst of trust fever at the end of the 19th century. When the states relaxed their incorporation laws, individuals such as John D. Rockefeller and J. P. Morgan were able to establish large monopolistic corporations that came to be known as trusts.

(continues)

THE TRUSTS (CONT.)

John D. Rockefeller was the first industrialist to overwhelm the competition—by means both legal and illegal—and thus corner the market on petroleum with Standard Oil. His corporate counsel soon devised a new method of trust management, whereby stockholders in competing enterprises would turn over control of their companies to a board of directors that would manage them to maximize their benefit. Thus the modern industrial megacorporation was born.

Other industries quickly followed suit: By 1890 there was a whiskey trust, a sugar trust, a tin-can trust, and a tobacco trust. J. P. Morgan managed to orchestrate mergers to form International Harvester and reorganized a number of railroads. His greatest triumph was in forming U.S. Steel, the nation's first billion-dollar corporation and, at the time, the largest in the world.

It seemed only a matter of time until a money trust formed, and indeed three large investment companies—Morgan, the National Bank of New York, and the National City Bank of New York—merged, putting control of what had previously been 112 separate financial organizations into the hands of a few directors.

Trust fever soon turned to antitrust fever, though, when muckraking journalists Ida Tarbell and Henry Demarest Lloyd took on the big businesses in a series of well-documented books and articles, creating a public outrage that forced the federal government to take action.

Basically there are three ways in which governments can deal with monopolies. They can break them up, regulate them, or, in a method favored in Europe and little liked in the United States, convert them to public ownership, an approach most Americans deem too socialistic. After 1890, the Sherman Anti-Trust Act could be used to break up the trusts, and regulation was accomplished through the establishment of government oversight agencies, such as the Interstate Commerce Commission.

The Sherman Anti-Trust Act proved relatively weak, however, partly for its ambiguity, somewhat rectified by the Clayton Anti-Trust Act of 1914. Ironically, one of the first applications of the Sherman Anti-Trust Act, which outlawed combinations "in restraint of trade," was against labor unions! In 1902, when the hatters' union launched a nationwide boycott against a nonunion manufacturer in Danbury, Connecticut, the company sued the union as an unlawful combination is restraint of trade, and the Supreme Court agreed. The Clayton Act, as a consequence, specified that antitrust law was not applicable to unions.

Antitrust laws did, however, force the breakup or restructuring of Swift and Company, Standard Oil, and American Tobacco, and suits were successfully brought against General Electric and Westinghouse for price-fixing, but not until 1982 was AT&T forced to break up.

Although the United States has more antitrust laws than any other nation, like most other nations it has been unable to stop the march of corporate progress. The ownership of many industries is heavily concentrated in the hands of a few persons, and in the late 1980s many American corporations became or were bought by international corporations.

1892   Boll weevils enter the United States in Texas. It annually destroys about 8 percent of the total cotton crop, resulting in a $200–$300 million loss.

    General Electric Company opens a corporate research and development division.

    Pinkerton detectives are called in to break a strike by steelworkers at Andrew Carnegie's steel plant in Homestead, Pennsylvania, and seven strikers are killed.

1893   Another panic sends the nation into a long depression.

1894   Henry Demarest Lloyd, a muckraking journalist, publishes his influential antitrust book, *Wealth Against Commonwealth*.

    When an American Railway Union strike at the Pullman factory outside of Chicago threatens to disrupt train travel across the nation, a federal court issues an injunction forbidding this interference with interstate commerce. Union leader Eugene V. Debs ignores the injunction and is arrested and jailed. Federal troops break up the strike, but not before 13 workers are dead and 50 wounded. Railroad workers in 26 more states protest, with additional violence and death.

Wheat prices bottom out, causing reverse immigration as prairie schooners head back east with the words "In God we trusted, in Kansas we busted" painted on their sides. But during the 1890s new strains of wheat promote recovery. Turkey, a hard, red, winter wheat first introduced by German Mennonites in 1873, is planted throughout the southern plains. Other red, spring wheats are favored on the northern plains. In the 1930s through the 1960s, other varieties are introduced. In the 20th century competition for the export market comes from Canada, Australia, and Argentina.

1897   The Klondike gold rush begins. Between 1885 and 1929 more than $175 million in gold is taken out of Alaska. Seward's purchase of the "Folly" is justified.

1898   The National Consumers' League, the first major watchdog group to oversee consumers' rights, is founded. It fights for labeling laws and criticizes workplace conditions.

1899   The Olds Motor Works is formed in Detroit. Its plant uses interchangeable parts, preparing the way for mass production.

1900   The Currency Act formally puts the United States on a gold standard.

Although the value of cotton exported has continued to rise since the days when it was "king," it now constitutes only 17 percent of exports.

The United States is first in the world in productivity. In the early 20th century it manufactures one-third of the world's goods. It is also first in iron and steel production.

THE GOLD STANDARD

One of the major problems confronting any nation is establishing and maintaining the value and stability of its money. From the date of its founding the United States proved to be no exception. Colonial America, for example, forbidden to mint its own coins or to import British money, traded largely in commodities. Foreign coins, especially ones from Spain, circulated freely. The initial coinage of the government under the Constitution was based on both gold and silver at a fixed ratio that tended to overvalue silver. By the late 19th century this inherent tension came to have political overtones in the struggle between agrarian and industrial interests. Finally in 1900 gold became the official standard. Not until the Great Depression did President Franklin D. Roosevelt, using his executive powers under the Emergency Banking Act, prohibit banks from paying in gold or from exporting gold, a gesture that, in effect, took the country off the gold standard. By the 1950s the dollar, in addition to other methods of payment such as the "paper gold" issued by the International Monetary Fund, had replaced gold as the international unit of exchange.

President Richard Nixon officially ended the nation's tie to gold in 1975. Henceforth, gold would be traded on the free market like any other commodity.

The Modern Era

1901   J. P. Morgan forms U.S. Steel by merging several other steel companies, including Andrew Carnegie's Carnegie Steel Company; it becomes the first billion-dollar corporation.

The discovery of oil at the Spindletop field spurs Texas industry and marks the beginning of the decline of ranching and farming in the state.

King C. Gillette organizes the Gillette Safety Razor Company. In 1903 he sells 51 razors and 168 blades. One year later he sells 90,000 razors and 12,400,000 blades.

Corbis-Bettmann

J. P. Morgan

1903   Maggie Lena Walker, an African American, becomes the first woman bank president.
Henry Ford founds the Ford Motor Company in Detroit.

The Department of Commerce and Labor is created as a cabinet-level post. In 1913 it is divided into two cabinet-level departments.

Secretaries of Commerce and Labor

Secretary	President	Appointed	Secretary	President	Appointed
George B. Cortelyou	Roosevelt, T.	1903	Oscar S. Straus	Roosevelt, T.	1906
Victor H. Metcalf	Roosevelt, T.	1904	Charles Nagel	Taft	1909

1904   Ida Tarbell publishes her two-volume, muckraking *History of the Standard Oil Company*. It had been published, serially, in *McClure's* magazine one year earlier.

1905   The first Rotary Club, a civic organization for business and professional people, is organized in Chicago.

1906   The agency later known as the Food and Drug Administration is established under the Pure Food and Drug Act, and the Meat Inspection Act sets standards. Both acts are strongly influenced by the revelations of corruption and disregard for safety and cleanliness from the pages of Upton Sinclair's *The Jungle*.

1908   Ford introduces the Model T car, which costs $850. More than 15 million are sold in the next 20 years.

Model T

The Supreme Court rules that the Sherman Anti-Trust Act applies to labor unions.

In *Muller v. Oregon*, the Supreme Court upholds a law that limits the work hours of women. Louis D. Brandeis represents Oregon and submits what comes to be known as a "Brandeis Brief," marshaling statistical and sociological evidence to bolster the state's case.

1909   Congress enacts the Payne-Aldrich Tariff, which lowers tariffs on imported goods almost 20 percent.

The National Conservation Commission makes the first systematic count of the nation's natural resources.

1911   Under the Sherman Anti-Trust Act, the Supreme Court orders Standard Oil and American Tobacco to restructure.

1913   The Sixteenth Amendment permits an income tax.

The Ford Motor Company sets up the first assembly line.

The Federal Reserve System replaces the Independent Treasury System. It creates 12 Reserve Banks and a Federal Reserve Board to direct the nation's credit and monetary affairs.

Congress divides the Department of Commerce and Labor into two separate cabinet-level departments.

Secretaries of Commerce

Secretary	President	Year Appointed	Secretary	President	Appointed
William C. Redfield	Wilson	1913	Luther H. Hodges	Johnson, L. B.	1963
Joshua W. Alexander	Wilson	1919	John T. Connor	Johnson, L. B.	1965
Herbert C. Hoover	Harding	1921	Alex B. Trowbridge	Johnson, L. B.	1967
	Coolidge	1923	Cyrus R. Smith	Johnson, L. B.	1968
William F. Whiting	Coolidge	1928	Maurice H. Stans	Nixon	1969
Robert P. Lamont	Hoover	1929	Peter G. Peterson	Nixon	1972
Roy D. Chapin	Hoover	1932	Frederick B. Dent	Nixon	1973
Daniel C. Roper	Roosevelt, F. D.	1933		Ford	1974
Harry L. Hopkins	Roosevelt, F. D.	1939	Rogers C. B. Morton	Ford	1975
Jesse Jones	Roosevelt, F. D.	1940	Elliot L. Richardson	Ford	1975
Henry A. Wallace	Roosevelt, F. D.	1945	Juanita M. Kreps	Carter	1977
	Truman	1945	Philip M. Klutznick	Carter	1979
W. Averell Harriman	Truman	1947	Malcolm Baldrige	Reagan	1981
Charles Sawyer	Truman	1948	C. William Verity, Jr.	Reagan	1987
Sinclair Weeks	Eisenhower	1953	Robert A. Mosbacher	Bush	1989
Lewis L. Strauss	Eisenhower	1958	Barbara H. Franklin	Bush	1992
Frederick Mueller	Eisenhower	1959	Ronald H. Brown	Clinton	1993
Luther H. Hodges	Kennedy	1961	William Daley	Clinton	1997

Secretaries of Labor

Secretary	President	Year Appointed	Secretary	President	Appointed
William B. Wilson	Wilson	1913	James D. Hodgson	Nixon	1970
James J. Davis	Harding	1921	Peter J. Brennan	Nixon	1973
	Coolidge	1923		Ford	1974
	Hoover	1929	John T. Dunlop	Ford	1975
William N. Doak	Hoover	1930	W. J. Usery, Jr.	Ford	1976
Frances Perkins	Roosevelt, F. D.	1933	F. Ray Marshall	Carter	1977
L. B. Schwellenbach	Truman	1945	Raymond J. Donovan	Reagan	1981
Maurice J. Tobin	Truman	1949	William E. Brock	Reagan	1985
Martin P. Durkin	Eisenhower	1953	Ann D. McLaughlin	Reagan	1987
James P. Mitchell	Eisenhower	1953	Elizabeth Hanford Dole	Bush	1989
Arthur J. Goldberg	Kennedy	1961	Lynn Martin	Bush	1991
W. Willard Wirtz	Kennedy	1962	Robert B. Reich	Clinton	1993
	Johnson, L. B.	1963	Alexis Herman	Clinton	1997
George P. Schultz	Nixon	1969			

1914   The Federal Trade Commission is established to maintain competition in the U.S. economy but prevent monopolies and unfair or deceptive trade practices.

The Clayton Anti-Trust Act strengthens the Sherman Anti-Trust Act by outlawing specific practices. It also forbids the use of antitrust law against labor organizations and the use of the injunction against labor.

At a time when skilled autoworkers are getting $2.50 per day and unskilled $1.80, Henry Ford raises wages to $5 per day and cuts the workday from nine to eight hours.

1915　Alexander Graham Bell places the first transcontinental telephone call, from New York to San Francisco.

1916　The Ford plant assembly line in Detroit rolls off its one-millionth car; it is producing 2,000 cars per day.

The Federal Farm Loan Act makes credit available to farmers.

Congress passes a child labor law, but it is ruled unconstitutional in 1918.

1917　To ensure that the railroads operate smoothly during World War I, President Woodrow Wilson orders the federal government to run them, which it does for 26 months.

1919　The Radio Corporation of America (RCA) is formed.

The Red Scare tarnishes the reputation of labor, as labor radicalism is associated with socialism, communism, and left-wing political agitation by immigrants and aliens, many of whom are deported.

1920　The Transportation Act returns control of the railroads to the owners.

KDKA, America's first commercial radio station, begins broadcasting from Pittsburgh, Pennsylvania.

Union membership totals 19.7 million, but only 28 percent of the workforce.

1924　A Child Labor Amendment passes Congress and is sent to the states but fails to be ratified.

1926　RCA, AT&T, and the British General Post Office hold the first transatlantic radiotelephone conversation between New York City and London.

RCA organizes the National Broadcasting Company (NBC) as the first radio network.

1927　The Columbia Broadcasting Company (CBS) is organized to compete with NBC.

The first television transmission from New York City to Washington, D.C., is accomplished by AT&T.

1928　Ford Motor Company assembly lines produce the 15-millionth—and last—Model T.

Clarence Birdseye applies his quick-freeze process to poultry, fish, and shellfish. In a few years frozen foods revolutionize American eating habits.

1929　The Agricultural Marketing Act establishes the Federal Farm Board, whose purpose is to encourage and promote marketing of farm products through cooperatives. Its programs were too timid and failed to deal with price fluctuations; it ceased to exist in 1933.

In October the stock market crashes, and the Great Depression begins. Within just four years national income drops by almost 50 percent and unemployment reaches 12.8 million, amounting to one-quarter of the civilian workforce. Bank suspensions number 659 in 1929; 1,352 in 1930; 2,294 in 1931; and 1,456 in 1932. Deposits in these banks total more than $3.5 billion.

1930　The Hawley-Smoot Act raises tariffs to an all-time high, with the result that international trade drops substantially. The American economy, on the other had, is quite self-sufficient. The year before the enactment of the tariff, imports amount to only 5 percent of national income.

Newspaper magnate William Randolph Hearst owns 33 newspapers whose circulation totals 11 million.

The worst bank failure to date occurs when the Bank of the United States in New York City collapses. With more than 400,000 depositors—many recent immigrants—the effect is devastating.

1932　The Norris–La Guardia Anti-Injunction Act forbids the use of the injunction in the majority of labor disputes.

1932   To aid those felled by the Great Depression, Wisconsin passes the first law establishing state-supported unemployment insurance.

1933   Within 100 days of his inauguration, Franklin D. Roosevelt ushers through Congress a series of legislation intended to ease the Great Depression. The Securities Act helps provide information about the stock market. The Emergency Banking Act provides for temporary insurance for depositors. The Federal Deposit Insurance Corporation becomes permanent in 1935. Relief measures, such as the Civilian Conservation Corps, the Agricultural Adjustment Administration, and the Federal Emergency Relief Administration are created. Funding is secured for the Tennessee Valley Authority, which is a project for flood control as well as massive electrification. The Emergency Farm Mortgage Act and the Home Owners' Loan Corporation provide help to farmers and homeowners.

In one of his first acts, Roosevelt declares a bank holiday, closing all banks from March 6 to March 12. In the first few days after the bank holiday about three-quarters of the banks are declared sound and reopened. Public confidence is restored.

When Roosevelt issues an executive order that banks cannot exchange money for gold, he in effect takes the United States off the gold standard.

1934   The Securities and Exchange Commission is established to regulate securities trading.

The Federal Communications Commission is established to regulate communication.

The Federal Farm Mortgage Corporation is created to help farmers refinance their debt.

The Trade Agreements Act enables the president to negotiate trade agreements with individual nations. By 1941, 22 agreements have been negotiated and signed. The overall effect lowers tariffs and stimulates American exports.

1935   The Rural Electrification Administration is created to bring electrical power to rural areas.

The Social Security Act establishes a federal pension for retirees.

The Revenue Act of 1935 (Wealth Tax Act) increases taxes on incomes above $50,000 and on corporations with incomes of more than $50,000 and profits greater than 10 percent.

Pan American airlines begins transpacific air service.

In *Schechter Poultry Corp. v. United States*, the Supreme Court finds the National Industrial Recovery Act unconstitutional.

The Committee for Industrial Organizations has great success organizing steelworkers.

1936   The Robinson-Patman Act encourages competition and discourages monopolies by making it illegal for businesses to collude on prices.

1937   William Randolph Hearst controls a publishing empire of 20 newspapers including the New York *Evening Journal,* the *Chicago Examiner,* and the *Los Angeles Examiner.*

1938   The Revenue Act reduces taxes on large corporations and raises taxes on small businesses, thus establishing a pattern that will persist for decades.

The Civil Aeronautics Board is created to oversee civil air transport.

Du Pont manufactures the first nylon product, a toothbrush. Wallace Carothers and a team of Du Pont scientists had been working on nylon for a decade. Nylon will be used in clothing and a host of other products.

1939   Regularly scheduled commercial television broadcasts begin.

1940   The first nylon stockings, which replace the far more expensive silk ones, are marketed.

1942   After the attack on Pearl Harbor, industry gears up for World War II. Government spending puts a complete end to the Depression. Unemployment virtually disappears, and by war's end 17 million jobs have been created. Industrial production increases 96 percent. Between 1941 and 1943 more than 5 million women enter the workforce, and in manufacturing hourly wages rise from 49¢ in 1940 to 79¢ in 1945, a 62 percent increase.

1945   World War II ends, and the United States enters a postwar economic boom.

1946   The Council of Economic Advisers is formed to shape domestic policy on employment.

1947   The United States produces 60 percent of the world's steel.

1950   Diners Club becomes the comprehensive credit card.

1952   To prevent a steel strike that could cripple the nation's businesses, President Harry Truman seizes the steel mills. The Supreme Court decides the seizure is unconstitutional.

1953   The first commercial color broadcast on television heralds a new market, but not until 1968 will color sets outsell black-and-white ones.

General Motors becomes the first corporation to report earnings of $1 billion annually. Six million cars roll off the assembly lines in Detroit each year.

1956   The Soil Bank is established to pay farmers not to plant certain crops in order to decrease production and to conserve the soil.

The Federal Highway Act authorizes a system of interstate highways that will make interstate commerce easier and cheaper.

1957   Electricity is produced by a nuclear reactor on an experimental basis in Shippingport, Pennsylvania.

1958   Pan American Airways introduces transatlantic jet travel.

1962   In the face of growing foreign competition, the Trade Expansion Act gives the president increased powers to cut tariffs.

Following the launch of *Telstar*, live intercontinental telecasts begin.

1963   The Office of the Special Representative for Trade Negotiations is established. In 1980 it becomes the Office of the U.S. Trade Representative.

1964   President Lyndon Johnson's War on Poverty raises millions of poor Americans out of poverty. It is the single biggest expansion of social services since the New Deal, the first to take place in a period of prosperity.

The Economic Opportunity Act provides funds for the Job Corps, VISTA, and other special programs for the poor and for youth.

1968   Automobiles built after this date must comply with the first government-mandated standards to improve car safety.

To fund the Vietnam War, President Lyndon Johnson requests a personal income tax surcharge of 10 percent.

In the largest merger to date in U.S. history, the New York Central and Pennsylvania Railroads form one company.

César Chávez, heading the United Farm Workers, launches a boycott of table grapes that wins widespread support. In 1970 grape workers get contracts from California growers.

1969   The Food and Drug Administration bans the sale of artificial sweeteners called cyclamates.

1970s   Even though real earnings have doubled since 1930, the nation experiences "stagflation," stagnant earnings combined with inflation, which reaches 13.5 percent by the end of the decade.

1970   Congress establishes the Environmental Protection Agency, which will, among other activities, regulate businesses' interactions with the environment.

When the National Air Quality Control Act calls for a 90 percent reduction in auto pollutants, the auto industry claims it cannot afford to meet these standards.

Postal workers walk out in a wildcat strike, the largest public-employee strike in the country's history.

1971   To slow down spiraling inflation, President Richard Nixon imposes a 90-day freeze on wages and prices and severs the dollar's tie to gold, which means the dollar will now float on the world currency market. To slow inflation, Nixon uses wage and price controls until 1973.

Amtrak, a quasi-governmental corporation, is created by Congress to operate many of the nation's remaining passenger trains.

1972   Out of fears for public health, the government bans the use of DDT, a common pesticide.

The Consumer Product Safety Commission is established.

Following a 1970 act of Congress, cigarette advertising is banned on radio and television.

César Chávez's United Farm Workers becomes a member of the AFL-CIO.

1973   The Arab oil embargo sends petroleum product prices soaring and leaves Americans waiting on gas lines.

1974   The oil embargo ends.

Regulations for food and household good labels go into effect.

Tony Boyle, president of the United Mine Workers, is convicted of the murder of rival Joseph A. Yablonski and his wife and daughter.

1975   In a pattern that will repeat in other state and local governments in the next two decades, New York City declares itself to be near bankruptcy and must take stringent measures, including the cutting of basic services, to restore its financial standing. It also receives a bailout loan from the federal government.

Long the world leader in steel production, the United States now produces only 16 percent of the world's steel.

When seven major northeastern railroads stand on the brink of bankruptcy, the Consolidated Rail Corporation, or Conrail, is formed, with a federal subsidy, to save them.

1977   Imports exceed exports by $29.2 billion, creating the largest trade deficit in U.S. history. This, however, is only the beginning of a chronic trade imbalance that mushrooms to well over $100 billion each year throughout the mid-1980s and into the 1990s.

The Alaskan oil pipeline, bitterly opposed by conservationists, begins operations.

The Department of Energy is created.

Secretaries of Energy

Secretary	President	Year Appointed	Secretary	President	Year Appointed
James R. Schlesinger	Carter	1977	John S. Herrington	Reagan	1985
Charles Duncan, Jr.	Carter	1979	James D. Watkins	Bush	1989
James B. Edwards	Reagan	1981	Hazel R. O'Leary	Clinton	1993
Donald P. Hodel	Reagan	1982	Frederico F. Pena	Clinton	1997

1978   In a move to "deregulate" industry, the Civil Aeronautics Board is scheduled for phaseout. The trucking industry is also deregulated.

Californians initiate tax revolt by adopting Proposition 13, a constitutional amendment cutting local property taxes by more than 50 percent.

1978-
1980   Inflation soars to a record-setting 10–13.5 percent.

1980   A windfall-profits tax is imposed on the oil industry.

Congress authorizes loan guarantees of more than $1.5 billion to prevent Chrysler, the third largest automobile manufacturer, from going under.

The United States produces one-fifth of the world's automobiles; in 1960, it had produced nearly half.

1981   In the first major revision of the tax code in decades, President Ronald Reagan cuts corporate and personal taxes. Domestic spending is severely cut at the same time that the military budget nearly doubles. Supply-side economics, which advocates a tax cut and reduced government spending to fix an ailing economy, replaces Keynesian economics, which has prevailed since the New Deal and favors government spending to stimulate the economy.

When air traffic controllers strike, President Reagan refuses to recognize their right to do so and replaces them, thus destroying their union.

1982   The country sinks into a recession, and unemployment reaches 9.5 percent, the highest since before World War II.

After a lengthy antitrust lawsuit, American Telephone & Telegraph (AT&T) is forced to break up into regional companies.

1983   The nation begins to recover, but unemployment drops only slowly; the stock market makes modest gains.

1985   The United States becomes a debtor nation. In 1986 it will be the world's number one debtor nation, with a debt of $220 billion.

1987   The stock market crashes, but federal protections and regulations initiated in the New Deal, plus an infusion from the Federal Reserve, keep the economy stable.

1989   A savings-and-loan scandal involving the abuse and misuse of bank funds, is scheduled for a bailout by Congress, costing taxpayers $180 billion.

The minimum wage is raised to $4.55 per hour, over President George Bush's veto.

1990   The country sinks into a recession that will soon prove to be worldwide.

Union membership stands at 16.7 million, 16 percent of the workforce.

1993   The North American Free Trade Agreement establishes Canada, Mexico, and the United States as a free-trade zone in which most goods and services are sold without tariffs.

1995   Republicans take over Congress and vow to cut spending even more and eradicate the deficit by the year 2000.

The Interstate Commerce Commission, the nation's first regulatory agency, is abolished.

THE DEBT: HOW IT GREW

The deficit, which is the amount the government spends beyond what it takes in during a fiscal year, is either good or bad, depending upon which group of economists one chooses to listen to. One school maintains that a deficit weakens the economy while another believes deficit spending serves as an important economic stimulus. In any event, the national deficit has grown and shrunk over the years in fairly regular cycles, never consuming more than about 10 percent of federal outlays (and sometimes consuming far less) until the 1980s—when it began to rise steadily to what more and more people consider to be alarming proportions.

(continues)

THE DEBT: HOW IT GREW (CONT.)

Public Debt of the United States

Year	Total Public Debt ($)	Per Capita Public Debt ($)
1791	75,463,000	—
1800	82,976,000	—
1810	53,173,000	—
1820	91,016,000	—
1830	48,565,000	—
1840	3,573,000	—
1850	63,453,000	—
1860	64,844,000	2.06
1870	2,436,453,000	61.06
1880	2,090,909,000	41.60
1890	1,122,397,000	17.80
1900	1,263,417,000	16.60
1910	1,146,940,000	12.41
1920	24,299,321,000	228.23
1930	16,185,310,000	131.51
1940	42,967,531,000	325.25
1950	257,357,352,000	1,696.67
1960	286,330,761,000	1,584.70
1970	370,918,707,000	1,811.12
1980	914,000,000,000	4,036.00
1985	1,827,000,000,000	7,655.00
1990	3,266,000,000,000	13,132.00
1995	4,974,000,000,000	18,930.00

1995- The White House and the Republican-dominated Congress reach an impasse over the
1996   fiscal year 1996 budget that shuts the government down for weeks. In a compromise mea-
       sure, a plan is enacted for eliminating the federal debt by the year 2002.

PANICS AND DEPRESSIONS

Until the Great Depression, the U.S. economy seemed to run in 20-year cycles. Following economic controls established by New Deal legislation, the downturns have been less severe in their effects.

1784- The new nation's first depression results from a shortage of currency and the war debt.
1786

1819   A panic is precipitated by wild speculation in western lands, followed by a sharp contraction of credit, led by the Second Bank of the United States. A six-year depression ensues.

1832   When President Andrew Jackson refuses to renew the charter of the Second Bank of the United States and transfers government funds to state banks, Nicholas Biddle, head of the National Bank, calls in commercial loans. A panic and recession follow. Eight hundred banks close, and the banking system collapses. One-third of manual laborers are out of work in New York City alone. Nationwide, unemployment reaches 10 percent.

1836   President Jackson precipitates another banking crisis by issuing the Specie Circular, declaring that the federal government will henceforth require hard currency for purchase of western public lands.

1837-   In response, English banks raise interest rates and reduce credit, sending shock waves through
1843   the cotton market that initiate a six-year depression.

1857-   This brief panic is notable for the role that telecommunications plays. When a branch of
1858   the Ohio Life Insurance and Trust Company fails, news that would formerly have taken weeks to crisscross the nation, its impact diminishing with time, is known within hours, thanks to the telegraph. The news induces one of the first waves of panic selling in the stock market. The underlying cause of the recession is a downturn in agricultural exports brought on by the end of the Crimean War in Europe, as well as overspeculation in railroads and real estate.

1873-   A major depression begins, precipitated by the failure of Jay Cooke and Company, which
1878   financed the Northern Pacific Railroad. Businesses topple, and the New York Stock Exchange closes for ten days. Before the depression is over, 100 banks and 18,000 businesses will fall.

1893-   A series of railroad bankruptcies causes banks to call in their loans. In all, 150 banks, 200
1897   railroads, and 15,000 small businesses succumb. Unemployment reaches 25 percent, and in New York City alone 20,000 are homeless. The depression lasts four years.

1929-   The Great Depression is set off by a stock market crash. Before it is over, 12.8 million
1941   people will have suffered unemployment and in 1930 and 1931, 2,300 banks fail.

1957-   In a short period of slow growth, this recession causes a 0.8 percent drop in the nation's
1958   gross national product (GNP) and causes 6.8 percent unemployment.

1973-   The GNP drops 1.3 percent, and unemployment rises to 8.3 percent.
1975

1981-   The GNP drops only 2.5 percent, but unemployment soars to 9.5 percent, the highest since
1982   before World War II. A decade of stagnant growth follows. The Midwest is hard-hit.

1990-   A worldwide recession occurs. In the United States it is regional, hitting the Northeast two
1992   years before the West Coast and leaving the usually hard-hit industrial Midwest virtually untouched.

THE RISE AND FALL OF LABOR

The rise of the factory system changed human relationships and work patterns. The paternalistic family work system, replicated in the apprenticeship system, disappeared as men and women left their homes and household shops to work in noisy factories at repetitive tasks under the sharp eye of a supervisor whose goal was increased production and higher profits for the factory owner—the capitalist. It did not take laborers long to realize that only their numbers gave them power and to band together to demand better working conditions and more pay. Factory owners—quite naturally—sought to suppress such unions, and the story of labor is a story of the long struggle for the right to organize and to assert some measure of control over the terms and conditions of work.

1741   Journeymen calkers in Boston combine in agreement not to accept notes for wages.

1768   An early organized strike takes place when New York tailors protest a cut in wages.

1791   Slater's mill employs nine operatives—seven boys and two girls—all between the ages of 7 and 12.

CHILD LABOR

When Slater's mill operated in the 1790s with a "work force" of children, no one objected. Children had always worked on the family farm, and if the family engaged in domestic industry, children carded wool and spun. Farm boys were sometimes hired out to neighbors, and by age 14 many were apprenticed.

The early textile mills of New England found young people suitable to the work. The machines needed only monitoring, and the work was not heavy. Girls put empty bobbins on the machines and took them off when they were full. Boys carried bobbin boxes where they were needed. The famous "Lowell girls" of a later generation were older, but the machinery was also more complex. Although all these young people worked long hours—sunup to sundown—so did most children of the farming and laboring classes of New England.

Factory owners were not inattentive to the welfare of the children in their care. Samuel Slater set up a Sunday school to teach reading and writing, and at Lowell the girls were housed in company boardinghouses where their leisure and morals were carefully supervised. As early as 1813 Connecticut required manufacturing establishments to provide for the education of child operatives, and in the next decades Massachusetts took the lead compulsory education for children and the limitation of their work hours.

But when, following the Civil War, the textile industry moved south, child labor took on a more sinister cast. Cheap, nonunion labor was the reason for building mills in the Carolina Piedmont, and these new factories relied on the labor of women and children. In 1880, 6 percent of American children between the ages of 10 and 15 were employed (not including agriculture). In 1900, one-quarter of southern mill operatives were children under 15, and half of these were below the age of 12.

The Knights of Labor had advocated that child labor be prohibited, and later unions recognized that, as children could not be unionized, only legislation could protect them. In the early years of the 20th century progressives made the abolition of child labor a pillar of their reform program. Seeking to publicize abuses, the National Child Labor Committee sent photographer Lewis Hine throughout the South to record the faces and sad fortunes of children who worked in the region's cotton mills, mines, and canneries. By 1920 most states had laws that forbade the employment of children under 14 and set an eight-hour day for workers under 16. Compulsory education laws also limited the availability of children for factory work.

But when the federal government sought to enact a nationwide ban on child labor, the Supreme Court struck it down as an unconstitutional interference in local labor conditions. Progressives countered with a constitutional amendment, which was sent to the states in 1924 but never ratified. Not until the Fair Labor Standards Act of 1938 was the employment of children under 16 prohibited in manufacturing and mining.

1794	Shoemakers in Philadelphia form the Federal Society of Journeymen Cordwainers, an early trade union that survives a strike in 1799.
	The Typographical Society of New York promotes higher wages, shorter hours, and better working conditions and sponsors benefits for sickness and burials.
1824	Women organize a strike in a Pawtucket, Rhode Island, textile mill.
1828	Workers in Philadelphia join together to seek political redress for some of their grievances. They promote a ten-hour workday, which becomes a chief aim for labor for the next two decades. By 1860, though not standard, the ten-hour day is widely accepted.
1833	When nine craft organizations in New York City join to form the General Trades Union, craft groups in other cities quickly follow suit. These workingmen's parties initiate a wave of strikes that sweep the nation and eradicate whatever bond previously existed between apprentices and journeymen and their masters.

1834	Local organizations of the General Trades Union form the National Trades Union, whose purpose is less to achieve workers' benefits than to overturn the wage system that has arisen along with factories.
	Women at the Lowell mills "turn out" to protest a wage cut. They do the same in 1836, again in vain, but these are the largest strikes in the country to date.
1837	The National Trades Union movement collapses under the weight of this year's financial panic.
1840	President Martin Van Buren gives labor at least a token victory when he signs an executive order establishing a ten-hour workday for certain federal government employees.
1842	In Massachusetts, child labor is limited to ten hours a day for children under the age of 12.
1845	In response to unionizing by men, women who work in the Lowell textile mills found the New England Female Labor Reform Association, which argues forcefully for a ten-hour workday.
1847	New Hampshire is the first state to pass legislation limiting the workday to ten hours.
1852	The National Typographical Union is founded, combining locals in the United States. It is an early, and long-lived, national craft union.
1860	Ten thousand workers in the Massachusetts shoe industry stage a six-week walkout.
1866	The National Labor Union is founded in Baltimore. In contrast to the labor organizations formed by specific craftspeople, who promote their own interests, its focus is general labor reform, that is, worker ownership of factories and opposition to the wage system.
1869	Philadelphia garment cutters found the Knights of Labor. This early union includes skilled and nonskilled workers and welcomes women and blacks. It calls for an eight-hour day. Membership peaks in 1886 at almost 1 million.
1877	The Great Railroad Strike occurs when workers on the Baltimore & Ohio in Martinsburg, West Virginia, stage a local strike that soon spreads across the country. For the first time, federal troops are used to quell a strike. Although more than 100 strikers are killed, this strike, the first nationwide work stoppage, gives labor a sense of its power.
1882	The first Labor Day is celebrated. Congress makes it a legal annual holiday in 1894.
1884	The new federal Bureau of Labor begins to compile labor statistics.
1886	The American Federation of Labor (AFL) forms to represent skilled workers, organized by craft. More disciplined than the Knights of Labor, which it supersedes, it excludes women, blacks, and immigrants, and works specifically for its members rather than for general labor reform. As it gains strength, it closes the labor-reform unions out of the negotiating process. Samuel Gompers is the influential first president.
1892	When silver miners in Coeur d'Alene, Idaho, refuse a wage cut, owners stage a lockout and bring in strikebeakers. Violence erupts, and federal troops are dispatched to the area.
1893	The Western Federation of Miners, a large and militant union, is organized.
1897	The American Federation of Labor has a half million members.
1901	The Socialist Party of America is formed.
1902	In Pennsylvania 150,000 United Mine Workers, led by John Mitchell, strike for five and one-half months, demanding a 20 percent increase in wages and an eight-hour workday. Under pressure from President Theodore Roosevelt to arbitrate, they settle for a 10 percent increase and no change in the workday.
	Maryland becomes the first state to enact workmen's compensation.
1904	The AFL claims 1.7 million members.

1904	The National Child Labor Committee is organized to promote legislation ending child labor.
1905	In an attempt to take the labor movement into a more inclusive and radical direction, workers in Chicago, with support from the Socialist party, found the Industrial Workers of the World (IWW), which briefly becomes a force among unskilled workers and immigrant laborers.
1909-1910	The militant "Uprising of the 20,000," a New York City shirtwaist workers' strike, brings previously unorganized, unskilled workers into unions.
1911	The Triangle Shirtwaist Factory fire in New York City kills 146 women workers. The tragedy underscores the terrible working conditions of urban sweatshops. Building codes, labor reform, and the International Ladies Garment Workers Union are all taken more seriously.
1912	During its brief heyday, the Industrial Workers of the World (known as the Wobblies) turns a walkout of textile workers in Lawrence, Massachusetts, into the famous "Bread and Roses" strike and forces union recognition.
1913	A six-month silkworkers' strike in Paterson, New Jersey, inspires a benefit at Madison Square Garden in which the strike's most dramatic moments are reenacted.
1914	In Ludlow, Colorado, a mining town dominated by the Colorado Fuel and Iron Company, the United Mine Workers strike for better safety, higher wages, and union recognition. When the state militia and private guards fire on the strikers, 14 persons, including 11 children, are killed. The Ludlow massacre arouses widespread protest against management policies.
1919	When Boston police go out on strike, Massachusetts governor Calvin Coolidge becomes famous for asserting, "There is no right to strike against the public safety by anybody, anywhere, anytime."
1919-1920	Steelworkers in Midwestern steel towns strike unsuccessfully to force management to recognize their union. In Gary, Indiana, a violent riot leaves 18 dead.
1920	The AFL claims 4 million members.
1929	Only 30 percent of the industrial labor force works more than 54 hours a week.
1932	The Democratic party earns the support—and votes—of labor.
1933	President Franklin D. Roosevelt, in recognition of the growing power of labor, appoints Frances Perkins as the first female head of the Department of Labor. She is an active supporter of workers and unions.
1935	The Wagner Act establishes the right of workers to join unions and bargain collectively and creates the National Labor Relations Board to oversee collective bargaining.
	The AFL claims 2.5 million members.
	Advocating the organization of workers by industry rather than craft, John L. Lewis and the United Mine Workers found the Committee for Industrial Organization to concentrate on organizing workers in mass-production industries such as rubber, cars, and steel. It is later expelled from the AFL and becomes the Congress of Industrial Organizations (CIO).
1936	The Walsh-Healy Act sets a minimum wage for workers at companies that hold government contracts. It also mandates an eight-hour day and 40-hour week, and bans child and convict labor.
1936-1937	Autoworkers initiate a sit-down strike at the General Motors plant in Flint, Michigan. When GM recognizes the United Auto Workers union, the stage is set for huge growth in the UAW and other mass-production industry unions.

1938	The Fair Labor Standards Act mandates a minimum wage and 40-hour week and forbids child labor in any business engaged in interstate commerce.
	The CIO claims 4 million members.
1941-1945	To support the war effort, unions are encouraged to sign no-strike pledges, and many do. Yet more strikes occur in this four-year period than in any other in American history.
1943	John L. Lewis and the United Mine Workers stage a walkout that resists government efforts to end it.
1945	Together the AFL and CIO claim 14.8 million members, or more than one-third of the nonagricultural workforce—an all-time high.
1946	The Employment Act establishes maximum employment as a government responsibility.
1947	The Taft-Hartley Act overrules many of the prolabor elements of the Wagner Act.
1952	To prevent a steel strike that could cripple the nation's businesses, President Harry Truman seizes the steel mills. The Supreme Court decides the seizure is unconstitutional, and the seven-week strike that follows puts 600,000 unionized steelworkers and 1.4 million workers in industries dependent on steel out of work.
1955	The American Federation of Labor and the Congress of Industrial Organizations merge to form the AFL-CIO.
1957	The federal government investigates racketeering in labor unions and finds Dave Beck, the head of the Teamsters Union and vice president of the AFL-CIO, guilty of misuse of funds. Teamsters vice president Jimmy Hoffa is also charged. Several unions are expelled from the AFL-CIO.
1959	A four-month steel strike ends only when a federal court invokes the Taft-Hartley Act and orders workers to return to their jobs.
1963	To combat discriminating wage scales, the Equal Pay Act mandates equal pay for equal work for industries engaged in interstate commerce.
1964	Although traditionally discriminatory toward minorities and women, labor unions endorse civil rights legislation.
	Jimmy Hoffa, head of the Teamsters, is convicted of jury tampering and fraudulent use of union funds; he receives a 13-year prison sentence. President Richard Nixon commutes his sentence. Shortly after he is released, he vanishes in Detroit.
1970	Workers' wages have tripled since 1945.
1975	In the first strike by physicians, doctors in New York and Chicago protest working conditions and long hours.
1978	President Jimmy Carter halts a coal miners' strike, citing the national interest.
1981	President Ronald Reagan, instituting strong antilabor policies, orders striking air traffic controllers to return to work or face dismissal. More than 11,000 are dismissed, and the union is decertified.
1984	For the first time, the AFL-CIO endorses a presidential candidate—Democrat Walter Mondale.
1992	Women represent 45 percent of the civilian labor force.
1993	Organized labor unsuccessfully opposes the North American Free Trade Agreement, fearing loss of U.S. jobs to cheaper labor in Mexico.
1994	Major-league baseball players go on strike in August and the rest of the season is canceled. The players object to owners' salary caps. This longest work stoppage in professional sports ends in April 1995.

MAJOR ACTS OF CONGRESS AFFECTING BUSINESS, COMMERCIAL AGRICULTURE, AND LABOR

1791   Bank Act. The Bank of the United States is chartered for 20 years. It will serve as the government's fiscal agent and depository for federal funds.

1807   Embargo Act. This act forbids almost all foreign commerce. It is repealed in 1809.

1816   Bank Act. The charter of the Bank of the United States having expired, a second bank is chartered, again for 20 years.

1840   Independent Treasury Act. This act, repealed in 1841 but passed again in 1846, orders public funds to be deposited in the Treasury building and in subtreasuries in various cities. It serves as the basis for the U.S. fiscal system until 1913.

1862   Legal Tender Act. This act empowers the federal government to print paper money.

1863   National Bank Act. This act prohibits state banks from printing paper money.

1873   Coinage Act. This act, which omits provision for coining silver dollars, demonetizes silver and puts the United States on the gold standard.

1875   Resumption Act. This act sets January 1, 1879, as the date for redemption of greenbacks in specie. But in 1878 gold reserves are so high that Congress agrees to allow the $347 million in outstanding greenbacks to remain in circulation.

1878   Bland-Allison Act. This act provides for the freer coinage of silver, requiring the U.S. government to purchase between $2 and $4 million of silver bullion to be coined into silver dollars.

1882   Chinese Exclusion Act. In reaction to an influx of cheap Chinese labor, this act denies Chinese laborers entry to the United States for ten years and is the first major attempt to regulate the immigrant labor force.

1887   Interstate Commerce Act. This act prohibits discriminatory rates and practices by railroads and establishes the first regulatory commission, the Interstate Commerce Commission.

1890   Silver Purchase Act. This compromise act requires the U.S. government to double its purchase of silver and adds to the amount of money in circulation.

Sherman Anti-Trust Act. This first federal attempt to regulate monopolies is ambiguous. It states that combinations "in restraint of trade" are illegal, and is actually used against labor unions as well as trusts.

1898   Erdman Act. This act provides for the voluntary mediation of labor disputes, but it is rarely used in the next decade. Its provision prohibiting railroads from requiring that employees promise not to join a union is overturned by the Supreme Court.

1900   Currency Act. This formally puts the United States on a gold standard.

1906   Pure Food and Drug Act. This act prohibits the sale of impure food and drugs and requires that food labels include contents; it also creates what is later called the Food and Drug Administration to oversee enforcement of the law.

Meat Inspection Act. This mandates improvements in the sanitary conditions at meat-packing plants and their enforcement through federal inspection.

1909   Income Tax Amendment. Congress passes this constitutional amendment, which authorizes a federal tax on incomes. It is ratified by the states and goes into effect as the Sixteenth Amendment in 1913.

1913   Federal Reserve Act. This act restructures the nation's banking and currency system and creates the Federal Reserve Board to direct the nation's credit and monetary affairs.

1914   Clayton Anti-Trust Act. This act strengthens the Sherman Anti-Trust Act and exempts labor organizations from antitrust laws.

Federal Trade Commission Act. This act establishes this independent agency charged with maintaining a competitive enterprise through preventing monopolies and unfair trade practices.

1916   Federal Farm Loan Act. This act makes credit available to farmers via a system of Farm Loan Banks.

Adamson Act. This act established the eight-hour day for railroads operating in interstate commerce.

1926   Railway Labor Act. Amended later to include all forms of transportation, this law protects the collective-bargaining rights of railroad employees. A 1934 amendment establishes the National Railroad Adjustment Board to arbitrate employee-employer grievances.

1929   Agricultural Marketing Act. This establishes the Federal Farm Board, whose purpose is to encourage and promote marketing of farm products through cooperatives.

1932   The Norris–La Guardia Anti-Injunction Act. This act forbids the use of the injunction in the majority of labor disputes.

1933   National Industrial Recovery Act. This act aims at preventing the contraction of business and reducing unemployment to end the Depression.

Emergency Banking Act. This stabilizes the banks during the Depression and provides the basis for the Federal Deposit Insurance Corporation, which becomes permanent in 1935.

The Farm Credit Act. This act protects farmers against foreclosures.

1934   Securities Exchange Act. This establishes the Securities and Exchange Commission to regulate securities trading.

Federal Communications Act. This establishes the Federal Communications Commission to regulate the communication industry.

Reciprocal Trade Act. This gives the president the power to negotiate trade agreements with individual countries.

1935   Social Security Act. This establishes a federal pension for retirees, to be funded with a payroll tax.

Wagner Act (National Labor Relations Act). This act recognizes labor's right to organize and to bargain collectively; it also creates the National Labor Relations Board to oversee collective bargaining.

1936   Robinson-Patman Act. By making it illegal for businesses to collude on prices, this act encourages competition and discourages monopolies.

Walsh-Healy Act. This sets a minimum wage for workers at companies holding government contracts.

1938   Fair Labor Standards Act. This act mandates a minimum wage and 40-hour week and forbids child labor in any business engaged in interstate commerce.

Revenue Act. This act reduces taxes on large corporations and raises them on small businesses, thus establishing a pattern that will persist for decades.

1946   Employment Act. This creates the Council of Economic Advisers to advise the executive branch and establishes that maintaining employment, production, and purchasing power is a role of government.

1947   Taft-Hartley Act. Passed over President Harry Truman's veto, this act, also called the Labor-Management Relations Act, revises the Wagner Act by outlawing the unfair practices of unions as well as management. It forbids closed shops, jurisdictional strikes, secondary boycotts, and political contributions by unions (overturned by the Supreme Court). Most important, it grants the president the power to delay by 80 days a strike that threatens the national interest. It also requires union leaders to swear under oath that they are not members of the Communist party.

1956　Agricultural Act. This establishes the Soil Bank, a program under which farmers are paid not to grow certain crops, in order to decrease production and to conserve soil.

1959　Landrum-Griffin Act, also known as the Labor-Management Reporting and Disclosure Act. Enacted after an extensive congressional investigation into labor racketeering, this law attempts to outlaw corrupt practices by unions and employers.

1962　Trade Expansion Act. This act gives the president increased powers to cut tariffs to promote world trade.

1963　Equal Pay Act. This act requires equal pay for equal work in industries engaged in interstate commerce.

1964　Civil Rights Act. Title VII forbids employers and unions to discriminate on the basis of race, color, religion, national origin, and sex.

　　　Economic Opportunity Act. This act funds the Job Corps and special programs for the poor and for youth.

1967　Fair Packaging and Labeling Act. The first important law to set standards for the advertising industry and for the packaging of consumer goods, this act results from pressure by the consumer movement.

1970　Air Quality Control Act. Calling for a 90 percent reduction in auto pollutants by 1975, this act is first passed in 1967 but is given real teeth in 1970.

1975　Energy Policy Conservation Act. A result of a major oil shortage, this act attempts to conserve and allocate energy resources.

1981　Economic Recovery Tax Act. This first significant rewriting of tax law in several decades reduces corporate and personal income taxes dramatically.

1985　Gramm-Rudman Act. To control the federal deficit, this act mandates across-the-board spending cuts if deficit-reduction goals are not met.

1993　Family Leave Act. This act permits workers in companies of 50 or more employees to have up to 12 weeks a year unpaid leave for family and medical purposes.

SUPREME COURT DECISIONS AFFECTING BUSINESS, COMMERCIAL AGRICULTURE, AND LABOR

1810　*Fletcher v. Peck.* In this first decision invalidating a state law as unconstitutional, the Court says a state cannot impair the obligation of contracts.

1819　*Dartmouth College v. Woodward.* In a major boost to commercial interests, the Court rules that a charter to a private corporation is a contract, and, again, states cannot interfere with contracts.

　　　McCulloch v. Maryland. In ruling that the federal government has a right to charter a national bank and that states may not tax a national bank, the Supreme Court greatly expands the scope of federal power.

1824　*Gibbons v. Ogden.* In the first of what will be a series of decisions on interstate commerce, the Court declares that states cannot grant monopolies that restrain interstate commerce and that the power of Congress to regulate interstate commerce is supreme.

1837   *Charles River Bridge v. Warren Bridge.* The Court rules that any ambiguities in the chartered rights of corporations should be resolved in favor of broader public interests, again undercutting the power of monopolies.

1877   *Munn v. Illinois.* The Court upholds an Illinois law establishing maximum rates for storing grains, one of the so-called Granger laws enacted by state legislatures in the Midwest at the insistence of the Grange. The decision establishes the constitutional principle of public regulation of private business involved in serving the public interest.

1895   *United States v. E. C. Knight Co.* The Court rules that the Sherman Anti-Trust Act does not apply to the sugar trust, even though it refines more than 90 percent of the sugar sold in the country.

   Pollock v. Farmers' Loan and Trust Co. The Court strikes down a general income tax law, setting the stage for a constitutional amendment that will make income taxes legal.

   In re Debs. The Court upholds the validity of the injunction ordering Eugene V. Debs and others to halt the 1894 Pullman strike. A lower court had upheld the injunction on the basis of the Sherman Anti-Trust Act, but the Supreme Court upholds it on the grounds of national sovereignty and federal authority to remove obstructions to interstate commerce and the transportation of the mails.

1904   *Northern Securities v. United States.* In an important antitrust decision, the Court decides that stock transactions like those J. P. Morgan is using to form a railroad merger are an illegal restraint of interstate commerce.

1905   *Swift and Co. v. United States.* In a case involving meatpackers who combined to fix prices on sales in the Chicago stockyards, the Court rules that Congress can regulate local commerce that is part of an interstate current of commerce. The ruling establishes the "stream of commerce" doctrine, explaining that the meatpackers in the stockyards are the middle link of an interstate transaction, with cattle shipped from out of state and packed meat shipped to other states for sale.

   Lochner v. New York. The Court overturns a New York law seeking to regulate the hours of workers by holding that it interferes with the right of free contract. Oliver Wendell Holmes writes a famous dissent in which he argues that the Constitution "is not intended to embody a particular economic theory" and that "the word 'liberty' is perverted when it is held to prevent the natural outcome of a dominant opinion."

1908   *Adair v. United States.* The Court rules that a law prohibiting railroads from requiring that workers promise not to join a union is unconstitutional.

   Danbury Hatters' Case. The Court rules that a labor union's boycott of an industry restricts trade; in other words, the Sherman Anti-Trust Act applies to labor unions.

   Muller v. Oregon. The Court for the first time upholds a law that limits work hours, in this case of women.

1917   *Bunting v. Oregon.* This decision overturns *Lochner* and extends *Muller* by declaring that the government does have the power to regulate work hours.

1918   *Hammer v. Dagenhart.* The Court strikes down the Keating-Owen Child Labor Law, which prohibits shipment in interstate commerce of goods produced by child laborers, thus setting the stage for a constitutional amendment outlawing child labor (which failed to ratify).

1923   *Adkins v. Children's Hospital.* The Court strikes down an act of Congress setting minimum wages for women and children workers in the District of Columbia, again interpreting this law as price fixing and in violation of the freedom of contract.

1935   *Schechter Poultry Corp. v. United States.* The Court finds the National Industrial Recovery Act unconstitutional.

1937   *NLRB v. Jones & Laughlin Steel Corp.* The Court upholds the Wagner Act (National Labor Relations Act), finding that the federal government has the power to regulate intrastate matters that affect interstate commerce.

West Coast Hotel Co. v. Parrish. The Court upholds the minimum-wage law for women and children, overturning *Adkins*.

1941   *United States v. Darby Lumber Co.* The Court overturns *Hammer*, ruling that Congress has the authority to prohibit shipment in interstate commerce of goods manufactured in violation of federal minimum wage and maximum hours standards.

1952   *Youngstown Sheet and Tube Co. v. Sawyer.* Following President Harry Truman's seizure of the steel industry to prevent a threatened strike during the Korean War, the Court rules that the president does not have the authority to make such a seizure.

1971   *Griggs v. Duke Power Co.* The Court rules even neutral employment practices may constitute discrimination if they have a discriminatory impact.

1975   *Goldfarb v. Virginia State Bar.* The Court states that antitrust laws apply to lawyers, specifically that bar associations adopting minimum fee schedules are in violation of price-fixing provisions.

1979   *United Steelworkers of America v. Weber.* Despite *Bakke*, which undermined the use of quotas, the Court upholds racial quotas in the workplace and states that employers may be required to reserve a specified percentage of jobs for protected workers but only for a limited period of time. The number must be tied to past discrimination and must not overly tread on the rights of nonprotected groups.

1986   *Sheet Metal Workers Local 28 v. EEOC.* The Court rules that courts may order unions to use quotas to overcome past discrimination.

Meritor Savings Bank v. Vinson. The court finds that sexual harassment in the workplace, either creating a hostile work environment or leading to loss of employment, may constitute discrimination.

1989   *Wards Cove Packing Co. v. Antonio.* The Court states that statistical imbalances in race or gender in the workplace are not in themselves proof of discrimination and that plaintiffs must prove that neutral employment practices have a discriminating effect.

SIGNIFICANT PEOPLE IN AMERICAN BUSINESS, LABOR, AND ECONOMICS

Astor, John Jacob (1763–1848).   One of the country's first business magnates, Astor began as a fur trader but made his fortune in real estate. Born in poverty in Germany, he was considered the richest man in America at the time of his death.

Ayer, Harriet (1849–1903).   The first woman to make a fortune selling cosmetics, Ayer associated herself with Madame Recamier, a famous beauty of the Napoleonic era, and claimed to have a special beauty cream that had been discovered in Paris.

Borlaug, Norman (1914–).   An agronomist, Borlaug attempted to reduce world hunger through agriculture; his efforts led to his being awarded the Nobel Peace Prize in 1970.

Brady, James B. (1856–1917).   Popularly known as "Diamond Jim" for the large jewels he liked to wear and for his flamboyant manner of living, Brady earned his money selling railroad supplies and later won fame as a philanthropist.

Burbank, Luther (1849–1926).   Burbank single-handedly raised plant breeding to a science. He developed many new varieties of plants, among them the Burbank potato and the Shasta daisy. He was the author of *How Plants Are Trained to Work for Man* (1921) and co-author of *Harvest of the Years* (1927) and *Partners of Nature* (1939).

Carnegie, Andrew (1835–1919).   This financier-entrepreneur started out as a bobbin boy and telegraph messenger, then honed his managerial skills with the Pennsylvania Railroad before turning to steel manufacturing. Eventually he sold his steel company to J. P. Morgan. He used his money to fund more than 2,800 libraries and other philanthropies across the country.

Carver, George Washington (1864?–1943).   As director of agricultural research at Tuskegee Institute, Carver, an African American, devised hundreds of uses for peanuts, soybeans, and sweet potatoes, as well as working on soil improvement and crop diversification.

Chávez, César (1927–1993).   The son of Mexican-American migrant farm workers, Chavez founded the National Farm Workers Association in 1972. His United Farm Workers (UFW) became a member of the AFL-CIO in 1972. Chavez used nonviolent tactics such as boycotts to gain better working conditions for migrant workers.

Commons, John (1862–1945).   An economist and social reformer, Commons taught at the University of Wisconsin, where he founded the field of industrial relations. Commons played a significant role in shaping the New Deal legislation. Before turning his attention to federal legislation, he helped to write much of Wisconsin's progressive reform legislation on such issues as workers' compensation and public utility regulation. These were the prototypes for other states and the federal government.

Cooke, Jay (1821–1905).   A financier and investment banker, Cooke helped to fund the Civil War for the North by mass-marketing federal bonds to individual Americans, thus pioneering the idea of paper wealth and also creating the first advertising campaign that relied on appeals to people's patriotism.

Debs, Eugene V. (1855–1926).   A strong leader and advocate of labor unions, pacifist, and founder of the Socialist party in the United States, Debs was the party's five-time candidate for president. Considered by many to be a martyr to the cause of labor, he was jailed briefly during the 1894 Pullman strike for ignoring an injunction and again in 1918–1921 for espionage.

Disney, Walt (1901–1966).   A filmmaker and animation pioneer, Disney created one of the first great entertainment empires devoted to providing "family" entertainment.

Eastman, George (1854–1932).   Eastman, who invented many of the elements that turned photography into a modern science, founded the Eastman Kodak Company in 1892. Like Carnegie, he gave most of his money away before he died.

Firestone, Harvey (1868–1938).   Firestone manufactured rubber tires and in 1900 founded Firestone Tire & Rubber Co., one of the largest tire manufacturers in the United States.

Fisher, Irving (1867–1947).   An economist, Fisher pioneered the idea of a "compensated dollar" and contributed to the development of index numbers, standard figures against which certain economic factors, such as inflation and the cost of living, are measured and then used to trigger increases in wages and Social Security.

Ford, Henry (1863–1947).   Ford founded Ford Motor Company and was among the first to use the assembly-line method of manufacturing, which in turn enabled him to turn out an inexpensive car, the Model T.

George, Henry (1839–1897).   This economist's thinking influenced tax legislation in many countries. As the leader of the single-tax movement, he proposed to levy a single tax on land, whose unearned gains he viewed as being the dividing line between rich and poor. The tax would then be used to operate governments. He elaborated on this theory in his book *Progress and Poverty* (1879).

Gleason, Kate (1865–1933).   Gleason became the first woman to head a national bank when she filled in for the bank president after he enlisted in the service during World War I. She served until 1919, and pioneered the large-scale development of low-cost housing.

Gompers, Samuel (1850–1924).   A cigar maker, Gompers was one of the founders of the American Federation of Labor and its longtime president. Gompers opposed labor-reform groups such as the Knights of Labor and also opposed what he considered Socialist elements in the labor movement. His success lay in his focus on more wages and shorter hours.

Gould, Jay (1836–1892).   Gould made his fortune in railroad speculation and at one time controlled the New York elevated, most of the railroads in the Southwest, and Western Union Telegraph Company. He later controlled the Erie Railroad and then the Union Pacific. Gould was feared for his stock manipulations and despotic management methods.

Green, Hetty (1834–1916).   After inheriting $10 million from her wealthy mercantile family, Green traded her way into a $100 million fortune and was widely held to be the richest woman of her time.

Hamilton, Alexander (1755–1804).   Among the many accomplishments of this politician and economic theorist, Hamilton was the first secretary of the treasury, serving under George Washington. Hamilton devised the U.S. fiscal program, supporting tariffs and excise taxes as a means of raising money for the new federal government. He advocated a financially strong federal government, while his opponents, led by Thomas Jefferson, wanted to leave the financing of government to state and local branches. He was killed by rival Aaron Burr in a duel.

Hearst, William Randolph (1863–1951).   Hearst, who built the first great publishing empire, at one time owned 20 newspapers and nine magazines. His primary goal was to sell a lot of newspapers, and to that end he sold them for a penny, thus undercutting the competition. He virtually invented tabloid journalism, which made use of oversized, outrageous headlines, shocking photographs, and sensational reportage.

Hughes, Howard (1905–1976).   The wealth of this tycoon came from the Hughes Tool Company, which he inherited from his father. Interested in aviation, he founded a company that made experimental planes and set many speed records. He also produced movies, the most prominent of which was *The Front Page*. Toward the end of his life, he became the country's most famous recluse.

Hunt, H. L. (1889–1974).   This Texas oil magnate once amassed enough silver to manipulate the entire U.S. market. Once one of the richest people in the United States, he held ultraconservative political views.

Jefferson, Thomas (1743–1826).   The third U.S. president, Jefferson was one of the leaders of the debate over the federal government's role in the country's finances; he preferred that fiscal power reside with state and local governments. His more specific contribution to the country's economic development was to devise the decimal system that is the basis for the U.S. currency system.

Johnson, Lyndon Baines (1908–1973). Under the banner of the Great Society, Johnson as president declared the "War on Poverty" and followed through with a series of social and economic programs that significantly raised the standard of living for millions of Americans. His programs included Medicare, Medicaid, and Head Start.

Jones, Mary Harris ("Mother") (1830–1930): A prominent figure in the labor movement, "Mother" Jones helped found both the Social Democratic party and the Industrial Workers of the World. She gained fame as an effective speaker during the Great Railroad Strike of 1877 and the Haymarket riots in 1886, after which she concentrated her efforts on organizing miners in the coal fields of West Virginia. At the age of 83 she was convicted of conspiracy and sentenced to 20 years in prison, but the sentence was commuted in time for her to be present at the Ludlow massacre and to lobby President Wilson on the miners' behalf. After World War I she continued as a union agitator and organizer and lived to enjoy a splendid celebration of her 100th birthday.

Kelley, Florence (1859–1932). As an associate of Jane Addams at Hull-House and a proponent of labor reform, Kelley went on to head the National Consumers' League, shaping it into an effective lobbying organization that played a seminal role in passing protective legislation for women and children. She helped develop the strategy behind the successful defense in *Muller v. Oregon*, a case involving the work hours of women.

Laughlin, James (1850–1933). An economist, Laughlin played an important role in devising the centralized Federal Reserve System.

Lloyd, Henry Demarest (1847–1903). Along with Ida Tarbell, Lloyd, a financial reporter at the *Chicago Tribune*, exposed the evils of monopolistic corporations. He wrote *Wealth Against Commonwealth* (1894), an exposé of big business.

McCormick, Cyrus (1809–1884). McCormick's mechanical reaper contained all the elements that are present in every reaping machine. Although there was a rival reaper, he built the more successful business, pioneering in areas such as repair and spare parts and installment buying. After his death, his firm merged with International Harvester to form the United States' largest farm-machinery manufacturer.

McWhinney, Madeleine (1922–). McWhinney was the first president of the First Women's Bank, chartered in 1975 and intended to counteract the prejudice women encountered in the world of finance. She later became the first woman to be named an assistant vice president in the Federal Reserve System.

Morgan, John Pierpont (1837–1913). Along with John D. Rockefeller, Morgan was one of the business entrepreneurs who earned the title "robber baron" in the late 1890s for his organization of trusts. Morgan was involved in railroad reorganization and the mergers that formed International Harvester. He also engineered the consolidation of U.S. Steel, the country's first billion-dollar corporation.

Morgenthau, Henry, Jr. (1891–1967). As secretary of the treasury from 1934 to 1945 Morgenthau supervised the sale of the U.S. bonds that largely financed World War II and later worked to establish the World Bank and International Monetary Fund.

Morris, Robert (1734–1806). Although Morris, a colonial merchant, initially voted against independence, he became known as the "financier of the Revolution" for the pivotal role he played in raising funds to support the war and in organizing the finances of the new nation after the war. After being appointed superintendent of finance, he worked to establish a national mint and a federal banking system.

Perkins, Frances (1882–1965). Perkins worked to eradicate child labor and to establish unemployment insurance and wrote much of the pro-labor legislation in New York State under governors Al Smith and Franklin Roosevelt. Roosevelt appointed her secretary of labor, and in that role she was responsible for the much of the New Deal labor legislation.

Powderly, Terence V. (1849–1924). A labor leader and reformer, Powderly was president of the Machinists and Blacksmiths National Union when he joined the Knights of Labor, which he led from 1879 to 1893. His program addressed labor reform generally, calling for worker-run factories, producers' and consumers' cooperatives, the regulation of trusts, and the abolition of child labor as well as for an eight-hour day.

Reagan, Ronald (1911–). During his presidency (1981–1989), Reagan reversed the activist fiscal policies of Roosevelt and Johnson, advocating reduced federal spending on social and educational programs and increased spending on the military. Despite supporting a balanced budget, he presided over the biggest peacetime buildup of U.S. debt in history and also sponsored a major rewriting of the federal income tax law.

Rockefeller, John D. (1839–1937). As the founder of the Standard Oil Trust, Rockefeller forged a new form of business organization, the horizontal corporation, whose goal was to control a single product—in his case, oil. At the time of his retirement in 1911, Rockefeller had a fortune estimated at $1 billion, much of which he gave to philanthropic enterprises.

Roosevelt, Franklin Delano (1882–1945). Elected to the presidency at the depth of the Great Depression, Roosevelt presided over major economic reforms, such as the National Recovery Administration and the Public Works Administration, that were intended to stabilize the nation's economy and restore it to health. He also instituted Social Security, the federal old-age pension, and the Federal Deposit Insurance Corporation (FDIC), which insures bank accounts.

Tarbell, Ida (1857–1944). Along with Henry Demarest Lloyd, Tarbell waged journalistic war on the trusts of the late 19th century. Her *History of the Standard Oil Company* (1904) resulted in federal action against the company. Lloyd and Tarbell were among the first journalists known as muckrakers.

Townsend, Francis (1867–1960). During the heart of the Great Depression, Townsend, a physician, proposed that the federal government establish an old-age pension. His idea was to give all retirees $200 a month in scrip out of funds raised by a federal sales tax. He popularized the idea enough to pave the way for the Social Security Act to be passed in 1935.

Vanderbilt, Cornelius (1794–1877). This industrial magnate and financier made his initial money in a steamship line and went on to make even more in railroads. Along with a handful of other industrial barons, like Gould and Carnegie, he was able to amass a nearly unheard-of fortune.

Veblen, Thorstein (1857–1929). Veblen merged economic and sociological theory, most successfully in his book *The Theory of the Leisure Class* (1899), in which he coined the term *conspicuous consumption*. Veblen was also interested in the conflict between technology, which he felt sought only efficiency and reduced costs, and commerce, or "business," whose primary goal was profit maximization.

Walker, Maggie Lena (1867–1934). Founder and president of the St. Luke Penny Savings Bank, Walker in 1903 was the first woman to be president of any U.S. bank. When her bank merged with several other African-American banks to form the Consolidated Bank and Trust Company, she became chairman of the board, a position she held until her death.

Walton, Sam (1918–1992). The founder of Wal-Mart, Walton pioneered in the development of superstores, huge "general" stores that provided an unprecedented array of goods at low cost.

Wanamaker, John (1838–1922). The founder of the Philadelphia department store bearing his name, Wanamaker was a pioneer in department-store management, especially in the area of customer service.

Ward, Aaron Montgomery (1844–1913). In 1872 Ward founded the first American mail-order company, which bears his name, and he pioneered the mass sales of low-priced goods.

Westinghouse, George (1846–1914). Westinghouse invented the air brake and automatic signal devices and introduced the high-tension, alternating-current system of electricity. His company was organized to manufacture the latter two devices. Westinghouse owned 400 patents.

Whitney, Eli (1765–1825). An inventor, Whitney is best known for the cotton gin, which quickly and mechanically separated the cotton fiber from the seed. Whitney also produced the first rifles with interchangeable, standardized parts, for which he is credited with anticipating mass production.

Woolworth, Frank V. (1852–1919). This innovative merchandiser created the "five and dime" store chain, which he expanded and internationalized. At one time there were more than 1,000 Woolworth stores in existence. In 1913 he built what was then the world's tallest building, in Manhattan.

ADDITIONAL SOURCES OF INFORMATION

Berry, Wendell. *Home Economics.* North Point, 1987.

Bluestone, Barry, and Bennett Harrison. *The Deindustrialization of America.* Basic Books, 1982.

Bovard, James. *The Farm Fiasco.* ICS, 1988.

Chandler, Alfred D., Jr. *The Visible Hand: The Managerial Revolution in American Business.* Harvard, 1977.

Critchfield, Richard. *Trees, Why Do You Wait? America's Changing Rural Culture.* Island, 1991.

Denby, Charles. *Indignant Heart: A Black Worker's Journal.* South End, 1978.

Dulles, Foster R., and Melvyn Dubofsky. *Labor in America: A History.* 4th rev. ed. Harlan Davidson, 1984.

Freeman, Richard B., and James L. Medoff. *What Do Unions Do?* Basic Books, 1984.

Galbraith, John Kenneth. *The Great Crash of 1929.* 3rd ed. Houghton Mifflin, 1972.

Gates, Paul W. *The Farmer's Age: Agriculture, 1815–1860.* M. E. Sharpe, 1977.

Green, James. *The World of the Worker: Labor in 20th Century America.* Hill & Wang, 1981.

Kessler-Harris, Alice. *Out to Work: A History of Wage-Earning Women in the United States.* Oxford University Press, 1982.

McElvaine, Robert S. *The Great Depression: America, 1929–1941.* University of North Carolina Press, 1983.

Noble, David F. *America by Design: Science, Technology and the Rise of Corporate Capitalism.* Oxford University Press, 1979.

Phillips, Kevin P. *The Politics of Rich and Poor.* Random House, 1990.

Rhodes, Richard. *Farm: A Year in the Life of an American Farmer.* Simon & Schuster, 1989.

Scharf, Lois. *To Work and to Wed.* Greenwood, 1980.

Schumacher, E. F. *Small Is Beautiful: Economics As If People Mattered.* HarperCollins, 1989.

Stewart, James B. *Den of Thieves.* Simon & Schuster, 1991.

Terkel, Studs. *Hard Times: An Oral History of the Great Depression.* Pantheon, 1970.

———. *Working.* Pantheon, 1974.

Trachtenberg, Alan. *The Incorporation of America: Culture and Society in the Gilded Age.* Hill & Wang, 1982.

Veblen, Thornstein. *Theory of the Leisure Class.* Repr. of 1899 ed., Kelly, 1975.

Wethheimer, Barbara M. *We Were There: The Story of Working Women in America.* Pantheon, 1977.

10

Education

311

SIGNIFICANT EVENTS IN AMERICAN EDUCATION

Within a hundred years of its founding, the United States was building one of the Western world's great public-education systems. Maintaining this system, though, has proven to be one of its more difficult undertakings, a task that is made more treacherous by the fact that the schools are administered by the individual states while oversight, such as it is, is typically left to the federal government. The United States remains one of the few modern, industrialized nations that does not have an established national curriculum.

The Colonial Era

1635-1636   Boston Latin School is established. This grammar school for boys is supported by the town of Boston.

1636   Harvard College is founded with a grant from the Massachusetts General Court and a bequest (1638) from John Harvard. Intended to train Puritan ministers, it grew to be a premier institution of higher learning.

1647   Massachusetts Bay requires towns of more than 100 families to establish grammar schools (for boys only).

1689   By this date, Connecticut, Plymouth, and New Hampshire also require grammar schools.

1690   The *New England Primer*, first published in the 1680s, becomes the most widely used reader in the colonies.

1693   The College of William and Mary in Virginia becomes the second institution of higher learning in the colonies.

1700   New England has the highest literacy rate in the colonies.

1701   New England has the highest literacy rate in the colonies. Yale College, named for benefactor Elihu Yale, is chartered. It moves to New Haven in 1716.

1746   The College of New Jersey is chartered at Princeton by New Light Presbyterians. It is renamed Princeton in 1896.

1776   Phi Beta Kappa, the honorary society for academic achievement, is founded at the College of William and Mary, originally as a social club.

The Early Republic

1782   Quakers organize the Philadelphia African School.

St. Mary's Church in Philadelphia opens the first Catholic school.

1783   Noah Webster publishes the *American Spelling Book*, standardizing American spelling as distinct from British usage. It sells millions of copies and is widely used in schoolrooms for a century.

1787   The Young Ladies Academy in Philadelphia opens. A prototype for female academies, it seeks to train the wives and mothers of the new republic to prepare their sons for citizenship.

1789   The University of North Carolina is chartered. In 1795 it is the first state university to begin instruction.

1792   Sarah Pierce opens a school for girls in her home in Litchfield, Connecticut. A quarter century later, the Litchfield Female Academy is drawing students from all over the Northeast.

Noah Webster

1807   Washington, D.C., founds its first school for blacks.

1809   Elizabeth Ann Seton founds a Catholic school in Emmitsburg, Maryland, and establishes the first American religious order, the Sisters of Charity of St. Joseph. She is elevated to sainthood in 1974.

THE RISE AND FALL OF PAROCHIAL EDUCATION

When the huge wave of immigrants arriving in the late 1800s found the public schools too "American," meaning too Protestant, for their tastes, they pushed the Roman Catholic church to institute a system of parochial schools. The U.S. Catholic church, however, having long enjoyed the protection that freedom of religion brought, established the schools only reluctantly and made sure to fold a heavy dose of patriotism into the curriculum.

There were advantages and disadvantages to a parochial school system. On the negative side, schools would absorb resources intended for churches, and church administrators were torn over which needs to fulfill first for their many new parishioners. Parochial schools would also enforce separatism for Catholics, which was seen as a disadvantage especially for those who were new to the country. But parochial schools also offered control over prayers, Mass, and Communion, all advantages in the eyes of the church.

Today, Roman Catholics are not the only denomination to sponsor their own schools. Nearly every Protestant denomination supports some schools, although in recent years many mainstream

(continues)

THE RISE AND FALL OF PAROCHIAL EDUCATION (CONT.)

denominational schools have closed while many new fundamentalist schools have opened. Jewish parochial education, especially among the very religious, has also experienced a renaissance since World War II. No other religion, though, has established the large nationwide network of parochial schools that the Catholic church has.

Nearly half of all private schools in the United States are Catholic. Enrollment in Catholic schools peaked in 1964, with 5.6 million children, and steadily fell off from there. By 1990 attendance had fallen to 2.5 million.

Some parochial schools, and a fair number of private schools, were founded in the wake of *Brown v. Board of Education of Topeka* (1954) and its order, a year later, that public schools be integrated with "all deliberate speed." In recent years vouchers that parents could use as money to help pay tuition in the school of their choice—public, private, or parochial—have been proposed as part of the school reform debate.

1818	Boston establishes public elementary schools.
1819	Emma Willard tries and fails to get New York State to fund higher education for women, largely as a means of training teachers.
1821	Emma Willard opens the Troy Seminary in Troy, New York. Intended to be a step up from the academies, seminaries offer more advanced education, although their primary purpose is still to train women as teachers.
	The first high school in the United States is established in Boston.
1822	Philadelphia organizes its first public school for blacks.
1823	Catharine Beecher, an important proponent of women's education, opens the Hartford Seminary in Connecticut.

WOMEN'S EDUCATION

Women's education, intimately tied to the status of women, long put women in a double bind: they recognized that education was the means to increased autonomy and higher status, but as the many restrictions on women's lives restricted their education, too, few educational opportunities were open to them.

In colonial America, most girls were taught at home, and their "education" consisted largely of domestic skills. In New England many girls learned to read as well, as Bible reading was deemed necessary for salvation. Toward the end of the colonial era the daughters of the wealthy attended schools that taught a few academic subjects but primarily emphasized female accomplishments such as music, art, and fancy needlework.

Following the Revolution new female academies trained women to be the mothers of the sons of the Republic, upon whose enlightened citizenship the new country was thought to depend. Accomplishments were still stressed, but academic subjects increased, and in the early 19th century leading educators such as Emma Willard and Catharine Beecher promoted girls' education at private seminaries. Increasing numbers of girls, especially in New England, attended public grammar schools.

At the same time, teaching as a profession became increasingly open and attractive to women, and many female seminaries specialized in training teachers. By the time of the Civil War, women predominated in teaching and were looking to enter other professions as well, especially as increasing numbers of schools of higher education were open to women.

Following the Civil War, the new black colleges established by the Freedmen's Bureau and missionary societies were largely open to women. Many all-male colleges opened women's affiliates, and by 1900 women constituted at least a quarter of all college students. On the high school level, girls actually outnumbered boys.

The growing predominance and assertiveness of women in education produced something of a backlash, as critics, enamored of the new Freudian psychology, pointed out that college women were less likely to marry and would bear fewer children than non-college-educated women. Did education make women unfit for their roles as wives and mothers?

In the early decades of the 20th century, while the number of women attending college continued to increase, the percentage of women enrolled in college, as opposed to the percentage of men, decreased, and fewer women, proportionally, received Ph.D.s than in 1900. This trend did not reverse until the late 1960s, with the resurgence of feminism, the introduction of women's studies programs, the opening of previously all-male schools to women, and federal laws prohibiting discrimination on the basis of sex. Since 1974, women college students outnumbered men.

In the 1990s, with 19 percent of women college educated and 59 percent in the workforce, the old debate was renewed again, with a new—and old—focus: the care of children. With women no longer "at home," were children in day care centers and unsupervised after school at risk? Was "supermom"—the bright, professional woman who was a success at work and in the evenings spent "quality time" with her children—a fraud? Did the new empowerment—the sense that women could do it all—come with a new set of demands that put women once again in the double bind?

1824	The first public high school for girls opens in Worcester, Massachusetts. Across the country, more will follow Massachusetts's example.
	Dartmouth College, founded in 1754 and moved to New Hampshire in 1769, admits its first black students.
	The Franklin Institute is founded in Philadelphia.
1826	The lyceum movement, promoting adult education and self-improvement, is initiated when Josiah Holbrook establishes a lyceum in Millbury, Massachusetts. In 1831 the National American Lyceum is established, and within a few years there are town lyceums in 15 states.
1827	Massachusetts becomes the first state to use taxes to support public education. Every town with a population of 500 or more families is required to have a high school.
1829	The first American encyclopedia, *Encyclopaedia Americana*, begins publication.
1833	Oberlin College opens the first coeducational college. A center of abolition, it also, after 1835, admits black students.
	Prudence Crandall converts her girl's school in Canterbury, Connecticut, into a school for black girls, despite a law restricting the education of black children. She is arrested, and although the verdict against her is reversed by a higher court, harassment and violence force her to close her school.
1836	The first McGuffey's Readers, a series of textbooks designed to promote moral improvement and patriotism, are published; they will sell an estimated 122 million copies and influence generations of elementary school children.
1837	Mary Lyon, an important advocate of women's education, opens Mount Holyoke Female Seminary, which will become the prestigious Mount Holyoke College.
	Horace Mann initiates school reform as the first secretary of the newly established Massachusetts Board of Education. He works to lengthen the school year, increase the numbers of public high schools, raise teachers' salaries, improve teacher training, and centralize authority. Believing that children learn best in nurturing environments, he also seeks to end the harsh punishments inherited from Puritan schoolrooms.
1838	Henry Barnard, appointed secretary of the Connecticut Board of School Commissioners, initiates similar reforms in Connecticut schools.

1839   Horace Mann establishes the first state normal school, for the training of teachers, in Lexington, Massachusetts.

1848   At the Seneca Falls Convention, the first public meeting in the United States held to advocate women's rights, women protest that they have not been permitted to obtain an equal education.

1850   Young unmarried women predominate as teachers in grammar. schools; most have been trained in seminary schools established by women.

1852   Massachusetts becomes the first state to enact compulsory school attendance laws.

1855   The first kindergarten opens as a special school for the children of German immigrants in Watertown, Wisconsin.

Boston public schools are integrated.

Berea College is founded in Berea, Kentucky, as a one-room district school. In 1869, it becomes a college offering black and white students the opportunity to work to pay for their education. In 1904 Kentucky law prohibits integration and, subsequently, Berea has to comply.

1856   In Wilberforce, Ohio, the African Methodist Episcopal Church opens a coeducational college that offers academic training to African Americans.

1857   Congress incorporates the Columbia Institution for the Instruction of the Deaf and Dumb and the Blind, under the direction of Edward Miner Gaullaudet. It is the predecessor of Gallaudet University.

1860   On the brink of the Civil War, more than 90 percent of the southern black population is illiterate, mostly because it is illegal to educate African Americans. Free blacks attempt to educate themselves and their children through small, informally organized schools.

The first formally organized kindergarten opens in Boston.

1861   Vassar chartered as a women's college. It opens in 1865.

The first Ph.D. in the United States is awarded at Yale University.

The American Missionary Association organizes the first school for free blacks in the South at Fortress Monroe, Virginia. In 1868 it becomes Hampton Institute.

1862   The Morrill Land-Grant Act sets aside public lands for support of state colleges emphasizing agricultural and mechanical subjects. Later they will also emphasize technology.

The Industrial Era

1865   The American Missionary Association organizes Atlanta University for black students.

1866   Fisk University in Nashville is founded by the American Missionary Association for black students.

1867   Henry Barnard is appointed the first U.S. commissioner of education, heading a new federal agency that would oversee the gathering of educational statistics and the dissemination of information about U.S. education. Barnard compares the U.S. and European systems and prepares many reports.

Howard University is founded by Oliver O. Howard, former union general and head of the Freedmen's Bureau, to educate the newly emancipated slaves. It is a coeducational, integrated college. In 1868 it opens a medical school and a law school. It becomes one of the first schools to admit women to medical training.

Morehouse, another prominent black school, is established in Atlanta.

1869   With the help of the Freedmen's Bureau, the federal agency established to serve the needs of former slaves after the Civil War, 3,000 schools are established, attended by more than 150,000 African-American students. Over half of the 3,300 teachers in these schools are black. The bureau also assists in the founding of several black colleges, including Hampton, Fisk, and Tougaloo.

1870   Across the country, colleges number 563, and women make up 21 percent of college enrollees.

1873-   The Chautauqua movement, whose goal is adult education, begins in Lake Chautauqua,
1874   New York. Thousands of people soon sign up for the correspondence courses, and the traveling circuit of lectures prove even more popular.

1873   Saint Louis opens the first public school kindergarten, and the idea quickly grows in popularity around the nation.

        Bellevue Hospital in New York City establishes a school of nursing.

1875   Smith and Wellesley are founded in Massachusetts as women's colleges.

1876   Johns Hopkins University establishes the prototype graduate-school curriculum, which is quickly taken up by other colleges and universities and is still the model of graduate education today.

1877   The Women's Educational and Industrial Union opens in Boston; it is devoted to the education of working-class women.

1879   The Carlisle School in Pennsylvania is established for Native American children. Like other nonreservation schools, it seeks to "Americanize" its students.

1881   Booker T. Washington founds the Tuskegee Institute in Alabama to provide practical education for black males and to train teachers.

        Spelman College, which will become a prestigious college for black women, is founded.

1884   As part of a nationwide trend to educate boys for the trades, the Chicago Manual Training School opens. Other cities will soon establish public vocational high schools.

VOCATIONAL EDUCATION

Teaching the trades in a formal school setting is relatively new. During the 18th century, young boys learning to be artisans worked as apprentices to master craftsmen in a structure that was maintained by guild regulations and by law. But the rise of industry "deskilled" many trades, and as the apprenticeship system declined concerns for the schooling of workers rose. By the end of the 19th century manual training schools and vocational course offerings in high schools were integrating vocational education in public schools, and in the 20th century vocational training began to receive support from by federal funds. Today this branch of education encompasses not only the traditional trades but new skills in technology and computer fields.

1885   Quakers found Bryn Mawr as a women's college, modeled on a curriculum plan developed at Johns Hopkins. It becomes one of the first women's colleges to offer graduate degrees.

Late 1880s   Literacy tests begin to be used to keep African Americans from voting.

1889   Barnard College is founded as an affiliate of Columbia University. It is incorporated into Columbia in 1900.

1890   Four percent of young people ages 14 to 17 are enrolled in school.

        Forty-seven percent of colleges and universities are coeducational.

1894   Radcliffe affiliates with Harvard.

1895   W.E.B. Du Bois becomes the first African American to earn a Ph.D. from Harvard.

All elementary and high schools in Chicago offer "shop" classes for working-class boys, although they are opposed by the unions, which prefer on-the-job training.

1896   George Washington Carver becomes director of agricultural research at the Tuskegee Institute, where he will build his reputation as a prestigious botanist-inventor.

George Washington Carver

1899   The Supreme Court permits the existence of separate educational facilities for black and white children.

1900   There are 6,000 public high schools in the United States, up from 160 in 1870. More than 4,000 kindergartens and similar programs serve children ages three to seven. There are more than 100 coeducational black colleges and universities.

Corporate leaders like Andrew Carnegie and John D. Rockefeller have begun to make large donations to universities.

Per-pupil spending in the South is at least 50 percent below that in the rest of the nation.

The Modern Era

1901   The first College Entrance Examination Board examinations are given.

1904   Mary McLeod Bethune, a prominent educator, founds the Daytona Normal and Industrial School in Daytona, Florida, to educate young black girls for a life more fulfilling than domestic service. The grammar school grows rapidly, first into a high school and then a four-year accredited college—Bethune-Cookman College.

1910   Colleges number nearly 1,000, but only 3 percent of the college-age population attends them. Women constitute 40 percent of enrollment.

When a Carnegie Foundation report by Abraham Flexner reveals that American medical schools are grossly inadequate compared to the great institutions of Europe, reforms in standards, organization, and curriculums are initiated.

1916   The Bureau of Education reports that southern states spend an average of $10.32 for white students and $2.89 for black children.

John Dewey publishes *Democracy and Education*, an examination of democratic ideas and their application to the enterprise of education.

DEMOCRACY AND EDUCATION

John Dewey's study of psychology led him to child development, to schooling, to the purpose of schools in a democratic society. When he published *Democracy and Education* in 1916, his theories were already well known. Education, Dewey said, should be a process whereby the child learns to solve problems effectively, thus enhancing the adult's capacity to improve not only his or her own life but, more important, society itself. Schools should serve society, and in *Democracy and Education* Dewey examined the democratic values that schools should promote.

Although his statement of the relationship between democracy and education was new, especially for its application of the emerging discipline of psychology, the connection itself was as old as the republic. Schools in America had long been expected to prepare young people for citizenship, to transmit democratic values, even to solve America's problems. When, in the late 19th century, nativists worried that the "new immigrants" from southern and eastern Europe might not be easily assimilated into American culture, they called on the schools to accomplish "Americanization." Schooling would also "Americanize" Indian peoples and teach former slaves how they could fit into society as free persons. Schools would teach not only the "Three Rs" but hygiene and etiquette, agriculture to rural children, and in cities the mechanical and industrial skills that working-class children would need in their occupations. Schools would teach the virtues of democratic government, the importance of law and order, and a sense of individual worth.

In retrospect it seems no accident that, in the middle of the 20th century, schools would become the focal point of the struggle for equal rights. *Brown v. Board of Education of Topeka* (1954), ruling school segregation unconstitutional, made schools the test tube and catalyst for the most significant restructuring of racial and social relations the country had yet experienced. It seems that when society fails, or politics, or even human nature, the schools are called on to provide the remedy.

In America, we still ask a lot of our schools. Schools are expected to be the great equalizers, the means by which every child gets a chance. In addition to all the academic subjects, schools teach socially acceptable behavior. Student governments train students for leadership; sports programs emphasize sportsmanship and physical fitness; music and art classes transmit culture and inspire creativity. Schools teach nutrition, health, sex education, and to say no to drugs. Schools screen students, identify physical and psychological difficulties, and give assistance. Schools promote multiculturalism and self-esteem.

Dewey believed that schools should not be just a training for life but the experience of life, builders of knowledge and builders of character. Debates in the 1990s over values education, functional literacy and cultural illiteracy, declining test scores, and comparisons with other industrial nations in which the United States does poorly are shaped by our notions of the many roles of the school in a democracy and still grounded in Dewey's assumptions that schools should be the means whereby society itself is improved.

1918   Every state has a compulsory education requirement.

1920s   Nursery schools are established. One of the earliest is the Ruggles Street Nursery in Boston.

1920   Thirty-two percent of young people ages 14 to 17 are enrolled in high school.

1921   The Association of Collegiate Alumnae becomes the American Association of University Women.

1925   The Scopes "Monkey Trial" rivets the nation. Several southern school districts, pressured by religious fundamentalists, have outlawed the teaching of evolution. When John T. Scopes, a teacher in Dayton, Tennessee, breaks the law to teach it, he is arrested. The trial is broadcast nationally over radio. Scopes is found guilty, but state statutes outlawing the teaching of evolution, though they remain on the books, are rarely enforced. The state statutes are not repealed, but no more lawsuits are brought over this issue for decades.

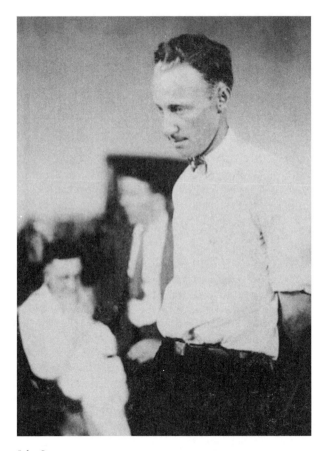

John Scopes

1930   Forty-seven percent of young people ages 14 to 17 are enrolled in high school.

1932   Howard University starts the *Journal of Negro Education*.

1935   A survey of elementary and secondary schools in ten southern states finds that public school systems in the South spend an average of $49 on each white child, compared to $17 on each black one.

1944   The GI Bill provides educational stipends for World War II veterans to attend vocational schools or colleges. By 1956 nearly 10 million veterans take advantage of these stipends, pushing university enrollments to all-time highs and changing the elitist character of higher education.

The United Negro College Fund is founded to support black institutions of higher learning.

1946   The Fulbright program establishes educational exchanges and fellowships for Americans studying and teaching abroad.

1947   The federal Office for Education launches a "Zeal for Democracy" campaign, designed to help teachers promote democratic values in the classroom and demonstrate, through education, the superiority of democracy over communism. It is implemented nationwide.

Early 1950s   In the midst of the "red scare" generated by the cold war, colleges and universities are special targets of those who fear Communists may be attempting a takeover. As a result, many teachers are fired, perhaps as many as 600 in colleges, universities, and public schools. Across the country, a chilling effect is felt on free speech on campuses. J. Edgar Hoover and the Federal Bureau of Investigation are active in this red scare.

1950   There are 2.6 million students enrolled in higher education. Women, who constituted 40 percent of all college graduates in 1940, are only 25 percent of this year's graduating class.

The University of North Carolina admits its first black students.

1953   The Department of Health, Education, and Welfare is established, with Oveta Culp Hobby named its first secretary.

Secretaries of Health, Education, and Welfare

Secretary	President	Year Appointed	Secretary	President	Year Appointed
Oveta Culp Hobby	Eisenhower	1953	Robert H. Finch	Nixon	1969
Marion B. Folsom	Eisenhower	1955	Elliot L. Richardson	Nixon	1970
Arthur S. Flemming	Eisenhower	1958	Caspar W. Weinberger	Nixon	1973
Abraham A. Ribicoff	Kennedy	1961		Ford	1974
Anthony J. Celebrezze	Kennedy	1962	Forrest D. Matthews	Ford	1975
	Johnson, L. B.	1963	Joseph A. Califano, Jr.	Carter	1977
John W. Gardner	Johnson, L. B.	1965	Patricia Roberts Harris	Carter	1979
Wilbur J. Cohen	Johnson, L. B.	1968			

1954   In *Brown v. Board of Education*, the Supreme Court orders American public schools desegregated. A quarter century of turmoil follows, as racial tensions in American society are played out in the schools. Some schools and school systems in the South close down altogether rather than integrate.

BROWN V. BOARD OF EDUCATION

In December 1952, when Thurgood Marshall argued the *Brown* case before the Supreme Court, he had been preparing for this moment for years. The National Association for the Advancement of Colored People had first developed its legal strategy in the early 1930s. The "separate-but-equal" doctrine, ruled constitutional by the Court in an 1896 decision, could be chipped away, NAACP lawyers believed, through attacks on violation of "equal protection of the laws" in schools. Southern states with segregated systems did not have law schools, medical schools, or other graduate school programs for blacks, and that's where the attack would begin.

(continues)

BROWN V. BOARD OF EDUCATION (CONT.)

In 1935, Marshall argued before a Maryland judge that Donald Murray, denied admission to the University of Maryland's all-white law school, should not be sent by the state to an out-of-state law school. This solution, said Marshall, was in violation of the Constitution's guarantee of equal treatment under the law. The Maryland judge agreed and ordered the University of Maryland law school to admit Murray.

Other successes followed. The Supreme Court ordered the University of Missouri School of Law to admit Lloyd Lionel Gaines (Missouri had proposed building a law school on a black campus instead). The Court declared that the basement rooms the University of Texas said it would set up for Herman Sweatt did not constitute a law school comparable to the law school for whites. The Court said that 68-year-old doctoral candidate John McLaurin, ordered by the University of Oklahoma to sit at a desk surrounded by a railing labeled "reserved for colored," was not getting an equal education either.

Finally the NAACP was ready to attack segregated education head-on—at the primary school level, where separate education had turned out to be patently unequal. The per capita spending for white students in South Carolina's Clarendon County—to give only one example—was $179 per year; for black students it was $43. There was one teacher for every 28 white students; one black teacher for every 47 black students. The net worth of the country's three black schools, for 808 children, was one-fourth the value of the two schools for the 276 white students.

But when Marshall argued the case of Linda Brown, the seven-year-old daughter of a minister in Topeka, Kansas, who had to travel 21 blocks to an all-black school although there was an all-white school just 4 blocks from her home, he did not concentrate on facilities. The facilities, in Topeka, even the plaintiffs agreed, were substantially equal. The case turned on an inequality far deeper. Marshall pointed to evidence from a series of studies conducted by psychologists Kenneth Clark and Mamie Phipps Clark, who had attempted to determine the mindset of black children in New York City, Washington, D.C., and the South. Using white and black dolls, and asking the children to describe their reaction to them, the Clarks reported that black children in the South had internalized a sense of inferiority. Of 16 children tested in Clarendon County, ten said they liked the white doll better. Nine said the white doll looked "nice," while 11 said the black doll looked "bad." When asked which doll was most like them, many of the children became emotionally upset as they pointed to the doll they had rejected.

Using this evidence, the NAACP argued that segregation *in itself* imposed serious social and psychological handicaps on black children and even retarded their educational and mental development. Because education, said the lawyers, encompasses the full development of children as human beings, segregated education could never be fair even if facilities were equal and excellent.

The Court agreed. When it handed down its historic decision on May 17, 1954, Chief Justice Earl Warren, who spoke for a unanimous court, declared: "We conclude that in the field of public education the doctrine of 'separate but equal' has no place. Separate educational facilities are inherently unequal." With that, the legal framework supporting segregation crumbled altogether, setting in motion a tense and monumental shift in America's race relations that would be played out for decades in the nation's public schools.

1957   The USSR launches the *Sputnik* satellite, and the impact is felt in education, where new emphasis is placed on science.

Central High School in Little Rock is integrated, but only after President Eisenhower sends federal troops to protect black students and ensure order.

1958   Ten thousand black students march on Washington, D.C., in support of integrated education.

Arkansas governor Orval Faubus closes the Little Rock, Arkansas, schools rather than continue integration.

1959   Following a Supreme Court ruling, the Little Rock schools open again, integrated in accordance with federal requirements.

1960s   Innovative school reforms include "new math," emphasizing abstract concepts rather than memory work; the "open classroom," with physical and pedagogical flexibility, and team teaching.

      Community colleges, with two-year programs that prepare students directly for an occupation or for transfer to four-year colleges, multiply rapidly.

1960   There are 3.2 million students attending higher-education institutions.

1962   James Meredith, an African-American veteran, attempts to register for classes at the University of Mississippi, and Governor Ross Barnett personally blocks his way in defiance of a federal court order. President John F. Kennedy mobilizes the Mississippi National Guard to protect Meredith from an angry mob of several thousand. After a night of violence, in which 2 persons are killed and more than 160 federal marshals are wounded, President Kennedy sends 5,000 troops to Mississippi. Meredith is guarded for a year, until he graduates.

James Meredith being escorted by federal marshals

1963   When Alabama governor George Wallace makes his famous "stand in the schoolhouse door" and personally blocks the admission of black students to the University of Alabama, President John F. Kennedy sends Attorney General Nicholas Katzenbach and federal officials to confront him. Wallace backs down.

1964   Perhaps in reaction to the conflict in the public schools over desegregation, parochial school enrollment reaches an all-time high of 5.6 million students.

      As the post–World War II baby boomers reach college age, college enrollments expand dramatically, from 784,000 in 1963 to 1,037,000 this year.

      President Lyndon Johnson starts the Job Corps to give vocational training to poor urban youth, which is not successful, and Head Start, a preschool program for urban youth, which is highly successful.

1966   The U.S. Office of Education reports that one-quarter of black students attend schools with white students.

1967-   Student protests against the Vietnam War escalate each year, peaking in May 1970 following
1970   the killing of four students at Kent State University by the Ohio National Guard. Two million students at 350 campuses demonstrate, and many colleges close early (see Chapter 5).

During the same period, militant blacks, galvanized by the Black Power movement, demand minority scholarships and black studies programs. Demand are "nonnegotiable."

1967   Federal funds for education are increasing dramatically, from $5.4 million in 1963 to $12.2 million this year.

1968   The Supreme Court orders all the public schools in the country to draw up desegregation plans.

Berkeley, California, buses students to schools out of their neighborhoods to achieve racial balance.

Teachers striking in New York City cite racial discrimination in hiring, wages, and facilities as major complaints.

The Children's Television Workshop is incorporated. Its *Sesame Street*, a pioneering model for children's television, premieres on PBS in 1969.

1969   A student strike at San Francisco State University that closes down the school ends with the administration's agreeing to fund a black studies program.

Princeton admits women. Within the next few years many traditionally male colleges open their doors to women.

1970   Colleges are expanding dramatically to handle the baby boomers, enlarging their campuses, building new ones, and planning extension schools.

There are 7.5 million students enrolled in higher education.

The number of women in college is up, this year 48 percent of the college population.

1971   President Nixon signs a $5 billion appropriation for the Office of Education, the largest to date. He also asks for an increase in funds for guaranteed loans for college students and that a larger proportion of low-interest bank loans go to students from low-income families.

The Supreme Court rules that busing is an appropriate means for achieving racial balance. Bitterly opposed for destroying neighborhood schools, busing becomes a hot political issue.

The Ford Foundation creates a $100 million, six-year scholarship program to aid private black colleges.

1972   President Richard Nixon orders a one-year moratorium on school busing, and Congress agrees.

1975   Parochial school enrollment sinks to 3.3 million.

About 150 women's studies programs have been established. By 1980 as many as 30,000 women's studies courses will be offered at colleges and universities.

Legislation barring discrimination by sex in college admissions, classes, financial aid, and athletics goes into effect.

A major clash breaks out in Boston over school busing when a federally mandated school busing program is instituted, but by the end of the 1970s there is little remaining controversy over busing because there are so few busing programs.

1978   The Supreme Court rules that racial quotas in admissions programs are illegal.

1979   The Department of Education is established, with Shirley Hufstedler named its first secretary.

Secretaries of Education

Secretary	President	Year Appointed	Secretary	President	Year Appointed
Shirley Hufstedler	Carter	1979	Lauro F. Cavazos	Bush	1989
Terrel Bell	Reagan	1981	Lamar Alexander	Bush	1991
William J. Bennett	Reagan	1985	Richard W. Riley	Clinton	1993
Lauro F. Cavazos	Reagan	1988			

1980   The U.S. Civil Rights Commission reports that nearly half of all minority schoolchildren are in "racially isolated" schools. Housing patterns, particularly "white flight" to the suburbs, perpetuate the pattern of "minority majority" schools.

The new U.S. Department of Education publishes *A Nation at Risk*, which argues that American education is in crisis and calls for reform.

1984   College enrollment peaks this year at 1,662,000. Black enrollment, which has been rising, constitutes more than 10 percent of college enrollment.

1990   College expenses reach a record high; an Ivy League education costs $20,000 a year.

Of the school-age population, ages 5 to 17, 91 percent are enrolled in school.

1991   The home school movement is growing, with more than 300,000 students being educated at home, most for religious reasons.

1993   Goals 2000, a new federal effort at educational reform, is supported by a series of new laws strengthening Head Start, creating programs to support college tuition, and otherwise promoting education through the setting of national goals.

The Costs of Education, 1900–1990

Average Annual Expenditure Per Student in Public Elementary and Secondary Schools

Year	$ per Student
1900	$20
1910	$33
1920	$64
1930	$108
1940	$105
1950	$260
1960	$471
1970	$955
1980	$2,491
1990	$5,532

Average Teacher Salaries

1900	$325
1910	$485
1920	$871
1930	$1,420
1940	$1,441
1950	$3,010
1960	$5,174
1970	$9,047
1980	$16,715
1990	$32,638

LITERACY: HOW AMERICANS READ

American colonists were more literate as a group than the population they left behind. During the 1700s when Europe's literacy rate hovered at 30 to 40 percent, half of the male colonists could read, as could a quarter of the women. Literacy tended to be highest in the New England colonies, undoubtedly because Puritans put great store in education. Eighty-five percent of the men and 50 percent of the women were literate.

Thanks largely to public schooling, by 1870 only 20 percent of Americans were illiterate, and at the turn of the century that figure was reduced to slightly over 10 percent. The rate of illiteracy continued to drop throughout the 20th century, from 6 percent in 1920 to an effective illiteracy rate of 1 percent in 1969.

At the very point at which it would have been easy to declare that the United States suffered no illiteracy, educators realized that the ability to read meant more than being able to make out letters on a page. In an increasingly technological world, functional literacy, that is, the ability not only to read words but to use them in cultural contexts, including the workplace, would be increasingly important. Throughout the 1970s until the present day, concern has grown over the number of Americans who read but not well enough to hold down one of the 80 percent of all new jobs that now require more than a high school education. Forty percent of U.S. high school graduates cannot read at a ninth-grade level, and more than 20 million Americans cannot read at a fourth-grade level. It has been estimated that functional illiteracy costs the United States $200 billion a year.

Numerous programs have been launched to improve American literacy, but in an age of dwindling funds and a push by some in Congress to eliminate the Department of Education, solutions to this problem seem increasingly scarce.

ACTS OF CONGRESS AFFECTING EDUCATION

1785   Land Ordinance. This legislation, passed by the Confederation Congress to provide for the survey and sale of public lands, reserves one lot in every township for "the maintenance for public schools."

1787   Northwest Ordinance. This legislation, passed by the Confederation Congress to establish the process whereby U.S. territories will qualify for statehood, declares: "Religion, morality, and knowledge, being necessary to good government and the happiness of mankind, schools and the means of education shall forever be encouraged."

1862   Morrill Land-Grant Act. This act sets aside public lands for endowing agricultural colleges that would also offer classes in home economics and engineering. Eventually more than 70 land-grant colleges are established.

1866   Supplementary Freedmen's Bureau Act. Set up to help recently emancipated slaves after the Civil War, the Freedmen's Bureau helps establish nearly 3,000 schools and contributes to the founding of black colleges.

1887   Dawes Severalty Act. This act provides funds to create boarding schools for Native American children, designed as much to assimilate as to educate them.

1917   Smith-Hughes Act. This act establishes federal grants to support agricultural home economics, vocational, and business education in public high schools.

1944   Servicemen's Readjustment Act. More popularly called the GI Bill, this mandates substantial educational stipends for returning World War II veterans to attend vocational schools or colleges.

1958   National Defense Education Act. This act provides funds to strengthen science, math, and modern language education and creates a federal low-interest student loan program.

1963   Vocational Education Act. This act provides federal funds for industrial education, and the field grows. Various amendments extend vocational education to adults, handicapped persons, and disadvantaged students.

1964   Civil Rights Act. This act prohibits discrimination on the basis of race, color, or national origin in federally assisted programs. As many schools and colleges receive federal money, it helps assure equal educational opportunity and provides the framework for affirmative action programs. By 1966 more than half of the school districts in 17 southern states are in compliance with federal regulations.

Equal Opportunity Act. This act creates Head Start, an educational program for preschool disadvantaged children; the Job Corps, which provides educational programs and vocational training for young people; and work-study programs that support the part-time employment of students from low-income families in institutions of higher education.

1965   Elementary and Secondary School Act. This act provides aid to elementary and secondary schools.

Higher Education Act. This act provides funds for scholarships for college undergraduates.

1975   Handicapped Children's Act. This act prohibits the segregation of handicapped children and requires all classrooms to be accessible.

SPECIAL EDUCATION

The United States has been a leader in the development of special education, which involves providing specialized schooling for learning- and physically disabled students. Thanks to the Handicapped Children's Act of 1975, many special programs have been set up for special-needs students, and more than 5 million students now receive some form of special education in the public schools. Unlike routine education, which is managed almost entirely by the states, standards for special education are mandated by the federal government, which also provides funds to research, institute, and carry out the programs.

Under the Handicapped Children's Act, public schools must educate special-needs children in the least restrictive environment. As a result, 90 percent of all special education now takes place in the regular classroom, and most special-education students attend special classes for only part of the day.

Federal funds provide for 15,000 specialized-education instructors, but students also have benefited from such technological aids as computers that convert written text to spoken for blind children and special wires in classrooms that relay information to hearing-impaired students wearing special hearing aids. Federal funds have made classrooms, physical education facilities, and school buses accessible to children in wheelchairs.

SUPREME COURT DECISIONS AFFECTING EDUCATION

Most Supreme Court decisions relating to education have dealt either with religion or with race.

1819   *Dartmouth College v. Woodward.* The Court rules that the New Hampshire legislature cannot amend Dartmouth's charter to make it a public institution. The case establishes the important principle that a charter is a contract.

1899   *Cumming v. Richmond County Board of Education.* In an early decision in support of the Jim Crow laws, the Court sanctions segregated public schools and by logical extension inherently unequal facilities.

1930   *Cochran v. Louisiana Board of Education.* Public school boards can supply secular textbooks to parochial schools. The Court holds that supplying schoolbooks to all children benefited the state. The plaintiff had brought the suit under the due process clause of the Fourteenth Amendment.

1938   *Missouri ex rel. Gaines v. Canada.* The Court rules that the University of Missouri Law School must either admit blacks or build a separate and equal facility for them.

1940   *Alston v. School Board of the City of Norfolk.* Black teachers and white teachers, according to this decision, are entitled to equal pay.

   Minersville School District v. Gobitis. The Court rules that flag saluting in public schools can be compulsory even for Jehovah's Witnesses, whose faith forbids them to worship graven images.

1943   *West Virginia State Board of Education v. Barnette.* The Court reverses the decision in the *Gobitis* case, saying that an individual cannot be forced to salute the flag against his or her will.

1947   *Everson v. Board of Education.* State reimbursement of money spent on busing to parochial schools does not constitute an infringement of the First Amendment.

1948   *McCollum v. Board of Education.* In a case where students were released from regular classes to attend religious ones taught in the public schools by private school teachers, the Court finds that public schools and public monies cannot be used to teach religion, nor can religion be promoted in the public schools.

1950   *McLaurin v. Oklahoma State Regents.* The Court agrees that equal physical facilities do not guarantee equality and overrides regulations that force a black student to live and eat separately from whites.

   Sweatt v. Painter. The Court rules that provisions made by the University of Texas Law School for a black student are unequal.

1952   *Zorach v. Clauson.* The Court reaffirms its 1948 ruling, reiterating that public schools cannot teach religion, but validates the right of students to receive religious education, off school property, during the school day.

1954   *Brown v. Board of Education of Topeka.* In a landmark ruling, the Court unanimously overrules the separate but equal doctrine established by *Plessy v. Ferguson* (1896) and states: "We conclude that in the field of education the doctrine of 'separate but equal' has no place. Separate educational facilities are inherently unequal."

1962   *Engel v. Vitale.* The Court outlaws prayer in public schools as a violation of the separation of church and state.

1963   *Abington Township v. Schempp.* The Court outlaws Bible readings and readings of the Lord's Prayer in public schools.

1971   *Swann v. Charlotte-Mecklenburg Board of Education.* The Court validates busing as a tool for desegregating the schools and achieving racial balance.

1972   *Wisconsin v. Yoder.* The Court rules that, despite compulsory education laws, Old Order Amish children cannot be required to attend school after the eighth grade. Parents assert that high schools engender values contrary to Amish beliefs.

1973   *Keyes v. School District #1, Denver.* The Court strikes down a lower court's order to achieve racial balance in schools by busing black children from a city jurisdiction to suburban schools.

   Committee for Public Education v. Nyquist. The Court strikes down reimbursement of tuition and tuition tax credits for parochial schools.

1974   *Milliken v. Bardley.* The court backtracks on busing, saying that inner-city schools (mostly black) and suburban districts (mostly white) do not have to engage in interdistrict busing to achieve racial balance.

Cleveland Board of Education v. La Fleur. The Court holds that mandatory maternity leave policies are unconstitutional.

1978   *University of California Regents v. Bakke*. The Court deals a blow to educational affirmative-action programs by ruling that quotas, such as the one Allan Bakke claimed kept him out of the medical school, are "reverse discrimination" and therefore illegal.

1980   *Stone v. Graham*. The Court strikes down a Kentucky law requiring the posting of the Ten Commandments in public-school classrooms.

1982   *Plyler v. Doe*. The Court rules that a state may not deny public education to the children of illegal aliens.

1984   *Grove City College v. Bell*. The Court rules that only specific departments receiving federal grants have to comply with federal requirements for nondiscrimination. The case weakens enforcement of civil rights laws until the Civil Rights Restoration Act of 1988 specifies that antibias provisions apply to the entire institution if any part receives federal funding.

1985   *Wallace v. Jaffree*. The Court rules that Alabama's "moment of silence" in school class-rooms is a violation of the First Amendment because the legislature had clearly provided for the moment to encourage prayer.

1987   *Edwards v. Aguillard*. The Court rules that a Louisiana statute requiring schools that teach evolution must also teach "creation science," is a violation of the First Amendment.

1988   *Hazelwood School District v. Kohlmeier*. The Court rules that school officials may censor the publications of a high school journalism class.

1992   *Lee v. Weisman*. The Court officially sanctioned prayer at graduation ceremonies in public schools violates the establishment clause of the First Amendment.

SIGNIFICANT PEOPLE IN AMERICAN EDUCATION

Adler, Felix (1851–1933).   An educator and founder of the Ethical Culture Society, or the Ethical movement, Adler was a child-welfare activist who promoted free kindergartens and vocational-training schools. He was an early adherent of progressive education.

Barnard, Henry (1811–1900).   Barnard worked to promote public school education in Connecticut through improved supervision of grammar schools. He later performed similar services in Rhode Island and Wisconsin and in 1867 was appointed the first U.S. commissioner of education. He published the *Journal of Education* for 25 years.

Beecher, Catharine (1800–1878).   A champion of women as grammar-school teachers, Beecher argued that women were naturally more nurturing and thus better suited to teaching. Beecher founded the Hartford Academy in 1823. In the 1840s she campaigned to send women west to teach.

Bethune, Mary McLeod (1875–1955).   The 17th child of former slaves, Bethune became an early advocate of education for black women. After being educated at the Moody Bible Institute in Chicago, Bethune taught in a series of mission schools before founding the Daytona Normal and Industrial Institute (now Bethune-Cookman College) for black girls. She helped found the National Association of Colored Women's Clubs and the National Council of Negro Women and served as a minority-affairs advisor to President Franklin Roosevelt.

Carver, George Washington (c. 1861–1943).   Born a slave, Carver received a B.A. and M.A. from Iowa State College. Starting in 1896 he headed Tuskegee Institute's agriculture department, where he built one of the nation's first productive agricultural laboratories and promoted soil improvement and crop diversification, discovering many uses for the peanut, sweet potato, and soybean. As an educator, he is best remembered for his "school on wheels," a mobile classroom dedicated to teaching poor southern farmers how to work their land more productively.

Dewey, John (1859–1952).   An educational theorist and psychologist, Dewey was the author of *The School and Society* (1899) and *Democracy and Education* (1916). Influenced by G. Stanley Hall, his teacher at Johns Hopkins, Dewey developed and promoted progressive education, a system of teaching in which children are nurtured and rewarded instead of disciplined and punished and there is great emphasis on creative thinking, experimentation, and practice. His philosophy of education continues to influence schools today. Dewey also believed schools should foster democracy and community spirit.

Du Bois, W.E.B. (1868–1963).   An educator, social reformer, and African-American leader, Du Bois was the first African American to be awarded a Ph.D. from Harvard. By urging the formation of a black politically oriented leadership elite, he stood in stark contrast to Booker T. Washington, who believed blacks should focus on learning trades and stay out of political skirmishes. Du Bois constantly promoted the cause of higher education for blacks. He taught history and education at Atlanta University and wrote many scholarly books about black culture, most notably *The Souls of Black Folk* (1903), *The Suppression of the African Slave Trade to the United States of America, 1638–1870* (1896), *and Black Reconstruction in America* (1935). In 1909 he co-founded the Niagara Movement and the National Negro Committee, the predecessor to the National Association for the Advancement of Colored People.

Galarza, Ernesto (1905–1984).   An education and labor activist and professor, Galarza was one of the few Mexican Americans to successfully navigate the American school system to his advantage. Although he could just as easily have excelled as a scholar, he spent his life trying to help his fellow Mexican Americans. From 1936 to 1947 he worked with the Pan-American Union on education issues, and in later years he organized farm workers and sought to improve public education in California. He spoke out against segregation, insensitive teachers, and overcrowding in barrio schools.

Gallaudet, Thomas Hopkins (1787–1851).   A pioneer in education for the hearing impaired, Gallaudet founded the first U.S. school for the deaf, in Hartford. His youngest son, Edward Miner Gallaudet (1837–1917) founded the school for the hearing impaired that is now Gallaudet University, in Washington, D.C.

Gesell, Arnold (1880–1961).   A psychologist who specialized in child development, Gesell garnered a lay as well as a professional audience for his ideas and helped to change the way Americans view child rearing, largely by teaching them how children think at various stages of their development. He elucidated his views in a series of books that include *The First Five Years of Life* (1940) and *The Child from Five to Ten* (1946), which to this day are widely read by teachers and parents alike.

Hall, G. Stanley (1844–1924).   A founder of developmental psychology, Hall established, at Johns Hopkins, one of the first psychology laboratories in the United States. He was also one of the first persons to apply psychology to education. In his books *The Contents of Children's Minds* (1883) and *Adolescence* (1904), he wrote about the thoughts of children. He was the founder and first president of the American Psychological Association and the first president of Clark University.

Johnson, Lyndon Baines (1908–1973).   As president from 1963 to 1969, Johnson, moved by his own experience teaching minority children, pushed Congress to increase funding for education. He began Head Start, a highly successful preschool program for disadvantaged children.

"Somehow you never forget what poverty and hatred can do when you see its scars on the hopeful face of a young child," he told Congress. "I want to be the president who educated young children." Johnson was the first of several presidents who tried to move public education from state control onto the national agenda.

Lyon, Mary (1797–1849).   Primarily interested in advancing higher education for women, in 1837 Lyon founded Mount Holyoke Female Seminary, the first U.S. college for women. As principal, she developed an academic program that emphasized service to others.

Mann, Horace (1796–1859).   Along with John Dewey, Mann is one of two towering figures in American education. Studying law, Mann fought for tax-supported, nonsectarian public education. As an elected official (member of the Massachusetts House, 1827–1833, the Massachusetts Senate, 1833–1837), he worked for compulsory education, which would also help to eradicate child labor, and he supported the establishment of public high schools, the education of women (including their training as teachers), and the abolition of corporal punishment in schools. Mann believed children should be nurtured rather than punished. He also advocated breaking schools down into classes by age groups and paying extra attention to the youngest learners. He was appointed secretary of the first board of education in the country and left politics to work on it. A staunch believer in educating people for democracy, he wrote: "The scientific or literary well-being of a community is to be estimated not so much by its possessing a few men of great knowledge, as its having many men of competent knowledge."

Rush, Benjamin (1745–1813).   In addition to being an innovative physician, Rush was an early advocate of women's education and in 1787 founded one of the first schools for women, the Young Ladies Academy in Philadelphia.

Seton, Elizabeth Ann (1774–1821).   A convert to Roman Catholicism, Seton established a school for Catholic children. She is also the first U.S.-born saint, having been canonized in 1974, and founded the first American religious order for women, the Sisters of Charity of St. Joseph.

Skinner, B. F. (1904–1990).   A psychologist, Skinner helped to develop and popularize behaviorism, which holds that people are known to respond to various external stimuli in ways that can aid learning. Out of this came programmed learning, a system of study in which students get immediate feedback (the reward). Skinner wrote many books, including *The Behavior of Organisms* (1938), *Walden Two* (1948), and *About Behaviorism* (1974).

Terman, Lewis (1877–1956).   A psychologist who pioneered in educational testing, Terman introduced the Binet Intelligence Test (later the Stanford-Binet) and refined it; it would later become the leading intelligence test for American children. Terman invented the term *intelligence quotient*, or IQ. In his book *Genetic Studies of Genius* (1925–1930), he traced the careers of 1,500 unusually bright children.

Thomas, Martha Carey (1857–1935).   An activist for educational equality, Thomas was one of the founders of Bryn Mawr College for women in 1885, and in 1894 she became its president. She led a movement to admit women to Johns Hopkins University, where her father was a trustee but she was banned from classes. She was the author of *The Higher Education of Women* (1900).

Thorndike, Edward (1874–1949).   As the theoretical link among psychologists William James, John Watson, and B. F. Skinner, Thorndike studied the measurement of mental accomplishment, especially the way that reward could function as an aid to learning. From 1922 to 1940 he directed the psychology division of the Institute of Educational Research at Columbia's Teachers College. He was the author of many books, including *Educational Psychology* (1903) and *Mental and Social Measurements* (1904).

Washington, Booker T. (1856–1915).   A firm believer in education, even when segregated, this African-American leader urged blacks to work in the trades. He founded Tuskegee Institute, a small black trade school that by the time of his departure was highly respected, training students in more than 35 trades and promoting economic independence. In addition to writing his autobiography, *Up from Slavery* (1901), Washington served as advisor to presidents Theodore Roosevelt and William Taft.

Watson, John B. (1878–1958).   Along with B. F. Skinner, Watson, a psychologist, popularized behaviorism and studied its effect on the educational process. He used children to explore his principles of behavior modification. A firm believer that environment is the determining factor in development, Watson put forth his ideas in *Psychology from the Standpoint of a Behaviorist* (1919) and *Psychological Care of Infant and Child* (1928), among other works.

Webster, Noah (1758–1843).   Webster wrote many early textbooks, including the first American dictionary. In 1783 he published the *American Spelling Book*. More popularly known as the "blue-backed speller," it sold millions of copies over its unusually long life. Webster also was a founder of Amherst College.

Willard, Emma (1787–1870).   Willard campaigned for equal educational opportunities for women, and in her own school, the Troy Seminary, founded in 1821, she introduced such subjects as hitherto "masculine" mathematics and philosophy. Willard published history textbooks and lobbied the state of New York unsuccessfully to fund higher education for women. Like many of the early female educators, she trained hundreds of teachers.

ADDITIONAL SOURCES OF INFORMATION

Bailyn, Bernard. *Education in the Forming of American Society*. University of North Carolina, 1960.

Cremin, Lawrence A. *American Education: The Colonial Experience, 1607–1783*. Harper & Row, 1970.

———. *American Education: The Metropolitan Experience, 1876–1980*. Harper & Row, 1988.

———. *American Education: The National Experience, 1783–1896*. Harper & Row, 1980.

Dewey, John. *Democracy and Education: An Introduction to the Philosophy of Education*. Darby, 1932.

Du Bois, W.E.B. *The Souls of Black Folk*. Dover, 1994.

Edelman, Marian Wright. *The Measure of Our Success*. HarperCollins, 1993.

Gardner, Howard. *The Unschooled Mind*. Basic, 1993.

Hofstadter, Richard. *Anti-Intellectualism in American Life*. Random House, 1966.

Karier, Clarence J. *The Individual, Society and Education: A History of American Educational Ideas*. 2d ed. University of Illinois Press, 1986.

Nasaw, David. *Schooled to Order: A Social History of Public Schooling in the United States*. Oxford University Press, 1979.

11
Science and Medicine

The early settlers of America had a whole new world of plants, animals, and landforms to explore and classify, and even before the 18th century small scientific communities had begun to form. The successful outcome of the Revolutionary War created a burst of new scientific energy. Museums, societies, and journals proliferated, helping to propel the nation to become the world's technological leader. In pure science, however, the United States still lagged behind Europe. But in the early 20th century Americans began catching up, winning their fist Nobel science prizes. By the 1940s the United States had become preeminent in both science and technology, with Americans capturing the most science Nobels. At century's end, America still leads the world in science, but other countries such as Japan and Germany are narrowing the gap. Throughout American history, the increasing interdependence of science and technology has accelerated the development of both.

Note: Often the date shown for an invention is that of its patent, although sometimes patents were delayed for years and in other cases may have preceded the development of a working model. For other inventions and discoveries, see Chapters 7, 9, and 12.

SIGNIFICANT EVENTS IN AMERICAN SCIENCE AND MEDICINE

1683   Boston clergyman Increase Mather and other Boston gentlemen establish the Philosophical Society "for conference upon improvements in philosophy and additions to the stores of natural history."

1721   Boston physician Zabdiel Boylston experiments with inoculation to combat a smallpox epidemic introduced from the West Indies; all but 6 of his more than 240 patients survive.

1730   Thomas Godfrey invents the reflecting quadrant, a device used for sea navigation.

1730-
1747   Mark Catesby publishes his *Natural History of Carolina, Georgia, Florida and the Bahama Islands*, one of the earliest books to describe the flora and fauna of the British colonies.

1735   First medical society in the colonies founded in Boston.

1742   Benjamin Franklin invents the Franklin stove, or Pennsylvania fireplace; it provides more heat while burning less fuel than other fireplaces.

1743   The American Philosophical Society is founded in Philadelphia, with Benjamin Franklin as its first secretary.

1752   Benjamin Franklin performs his famous kite experiment, showing that lightning is a form of electricity. Franklin also invents the lightning rod, a metal conductor that prevents houses from being struck by lightning.

Thomas Bond open the first general hospital in the colonies, in Philadelphia. The hospital also cares for mental patients.

1753   Mathematician, astronomer, and surveyor Benjamin Banneker fashions a wooden striking clock that keeps time accurately for more than 50 years.

1762   William Shippen, Jr., begins giving anatomy lessons in Philadelphia.

1765   The College and Academy of Philadelphia opens the first medical school in the colonies, which becomes the College of Physicians and Surgeons.

John Bartram is appointed Botanist to the King. In his travels throughout the colonies he will catalogue the flora and fauna of North America.

BENJAMIN BANNEKER (1731–1806)

Banneker, the son of a former slave, was largely self-taught, although for several winters when he was a child he attended school. There he first showed a talent for mathematics. At the age of 21, Banneker became famous for devising a striking wooden clock, using a borrowed pocket watch as a model. The clock kept accurate time for more than 50 years. Using borrowed books, Banneker studied astronomy, mathematics (he later taught himself calculus and spherical trigonometry), and surveying. His gifts as a surveyor were so noticeable that he was selected to assist Andrew Ellicott in surveying the site of the nation's new capital, Washington, D.C. Throughout most of the 1790s he published almanacs containing scientific data and observations.

In 1792 Banneker sent an almanac to Thomas Jefferson, enclosing a letter protesting the low esteem in which African Americans were held and affirming "that one universal Father . . . hath made us all of one flesh . . . that He hath afforded us all the same sensations and endowed us all with the same faculties and that however variable we may be in society or religion, however diversified in situation or color, we are all of the same family and stand in the same relation to Him." Jefferson responded with warm thanks and a wish that the "degraded condition" of African Americans be ended and "a good system commenced for raising the condition both of their body and mind to what it ought to be."

1767	Medical instruction is inaugurated at King's College (Columbia University) in New York.
1773	The Eastern Asylum opens in Williamsburg, Virginia, to care for the mentally ill exclusively.
1775	John Lorimer develops the first dipping needle compass.
1780	The American Academy of Arts and Sciences is founded in Boston.
1783	Medical Institution of Harvard opens for classes.
1784	Benjamin Franklin invents bifocal spectacles.
1786	Physician Benjamin Rush opens the first free dispensary in the United States.
1790	The first federal patent is issued to Samuel Hopkins of Vermont for manufacturing process for pot and pearl ash. Jacob Perkins of Massachusetts gets a patent for cutting and heading nails in a single operation.
1794	Charles Willson Peale, portrait painter, naturalist, and inventor, moves his gallery into the hall of the American Philosophical Society.
1803-1806	President Thomas Jefferson commissions Captain Meriwether Lewis and Lieutenant William Clark to explore the Louisiana Purchase territory and the lands westward to the Pacific. Besides mapping the most accessible routes through the Rockies, the two are also asked to collect data on the region's natural resources, geography, wildlife, and climate. The expedition seeks the headwaters of the Missouri River, and any connection with the Columbia. By spring of 1805 the party reaches the Pacific Ocean. They recross the Rockies and return to Saint Louis in September 1806, with much of the scientific data Jefferson requested.
1804	Ornithologist John James Audubon does the first banding studies on wild American birds.
1809	In the first operation of its kind recorded in the United States, Kentucky doctor Ephraim McDowell successfully removes an ovarian tumor.
1812	The *New England Medical Review and Journal*, now the *New England Journal of Medicine*, begins publication.
1818	Benjamin Silliman, first professor of chemistry and natural history at Yale, founds *American Journal of Science and Arts*, which he edits until 1846.
1822	Physician William Beaumont, while employed by the U.S. Army, begins groundbreaking investigations into the nature of human gastric juices.

1829 Physicist Joseph Henry improves the electromagnet to make it practical for use.

1831 Samuel Guthrie discovers chloroform, which will be used throughout the world as an anesthetic.

1836 Inventor Samuel Colt receives a patent for his invention of the revolver.

1840 Dentists Horace Hayden and Chapin Harris establish the world's first dental school, the Baltimore College of Dental Surgery.

1842 Physician Crawford Long removes a cyst from the neck of a patient under ether anesthesia. The operation is the first recorded use of general anesthesia during surgery.

Dorothea Dix presents a memorial to the Massachusetts legislature detailing the cruel treatment of the insane in jails and almshouses and calling for the separation of the criminal and the insane. Her advocacy leads to the establishment of state-supported hospitals for the insane in many states.

1844 The Association of Medical Superintendents of American Institutions for the Insane (today the American Psychiatric Association) is founded.

1845 The periodical *Scientific American* begins publication.

1846 Congress establishes the Smithsonian Institution in Washington, D.C., with a bequest from the late James Smithson. Physicist Joseph Henry is named first secretary and director.

The American Association for the Advancement of Science (AAAS) is established in Philadelphia.

Inventor Elias Howe patents the lock-stitch sewing machine.

William Morton demonstrates the use of ether during surgery at Massachusetts General Hospital.

1847 Physician Nathan Davis founds the American Medical Association (AMA).

Astronomer Maria Mitchell discovers a comet and determines its orbit.

1848 Astronomer George Bond discovers Saturn's eighth satellite.

Maria Mitchell is the first woman elected to the American Academy of Sciences.

MARIA MITCHELL (1818–1889)

Maria Mitchell was introduced to science early by her father, a lover of science. As a young girl, she helped him chart the stars. At the age of 12, she observed an eclipse, which deeply impressed her. But if Maria Mitchell wanted to become a scientist, 19th-century America offered women virtually no opportunities. So Mitchell opened her own school in 1835, before assuming a year later the position of librarian of the Nantucket Athenaeum. In October 1847, appropriating the telescope her father had installed on the roof of the bank where he was employed, she discovered a new comet. This extraordinary feat brought her international recognition. In 1848 she became the first woman member of the American Academy of Arts and Sciences. (For nearly 100 years no other woman was elected.) In 1857 a group of women gave her a five-inch telescope, which she used to study sunspots, nebulae, and planets. Taking daily photographs of the sun, she made numerous discoveries about sunspots. In 1865 she became professor of astronomy at the newly founded women's college, Vassar. Several student became astronomers. A feminist, Mitchell helped establish the Association for the Advancement of Women, of which she served as president in 1870.

1849 Elizabeth Blackwell is the first American women to receive an M.D. degree; it is awarded by Geneva Medical College in Syracuse, New York.

Walter Hunt devises the modern safety pin.

1850   Astronomers William and George Bond discover the Crêpe Ring of Saturn.

1851   Inventor Isaac Singer patents a continuous-stitch sewing machine.

1854   Inventors Horace Smith and Daniel Wesson devise a new type of repeating device for pistols and rifles.

1857   Elizabeth Blackwell opens the New York Infirmary for poor Women and Children: the new hospital will be staffed only by female doctors.

Charles Darwin outlines his theory of evolution to Harvard botanist Asa Gray, who will later write a favorable review of *Origin of Species* (1859) for the *American Journal of Science* and a series of articles popularizing Darwin's theories for the *Atlantic Monthly*.

THE EVOLUTION REVOLUTION

Charles Darwin spent more than a decade interpreting the notes he had made during five years aboard HMS *Beagle*. He formulated and documented his concept of evolution meticulously. When he published his ideas as *Origin of Species* in 1859, evolution shook the scientific world with reverberations for philosophy, religion, and all of human society. This theory of natural selection as the explanation for the diversification of species threatened to separate science forever from traditional assumptions about divine creation.

Castigated as atheism, as testimony that man descended from apes, as evidence that there is no God, Darwinism was not popular with everyone in America. While the nation's paleontologists, naturalists, and biologists accepted the theory, its religious thinkers struggled with the idea. Did survival of the fittest mean that only the best got to heaven? Did Darwin's evidence repudiate all biblical teachings?

Herbert Spencer's application of Darwin's theories to the evolution of society did gain ready acceptance in America, however. The industrial tycoons and robber barons who praised the virtues of free enterprise found in this new social Darwinism justification for not interfering in the social order that seemed to benefit them. John D. Rockefeller recited Spencer to Sunday school classes, instructing children to think of giant corporations (like his Standard Oil) as evidence of the survival of the fittest. And if only the fittest survived, reasoned many, then the poor were simply not fit and attempts to improve their condition were only a misguided tinkering with the natural order. This thinking, which dominated domestic social and economic policy until the end of the 19th century, became influential in foreign policy as well, as it seemed to justify the conquest or economic management of weak countries, particularly in Latin America, that could not—to American standards—manage themselves. While rarely cited today, social Darwinism still haunts debates over welfare and public assistance.

In a bizarre footnote to Darwin's revolution, creationists and evolutionists confronted each other directly in 1925 at the so-called Monkey trial in Dayton, Tennessee. When John T. Scopes was arrested for breaking Tennessee law by teaching evolution to his high school biology class, Clarence Darrow and the American Civil Liberties Union came to his defense. Arguing the state's case was William Jennings Bryan, populist, secretary of state, and three-time presidential candidate. Although the judge found Scopes guilty, it was no victory. Bryan, humiliated on the witness stand by Darrow's scorching examination, died a few days later; Tennessee's creationism law was never again enforced; and the revolution wrought by evolution, if not complete, was certainly secure.

1859   Naturalist Louis Agassiz establishes the Museum of Comparative Zoology at Harvard.

1860   Astronomer Alvan Clark discovers that Sirius is a double star.

1861   The U.S. Sanitary Commission is set up by Simon Cameron, the secretary of war.

1862   Inventor Richard Gatling patents his rapid-fire Gatling gun, the predecessor of the machine gun.

Clara Barton volunteers as a nurse for the Union Army, serving at the Battle of Cedar Mountain. At the Second Bull Run, she distributes coffee, crackers, and supplies to the wounded.

The National Archives/Corbis

Clara Barton

CLARA BARTON AND THE AMERICAN RED CROSS

In April 1861, Clara Barton, a clerk in the U.S. Patent Office, welcomed the Massachusetts Sixth Regiment to Washington. The boys were from her hometown, and she knew some of them. She saw immediately what they lacked: towels, handkerchiefs, serving utensils, thread, needles, preserved fruits, blankets, candles—all the necessities basic for comfort that the army seemed unable to supply. After a year of devoting herself to soliciting supplies, she volunteered as a nurse, and on the battlefield she saw how truly unprepared the Union Army was to cope with the slaughter of war. "I saw many things that I did not wish to see and I pray God I may never see again," she told a friend. The wounded whose needs she attended to called her "the Angel of the Battlefield."

After the war, on a "rest cure" in Europe during the Franco-Prussian War, Barton participated in relief efforts organized by the International Red Cross. When she returned to the United States, she was determined to found an American branch of this organization that gave aid to war victims and provided medical supplies and services at the front. In 1881 she formed the American Association of the Red Cross, and a year later the U.S. Senate ratified the Geneva Convention for the Amelioration of the Condition of the Wounded and Sick of Armies in the Field. Under its terms, the neutrality and safety of medical personnel and civilian volunteers, as well as the humane treatment of the wounded, were guaranteed.

Under Barton's leadership, the domestic program of the Red Cross provided peacetime relief during forest fires, epidemics, and earthquakes. Its work following the Johnstown, Pennsylvania, flood in 1889 won national recognition. Overseas, the Red Cross sent money and supplies to victims of religious wars in Turkey and Armenia, and during the Spanish-American War it made sure that trained nurses, doctors, and supplies were on hand in Cuba.

Although her last years as head of the American Red Cross were marked by controversy, Barton left a legacy of volunteer nursing, female humanitarism, and organized aid for the care of victims of war and disaster that would give comfort and hope to millions.

1865	Linus Yale, Jr., invents the pin-tumbler cylinder lock.
1866	Othniel Marsh, first professor of paleontology in the United States, leads a bone-hunting expedition for Yale. This and a later expedition for the U.S. Geological Survey yield 500 new species, including the pterodactyl, which Marsh is the first to identify.
1869	The first state board of health is established in Massachusetts.
1870	J. W. Hyatt invents celluloid.
1871	Horticulturist Luther Burbank begins to experiment with plant breeding and hybrids.
1872	*Popular Science* magazine begins publication.
	Robert Chesebrough patents Vaseline® (petroleum jelly).
1873	Florence Nightingale's nurses' training program is implemented at Bellevue Hospital in New York City.
1874	Ophthalmologist Samuel Theobald and others found the Baltimore Eye & Ear Dispensary. Eight years later he founds the Baltimore Eye, Ear, and Throat Charity Hospital with which he is associated the remainder of his life.
	Kansas doctor Andrew Still pioneers osteopathy, a therapeutic system based on the premise that restoring or preserving health can be accomplished by manipulating the skeleton and muscles.
1875	Inventor George Green patents an electric dental drill.
1876	Physicist Josiah Willard Gibbs publishes a paper on thermodynamics that will become the foundation of physical chemistry. Gibbs, unlike most American scientists who are experimenters, was the outstanding theoretician produced by the United States in the 19th century.
	Physicist Henry Rowland uncovers the magnetic effect of electric convection.
1877	Astronomer Asaph Hall discovers two moons of Mars.
1879	Ira Remsen and Constantin Fahlberg, at Johns Hopkins University in Baltimore, formulate the sugar substitute saccharine.
	The Archeological Institute of America is founded.
	Inventor Thomas Edison devises the incandescent electric lamp.

THOMAS ALVA EDISON

In some ways, Thomas Alva Edison typifies the self-made man and the Yankee inventor who specialized in practical applications for science. Born in 1847 to a family of declining fortunes in a small Ohio town, he overcame the adversities of limited schooling and hearing loss to become an American hero, the "Wizard of Menlo Park," whose incandescent lamp transformed the patterns of daily life around the world.

Edison knew how to work hard, and he knew how to organize others to do so, too. His laboratory in Menlo Park, New Jersey, was an "invention factory," and Edison's staff included mechanics who could take his endless questioning as well as his demands on their time. Under pressure to eliminate the "bugs" in one of his stock printer devices to fill a big order, he told his assistants, "I've locked the door and you'll have to stay here until this job is completed. Well, let's find the bugs." It took 60 straight hours.

Edison knew how to make the most of his inventions, too. He wasn't the first to dream of an incandescent lamp. Inventors had been working on the idea for years. The problem was to find the right material—a filament that would glow, and not burn up, when a current of electricity was passed through it. Edison pressed his assistants and Francis Upton, a theoretical mathematician who supplied the gaps in Edison's understanding, for more than a year. When the team found that carbonized cotton thread burned for 40 hours, Edison staged a demonstration. On New Year's Eve, 1879, he invited the public to Menlo Park, illuminated with 150 bulbs. Then he set about, as he put it, making "electric light so cheap that only the rich will be able to burn candles."

In 1887 Edison built a new laboratory in West Orange. Its brick buildings housed precision machinery; its library had 10,000 books. There was a music room, a darkroom, and a stockroom. A picket fence and guards kept interlopers out. Edison was less often in the lab than at his desk, directing a staff of 50. In his lifetime, the Edison labs boasted more than a thousand patents. Most served useful and practical purposes.

While Edison's inventive genius clearly contributed to technology and human comfort, his genius for organization may have been equally important. Although he was the inspiration—the wizard—his team structure and regimen for orchestrating the work of mechanics, technicians, and theoreticians would become standard practice in the complex industrial research laboratories of the next century.

1880   Telephone inventor Alexander Graham Bell along with his father-in-law founds the magazine *Science*.

George Eastman patents a dry plate photographic process.

1881   Physicist Albert Michelson invents the interferometer, a device that measures distance by the length of light waves.

The American Society of Mechanical Engineers is founded.

George Sternberg, a U.S. Army bacteriologist, isolates the pneumococcus bacterium that is responsible for pneumonia. Sternberg's announcement of his discovery comes almost simultaneously with Louis Pasteur's statement of the same information.

The American Association of the Red Cross is founded by Clara Barton.

1882   Nikola Tesla's discovery of the rotating electromagnetic field will lead to devices using alternating current.

1884   Physician Edward Trudeau, who advocates sanitariums for the treatment of tuberculosis patients, establishes one at Saranac Lake, N.Y.

Surgeon William Halsted begins to administer cocaine as a local anesthetic.

1885   In Davenport, Iowa, physician William Grant performs the first successful appendectomy in the United States.

Engineer William Stanley invents the electric transformer.

Alvan Clark and his sons build the Lick Observatory on Mount Hamilton, California, and help propel American astronomy into the front ranks.

1887 Physicists Albert Michelsen and Edward Morley show that there is no absolute motion of the earth relative to an ether, an experiment that paves the way for the development of Einstein's theory of relativity.

The National Geographic Society is founded.

1888 John Loud invents the ballpoint pen.

Inventor William Burroughs develops the first successful recording adding machine.

Chemist Herbert Dow devises a new method for the effective production of bromine. Dow's work with brines led to the creation of the Dow Chemical Company in 1897.

1889 Biophysicist Jacques Loeb pioneers artificial parthenogenesis.

1891 Herman Frasch begins work on an economical process for the extraction of sulfur from underground deposits.

Astronomer James Keeler proves that Saturn's rings are composed of tiny meteor particles.

Nikola Tesla invents the Tesla coil, which produces high-frequency, high-voltage electric current; it will later be used in radios and televisions.

Jesse Reno devises the escalator.

1892 Pathologist Theobald Smith detects that ticks spread Texas cattle fever; this paves the way for the discovery of how diseases like malaria, typhus, and Lyme disease are spread.

Physician Andrew Still founds the American School of Osteopathy.

George Eastman incorporates Eastman Kodak Company and develops daylight loading film cartridge and processing. Late in life, he will give his fortune away, establishing, among other donations, The Eastman School of Medicine and Dentistry at the University of Rochester.

1893 Albert Michelson measures a meter, based on the wavelength of cadmium light; in 1925, this measurement is universally accepted.

Geologist Thomas Chambers establishes the *Journal of Geology*.

Daniel Williams, a Chicago surgeon, performs the world's first open-heart surgery.

Johns Hopkins University opens its medical school and affiliated hospital in Baltimore, Maryland.

1895 Chemist Edward Morley determines the atomic weight of oxygen.

Daniel Palmer establishes chiropractics; by 1930 there are 16,000 practitioners.

King Gillette invents the safety razor.

1897 Wisconsin's Yerkes Observatory installs a refracting telescope with a 40-inch lens.

1898 Physicist Wallace Sabine devises a reverberation equation that will form the basis of the science of architectural acoustics.

1900 Chemist Charles Palmer devises a new process for producing gasoline from petroleum.

1901 Industrialist John D. Rockefeller establishes the Rockefeller Institute for Medical Research in New York City.

Headed by Walter Reed, an army commission identifies the *Aëdes aegypti* mosquito as the transmitter of the yellow-fever virus.

Adrenaline becomes the first hormone to be isolated and purified in the research of chemist Jokichi Takamine, at the Johns Hopkins Medical School.

The National Bureau of Standards is established.

1902   Arthur Little receives a patent for his rayon-production process.

Engineer Willis Carrier invents air-conditioning.

Eugene Opie proves that diabetes results from the destruction of parts of pancreatic tissue called the islets of Langerhans.

Chemists Albert Barnes and Herman Hille discover an antiseptic that, marked as Argyrol, will protect newborns from blindness.

Geneticist Walter Sutton proves that chromosomes come in pairs and carry the units of inheritance; his work becomes the basis for the chromosomal theory of heredity.

1904   Astronomer Charles Perrine detects the sixth moon of Jupiter and will discover the seventh the next year.

1905   The legality of compulsory vaccination laws is upheld by the Supreme Court.

Clarence McClung discovers that females have XX chromosomes and males, XY.

1906   Pathologist Howard Ricketts isolates the cattle tick as the carrier of Rocky Mountain spotted fever.

1907   Zoologist Ross Harrison develops the first successful animal-tissue cultures.

Scientist Bertram Boltwood finds that the age of rocks containing uranium can be determined by measuring the ratio of uranium to lead.

1909   Chemist Leo Baekeland produces Bakelite, the first thermosetting plastic.

Geneticist Thomas Morgan proposes a new, innovative theory of the gene.

Chemist Phoebus Levene discovers that nucleic acid is of two kinds (RNA and DNA).

1910   Physician James Herrick is the first to diagnose sickle-cell anemia.

Thomas Morgan discovers that some inherited sex characteristics are sex-linked.

1911   Physicist Robert Millikan measures an electron's electric charge.

1912   James Herrick, in a written report that is the first diagnosis of a heart attack in a living patient, demonstrates that heart attacks are not always fatal.

Biochemists Elmer McCollum and Marguerite Davis isolate vitamin A.

William and Charles Mayo, brothers and physicians, build their own medical center in Rochester, Minnesota; the Mayo Clinic becomes one of the world's biggest medical centers.

1913   Biologist Alfred Sturtevant finds that genes line up in a row on chromosomes and pioneers chromosome mapping.

William Coolidge devises the modern X-ray tube.

The American Cancer Society is founded.

Pediatrician Béla Schick devises the Schick test to determine diphtheria immunity.

John B. Watson introduces behaviorism in psychology.

BEHAVIORISM

Psychology had a long gestation—first in philosophy and then in physiology. In the 19th century German and French scientists established psychology as a separate scientific discipline and, especially after Freud, Europeans seemed to dominate the field. But it was an American, William James, who first applied Charles Darwin's theory of natural selection to consciousness, and another American, John B. Watson, gave psychology a new direction. The recipient of the University of Chicago's first Ph.D. in psychology, for a dissertation entitled "Animal Education: The Psychical Development of the White

Robert Millikan

Rat," Watson was professor and director of the psychological laboratory at Johns Hopkins when he delivered an important address at Columbia University in 1913. "Psychology as the Behaviorist Views It" became a manifesto of a new, behaviorist approach to psychology that would be highly influential for half a century.

"Psychology as the behaviorist views it is a purely objective experimental branch of natural science," proclaimed Watson. "Its theoretical goal is the prediction and control of behavior." Concerned largely with external and sensory stimuli and behavioral reaction or physiological response, behaviorists sought to explain animal and human behavior through objective observation and in measurable terms. Applying this approach to the study of learning in rats, B. F. Skinner at Harvard concluded that learning is a series of patterned responses to stimuli and rewards.

From these theories emerged therapeutic approaches focused on behavior modification. Through conditioning, clients are desensitized to anxieties and fears or, through exposure to a system of rewards and punishments, engineered to change their actions.

1914   Biochemist Edward Kendall isolates the thyroid hormone thyroxin.

1916   The National Research Council (NRC) is founded by the United States National Academy of Sciences.

Elmer McCollum isolates vitamin B.

1916   Margaret Sanger opens the first birth-control clinic in the United States, in Brooklyn.

1918-   A worldwide influenza epidemic comes to the United States, killing half a million people.
1919

1920   Physician Karl Menninger establishes the Menninger Clinic in Topeka, Kansas. The clinic will pioneer a "total-environment" approach that will change the methods for treatment of mental illness.

Robert H. Goddard demonstrates the lifting power of rockets.

1922   Elmer McCollum isolates vitamin D in cod-liver oil and discovers its effectiveness in combating rickets.

1923   Physicist Peter Debye provides a mathematical description of electrolysis.

Margaret Sanger's birth-control clinic in New York City regularly dispenses contraceptive devices.

Harry Steenbock of the University of Wisconsin proposes that exposing foods to ultraviolet light can turn them into better sources of vitamin D.

Robert Millikan receives the Nobel Prize for his experiments that prove Albert Einstein's work and theories on the photoelectric effect.

Jacob Schick invents the electric razor; he obtains a patent in 1928.

1923   Researchers George and Gladys Dick, husband and wife, identify the streptococcus responsible for scarlet fever and devise a serum for the disease.

1925   Chemist Julius Nieuwland pioneers synthetic rubber.

Physician Thomas Cooley describes a type of anemia that will take his name; Cooley's anemia is a hereditary blood disease with no cure.

1926   Geneticist Hermann Muller discovers that mutations can be produced by X rays.

Biochemist James Sumner shows that enzymes are proteins.

1927   Harvard professor Philip Drinker creates the "iron lung," a device for mechanical artificial respiration.

1929   The progenitor of the Blue Cross nonprofit health insurance association is founded in Dallas, Texas.

Edwin Hubble establishes that the universe is expanding.

1930   In Flagstaff, Arizona, Lowell Observatory astronomers led by Clyde Tombaugh discover the planet Pluto.

The Adler Planetarium, the first in the United States, opens in Chicago.

Inventor Clarence Birdseye, inspired by a visit to the Eskimo people in Alaska, receives a patent for freezing as a way of preserving food.

1931   The Food and Drug Administration is established, charged with protecting the health of the nation against impure and unsafe foods, drugs, cosmetics, and other potential hazards.

Physicist Harold Urey and two colleagues discover heavy water (deuterium oxide), leading to the production of atomic energy.

Astronomer Karl Jansky discovers that radio waves come from space, paving the way for the science of radio astronomy.

Physicist Ernest Lawrence constructs the world's first effective cyclotron; his success will speed the development of atomic knowledge.

1932   Biochemist Charles King isolates vitamin C.

Physicist Carl Anderson discovers the positron.

1933　Albert Einstein accepts a post at Princeton's Institute for Advanced Study. The Nazi government will shortly confiscate his property and revoke his German citizenship because he is Jewish.

QUANTUM MECHANICS AND REFUGEE SCIENTISTS

Throughout the 19th century American science had a bent for the practical. While Americans excelled in technology and in scientific work that was useful and profitable, basic research was neglected and unappreciated. Josiah Willard Gibbs, a professor of mathematical physics at Yale who was publishing a series of papers on thermodynamics, for example, was not paid a salary until he was on the verge of moving to Johns Hopkins.

Between 1910 and 1920 leaders in American physics, aware of the ferment in theoretical physics—particularly quantum mechanics—in Europe, made a concerted effort to interest American students in the subject. Particularly after World War I, some believed that the national interest depended on it. Between 1920 and 1930 degrees in physics nearly tripled. Funds from the Rockefeller fortune supported research programs. Lecture series brought Europe's most distinguished physicists to the United States. Harvard, Berkeley, Chicago, Princeton, and the California Institute of Technology emerged as thriving centers for the study of quantum theory.

Young Americans often went to Germany to study with leaders in the field, but now more frequently young European physicists, particularly Jews blocked by quotas on Jews in faculties, found positions in American universities attractive. Many left Europe for the greater opportunities life in America offered. Paul Epstein of Munich was one of the first, taking a position at Caltech in 1921. Others who came in the 1920s included John von Neumann, Fritz Zwicky, and Eugene Wigner.

After the rise of fascism in the 1930s and the enforcement of Hitler's racial laws, Jewish scientists were dismissed from German universities. Now escape from Europe became a stronger push than the pull of American research opportunities, which were considerable. Among the refugees were Hans Bethe, Edward Teller, Albert Einstein, Enrico Fermi, and Leo Szilard, whose effect on American physics and America itself cannot be underestimated. After World War II, Szilard joked that he, Fermi, and other physicists should receive the Nobel Peace Prize for *not* having conducted, before they fled fascism, the uranium experiments that would have allowed Hitler to conquer the world.

1934　Biochemist Robert Williams isolates a substance in rice husks that prevents beriberi.

1935　Du Pont chemist Wallace Carothers invents nylon.

Biochemist Wendell Stanley isolates the first crystalline virus.

Biochemists Herbert Evans and Oliver and Gladys Emerson isolate vitamin E.

Vitamin K is isolated by Danish biochemist Henrik Dam and American biochemist Edward Doisy.

1936　Researchers H. Houston Merritt and Tracy Putnam produce Dilantin, a drug that can be used to treat epilepsy and irregular heartbeats.

Robert Williams names his synthesized vitamin B_1 compound thiamine.

1937　Physicist Isidor Rabi develops a new method for studying the spectra of atoms in the radio-frequency range.

Carl Anderson discovers the muon, now know as a subatomic particle, with more mass than the electron.

The first radio telescope in the world is constructed by astronomer Grote Reber.

The first blood bank is opened in Chicago.

1937   Congress funds a National Cancer Institute to sponsor research into the disease.

1938   Du Pont researcher Roy Plunkett produces the plastic Teflon.

The March of Dimes organization for research into poliomyelitis is founded.

1939   John Dunning's cyclotron at Columbia University is the first in America to split an atom; the reaction emits gamma rays, and Albert Einstein suggests in a letter to President Franklin Roosevelt that reactions of this kind could lead to the generation of "vast amounts of power" and also to the "construction of bombs."

Chemist Linus Pauling publishes his theory of the chemical bond by which it is possible to construct accurate models for some anomalous molecules. *The Nature of the Chemical Bonds* is still highly regarded.

LINUS PAULING

It would be hard to find a 20th-century equivalent of Benjamin Franklin—printer, inventor, scientist, statesman—but Linus Pauling comes close. Pauling, born in Oregon in 1901, received his Ph.D. in chemistry from the California Institute of Technology and taught and directed laboratories there for a large part of his career. His contributions are many and notable: application of the quantum theory to calculations of molecular structure; development of a theory of resonance to explain certain bonds in organic chemicals; determination of the molecular structure of antitoxins, amino acids, and proteins; production of synthetic antibodies. In 1954 he was awarded the Nobel Prize for discovering the forces holding proteins and molecules together, thus laying the groundwork for later descriptions of the structure of DNA.

But Pauling was not always to be found in his lab. In the early 1970s he stirred controversy for his advocacy of massive doses of vitamin C as preventing cancer and the common cold. He also took a great interest in public affairs and was especially active in the movement for nuclear disarmament. In 1957 he organized an international test-ban petition eventually signed by 11,000 scientists in 49 countries. The next year he wrote *No More War*, a compelling case for international peace. He was also an outspoken critic of the Vietnam War, continuously urging scientists to join their voices in protest. In 1963 he became one of the few recipients of two Nobel Prizes, his second a peace prize for his work on world disarmament.

1940s   Biologists Max Delbrück, Alfred Hershey, and Salvador Luria found the field of molecular biology with their discoveries about bacterial and viral reproduction.

1940   A research team at Columbia University separates the uranium-235 isotope from the more plentiful uranium-238 isotope using a gaseous diffusion process devised by physicist John Dunning and his colleagues; this newly isolated isotope will be the source of atomic energy.

Physicist Edwin McMillan discovers a radioactive element heavier than uranium, which he names neptunium. The following year, along with Glenn Seaborg, he will discover an even heavier element, to be named plutonium, which is suspected of having a greater energy yield than uranium.

Biochemist Martin David Kamen isolates the carbon-14 isotope.

Engineers at RCA publicly test an electron microscope.

Immunologist Karl Landsteiner discovers the Rh factor in blood.

1941   Physicist Vannevar Bush is the head of the new Office of Scientific Research and Development set up by President Franklin Roosevelt.

Microbiologist Selman Waksman coins the term *antibiotic*.

1942   Chemist Louis Fieser produces napalm for the U.S. Army.

Physicist Enrico Fermi and others invent the nuclear reactor.

Physician George Nicholas Papanicolaou's "Pap" test for cervical cancer is accepted by the medical profession.

Chemist Russell Marker makes oral contraceptives possible with his discovery that the wild Mexican barbasco plant is a cheap source of the hormone progesterone.

1944   Chemists William Doering and Robert Woodward synthesize quinine.

Surgeon Alfred Blalock performs the first operation to save a "blue baby."

Selman Waksman produces the antibiotic streptomycin, which will be used against tuberculosis. This disease, greatly feared as consumption during the 19th century, becomes curable.

Researchers Oswald Avery, Colin MacLeod, and Maclyn McCarty demonstrate that deoxyribonucleic acid (DNA) is the blueprint of heredity, determining the way an organism develops.

1945   In New Mexico, a government-funded team of scientists led by physicist Robert Oppenheimer explodes the first atomic bomb.

Grand Rapids, Michigan, is the first American community to experiment with the fluoridation of its drinking water.

THE MANHATTAN PROJECT

In 1939 Albert Einstein and other famous physicists, concerned that German scientists might build an atomic bomb, began campaigning to persuade President Franklin Roosevelt to beat Germany to the punch. Realizing that the bomb might hold the key to victory in World War II, Roosevelt established a small research project on atomic fission. The project soon expanded to include research teams at universities including Princeton, California, Columbia, and Chicago.

In 1942 the researchers found that a chain reaction in uranium produced atomic fission. The discovery by physicist Ernest Lawrence that a common uranium isotope, U-238, could be changed into a new fissionable element, plutonium, made building a bomb practicable. When informed of this development, Roosevelt approved the creation of a section of the army, with the code name "the Manhattan District," to oversee the project. Late in 1942, physicists Arthur Compton, Enrico Fermi, and colleagues produced the first small uranium chain reaction under the bleachers of Stagg Field at the University of Chicago.

Now the focus turned to producing an actual bomb. Plutonium was produced in Hanford, Washington, uranium at Oak Ridge, Tennessee. In Los Alamos, New Mexico, a new laboratory, directed by physicist J. Robert Oppenheimer, was organized to build the bomb. During the next three years more than $2 billion in federal money was spent on research and to produce the components of the bomb.

On July 16, 1945, the atom bomb was successfully tested at Alamogordo, New Mexico. Observers were thunderstruck at the sight of the first mushroom cloud created above the explosion. On August 6 an atom bomb was dropped by order of President Harry Truman from the B-29 bomber *Enola Gay* on Hiroshima, Japan. The bomb destroyed the city, killing almost 80,000 people. Three days afterward, a second bomb was dropped on another Japanese city, Nagasaki, killing 40,000 (with burns and radiation poisoning, the death toll from the bombs would reach 200,000). The Japanese surrendered five days later. World War II had ended and the nuclear age had begun.

1946   Congress establishes the Atomic Energy Commission.

1947   Edward Tatum and Joshua Lederberg find that sexual reproduction occurs in bacteria.

1947   Chemist Willard Libby finds that all organic material contain some carbon-14 atoms, which decay at a constant rate, a discovery that paves the way for the carbon-dating of archaeological evidence.

Chloromycetin, developed by Park-Davis chemists, is used to treat typhus patients, marking the first us a "broad-spectrum" antibiotic.

1948   Physicist Richard Feynman and Julian Schwinger propose a new theory of quantum electrodynamics.

Biochemists Edward Kendall and Philip Hench synthesize the adrenal hormone cortisone and find that it is an effective treatment for arthritis.

The anti–motion-sickness properties of the drug dymenhydrinate (marketed as Dramamine) are accidentally discovered by Johns Hopkins physicians who had thought that they were working with an antiallergy drug.

George Gamow, Ralph Alpher, and Robert Herman devise the big bang theory of the origin of the universe.

John Bardeen, Walter Brattain, and William Shockley invent the transistor.

Zoologist Alfred Kinsey publishes *Sexual Behavior in the Human Male*; based on his interviews with 18,500 American men, it suggests that many acts thought to be perverse are in fact normal because they occur so commonly.

1949   Researchers at the Merck laboratory synthesize the adrenocorticotropic hormone ACTH; it will be used later in treating AIDS.

1950   Du Pont manufactures the synthetic fiber Orlon.

The U.S. Atomic Energy Commission constructs the first nuclear reactor for power production.

The National Science Foundation is established to support basic research and education.

1952   Chemist H. Herbert Fox develops isoniazid, a drug to combat tuberculosis.

Scientist Eugene Aserinsky finds that sleep with rapid eye movements (REMS) is a distinct stage of sleep, which is later discovered to be associated with dreams.

A government team of scientists, led by physicist Edward Teller, develops the first hydrogen bomb.

1953   American researcher James Watson and his English partner, Francis Crick, identify the basic double-helix structure of DNA and its self-duplicating process; the discovery begins a new era in the study of genetics.

Congress passes legislation to establish a cabinet-level Department of Health, Education and Welfare. Oveta Culp Hobby is named the first secretary.

Secretaries of Health, Education, and Welfare

Secretary	President	Year Appointed	Secretary	President	Year Appointed
Oveta Culp Hobby	Eisenhower	1953	Robert H. Finch	Nixon	1969
Marion B. Folsom	Eisenhower	1955	Elliot L. Richardson	Nixon	1970
Arthur S. Flemming	Eisenhower	1958	Caspar W. Weinberger	Nixon	1973
Abraham A. Ribicoff	Kennedy	1961		Ford	1974
Anthony J. Celebrezze	Kennedy	1962	Forrest D. Mathews	Ford	1975
	Johnson, L. B.	1963	Joseph A. Califano, Jr.	Carter	1977
John W. Gardner	Johnson, L. B.	1965	Patricia Roberts Harris	Carter	1979
Wilbur J. Cohen	Johnson, L. B.	1968			

Secretaries of Health and Human Services

Secretary	President	Year Appointed	Secretary	President	Year Appointed
Patricia Roberts Harris	Carter	1979	Otis R. Bowen	Reagan	1985
Richard S. Schweiker	Reagan	1981	Louis W. Sullivan	Bush	1989
Margaret M. Heckler	Reagan	1983	Donna E. Shalala	Clinton	1993

Surgeon John Gibbon employs a heart-lung machine he has invented to perform successful open-heart surgery.

Researchers at New York's Sloan-Kettering Institute of Cancer Research provide early evidence of the link between tobacco products and cancer.

1954 Microbiologist Jonas Salk's polio vaccine is tested in mass trials. Pronounced safe the next year, it is distributed in a mass immunization program that will virtually wipe out the disease and fear that accompanied it.

Physician Clarence Lillehei builds pumps that can maintain circulation during open-heart surgery.

Jonas Salk

1954   The first successful kidney transplant in the world is performed by a Harvard surgery team.

Researchers William Masters and Virginia Johnson begin their revolutionary investigations into the physiology of human sexual response; in 1966 they will publish *Human Sexual Response*, based on observations of 382 women and 312 men in more than 10,000 cycles of sexual arousal.

A study of nearly 200,000 American men done by researchers Edward Hammond and Daniel Horn strongly suggest that smoking is hazardous to health.

Gregory Pincus and John Rock develop the first oral contraceptive pill.

1955   Biochemist Severo Ochoa is the first to synthesize RNA (ribonucleic acid).

Researchers discover that reserpine is effective in the treatment of schizophrenia and other mental disorders.

Physicists Owen Chamberlain and Emilio Segre discover the antiproton.

Physicists Clyde Cowen, Jr., and Frederick Reines discover the neutrino, a subatomic particle with no mass or charge.

1957   Biochemist Arthur Kornberg and his colleagues at Stanford University devise a method for synthesizing a biologically inactive form of DNA.

1958   Astronomer James Van Allen discovers radiation belts, now known as the Van Allen belts, surrounding the earth in space.

The National Aeronautics and Space Administration is established to conduct research and space exploration.

1959   Researchers William Stein, Stanford Moore, and their assistants code a complete amino-acid sequence of the biologically important enzyme ribonuclease.

1960   Laser technology is perfected by Theodore Maiman, who builds upon the earlier efforts of other scientists, such as R. Gordon Gould, Charles Townes, and Arthur Schawlow.

1961   Physician Frances Kelsey of the Food and Drug Administration blocks the marketing in the United States of thalidomide, a sleep-inducing drug that causes serious birth defects.

Scientist Marshall Nirenberg reads one of the "letters" of the genetic code.

Physicist Murray Gell-Mann and others develop method of classifying subatomic particles.

1962   Physician John Enders devises the first effective measles vaccine.

Biologist Rachel Carson's *Silent Spring*, an attack on pesticides, launches the environmental movement.

1963   Astronomer Maarten Schmidt is the first to identify a quasar.

The first liver transplant is performed by surgeon Thomas Starzl.

1964   The surgeon general issues a report that concretely connects cigarette smoking to lung cancer.

Murray Gell Mann identifies quarks, components of heavy subatomic particles, like protons and neutrons.

Surgeon James Hardy performs the first transplant of an animal heart into a human.

Congress passes the Medicare Act, establishing the first government-run program to provide health insurance for citizens aged 65 and over.

THE FEDERAL GOVERNMENT AND HEALTH CARE

Beginning in 1964 with the passage of Medicare, the U.S. government began to assume direct responsibility for the health care of Americans ages 65 and older. The next year Medicaid was instituted to provide medical aid to the poor. These programs, as well as veterans' hospitals, now cover millions of Americans.

But these were not the first U.S. government programs to address the health and medical needs of America's citizens. In 1798, partly to encourage young men to join the merchant marine despite risks encountered in the Atlantic from warring Britain and France, Congress authorized the establishment of marine hospitals. From this beginning grew the U.S. Public Health Service, which today collects vital statistics on the health of Americans, manages health services for Indians and Alaska natives, and oversees the National Library of Medicine and the Food and Drug Administration.

Government responsibility for the purity of food and drugs manufactured and sold in the United States stems partly from the outrage following Upton Sinclair's *The Jungle* (1906), which exposed practices in the Chicago stockyards. The Pure Food and Drug Act and the Meat Inspection Act, both passed that same year, forbade adulteration and enforced sanitary regulations in the meat-packing industry. Today the Pure Food and Drug Administration conducts research and develops standards with regard to food, drugs, and cosmetics.

Other federal units include the Centers for Disease Control, which administers programs for the prevention of communicable diseases, and the National Institutes of Health, which conducts and supports biomedical research into the causes, prevention, and cure of diseases. In fact, the federal government, through its programs supporting research, regulating drugs, promoting maternal and child welfare services, giving grants for the construction of hospitals and research facilities, and underwriting some costs of training for doctors, nurses, and other medical personnel, has a role in all health-care policies and issues with a public dimension.

1965	Congress legislates that all cigarette packaging be labeled with health warnings.
	Astronomers Arno Penzias and Robert Wilson find radio waves produced by the big bang.
1966	Researchers Paul Parkman and Harry Myer devise a rubella (German measles) vaccine.
	Heart surgeon Michael De Bakey implants the first artificial heart in a human.
1967	New York surgeon Adrian Kantrowitz attempts the first American transplant of a human heart, but his patient does not survive beyond a few hours.
	Arthur Kornberg and co-workers synthesize biologically active DNA.
1969	Three Apollo Program astronauts land on the moon, taking rock and soil samples.
	Following the signing of the Nuclear Nonproliferation Treaty, President Richard Nixon orders stockpiles of bacteriological weapons destroyed and renounces the use of chemical weapons except for defense.
	Biochemist Jonathan Beckwith and co-workers are the first to isolate a single gene.
	Surgeon Denton Cooley implants the first artificial heart for temporary use in a human.
1970	Biochemist Hamilton Smith finds a restriction enzyme that splits certain DNA strands at specific sites.
	Microbiologist David Baltimore discovers "reverse transcriptase," a viral enzyme capable of reversing the usual DNA-to-RNA transcription, a key development in genetic engineering.
	Har Khorana and co-workers produce the first artificial gene.
	The National Oceanic and Atmospheric Administration is established, to explore and chart the global ocean and its living resources; to monitor and predict weather conditions and issue warnings; and to assess environmental modification.

1971 Choh Hao Li synthesizes somatropin, a growth hormone that is produced naturally by the pituitary gland.

Researcher Raymond Damadian applies for a patent on the magnetic resonance imaging (MRI) scanner; it will be used to detect abnormalities inside the body.

The Food and Drug Administration tells doctors to stop prescribing diethylstilbestrol (DES) to ease morning sickness in pregnant women because evidence suggests that the drug predisposes their daughters to reproductive tract cancers.

Legislation providing $1.6 billion for cancer research is approved by Congress.

1972 The surgeon general issues a report warning that the health of nonsmokers is endangered by other people's smoking around them.

1973 In the first example of genetic engineering, Stanley Cohen and Herbert Boyer put a specific gene into bacterium.

The CAT scanner is introduced after having been developed by Allan Cormack and Godfrey Hounsfield.

1974 Physician Henry Heimlich demonstrates the Heimlich maneuver, which will become the standard emergency treatment for choking victims.

In Ethiopia, U.S. anthropologist Donald Johanson and co-workers discover the nearly complete skeleton of *Australopithecus afarensis*, an early relative of humans.

1975 Lyme disease is identified in Lyme, Connecticut, and is found to be carried by ticks that live on animals in wooded areas, primarily in the Northeast.

1976 The National Institutes of Health suggest regulating some kinds of genetic testing to avoid the creation of dangerous new organisms.

Har Khorana announces that he and his colleagues have successfully synthesized a bacterial gene, analine-transfer RNA, and inserted it into a living cell, where it has functioned successfully.

1977 The bacterium that causes Legionnaire's disease is identified.

Using techniques from the recent developments in genetic engineering, American scientists successfully produce insulin from bacteria.

Congress creates the U.S. Department of Energy. James R. Schlesinger is named the first secretary.

1979 The Department of Health, Education and Welfare is redesigned as the Department of Health and Human Services.

1980 Physicist Luis Walter Alvarez develops the theory that dinosaurs became extinct because of the impact of a large meteorite or comet on Earth.

Researcher Martin Cline and co-workers transfer a functioning gene from one mouse to another.

1982 The first total replacement of a human heart with an artificial one is performed at the Utah Medical Center in Salt Lake City, by surgeon William DeVries.

1984 American and French researchers isolate the first AIDS-inducing viruses.

A surgery team performs the first successful operation on a fetus.

1985 Construction begins in Hawaii on the world's largest telescope, the Keck, whose mirror will have a diameter of 33 feet (10 meters).

1986 The FDA-approved hepatitis B vaccine is the first accepted genetically engineered vaccine.

1987 AZT, a drug designed for the treatment of AIDS victims, is approved by the FDA.

The FDA approves Lovastatin, a drug that lowers the cholesterol level.

The National Aeronautical and Space Administration determines that the continents are moving in patterns predicted by the theory of plate tectonics.

1990   The Hubble space telescope goes into orbit.

National Institutes of Health researchers put a foreign gene into a human for the first time.

1992   Astrophysicist George Smoot supports the big bang theory of the creation of the universe; using microwave and satellite technology, he has located the exact places where galaxies began to form.

1993   The Clinton administration unveils a plan to reform medical care in the United States by introducing "managed competition" among insurers, but it is defeated by vigorous opposition from many sides.

1994   Data collected by the repaired Hubble space telescope leads astronomers to question the age, size, and origin of the universe.

A team of U.S. scientists reports it has isolated and cloned a gene in mice that causes obesity when it malfunctions; this mouse gene has a counterpart in humans.

1995   President Clinton authorizes proposed Food and Drug Administration regulations intended to curb tobacco use by teenagers.

1996   The National Aeronautics and Space Administration reports that a meteorite from Mars reveals signs of ancient microscopic life.

AMERICAN NOBEL PRIZES IN THE SCIENCES (THROUGH 1996)

Chemistry

1914	Theodore Richards
1932	Irving Langmuir
1934	Harold Urey
1946	James Sumner
	John Northrop
	Wendell Stanley
1949	William Giauque
1951	Edwin McMillan
	Glenn Seaborg
1954	Linus Pauling
1955	Vincent du Vigneaud
1960	Willard Libby
1961	Melvin Calvin
1965	Robert Woodward
1966	Robert Mulliken
1968	Lars Onsager
1972	Christian Anfinsen
	Stanford Moore
	William Stein

1974	Paul Flory
1976	William Lipscomb
1979	Herbert Brown
1980	Paul Berg
	Walter Gilbert
1981	Roald Hoffman
1983	Henry Taube
1984	Robert Merrifield
1985	Herbert Hauptman
	Jerome Karle
1986	Dudley Herschbach
	Yuan Lee
1987	Donald Cram
	Charles Pedersen
1989	Sidney Altman
	Thomas Cech
1990	Elias James Corey
1992	Rudolph A. Marcus
1993	Kary B. Mullis
1994	George A. Olah

1995	F. Sherwood Rowland
	Mario Molina
1996	Richard E. Smalley
	Robert F. Curl, Jr.

Physics

1907	Albert Michelson
1923	Robert Millikan
1927	Arthur Compton
1937	Clinton Davisson
1939	Ernest Lawrence
1943	Otto Stern
1944	Isidor Rabi
1946	Percy Bridgman
1952	Felix Block
	Edward Purcell
1955	Willis Lamb
	Polykarp Kusch
1956	William Shockley
	John Bardeen
	Walter Brattain
1959	Emilio Segre
	Owen Chamberlain
1960	Donald Glaser
1961	Robert Hofstadter
1963	Eugene Wigner
	Maria Goeppert-Mayer
1964	Charles Townes
1965	Julian Schwinger
	Richard Feynman
1967	Hans Bethe
1968	Luis Walter Alvarez
1969	Murray Gell-Mann
1972	John Bardeen
	Leon Cooper
	Robert Schrieffer
1973	Leo Esaki
	Ivar Giaever
1975	James Rainwater
1976	Burton Richter
	Samuel Ting
1977	Philip Anderson
	John Van Vleck

1978	Arno Penzias
	Robert Wilson
1979	Sheldon Glashow
	Steven Weinberg
1980	James Cronin
	Val Fitch
1981	Nicolaas Bloembergen
	Arthur Schawlow
1982	Kenneth Wilson
1983	Subrahmanyam Chandrasekhar
	William Fowler
1988	Leon Lederman
	Melvin Schwartz
1989	Hans Dehmelt
	Norman Ramsey
1990	Jerome Friedman
	Henry Kendall
1993	Joseph H. Taylor
	Russell A. Hulse
1994	Clifford G. Shull
1995	Martin L. Perl
	Frederick Reines
1996	David M. Lee
	Robert C. Richardson

Physiology or Medicine

1933	Thomas Morgan
1934	George Whipple
	George Minot
	William Murphy
1943	Edward Doisy
1944	Joseph Erlanger
	Herbert Gasser
1946	Hermann Muller
1947	Carl Cori
	Getty Cori
1950	Edward Kendall
	Philip Hench
1952	Selman Waksman
1953	Fritz Lipmann
1954	John Enders
	Thomas Weller
	Frederick Robbins

1956	Andre Cournand Dickinson Richards	1977	Roger Guillemin Andrew Schally Rosalyn Yalow
1958	George Beadle Edward Tatum Joshua Lederberg	1978	Werner Arber Daniel Nathans Hamilton Smith
1959	Severo Ochoa Arthur Kornberg	1979	Allan Cormack
1961	Georg von Bekesy	1980	Baruj Benacerraf George Snell
1962	James Watson	1981	Roger Sperry David Hubel
1964	Konrad Bloch	1983	Barbara McClintock
1966	Peyton Rous Charles Huggins	1985	Michael Brown Joseph Goldstein
1967	Haldan Hartline George Wald	1986	Stanley Cohen Rita Levi-Montalcini
1968	Robert Holley Har Khorana Marshall Nirenberg	1987	Susumu Tonegawa
1969	Max Delbruck Alfred Hershey Salvador Luria	1988	Gertrude Elion George Hitchings
1971	Earl Sutherland, Jr.	1989	J. Michael Bishop Harold Varmus
1972	Gerald Edelman Rodney Porter	1990	Joseph E. Murray E. Donnall Thomas
1974	George Palade	1992	Edmond H. Fischer Edwin G. Krebs
1975	David Baltimore Renato Dulbecco Howard Temin	1993	Philip A. Sharp
		1994	Alfred G. Gilman Martin Rodbell
1976	Baruch Blumberg Carleton Gajdusek	1995	Edward B. Lewis Eric F. Wieschauf

SUPREME COURT CASES AND ACTS OF CONGRESS AFFECTING SCIENCE AND MEDICINE

1789 U.S. Constitution. This founding document gives Congress the power "to promote the Progress of Science and the useful arts by securing for limited Times to Authors and Inventors the exclusive Right to their respective Writings and discoveries." In its first session (1790), Congress passed a patent law.

1906 Pure Food and Drug Act. This act defines food adulteration and forbids the manufacture, sale, or transportation of adulterated food and drugs involved in interstate commerce. A Meat Inspection Act, passed the same year, enforces sanitary regulations in the meat-packing industry.

1921 The Sheppard-Towner Act. This establishes the first federally funded health care program granting the states matching funds to set up prenatal and child health care centers.

1938   Food, Drug, and Cosmetic Act. This act expands the scope of the Pure Food and Drug Act, prohibiting the misbranding of products and providing for factory inspections.

1944   Public Health Service Act. This act consolidates and revises all legislation relating to the Public Health Service.

1964   The Medicare Act. This establishes the first federally controlled health insurance program for Americans aged 65 or over. The next year, Congress attaches Medicaid, a national health insurance program for low-income Americans, to the Social Security Amendments.

1973   *Roe v. Wade*. The Court rules that the right to privacy protects a woman's decision whether to bear a child. State laws that make abortion a crime are overturned.

1974   The National Research Act. Congress establishes guidelines for research on humans.

1976   The Toxic Substances Control Act. This act prohibits the marketing of new chemical compounds before their impact on the environment is tested.

1980   *Diamond v. Chakrabarty*. The Court rules that manufactured biological products can be patented.

1990   *Cruzan v. Director, Missouri Department of Health*. The Court acknowledges an individual's right to die by refusing life-sustaining treatment.

SIGNIFICANT PEOPLE IN SCIENCE AND MEDICINE

Agassiz, Jean Louis (1807–1873).   Agassiz was professor of natural history at Harvard between 1848 and 1873. In 1859 his collections formed the basis for the Harvard Museum of Comparative Zoology.

Alvarez, Luis Walter (1911–1988).   A physicist, Alvarez was part of the atomic-bomb project team at Los Alamos, New Mexico. He also won the 1968 Nobel Prize in physics for employing bubble chambers to find subatomic particles. With his son Walter, Alvarez expounded the theory that some 65 million years ago a large meteorite or a comet hit the earth, with its impact causing the extinction of dinosaurs and other species.

Audubon, John James (1785–1851).   Ornithologist Audubon made the first American bird-banding experiments, starting in 1804. His drawings of birds, based on firsthand observation, appeared in his *Birds of America*, which was published in parts between 1827 and 1838. This work, a significant scientific achievement, is still impressive today.

Baekeland, Leo (1863–1944).   In 1909 Baekeland invented Bakelite, the first thermosetting plastic. From 1893 to 1899, he successfully worked on producing the first commercial photographic paper.

Barton, Clara (1821–1912).   Barton, a nurse, solicited and distributed supplies during the Civil War and aided the wounded on the battlefield. Between 1870 and 1871 she helped the International Red Cross in Europe during the Franco-Prussian War. After establishing the American Red Cross in 1881, Barton served as its first president until 1904.

Bartram, John (1699–1777).   A botanist, Bartram created the first botanical garden in America at his home along the Schuylkill River near Philadelphia. He journeyed throughout the Alleghenies and Catskills, and as far south as the Carolinas and Florida, in search of new plants, often accompanied by his son William, who published *Travels* in 1791. John Bartram was also a keen observer of Indian life.

Blackwell, Elizabeth (1821–1910).   Blackwell became the first American woman doctor after she graduated from New York State's Medical College in 1849. In 1853 she co-founded a private dispensary in New York, which later became the New York Infirmary for Poor Women and Children. This was later expanded to include the Women's Medical College to train doctors, the first such institution. In 1869 Blackwell moved to England, where she helped found the London School of Medicine for Women.

Burbank, Luther (1849–1926).   A horticulturist, Burbank developed more than 800 new varieties of plants and flowers, including superior varieties of lilies, roses, corn, squash, potatoes, and the Shasta daisy.

Burroughs, William (1855–1898).   Burroughs invented the recording adding machine in 1888.

Cannon, Annie (1863–1941).   A staff member at the Harvard College Observatory between 1896 and 1940, Cannon discovered 300 variable stars and 5 novae and catalogued more than 225,000 stellar spectra for the *Henry Draper Catalogue*, published from 1918 to 1924.

Carothers, Wallace (1896–1937).   Carothers was the director of organic chemical research for the Du Pont Company from 1928 until his death. While there, he invented nylon, but the patent was issued to Du Pont after his death in 1937. Carothers also helped to develop the first commercially successful synthetic rubber.

Carrier, Willis (1876–1950).   Carrier invented air-conditioning, the dehumidifier, and centrifugal refrigeration.

Carson, Rachel (1907–1964).   Carson, a biologist, wrote three popular books of meticulous observation of sea life: *Under the Sea Wind* (1941), *The Sea Around Us* (1951), and *The Edge of the Sea* (1954). But her most famous book, generally acknowledged to have ushered in the modern environmental revolution, is *Silent Spring* (1962), an attack on the use of insecticides.

Carver, George Washington (1864–1943).   Carver, an agricultural chemist, produced more than 300 derivatives from peanuts and 118 from sweet potatoes. The son of slaves, he encouraged southern farmers to plant soil-enriching crops like soybeans and peanuts rather than soil-destroying crops like cotton.

Colt, Samuel (1814–1862).   Colt invented the revolver, for which he received a patent in 1836. His pistol became so popular that the name Colt is synonymous with the revolver.

Coolidge, William (1875–1975).   A physical chemist, Coolidge did his research for General Electric beginning in 1905. In 1910 he invented the modern tungsten-filament electric light. He also invented a new tube (called the Coolidge tube) for X-ray production (1913), portable X-ray units, high-powered X rays for treating cancer, and, with Irving Langmuir, the first submarine-detecting device.

Cushing, Harvey (1869–1939).   As a neurosurgeon, Cushing introduced major advances in diagnostic and surgical technique. He was also a distinguished teacher and author of medical works.

De Bakey, Michael (1908–).   As head of surgery at Houston's Baylor College of Medicine, De Bakey performed the first successful carotid endarterectomy in 1953. He developed an "assisting" heart and did early work on heart transplants.

Debye, Peter (1884–1996).   A native of the Netherlands, Debye won the 1936 Nobel Prize for chemistry, before coming to the United States where he studied the structure of molecules and the conductivity of electricity by salt solutions.

Delbrück, Max (1906–1981).   With Salvador Luria and Alfred Hershey, German-born biologist Delbrück did ground-breaking research on bacteriophages that furthered knowledge about DNA. The three were awarded the 1969 Nobel Prize for physiology or medicine.

Dix, Dorothea (1802–1887).   A social reformer, Dix exposed the cruelty of incarcerating the insane and mentally ill in county jails and state penitentiaries, which she visited throughout Massachusetts before presenting her famous memorial to the Massachusetts legislature in 1842. Her work led to the founding of state hospitals for the insane in many states. During the Civil War she served as superintendent of women nurses for the Union forces.

Doisy, Edward (1893–1986).   A biochemist, Doisy isolated female sex hormones estrone (1929) and estradiol (1936). He also determined the chemical nature of vitamin K (1939) and isolated K, a variant form. He shared the 1943 Nobel Prize in physiology or medicine with Henrik Dam.

Draper, Charles (1901–1987).   An aeronautical engineer, Draper is known as the father of inertial guidance. He invented gyroscope-stabilized gunsights, which helped antiaircraft guns and aerial bombs hit their targets during World War II and subsequent wars. Draper also developed the guidance technology for marine and air navigation and for guided missiles.

Edison, Thomas (1847–1931).   Edison patented more than a thousand inventions. Some of the most significant were the incandescent electric lamp, the electric valve, the alkaline storage battery, and an improved movie projector. His Edison General Electric Company became the General Electric Company.

Einstein, Albert (1879–1955).   German-born Einstein revolutionized the study of physics when he formulated his theory of relativity. Fleeing Nazi Germany, he settled in the United States and was among a group of distinguished scientists who urged development of the atomic bomb. Horrified by the two bombs dropped on the Japanese cities of Hiroshima and Nagasaki in 1945, Einstein later became a leading figure in the movement to control nuclear weapons. He won the 1921 Nobel Prize in physics for his discovery of the law of the photoelectric effect.

Enders, John (1897–1985).   A virologist, Enders helped discover a measles vaccine. He shared the 1954 Nobel Prize for physiology or medicine with Frederick Robbins and T. H. Weller for their work cultivating polio viruses in tissue culture.

Evans, Herbert (1882–1971).   Anatomist Evans, with Oliver and Gladys Emerson, isolated vitamin E in 1935.

Fermi, Enrico (1901–1954).   Italian-born physicist Fermi is known as one of the founders of the nuclear age. He won the 1938 Nobel Prize for physics for his discovery of neutron-induced nuclear reactions (1934–1937), and after traveling to Stockholm to receive the prize he continued to the United States as his wife was Jewish and they sought to escape Fascist Italy. In 1942 he directed the first controlled nuclear chain reaction. Fermi also worked on the atomic-bomb project at Los Alamos, New Mexico. The element fermium is named after him, and the prestigious Fermi Award for physics is given in his honor.

Franklin, Benjamin (1706–1790).   Inventor, scientist, statesman, and philosopher, Franklin founded the Junto (1727), a discussion club that became the American Philosophical Society in 1743. Among his inventions were the Franklin stove, bifocal glasses, and the lightning rod. Around 1746 he began experimenting with electricity. His famous kite experiment occurred in 1752.

Gamow, George (1904–1968).   Physicist Gamow devised the theory of radioactive decay in 1928. He proposed the big bang theory of the origin of the universe. Born in Russia, Gamow came to the United States in 1934.

Gatling, Richard (1818–1903).   Gatling invented a rapid-fire gun, which he patented in 1862; it was the precursor of the modern machine gun.

Gibbs, Josiah Willard (1839–1903).   Gibbs's work while he was a professor of mathematical physics at Yale became the basis for the science of quantum mechanics.

Gorgas, William (1854–1920).   An army officer and doctor, Gorgas was chief sanitary officer in Havana, Cuba, from 1898 to 1902. By using strict measures to destroy mosquitos, he virtually ended yellow fever in Havana. As chief sanitary officer of the Panama Canal Commission between 1904 and 1913, he applied the same tactics, thereby making the canal's completion possible.

Henry, Joseph (1797–1878).   A physicist, Henry improved the electromagnet, and his contributions to electromagnetism were indispensable to the development of the commercial telegraph. In 1846 he was appointed the first secretary and director of the new Smithsonian Institution, and he established its broad policies for the diffusion of knowledge.

Hubble, Edwin (1889–1953).   Astronomer Hubble showed that some nebulae are independent galaxies, discovered the "red shift" of light, and proved that all galaxies beyond the Milky Way are receding from ours and therefore the universe is expanding.

James, William (1842–1910).   The brother of writer Henry James, William James was a psychologist and a philosopher. His classic book *The Principles of Psychology* (1890) examines the relationship among thought, experience, and action.

Kendall, Edward (1886–1972).   Kendall headed the biochemistry section of Minnesota's Mayo Clinic, where he isolated the steroid hormone cortisone and, with Philip Hench, used it successfully to treat rheumatoid arthritis (1948). Kendall and Hench shared the 1950 Nobel Prize for physiology or medicine for their work with Switzerland's Tadeus Reichstein.

Landsteiner, Karl (1868–1943).   An Austrian-born immunologist and pathologist, Landsteiner discovered the A, B, and O human blood types (1901), created the ABO system of blood typing, discovered the M and N blood groups, and, with Alexander Weiner, discovered the Rhesus factor (1940). He received the 1930 Nobel Prize for physiology or medicine.

Lawrence, Ernest (1901–1958).   A physicist, Lawrence invented the cyclotron, produced radioactive isotopes, and used radioactivity to investigate medical and biological problems. He taught at the University of California, and he won the 1939 Nobel Prize for physics.

Lederberg, Joshua (1925–).   With George Beadle and Edward Tatum, Lederberg proved that sexual recombination occurs in bacteria, via processes that cause the exchange of genetic material. The three geneticists shared the 1958 Nobel Prize in physiology or medicine for their work.

Levene, Phoebus (1869–1940).   A chemist, Levene did pioneering work on nucleic acids. He determined the formation of nucleotides and the way they combine in chains. He also isolated the sugar ribose (1909) and discovered 2-deoxyribose (1929).

Libby, Willard (1908–1980).   A chemist, Libby devised the radioactive carbon-14 dating technique of objects in the 1940s. He received the 1960 Nobel Prize for chemistry for this work.

Long, Crawford (1815–1878).   Long was the first surgeon to use ether as an anesthetic, beginning in 1842.

Luria, Salvador (1912–1991).   With Max Delbrück, Italian-born microbiologist Luria researched bacteriophages, creating a fluctuation test and finding evidence that spontaneous mutations cause phage-resistant bacteria.

McClintock, Barbara (1902–1992).   McClintock, a geneticist studying the cells of successive generations of growing corn, discovered that genes are not permanently arranged on the chromosome but sometimes "jump," or move around, possibly changing inheritance. For years McClintock's discovery was either ignored or ridiculed by other scientists. But in 1983 she won the Nobel Prize for physiology or medicine for her research into the mechanisms of genetic inheritance.

McClung, Clarence (1870–1946).   McClung published the hypothesis that sex is determined by the chromosomes (1899–1902).

McMillan, Edwin (1907–1991).   Physicist McMillan, with Philip Abelson, discovered neptunium, element 93, and with Glenn Seaborg and others he discovered plutonium. During World War II McMillan helped the navy develop radar and sonar, before joining the Manhattan Project for the development of the atomic bomb at Los Alamos, New Mexico.

Mead, Margaret (1901–1978).   An anthropologist, Mead lived among the peoples of the Pacific Islands to study how cultures differ and how this difference affects personality development. Her most famous book, *Coming of Age in Somoa* (1928), compares the lives of Samoan adolescents with those of their peers in Western societies.

Menninger, Karl (1893–1990).   Menninger was one of the first American doctors to be psychoanalytically trained. In Topeka, Kansas, he founded a psychiatric clinic (1920) and a foundation (1941), where psychiatrists received psychiatric training.

Michelson, Albert (1852–1931).   A German-born physicist, Michelson devised a way of very accurately measuring the speed at which light travels; invented (1881) an inferometer for determining distances via the length of light waves; measured a meter in relation to the wavelength of cadmium light; performed an experiment (1887), with Edward Morley, that by demonstrating that the earth has no absolute motion relative to an ether paved the way for the theory of relativity. Michelson won the 1907 Nobel Prize for physics.

Millikan, Robert (1868–1953).   A physicist, Millikan measured the electron's charge and did important research on the photoelectric effect. He received the 1923 Nobel Prize for physics.

Morgan, Thomas (1866–1945).   Beginning in 1909, Morgan studied heredity in *Drosophila* fruit flies. He established that genes exist for specific traits located at specific sites on chromosomes. For this discovery, he was awarded the 1933 Nobel Prize for physiology or medicine.

Morley, Edward (1838–1923).   A chemist and physicist, Morley is most known for his work with Albert Michelson on the ether-drift experiment (1887), which led to Einstein's theory of relativity.

Muller, Hermann (1890–1967).   A geneticist, Muller won the 1946 Nobel Prize for physiology or medicine for his work on the artificial transmutation of genes, using X rays, produced first in 1926.

Nieuwland, Julius (1878–1936).   A chemist and a Catholic priest, Nieuwland did pioneering work in the synthesizing of rubber.

Oppenheimer, Robert (1904–1967).   Oppenheimer headed the team of scientists working on the Manhattan Project in Los Alamos, New Mexico, to develop the atomic bomb. Oppenheimer also was the director of the Institute for Advanced Study at Princeton University. He strongly opposed the development of the hydrogen bomb.

Pauling, Linus (1901–1994).   A chemist, Pauling was one of the first to apply the quantum theory to calculating molecular structures. He devised the idea of resonance to explain covalent bonds in certain organic compounds. He also determined the three-dimensional structures of numerous amino acids, proteins, and antitoxins. For his work he won the 1954 Nobel Prize for chemistry. He also was awarded the 1962 Nobel Peace Prize for his work in favor of nuclear disarmament.

Rabi, Isidor (1898–1988).   In 1937 Rabi, an Austrian-born physicist, invented a method for registering the magnetic properties of atomic nuclei. This discovery led to the laser, maser, atomic clock, and nuclear-resonance magnetic imaging. Rabi won the 1944 Nobel Prize for physics.

Reed, Walter (1851–1902).   Reed, a surgeon, headed the U.S. Army commission sent to Cuba in 1900 to find the cause and transmission mode of yellow fever. The commission's 1901 report proved that the mosquito *Aëdes aegypti* transmitted the disease. The disease was then virtually eradicated by destroying the insects. Washington, D.C.'s Walter Reed Hospital was named after him.

Rush, Benjamin (1745–1813).   Rush, a physician, founded the first free dispensary in the United States (1786) and wrote the first American chemistry textbook (1770) and the first psychiatric treatise in the United States (1812).

Sabin, Albert (1906–1993).   In the late 1950s Sabin, a physician and medical researcher, developed an attenuated-virus oral polio vaccine.

Sabine, Wallace (1868–1919).   Sabine created the science of architectural acoustics. He also founded and was the dean of Harvard's Graduate School of Applied Science (1906–1915). In his honor, the unit of sound-absorbing power is called the sabin.

Salk, Jonas (1914–1995).   A physician and microbiologist, Salk was known for his development, in 1952, of the Salk vaccine against polio.

Sanger, Margaret (1883–1966).   As a public health nurse, Sanger clearly saw the need for family limitation, especially in the face of poverty, and the frequent death of women from self-induced abortions. She advocated "birth control," a term she coined, and opened the first birth control clinic in the United States. In 1921 she founded the Birth Control League, now Planned Parenthood. By the 1930s her once scandalous notions had gained wide public acceptance.

Schick, Béla (1877–1967).   A Hungarian-born physician, Schick developed the Schick test to detect susceptibility to diphtheria in 1913.

Seaborg, Glenn (1912–).   Seaborg co-discovered the elements americium, berkelium, californium, curium, einsteinium, fermium, mendelevium, nobelium, and plutonium. He shared the 1951 Nobel Prize in chemistry with Edwin McMillan. During World War II he worked on the development of the atomic bomb.

Segre, Emilio (1905–1989).   Segre worked with Enrico Fermi on neutron experiments that helped establish nuclear physics. With Fermi, he detected slow neutrons (1935). He also developed technetium, the first artificially made element. In 1940 he discovered astatine and plutonium with Glenn Seaborg (1941). He shared with Owen Chamberlain the 1959 Nobel Prize for their discovery of the antiproton.

Silliman, Benjamin (1779–1864).   Professor of chemistry and natural history at Yale for half a century, Silliman studied petroleum products and made discoveries regarding carbon, hydrofluoric acid, and bromine, but his greatest contributions were as a teacher and popular lecturer on scientific subjects. He founded the *American Journal of Science and Arts* and the National Academy of Sciences and was the first president of the Association of American Geologists, precursor to the American Association for the Advancement of Science.

Steinmetz, Charles (1865–1923).   An electrical engineer, Steinmetz patented more than 200 improvements in electrical apparatus. He derived the law of hysteresis and worked on the theory and calculation of alternating currents.

Sturtevant, Alfred (1891–1970). Sturtevant was the first scientist to map genes on chromosomes (1913).

Sutton, Walter (1877–1916). A geneticist, Sutton demonstrated that chromosomes carry units of inheritance and exist in distinct pairs (1902–1903). His work formed the basis for the chromosomal theory of heredity.

Tatum, Edward (1909–1975). With George Beadle and Joshua Lederberg, Tatum discovered that genes transmit hereditary characters by controlling specific chemical reactions. Along with his co-researchers, he received the 1958 Nobel Prize for physiology or medicine.

Teller, Edward (1908–1993). Teller, a Hungarian-born physicist, worked on the atomic bomb during World War II. He was one of the key figures in the development of the hydrogen bomb (1952).

Temin, Howard (1934–1994). Temin, an oncologist, proved that a cancerous sarcoma virus translates its RNA into DNA, which then reinstructs the reproductive activity of the cell, changing it to a cancer cell. He also identified reverse transcriptase as the viral enzyme that synthesizes the DNA containing the information in viral RNA. Temin's discovery, also independently made by David Baltimore, helped to identify the AIDS virus and aided genetic engineering. Temin shared the 1975 Nobel Prize for physiology or medicine with Renato Dulbecco and Baltimore.

Urey, Harold (1893–1981). For his discovery of deuterium, or heavy water, in 1931, chemist Urey was awarded the 1934 Noble Prize for chemistry. He also worked on the development of the atomic bomb.

Waksman, Selman (1888–1973). In 1944 Waksman, a Russian-born biochemist, discovered the antibiotic streptomycin, which became widely used in the treatment of tuberculosis. For this discovery he won the 1952 Nobel Prize for physiology or medicine.

Watson, James (1928–). While a graduate student at England's Cambridge University in 1953, Watson, a biologist, codiscovered with Francis Crick the molecular structure of deoxyribonucleic acid (DNA). For this discovery they received the 1962 Nobel Prize in physiology or medicine.

ADDITIONAL SOURCES OF INFORMATION

Bruce, Robert V. *The Launching of Modern American Science, 1846–1876.* Knopf, 1987.

Daniels, George H. *Science in American Society: A Social History.* Knopf, 1971.

Hughes, Thomas P. *American Genesis: A Century of Invention and Technological Enthusiasm, 1870–1970.* Viking, 1989.

Josephson, Matthew. *Edison.* McGraw-Hill, 1959.

Kohlstedt, Sally Gregory, and Margaret W. Rossiter, eds. *Historical Writing on American Science: Perspectives and Prospects.* Johns Hopkins University Press, 1985.

Marcus, Alan I., and Howard P. Segal. *Technology in America: A Brief History.* Harcourt Brace Jovanovich, 1989.

Noble, David F. *America by Design: Science, Technology and the Rise of Corporate Capitalism.* Knopf, 1977.

Pursell, Carroll W., Jr., ed. *Technology in America.* 2d ed. MIT Press, 1990.

Williams, Trevor I. *Science: A History of Discovery in the 20th Century.* Oxford University Press, 1990.

12

Transportation and Communication

America's short history has been shaped in part by revolutions in transportation and communication. These both stimulated commercial enterprise and helped reduce the physical and psychological isolation of local communities, especially those in the West, thereby strengthening national identity and pride.

SIGNIFICANT EVENTS IN TRANSPORTATION AND COMMUNICATION

1539	The first printing press in the New World is set up in Mexico City.
1639	At Harvard College in Cambridge, Massachusetts, the first colonial printing press is used.
1685	Maps of the Middle English colonies and Virginia are printed.
1690	The first newspaper in America, the Boston news sheet *Publick Occurrences Both Forreign and Domestic*, appears just once.
1693	William Bradford sets up a printing press in New York City.
1704	The *Boston News-Letter* becomes the first regularly published American newspaper.
1730	Benjamin Franklin buys *The Pennsylvania Gazette* from Samuel Keimer.
1732	Benjamin Franklin publishes the *Philadelphia Zeitung*, the first foreign-language newspaper in the English colonies.
1734	New York printer John Peter Zenger is arrested for libel; the charges against him are based on his legal responsibility for articles written mostly by others but appearing in his newspaper, the *New York Weekly Journal*.

THE TRIAL OF JOHN PETER ZENGER

John Peter Zenger was a successful printer in New York City. In 1733 he began printing the *New York Weekly Journal*, which attacked the politics of another paper, the government-controlled *New York Gazette*. Although Zenger himself did not write the articles attacking the administration of Governor William Cosby, he was legally responsible for them and was arrested on libel charges in 1734. In the famous trial that took place in 1735, Zenger was defended by Alexander Hamilton, who sought to establish truth as a defense in libel cases. Hamilton's arguments proved persuasive, and Zenger was acquitted. The Zenger case laid the foundation for freedom of the press in America.

1735	John Peter Zenger is acquitted of libel; the verdict helps establish freedom of the press in America.
1741	The first two magazines published in the colonies are the *American Magazine* and *Benjamin Franklin's General Magazine*, both published in Philadelphia. These two forerunners of later periodicals are regional and expensive.
1756	A major stagecoach line operates between Philadelphia and New York City.
1764	In Hartford the *Connecticut Courant*, a weekly, begins publication.
1773	Regular mounted mail service is established between Boston and New York.

1784   Abel Buell engraves and prints the first map of the United States; it shows the boundaries established by the Treaty of Paris (1783), which formally recognizes the new nation.

1785   Regular stagecoach routes between New York, Boston, and Philadelphia are established.

1787   Having obtained from New Jersey, Pennsylvania, New York, Delaware, and Virginia exclusive rights to build and operate steamboats on their waterways, inventor John Fitch launches the first American steamboat on the Delaware River.

James Rumsey's jet-propelled steamboat, demonstrated on the Potomac in Maryland, shoots a stream of water through its stern.

1789   The first American road map is published by Christopher Colles.

1792   The Essex Merrimac Bridge, a covered timber truss construction, is built in Massachusetts by Timothy Palmer.

Work is begun on South Carolina's Santee Canal, to be completed in 1800.

1794   Construction begins on Massachusetts's Middlesex Canal, which is completed in 1803.

1795   Robert Fulton patents the first power shovel, to be used in digging canals.

A 62-mile stretch of road is opened for traffic between Philadelphia and Lancaster, Pennsylvania. This first significant turnpike is also the first macadam road.

1796   James Finley builds the first American suspension bridge, across Jacob's Creek in Westmoreland, Pennsylvania.

Congress approves the construction of a road from present-day Wheeling, West Virginia, to present-day Maysville, Kentucky. Called Zane's Trace, it will become one of the routes most traveled by settlers going west.

1800   The *Nautilus*, a hand-operated submarine, is invented by Robert Fulton, but he fails to interest any government in it.

Semaphore, or visual signaling, communications are established on "telegraph hills" between Martha's Vineyard, Massachusetts, and Boston.

1801   *The New York Evening Post*, founded by Alexander Hamilton, begins publication.

1802   A screw-driven steamboat is invented by John Stevens. This is the first powered screw applied to ship propulsion.

1804   John Stevens crosses New York's Hudson River in a twin-screw steamboat.

1807   Robert Fulton's 150-foot-long steamboat, the *Clermont*, steams from Albany to New York City and back on the Hudson River. Although not the first steamboat, the *Clermont* is the first one built economically enough to make this mode of transportation commercially viable.

1808   John Stevens invents the *Phoenix*, a steamboat powered by a low-pressure engine.

1809   The *Phoenix* becomes the world's first seagoing steamboat as it travels from New York to Philadelphia.

1811   The SS *New Orleans*, the first steamboat traveling down the Mississippi River, leaves Pittsburgh and reaches New Orleans. Subsequently it begins a regular run between New Orleans and Natchez, Mississippi.

One popular form of overland travel for settlers is the Conestoga wagon; about 60 feet long, it is drawn by four to six horses and decorated with bells.

The Weekly Register, an early attempt at a news magazine, begins publication. It will publish for four decades.

1814   The USS *Fulton*, the first steam warship, is launched by Robert Fulton.

Robert Fulton

1815   The *North American Review* begins publication.

The Cumberland Road, which is to become a widely used route for westward-bound settlers, is begun at Cumberland, Maryland.

1817   Construction on the Erie Canal begins. This project has been promoted chiefly by New York governor De Witt Clinton to connect New York City with the Great Lakes via the Hudson River and a 364-mile canal from Albany to Buffalo. Building the 40-foot-wide, 4-foot-deep canal with 83 locks and more than 300 bridges will be a great technological challenge.

1818   The Black Ball Line establishes the first regularly scheduled clippership service from New York to Liverpool, England. These sailing ships carry packets of mail along with cargo and passengers. The average transatlantic voyage takes 30 days.

1820   Daniel Treadwell invents the horse-powered printing press.

1821   *The Saturday Evening Post,* which features middlebrow fiction and American nostalgia, is the first periodical designed for the masses.

1822   The first steamboat voyage from New York to New Orleans is completed by the SS *Robert Fulton.*

1825   The Erie Canal is completed in only eight years; the first boat to use the canal, the *Seneca Chief,* is launched at Buffalo and speeds at 4 miles per hour toward New York City. The canal will be a phenomenal success, providing an easy passage for westbound settlers and for commercial goods moving from the East to the Ohio and Mississippi valleys. Soon nearly every state will build canals, with most promoting east-west links.

John Stevens builds the first American steam locomotive, the *Action*.

1826   Connecticut inventor Samuel Morey patents an internal combustion engine.

The first railroads are constructed; powered by horses, sails, or cables, they are used to transport such items as coal or granite for short distances.

1827   Isaac Adams invents the Adams press, which will become the standard in the printing industry for the next half century.

1829   The *Encyclopaedia Americana*, the first American encyclopedia, is published in Philadelphia.

The *Philadelphia Inquirer* starts out as *The Pennsylvania Inquirer*.

Joseph Henry builds the first electric motor.

William Burt invents an early prototype of a typewriter.

Railroad Construction, 1830–1920

Miles of Track	Approximate Miles
1830–1840	~2,000
1841–1850	~4,000
1851–1860	~20,000
1861–1870	~15,000
1871–1880	~40,000
1881–1890	~70,000
1891–1900	~30,000
1901–1910	~47,000
1911–1920	~8,000

1830   The first passenger line, the Baltimore & Ohio Railroad, opens with 13 miles of track.

Best Friend of Charleston, the first American-built commercial locomotive, is designed by Horatio Allen and run on a track in Honesdale, Pennsylvania.

Peter Cooper builds *Tom Thumb*, the first commercially viable steam locomotive, but it races against a horse and loses due to an engine breakdown.

The *Boston Transcript* begins publication; it will survive until 1940.

Godey's Lady's Book, the first periodical for women, begins publication. It features light fiction, poetry, and essays and keeps women updated on current fashions.

1831   After buying a horse-powered English locomotive called the *John Bull*, Robert Stevens establishes America's first steam railway service in New Jersey. He also invents the inverted-T rail, a flanged railroad track.

1832   The *Ann McKim*, the first American sailing clipper ship, is launched in Baltimore, Maryland.

In New York City, the New York & Harlem Railroad begins operating the first streetcar in the world. Built by John Mason, the horse-drawn car runs along part of Fourth Avenue.

1833   The *New York Sun*, the city's first successful penny daily paper, is launched.

1834   Zachariah Allen invents an automatic steam-engine cutoff valve.

Thomas Davenport invents a primitive electric motor, which he uses the following year to power the first electric locomotive.

1835   In Brownsville, Pennsylvania, America's first cast iron bridge is constructed over Dunlap Creek.

The *New York Herald*, a one-cent daily, is first printed. The newspaper, started by editor James Bennett, will pioneer in publishing financial reports, crime stories, and society news and in using the telegraph and European correspondents.

1836   The *Philadelphia Public Ledger*, a penny daily, is founded.

1837   Samuel Morse patents the Morse code for use with the telegraph and demonstrates his invention.

The *Baltimore Sun*, a penny daily, begins publication.

The *New Orleans Picayune* is established.

1839   Charles Goodyear makes rubber resistant to heat and cold through the process of vulcanization.

1840   In Ohio, the *Toledo Blade* starts publication.

1841   Horace Greeley establishes the *New York Tribune*, a daily that becomes very influential in molding the thought of Northerners before the Civil War.

1842   The *Pittsburgh Post-Gazette* begins publication.

1843   Samuel Morse receives federal money to build a telegraph line between Baltimore and Washington, D.C.

1844   After construction of the first telegraph line is completed, Morse sends the first telegraph message, "What hath God wrought!" from Washington, D.C., to Baltimore.

1845   A weekly scandal sheet, the *Police Gazette*, is founded.

1846   The *Pittsburgh Dispatch* begins publication.

The *Boston Herald* is founded.

1847   Industrialist Richard Hoe invents the rotary press and web press; these inventions make possible the development of mass-circulation daily newspapers.

The *Chicago Tribune* begins publication, as does the *Philadelphia Evening Bulletin*.

1848   The New York News Agency is founded; it will change its name to the Associated Press in 1856.

1849   In Minnesota Territory, the *St. Paul Pioneer* is first published.

The Pacific Railroad Company, the first charted railway west of the Mississippi, begins laying track; the first section opens in 1852.

George Corliss patents a four-valve steamship engine, a vast improvement over the one-valve model.

1850　The first overland mail delivery west of the Missouri River begins from Independence, Missouri, to Salt Lake City, Utah.

　　　In New York, *Harper's Monthly,* a respected journal of opinion, fiction, and essays, begins publication.

　　　The *Portland Oregonian* is founded.

　　　Congress makes the first federal land grants to promote railroad development.

1851　*The New York Times* publishes its first issue.

1852　A passenger elevator is designed by Elisha Otis. The following year, Otis invents an elevator safety device to stop a car from plunging if the cable breaks.

　　　Work on the Baltimore & Ohio Railroad is completed to the Ohio River, and it begins operating from Baltimore to Wheeling, West Virginia. Because of the railroad, Chicago is now connected by rail to the East.

1853　The New York Central Railroad, formed by joining ten small railroads, links New York City and Buffalo, New York.

1855　At Niagara Falls, New York, a railroad suspension bridge is constructed; a year later it is crossed by a train for the first time.

　　　Frank Leslie's Illustrated Newspaper, the most successful early illustrated periodical, is founded in New York City.

1856　The Western Union Company is founded.

　　　A printing telegraph is patented by David Hughes.

1857　*Atlantic Monthly* magazine begins publication.

1858　Financier Cyrus Field builds the first submarine telegraph cable between America and Europe.

　　　Stagecoach service with mail delivery begins between San Francisco and Saint Louis, Missouri.

1859　The first passenger elevator in an American hotel is installed in New York City's Fifth Avenue Hotel.

　　　The *Rocky Mountain News* is the first paper to be published in the soon-to-be Montana Territory.

1860s　Sylvester Roper develops a steam-powered vehicle.

1860　The Pony Express begins speedy overland mail service from Saint Joseph, Missouri, to Sacramento, California.

THE PONY EXPRESS

In 1859 railroads delivered mail to the eastern part of America and as far west as Missouri. In Missouri, wagon trains and stagecoaches took over the task of carrying mail to the West. But the stagecoach journey to California was long—about 22 days. In 1860 this situation dramatically improved, with the establishment of the Pony Express, which cut the time of mail delivery to the West by more than half. A Pony Express rider, mail pouches strapped to his horse, galloped between 35 and 75 miles before passing the mail to a fresh rider, waiting at one of the 190 stations along the way. Although the Pony Express became legendary for its exploits, the company was short-lived. The completion in the early 1860s of the first transcontinental telegraph, capable of virtually instantaneous message transmission, cut short the colorful life of the Pony Express.

1861   There are 31,000 miles of railroad track in the United States.

Elisha Otis patents the steam elevator, which will become the basis of the Otis elevator business.

Telegraph wires link New York to San Francisco, making immediate bicoastal communication possible.

1862   John Ericsson launches the *Monitor*, an ironclad steam warship—a wooden ship covered by metal plates. Its revolving turret will become a feature of battleships.

Congress passes the Pacific Railroad Act, granting the Union Pacific and Central Pacific railways vast lands from Omaha, Nebraska, to Sacramento, California, on which to build the first transcontinental railroad.

1864   Steel rails are used on the Pennsylvania Railroad.

George Pullman builds the first comfortable railroad sleeping car. The Pullman car has a folding upper berth and extendible seat cushions to create a lower berth.

1865   William Bullock improves the rotary press, which can now cut sheets as they are printed. Both Hoe's web press and Bullock's rotary press make possible the development of mass-circulation daily newspapers.

The *San Francisco Chronicle* begins as the *San Francisco Dramatic Chronicle*. The *Nation*, a liberal weekly magazine, is founded by Edwin Godkin.

1866   The first refrigerated railroad car in America is constructed in Detroit.

Henry House invents a 12-horsepower steam car.

The first truly functional transatlantic cable is completed.

1867   Alfred Beach invents a pneumatic passenger subway system. The idea is picked up and was still used, with modifications, 90 years later.

In New York City, the first elevated railroad is established, running from downtown Manhattan to Thirtieth Street.

1868   George Westinghouse invents railroad air brakes.

Christopher Sholes invents the typewriter.

The *Atlanta Constitution* begins publication.

1869   The transcontinental railroad is completed. The last, and golden, spike is planted by California governor Leland Stanford at Promontory Point, Utah. A telegraph operator signals the completion to a waiting nation.

Cyrus Field builds a successful telegraph cable between France and Massachusetts.

THE GOLDEN AGE OF U.S. RAILROADS

During the 50 years following the Civil War, American railroads were the dominant mode of transportation. The railway network expanded from 35,000 miles (56,000 km) in 1865 to 254,000 miles (406,400 km) in 1916. Some factors that contributed to this expansion were:

- The completion of five transcontinental railroads from 1869 to 1894.
- Federal land grants to railroads. Between 1862 and 1872, for example, Congress granted more than 100 million acres of public lands to railroad companies and also provided them with more than $64 million in loans and tax incentives.
- The period's technological innovations, which made railway service more economical, included more powerful engines, refrigerated cars, and air brakes.

- The adoption of a standard track gauge (size of track), which allowed trunk lines (main long-distance lines) to link the many smaller systems in the Northeast and the South.
- The introduction in 1883 of four standard time zones, which permitted an orderly national scheduling system.

1870   The first asphalt-paved road is created in Newark, New Jersey, by scientist Edward DeSmedt.

1871   An improved rotary press prints both sides of a page simultaneously.

1872   Motion-picture pioneer Eadweard Muybridge invents the zoopraxiscope, which by reproducing moving pictures on a screen is a forerunner of the movie projector.

        In Chicago the first mail-order house, Montgomery Ward & Company, is established.

        The *Boston Daily Globe* begins publication.

1873   The first penny postcards are issued.

        Free mail delivery is provided in cities with a population of 20,000 or more.

        St. Nicholas Magazine, a children's magazine, begins publication.

        Andrew Hallidie invents cable cars to traverse San Francisco's hills.

1874   In San Francisco Thomas Edison develops a telegraph system enabling four messages to be sent simultaneously over one wire.

1876   Scottish American Alexander Graham Bell patents the telephone. The first words transmitted over the telephone wire are to his assistant: "Mr. Watson, come here. I want you." Bell's invention signals America's rise to international leadership in industrial technology.

1877   Emile Berliner invents a microphone for the telephone.

        The first Bell telephone is bought.

        Charles Glidden organizes the world's first telephone exchange in Lowell, Massachusetts.

        The first intercity telephone communication is between Chicago and Milwaukee and between Salem, Massachusetts, and Boston. Boston has the first telephone switchboard.

        In Newark, New Jersey, electrical engineer Edward Weston sets up an electric streetlight.

        The *Washington Post* is founded.

        The Great Railway Strike interrupts transportation across the country.

1878   Augustus Pope manufactures the first bicycles in America.

        Thomas Edison demonstrates the phonograph. On a tinfoil-wrapped cylinder, he records "Mary had a little lamb."

1879   George Selden applies for a patent on a gasoline motor-driven vehicle.

1880   George Eastman markets a process for making photographic dry plates, which do not have to be exposed and developed immediately.

        The *Kansas City Evening Star* begins publication.

1881   Frederic Ives produces the first color photograph.

1883   Canada and the United States agree on four standard time zones.

        The Brooklyn Bridge, at the time the world's largest suspension bridge, is completed, stretching from Brooklyn to lower Manhattan. The designer of the bridge, John Roebling, dies during its construction.

        The *Ladies' Home Journal* begins publication.

        Joseph Pulitzer, the publisher of the *St. Louis Post-Dispatch*, buys the *New York World*.

        Thomas Edison devises a trolley that runs on an electrified third rail; it is still used by the New York subway system.

Thomas Edison

1884   Lewis Waterman manufactures the first fountain pen.

        Ottmar Mergenthaler patents the Linotype typesetting machine, which casts one line of characters at a time, greatly increasing the speed of newspaper and magazine composition.

        New York and Boston are linked by telephone wires.

1885   The Dictaphone, a device for recording dictation, is invented by Charles Tainter.

        The electric transformer is invented by William Stanley.

        Good Housekeeping magazine is founded.

1887   An electrically lit train on the Pennsylvania Railroad begins service between New York and Chicago.

        Congress passes the Interstate Commerce Act, which regulates commerce extending beyond state borders.

        Celluloid photographic film is developed by clergyman Hannibal Goodwin.

        In Richmond, Virginia, the first electric trolley line is constructed.

1888　The Pullman Car Company constructs an electric freight-hauling locomotive.

The *National Geographic* magazine offers armchair travelers a glimpse of the world.

Herman Hollerith devises the first successful computer, a punched-card tabulating machine; Hollerith's machines will tabulate the results of the 1890 census.

George Eastman invents the Kodak box camera, the first camera using roll film, ushering in the age of amateur photography.

1889　In New York City, Otis Brothers installs an electric elevator.

New York World reporter Nellie Bly begins an around-the-world ship voyage in an attempt to beat the record of Phineas Fogg, the hero of Jules Verne's novel, *Around the World in 80 Days*. She returns home in 72 days, 6 hours, and 11 minutes, setting a record time.

Thomas Edison invents the kinetograph, the first sound camera.

Railroad Network, 1890

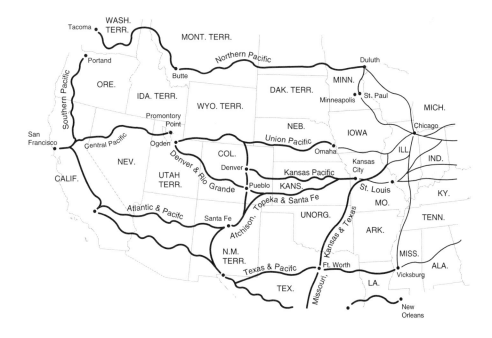

1891　Thomas Edison patents his kinetoscopic camera, which takes moving pictures on a strip of film. A single viewer looking into a lighted box, which is turned by a crank, can see the film.

In Des Moines, Iowa, William Morrison builds an electrically powered car for six passengers.

1892　George Eastman invents daylight-loading film.

1893　The Edison Laboratories builds a film studio in West Orange, New Jersey.

Franklin and Charles Duryea build the first successful gasoline car.

McClure's magazine begins publication.

1894   The first movie projector publicly shows two kinetoscopic films.

1895   George Selden's patent for a "road engine," the first in America for a gasoline-powered car, is granted.

The Baltimore & Ohio Railroad uses electric locomotives.

Connecticut's Hart Rubber Works produces the first American pneumatic, or air-filled, tires.

The first American car race is run between Chicago and Waukegan, Illinois.

1896   Rural free mail delivery begins.

In New York City, the first moving picture is shown to the public at Koster and Bial's Music Hall.

Samuel Langley flies a steam-powered model plane.

Henry Ford constructs his first successful gasoline-powered car.

1897   The *Argonaut II*, a gasoline submarine with wheels for moving on the ocean floor, is launched by Simon Lake and becomes the first submarine to travel in the open seas.

In Boston the Boylston Street subway line begins operating; it is the first American subway.

In New York City the *Jewish Daily Forward* begins publication; it will soon become the most influential Jewish newspaper in America.

1898   The *Holland*, the first practical submarine, which is powered by electricity underwater and gasoline on the surface, is launched by John Holland.

1900   The Olds Motor Works, founded the previous year by Ransome Olds, begins the first mass production of cars in Detroit.

Physicist Reginald Fessenden uses radio waves to transmit spoken words for the first time.

Work is begun on the New York subway.

More than 1 million miles of telephone line are now strung across the United States.

In Boston, trolleys replace horsecars.

1901   In Philadelphia, Otis Brothers installs what comes to be called an escalator in Gimbel's Department Store.

1902   The American Automobile Association (AAA) is founded to help members organize automobile tours and provide them with emergency road service.

1903   In Kitty Hawk, North Carolina, Orville and Wilbur Wright make the world's first successful sustained manned flights in a gasoline-powered aircraft. In the longest of their four flights this day, Wilbur stays in the air 59 seconds, as his plane, *Flyer I*, covers 852 feet.

The Pulitzer Prizes are established by *New York World* publisher Joseph Pulitzer.

Linking Honolulu with San Francisco, the first Pacific cable is completed, with President Theodore Roosevelt's opening message relayed around the world in 12 minutes.

The United States and Panama sign the Hay-Bunau-Varilla Treaty, giving the United States a renewable 99-year lease on a ten-mile strip of land across the Isthmus of Panama in exchange for $10 million and an annual payment of $230,000. The United States wants to use this land to build a canal to make ocean travel from the Atlantic to the Pacific easier.

Henry Ford founds the Ford Motor Company.

Massachusetts issues the first automobile license plates; soon all states will follow.

The Harley-Davidson motorcyle is devised by William Harley.

1905   The Long Island Railroad installs a third rail, becoming the first American railroad to have no steam locomotives running on its tracks.

The *Chicago Defender*, the first significant black newspaper, begins publication.

Joseph Pulitzer

The first movie theater is built in Pittsburgh; it charges a nickel for admission and is called a nickelodeon.

AT&T introduces rotary dialing.

1906   Directed by the U.S. Army Corps of Engineers, construction of the Panama Canal begins. The cost of the 40-mile canal will be over $300 million.

From a station in Brant Rock, Massachusetts, Reginald Fessenden broadcasts the first radio program combining voice and music.

Lee De Forest, "Father of the Radio," invents a three-electrode vacuum-tube amplifier that forms the basis for the development of the radio.

1907   The first taxis, imported from Paris, arrive in New York City.

The United Press (UP) is founded to compete with the Associated Press (AP), established in 1848.

1908   Henry Ford introduces the Model T, soon to be the most popular contemporary motor car.

The Cadillac Automobile Company is the first to use interchangable parts in assembling cars.

The General Motors Company is founded by William Durant.

The University of Michigan establishes the first professional school of journalism.

Mutt and Jeff becomes the first comic strip to appear each day with the same characters.

Glenn Curtiss makes the first official American public flight of over one kilometer.

1909   In New York City the *Amsterdam News* begins publication; it will become America's largest secular black weekly newspaper.

1909   Thomas Edison creates the Motion Pictures Patents Company to prevent unlicensed film-making companies from producing motion pictures.

1911   Cartoonist John Bray develops animated motion picture cartoons. All future animators will employ his "cel" system, in which each frame is composed of layers of celluloid transparencies, with only those layers showing figures in motion changing from frame to frame.

The introduction of *Photoplay*, the first fan magazine, allows Americans to keep close tabs on such adored Hollywood stars as Charlie Chaplin, Rudolph Valentino, Theda Bara, and Clara Bow.

Charles Kettering's electric self-starter for cars enables engines to be started without being manually cranked.

The Keystone Company is formed by motion-picture pioneer Mack Sennett.

1912   Albert Howell invents a continuous printer that automatically copies motion pictures, making possible their mass distribution.

The seaplane is invented by Grover Loening.

1913   The assembly line is introduced at the Ford Motor Company; by 1925 Ford is turning out more than 9,000 cars a day.

U.S. Parcel Post begins operating. Approximately 300 million packages have been mailed by year's end.

The Dodge Brothers, John and Horace, begin making their own cars, which are among the first U.S. automobiles with all-steel bodies.

1914   The Panama Canal, linking the Atlantic and Pacific oceans, is completed.

In Cleveland the world's first red-green traffic lights are installed.

Gulf Oil produces and then distributes the first American automobile maps; soon free maps given away at gas stations will encourage car travel.

Charles Lawrence develops an air-cooled airplane engine that will make long-distance flight possible.

1915   The Federal Trade Commission is established to regulate interstate commerce.

Long-distance telephone service starts between San Francisco and New York.

The first transatlantic telephone communication is transmitted; it is between Virginia and Paris.

The Ford Motor Company produces its 1 millionth car.

The Chevrolet Motor Company is founded by William Durant.

1916   Lee De Forest broadcasts the first radio news.

Work on a nationwide U.S. highway system is begun.

The first mechanical windshield wipers are introduced in America.

Teletype is invented by Markrun Company of Chicago; it will become operational in 1928.

1917   Edwin Armstrong invents the superheterodyne circuit, which will be the design for amplitude modulation (AM) radios.

A new barge canal replaces New York's Erie Canal, which has become obsolete because of steam power.

President Woodrow Wilson orders the federal government to run the railroads to ensure their smooth operation during World War I.

1918   The first U.S. airmail stamps are introduced as the Post Office opens airmail service; the first route is New York-Philadelphia-Washington.

Louis B. Mayer Pictures is founded.

1919   The NC-4 aircraft completes the first transatlantic flight by a heavier-than-air machine from Newfoundland to Lisbon.

The Radio Corporation of America (RCA) is founded.

The first successful tabloid, The New York *Daily News*, starts publication.

With director D. W. Griffith, actors Mary Pickford, Charlie Chaplin, and Douglas Fairbanks found United Artists.

1920   The first regular radio broadcasts begin.

The first transcontinental airmail route is established between New York City and San Francisco.

International Telephone and Telegraph (ITT) is founded.

The Transportation Act gives control of the railroads back to their owners.

1921   The first transcontinental U.S. day-night flight is completed from North Platte, Nebraska, to New York City.

The first transcontinental airmail flight from New York City to San Francisco takes 27 hours.

Congress passes a Federal Highway Act, coordinating state highways and standardizing U.S. road building.

1922   James Doolittle completes the first single-day bicoastal flight between Pablo Beach, Florida, to San Diego.

The *Reader's Digest* begins publishing monthly; pocket-sized, it features articles condensed from magazines and books.

William Stout develops the first completely metal aircraft.

The first radio commercials are aired by New York's WEAF.

1923   The Hertz Drive-Ur-Self System, which will become the world's largest rental-car company, is founded.

Warner Bros. Pictures is incorporated.

Time magazine begins publication.

Juan Trippe and John Hambleton buy some flying boats; through mergers their venture will eventually become Pan American Airways.

Vladimir Zworykin patents the iconoscope, an early type of television.

1924   Two U.S. Army planes complete the first round-the-world-flight.

RCA transmits photographs by radio from New York City to London; transmission time per photo is about 25 minutes.

The first American diesel electric locomotive begins running on New Jersey's Central Railroad.

The *New York Herald Tribune* starts publication; it will compete with *The New York Times* until the *Tribune* ends publication in 1966.

The Computing-Tabulating-Recording Company, created in 1911, renames itself International Business Machines (IBM).

Metro-Goldwyn-Mayer (MGM) is formed through merger by Marcus Loew, Samuel Goldwyn, and Louis B. Mayer.

1925   *The New Yorker* magazine begins publishing; the editor, Harold Ross, will feature the work of such talented young cartoonists as Peter Arno and James Thurber and urbane writers such as Dorothy Parker and Robert Benchley.

The first Lockheed Vega, a single-engine transport plane, is introduced and goes on to become one of the most widely used transport planes through the early 1930s.

1926   Francis Davis patents power steering; it will be installed by commercial automakers in 1951.

Richard Byrd and Floyd Bennett make the first flight over the North Pole.

David Sarnoff establishes the National Broadcasting Company (NBC).

The *National Enquirer* begins publishing; after Genesco Pope assumes control in 1952, it will emphasize sensationalism, a focus that will enable it to increase weekly circulation to more than 400 million by 1975.

Robert Goddard launches the first liquid-fueled rocket.

1927   Charles Lindbergh completes the first nonstop solo transatlantic flight from New York to France in the *Spirit of St. Louis*; the flight, which makes "The Lone Eagle," or "Lucky Lindy," a world hero, covers 3,600 miles in $33^1/_2$ hours.

Built under the Hudson River, the Holland Tunnel opens, connecting New York City with New Jersey.

The Jazz Singer, the first successful feature-length motion picture with sound, is released. Its success marks the beginning of the end for silent films.

William S. Paley buys United Independent Broadcasters, changing its name one year later to the Columbia Broadcasting System (CBS).

1928   The first bicoastal bus service, the Pioneer Yelloway Bus Line, begins operating from Los Angeles to New York City.

Charles Smith and his crew make the first flight across the Pacific Ocean.

The last Model T is produced by the Ford Motor Company.

Vladimir Zworykin receives a patent for color television.

In Schenectady, New York, the General Electric station broadcasts the world's first regularly scheduled television programs.

William S. Paley establishes the Columbia Broadcasting System (CBS).

Walt Disney's *Steamboat Willie*, which introduces Mickey Mouse, is the first animated cartoon with a soundtrack.

Vannevar Bush builds the differential analyzer, the first computer to use electronic parts, that is, vacuum tubes for storing values as voltages.

1929   Ford produces the first station wagon.

Glenn Curtis designs the first mobile home.

Delta Air Lines begins operations.

The first commercially successful car radio is invented by Paul Galvin.

The FM radio is introduced.

The first instrumented rocket is launched by Robert Goddard.

Richard Byrd and his crew make the first flight over the South Pole.

1930   The first successful transcontinental glider flight, from San Diego, California, to New York City, is made by Captain Frank M. Hawks.

Both Transcontinental and Western Air (TWA) and United Airlines are formed by mergers.

Henry Luce's *Fortune* magazine begins publication.

The Hays Office, a self-monitoring and enforcement organization established by the film industry in 1922, develops a strict censorship code prohibiting motion-picture depictions of cohabitation and seduction, among other things.

1931   The world's largest suspension bridge, the George Washington Bridge, is completed, connecting New York City to New Jersey.

Clyde Pangborn and Hugh Herndon make the first nonstop flight across the Pacific Ocean.

1932   U.S. Route 66 opens; this 2,200 mile highway links Chicago and Los Angeles.

New York City's Radio City Music Hall opens.

The first "walkie-talkie" portable two-way radio sets are invented by the U.S. Army Corps of Engineers, assisted by Motorola's Paul Galvin.

A television receiver with a cathode-ray picture tube is demonstrated by RCA.

Amelia Earhart is the first woman to make a solo flight across the Atlantic Ocean.

Paramount Pictures is formed through a merger.

1933   Edwin Armstrong perfects frequency modulation (FM) radio.

Wiley Post makes the first solo round-the-world flight.

The first modern airliner, the Boeing 247, begins operating.

Esquire magazine begins publishing; it will become an important arbiter of men's tastes.

The World's Fair, celebrating a century of progress, opens in Chicago.

1934   American Airlines is created by reorganizing the American Airways Company, established four years earlier.

Chrysler Motors produces the world's first curved single-piece windshield.

The new Burlington *Zephyr*, the first diesel-powered streamlined passenger train, operates between Chicago and Denver, marking the end of steam engines on American tracks.

Introduced by Chrysler, the Airflow is the first streamlined car.

Congress creates the Federal Communications Commission (FCC) to oversee the radio, telephone, and telegraph industries; radio stations must now receive their operating license from the FCC.

1935   Boeing's B-17 bomber is the first low-wing, four-engine, all-metal aircraft.

Becky Sharp is the first full-length film shot in three-color and Technicolor.

Congress passes the Motor Carrier Act, putting the Interstate Commerce Commission in control of interstate bus and truck lines.

Statistician George Gallup founds the American Institute of Public Opinion (the Gallup poll).

Kodachrome, a film sensitive to three primary colors, is invented by Leopold Mannes and Leopold Godowsky.

1936   Henry Luce founds *Life* magazine, a weekly photographic news and feature publication.

Pan American Airways begins transpacific flights from San Francisco to Manila.

Douglas DC-3 transport planes are introduced; they become the most popular airplanes in history.

1937   Filled with dangerous hydrogen gas, the dirigible *Hindenburg* explodes at Lakehurst, New Jersey, killing 36, including 13 passengers.

Amelia Earhart vanishes during a Pacific Ocean flight from New Guinea to Howland Island.

Frank Whittle constructs the first working jet engine.

The Golden Gate Bridge, spanning San Francisco Bay and linking San Francisco with Marin County, is completed; until 1964 it is the world's longest suspension bridge.

1937   *Newsweek* and *Woman's Day* magazines start publication.

Walt Disney's *Snow White and the Seven Dwarfs* is the first feature-length animated film.

1938   The Civil Aeronautics Board is established to regulate air transportation.

Chester Carlson invents xerography; the process will revolutionize duplication of papers, which has until now been achieved by carbon copying.

1939   Igor Sikorsky develops the first practical helicopter.

John Atanasoff begins developing the first electronic computer.

Pan American begins regularly scheduled transatlantic passenger flights.

New York City's La Guardia Airport opens.

New York publisher Simon & Schuster introduces the pocket book, or paperback, to U.S. readers.

1940   The first commercial plane using pressurized cabins is the Boeing 307-B.

The Pennsylvania Turnpike becomes the first tunneled American superhighway.

The first Los Angeles freeway, the Arroyo Seco Parkway, opens to traffic.

Peter Goldmark invents the first successful color television system.

General Motors introduces the first automatic transmission in American cars.

1941   The FCC approves TV broadcasting.

The Atchinson, Topeka, and Santa Fe Railroad begins operating the first American diesel freight locomotives.

1942   Built by the Bell Aircraft Company, the first American jet airplane is flown by Robert Stanley.

1943   The American Broadcasting Company (ABC) is established by millionaire Edward Noble.

1944   Aided by a grant from IBM, Howard Aiken develops the second electronic digital computer, the Mark I Automatic Sequence Controlled Calculator, but it often breaks down.

Walter Annenberg founds *Seventeen* magazine for female teens.

1945   *Ebony* magazine, a monthly picture magazine for blacks, is started by John Johnson.

1946   Douglas Aircraft's DC-6 is introduced; it can fly 300 miles per hour and carry 48 to 52 passengers.

A pilotless rocket missile is built by the Farey Aviation Company.

ENIAC, the first electronic computer, is developed by John Eckert and John Mauchly.

1947   B. F. Goodrich produces the first tubeless car tires.

U.S. Air Force captain Chuck Yeager makes the first supersonic flight in a U.S. Bell X-1 rocket plane.

William Shockley, Walter Brattain, and John Bardeen develop the transistor, which will become the essential semiconductor device used on microprocessors and other chips.

The advent of television and the mass exodus to the suburbs (where there are, at least initially, few movie theaters) leads to the decline of movies as America's favorite entertainment.

1948   In New York City, Idlewild International Airport (later Kennedy International Airport) opens; at the time it is the world's largest commercial airport.

U.S. News & World Report magazine starts weekly publication.

Peter Goldmark invents the 33 1/3-rpm phonograph record, the first long-playing record.

Edwin Land invents the Polaroid Land Camera; it develops photographs inside the camera in approximately 60 seconds.

The first chess-playing computer is built at the Massachusetts Institute of Technology (MIT).

One million homes have television sets.

1949   U.S. Air Force pilots complete the first nonstop flight around the world.

The Department of Justice, charging that AT&T has monopolized the telephone industry in violation of the Sherman Anti-Trust Act of 1890, requests that AT&T break up its Western Electric division into separate companies, thereby permitting competition in telephone production and installation.

John Mauchly and John Eckert build BINAC, the first American electronic-stored program computer.

1950   New York City's Port Authority opens and will become the world's busiest bus terminal.

The first Xerox copier is produced by Rochester, New York's Haloid Company.

The FCC licenses CBS to make color TV broadcasts, which it begins doing a year later.

1951   The first transcontinental television broadcast is made; it's of an address by President Harry Truman in San Francisco.

John Mauchly and John Eckert build UNIVAC I, the first commercial electronic computer; it stores data on magnetic tape. (The U.S. Census Bureau installs the first UNIVAC I.)

Wang Laboratories is established by An Wang, who hopes to produce small business calculators.

Three-dimensional motion pictures are shown for the first time.

1952   On her maiden voyage, the passenger ship SS *United States* sets a new record, making the transatlantic crossing in 3 days, 10 hours, and 40 minutes.

The first videotape, invented by John Mullin and Wayne Johnson, is demonstrated.

CBS relies on a UNIVAC computer to predict the results of the presidential election; the computer correctly predicts a landslide victory by Republican candidate Dwight Eisenhower.

Mad comic strip, which will evolve into *Mad* magazine, presents a satirical take on life that appeals primarily to adolescents.

1953   The first IBM computer, the IBM 701, is introduced, and the first high-speed printer is linked to a computer.

TV Guide, with weekly program listings, begins publication.

Hugh Hefner begins publishing *Playboy* magazine, which features photographs of nude women as well as serious fiction.

The first operational supersonic fighter, the North American F-100 Super Sabre, is introduced.

1954   The first practical silicon transistors are introduced by Texas Instruments.

RCA produces the first American color television sets. It also produces the first video recorder.

The *Nautilus*, the first nuclear-powered submarine, is launched at Groton, Connecticut.

The 559-mile-long New York State Thruway opens.

Sports Illustrated magazine begins to publish.

1955   At Tarrytown, New York, the Tappan Zee Bridge, a cantilever span across the Hudson River, opens.

New York's Long Island Expressway opens to traffic.

IBM introduces its first business computer, the IBM 752.

In New York City, *The Village Voice*, a liberal weekly paper, begins publication.

1955 William F. Buckley, Jr., founds the *National Review*, a biweekly journal of conservative political thought.

1956 The first nonstop transcontinental helicopter flight is made from San Diego to Washington, D.C.

The Federal Aid Highway Act allocates 90 percent of the estimated $33.5 billion needed to construct a 42,500-mile network of roads connecting the nation's major urban centers.

An IBM team led by John Backus invents FORTRAN, the first computer-programming language.

late 1950s John McCarthy creates Lisp, the computer language of artificial intelligence.

1957 At Mackinaw City, Michigan, the Mackinac Straits Bridge, the world's longest suspension bridge to date, opens.

New York City's last trolley car is removed from service, with motorbuses substituted for streetcars in most major American cities.

1958 Pan Am and England's BOAC begin transatlantic jet service.

The first American-manufactured commercial jet, the Boeing 707, begins service; it can seat 211.

The National Aeronautics and Space Administration (NASA) is formed, and the first U.S. Earth satellite launched.

United Press International (UPI) is created by a merger of the United Press and the International News Service.

The Control Data Corporation introduces the first completely transistorized computer, developed by Seymour Cray.

The Ampex Corporation develops the first color video recorder.

1959 Xerox produces its first commercial copier.

Jack Kilby and Robert Noyce independently invent the microchip, paving the way for miniature products and electronic wristwatches.

Launched at Camden, New Jersey, the *Savannah* is the first nuclear-powered merchant ship.

NASA chooses seven astronauts.

1960 The Digital Equipment Company develops the first minicomputer, the PDP-1.

The Bulova Accutron is the first electronic wristwatch.

Echo I, the first communications satellite, is launched.

The auto industry starts producing compact cars to better compete against foreign economy and sports cars.

Edwin Land invents black-and-white Polaroid film.

1961 Navy commander Alan Shepard, Jr., makes the first American manned space voyage, reaching an altitude of 115 miles in a 15-minute flight.

The IBM Selectric typewriter, with a moving-ball cluster of interchangeable type, is introduced.

1962 Marine Corps pilot John Glenn is the first American to orbit the earth, in the Mercury capsule *Friendship 7*.

Virgil "Gus" Grissom becomes the second American in space, making a 15-minute flight aboard the Mercury Mission's *Liberty Bell 7*.

Telstar, the first active communications satellite, is launched and transmits the first live transatlantic telecasts.

John Glenn

Congress creates a private company, the Communications Satellite Corporation (COMSAT), to oversee the role of the United States in developing a worldwide system of communication satellites.

Near Washington, D.C., John Foster Dulles International Airport, the first civilian airport designed to accommodate jets, opens.

The Lear jet is developed by William Lear.

1963   The Post Office inaugurates five-digit zip codes.

AT&T produces transistorized electronic Touch-Tone phones.

Edwin Land introduces Polaroid color film.

A satellite relays color TV for the first time.

Touch-Tone telephone service begins.

1964   The Verrazano-Narrows Bridge between Brooklyn and Staten Island, New York, opens; it is at present the world's longest suspension bridge.

John Kemeny and Thomas Kurtz invent BASIC, a computer language for beginners, which becomes the main programming language for personal-computer owners.

The Boeing 727, seating 145, is introduced.

1965 *Early Bird*, the first commercial communications satellite, is put into orbit by COMSAT.

In New York City, radio station WINS pioneers all-news programming.

Astronaut Edward White is the first American to walk in space, spending approximately 20 minutes outside the *Gemini 4* spacecraft, which is in the process of orbiting the earth three times.

IBM introduces its first integrated circuit-based computer, the 360.

Ralph Nader publishes *Unsafe at Any Speed,* an indictment of the American auto industry for its focus on profits rather than safety; the book encourages Congress to pass new safety regulations for cars.

1966 Congress passes the Freedom of Information Act, giving greater public access to public information.

The Department of Transportation is established.

Secretaries of Transportation

Secretary	President	Year Appointed	Secretary	President	Year Appointed
Alan S. Boyd	Johnson, L. B.	1966	Andrew L. Lewis, Jr.	Reagan	1981
John A. Volpe	Nixon	1969	Elizabeth Hanford Dole	Reagan	1983
Claude S. Brinegar	Nixon	1973	James H. Burnley	Reagan	1987
	Ford	1974	Samuel K. Skinner	Bush	1989
William T. Coleman, Jr.	Ford	1975	Andrew H. Card, Jr.	Bush	1992
Brock Adams	Carter	1977	Federico F. Pena	Clinton	1993
Neil E. Goldschmidt	Carter	1979	Rodney Slater	Clinton	1997

1967 Astronauts Virgil Grissom, Edward White, and Roger Chaffee are killed when fire traps them in the capsule of the Saturn 1-B rocket while it is on the ground.

Rolling Stone magazine is founded by Jann Wenner.

Congress creates a Corporation for Public Broadcasting to increase noncommercial radio and television broadcasting.

A Commission on Obscenity and Pornography is created by Congress; it finds that pornography does not influence crime or sexual deviance.

The Federal Communications Commission orders all radio and TV cigarette commercials to warn of the possible danger in smoking.

1968 The 911 emergency phone number is inaugurated in New York City, with most large cities following suit.

The Penn Central Railroad is created by a merger between the New York Central and the Pennsylvania railroads; it is at present the biggest merger in United States history.

Apollo 8, the first manned space mission to orbit the moon, is launched.

Front-seat shoulder belts are now required equipment in cars.

1969 Astronaut Neil Armstrong becomes the first human to walk on the moon; as he steps onto it from the lunar module *Apollo 11*, Armstrong is joined by fellow astronaut Edwin "Buzz" Aldrin, while millions worldwide watch on television.

Cigarette advertising will be gradually eliminated from radio and television during the next three years, according to a decision announced by the National Association of Broadcasters.

Reversing a Georgia antipornography law, the Supreme Court rules that in the privacy of their own homes people may read or view films without censorship.

Penthouse magazine, established by Robert Guccione, begins publication.

1970   Pan Am puts the first jumbo jet, the Boeing 747, into service. It is capable of carrying 490 passengers.

The Burlington Northern, Inc. is created by a merger of the Chicago, Burlington & Quincy and the Great Northern, Northern Pacific, and Chicago railroads.

The floppy disk is invented for storing computer-originated data.

Lexitron introduces the first word processor, a computer for handling written text.

The Post Office Department becomes an independent agency rather than a federal agency and is renamed the Postal Service.

Ms. magazine is founded; feminist Gloria Steinem is its first editor.

1971   Amtrak (The National Railroad Passenger Corporation) assumes control of nearly all the nation's passenger railway service after being authorized by Congress to operate intercity passenger trains.

The Picturephone is introduced by Bell Telephone.

Direct telephone dialing is now possible between parts of the United States and Europe.

Texas Instruments develops the first pocket calculator.

Intel introduces the first microprocessor, several integrated circuits on a single silicon chip.

1972   *Pioneer 10*, an unmanned United States spacecraft, begins a nearly two-year journey past the planet Jupiter; the probe will be the first human-made object to go beyond the solar system.

Frederick Smith founds Federal Express.

The Polaroid SX system develops a color print outside the camera in front of the photographer's eyes.

1973   Intel markets the 8080 microprocessor, which becomes the central processing unit (CPU) of several microcomputers.

1974   *People* magazine is first published by Time, Inc.

The first personal computer, the Altair, is developed.

A nationwide speed limit of 55 mph (89 kph) is established.

1975   In the final Apollo mission, the first United States–Soviet space link occurs 140 miles above the earth, as astronauts Thomas Stafford, Vance Brand, and Donald Slayton meet up with cosmonauts Valery Kubasov and Aleksei Leonov.

The probe *Viking 1* is launched. With a second probe, *Viking 2*, it will land on Mars in 1976, sending back data and photos.

William Gates and Paul Allen found the Seattle-based Microsoft Company; the company will produce MS-DOS, the operating system for IBM's first personal computer.

1976   The federal government restructures six bankrupt railroads as a private corporation called the Consolidated Rail Corporation (Conrail); the government is to become Conrail's biggest stockholder.

A small strip of Washington, D.C.'s Metro subway opens.

Wang Laboratories develops office work stations with shared central computers.

Fax (facsimile transmission) machines are first used by businesses.

Steven Jobs and Stephen Wozniak found Apple Computer to develop personal computers.

1977   In West Virginia, the 1,817-foot New River Gorge Bridge is the world's longest steel arch bridge.

The Trans-Alaska oil pipeline opens.

Apple introduces the Apple II, the first assembled personal computer.

The probe *Voyager 2*, is launched; it will photograph Jupiter in 1979, Saturn in 1981, Uranus in 1986, and Neptune in 1989.

1978   *Self* and *Working Woman* magazines begin publication.

The Air Transport Deregulation Act phases out federal regulation of the airlines industry.

Apple introduces the first disk drive for personal computers.

Hayes markets the first microcomputer-compatible modem.

The Panama Canal treaties cede control of the canal to Panama, through a 20-year transition, beginning in 1979 and ending December 31, 1999, but with the canal's neutrality guaranteed.

Cellular phones are developed by AT&T Bell Labs; by 1981 they are in use nationwide.

The first spreadsheet for personal computers, which allows computers to be used for accounting functions, is developed by VisiCalc.

1979   Congress passes the Chrysler Loan Guarantee Bill, which saves the company from bankruptcy.

1980   The *Voyager I* spacecraft explores Saturn.

Atlanta's Hartsfield International Airport opens.

Easing some of the restrictions imposed by the Interstate Commerce Act (1887), the Staggers Rail Act deregulates the railways in various ways, such as giving them more freedom in setting rates.

The newly created (by merger) CSX Corporation's 27,000 miles of track make it the largest American railroad.

Ted Turner's Atlanta-based Cable News Network (CNN) starts operating.

1981   The IBM personal computer, using the Microsoft disk-operating system (MS-DOS), is introduced and soon becomes the industry standard.

The first portable computer, the Osborne 1, is developed.

The space shuttle *Columbia*, the first reusable manned spacecraft, is launched.

1982   Compaq develops the first clone of the IBM personal computer.

Compact-disc players are designed. CDs will almost entirely replace long-playing records.

AT&T agrees to spin off 22 regional and local companies but will keep its long-distance lines, Western Electric manufacturing facilities, and Bell Laboratories research facilities.

The Boeing 767, capable of seating 211, is introduced.

The space shuttle *Columbia* makes its first commercial flight.

The color daily *USA Today* begins publication.

Eastman Kodak introduces the film-disk, a flat plastic cartridge containing a film disk that turns in front of an exposure window situated behind a camera lens.

1983   Apple's Lisa personal computer introduces pull-down menus and the mouse, a hand device that moves the cursor on the screen.

IBM builds the first hard-disk drive into its PC-XT personal computer.

Astronaut Sally Ride becomes the first woman in space.

1984   IBM introduces a one-megabyte RAM memory chip, with four times the memory of earlier chips.

The Supreme Court declares that videotape recording for home use only does not violate copyrights.

Auto-focus cameras are developed.

1985 Bell Laboratories transmits over a single optical fiber the equivalent of 300,000 simultaneous telephone conversations.

Apple's LaserWriter printer and Aldus Corporation's PageMaker make desktop publishing possible.

1986 The space shuttle *Challenger* explodes after liftoff, killing the seven astronauts aboard.

Experimental aircraft *Voyager* circles the earth without refueling.

IBM's OS/2 operating system enables personal computers to run several programs at once.

1987 The federal government sells its Conrail stock to private investors.

1988 Ted Turner founds Turner Network Television (TNT).

Steven Jobs introduces a "computer workstation," with an optical disk drive that stores 250 times more data than IBM and Apple floppy disks.

1989 Intel introduces the 8086 chip, which, capable of containing 1 million transistors, gives the microcomputer the power and speed of a supercomputer.

1990 The space probe *Magellan* begins orbiting Venus, sending back radar images of the surface of the planet.

1992 The probe *Mars Observer* is launched to map the planet.

AFTER THE WRIGHT BROTHERS: FAMOUS AMERICAN AIRPLANE FLIGHTS

1908 Glenn Curtiss completes the first official American public flight of over one kilometer.

1911 In a series of short flights, Calbraith Rodgers takes 49 days to make the first transcontinental flight across America—from Sheepshead Bay, New York, to Pasadena, California.

1924 Two U.S. Army planes take almost six months to make the first round-the-world flight of 26,345 miles (42,398 kilometers).

1926 Explorers Richard Byrd and Floyd Bennett make the first flight over the North Pole.

1927 Charles Lindbergh makes the first solo nonstop transatlantic flight. The 3,610-mile (5,810-kilometer) journey from Garden City, New York, to Paris takes 33 1/2 hours.

1928 Charles Smith and his crew make the first flight across the Pacific Ocean from Oakland, California, to Brisbane, Australia. They make stops at Honolulu, Hawaii, and Fiji.

1929 Richard Byrd and his crew make the first flight over the South Pole.

1931 Clyde Pangborn and Hugh Herndon make the first nonstop flight across the Pacific Ocean—from Misawa, Japan, to Wenatchee, Washington.

1932 Amelia Earhart becomes the first woman to fly solo across the Atlantic Ocean. Starting from Harbour Grace, Newfoundland, she lands in a pasture in Wales, in 15 hours and 18 minutes.

1933 Wiley Post makes the first solo round-the-world flight, journeying 15,596 miles (29,099 kilometers) in 4 days, 19 hours, and 36 minutes.

1949 A U.S. Air Force plane makes the first nonstop round-the-world flight, traveling 23,452 miles (37,742 kilometers) in 3 days, 22 hours, and 1 minute.

1986   Richard Rutan and Jeana Yeager make the first round-the-world flight without refueling, starting and ending their journey at Edwards Air Force Base, California.

1988   Clay Lacy, his crew, and 36 passengers fly around the world in the record time of 36 hours, 54 minutes, 15 seconds.

SIGNIFICANT EVENTS IN AMERICAN SPACE EXPLORATION

1926   Robert Goddard launches the first liquid-propelled rocket.

1958   The National Aeronautics and Space Administration (NASA) is established.

1961   Alan B. Shepard, Jr., is the first American astronaut in space.

1962   John Glenn, Jr., is the first American astronaut to orbit the earth.

1965   Edward White becomes the first American to walk in space, spending approximately 20 minutes outside the *Gemini 4* spacecraft.

1968   America launches *Apollo 8*, the first manned spaceship mission that orbits the moon.

1969   American astronauts Neil Armstrong and Edwin Aldrin, Jr., achieve the first manned landing on the moon.

1971   The American spacecraft *Mariner 9* is the first to orbit another planet, Mars.

1975   The United States and the Soviet Union launch the first international manned space mission, the Apollo-Soyuz Test Project.

America launches the probe *Viking 1*. It and a second probe, *Viking 2*, will land on Mars the next year, transmitting pictures of the planet's surface.

1977   America launches the probe *Voyager 2*; it flies past Jupiter in 1979, Saturn in 1980, Uranus in 1986, and Neptune in 1989, sending back photos.

1981   America launches the space shuttle *Columbia*, the first reusable manned spacecraft.

1983   Astronaut Sally Ride becomes the first woman in space.

1986   The American space shuttle *Challenger* tears apart soon after launch; all seven crew members die in the accident.

1990   The American space probe *Magellan* begins its orbit around Venus, sending back radar images.

1992   America launches the probe *Mars Observer*; it reaches Mars in 1993, sending back photos and data more detailed than ever.

ACTS OF CONGRESS AFFECTING TRANSPORTATION AND COMMUNICATION

1798   Alien Acts. In two acts, Congress empowers President John Adams to arrest and deport "dangerous" aliens during wartime.

Sedition Act. This act suppresses editorial criticism of the president and his administration.

1862	Pacific Railroad Act. Congress grants to the Union Pacific and the Central Pacific railroads subsidies in land and money for the construction of a transcontinental railroad.
1887	Interstate Commerce Act. Congress establishes the Interstate Commerce Commission (ICC) to regulate the railway industry, specifically to require the railroads to charge "reasonable and just" freight rates.
1903	Elkins Act. This forbids railroads to charge rates different from their published rates and holds railroad officials personally liable if rebating occurs.
1906	Hepburn Act. This authorizes the Interstate Commerce Commission (ICC) to fix railroad rates and inspect financial records.
1910	Mann-Elkins Act. Congress extends the Interstate Commerce Commission's power over railroads and also places telegraph, cable, and telephone companies under ICC control.
1917	Espionage Act. This makes it illegal to interfere with recruiting or drafting soldiers or to do anything that negatively influences military morale.
1920	Transportation Act. This returns the railroads to their owners after President Woodrow Wilson placed them under federal control during World War I.
1926	Air Commerce Act. For the first time Congress imposes safety regulations on aircraft, requiring registration and licensing of planes and pilots.
1934	Communications Act. This creates the Federal Communications Commission (FCC) to regulate broadcasting, basically through its power to license stations.
1940	Smith Act. Congress makes it unlawful to advocate the overthrow of the government by either force or violence.
1956	Federal Aid Highway Act. This calls for construction of a system of interstate highways covering 41,000 miles (66,000 kilometers).
1965	Clean Air Act. Congress orders the automobile industry to decrease the pollution produced by new cars.
1966	Highway Safety Act. In the first of a number of acts addressing motor-vehicle safety, Congress allows federal agencies to set mandatory safety standards for motor vehicles.
	Freedom of Information Act. This act requires that federal agencies make most of their records available to the public. Nine classes of records are exempt, including documents related to national security or trade secrets.
1967	Public Broadcasting Act. Congress establishes noncommercial radio and television.
1971	Amtrak Act. This establishes Amtrak passenger service to operate nearly all American intercity passenger railway service.
1974	Privacy Act. This act requires federal agencies to give individuals any information in their files about them and to correct incorrect records.
1976	Conrail Act. Congress creates Conrail to provide freight service for six bankrupt railroads in the Northeast.
1978	Air Transport Deregulation Act. Congress virtually deregulates domestic airlines.
1980	Staggers Rail Act. This act deregulates railroads in various ways, such as permitting them increased flexibility in setting rates and greater authority to form long-term contracts with freight shippers.
	Privacy Protection Act. This declares that before newspaper premises are searched, the police must obtain subpoenas.

SUPREME COURT DECISIONS AFFECTING TRANSPORTATION AND COMMUNICATION

1824   *Gibbons v. Odgen.* In a decision that helps prevent interstate trade wars, the Court rules that states cannot restrain interstate commerce and that the power of Congress to regulate interstate commerce does not stop at the jurisdictional lines of several states.

1876   *Munn v. Illinois.* The Illinois legislature has set maximum rates that could be charged by grain warehouses and elevators. After Ira Munn, a grain elevator operator, is sued by the state for refusing to obey the statute, he contends that the state law conflicts with the interstate commerce powers of Congress. The Court rules that because elevators and warehouses engage in local transactions, they are subject to state control. The decision triggers numerous cases in which the Court is requested to overturn state regulatory laws.

1964   *New York Times Company v. Sullivan.* The Court declares that the First Amendment protects critics of public officials, even if the charges are false.

1971   *New York Times Company v. United States.* In 1971 *The New York Times* publishes the secret Pentagon Papers. The Nixon administration obtains an injunction against the paper, alleging it breached national security. In an unauthored opinion, the Court observes that the government, in this instance, has not met "the heavy burden of showing justification" for "prior restraint" on the freedom of the press.

1973   *Miller v. California.* Communities gain greater control over pornographic and obscene films, magazines, and books. The decision also defines "contemporary community standards" as local, not national.

1976   *Nebraska Press Association v. Stuart.* The Court holds that injunctions against the press publishing information about pending criminal trials are permitted only when all other means of insuring a fair trial prove inadequate.

1978   *Zurcher v. Stanford Daily.* The Court holds that newspaper offices may be searched by police with warrants.

1979   *Gannett v. DePasquale.* Judges may bar the press and the public from criminal proceedings.

SIGNIFICANT PEOPLE IN TRANSPORTATION AND COMMUNICATION

Armstrong, Edwin (1890–1954).   Armstrong's electrical inventions pioneered radio. They included regenerative circuits, superheterodyne circuits, superregenerative circuits, and the frequency-modulation system of radio.

Bardeen, John (1908–).   With William Shockley and Walter Brattain, Bardeen invented the transistor, for which they received the 1956 Nobel Prize in physics.

Bell, Alexander Graham (1847–1922).   Bell founded a training school for teachers of the deaf in Boston in 1872. Two years later he invented a telegraph multiplexing system. In 1875 he transmitted the first intelligible words over the telephone to his assistant, Thomas Watson. Bell patented the telephone the next year. With others, he founded the Bell Telephone Company.

Bennett, James Gordon (1795–1872).   Scottish-born Bennett founded the *New York Herald*, a one-cent daily, in 1835, editing it until his death. He pioneered in publishing society news and Wall Street financial news, and in employing European correspondents and the telegraph.

Brattain, Walter (1902–1987).   With physicists William Shockley and John Bardeen, Brattain coinvented the transistor in 1947 at the Bell Research Laboratory.

Bush, Vannevar (1890–1974).   An electrical engineer, Bush devised the differential analyzer in 1928, thereby pioneering the analogue computer.

Carlson, Chester (1906–1968).   Carlson invented the electrostatic process of xerography in 1938 and patented it two years later. Xerox copiers were not introduced to the public until 1958.

Clinton, De Witt (1769–1828).   A two-term governor of New York (1817–1823 and 1825–1828), Clinton used the power of his office to become the chief promoter of the Erie Canal.

De Forest, Lee (1873–1961).   Forest, known as "the Father of Radio," patented more than 300 inventions. Among his most important achievements are the invention of the Audion, the first grid-triode vacuum tube, which made it possible to amplify radio waves; the introduction of the radio news broadcast; and the establishment of the first radio station.

Disney, Walter (1901–1966).   Disney created animated cartoons and produced the first animated movie with sound as well as the first feature-length animated films. His animated films remain popular worldwide today.

Durant, William (1861–1947).   Durant controlled the Buick Motor Car Company and subsequently founded General Motors Company and Chevrolet Motor Company (with Louis Chevrolet).

Earhart, Amelia (1897–1937).   Flying from Newfoundland to Wales in 1928, Earhart became the first female to cross the Atlantic Ocean in an aircraft. In 1932 she was the first woman to fly the Atlantic solo. In 1935 Earhart achieved two solo firsts—Hawaii to the mainland and Mexico City to New York. Earhart vanished during a round-the-world flight in 1937.

Eastman, George (1854–1932).   Eastman developed the process for producing photographic dry plates in 1880. Four years later he received a patent for flexible film. Eastman also invented the Kodak hand camera, daylight-loading film, and the Brownie camera. He founded the Eastman Kodak company in 1892.

Edison, Thomas (1847–1931).   Edison patented more than 1,000 inventions. Some of the most significant related to transportation and communication were the quadruplex telegraph, the mimeograph, the microphone, the phonograph, the incandescent electric lamp, and the kinetoscope, a machine for making movies.

Fessenden, Reginald (1866–1932).   A radio pioneer, Fessenden devised the electrolytic detector, high-frequency alternator, and the heterodyne receiver. He also made the first radio broadcast of voice and music and patented 300 inventions.

Ford, Henry (1863–1947).   Ford built his first practical gasoline car in 1896 and founded the Ford Motor Company seven years later. He introduced his Model T in 1908. Through the moving assembly line, which he created, Ford was able to produce more than 240,000 Model T's a year. For almost 20 years the Model T was the best-selling car; it made America into a nation on wheels.

Franklin, Benjamin (1706–1790).   As well as being a statesman, scientist, and philosopher, Franklin was a printer, having apprenticed to his brother James, a Boston printer, in 1718. On moving to Philadelphia he pulished an early newspaper, the *Pennsylvania Gazette*, from 1730 to 1748.

Fulton, Robert (1765–1815).   Fulton invented the submarine at Le Havre the winter of 1800–1801, but no government showed any interest. In 1801, minister to France Robert Livingston commissioned him to build a steamboat. Fulton returned to the United States in 1806, and the next year his steamboat, the *Clermont*, steamed from New York to Albany. Although it was not the first steamboat, it was the first of a line of commercially viable steamboats. In 1814 Fulton launched the world's first steam warship.

Gates, William, III (1955–).   At the age of 19, Gates, along with Paul Allen, formed the Microsoft Company, which produced MS-DOS, the operating system for IBM's first personal computer. That system and other Microsoft programs such as OS/2 and Windows made Microsoft the world's largest manufacturer of microcomputer software.

Goddard, Robert (1882–1945).   Among Goddard's pioneering rocket experiments are the design and testing of the first successful liquid-fueled rocket. He also became the first person to exceed the speed of sound. Goddard received more than 200 rocketry patents.

Goldmark, Peter Carl (1906–1977).   At the Columbia Broadcasting Systems Laboratories, Goldmark, an engineer, invented the color television system and the $33^1/_3$-rpm phonograph, the first long-playing record.

Goldwyn, Samuel (1882–1974).   Poland-born Goldwyn founded Goldwyn Pictures in 1917, later merging with Metro Pictures to form Metro-Goldwyn-Mayer. He produced the first feature film, *The Squaw Man*, in 1913 and went on to produce many memorable films throughout the thirties, forties, and fifties.

Gould, Jay (1836–1892).   A financier and speculator, Gould controlled the New York elevated, most of the southwestern railroads, and the Western Union Telegraph Company.

Greeley, Horace (1811–1872).   A journalist and political leader, Greeley, with Jonas Winchester, established and edited the weekly magazine *The New Yorker* from 1834 to 1841. In 1841 he founded the *New York Tribune*, which became tremendously influential in the North, especially before the Civil War. The paper supported abolitionism, free common-school education, and various other reforms.

Harriman, Edward (1848–1909).   A railroad magnate and financier, Harriman owned several railroads, including the Lake Ontario Southern Railroad and the Illinois Central. He reorganized the Union Pacific and then acquired Southern Pacific and Central Pacific, which enabled him to dominate western rail service. He later lost a hard-fought battle against James Hill for control of the Northern Pacific Railroad.

Hearst, William Randolph (1863–1951).   Hearst built the first great publishing empire, publishing 28 major newspapers and 18 magazines in 1935. To sell his newspapers to the mass market, he charged a penny for them and pioneered many techniques of tabloid journalism such as oversized, outrageous headlines, shocking photographs, and stories that were sometimes more sensationalistic than accurate.

Hill, James (1838–1916).   With associates, Hill acquired the St. Paul and Pacific Railroad, reorganizing and extending it. He created the Northern Railway Company to merge all his lines. Hill won an epic battle against Edward Harriman for control of the Northern Pacific.

Hughes, Howard (1905–1976).   An industrialist, aviator, and motion-picture producer, Hughes founded a company that made experimental planes and set many speed records.

Jobs, Steven (1955–).   With Stephen Wozniak, Jobs introduced the Apple computer, helping launch the personal-computer revolution. Jobs created in Apple a user-friendly alternative to IBM's personal computer. After resigning from Apple in 1985, he founded the NeXT Computer Company.

Kemeny, John (1926–1992).   Kemeny, with Thomas Kurtz, invented the BASIC computer language.

Kettering, Charles (1876–1958).   An electrical engineer, Kettering invented the automotive electric self-starter and lighting and ignition systems for cars.

Land, Edwin (1909–1991).   Land, who was mainly self-taught, invented the first Polaroid Land Camera, which developed photographs inside the camera in about 60 seconds. He also invented black-and-white Polaroid film and color film. Land received patents for more than 530 inventions.

Lindbergh, Charles (1902–1974).   Lindbergh completed the first solo nonstop transatlantic flight from New York to Paris in the Spirit of St. Louis in 1927, becoming an instant hero.

Luce, Henry (1903–1967).   Editor and publisher. With Briton Hadden, Luce founded and edited the weekly magazine *Time*. He also established the monthly *Fortune*, the weekly picture magazine *Life*, and *Sports Illustrated*.

Mauchly, John (1907–1980).   A physicist and engineer, Mauchly, with John Eckert, devised the first electronic computer, the Electrical Numerical Integrator and Computer (ENIAC). They also co-invented two later models, BINAC and UNIVAC I.

Mayer, Louis B. (1885–1957).   Russian-born Mayer, after having formed the largest theater chain in New England, founded Metro Pictures and Louis B. Mayer Pictures in 1918. In 1924 these merged with the Goldwyn Company to become Metro-Goldwyn-Mayer, with Mayer as vice president and general manager until 1951. Under Mayer's reign, MGM produced slick, star-studded entertainments, and in the thirties and forties Mayer was the most powerful magnate in Hollywood.

Mergenthaler, Ottmar (1854–1899).   Mergenthaler patented the first Linotype typesetting machine in 1884; it was the first major improvement in setting type since Gutenberg's invention of moveable type in about 1440. Mergenthaler later patented improvements such as automatic justification.

Morse, Samuel (1791–1872).   Morse conducted experiments on a magnetic telegraph beginning in 1832. He invented the Morse code, which he filed a patent for in 1837, to be used in a telegraph. Congress granted him $30,000 to oversee the construction of a telegraph line between Baltimore and Washington, D.C. In May 1844 Morse sent the first telegraphic message ever over this line: "What hath God wrought!" His telegraph signals made possible instantaneous long-distance communication.

Muybridge, Eadweard (1803–1904).   Asked to use photography to prove that a running horse has four feet off the ground at one point in its stride, Muybridge went on to make photographic studies of motion. He invented the zoopraxiscope, a forerunner of the movie projector.

Noyce, Robert (1927–1990).   An engineer, Noyce coinvented the integrated circuit, a system of interconnecting transistors on a single silicon microchip. The invention led to the development of pocket calculators and microcomputers. Noyce and Gordon Moore founded the Intel Corporation, which became a leading manufacturer of semiconductors.

Olds, Ransome (1864–1950).   An inventor and manufacturer, Olds helped establish Detroit's Olds Motor Works. In 1901 he built 425 Oldsmobiles, beginning mass production of American cars.

Otis, Elisha (1811–1861).   Otis invented the safety device that kept hoisted machinery safely in the air, making possible the first passenger elevator. Otis received a patent for a steam elevator in 1861 and established the Otis elevator business, which became the major manufacturer of passenger elevators. These, in turn, permitted the building of skyscrapers.

Paley, William S. (1901–1990).   Paley bought United Independent Broadcasters Inc. in 1927, renaming it the Columbia Broadcasting System (CBS). With the coming of television, he formed CBS Television, which under his guidance became a communications giant.

Pullman, George (1831–1897).   Pullman designed the first Pullman railroad car, with a folding upper berth and a lower berth formed from extendible seat cushions. He established the Pullman Palace Car Company in 1867 to build his cars. Pullman also designed the Pullman dining car and built the town of Pullman, near Chicago, for his workers.

Sarnoff, David (1891–1971).   A radio and television pioneer, Sarnoff was the first to suggest a commercially marketed radio receiver (1915). He went on to found the National Broadcasting Company (NBC) and to create an experimental television station.

Scripps, Edward (1854–1926).   With his half-brother George Scripps and Milton McRae, Scripps organized the Scripps-McRae League of Newspapers in 1894 and the Scripps-McRae Press Association in 1897. He also bought Publishers' Press and merged it into the United Press.

Selden, George (1846–1922).   In 1895 Selden was granted the patent for a "road engine," the first American gasoline-engined car, which he had invented in 1879.

Sennett, Mack (1880–1960).   A motion-picture pioneer, Sennett first worked under the director D. W. Griffith at Biograph Studios from 1910 to 1911, before leaving to form the Keystone Company, one of the early movie picture companies in America.

Shockley, William (1910–1989).   At Bell Telephone Laboratory Shockley co-invented (with John Bardeen and Walter Brattain) the transistor, for which they won the 1956 Nobel Prize for physics. In 1954 he started his own semiconductor factory, which ignited the electronics boom and helped create "Silicon Valley," after ex-employees began their own companies.

Sholes, Christopher (1819–1890).   Along with Carlos Glidden and Samuel Soulé, Sholes patented the typewriter. In 1873, after Glidden and Soulé gave up their rights to the invention, Sholes sold his to the Remington Arms Company for $12,000.

Sikorsky, Igor (1889–1972).   A Russian-born aeronautical engineer and inventor, Sikorsky invented the helicopter in 1909. Four years later he designed, built, and flew the world's first successful multimotored aircraft. In 1931 Sikorsky developed the amphibian *American Clipper*, which pioneered in transoceanic commercial flights.

Stevens, John (1749–1838).   Stevens built the first screw-driven steamboat; it marked the first time the powered screw was used in ship propulsion. He also designed the *Phoenix*, which by steaming from New York to Philadelphia in 1809, became the first seagoing steamboat in the world. In 1811 Stevens started the world's first steam ferry service. In 1825 he built the first American steam locomotive.

Turner, Ted (1938–).   In 1980 Turner founded the Cable News Network, the first network to broadcast news 24 hours a day. Turner also established the new movie channel TNT.

Vanderbilt, Cornelius.   Known as **Commodore Vanderbilt** (1794–1877). Vanderbilt established a controlling interest in a number of eastern railroads, including the New York and Harlem Railroad, the Hudson River Railroad, and the New York Central Railroad. His acquisition of the Lake Shore & Michigan Southern line extended his rail network to Chicago. Vanderbilt built New York City's Grand Central Terminal.

Warner, Harry (1881–1958).   With his brothers, Samuel, Albert, and Jack, Warner established motion-picture studios in Hollywood in 1918. Five years later these were incorporated into Warner Bros. Pictures.

Westinghouse, George (1846–1914). Westinghouse patented the railroad air brake in 1869 as well as automatic railroad signal devices. He founded Westinghouse Electric Company to manufacture these inventions. Interested in electric and natural gas innovation, he held more than 400 patents.

Wright, Wilbur (1867–1912) and his brother Orville (1871–1948). Aviation pioneers, the Wright brothers made the world's first successful flights in a motorized aircraft near Kitty Hawk, North Carolina. Orville completed the first flight, followed the same day by Wilbur, whose flight lasted 59 seconds and covered 852 feet. In 1908 the Wright brothers developed the first plane for the U.S. Army, which successfully tested the following year.

Zworykin, Vladimir (1889–1982). In the 1920s, while working for Westinghouse, Russian-born engineer Zworykin patented two inventions, the iconoscope and the kinescope; together they became the first television system. Later he became director of electronic development for RCA.

ADDITIONAL SOURCES OF INFORMATION

Barnouw, Erik. *A Tower of Babel: A History of Broadcasting in the U.S. to 1933*. Oxford University Press, 1966.

———. *Tube of Plenty*. Rev. ed. Oxford University Press, 1982.

Bilstein, Roger. *Flight in America, 1900–1983*. Johns Hopkins University Press, 1984.

Flink, James J. *The Car Culture*. MIT Press, 1975.

Goodrich, Carter, ed. *Canals and American Economic Development*. Kennikat Press, 1961.

Jackson, Kenneth T. *Crabgrass Frontier: The Suburbanization of the United States*. Oxford University Press, 1985.

Jensen, Oliver. *The American Heritage History of Railroads in America*. McGraw-Hill, 1975.

Lewis, D. L., and Laurence Goldstein, eds. *The Automobile and American Culture*. University of Michigan Press, 1984.

Marchand, Roland. *Advertising the American Dream: Making Way for Modernity*. University of California Press, 1985.

Morrison, Samuel Eliot. *The Maritime History of Massachusetts, 1783–1860*. Houghton Mifflin, 1961.

Rogers, Everett M., and Judith K. Larsen. *Silicon Valley Fever: Growth of High-Technology Culture*. Basic Books, 1984.

Sklar, Robert. *Movie-Made America: A Cultural History of American Movies*. Random House, 1976.

Sterling, Christopher, and John Kittross. *Stay Tuned: A Concise History of American Broadcasting*. Wadsworth Publishing, 1978.

Stover, John F. *American Railroads*. University of Chicago Press, 1961.

Summers, Mark W. *Railroads, Reconstruction, and the Gospel of Prosperity*. Princeton University Press, 1984.

Taylor, George Rogers. *The Transportation Revolution, 1815–1860*. Holt, Rinehart and Winston, 1951.

13
Religion

SIGNIFICANT EVENTS IN AMERICAN RELIGION

The United States was the first modern, Western nation founded by Protestants. Although it has no established religion, and has generally been tolerant of people of all faiths, much of the country's history has been shaped by its Protestant heritage.

1565   The Spanish found the city of St. Augustine in Florida; the first Catholic parish in what will be the United States is established there.

1579   Sir Francis Drake and crew hold the first Protestant service in California.

1609   The Church of England becomes the established church of Virginia.

1612   Pocohontas is converted to Christianity in Virginia.

1620   The first Pilgrims arrive in North America. Religious dissidents, they set sail from England on the *Mayflower* and are headed for Virginia, but instead they reach Plymouth, Massachusetts, where they begin a colony.

1628   Dutch colonists establish the first Reformed congregation in New Amsterdam, later New York.

       The first Puritans, led by John Endecott, arrive from England and settle in Salem, Massachusetts.

1630   John Winthrop founds a new community in Boston, thus beginning the Puritan Great Migration to New England.

1634   Under charter of Charles I of England, Lord Baltimore and his sons settle Maryland, which they intend to be a refuge for persecuted Roman Catholics.

1635   The Puritan colony at Salem, Massachusetts, banishes clergyman Roger Williams, who is at odds with its union of church and state.

1636   Williams founds Rhode Island as a colony that will welcome religious dissidents and practice religious tolerance.

       Thomas Hooker, a minister who is unhappy with the strictness of life in Massachusetts, founds Hartford, Connecticut.

1637   Anne Hutchinson, a popular lay theologian, is branded a heretic for her teachings on grace and justification. Accused of claiming to receive direct divine revelation, she is banished from Massachusetts Bay.

1639   The first Lutheran congregation in the New World is established at Fort Christiana, a Swedish colony in what is now Delaware.

1647   Rhode Island drafts the first civil code in the colonies calling for separation of church and state.

1654   The first Jewish immigrants land at New Amsterdam.

1656   Quakers arriving in Massachusetts are imprisoned and deported. When two return in 1659, they are hanged on Boston Common.

1661   Massachusetts ends persecution of Quakers.

1662   The Massachusetts clergy adopt the Half-way Covenant, allowing the baptism of the children of those who are baptized but have not had the conversion experience necessary for full church membership.

       Baptism of children is made mandatory in Virginia.

1668   The French establish a Jesuit mission at Sault Sainte Marie, Michigan.

1670　The Act of Virginia decrees that indentured servants who are not Christian must remain servants for life; it is not repealed until 1682.

1677　English Quakers settle in New Jersey.

1681　Quaker William Penn receives a charter from King Charles II of England for lands that will become Pennsylvania. He founds Philadelphia.

1683　Mennonites from Germany emigrate to America and settle near Philadelphia in Germantown.

1684　Francis Makemie establishes the first Presbyterian congregation in America at Snow Hill, Maryland.

1685　Louis XIV of France renounces the Edict of Nantes, thus denying religious freedom to French Protestants, many of whom emigrate to the colonies.

1687　Eusebio Kino, a Jesuit missionary, begins his work in Arizona. By his death in 1711, the mission has made 30,000 converts.

1690s　Franciscans begin to build missions in Arizona.

1692　The witchcraft trials are held in Salem, Massachusetts, resulting in the execution of 20 women over the next two years.

Salem witch trials

THE SALEM WITCH TRIALS

One of the more bizarre chapters in American history is the Salem witch trials. In Europe, people, mostly women, had been persecuted as witches for hundreds of years, and the Puritans brought a belief in witchcraft to the New World. Occasional persecutions occurred throughout the colonies, but none rivaled the witch trials in Salem, Massachusetts.

(continues)

THE SALEM WITCH TRIALS (CONT.)

In 1692 a number of teenage girls began to behave strangely, gathering to meet and murmur incantations, suffering from minor fits and displaying an uncanny ability to foretell the future. Initially they blamed no one for their behavior, but under pressure from the community and questioning by various clergymen, they pointed a finger at various people, mostly middle-aged women, who lived among them.

Hundreds were accused, 27 were tried, and 20 were executed—19 by hanging, one by being pressed to death with stones. Within a few months of the initial trials, even those who believed in witchcraft began to question the procedures, specifically the mass hysteria that surrounded these events.

A new governor of the Massachusetts Bay Colony, Sir William Phipps, forbade any further trials. A new court was convened for the 52 people who awaited trial, and all were eventually exonerated.

Aside from mass hysteria, some historians would attribute this erratic episode to social changes that were occurring within the staunchly religious community and also to class divisions within it.

1702	Cotton Mather, an important Massachusetts minister, publishes *Magnalia Christi Americana*, a major history of American religious development.
1706	Francis Makemie organizes the Synod of Philadelphia, uniting Presbyterians of different backgrounds.
1707	Baptists organize what may be the first North American church umbrella group, the Philadelphia Baptist Association, which brings together five churches in three states (Pennsylvania, Delaware, and New Jersey).
1714	In King's Chapel in Boston the first pipe organ is played in an American church and is denounced by Puritans.
1719	*The Psalms of David Imitated* becomes the primary hymnal used in Protestant churches.
1730s–1760s	The Great Awakening, the first wave of revivalism, starts in New England and soon spreads across the colonies.
1730	The first Jewish synagogue in North America is built.
1735	John Wesley, the founder of Methodism in England, brings the first Methodists to the colonies; they settle in Georgia.
1737	Jonathan Edwards publishes his *Faithful Narrative of the Surprising Work of God in the Conversion of Many Hundred Souls in Northampton*, his first widely read work, describing the extraordinary renewal that followed his preaching on justification by faith.
1740s	The Great Awakening sweeps New England.
1740	George Whitefield, English Evangelical leader, preaches to huge crowds from Georgia to Maine; his tour is the key event in New England's Great Awakening.
1741	Evangelical leader Jonathan Edwards preaches his Great Awakening sermon, "Sinners in the Hands of an Angry God."

REVIVALISM

Four great waves of revivalism have swept the nation since the colonial era. Each of these outbreaks of evangelical religious fervor has been a reaction to a perceived apathy in the churches and the growing secularization of society, and each has had at its heart an emphasis on personal conversion and the emotional aspects of religious commitment.

The first wave, called the Great Awakening, began in the 1730s and reached its peak in the early 1740s, when the Anglican evangelist George Whitefield preached to thousands, and Jonathan Edwards published accounts of revival in New England and preached his famous sermon, "Sinners in the Hands of an Angry God."

The advocates of the awakening, known as the "New Lights," were opposed by "Old Light" ministers like Charles Chauncy of Boston, who accused the revival movement of emotionalism and irrationalism. By the time of the Revolution, this first wave of revivalism was over, although Evangelicalism would remain an important part of American religious life.

The Second Great Awakening, which has been called "the most influential revival of Christianity in the history of the United States" (Mark Noll) began during the late 1790s and ran its course through the 1820s. In the aftermath of the Revolution, church membership had declined to under 10 percent of the population, and in frontier regions, Christian influence was almost nonexistent.

The Awakening was characterized by great camp meetings, like that held at Cane Ridge, Kentucky, in 1801, where participants barked like dogs, jerked about, and danced in ecstasy, and by the efforts of circuit-riding Methodist ministers and Baptist farmer-preachers, who planted churches throughout the South and West.

The latter part of the Awakening saw the beginning of the ministry of Charles G. Finney, who established many of the features of the typical revival meeting and accelerated the move away from classical Calvinist theology of the First Great Awakening to one that recognized the place of free will in salvation.

The Second Great Awakening solidified the position of evangelicals in American religious life and provided the matrix from which reform movements such as abolitionism, prohibitionism, and the women's rights movement would come.

The third wave of revivalism got under way in the 1890s, with the revival meetings of Billy Sunday, a former professional baseball player who had had a conversion experience in 1886. Sunday used his pulpit to denounce Darwinism and to promote Prohibition. In 1917, he preached a revival in New York during which almost a hundred thousand people responded to his altar calls. The wave of revival came to an end with the publicity surrounding the Scopes "monkey trial," and antimodernist evangelicals, now known as fundamentalists, separated themselves from public and political life.

The present wave of revivalism began in the 1950s with Billy Graham, who began as a classic tent-meeting revivalist, and went on to hold gigantic televised stadium revivals around the world. As his ministry evolved, Graham managed to separate his evangelical message from much of the combativeness and histrionic excess that had discredited his fundamentalist forebears. Closely associated with American leaders from Eisenhower on, Graham and the institutions that grew up around him helped to restore evangelicals as active players in American public life.

1743   Boston Congregationalist minister Charles Chauncy, a theological liberal, takes on the Evangelicals in "Seasonable Thoughts on the State of Religion in New England," which decries the emotionalism and irrationalism of revivalist religion. The "battle of the pamphlets" begins between Chauncy and Jonathan Edwards, ending only with Edwards's death in 1758.

1748   Henry Melchior Muhlenberg establishes the Pennsylvania Ministerium, the first permanent governing body for Lutherans in America.

1755   Shubal Stearns and Daniel Marshall set the stage for Baptist growth in the South when they found their Sandy Creek, North Carolina, church during the Great Awakening.

1757   The Philadelphia Quakers ban slaveholding among their members, thus initiating the religious debate over slavery.

1759   The Franciscan friar Junípero Serra establishes Mission San Diego, the first of his nine California missions.

1763   A synagogue, the oldest still standing in the United States, is built in Newport, Rhode Island. It becomes known as the Touro Synagogue after its first rabbi.

1771   Francis Asbury (1741–1816), a blacksmith and Methodist minister, introduces the circuit-rider system of preaching, already practiced in England. A circuit-riding preacher can tend to 30 to 40 communities rather than just one; it proves to be an invaluable way of preaching on the American frontier.

1773   The first annual conference of Methodists is held in Philadelphia.

1774   Ann Lee, an English immigrant, organizes the first American Shaker colony in upstate New York.

1776   At the time of the country's founding, 9 of the 13 colonies have established religions.

1780s   African Americans George Liele and David George become the first American missionaries. Liele founds churches in Jamaica, and George serves in Nova Scotia and helps found Sierra Leone.

1780   The first Universalist church, emphasizing the unity of the divine, opens in Gloucester, Massachusetts.

1783   Philadelphia Quakers vote to admit African Americans as members.

1784   John Wesley decides to allow Methodists in America to set up their own church, independent of the Church of England. The Methodist Episcopal church is organized in Baltimore; Francis Asbury becomes its first bishop.

        Samuel Seabury, a Connecticut Anglican, is consecrated a bishop by bishops of the Scottish Episcopal Church, assuring that American Anglicanism will survive the Revolution.

1785   Boston's Anglican King's Chapel adopts an edition of *The Book of Common Prayer* without references to the doctrine of the Trinity, becoming America's first Unitarian congregation.

1786   Thomas Jefferson's Virginia Bill for Establishing Religious Freedom, a prototype for the First Amendment, is passed, over the opposition of conservatives who would like established religion to continue.

1789   The Protestant Episcopal Church is officially founded in America to succeed the Church of England in the aftermath of the Revolution. *The Book of Common Prayer* and the Constitution and Canons of the Church are adapted to suit Americans.

        The First General Assembly of Presbyterians meets in America.

1790s   The Second Great Awakening begins.

1790   John Carroll, the first Roman Catholic bishop in the United States, is installed as bishop of Baltimore.

1791   The Bill of Rights is ratified, adding ten amendments to the Constitution. The First Amendment guarantees, among other rights, freedom of religion.

1793   The first independent Methodist church for African Americans is established in Philadelphia by Richard Allen.

1794   The first Eastern Orthodox church is consecrated in North America on Kodiak Island, Alaska, by Russian monks.

1796   Black members of the John Street Methodist Church in New York, protesting discrimination, form their own congregation. It later grows into the African Methodist Episcopal Zion church.

1800   The first recorded camp meeting, a staple of revivalism, is held in Logan County, Kentucky.

1801   In the Plan of Union, Presbyterians and Congregationalists on the frontier agree to unite small groups from both churches and accept the ministers of either.

        At Cane Ridge, Kentucky, thousands hear the gospel from Presbyterian, Methodist, and Baptist preachers. The fervor and the unusual behavior of many in the crowds electrify the country.

1805   Henry Ware, a liberal Congregationalist, is elected Hollis Professor of Divinity at Harvard, signaling the liberal ascendancy in Massachusetts Congregationalism.

1806   Massachusetts Congregationalists, protesting liberal trends at Harvard, found Andover Seminary to preserve Calvinist orthodoxy.

1808   The first Bible Society is established in Philadelphia by Episcopal bishop William White.

1809   Elizabeth Bayley Seton, a young widow and convert to Catholicism, founds the Sisters of Charity of St. Joseph in Baltimore. In 1975, she becomes the first Catholic saint born in the United States.

1811   Alexander Campbell, an Irish immigrant, starts the Brush Run Church in Pennsylvania. Calling for a return to a non-creedal New Testament Christianity, Campbell organizes his followers as the Disciples of Christ.

1814   The Rappites, under the leadership of George Rapp, found a utopian colony in New Harmony, Indiana.

1816   The African Methodist Episcopal church becomes an independent church in Philadelphia.

With 214,235 members, there are now more Methodists in the United States than in England.

The American Bible Society is founded in New York.

1819   Unitarianism, which affirms the unity of God, is founded in Boston by William Ellery Channing.

1820s Shaker colonies thrive throughout New England.

1820   King Kamehameha II welcomes the first Christian missionaries to Hawaii.

The General Synod of the Evangelical Lutheran church unites Lutherans in the eastern United States.

1824   The American Sunday School Union organizes to promote Sunday schools across the country.

The Baptist General Missionary Convention becomes the first national Baptist association; it coordinates the church's active missionary program.

The Reformed Society of Israelites, a precursor of Reform Judaism, is founded in Charleston, South Carolina.

1825   The Owenites, organized by Robert Dale Owen, establish themselves in New Harmony, Indiana, when Owen buys the community from the Rappites.

The American Unitarian Association is founded in Boston.

1829   The First Provincial Council of Baltimore brings together the Roman Catholic bishops of the United States.

1830   The Church of Jesus Christ of Latter-day Saints (Mormons) is founded at Fayette, New York, by Joseph Smith, Jr. A year later it establishes its headquarters at Kirtland, Ohio.

1832   The California missions are secularized.

1833   The Congregational Church is disestablished in Massachusetts, ending the religion's establishment in the United States.

1836   Ralph Waldo Emerson's *Nature* is published, and the Transcendental Club meets for the first time in Boston. Transcendentalism, a philosophical and cultural movement stressing people's innate ability to discover religious truth outside the bounds of Christianity, will dominate American thought for a decade. In addition to Emerson, its champions include Henry David Thoreau, Margaret Fuller, Bronson Alcott, and, for a time, Orestes Brownson.

1838   Following the economic collapse of their Kirtland, Ohio, community, Joseph Smith and his followers flee to western Missouri, where Smith plans to build the city of Zion at Independence.

1839   John Humphrey Noyes founds the Putney Community in Vermont, a group that preaches the communism it believes existed in the early Christian church.

Persecuted by Missourians, Joseph Smith takes his Mormon followers to Nauvoo, Illinois.

German immigrants in Perry County, Missouri, form the nucleus of what will become the Lutheran Church–Missouri Synod.

1840   In Alaska, Russian priest John Veniaminov becomes the first Orthodox bishop to serve in the Americas.

1843   The Methodist Episcopal church splits over the issue of slavery. The abolitionists form the Wesleyan Methodist church.

1844   Joseph Smith, the founder of Mormonism, and his brother Hyrum are murdered by a mob at the Carthage, Illinois, jail. Brigham Young, the senior Mormon apostle, succeeds Smith as president of the church.

Orestes Brownson, after a spiritual pilgrimage that takes him from Presbyterianism through Unitarianism and Transcendentalism to his own Church of the Future, is baptized a Roman Catholic in Boston. Until his death in 1876, Brownson is America's leading Catholic journalist and lay apologist.

1845   Splitting with their northern brethren over the issue of slavery, Baptists in the South form the Southern Baptist Convention. By the 1990s, the SBC is the largest Protestant church body in the United States.

1847   Under the leadership of Brigham Young, the Mormons migrate again, this time to the western frontier, where they found Salt Lake City, Utah, as a religious community.

Liberal Congregational theologian Horace Bushnell publishes *Christian Nurture*, a precursor of Protestant modernism.

THE LAND OF UTOPIA

From the time of its discovery, the New World has held the promise of a fresh start. Blessed with an abundance of land and imposing few restraints on religion America has been the home to many utopian communities, idealistic if impractical attempts to perfect human nature in a harmonious society.

Among the first utopian groups was the Shakers, whose founder, Mother Ann Lee, settled in Watervliet, New York, in 1774. Her followers, who believed she was the second coming of Christ, lived a celibate life in communities where the sexes were strictly separated and all property was held in common. At the height of their popularity in the 1840s, the Shakers supported 19 communities in eight states and had about 6,000 adherents. Shaker worship, at first ecstatic, with trances, dancing, and shouting announcing the presence of the Holy Spirit, later became ritualized, with ordered singing and dancing. Although only a few Shakers survive today, the Shaker legacy survives on the simple, beautiful, and well-crafted furniture and other products they made, which today are highly prized by collectors and are often reproduced.

Central New York produced several other notable experimental communities. In 1848, the radical social reformer John Humphrey Noyes moved his community from Vermont to the town of Oneida, New York. Like the Shakers, Noyes was interested in reshaping relations between men and women, but instead of celibacy, his followers practiced a complex system of communal marriage that shocked the outside world. The Oneida Community, which numbered more than 300 at its height, was successful commercially and agriculturally but broke apart in 1881. Oneida Silver, a company Noyes founded, still survives.

The Mormons, also born in central New York, also sought to be a utopian community in the early days of their existence. In planned communities like Nauvoo and Salt Lake City, they practiced polygamy and shared economic resources. Although they have survived and prospered as a church, their dreams of building a Western Zion were undermined by the gold rush of 1849, further weakened during the Civil War, and finally ended when polygamists were disenfranchised by Congress in 1882.

In 1842 a group of German Pietists, the Community of True Inspiration, immigrated to New York. They founded a village near Buffalo. Fleeing urban corruption, they moved to Iowa between 1855 and 1864, establishing seven villages as the Amana Society. In 1932, internal strife and outside pressure resulted in the dissolution of the community. Its assets, in the form of shares in a new corporation, were divided among the members. It is now best known as a manufacturer of kitchen appliances.

In 1805, another German immigrant, George Rapp, sought to build a cooperative, celibate community in Harmony in western Pennsylvania. In 1814, the community moved to New Harmony in southern Indiana. In 1824, Rapp and his followers sold the village to the industrialist Robert Owen and moved back to Pennsylvania. Owen tried to build a "Community of Equality" at New Harmony, but communal living ended in 1827. Today New Harmony's 26 historic buildings have been restored.

Brook Farm, a 200-acre farm in Roxbury, Massachusetts, was founded by George Ripley and 17 others in 1841. Its visitors and members included many leading Transcendentalists, including Emerson, Thoreau, and Bronson Alcott. In 1844, Brook Farm came under the influence of the French socialist Charles Fourier. It was disbanded after a fire in 1847.

Despite their failure to survive in their communal form, these remarkable movements have left their mark on American culture.

1848	John Humphrey Noyes establishes his Perfectionist Community in Oneida, New York.
	Mysterious rappings are heard in the house of the Fox family in Hydesville, New York, initiating spiritualism, the belief that the living can contact the spirits of the dead through mediums.
1852	The Reorganized Church of Jesus Christ of Latter-day Saints is established. Rejecting the leadership of Brigham Young and such Mormon doctrines as polygamy, it is headquartered at Independence, Missouri.
1853	Isaac Mayer Wise becomes rabbi of Congregation Bene Yesherun in Cincinnati, Ohio. Committed to the transformation of Judaism, Wise publishes a revised prayerbook, *Minhag America* (American Ritual), and discontinues observance of the dietary laws and other traditional Jewish practices.
1854	James Augustine Healy is ordained as the first African-American Roman Catholic priest; in 1875, he will become a bishop.
1858	The United Presbyterian Church of North America is founded.
	Isaac Hecker, a convert from Transcendentalism to Roman Catholicism, founds the Paulist Fathers.
1859	*On the Origin of Species* by Charles Darwin makes the scientific argument for evolution.
c. 1861	The Old School Presbyterian church splits over slavery. The proslavery forces reorganize as the Presbyterian Church in the Confederate States of America.
1863	The Seventh-day Adventist church, which believes in the imminent second coming of Christ and observes Saturday as the sabbath, is founded in Battle Creek, Michigan, by followers of religious leader William Miller.
	President Abraham Lincoln begins the practice of annual Thanksgiving Days.
1866	Mary Baker Eddy begins teaching the Christian Science form of faith healing.
1867	The first collection of African-American spirituals, *Slave Songs of the United States*, is published.

1870s   The Holiness movement sweeps through American Protestantism. Growing out of the Methodist churches, the movement teaches that "entire sanctification," complete surrender to God, is possible for believers in this life.

1870   The Colored Methodist Episcopal church is established and soon becomes the Christian Methodist Episcopal Church, South.

1872   Bible teacher Charles Russell, who will later found the Jehovah's Witnesses, announces that Christ will return in 1874 without anyone being aware of his presence.

1875   Mary Baker Eddy publishes *Science and Health with Key to the Scriptures*, an explanation of her theology.

Dwight Moody begins his American revival tour after successfully converting thousands in Britain.

The Theosophical Society, which combines occultism and spiritualism with elements of Eastern religion, is founded in New York by Helena Blavatsky and Henry S. Olcott.

1876   Felix Adler founds the Ethical Culture Society.

1879   The Supreme Court, upholding the antipolygamy law, rules that religion cannot be used as a defense against behavior that is criminal or even morally offensive to most persons.

Mary Baker Eddy formally founds the Church of Christ (Scientist).

Mary Baker Eddy

1880   The Salvation Army begins its work in the United States.

1880-   When pogroms threaten their existence in Russia and Eastern Europe, many Jews immi-
1917   grate to the United States.

1883   Nonkosher food is served at the banquet celebrating the first graduating class at Hebrew Union College in Cincinnati; in the aftermath, more traditional Jews separate themselves from the Reform movement, eventually forming Conservative Judaism.

1884   The Third Plenary Council of Baltimore begins the intensive development of Roman Catholic parochial schools in response to the influx of Catholic immigrants and the spread of secular education.

      Charles Russell founds the Zion's Watch Tower Tract Society.

1887   The Jewish Theological Seminary, the first institution of Conservative Judaism, is founded in New York.

1890   The Mormons officially disown the practice of polygamy so that Utah can become a state, which it does in 1896.

1895   Billy Sunday, an enormously popular revivalist, begins his preaching career, and a third wave of revivalism sweeps the country.

      The National Baptist Convention, U.S.A. is organized to accommodate the growing number of black Baptist churches that form in the aftermath of the Civil War.

1897   The Rabbi Isaac Elchanan Theological Seminary is founded to train rabbis for Orthodox Jewish congregations.

1898   Gideons International is founded by traveling salesmen John Nicholson and Sam Hill in Boscobel, Wisconsin. Ten years later the Gideons will have placed 25 Bibles in hotel rooms in Montana; 75 years later, at their peak, they will be placing 16 million Bibles in hotel rooms every year.

1900   The Roman Catholic church in the United States has 12 million members, and there are 6 million Methodists, 5 million Baptists, 1.5 million Lutherans, 1.5 million Presbyterians, and 1 million Jews.

1901   The American Standard Version of the Bible is published. Based on the King James version of 1611, it will be recognized by most Protestant denominations.

      The Pentecostal movement is born when the "gift of tongues," ecstatic speech, breaks out at Charles Fox Parham's Bible school in Topeka, Kansas. Parham identifies speaking in tongues as the primary sign of Spirit baptism.

1906   William J. Seymour begins the Azusa Street Revival in Los Angeles and the Pentecostal movement spreads across the country.

1907   Walter Rauschenbusch publishes *Christianity and Social Crisis*, the major work of the Social Gospel movement that seeks to apply Christ's teachings to social problems.

1908   Mary Baker Eddy founds *The Christian Science Monitor*, a daily newspaper.

      The Church of the Nazarene, the largest to grow from the Holiness movement, is formed through the union of several Holiness church bodies.

      Thirty-three Protestant denominations with 18 million members form the Federal Council of Churches, the precursor of the National Council of Churches.

1909   C. I. Scofield publishes *The Scofield Reference Bible*, which codifies the teachings of premillennial dispensationalism, and makes a powerful impact on the nascent fundamentalist movement.

1916   Stephen Wise, a prominent Reform rabbi, organizes the American Jewish Congress to respond to pogroms in eastern Poland.

1917-
1919
World War I stimulates cooperation among churches.

1918   Evangelist Aimee Semple McPherson begins her radio broadcasts.

1919   Father Divine organizes an evangelical communal colony on Sayville, Long Island, devoted to renunciation of personal property and racial equality.

1922   Mordecai Kaplan founds the Society for the Advancement of Judaism and begins to write about Judaism as a culture rather than a religion, thus laying the foundation for the Reconstructionist movement.

1923   Pentecostal preacher Aimee Semple McPherson builds the Angelus Temple in Los Angeles, whose large rotating illuminated cross can be seen for 50 miles.

The Auburn Affirmation, a liberal protest against enforced orthodoxy, is signed by 1,300 Presbyterian ministers.

J. Gresham Machen of the Princeton Theological Seminary, the intellectual leader of fundamentalism, publishes *Christianity and Liberalism*, his most influential work. In 1929, he leaves Princeton to found Westminster Theological Seminary in Philadelphia.

1926   Father Charles Coughlin, a Catholic priest in Royal Oak, Michigan, broadcasts his first radio show. By 1930, he has turned to politics, and attracts an audience of some 40 million. During the 1930s, he becomes increasingly anti-Semitic and anti-Roosevelt. In 1942, he is silenced by the bishop of Detroit.

1930s   The Black Muslims begin to gain a following under W. D. Fard and Elijah Muhammad, in Detroit, Michigan.

1932   Reinhold Niebuhr's book *Moral Man and Immoral Society* is published.

1933   Dorothy Day, founder of the national Catholic Worker movement, publishes *The Catholic Worker*, a newspaper that weds religious feeling to radical politics.

1939   Three branches of Methodism—The Methodist Episcopal church; the Methodist Episcopal church, South; and the Methodist Protestant church—unite.

1940   In a case involving the Jehovah's Witnesses, the Supreme Court decides that the states must extend and protect all the rights regarding religion guaranteed under the First Amendment.

1948   Thomas Merton, an ascetic Trappist monk and author, publishes *The Seven Storey Mountain*, his autobiography.

1949   Evangelical leader Billy Graham holds his first tent crusade in Los Angeles and converts some prominent Hollywood stars.

1950s   The fourth (and present-day) wave of religious revivalism begins.

1950   Twenty-five Protestant and four Eastern Orthodox groups, with membership totaling 33 million, form the National Council of Churches.

1952   The Revised Standard Version of the Bible, based on the King James version of 1611, is introduced.

1953   The Church of Scientology, which believes people are immortal, is founded in Washington, D.C., by L. Ron Hubbard, best-selling author of *Dianetics: The Modern Science of Mental Health*.

1954   By order of President Dwight Eisenhower, the words "under God" are added to the Pledge of Allegiance.

Oral Roberts, an itinerant faith healer and evangelist, begins to broadcast his healing services on television.

1955   The Presbyterian church becomes the first mainline Protestant denomination to approve the ordination of women.

Martin Luther King, Jr., leads the Montgomery bus boycott, the first battle in the modern civil rights struggle.

1956   The Methodist church, at its annual conference, becomes the first mainkine Protestant denomination to ban racial segregation.

1957   Martin Luther King, Jr., becomes president of the Southern Christian Leadership Conference.

The United Church of Christ is formed by the merger of the Evangelical and Reformed church and the Congregational Christian churches.

1960s- In the wake of the changes introduced by the Second Vatican Council and the renewed
1970s   condemnation of artificial contraception by Pope Paul VI, issues of sexuality increasingly come to preoccupy American Catholics.

1961   Universalist and Unitarian churches merge.

1962   The Supreme Court decides that mandated prayer in the public schools is unconstitutional.

THE ESTABLISHMENT CLAUSE

The United States is one of the few nations to try to institutionalize freedom of religion. Other countries guarantee and protect the right to practice religion freely, but no other country has expended the time and energy the United States has on maintaining what Thomas Jefferson called a "wall of separation between church and state."

The earliest bill mandating separation, which Thomas Jefferson called his proudest achievement, was a Bill for Establishing Religious Freedom, introduced in 1776 even though another ten years would be required to pass it.

Jefferson was not without his reasons for believing that the new nation needed laws regarding the establishment of religion. In 1776, 9 of the 13 colonies had established religions. Massachusetts, Rhode Island, and New Hampshire supported Congregationalism and, Jefferson's bill notwithstanding, continued to do so well into the 19th century. In New York and the southern colonies, the Anglican faith (later Episcopalianism) was established. New York required officeholders to renounce the Pope, and even Pennsylvania, otherwise a bastion of religious freedom, required elected officials to sign an oath subscribing to their belief in the Scriptures. There were patriots, among them Patrick Henry, who wanted an official state religion to be paid for with tax moneys.

Eventually Jefferson's establishment bill (or disestablishment bill, as it might more properly have been called) was codified in the Bill of Rights, specifically in the First Amendment, which reads, in part: "Congress shall make no law respecting an establishment of religion, nor prohibiting the free exercise thereof."

In truth, though, the wall that Jefferson tried so hard to build is permeable and at times blurry, more like what James Madison described as a "line of separation between the rights of religion and civil authority." For example, churches are traditionally exempt from paying taxes, yet the taxpayers support military chaplains. Since the 1940s, the Supreme Court has regularly and continuously been called upon to settle various religious disputes such as, for example, whether federal moneys can be used to bus children to parochial schools (they can), whether Nativity scenes and other religious symbols can be displayed on public property (they can), and whether the Ten Commandments can be posted in public schools (they cannot).

Perhaps the greatest accomplishment of the nation is not that it has built a wall or drawn a line between church and state but that it has displayed such an amazing amount of flexibility on the subject.

1963   Martin Luther King, Jr., leads the March on Washington, a cleric-inspired protest against the denial of civil rights to millions of black Americans.

In a second decision, the Supreme Court bans Bible reading in public schools.

1963   The Roman Catholic liturgy is changed in the United States to include the use of some English.

1965   Elijah Muhammad publishes *Message to the Black Man in America*, a religious treatise on the Nation of Islam.

Faith healer Oral Roberts opens Oral Roberts University in Tulsa, Oklahoma.

1966   The International Society for Krishna Consciousness, which appeals to many American youths, is founded in New York by Swami Prabhupada, a Calcutta Hindu scholar and teacher.

The Methodist church and the United Church of the Brethren unite to form the United Methodist church.

1967   Presbyterians adopt their first new confession since 1647.

1970s   Cults, such as that headed by Korean reverend Sun Myung Moon, win thousands of converts, especially among the young. Moon's financial empire is vast; he publishes a conservative newspaper called the *Washington Times* and owns and operates many retail businesses. When he stages huge mass wedding ceremonies for members whose mates the church has selected, some parents protest and hire private detectives to kidnap and deprogram their "Moonie" children, whom they view as brainwashed.

1970   The entire Roman Catholic Mass is now said in the vernacular.

The Supreme Court validates the right of religious organizations to remain tax-exempt.

1971   The Supreme Court rules that federal funds cannot be used to support parochial schools.

1972   Four Episcopal bishops defy church law to ordain 11 women priests.

The first woman rabbi is ordained by the Reformed branch of Judaism.

1973   The Conservative branch of Judaism permits women to be counted when forming a quorum for worship.

In the aftermath of *Roe v. Wade*, the Roman Catholic church begins to mount organized opposition to abortion.

1974   Jim Bakker founds the Praise the Lord (PTL) ministry, which will become, ten years later, a multimillion-dollar telemedia religious organization.

1975   Pope Paul VI canonizes Elizabeth Seton, the first U.S.-born Catholic saint.

1978   Following a U.S. government investigation into allegations of abuse of congregants, followers of San Francisco clergyman Jim Jones of the People's Temple flee to Guyana, where 911 persons commit mass suicide by drinking Kool-Aid laced with cyanide.

1979   The Moral Majority is founded in Lynchburg, Virginia, by Baptist minister Jerry Falwell. It is the first evangelical group to become politically active, advocating conservative moral and political positions.

Reaching an audience of more than 20 million, approximately 1,400 radio stations and 30 television stations are dedicated to religious programming.

1980s   After several centuries of domination by the mainstream Protestant churches, more Christians now belong to evangelical churches than to mainstream Protestant churches.

1980s–   Brought together in the Right to Life movement, evangelical and Roman Catholic conser-
1990s   vatives begin to cooperate more broadly in the political arena.

1983   The two branches of the Presbyterian church (the United Presbyterian Church of North America and the Presbyterian Church of the United States), which split over slavery, merge to form the Presbyterian Church (U.S.A.).

Jim and Tammy Bakker

The Supreme Court denies tax-exempt status to private religiously affiliated universities that practice racial discrimination.

Northern and southern Presbyterians unite in the Presbyterian Church (U.S.A.).

1985   The Conservative branch of Judaism ordains its first woman rabbi.

1987   Televangelist Jim Bakker resigns his pulpit after confessing that he cheated on his wife with a church secretary and then used church money to buy the secretary's silence.

1988   Assembly of God televangelist Jimmy Swaggart is defrocked after he confesses to having sexual relations with a prostitute. Ordered to stay off television for one year, he is back on the airwaves after three months.

The Reverend Jerry Falwell resigns from the Moral Majority in the wake of the scandal involving Jim and Tammy Bakker and the PTL Club.

The Lutheran Church in America, the American Lutheran church, and the Association of Evangelical Lutheran Churches merge to form the Evangelical Lutheran church in America.

1993   The Supreme Court invalidates a local Florida law that bans the use of animals in religious rites but still permits hunting and fishing.

1997   Episcopalians and Lutherans vote on a concordat providing intercommunion between the Episcopal church and the Evangelical Lutheran church in America.

RELIGIONS FOUNDED IN AMERICA

Although several religions are closely identified with America—Puritanism, Shakerism, and Methodism come to mind—these were actually founded in England, and their followers came here to escape persecution. What follows is a list of purely indigenous American religions. Some flared only briefly before burning out, while others proved to be enduring. The religions are as idiosyncratic as Americans themselves, and if they share anything in common, it is only that each, in its own unique way, seems to speak to our national character.

1819   William Ellery Channing publishes *Unitarian Christianity*. Unitarians reject the traditional Christian doctrine of the Trinity. The American Unitarian Association is founded in Boston in 1825.

1830   The Church of Jesus Christ of Latter-day Saints is founded by Joseph Smith in Fayette, New York. After suffering much persecution, Mormons will eventually migrate to Utah.

1839   John Humphrey Noyes founds the Putney Community in Vermont. The group hopes to duplicate the free love and communism it believes existed in early Christian communities. It moves to Oneida, New York, in 1848, but dies out within a few years.

1863   The Seventh-day Adventist church, which believes in the imminent second coming of Christ, is founded in Battle Creek, Michigan.

1866   Mary Baker Eddy begins preaching the teachings of what will become the Christian Science religion, which practices faith healing. In 1879 she establishes the Church of Christ (Scientist).

1872   Jehovah's Witnesses, a millennialist group, is organized in Pittsburgh by Congregationalist minister Charles Russell.

1876   The Ethical Culture Society, or the Ethical movement, which believes that all societies share an ethical culture that is not necessarily religious in its origins, is founded by Felix Adler in New York City.

1922   The Reconstructionist movement in Judaism, the only Jewish denomination that originated entirely in America, is founded by Mordecai Kaplan.

1930s   The Black Muslims, also known as the Nation of Islam—a black nationalist group that adheres to the principles of Islam—is founded in Detroit by W. D. Fard.

RELIGION AND HIGHER EDUCATION

Many of the oldest and most important universities and colleges in the country were established by religious denominations.

Year	College/University	City, State	Denomination
1636	Harvard University (founded as Harvard College)	Cambridge, Massachusetts	Congregational
1693	College of William and Mary	Williamsburg, Virginia	Anglican
1701	Yale University (founded as the Collegiate School)	New Haven, Connecticut	Congregational
1746	Princeton University (founded as the College of New Jersey)	Princeton, New Jersey	Presbyterian
1754	Columbia University (founded as King's College)	New York, New York	Anglican

Year	College/University	City, State	Denomination
1764	Brown University (founded as Rhode Island College)	Providence, Rhode Island	Baptist
1769	Dartmouth College	Hanover, New Hampshire	Congregational
1787	Cokesbury College	Abingdon, Maryland	Methodist
1789	Georgetown University	Washington, D.C.	Roman Catholic
1813	Colby College	Waterville, Maine	Baptist
1842	University of Notre Dame	South Bend, Indiana	Roman Catholic
1875	Brigham Young University	Provo, Utah	Mormon
1891	University of Chicago	Chicago, Illinois	Baptist
1910	Southern Methodist University	Dallas, Texas	Methodist

AFRICAN AMERICANS AND RELIGION

The relationship between Christianity and African Americans is a unique and fascinating aspect of American history. At first denied the right to practice either their own African faiths or the Christianity that prevailed in America, blacks were later alternately welcomed and rejected by various Protestant denominations. In the years before the Civil War, many Protestant clergymen supported slavery from their pulpits. After the Civil War, black clergy, who had always been influential in American culture, formed their own churches, which quickly became the backbone of many black communities. During the 1950s and 1960s, these churches spearheaded the civil rights movement.

1730s–1770 The Great Awakening prompts the conversion of many blacks, most of whom are slaves. Blacks and whites worship together.

1780s African Americans George Liele and David George become the first American missionaries when they found churches in, respectively, Jamaica and Sierra Leone.

1794 In Philadelphia, two important and influential black churches are founded: The Bethel African Methodist church by Richard Allen and the St. Thomas African Episcopal church by Absalom Jones.

1800s Black churches form throughout the North. In the South, as slaveowners react to their fears about letting their slaves assemble, slaves are sometimes permitted to worship in groups and sometimes denied the right to do so.

1808 The Abyssinian Baptist church, which will become one of the most influential houses of worship in Harlem and at times nationally, is founded. It will one day be the home pulpit of Adam Clayton Powell, Sr., and, briefly, Adam Clayton Powell, Jr.

1809 The first black Baptist church is founded in Philadelphia. Black Baptists will soon become one of the largest Protestant denominations.

1816 The African Methodist Episcopal church, the first major black denomination, is established by Richard Allen.

1829 Although few African Americans have been exposed to Roman Catholicism, and thus few have converted, a black order, the Oblate Sisters of Providence, is founded.

1842 A second African-American Roman Catholic order, the Holy Family Sisters, is founded.

1854 James Augustine Healy is the first African American ordained as a Roman Catholic priest.

1863–1865 Northern missionaries follow the Union army into the South and convert many of the newly freed slaves to Protestantism. Many blacks join white churches.

1870   The Colored Methodist Episcopal church is founded by blacks who leave the predominantly white Methodist Church, South.

During Reconstruction, blacks are driven out of the white churches and found their own. Some black denominations such as the African Methodist Episcopal church promote the return to Africa, but few choose to do this. Out of this movement comes, however, a commitment on the part of the black churches to build missions and seek converts in Africa.

Late 1870s   The majority of blacks have withdrawn from white churches to establish their own. The primary denominations are the African Methodist Episcopal church and the black Baptist churches.

1875   James Augustine Healy becomes the first American Catholic black bishop and presides for 25 years over a diocese that includes Maine and Rhode Island.

1890s-   Large numbers of southern blacks emigrate to northern cities, where many are converted to
1920s   Roman Catholicism. Black enrollment in parochial schools increases.

Black sects of Islam and Judaism begin to form.

1895   The National Baptist Convention of the U.S.A. is formed by the merger of the Foreign Mission Baptist convention of the U.S.A., the American Baptist Convention, and the Baptist National Education Convention. It is the largest of the African-American churches.

1900   The African-American churches that have formed in the wake of the Civil War are, and will remain, a major influence in black cultural and social life. Of 8.3 million blacks, the census shows that 2.7 are affiliated with a black church.

1906   William J. Seymour, a black preacher, leads multiracial congregations in the Azusa Street Revival in Los Angeles and thus starts the Pentecostal movement, which will become known for its members' ability to speak in tongues.

1930s-   From their pulpits, black clergy begin to mobilize their congregants for the civil rights
1960s   movement.

1955   Baptist minister Martin Luther King, Jr., organizes the Montgomery, Alabama, bus boycott, which in turn sets off the nationwide civil rights movement. An advocate of nonviolence, King will remain, until his assassination in 1968, the preeminent black civil rights leader.

1957   Martin Luther King, Jr., Bayard Rustin, and black ministers form the Southern Christian Leadership Conference (SCLC), which will play a major role in coordinating the work of black churches during the civil rights movement.

1960s   Elijah Muhammad, the head of the Nation of Islam, calls for the creation of an all-black nation-within-a-nation. As black militants denounce Christianity as a white religion, Malcolm X, a charismatic Muslim leader, is able to convert many blacks to the Nation of Islam. Black Muslims, who number about 100,000, support 33 temples.

1964   Malcolm X breaks with the Nation of Islam to found the Organization for Afro-American Unity, a splinter group of Black Muslims.

1965   Malcolm X is assassinated at a religious rally in New York City.

1968   Martin Luther King, Jr., is assassinated in Memphis, Tennessee.

1975   Elijah Muhammad, the moving force behind the Nation of Islam, dies in Chicago.

1989   In Massachusetts, Barbara Harris, an African American, becomes the first woman bishop of the Episcopal church.

1990   The census shows that black Baptists are the fourth-largest U.S. denomination, with 8.7 million members.

George Stallings, a dissident Roman Catholic, breaks with the church to found the African-American Catholic church.

1991   Mary Ann Coffey becomes the first black and the first woman to head the National Conference of Christians and Jews.

SUPREME COURT DECISIONS AFFECTING RELIGION

1879   *Reynolds v. United States.* In a ruling that some would argue does not protect religious interests, the Court decides polygamy is illegal even though Mormons claim it is their religious right. The Court reasons that criminal or even morally offensive practices conducted under the auspices of religion are not protected by the First Amendment.

1940   *Cantwell v. Connecticut.* The protection of the First Amendment extends to the practices of state governments.

1948   *McCollum v. Board of Education.* In a case in which students are released from regular classes to attend religious ones taught in the public schools by public-school teachers, the Court finds that public schools and public moneys cannot be used to teach religion, nor can religion be promoted in the public schools.

1952   *Zorach v. Clauson.* The Court validates the right of students to receive religious education, off public-school property, during the school day.

1962   *Engel v. Vitale.* In an 8–1 decision the Court finds denominational or nondenominational prayer in schools an unacceptable breach of church-state separation.

1963   *School District of Abington v. Schempp.* The Supreme Court expands its ban on school prayer to include Bible reading.

1968   *Board of Education of Central School District No. 1 v. Allen.* The Court decides that tax moneys can be used to buy textbooks in parochial schools because the benefit goes to students and not to any religion.

1970   *Walz v. Tax Commission.* The Court reaffirms the exclusion of church property from taxation.

1972   *Cruz v. Beto.* The Court rules that prisoners have a right to practice their religions while incarcerated.

1981   *Thomas v. Review Board of the Indiana Employment Security Division.* In a decision that affirms the right of the legal system to protect religious beliefs, a Seventh-day Adventist woman who was fired for refusing to work on Saturdays is found to be entitled to unemployment benefits.

1983   *Bob Jones University v. United States.* The Court denies tax-exempt status to private schools practicing racial discrimination.

1984   *Lynch v. Donnelly.* A city is not showing a preference for one religion when it maintains a customary Christmas display of a Nativity scene on public property.

1985   *Wallace v. Jaffree.* The Court rules that Alabama's "moment of silence" in school classrooms is a violation of the First Amendment.

1987   *Edwards v. Aguillard.* The Court rules that a Louisiana statute requiring schools that teach evolution to also teach "creation science," a biblical view of the origins of the universe, is a violation of the First Amendment.

1992   *Lee v. Weisman.* Officially sanctioned prayer at graduation ceremonies in public schools violates the establishment clause of the First Amendment.

1993   *Church of the Lukumi Babalu Aye v. City of Hialeah.* The Court overrules a local Florida law that bans the use of animals in religious rites.

SIGNIFICANT PEOPLE IN AMERICAN RELIGION

Adler, Felix (1851–1933).   Adler founded the Ethical Culture Society, or the Ethical movement, which holds that an ethical culture can exist in a society independent of religious beliefs. Under Adler's direction, the Ethical Culture Society took stands on labor relations, child welfare, and better services for the poor.

Allen, Richard (1760–1831).   Founder of the African Methodist Episcopal church and a prominent African-American clergyman, Allen, who was the son of slaves, organized the Free African Society, an important precursor to abolitionist and black self-reliance societies that became common in the mid-19th century. During the War of 1812 he led a group of blacks in the defense of Baltimore and probably kept the city from being burned by the British. In 1794 he founded Bethel Church, the first A.M.E. congregation, and in 1816, when the church was formally established, he became its first bishop. A statue of Allen, erected in Philadelphia's Fairmount Park, was the first public statue erected to honor a black American.

Asbury, Francis (1745–1816).   Asbury established the Methodist church in the United States. Following a format established by John Wesley in England, he introduced the circuit-rider system, which proved to be a highly effective way to preach on the frontier. Circuit-rider preachers routinely attended to as many as 20 to 40 congregations at a time, traveling on horseback among the communities assigned to them.

Beecher, Lyman (1775–1863).   A prominent Presbyterian and Congregational preacher and founder of the American Bible Society, Beecher was a leader in several liberal 19th-century reform movements, including abolitionism. He had 13 children, among them Harriet Beecher Stowe, Catharine Beecher, and Henry Ward Beecher.

Channing, William Ellery (1780–1842).   Founder of Unitarianism, a faith that does not accept the Christian doctrine of the Trinity, Channing also preached in favor of religious tolerance and against slavery. A noted author on social issues, he wielded influence over the Transcendentalists, including Ralph Waldo Emerson.

Chauncy, Charles (1705–1787).   A Congregational minister, Chauncy led the liberal opposition to the Great Awakening on grounds that revivalism was too emotional and irrational.

Day, Dorothy (1897–1980).   Day founded the Catholic Worker movement, which combined religious devotion with radical politics. She was a committed pacifist. With Peter Maurin, he started *The Catholic Worker* newspaper in 1933. Considered an outsider most of her life, by the time of her death Day was recognized as a significant religious leader.

Eddy, Mary Baker (1821–1910).   In 1879 Eddy established the Christian Science church, which believes that sickness is an illusion of "mortal mind" and rejects medical treatment. In 1908 she began publishing *The Christian Science Monitor*, a widely respected newspaper still published today.

Edwards, Jonathan (1703–1758).   Considered by many to be the greatest religious thinker produced by America, Edwards was a seminal force in the First Great Awakening. An exponent of orthodox Calvinism, Edwards used the resources of the new learning to argue for his views. In *A Treatise Concerning Religious Affections*, he defended the role of experience and feeling in religious life. In 1757, he became president of the College of New Jersey, later Princeton University. In 1758, believing in the efficacy of the newly introduced smallpox inoculation, he allowed himself to be inoculated and died of the resulting complications. A multifaceted and subtle thinker and writer, he is unfortunately remembered chiefly for his powerful (and uncharacteristic) sermon, "Sinners in the Hands of an Angry God."

Father Divine (1878–1965). Born George Baker, Father Divine established an evangelical communal colony on Sayville, Long Island, from which he held forth, preaching a renunciation of personal property and racial equality, for 45 years. He established 170 missions, or "heavens," for his largely African-American followers.

Graham, Billy (1918–). A prominent and widely respected Southern Baptist minister and author, Graham took American revivalism abroad by leading highly successful international evangelical crusades. He also used radio and television to convey his message of redemption. His books include *Peace with God* (1953), *World Aflame* (1965), and *Answers to Life's Problems* (1988).

Hutchinson, Anne (1591–1643). An influential Puritan lay leader and midwife at a time when women rarely spoke out regarding church affairs, Hutchinson is best known for her role in the Antinomian Controversy, a theological crisis that occurred between 1636 and 1638. She and her supporters argued that working hard and living a moral life did not, as most Puritans advocated, provide evidence of election. She also seemed to believe that a person could have immediate knowledge of his or her salvation. Tried and excommunicated for her beliefs, Hutchinson left the Massachusetts Bay Colony and founded Portsmouth, Rhode Island.

Kaplan, Mordecai (1881–1983). A rabbi, Kaplan originated Reconstructionist Judaism, which holds that Judaism is an evolving religion and culture, and that people, not Scripture, determine its practices. He founded the Society for Advancement of Judaism, the major Reconstructionist umbrella organization.

King, Martin Luther, Jr. (1929–1968). A moving force behind the civil rights movement in the United States, Reverend King insisted on nonviolent reform. Using his Dexter Street Baptist Church as his base of operations, he and his followers launched the Montgomery (Alabama) bus boycott in 1955, which in turn led to the civil rights movement of the 1960s. He co-founded the Southern Christian Leadership Conference and led an important antiwar march on Washington in 1963, which culminated with his famous "I Have a Dream" speech at the Lincoln Memorial. King's death by assassination, along with that of President John F. Kennedy and his brother Robert Kennedy, was one of three that deeply scarred the nation in the 1960s. He was awarded the Nobel Peace Prize in 1964.

Lee, Ann (1736–1784). A religious mystic, Lee brought the Shaker faith to America from England and founded its first community in 1776 in Watervliet, New York. When she died, her followers were severely disappointed, since they had believed she was immortal.

Makemie, Francis (1658–1708). An Irish-born minister, Makemie established the Presbyterian church in the United States. He preached up and down the East Coast, formed two Presbyterian churches in Maryland, and established the first presbytery in Philadelphia.

Malcolm X (1925–1965). This prominent Black Muslim leader initially demonized whites, but after visiting Mecca and learning that Islam preached equality of races, he changed his views. Malcolm X remained a staunch believer in self-help for blacks and advocated violence, only when necessary, as a form of self-defense. He is widely viewed as the father of the Black Power movement. After he broke away from Elijah Muhammad, he was assassinated, many believe, by other Muslims. His *Autobiography of Malcolm X* is widely read to this day.

Mather, Cotton (1663–1728). A prolific Puritan minister in the Massachusetts Bay Colony and the son of Increase Mather, he produced hundreds of sermons and at least several major books, among them *Magnalia Christi Americana* (1702), a religious history of New England, and *The Wonders of the Invisible World* (1693), a defense of the Salem witch trials. Apart from supporting the Salem trials, Mather was an enlightened man who liked to disseminate scientific information and who played an important role in introducing the smallpox vaccine to the colonies.

McPherson, Aimee Semple (1890–1944).   A charismatic faith healer and radio evangelist, McPherson developed a large following composed mostly of midwesterners and southerners who had recently immigrated to Southern California. She founded the International Church of Foursquare Gospel, and in 1923 she built the Angelus Temple in Los Angeles. After a mysterious disappearance and reemergence, coupled with a claim that she was kidnapped, McPherson was tried for fraud and acquitted. Other charges were later brought against her for other business dealings. She died from an overdose of sleeping medicine.

Merton, Thomas (1915–1968).   A Trappist monk, Merton was also a religious theorist, scholar, author, and social critic. He was one of the first Christians to see a connection between Eastern and Western religions. The son of an Australian father and an American mother, Merton only gradually became interested in religion. In 1941, he entered a Trappist monastery, largely because of the order's vows of silence and solitude. Merton's autobiography, *The Seven Storey Mountain* (1948), became a best-seller.

Moody, Dwight (1837–1899).   A prominent evangelist, Moody ran what may have been the first transcontinental revival campaigns, encompassing both the United States and England. Studiedly nondenominational, he converted millions in the last decades of the 19th century, who were then told to join the denomination of their choice. Moody founded the Moody Bible Institute as well as a theological preparatory school, both in Chicago.

Muhammad, Elijah (1897–1975).   Under Elijah Poole, who took the name Elijah Muhammad, the Black Muslims first gained a large and significant following in Detroit. A follower of W. D. Fard, who founded the Nation of Islam, Muhammad founded the second Temple of Islam in Chicago, which became a prominent center for Black Muslim activities. When Fard mysteriously vanished at about the time the Chicago temple was founded, Muhammad became the sole leader of the religion. He published *Message to the Blackman*, a treatise on the religion, in 1964.

Niebuhr, Reinhold (1892–1971).   A prominent professor of Christian ethics, theologian-philosopher Niebuhr, after many years as a Detroit pastor, spent most of his professional career at Union Theological Seminary in New York City. Early in his career he despaired about his Protestant faith's ability to maintain moral rule and became a social activist. Later he returned to his faith and tried to confront the ways in which Christianity might accommodate contemporary issues. He was the author of *Moral Man and Immoral Society* (1932), *Christianity and Power Politics* (1940), and *The Nature and Destiny of Man* (1941–1943), as well as *The Structure of Nations and History* (1951).

Penn, William (1664–1718).   Penn created the Quaker state of Pennsylvania and founded the city of Philadelphia. A convert to Quakerism as a young man, Penn was jailed in England for his beliefs. While there he wrote *No Cross, No Crown*. He advocated religious tolerance and had hoped that Pennsylvania could become a utopian community that would welcome all religions.

Roberts, Oral (1918–).   One of the nation's leading faith healers and probably the first evangelical minister to amass a large congregation via television, Roberts founded Oral Roberts University in Tulsa, Oklahoma, a conservative fundamentalist school. He briefly became controversial in 1987 when he announced that God would take his life if he didn't receive $8 million in donations. He later claimed that goal was met.

Smith, Joseph (1805–1844).   Founder of the Church of Latter-day Saints, also known as the Mormon church, Smith began to organize the religion after undergoing a series of mystic visions, one of which included the appearance of an angel named Moroni who gave him the Book of Mormon, which Mormons today add to their Bible. In 1830 Smith established the Church of Jesus Christ of Latter-day Saints. Almost from the beginning he and his followers were persecuted for their beliefs and forced to move, first to western Missouri, then to Illinois, where Smith was jailed for treason. When he was hauled out of jail and killed by an anti-Mormon mob, he left behind 35,000 converts.

Sunday, Billy (William Ashley) (1862–1935). A popular evangelical preacher, Sunday employed highly dramatic (and high-pressure) tactics at his revival meetings. He began preaching in 1895 and reached the peak of his popularity during World War I. He preached in support of Prohibition and was also associated with attempts to restrict immigration. Sunday sponsored more than 300 revival meetings in all major cities and had preached to 100 million people at the time of his death.

Williams, Roger (1603?–1683). The founder of Rhode Island and an influential colonial preacher, Williams was a religious dissenter who opposed both the Puritans and the Quakers and argued in favor of a personal God. He was an early supporter of religious tolerance and separation of church and state.

Winthrop, John (1588–1649). An influential Puritan minister and the founder of the Massachusetts Bay Colony, Winthrop presided over the Antinomian crisis and was the chief persecutor of Anne Hutchinson. Like many Puritans, he believed America could be a model of a godly society, a view he articulated in his most famous sermon, "The Model of Christian Charity."

Wise, Isaac Mayer (1819–1900). Founder of the Union of American Hebrew Congregations, the Hebrew Union College, and the Central Conference of American Rabbis, Rabbi Wise was a major influence on the shape and growth of Reform Judaism in the United States. Wise, who headed a congregation in Cincinnati, was an assimilationist who believed Jews should not be bound by what he viewed as archaic religious laws.

Young, Brigham (1801–1877). After inheriting the leadership of the Mormon church from Joseph Smith, Young greatly enlarged the membership, was a major force in shaping it theologically, and in 1846 and 1847 led the Mormon migration to their permanent settlement in Utah. He helped to found Salt Lake City and also served as Utah's territorial governor.

ADDITIONAL SOURCES OF INFORMATION

Frazier, E. Franklin. *The Negro Church in America*. Rev. ed. Schocken, 1974.

Handy, Robert. *A History of the Churches in the United States and Canada*. Oxford University Press, 1977.

Herberg, Will. *Protestant, Catholic, Jew: An Essay in American Religious Sociology*. Doubleday, 1955.

Lesser, M. X. *Jonathan Edwards*. Macmillan, 1988.

Lincoln, C. E., and L. H. Mamiya. *The Black Church in the African-American Experience*. Duke University Press, 1990.

Middlekauff, Robert. *The Mathers: Three Generations of Puritan Intellectuals, 1596–1728*. Oxford University Press, 1971.

Neuhaus, Richard John. *The Naked Public Square: Religion and Democracy in America*. Eerdmans, 1984.

Noll, Mark. *A History of Christianity in the United States and Canada*. Eerdmans, 1992.

Queen, Edward L., Stephen R. Prothero, and Gardiner H. Shattuck, Jr., eds. *The Encyclopedia of American Religious History*. Facts on File, 1996.

Rosten, Leo. ed. *Religions in America*. Simon & Schuster, 1975.

14

American Culture

SIGNIFICANT EVENTS IN AMERICAN LITERATURE

1650   Poet Anne Bradstreet, a Puritan housewife, publishes *The Tenth Muse Lately Sprung Up in America*, considered by many to be the best of Puritan literature.

1747   Jonathan Edwards delivers his sermon "Sinners in the Hands of an Angry God," perhaps his most famous sermon. Essays and sermons by Puritan preachers are the primary literature of the colonies.

1773   Phillis Wheatley, an African-American slave, publishes *Poems on Various Subjects*.

1776   Thomas Paine, in *Common Sense*, produces some of the finest political discourse in the colonies.

1800   The Library of Congress is established.

1820   Washington Irving's *Sketch Book* is published, with two classic American tales: "The Legend of Sleepy Hollow" and "Rip Van Winkle."

1823   James Fenimore Cooper begins publishing the Leatherstocking Tales. The most popular and enduring novels of the series are *The Deerslayer* and *The Last of the Mohicans*.

1836   Ralph Waldo Emerson states the principles of Transcendentalism in his essay *Nature*.

1837   Ralph Waldo Emerson's "The American Scholar," a Phi Beta Kappa speech at Harvard, calls for a distinctly American literature.

1841   Ralph Waldo Emerson begins a seminal series, called *Essays*, which is published in the literary journal *The Dial*. In them are "The Over-Soul," "Self-Reliance," and "Compensation."

1843   With "Murders in the Rue Morgue," Edgar Allan Poe creates modern detective stories.

1850   Nathaniel Hawthorne publishes *The Scarlet Letter*.

1851   Herman Melville publishes *Moby-Dick*, perhaps the first enduring masterpiece of American literature; it is a symbolic story of life on a whaling vessel.

1854   Henry David Thoreau's *Walden* is published, a treatise on nature and self-reliance.

1855   Walt Whitman anonymously publishes *Leaves of Grass*.

1884   Satirist Mark Twain publishes the book that is widely regarded as his masterpiece, *The Adventures of Huckleberry Finn*. It and *Tom Sawyer*, published in 1876, influence writers as diverse as William Faulkner and Ernest Hemingway.

1885   William Dean Howells publishes *The Rise of Silas Lapham*.

1886   Henry James publishes one of his early realistic novels, *The Bostonians*.

1890   Emily Dickinson's poems are collected, and published, after her death.

1895   Stephen Crane publishes his masterpiece, a searing novel about the Civil War, *The Red Badge of Courage*.

1900   Theodore Dreiser's *Sister Carrie* shocks the public.

1903   Henry James produces the first of his great psychological novels, *The Ambassadors*.

1905   Edith Wharton in *The House of Mirth* produces a riveting psychological examination of class in America.

1913   Willa Cather tries out her sparse prose style in *O Pioneers!*

Herman Melville

1915   In *America's Coming of Age*, critic Van Wyck Brooks draws a distinction between "low-brow" and "high-brow" culture. This is both recognition of the fact that America now produces a literature that stands against the best in Europe and a bow to the popular mass culture that exists alongside it.

1921   Marianne Moore, a major poet of the era, publishes *Poems*.

1922   The first of the Harlem Renaissance writers to publish is Claude McKay, who writes *Harlem Shadows*. During the 1920s, Harlem writers, poets, journalists, intellectuals, artists, and musicians produce an expressive literary and artistic movement rooted in black culture.

         T. S. Eliot, an American expatriate who becomes a British subject, writes *The Waste Land*, a work that changes the face of poetry with its stark modernism.

1923   Wallace Stevens, one of the few American writers who never goes to Europe, publishes *Harmonium*, which contains most of his important poems.

         Harlem Renaissance novelist Jean Toomer publishes *Cane*.

         e. e. cummings's first volume of poetry, *tulips and chimneys*, is published.

         Ezra Pound publishes the first collection of his *Cantos*; he continues to work on this modern epic poem for the rest of his life.

1925   F. Scott Fitzgerald publishes *The Great Gatsby*, which many regard as his masterpiece.

1926   Ernest Hemingway publishes *The Sun Also Rises*.

1929   Ernest Hemingway writes *A Farewell to Arms*.

William Faulkner, whose creative fiction analyzes the South, publishes *The Sound and the Fury*, regarded by many as his masterpiece.

1934   F. Scott Fitzgerald's last major novel, *Tender Is the Night*, is published.

1936   William Faulkner's novel *Absalom! Absalom!* is published.

1938   Delmore Schwartz's *In Dreams Begin Responsibilities* is published.

1940   John O'Hara publishes *Pal Joey*.

In *Native Son*, Richard Wright portrays the new urban conditions of black political and social life.

1946   Southern writer Carson McCullers writes her classic *Member of the Wedding*, and Eudora Welty publishes *Delta Wedding*.

Robert Penn Warren produces his masterpiece, *All the King's Men*.

1948   Norman Mailer becomes an overnight success with his war classic, *The Naked and the Dead*.

1950   Carl Sandburg publishes *Complete Poems*, which will win the Pulitzer Prize.

1951   Novelist Kurt Vonnegut establishes his offbeat, witty style in *Piano Player*.

J. D. Salinger publishes the classic novel of adolescent alienation, *The Catcher in the Rye*.

1952   African-American writer Ralph Ellison publishes *Invisible Man*.

1953   James Baldwin publishes his masterpiece of black rage in *Go Tell It on the Mountain*.

Saul Bellow publishes *The Adventures of Angie March*.

1954   Wallace Stevens publishes *Collected Poems*, for which he will win the Pulitzer Prize.

1955   Elizabeth Bishop will win the Pulitzer for her *Poems: North and South—A Gold Spring*, published this year.

1956   *Howl* makes Allen Ginsberg famous as a Beat poet.

1957   Jack Kerouac publishes *On the Road*.

1959   Poet Robert Lowell writes *Life Studies*.

1961   John Updike begins his series of Rabbit novels with *Rabbit, Run*.

Walker Percy, a southern writer, publishes his critically acclaimed novel *The Moviegoer*.

Joseph Heller's *Catch-22* is published.

1963   Williams Carlos Williams publishes *Pictures from Brueghel, and Other Poems*.

1964   Robert Lowell's *For the Union Dead* is published.

1966   Poet Anne Sexton writes *Live or Die*, which will win the Pulitzer Prize.

Novelist Truman Capote writes *In Cold Blood*, a work of nonfiction that creates a new literary genre, literary journalism.

1967   William Styron writes what many regard as his finest work, *The Confessions of Nat Turner*.

1968   Gore Vidal's novel *Myra Breckinridge* shocks with its sexual content.

Poet Sylvia Plath's *Ariel* is published posthumously.

1969   Kurt Vonnegut's masterpiece, *Slaughterhouse Five*, is published.

Philip Roth's *Portnoy's Complaint* shocks with its sexual frankness.

1972   Eudora Welty's *The Optimist's Daughter* is published; it will win the Pulitzer Prize.

1973   *Sula*, by African-American novelist and Nobelist Toni Morrison, is published.

1975   Nobelist Saul Bellow produces *Humboldt's Gift*.

   E. L. Doctorow's novel *Ragtime* is published.

1977   John Cheever, who has previously written novels and stories of WASP life, writes *Falconer*, a novel about prison life that may be his finest.

1982   African-American novelist Alice Walker publishes *The Color Purple*.

1985   Larry McMurtry, widely perceived as a western writer, publishes *Lonesome Dove*.

1992   Cormac McCarthy publishes *All the Pretty Horses*.

1993   E. Annie Proulx writes *The Shipping News*.

1994   The collected short stores of Grace Paley, one of the most accomplished writers in this form, are published.

POETS LAUREATE OF THE UNITED STATES

In 1985 Congress created the post of poet laureate. By tradition, poets laureate write commemorative poetry for special occasions of the government (or monarch), but the American poet laureate, who is appointed for a yearly term by the Librarian of Congress, is asked to give a lecture on poetry and a poetry reading. The American poets laureate are:

1986–1987 Robert Penn Warren	1991–1992 Joseph Brodsky
1987–1988 Richard Wilbur	1992–1993 Mona Van Duyn
1988–1989 Howard Nemerov	1993–1995 Rita Dove
1990–1991 Mark Strand	1995– Robert Haas

AMERICAN NOBELISTS

The Nobel Prize for literature, which honors a body of work rather than a single book or play, has been awarded ten times to American writers. Here are the winners:

1930 Sinclair Lewis	1962 John Steinbeck
1936 Eugene O'Neill	1976 Saul Bellow
1938 Pearl Buck	1980 Czeslaw Milosz
1949 William Faulkner	1987 Joseph Brodsky
1954 Ernest Hemingway	1993 Toni Morrison

SIGNIFICANT PEOPLE IN AMERICAN LITERATURE

Baldwin, James (1924–1987).   Baldwin was one of the first writers to explore black rage and racism in novels such as *Go Tell It on the Mountain* (1953), and collections of essays such as *Nobody Knows My Name* (1961), and *The Fire Next Time* (1963). His eloquent novel *Giovanni's Room* (1956) examines the life of a white American who tries to come to terms with his homosexuality.

Bellow, Saul (1915–).   A Canadian-born novelist, Bellow explores in such works as *Herzog* (1964), *Mr. Sammler's Planet* (1970), and *Humboldt's Gift* (1975) the apathy of the modern world. His writing produced a new Jewish tradition in fiction. Bellow was awarded the Nobel Prize in 1976.

Bradstreet, Anne (c. 1612–1672).   A significant colonial author, Bradstreet wrote several books of poetry, including *The Tenth Muse Lately Sprung Up in America* (1650) and *Several Poems*.

Cather, Willa (1876–1947).   Long considered a regional novelist because she wrote about frontier life, Cather is today also recognized for her attention to the craft of fiction. Her novels include *O Pioneers!* (1913), *My Ántonia* (1918), and perhaps her masterpiece, *Death Comes for the Archbishop* (1927).

Cooper, James Fenimore (1789–1851).   America's first major novelist, Cooper idealized both American life and Native Americans in such books as *The Deerslayer* (1841) and *The Last of the Mohicans* (1826).

Crane, Stephen (1871–1900).   Crane was one of the first American novelists to experiment with naturalism. He is best known for his Civil War novel, *The Red Badge of Courage* (1895).

Dickinson, Emily (1830–1886).   Dickinson's unique and inventive style is revealed in the more than 1,700 poems she wrote on such topics as love, death, religion, and nature. Dickinson was a recluse, and only a handful of her poems were published in her lifetime.

Dreiser, Theodore (1871–1945).   Author of *Sister Carrie* (1900) and *An American Tragedy* (1925), Dreiser was a moving force behind the development of naturalism.

Eliot, Thomas Stearns (1888–1965).   One of the great modern poets, Eliot published *The Waste Land*, one of the landmarks of modernism in 1922. He became a British citizen in 1927.

Emerson, Ralph Waldo (1803–1832).   A leader in the social and literary movement known as Transcendentalism, which stressed the mysticism of nature, Emerson wrote essays entitled "Compensation" and "Reliance" and is also known for such poems as "Threnody" and "Brahma." His essays and literary connections also made him a leading figure in American literature.

Faulkner, William (1897–1962).   Forging a unique fiction style, Faulkner explored the decay of traditional values in American society, invariably using the South as the setting. Considered one of a handful of truly major American writers, Faulkner is remembered for *The Sound and the Fury* (1929), *Light in August* (1932), and *The Reivers* (1962). He was awarded a Nobel Prize in 1949.

Fitzgerald, F. Scott (1896–1940).   Fitzgerald was the most representative fiction writer of the "lost generation," a period of disillusionment when American intellectuals sought solace in Paris. Writing about the dissoluteness of the period between the two world wars, Fitzgerald produced well-known novels such as *The Great Gatsby* (1925), *Tender Is the Night* (1934), and *The Last Tycoon* (left unfinished, but published in 1941).

Frost, Robert (1874–1963).   One of the great American poets, who took as his subject the land, language, and people of New England, Frost published several books, most notably *A Boy's Will* (1913), *Steeple Bush* (1947), and *In the Clearing* (1962).

Hawthorne, Nathaniel (1804–1864).   A masterful American novelist, Hawthorne produced such memorable novels as *The Scarlet Letter* (1850) and *The House of the Seven Gables* (1851).

Hemingway, Ernest (1899–1961).   Along with Fitzgerald, a figure of the "lost generation," Hemingway lived in Paris after World War I and wrote such novels as *The Sun Also Rises* (1926), *A Farewell to Arms* (1929), and *For Whom the Bell Tolls* (1940). His masterpiece may be *The Old Man and the Sea* (1952).

Hughes, Langston (1902–1967).   One of the most famous writers associated with the Harlem Renaissance, Hughes was a novelist and poet. His first volume of poetry was The Weary Blues (1926).

Hurston, Zora Neale (1901–1960).   Hurston began her career as a folklorist, collecting black traditions of the American South. Her most famous novel is *Their Eyes Were Watching God* (1937).

Irving, Washington (1783–1859).   Irving wrote both fiction and nonfiction and is best remembered for *The Sketch Book* (1820), which contains "Rip Van Winkle" and "The Legend of Sleepy Hollow," two classic stories in American literature. Irving also wrote about the American West in A *Tour on the Prairies* (1835) and produced a biography of George Washington.

James, Henry (1843–1916).   An American expatriate who became a British subject, James wrote novels about America, most notably contrasting the innocence of Americans to the cynicism of Europeans. His work includes *The Portrait of a Lady* (1881), *The Bostonians* (1886), and *The Golden Bowl* (1904). His complex and subtle novels are now classics in American literature.

Longfellow, Henry Wadsworth (1807–1882).   One of the first important poets to use American subject matter, Longfellow is remembered for his narrative poems *Evangeline* (1847) and *The Song of Hiawatha* (1855).

Lowell, Robert (1917–1977).   The leader of an extraordinary generation of poets, Lowell himself is known for his exploration of evil and violence and his rich, skillful, symbolic style in such works as "The Quaker Graveyard at Nantucket," "Skunk Hour," and "For the Union Dead."

McCullers, Carson (1917–1967).   A southern writer, McCullers wrote about human despair in such works of fiction as *The Heart Is a Lonely Hunter* (1940), *Reflections in a Golden Eye* (1941), and *The Ballad of the Sad Cafe* (1951).

Mailer, Norman (1923–).   With the publication of his superb war novel, *The Naked and the Dead* (1948), Mailer was sprung overnight into literary stardom at a young age. He went on to publish fiction and nonfiction, and pioneered the "new journalism," a blend of reportage and fiction, stunningly exemplified in his 1979 *The Executioner's Song*, for which he won his second Pulitzer Prize.

Melville, Herman (1819–1891).   Taking nothing less than good and evil as his subject, Melville wrote several novels and is best remembered for his 1851 masterpiece, *Moby-Dick*.

Morrison, Toni (1931–).   This Nobelist author writes about black life in such novels as *Song of Solomon* (1977), *Beloved* (1987), *Sula* (1973), *Tar Baby* (1981), and *Jazz* (1992).

Poe, Edgar Allen (1809–1849).   A brilliant but erratic writer of fiction and poetry, Poe explored mystery and emotions. Some of his contributions appeared in the *Southern Literary Messenger*, which he edited. Among his best-known works are "Murders in the Rue Morgue" (1843) and *The Raven and Other Poems* (1845).

Steinbeck, John (1902–1968).   A full-blown realist who is remembered for writing about the Great Depression and what it did to Dust Bowl farmers, Steinbeck is best remembered for *The Grapes of Wrath* (1939). He also wrote *Of Mice and Men* (1937) and *Tortilla Flat* (1935). He won the Pulitzer and Nobel prizes.

Stevens, Wallace (1879–1955).   One of the major American poets, Stevens created brilliant physical images but was also concerned with exploring inner life, which he did eloquently in such books as *Harmonium* (1923), *Collected Poems* (1954), and *Opus Posthumous* (1957).

Thoreau, Henry David (1817–1862).   Thoreau's *Walden* (1854) is famous for its depiction of the solitary life in harmony with nature. His essay "Civil Disobedience," (1849) written to protest the Mexican War, influenced reformers such as Gandhi and Martin Luther King, Jr.

Twain, Mark (Samuel Langhorne Clemens) (1835–1910).   A novelist, newspaperman, and essayist, Twain was a brilliant satirist and a keen social observer. He is remembered for such American classics as *The Adventures of Tom Sawyer* (1876), *The Adventures of Huckleberry Finn* (1884), and *A Connecticut Yankee in King Arthur's Court* (1889).

Warren, Robert Penn (1905–1989).   A southern poet, novelist, and critic, Warren is best remembered for *All the King's Men*, his masterful roman à clef about the despotic southern politician Huey Long. Warren also co-authored two volumes of seminal criticism, *Understanding Poetry* (1938) and *Understanding Fiction* (1943), which pioneered a new, more purely textual form of criticism. He won Pulitzers for both fiction and poetry, cofounded *The Southern Review* with Cleanth Brooks, and in 1986 became the first poet laureate in America.

Wharton, Edith (1862–1937).   A chronicler of American society and the constrictions it imposed on women, Wharton wrote such novels as *The House of Mirth* (1905) and *The Age of Innocence* (1920). In an entirely different vein, she wrote a stunning novel of sexual repression in *Ethan Frome* (1911).

Wheatley, Phillis (c. 1753–1784).   Brought to America as a slave, Wheatley rose above her circumstances to produce remarkable poetry, most notably in her book *Poems on Various Subjects* (1773).

Whitman, Walt (1819–1892).   An innovative and major poet, Whitman also wrote about sexuality at a time when it was still considered taboo to do so. His masterpiece is *Leaves of Grass* (1855).

Williams, William Carlos (1883–1963).   One of the first and most important modern poets, Williams wrote eloquently about ordinary subjects. His work is published in *Collected Poems* (1934) and *Pictures from Brueghel* (1963). He was also a novelist and essayist.

Wright, Richard (1908–1960).   One of the most important African-American fiction writers, Wright explored the pain of being black in such works as *Native Son* (1940) and *The Outsider* (1953).

SIGNIFICANT EVENTS IN AMERICAN ART

1772	Charles Willson Peale paints the first known portrait of George Washington.
1774	European-trained John Singleton Copley leaves America for good, having achieved a reputation as a portraitist, although most of his fellow colonists prefer to have their likenesses done by the more prestigious European artists.
1781	John Singleton Copley paints *The Death of Lord Chatham*.
1795-1796	Gilbert Stuart, another well-known portraitist, paints *George Washington*.
1836	Hudson River artist Thomas Cole paints *The Course of Empire*.
1827	John James Audubon, who has traveled throughout the United States viewing its flora and fauna, begins publishing his illustrations in *Birds of America*.
1840	America's first art scandal occurs when the public ridicules sculptor Horatio Greenough's *George Washington*. The statue of the first president, shown in a Roman toga, is never permanently displayed in the Rotunda of the Capitol for which it was created.

1875   Thomas Eakins's *Surgical Clinic of Professor Gross* introduces a scientific interest to the subject matter of art.

1881   Sculptor Augustus Saint-Gaudens's statue of Admiral David Farragut is installed in Madison Square.

1884   Portraitist John Singer Sargent settles in London, where he paints stunning portraits that are much sought after by the rich.

1890   Childe Hassam, an American Impressionist, paints *Washington Arch, Spring.*

1895   Winslow Homer paints *The Northeaster,* one of his many fine depictions of the power of the sea.

1905   American Impressionist Mary Cassatt paints *Mère et enfant,* which hangs in the Louvre, one of her many studies of mothers and children.

      The Spielers, by George Luks, defines a new subject matter that some call vulgar.

1908   A group of artists form to exhibit their paintings. They call themselves The Eight but become known as the Ashcan School. They are Arthur B. Davies, Maurice Prendergast, Ernest Lawson, William Glackens, Everett Shinn, Robert Henri, John Sloan, and George Luks.

1912   John Sloan produces a portrait of working-class life called *McSorley's Bar.*

1913   Overnight the New York Armory Show changes the direction of American painting, creating a sensational new style known as modernism. The first generation of modern painters includes Max Weber, Man Ray, John Marin, and Alfred Maurer.

1914   William Glakens's *Washington Square* exemplifies a kind of social realism aligned with the Ashcan School.

1922   Daniel Chester French's famous statue of Lincoln is installed in the Lincoln Memorial in Washington, D.C.

1925   Man Ray creates *Clock Wheels,* one of the few American surrealist paintings.

1926   Alexander Calder, the preeminent sculptor of his day, exhibits one of his masterpieces, *The Circus,* a display of motorized wire sculptures.

1930   Edward Hopper paints one of his masterpieces, *Early Sunday Morning.*

      Grant Wood paints *American Gothic,* a classic portrait of an American farmer and his wife.

1931   Stuart Davis, who belongs to the second wave of modernists, paints *House and Street.*

      Georgia O'Keeffe's *Cow's Skull* is a characteristic study of shape and form in a southwestern setting.

1931-   Ben Shahn paints a series of gouaches on the Sacco-Vanzetti trial.
1932

1932   Alexander Calder exhibits a new art form, stabiles, which are movable, often motorized pieces of sculpture. These he follows with mobiles, delicately balanced hanging pieces that are moved by air currents.

1940   When Nazi Germany occupies France, Paris collapses as the center or the art world. Fleeing expatriates, combined with the American artists who were deeply influenced by the Armory Show, turn New York City into the new art capital of the world.

      Former social realist Ben Shahn paints the melancholy solitude of the lonely city in *Willis Avenue Bridge.*

      At the age of 80 Anna Mary Robertson Moses, known as Grandma Moses, has a one-woman show in New York. An untrained farmer's wife, she wins attention for her naive painting and after World War II gains widespread popularity. In 1949 President Truman invites her to the White House.

Alexander Calder

1943   Thomas Hart Benton paints *July Hay*.

Milton Avery, an individualistic painter who produces canvases of stunning simplicity, creates *Swimmers* and *Sunbathers*.

1945   Sculptor Isamu Noguchi completes *Kouros*. Later he is better known for his integrated environmental sculptures and stone sculpture gardens.

1948   Barnett Newman makes his first stripe paintings.

Realist Andrew Wyeth produces what will become one of the world's most widely reproduced paintings, *Christina's World*.

1952   Jackson Pollock shocks the art world with his drip paintings such as *Lavender Mist*.

1953   Willem de Kooning paints *Woman VI*, one of his most masterful works.

1954   Jasper Johns's flags and target images inaugurate pop art.

1956   Abstract expressionist Franz Kline paints *Mahoning*.

Robert Rauschenberg incorporates images and found objects into collages, such as *Gloria*.

1959   Field painters cause a stir with their brightly colored, vaguely Zen-like works of art: Kenneth Noland creates *Virginia Site*; Jasper Johns paints *Numbers in Color*; and Frank Stella paints *Jill*.

1961   Color field painter Kenneth Noland paints *A Warm Sound in a Gray Field*.

1962   Andy Warhol paints one of the masterpieces of pop art, *Campbell's Soup Can*.

1963   Roy Lichtenstein creates huge, comic-strip–like paintings, such as *Whaam!*

1964   Romare Bearden paints *The Prevalence of Ritual: The Baptism*.

1965   David Smith redefines contemporary sculpture with monumental steel and iron works that look like abstract drawings in the air. He is painting his *Cubi* series.

Frank Stella paints *Empress of India*.

1966   Louise Nevelson's *World*, a huge work, explores sculpture as environment.

1969   Pop art sculptor Claes Oldenburg's giant monument *Lipstick* is erected at Yale.

1975   Frank Stella paints *Montenegro I*.

1977   Georgia O'Keeffe is awarded the Medal of Freedom by President Carter.

1981   African-American collagist Romare Bearden creates *Artist with Painting and Model*.

Art Movements in the United States

Name	Dates	Description	Examples
Romanticism	Late 1700s–early 1800s	Revolt against formalism; main theme is man against nature, often portrayed in sentimental manner; colors light	Copley's *Watson and the Shark*
Realism	Mid- to late 1800s	Revolt against romanticism; no sentiment or pathos in content; deeper, darker palette	Eakins's *Gross Clinic*
Impressionism	Late 1800s	Breakthrough in painting: perspective no longer important, nor is subject; artist paints for sake of painting and to depict light and color	Cassatt's *Mother and Child*
Ashcan	Pre–World War I	Urban subject matter, such as boxing, gritty city life	Glackens's *Washington Square*
Social realism	1920s	Subject matter elevates working class; themes are intended to raise social consciousness	Shahn's *Passion of Sacco and Vanzetti*
Cubism	1920s	Much more popular in Europe, this expands on Impressionism and predates modern art; object is depicted from several angles at once; analytical	Feininger's *Steamer Odin*
Surrealism	1920s–1930s	Heavily psychoanalytic; attempt to paint using subconscious	Ray's *Clock Wheels*
Regionalism	1930s	Artists whose themes consciously depict aspects of American life, such as farming or New England	Grant Wood's *American Gothic*
Abstract expressionism	Post–World War II	Major movement of the era and the first to begin in the United States. Reaction to the chaos of the atomic bomb and war; violent colors, frenetic gestures; no object—just color	Pollock's *Lavender Mist*
Pop art	Mid-1950s	London-based but uses American icons almost exclusively. Lowbrow images used in art; realistic depiction	Johns's *Three Flags*
Color field	Late 1950s	Seeks order and control that is lacking in abstract expressionism; intense, poetic interest in color	Stella's *Empress of India*

SIGNIFICANT PEOPLE IN AMERICAN ART

Audubon, John James (1785–1851).   An illustrator-ornithologist, Audubon produced a stunningly beautiful and still unsurpassed collection of bird drawings and paintings, which were published in *Birds of America* beginning in 1827.

Bearden, Romare (1914–1988).   Bearden created colorful collages such as *Artist with Painting and Model*. He also worked to support other African-American artists by forming the group Spiral, whose purpose was to promote black artists, and by opening a gallery devoted to African-American art.

Calder, Alexander (1898–1976).   A rare artist who invented two new forms, the stabile and the mobile, Calder produced sculpture that was both amusing and iconoclastic.

Cassatt, Mary (1845–1926).   Influenced by French painters, Cassatt was one of the few major American Impressionists. Women and children were among her favorite subjects.

Copley, John Singleton (1738–1815).   Copley is considered the first great American portraitist; his subjects included Samuel Adams and Paul Revere.

Eakins, Thomas (1844–1916). A foremost portrait painter, he worked from live models and studied anatomy to produce his portraits and studies of American life.

Frankenthaler, Helen (1928–).   One of the iconoclastic painters who does not easily fit into any school, although she is associated with the abstract expressionists and studied with Jackson Pollock, Frankenthaler is known for her large, beautifully color-stained canvases.

Homer, Winslow (1836–1910).   An American realist who eschewed Europe at a time when his most famous contemporaries were painting there, Homer created such dramatic indigenous works as *Eight Bells* (1886), *Gulf Stream* (1899), *Life Line* (1884), and *Early Morning After a Storm at Sea* (1902). He was a master watercolorist and a lithographer as well as a painter in oils.

Johns, Jasper (1930–).   Rebelling against the total formlessness of the abstract expressionists, Johns returned to form but still managed to shock with his huge paintings of American flags and targets. His goal was to show that any subject could—and should—be viewed as art.

Kline, Franz (1910–1962).   This abstract expressionist painter from New York is remembered for his stark black-and-white canvases, among them *Mahoning*, painted in 1956.

Lichtenstein, Roy (1923–).   Lichtenstein's subjects—comic strips—belie their enormous artistic sophistication. Lichtenstein is most often associated with the pop art movement.

Luks, George (1867–1933).   A founding member of the Ashcan School, Luks was a social realist known for his spirited portraits.

Motherwell, Robert (1915–1991).   One of the moving forces behind abstract expressionism, Motherwell filled large canvases with huge blocks of color.

Nevelson, Louise (1900–1988).   In her sculpture Nevelson pioneered in the use of found materials. She is best known for her wood box sculptures.

Noguchi, Isamu (1904–1988).   Noguchi produced abstract stone sculptures that were often specifically designed for their setting, either gardens or buildings.

O'Keeffe, Georgia (1887–1986).   A highly individualistic painter, O'Keeffe's often huge and very precise canvases are frequently magnifications of such objects as flowers or skulls. Associated with New Mexico, she also painted New York City scenes.

Peale, Charles Willson (1741–1827).   After Copley, Peale was the most popular portraitist of the colonial era. He painted George Washington, Benjamin Franklin, Thomas Jefferson, and John Adams.

Pollock, Jackson (1912–1956).   One of the giants of abstract expressionism, Pollock dripped paint directly on the canvas, as in *Lavender Mist*. This technique called for and gave his work unusual dynamism, so that it was dubbed "action" painting.

Rauschenberg, Robert (1925–).   Rauschenberg, like Johns, rebelled against the abstractionists by painting everyday figures. He created sculptures, or combines, as he called them, of everyday objects put together in shocking ways. One, called *Monogram*, consists of a lifelike model of a sheep with a tire around its middle.

Ray, Man (1890–1976).   As well known for his photographs as for his other art, Man Ray presented everyday objects as art. He is often associated with surrealism.

Remington, Frederic (1861–1909).   Remington grew famous for his heroic paintings of life in the American "Wild West." He also sculpted in bronze. His *Bronco Buster*, of which there are more than 300 castings, gained wide popularity.

Rothko, Mark (1903–1970).   Like Pollock and Motherwell, Rothko was one of the pioneers of abstract expressionism. His large, rectangular bands of color influenced later painters.

Sargent, John Singer (1856–1925).   Although Sargent painted many watercolor landscapes, the largest body of his work consists of portraits of the rich. His ability to depict texture, whether in fabric or the flush of a woman's skin, was his forte.

Smith, David (1906–1965).   The preeminent sculptor of his day, Smith made sculptures that literally were abstract drawings in the air. Much of his work is public and monumental.

Stella, Frank (1936–).   Considered one of the foremost painters of his era, Stella has experimented with many styles, ranging from minimalist black works to color field canvases. In the 1970s, he created paintings that were three-dimensional.

Stuart, Gilbert (1755–1828).   Along with Copley and Peale, Stuart was one of the leading portrait painters of the colonial era. He is best known for his portrait of George Washington.

Warhol, Andy (1928–1987).   A leader of the pop art movement, Warhol created huge silk-screened canvases of popular cultural icons such as Marilyn Monroe and Mao Zedong. He also created paintings of such icons as Brillo boxes and Campbell's Soup cans, and was recognized as a talented filmmaker.

West, Benjamin (1738–1820).   West was the first American painter to win acclaim abroad. He settled in London in 1763, opening a school in which he taught and encouraged other American artists. In his historical paintings *The Death of General Wolfe* and *Penn's Treaty with the Indians*, he broke with tradition by depicting the figures in period dress instead of classical garb. In 1792 West became president of the Royal Academy.

Whistler, James (1834–1903).   Working mainly in England, Whistler painted many studies of the Thames, such as *Chelsea: Nocturne in Blue and Green* (1870). He championed the idea that a painter should produce a composition that, like music, existed for its own sake, without regard to moral or didactic values. Whistler is viewed as a precursor of abstract artists.

Wood, Grant (1891–1942).   In an age of modernism, Wood painted realistically, and in an age deeply influenced by European art, he was a populist, regional painter. Influenced by German and French primitivists, Wood produced stylized landscapes of the Midwest and portraits of its people.

THE NATIONAL ENDOWMENT FOR THE ARTS

The National Endowment for the Arts was established in 1965. Although the nations of Europe have always heavily subsidized their cultural activities, this belated attempt to support American art and culture was the first such effort in the United States, and there was little consensus that it was an appropriate government function. Despite this, the endowment managed to survive its initial three-year funding period and even proceeded to grow.

Over the years the NEA has had its hand in nearly every aspect of American culture, from fine art to dance to theater to opera. It is actively involved in educating teachers about culture. It insures fine art and cultural artifacts so they can travel to the United States from other countries, and, by insuring art going the other way, it helps to carry U.S. culture abroad. It sponsors artists- and writers-in-residence programs, funds theaters and museums, aids libraries, and reaches out to youth. The endowment works with both individuals and organizations.

Other than a perpetual shortage of funds, which must be provided by a sometimes reluctant Congress, the NEA encountered no serious difficulties in its first two decades. But in the late 1980s the Moral Majority began to raise objections to its existence on grounds that it was promoting art that the Moral Majority believed should not be funded with tax dollars.

So intense was the pressure that in one case the Corcoran Gallerey of Art in Washington, D.C., canceled a show of photographs by the late Robert Mapplethorpe because it contained a few examples of homoerotic themes. Senator Jesse Helms introduced legislation that would bar the NEA from funding "obscene" work, and Congress vowed to establish a panel that would evaluate art for obscene content. The furor died down, but the NEA remains a target of the conservative right.

In actuality, the NEA's involvement in cutting-edge projects is only a fraction of what it does. Much of its work revolves around the preservation of American folk art, crafts, and traditions. Some of its projects are as small as the collection and preservation of cowboy songs and poetry, a minor oral art that might nevertheless be entirely lost to us without the NEA's efforts. Other projects are more extensive, such as its efforts to preserve an entire range of Appalachian crafts.

SIGNIFICANT EVENTS IN AMERICAN MUSIC

1600s	The indigenous music in the Americas is that of the American Indian, which includes chanting and singing in a five-note scale. Colonists bring European music with them, much of it religious in purpose.
1770	William Billings publishes what is widely believed to be the first American composition, "The New England Psalm Singer."
1794	James Hewitt composes "Tammany, or the Indian Chief." Its theme is American, but its musical structure is European.
1818	Boston's Handel and Haydn Society, founded in 1815, gives its first performance of *Messiah*.
1842	The New York Philharmonic Orchestra is founded.
1865	Chicago supports an opera company in its newly built Crosby Opera House.
1878	The Central City Opera House in the Colorado mining town of the same name opens.
1881	The Boston Symphony is founded.
1883	The New York Metropolitan Opera gives its first performance, Charles Gounod's *Faust*.
1891	The Chicago Symphony is founded.
1892	The Czech composer Antonín Dvořák arrives in the United States to direct New York City's National Conservatory of Music. While in America he writes the "New World"

Symphony No. 9 in E Minor and exhorts American composers to draw on their rich cultural heritage, including Indian and African-American music. He trains several black musicians, most notably H. T. Burleigh, who goes on to arrange spirituals and other black music. Edward MacDowell, a member of this movement despite his European training, writes *Indian Suite* between 1891 and 1895.

1896   Edward MacDowell writes *Woodland Sketches* for piano.

1902   Charles Ives, a pioneer in "modern" music, completes his iconoclastic Second Symphony, but it will not be performed publicly until 1951.

1903   Victor Herbert composes *Babes in Toyland,* one of the first American operettas.

1908   Italian conductor Arturo Toscanini takes over the baton at the Metropolitan Opera, where he will reign until 1914.

1924   George Gershwin composes *Rhapsody in Blue.*

Aaron Copland composes his Symphony for Organ and Orchestra.

Aaron Copland

1928   Arturo Toscanini assumes leadership of the New York Philharmonic and turns it into one of the world's great symphony orchestras.

George Gershwin writes *An American in Paris.*

Virgil Thomson and Gertrude Stein create an American opera, *Four Saints in Three Acts.*

1935   George and Ira Gershwin's *Porgy and Bess,* an opera based on African-American music and themes, is performed on Broadway.

UNIQUELY AMERICAN: JAZZ

Jazz, which began in the late 19th century, is the only uniquely American contribution to the musical composition. Drawing its inspiration mostly from African music and also from indigenous American music such as spirituals, work songs, blues, and field hollers, jazz originated in the South and rather quickly worked its way north and west. Some romanticists say it traveled along the rivers, but in any event, by the 1940s jazz, helped along by swing, was a permanent part of the American musical scene.

Jazz differs from other Western music in two important ways, first in its use of improvisation, which refers to the spontaneous creation of variations on the melody, and second, through syncopation, a stress on a normally weak beat. Although all jazz shares these characteristics to a greater or lesser degree, jazz has progressed through a variety of styles, all of which are still in existence today.

The earliest jazz was Dixieland. This featured a clearly defined melody, produced by a horn, and a beat, or rhythm, supplied by piano or drums. The best of the early practitioners of Dixieland were King Oliver's Creole Jazz Band, which included such illustrious names as Louis Armstrong and Honoré Dutrey; the Wolverines, led by Bix Beiderbecke; and the New Orleans Rhythm Kings. A variation of Dixieland is ragtime, whose best-known advocate was Scott Joplin. With its distinctive style, produced mostly through marked syncopation, ragtime was spread by sheet music and piano rolls, in contrast to Dixieland, for which there typically was no written music.

Swing, which featured the big-band sounds of Count Basie, Duke Ellington (considered one of America's greatest composers), Glenn Miller, Tommy and Jimmy Dorsey, and Benny Goodman, helped to move jazz into the mainstream and to introduce it to whites. Swing featured call-and-response playing, lots of improvisational riffs (although often of the rehearsed kind), and no written music—with the exception of Duke Ellington, who was as much composer as bandleader.

Bebop, or bop, arose in the 1950s in reaction to swing and thus strove to be everything swing was not. Where swing was easy listening, bop was complex. Where swing was big bands, bop marked a return to the small group. Where swing emphasized melody, bop cared only about rhythm. Bop was created by such consummate musicians as Dizzy Gillespie and Charlie Parker. The best bop was never particularly mainstream, since it was so sophisticated and musically complex.

Related to bop is third stream, a fusion of jazz and classical music of the kind pioneered by the Modern Jazz Quartet, and cool jazz, whose chief proponents are Miles Davis and Charlie Parker. Third stream, jazz played for the first time by academically trained musicians, adheres (on occasion) to written scores and employs such classical forms as the rondo, the fugue, and even symphonic development. Cool jazz resembles swing but without the call-and-response and the riffs. Definitely experimental, it introduced to jazz such instruments as the flute, French horn, and the baritone sax.

Jazz in the sixties sounded like the era—wailing, angry and full of protest, and was played at its best by such artists as Ornette Coleman, Archie Shepp, and Sam Rivers. A new avant-garde jazz also emerged, featuring atonal music of the kind played by John Coltrane.

The 70s and 80s saw a renaissance of jazz, with fusion performers such as Herbie Hancock and Chick Corea trying to find ways to merge jazz and rock. This was accomplished largely through the introduction of heavy drums and electronic instruments. By the late 80s and early 90s, musicians like Wynton Marsalis were bringing jazz full circle. They embarked on a new classical—or as some said, neoclassical—age of jazz. Melody reigned once more, and elegant old tunes—by the likes of Ellington, George Gershwin, and Cole Porter—were once again heard.

1937   The NBC Symphony for the radio is created for Arturo Toscanini, one of the great conductors of his era.

1938   Two American ballets are performed for the first time: Walter Piston's *The Incredible Flutist* and Aaron Copland's *Billy the Kid*.

1942   Aaron Copland's ballet *Rodeo* and his *Lincoln Portrait* are staged.

Experimental composer John Cage creates *Imaginary Landscape No. 3*, scored for Balinese gongs, generator whine, an electric oscillator, buzzers, coil, and tin cans, among other "instruments."

1944   Aaron Copland's *Appalachian Spring* is first performed.

1947   Walter Piston writes his Pulitzer Prize–winning Third Symphony.

1948   Samuel Barber composes *Knoxville: Summer of 1915*.

1951   John Cage scores *Imaginary Landscape No. 4*, which consists of 12 radios randomly tuned.

1952   John Cage scores *4'33"*, his first major aleatory, or "chance" composition, which consists of a silent pianist on stage. The audience is supposed to listen to the sounds of the music hall.

1956   Leonard Bernstein writes the score for *Candide*.

Douglas Moore's opera *The Ballad of Baby Doe* is premiered at the Colorado Central City Opera House.

William Schuman composes *New England Triptych*.

1958   Samuel Barber's opera *Vanessa* wins the Pulitzer Prize.

1959   Walter Piston writes *Three New England Sketches*, a suite for orchestra.

1971   Leonard Bernstein composes *Mass*, a secular piece of music that is played for the first time at the opening of the John F. Kennedy Cultural Center in Washington, D.C.

1975   Philip Glass writes a strikingly modern opera, *Einstein on the Beach*.

Known for her innovative productions, Sarah Caldwell, who founded her own opera company in Boston, becomes the first woman to conduct the Metropolitan Opera.

SIGNIFICANT PEOPLE IN AMERICAN MUSIC

Barber, Samuel (1910–1981).   This traditionalist composer wrote, among other pieces, the operas *Vanessa* (1957) and *Antony and Cleopatra* (1966), commissioned for the opening of the Metropolitan Opera in its new location at Lincoln Center.

Berlin, Irving (1881–1989).   Although unable to read or write music, Berlin became one of the most successful composers of popular song in the 20th century. One of his first hits was "Alexander's Ragtime Band" in 1911. He wrote the music and lyrics for several musical comedies including *Annie Got Your Gun* (1946) and *Call Me Madam* (1950).

Bernstein, Leonard (1918–1990).   A composer and conductor, Bernstein was an overnight sensation when he substituted for Arturo Toscanini at the podium of the New York Philharmonic in 1943. He later conducted both the New York Philharmonic and the New York City Symphony Orchestra. Bernstein bridged the gap between classical and popular music with such works as *West Side Story* (1957) and *On the Town* (1944), both Broadway musicals, in addition to his more traditional classical works such as the symphony *Kaddish* (1963) and *Chichester Psalms* (1965).

Cage, John (1912–1992).   A pioneering experimental musician and composer, Cage sought to push the definitions of music, most notably with works such as the *Imaginary Landscape* series.

Copland, Aaron (1900–1990).   Perhaps the most "American" of the American composers, Copland is known for ballets such as *Rodeo* (1942), *Billy the Kid* (1938), and *Appalachian Spring* (1944).

Ellington, Duke (1899–1974).   Ellington was bandleader, pianist, and composer of such popular songs as "I Got It Bad and That Ain't Good" and "Don't Get Around Much Anymore." His jazz band toured the United States and Europe to great reviews.

Foster, Stephen (1826–1864).   During his short life Foster wrote a substantial number of songs that were popular in his own day and that are still sung at the end of the 20th century. Among the best known are "My Old Kentucky Home" (1853), "Jeannie With the Light Brown Hair" (1854), and "Beautiful Dreamer, Wake Unto Me" (1863).

Gershwin, George (1898–1937).   A composer of original and popular works and classical music, Gershwin wrote musicals such as *Lady, Be Good!* (1924) and music that combined elements of classical and jazz such as *Rhapsody in Blue* (1923) and *An American in Paris* (1924).

Glass, Philip (1937–).   This composer of modern music was influenced by Ives, and he blends traditional and untraditional tonality. He is perhaps best known for *Einstein on the Beach*, first performed in Paris in 1976.

Ives, Charles (1874–1954).   Although Ives is often called the grandfather of modern music, his compositions were not much played in his lifetime. His Third Symphony (1901–1904) won the Pulitzer Prize in 1947.

MacDowell, Edward (1860–1908).   A traditionalist composer who tried to use "American" themes, MacDowell wrote *Indian Suite* (1897) and *Woodland Sketches* (1896). His widow founded the MacDowell Artists' Colony.

Moore, Douglas (1893–1969).   This composer of highly theatrical works wrote a children's opera called *The Headless Horseman* (1937) and an adult opera, *Giants in the Earth* (1951).

Piston, Walter (1894–1976).   This traditional composer sometimes incorporated jazz rhythms. He wrote many symphonies, concertos, and string quartets, most notably his Third Symphony (1948), for which he won a Pulitzer.

Rodgers, Richard (1902–1979).   Rodgers composed the music for more than a dozen successful musical comedies, first with Lorenz Hart as lyricist and later with Oscar Hammerstein II as lyricist. He also wrote the music for the documentary film *Victory at Sea* (1952).

Sousa, John Philip (1854–1932).   Renowned for his marches, Sousa led the U.S. Marine Corps band from 1880 to 1892 when he organized his own band. His works include "Semper Fidelis" (1888), "The Washington Post March" (1889), and "Stars and Stripes Forever" (1897).

Stravinsky, Igor (1882–1971).   A native of Russia, Stravinsky came to the United States in 1939 and lived in America until his death. He composed ballet music (*The Fire-Bird* [1910] and *The Rite of Spring* [1913]) and operas (*The Rake's Progress* [1951]), as well as piano and symphonic music.

Thomson, Virgil (1896–1989).   This experimental composer and critic wrote, among other pieces, *The Mother of Us All* (1947), an opera, and film music for *The River* (1937). He wrote pieces for the organ, piano, and chamber ensembles.

Weill, Kurt (1900–1950).   A composer, Weill was born in Germany, where he was best known for his operas *The Threepenny Opera* (1928) and *The Rise and Fall of the City of Mahogany* (1927). Condemned as decadent by the Nazis, Weill left Germany for France and then the United States, where he mostly composed for musicals, although he did one last serious piece, *Street Scene* (1947).

SIGNIFICANT EVENTS IN AMERICAN ARCHITECTURE

1600s   Indigenous Native American architecture includes the rubble-and-clay, flat-topped cliff dwellings of the Pueblos, such as those located at Chaco Canyon, New Mexico (c. A.D. 1300).

1636   The San Miguel Mission is built in Santa Fe, New Mexico.

1699   The old adobe church and of San Estaban in Acoma, New Mexico, is remodeled. Its walls are 60 feet high and 10 feet thick.

1700   The Mission of San Xavier del Bac is founded just south of the Indian village of Tucson. Its church, known as the White Dove of the Desert, still stands as an outstanding example of Spanish colonial architecture.

1718   The French Quarter in New Orleans recalls that the old city, below Canal Street, was first platted in this year by the French.

1770   Thomas Jefferson begins building Monticello in Charlottesville, Virginia. Designed by Jefferson, it is a fine example of American classical revival.

1791   The Cabildo in New Orleans is erected as a government building by the Spanish. Today it is the Louisiana State Museum.

1792   The U.S. Capitol follows the Palladian form then popular in England. Initially designed by William Thornton, it is burned by the British during the War of 1812. B. H. Latrobe supervises the final reconstruction, and Boston architect Charles Bulfinch continues his work.

1799   Charles Bulfinch completes the Massachusetts State House in Boston. Its neoclassic design will influence statehouses across the country.

1819   Andrew Jackson begins constructing the Hermitage in Nashville, Tennessee. Today open to the public, it is both a typical plantation home and an excellent example of Greek revival architecture.

1872   H. H. Richardson begins building Trinity Church in Boston. Romanesque in spirit, it also displays a stripped-down modernism that many people believe marks the beginning of a new era of uniquely American design.

1883   The Home Insurance Building in Chicago stirs excitement. It is the first U.S. building in which a metal skeleton rather than the walls carries the weight and therefore is a prototype for modern skyscrapers.

1885   In Chicago, H. H. Richardson begins building the Marshall Field Wholesale Store (now demolished), another pioneering building that features little ornament and a new emphasis on functionality.

1886   The Auditorium in Chicago is begun by Louis Sullivan and his partner Dankmar Adler. The building is marked by its lack of ornament and wide generous arches that are the main architectural detail.

1888   New York's McKim, Mead, & White preserves classical architecture and Renaissance styles in, among others, the Boston Public Library, begun this year.

1890   Louis Sullivan builds the landmark Wainwright Building in Saint Louis. Steel-framed and modern by virtue of its emphasis on function over form, it is nevertheless decorated with one of Sullivan's characteristic friezes.

1891   As architects begin to experiment with building skyscrapers, the Monadnock Building in Chicago, built by the firm of Burnham & Root, at 16 stories becomes the last tall building constructed of load-bearing walls.

Louis Sullivan

1893   Frank Lloyd Wright, a disciple of Sullivan, begins to build the "prairie" houses, an icono-clastic new form of domestic architecture. The houses are radical by virtue of their empha-sis on the horizontal rather than the vertical plane. The apex of the prairie style is the Robie House in Chicago, built in 1909.

1902   The familiar landmark, the Flatiron Building, is completed by Daniel Burnham in New York City.

1904   Frank Lloyd Wright designs the Larkin Soap Building in Buffalo, New York. With its central courtyard and sealed windows, it is a radical design in institutional building.

1929   Buckminster Fuller builds the innovative Dymaxion House, one of the first prefabricated structures.

1931   The Philadelphia Savings Fund Society, built by George Howe, exhibits one of the primary characteristics of modernism, with glass walls replacing traditional windows.

1936   Frank Lloyd Wright begins to build a masterpiece of modern design, a house in Pennsylvania called Falling Water. By siting the spectacular cantilevered structure on a waterfall rather than on a hill overlooking the waterfall, Wright exemplifies his principles of naturalism.

1937   Ludwig Mies van der Rohe relocates the pioneering Bauhaus School in Chicago and starts the international style in the United States.

1949   Ludwig Mies van der Rohe begins to build nos. 845-60, two black steel, glass-walled apartment towers situated on Lake Shore Drive in Chicago.

1950   Ludwig Mies van der Rohe builds the Farnsworth House near Plano, Illinois, a strikingly modern building with its flat roof and glass walls.

1952   Gordon Bunshaft designs the first glass-walled high-rise in New York City, the strikingly spare and elegant Lever House.

1964   The CBS Building in New York City is completed. Designed by Eero Saarinen, it is supported by a central core.

1968   When other architects turn to postmodernism, Richard Neutra continues to adhere to the principles of functionalism and modernism with such innovative structures as the Northridge Medical Arts Building in Los Angeles.

1978   Philip Johnson sparks debate with his unabashedly neo-Georgian design for the AT&T Building (today Sony headquarters) in New York City.

1983   Frank Gehry completes the Norton House, in Venice, California. He successfully explodes the traditional rectilinear shape of most buildings to create asymmetrical buildings with great dynamism.

1990   Eighty-three years after construction was initially begun, the Neo-Gothic National Cathedral in Washington, D.C., is completed.

SIGNIFICANT PEOPLE IN AMERICAN ARCHITECTURE

Bulfinch, Charles (1763–1844).   Bulfinch designed the Massachusetts State House, the U.S. Capitol, and Massachusetts General Hospital. He pioneered the neoclassical style that became known in the United States as Federalist.

Bunshaft, Gordon (1909–1990).   Head designer at the pioneering firm of Skidmore, Owings, and Merrill, Bunshaft designed many classic modern buildings such as the Lever House in New York City (1952), the Albright-Knox Art Galley in Buffalo, New York, and the Hirshhorn Museum in Washington, D.C.

Burnham, Daniel (1846–1912).   With his partner, John Root, Burnham built many important buildings in Chicago and New York, including the Flatiron in New York City (1902), the Masonic Temple in Chicago, and Union Station in Washington, D.C. (1909). Burnham and Root did the general design for the 1893 World's Columbian Exposition in Chicago, which was largely responsible for inspiring several decades of neoclassical design in the United States.

Fuller, R. Buckminster (1895–1983).   This architect, engineer, and author is best remembered for designing the geodesic dome, a revolutionary new shape intended to provide maximum strength from a minimum amount of energy.

Johnson, Philip (1906–).   Heavily influenced by the Bauhaus School, Johnson built his well-known glass house in New Canaan, Connecticut (1949), and also worked on the Seagram Building in New York City (1958) and the New York State Theater at Lincoln Center (1962–1964). Later he joined the postmodern movement and built the AT&T Building (now the Sony Building) in New York City. In 1932 he wrote a classic text on modern architecture called *The International Style*.

Kahn, Louis (1901–1974).   Widely influential as a teacher, Kahn designed the Yale University Art Gallery in New Haven, Connecticut (1953), and the Kimbell Art Museum in Fort Worth, Texas (1972).

Latrobe, Benjamin (1764–1820).   Perhaps the first professional architect in the United States, Latrobe worked on the U.S. Capitol as well as the nation's first cathedral, the Roman Catholic Cathedral in Baltimore. Latrobe was a leader of the classic revival.

Mies van der Rohe, Ludwig (1886–1969).   Director of the Bauhaus in Germany from 1930 to 1933, he continued its principles in the United States in Chicago at the Illinois Institute of Technology, whose campus he designed. He collaborated with Philip Johnson to build the classic Seagram Building in New York City (1958).

Neutra, Richard (1892–1970).   As the creator of the Northridge Medical Arts Building and the Lovell Health House in Los Angeles, he continued the functional approach in modern design.

Pei, I. M. (1917–).   Although born in China, the American-trained architect has practiced in Boston and New York. His best-known American projects include the John Hancock Tower in Boston (1973) and the East Building of the National Gallery of Art in Washington, D.C. (1978).

Richardson, Henry H. (1838–1886).   Initially a Romanesque revivalist, Richardson later designed buildings that were harbingers of modernism. He is remembered for the Marshall Field Wholesale Store (demolished) and the Trinity Church in Boston (completed in 1877).

Saarinen, Eero (1910–1961).   This inventive Finnish-born architect was a proponent of the international style. Among his best-known projects are the Gateway Arch (1965), the Trans World Airline terminal at Idlewild (today Kennedy) Airport, New York City (1962), and Dulles International Airport outside Washington, D.C., completed after his death.

Sullivan, Louis (1856–1924).   Sullivan played a key role in the development of modern architecture with such buildings as the Wainwright in Saint Louis (1890) and the Auditorium in Chicago (completed 1889).

Wright, Frank Lloyd (1867–1959).   A key American architect, Wright both pioneered the modern style and developed his own unique style, as epitomized by such buildings as the Robie House (1909), Falling Water (completed 1937), and the Guggenheim Museum in New York City (completed 1959).

SIGNIFICANT EVENTS IN AMERICAN THEATER

1752   Lewis Hallam's troupe of English actors comes to Williamsburg.

1787   Typical of the melodramas so loved during the Federalist era is *The Contrast* by Royall Tyler.

1798   Another melodrama, William Dunlap's *Andre*, is popular.

1829   Plays like John Augustus Stone's *Metamora* introduce the stereotypes that abound in American theater, although few are as flattering as this tale of a noble American Indian. More common are images of the drunken Irishman or the savage Indian. Theater, especially minstrel shows, reinforce a stereotype of blacks as suited for menial work.

1849   American actors hold their own against the British stars, so much so that at Astor Place Opera House in New York riots break out between two rival factions, those who admire

American actor Edwin Forrest and those who love English actor William Macready, the two leading Shakespearean actors of their day. Twenty-two people are killed.

1852   A staged version of Harriet Beecher Stowe's influential novel, *Uncle Tom's Cabin*, is one of the first plays with a social conscience. Its goal is to show the evil of slavery.

1880   Steele MacKaye's melodrama *Hazel Kirke* is presented at Madison Square Theatre.

1905   David Belasco's *Girl of the Golden West* is staged.

1920   Eugene O'Neill's drama *Beyond the Horizon* is widely hailed as the first major American tragedy.

1921   Eugene O'Neill follows one success with another, the play *Anna Christie*.

1924   *Desire Under the Elms* becomes another success for Eugene O'Neill.

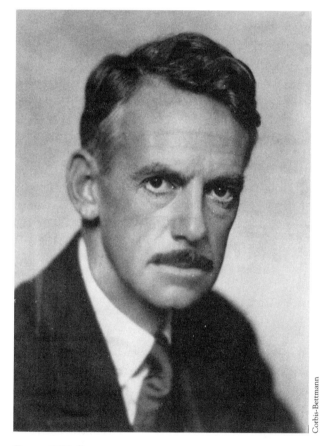

Eugene O'Neill

1931   *Mourning Becomes Electra* by Eugene O'Neill opens on Broadway.

1933   Eugene O'Neill's only light play, *Ah! Wilderness*, opens on Broadway.

1935   In one season, New York theatergoers can see Clifford Odets's *Waiting for Lefty* and *Awake and Sing* as well as Maxwell Anderson's *Winterset*, plays that exhibit a social consciousness not previously seen in American theater.

1935   Sinclair Lewis writes *It Can't Happen Here.*

The Federal Theater Project, begun this year, spurs much activity in serious theater by promoting minority theater (it funds 16 African-American companies) and staging exciting—and often controversial—new plays.

1938   Thornton Wilder's *Our Town* wins the Pulitzer Prize.

1939   Under attack from a group in the House of Representatives later formalized into the House Un-American Activities Committee, the Federal Theater Project is closed, but not before it presents T. S. Eliot's *Murder in the Cathedral* and an all-black cast in *Macbeth.*

1945   Tennessee Williams's *The Glass Menagerie* is staged.

1946   *The Iceman Cometh,* by Eugene O'Neill, plays on Broadway.

1947   Eugene O'Neill's *A Moon for the Misbegotten* is produced.

With the introduction of Tennessee Williams's powerful and very American play *A Streetcar Named Desire,* a new, postwar flowering of American theater gets under way.

1949   Arthur Miller's powerful *Death of a Salesman* is produced.

1953   Arthur Miller's *The Crucible* receives its first production. Ostensibly about the Salem witch trials, it is actually a parable about Senator Joseph McCarthy's modern-day witchhunt.

1955   *Cat on a Hot Tin Roof* by Tennessee Williams is staged.

1956   Eugene O'Neill's complex family drama *Long Day's Journey into Night* is staged.

1959   *Sweet Bird of Youth* by Tennessee Williams is produced.

A less realistic, absurdist form of drama is introduced with Edward Albee's *The Zoo Story.*

Lorraine Hansberry's riveting drama of black life, *A Raisin in the Sun,* draws large audiences.

1961   Tennessee Williams's play *Night of the Iguana* opens on Broadway.

1962   *Who's Afraid of Virginia Woolf?* is Edward Albee's first full-length play.

1964   Arthur Miller's *After the Fall* is produced.

1976   Ntozake Shange's play *For Colored Girls Who Have Considered Suicide/When the Rainbow Is Enuf* becomes the first black drama to be a success on Broadway since *A Raisin in the Sun.*

OPENING THE THEATRICAL DOOR TO EVERYONE

Theater, long considered, at least by the players, to be the most egalitarian art form, has nevertheless been a closed club to both women and minorities for much of its existence. The Pulitzer Prize for drama, to take but one example, has been given to women only seven times since its inception in 1918, and even more rarely to minorities. It was not won by a woman for all the years that encompassed the rise of both the civil rights and women's rights movements.

In 1981 dramatist Beth Henley broke the losing streak with her play *Crimes of the Heart,* which was initially produced by a regional theater. The next year, African-American dramatist Charles Fuller won for his poignant play *A Soldier's Story.* Since then two women—Marsha Norman and Wendy Wasserstein—and one black, August Wilson—have been honored with the prize. Passed over for it have been such esteemed African-American playwrights as Lorraine Hansberry, who wrote *A Raisin in the Sun,* and Ntozake Shange, who wrote *For Colored Girls Who Have Considered Suicide/When the Rainbow Is Enuf.*

1977   Sam Shepard's *Curse of the Starving Class* is produced, introducing a new—and at the time shocking—countercultural sensibility to American theater.

1978   Sam Shepard's new play, *Buried Child*, is produced off-Broadway.

1981   Beth Henley wins the Pulitzer Prize for drama. Her play *Crimes of the Heart* is also noteworthy for having been produced not on Broadway but rather in a regional theater.

1982   *A Soldier's Story* by African American Charles Fuller wins the Pulitzer Prize.

1983   Marsha Norman wins the Pulitzer Prize for drama for her play *'Night, Mother*.

1984   David Mamet's *Glengarry Glen Ross* is staged.

1990   African-American dramatist August Wilson wins the Pulitzer Prize for *The Piano Lesson*.

1991   After several years of eclipse, Edward Albee stages a comeback with *Three Tall Women*. But the Pulitzer Prize–winning play is premiered outside New York and produced off-Broadway.

1992   Richard Nelson, the only American dramatist whose work is regularly produced by the Royal Shakespeare Company in London, receives a Broadway production of his newest play, *Two Shakespearean Actors*, which describes the politics behind the 1849 Astor Place riot.

AN AMERICAN INVENTION: MUSICAL THEATER

1866   *The Black Crook*, which opens on Broadway, is the first American musical. It would hardly be to theatergoers' taste today, but it presages the popularity of this form in America.

1903   Victor Herbert stages the first of his operettas, *Babes in Toyland*.

1904   George M. Cohan, one of the giants of American musical theater, writes, produces, and stars in his own show, *Little Johnny Jones*, introducing favorites such as "I'm Yankee Doodle Dandy" and "Give My Regards to Broadway."

1906   Another musical starring George M. Cohan, *Forty-five Minutes from Broadway*, is a hit.

1907   Florenz Ziegfeld stages the first of his 24 annual *Follies*, a pastiche of vaudeville and musical theater that makes stars of such performers as Fanny Brice, Will Rogers, and Eddie Cantor.

1910   *Naughty Marietta*, another Victor Herbert operetta, successfully woos audiences.

1925   The musical *No! No! Nanette!* introduces a craze for tap dancing.

1927   More sophisticated fare is presented by George and Ira Gershwin in *Funny Face*.

       The first "modern" musical, successfully merging song and story, is *Show Boat*, by Jerome Kern and Oscar Hammerstein II.

1931   Fred and Adele Astaire make their last joint appearance on Broadway in *The Bandwagon*.

1932   Cole Porter writes the score for *The Gay Divorcée*.

1933   Irving Berlin's hit, *As Thousands Cheer*, leaves audiences—or rather all of America—singing "Easter Parade."

1935   George and Ira Gershwin's *Porgy and Bess*, a folk opera about African-American life, is presented with an African-American cast.

1943   *Oklahoma!* by Richard Rodgers and Oscar Hammerstein II, is the first musical to feature dancing that is fully integrated into the story, thanks to choreographer Agnes de Mille.

1949   Capitalizing on their success in *Oklahoma!*, Rodgers and Hammerstein present a serious story in musical format in *South Pacific*.

1951   Rodgers and Hammerstein present *The King and I*.

1956   Alan Jay Lerner and Frederick Loewe introduce the classic and much loved *My Fair Lady*.

1957   Composer Leonard Bernstein, choreographer Jerome Robbins, and lyricist Stephen Sondheim collaborate brilliantly on *West Side Story*, which introduces tragedy into musical theater in the form of an updated *Romeo and Juliet*.

1959   The last great Rodgers and Hammerstein musical is *The Sound of Music*.

1960   Capping out a golden age of musicals is Camelot, another Lerner and Loewe production.

1967   *Hair* is billed as an "American Tribal Love-Rock Musical." It moves to Broadway in 1968 as the first rock musical and the first mainstream musical to contain nudity.

1970   Composer Stephen Sondheim introduces a more complex musical in *Company*.

1975   *The Wiz*, a rock musical, reimagines *The Wizard of Oz*, with an all-black cast.

1978   *Ain't Misbehavin'*, featuring music by Duke Ellington, brings more sophisticated black music to Broadway audiences.

1986   Stephen Sondheim's *Into the Woods* gives depth and complexity to fairy tales.

1990   *A Chorus Line* closes after 6,137 performances.

1996   Within months of each other, two innovative musicals, *Rent* and *Bring in 'Da Noise, Bring in 'Da Funk* open on Broadway.

SIGNIFICANT PEOPLE IN AMERICAN THEATER AND MUSICAL THEATER

Albee, Edward (1928–).   Author of *The Zoo Story* (1959), *Who's Afraid of Virginia Woolf?* (1962), and *Three Tall Women* (1991), Albee pioneered in absurdist theater, then composed serious drama.

Anderson, Maxwell (1888–1959).   A dramatist concerned with social problems, Anderson wrote *What Price Glory?* (1924), *Both Your Houses* (1933), and *Lost in the Stars* (1949).

Barrymore, Ethel (1879–1959).   Part of a famous theatrical family, Barrymore made her name acting in such plays as *The Corn Is Green* and *The Second Mrs. Tanqueray*.

Barrymore, John (1882–1942).   The brother of Ethel, Barrymore is remembered for his riveting interpretation of Hamlet. He later became a matinee idol.

Cohan, George M. (1878–1942).   Cohan wrote, produced, directed, and acted in his own shows, which included *Little Johnny Jones* (1904) and *Forty-five Minutes from Broadway* (1906).

Drew, John (1827–1862).   An Irish comedian, Drew was the leading actor of his era, playing both comedy and Shakespeare.

Forrest, Edwin (1806–1872).   Widely regarded as the first great American actor, Forrest became famous for doing Shakespeare's tragedies. His rivalry with English actor W. C. Macready was at least partly the cause of the Astor Place riot in 1849, which killed 22 people.

Hammerstein, Oscar, II (1895–1960).   A lyricist and librettist, Hammerstein was the father of modern American musicals. Hammerstein's best-remembered works are *Show Boat* (1927) and *Oklahoma!* (1943).

Inge, William (1913–1973).   Inge made a name for himself in the American theater by writing plays about life in small Midwestern towns: *Come Back, Little Sheba* (1950), *Picnic* (1953), and *Bus Stop* (1955).

Kern, Jerome (1885– 1945). With Oscar Hammerstein II, Kern produced *Show Boat* (1927) and composed many songs for musical theater that remain popular.

Lerner, Alan Jay (1918–1986). Collaborating with composer Frederick Loewe, Lerner wrote the book and lyrics for the hit Broadway musicals *Brigadoon* (1947), *Paint Your Wagon* (1951), *My Fair Lady* (1956), and *Camelot* (1960), and for the film *Gigi* (1958). Lerner also wrote scripts for films, including *An American in Paris* (1952).

Mamet, David (1947–). This contemporary playwright is known for his crisp dialogue and strong male characters. His best-known plays are *American Buffalo* (1975) and *Glengarry Glen Ross* (1983), for which he received the Pulitzer Prize in 1984.

Miller, Arthur (1915–). One of the great playwrights of the post–World War II era, Miller has written such modern tragedies as *Death of a Salesman* (1949), *The Crucible* (1953), and *A View from the Bridge* (1955).

Odets, Clifford (1906–1963). Epitomizing the social protest school of drama, Odets wrote *Waiting for Lefty* (1935), *Awake and Sing* (1935), and *Golden Boy* (1937).

O'Neill, Eugene (1888–1953). A giant in American theater, O'Neill wrote such bleak and innovative psychological dramas as *Beyond the Horizon* (1920), *Desire Under the Elms* (1924), *Anna Christie* (1921), and the autobiographical *Long Day's Journey into Night* (produced in 1956). He was awarded the Nobel Prize in literature in 1936.

Porter, Cole (1891–1964). Porter began writing songs and musical reviews when he was an undergraduate at Yale University. He made his Broadway debut with *See America First* (1916). His mature work was notable for its wit and sophistication as exemplified in the musicals *Anything Goes* (1934) and *Kiss Me Kate* (1948).

Shepard, Sam (1943–). The leading countercultural playwright, Shepard wrote *Curse of the Starving Class* (1977), *Buried Child* (1978), and *True West* (1980). He wrote the screenplay for the movie *The Right Stuff*, in which he played Chuck Yeager.

Sherwood, Robert (1896–1955). This Pulitzer Prize–winning playwright wrote in several genres, producing the comedy *Reunion in Vienna* (1931) as well as the drama *The Petrified Forest* (1935).

Sondheim, Stephen (1930–). Sondheim launched his career as a lyricist by collaborating with Leonard Bernstein on *West Side Story* (1957). With Jule Styne he created *Gypsy* in 1959. On his own he has composed more than ten musicals that have broken new ground in terms of unconventional themes and complex melodies. Sondheim won the Pulitzer Prize in 1984 for *Sunday in the Park with George*.

Strasberg, Lee (1901–1982). As an acting teacher/director associated with the Actors' Studio in New York, Strasberg shaped several generations of actors by teaching "the method," based on an approach created by Russian Konstantin Stanislavsky.

Williams, Tennessee (1911–1983). Considered one of the foremost dramatists of the post–World War II era, Williams wrote plays about violence, loneliness, and anxiety. Women—especially southern women—were the great subject of this playwright, and gave women unforgettable roles in plays such as *A Streetcar Named Desire* (1947), *Sweet Bird of Youth* (1959), and *Night of the Iguana* (1961).

SIGNIFICANT EVENTS IN AMERICAN DANCE

1835	*La Sylphide* is performed for the first time in the United States, in Philadelphia.
1846	*Giselle* makes its American debut at the Howard Atheneum at the Howard Atheneum in Boston.
1908	Isadora Duncan, an American pioneer in modern dance who has made her name in Europe, tours the United States to great acclaim.
1910	Anna Pavlova makes her first American appearance at the Metropolitan Opera House, in *Coppélia*.
1915	Denishawn, the company of Ted Shawn and Ruth St. Denis, performs. Its dancers include Martha Graham and Doris Humphrey.
1929	Martha Graham, one of the pioneers of modern dance, forms her own dance troupe.
1934	The School of American Ballet, with George Balanchine at its head, is founded.
1937	The Mordkin Ballet, predecessor of the Ballet Theatre, is founded by Lucia Chase and Richard Pleasant. Along with City Ballet, it is one of two major companies performing classical ballet in the United States. It will soon be renamed the American Ballet Theatre.
1942	Agnes de Mille creates the first important American classical ballet, *Rodeo*.
1944	Martha Graham creates the classic modern-dance masterpiece *Appalachian Spring*.
1946	The New York City Ballet (originally the Ballet Society), the second major classical dance company in the United States, is founded by Russian-born George Balanchine, formerly of the Ballets Russes, and Lincoln Kirstein.
1950	Merce Cunningham, a seminal second-wave modern dancer, founds his own company, which will largely perform his own creations.
1954	Robert Joffrey founds the Joffrey Ballet, which is devoted to performing modern classical ballet.
1955	Paul Taylor, an innovative modern-dance choreographer, forms his own company, which performs mostly his own works.
1957	Ballet dancer-choreographer Jerome Robbins creates the dancing in *West Side Story*, a pivotal Broadway musical that bridges the gap between popular musical theater and classical ballet.
1958	Choreographer Alvin Ailey founds a dance company bearing his name. It is dedicated to performing modern dance with African and African-American themes.
1960	Alvin Ailey creates his masterpiece, a modern dance called *Revelations*.
1965	Modern-dance choreographer Twyla Tharp, who innovates dance without music and other experimental forms, establishes her own company.
1968	The Dance Theatre of Harlem, the first African-American classical company, is begun by Arthur Mitchell.
1969	Jerome Robbins creates *Dances at a Gathering*, perhaps the first major ballet with overtones of rock music. Robbins succeeds Balanchine as ballet master at City Ballet in 1983.
1974	The great Russian ballet dancer Mikhail Baryshnikov defects to the United States, where he dances with the American Ballet Theatre. He breaks new ground when he dances both classical and modern ballets.
1980	After working for several years in Europe and winning recognition there, choreographer Mark Morris establishes his own dance company, which shows off his very modern yet still classical ballets.

1988   Twyla Tharp becomes resident choreographer at the American Ballet Theatre and begins to expand the classical repertory to include many more modern dances.

1995   The Joffrey Ballet ceases to exist due to lack of funds. It will reorganize and reopen in Chicago, which many see as a sign that New York City's heyday as the ballet capital of the world has come to an end.

INFLUENTIAL AMERICAN DANCE COMPANIES

Alvin Ailey Dance Theater, New York: African-American themes

American Ballet Theatre, New York: Excellent dancing and repertoire; performs classical ballet with a smattering of modern dance

Ballet Hispanico, New York: Classical ballet with a Latin edge

Trisha Brown Company, New York: Modern dance

Lucinda Childs Dance Company, New York: Innovative modern dance

Cunningham Dance Foundation, New York: Avant-garde modern dance

Dance Theatre of Harlem, New York: Major African-American troupe; classical ballet

Martha Graham Dance Company, New York: Classic and new modern dance

Joffrey Ballet (now defunct, formerly of New York): Mounted revivals of classic, rarely done ballets, plus new repertory

Mark Morris Dance Group, New York: Cutting-edge dancing that merges classical and modern technique

New York City Ballet, New York: Along with American Ballet Theatre, the preeminent dance company in the country. Founded by George Balanchine and Lincoln Kirstein, its repertory includes classical ballet (performed in the company's own inimitable style) and some modern compositions.

Paul Taylor Dance Company, New York: Along with Cunningham Foundation, preeminent modern dance

Twyla Tharp, New York: Founder of various companies that dance her choreography, which is modern.

IMPORTANT CHOREOGRAPHERS IN AMERICAN DANCE

Ailey, Alvin (1931–1989).   A modern dancer and choreographer, in 1958 Ailey formed the Alvin Ailey Dance Theatre, a primarily black modern dance troupe featuring many African-American themes. Ailey's masterpiece is *Revelations* (1960).

Balanchine, George (1904–1983).   Considered by many critics to be the preeminent American choreographer, Balanchine trained in Russia and danced for years with Paris's innovative Ballets Russes. He became the first director of the New York City Ballet in 1948. His dances created a new trend in world ballet, one in which ballet became simpler, streamlined, and even abstract. Among his many great ballets are *Apollo* and *Serenade*. He created the original *Slaughter on Tenth Avenue*.

Cunningham, Merce (1919–).   This pioneering modern-dance choreographer began his career dancing with Martha Graham but went on to develop his own unique innovations, the most famous of which was to create dances that were independent of, or incidental to, the music that accompanied them. Cunningham often worked with avant-garde composer John Cage.

de Mille, Agnes (1905–1993).   An innovator in classical ballet, de Mille choreographed *Rodeo*, the first major American ballet. Working in musical theater, she sought to bring many of the techniques of ballet to the modern musical theater. Her pioneering techniques can be seen in the musical *Oklahoma!* (1943). She is also remembered for the ballet *Fall River Legend* (1948).

Duncan, Isadora (1877–1927).   A pioneering choreographer who rejected the restraints of classical ballet to create her own loose, free-form dances, Duncan set the stage for future and more classical modern dancers and choreographers.

Graham, Martha (1894–1991).   Martha Graham's troupe, more than any other force, made modern dance popular with American audiences. Her masterpiece is *Appalachian Spring* (1944).

Joffrey, Robert (1930–1988).   As a choreographer, Joffrey created notable works like *Remembrances* (1973) and *Postcards* (1980). In 1956 he founded the Joffrey Ballet, which became known for its eclectic repertoire, drawing on classics, new works, and fusions of modern dance.

Kirstein, Lincoln (1907–1996).   Kirstein was an impresario and businessman who worked with George Balanchine to found and direct the various ballet companies that eventually became the New York City Ballet. In addition, he helped establish the School of American Ballet.

Mitchell, Arthur (1934–).   A dancer and choreographer, Mitchell broke away from the New York City Ballet to found the Dance Theatre of Harlem. His own choreography, of which *Rhythmetron* is among the best known, combines elements of jazz and ethnic dance with classical ballet.

Morris, Mark (1956–).   Exemplifying perhaps the third wave of modern dance and the inevitable merging of modern and classical technique, Morris is best known for choreographing *L'Allegro* and *The Hard Nut*. Unlike Balanchine, who demanded physical perfection of his dancers, Morris's superb dancers often have far-from-classically shaped bodies.

Page, Ruth (1899–1991).   This choreographer was for many years the moving force behind ballet in Chicago, where she was director-choreographer of the Chicago Opera Ballet, the Page-Stone Ballet, and the Chicago Lyric Opera's ballet company. She also ran an acclaimed ballet school. Among her best-known creations are *Frankie and Johnny* and *Billy Sunday*.

Robbins, Jerome (1918–).   Dancer and choreographer Robbins attracted critical attention in 1944 when he created the ballet *Fancy Free*. He worked on many Broadway musicals including *West Side Story* and *Fiddler on the Roof*. Robbins was ballet master of the New York City Ballet with Peter Martins from 1983 to 1990.

Shawn, Ted (1891–1972).   With his wife, Ruth St. Denis, Shawn helped to forge a uniquely American form of modern dance by drawing on American and ethnic themes in his choreography. Shawn also helped to expand men's roles in dance. He and St. Denis formed their own company, Denishawn, and Shawn served as director of the dance festival at Jacob's Pillow, Massachusetts.

St. Denis, Ruth (1877–1968).   Drawing on theatrical roots, St. Denis created several dances, but her more important role was the creation and expansion of interest in American modern dance at a time when it was considered a minor theatrical form.

Tharp, Twyla (1941–).   Tharp's choreography combines elements of classical ballet and modern dance and has been an important force in moving these formerly opposing forms of dance closer to one another. In the 1960s, she performed her dances in a series of companies she formed; after that, her choreography was performed by the major ballet companies. Two of her most acclaimed dances are *Deuce Coup* and *Push Comes to Shove*.

THE DEVELOPMENT OF ART PHOTOGRAPHY

Although photographic methods had been developed by 1840, art photography as an art form did not emerge until the late 19th century. Not surprisingly, art photography was initially seen as competitive with painting, and even today some question whether photography can in fact be considered art. Early photographers often drew inspiration from painting, and when artists began painting abstract canvases, photographers began to explore abstraction in photographs. Unlike painting, where artists tend to join a movement and then leave it en masse to move on to something else, movements or schools in photography tend to exist concurrently.

1860   Mathew Brady photographs Abraham Lincoln. In the five years that follow, this first great American photodocumentarian will become well known for his daguerreotypes depicting the horrors of the Civil War. Brady-trained photographers such as Alexander Gardner are also active.

1873   Timothy O'Sullivan takes a magnificent photo, *Ancient Ruins in the Canyon de Chelly, New Mexico, in a Niche Fifty Feet above the Present Canyon Bed*. Other photographers who accompany expeditions exploring the American West are J. K. Hillers and W. H. Jackson.

1890   Jacob Riis publishes *How the Other Half Lives*. Riis's photographs, such as *Bandits' Roost*, are documentary. Unlike photojournalists who seek to capture a moment in time simply because it is there to record, Riis and other documentary photographers want to capture the moment for the purpose of promoting reform.

1902   Alfred Stieglitz begins publication of *Camera Work*, a forum for the Photo-Secession movement, which rebels against "salon" photography that imitates genre painting.

1908   Alfred Stieglitz and Edward Steichen open the "291 Gallery," where photography is displayed as art.

1922   In a series called *Equivalents*, Alfred Stieglitz photographs clouds, an attempt to show that photography can be as abstract as painting. Stieglitz, who is fascinated with the modern city, is also the first photographer to shoot skyscrapers as pure objects.

1923   Berenice Abbott, influenced by Man Ray, turns from sculpture to photography. She will produce a series of portraits of celebrities of the 1920s.

1927   Edward Weston merges realism and abstraction, in photographs such as *Shell*. Images like this are soon referred to as "pure" photography. In the 1930s Weston and Ansel Adams will found the f/64 group, the name taken from the smallest lens opening, which permits great precision and detail.

1928   Man Ray takes *Rayograph*, a purely abstract photograph.

1930   Ansel Adams publishes *Taos Pueblo*, a book of his photographs. His goal is to make unsentimental photographs, without any manipulation.

1933   Dorothea Lange's *White Angel Breadline* exemplifies the powerful images of people, in place and time, her camera will record.

1936   Dorothea Lange shoots the moving *Migrant Mother* in California.

1937   Margaret Bourke-White publishes *You Have Seen Their Faces*. Known for her series on the rural South during the Depression, Bourke-White also shares Stieglitz's fascination with the new city and invents a school of industrial photography, which in turn leads to commercial photography. Some of her work is sculptural in tone. This is a new kind of photojournalism, and Bourke-White is the first photographer hired for the new magazines *Fortune* and *Life*.

    The New Deal's Farm Security Administration sends photographers such as Dorothea Lange across the country to document rural America, recording the farms ravaged by drought and depression and the gaunt faces of farm men and women.

1938   The Museum of Modern Art publishes *American Photography*, coinciding with its retrospective on Walker Evans.

1939   Berenice Abbott publishes *Changing New York*, a ten-year project to document the city.

1941   Walker Evans's stunning black-and-white photographs of rural poverty accompany the text of James Agee's influential book *Let Us Now Praise Famous Men*.

1946   Robert Capa founds Magnum, an agency for photojournalists. In 1954, at age 41, he dies in a land mine explosion in Indochina, where he is photographing French combat troops.

1949   Aaron Siskind produces *Water Stains on Wall*, a photograph reminiscent of abstract art.

1953-   Edward Steichen's exhibition "The Family of Man" presents the work of 273 photo-
1955   graphers in 70 countries.

1958   Berenice Abbott produces scientific photographs for a high school physics text.

1962   Minor White creates *Capital Reef, Utah*, in which natural shapes make abstract composition.

1972   The photographs of Diane Arbus are published, revealing her uncanny ability to show the sad and strange side of life.

   Jerry Uelsmann revives fantasy photographs, which had a brief heyday in the 1920s. His *Untitled*, which superimposes the body of a nude woman on a landscape, is an excellent example of this genre. Similarly, W. Eugene Smith revives documentary photography with works such as *Tomoko in Her Bath*, a stunning *Pietà*-like image of a mother holding her daughter.

1976   *Imogen Cunningham: Photographs* is published, introducing the general public to the varied styles—both classic and romantic—of photography.

SIGNIFICANT EVENTS IN AMERICAN POPULAR CULTURE

American popular culture has been, in recent decades, the nation's most significant export. It consists primarily of the movies made by Hollywood, the world movie capital; television; best-selling books; and, most of all, rock music. In the following all-too brief and admittedly extremely selective chronology are some memorable moments and highlights of American popular culture.

1640   The *Bay Psalm Book*, published this year, will reach 27 editions by 1750.

1682   Mary Rowlandson's account of her capture by Native Americans becomes the most popular captivity account.

1707   Colonists enjoy reading *The Redeemed Captive*, Reverend John Williams's account of his capture by Native Americans during the Deerfield raid.

1731   The first public concert of secular music in the colonies is presented in a Boston home; admission is charged.

1732   Benjamin Franklin publishes *Poor Richard's Almanack*, which becomes a perennial best-seller.

1744   The Moravian community establishes a Collegium Musieum for the performance of nonreligious music such as chamber music and symphonies.

1767   On the eve of the American Revolution, "Yankee Doodle," a parody of the colonial soldier, appears in print.

1777   The first Independence Day is celebrated.

1783   Noah Webster publishes the *American Spelling Book,* which becomes one of the most `enduring best-sellers ever published.

1790s	The origins of "women's fiction" are rooted in popular novels such as *The Power of Sympathy* by William Hill Brown, *Charlotte Temple* by Susanna Rowson, and *The Coquette* by Hannah Foster.
1794	Charles Willson Peale moves his gallery into the hall of the American Philosophical Society in Philadelphia. It is one of the first American museums.
c. 1800	Johnny Appleseed (born John Chapman) roams the Midwest planting apple trees. He will become an American folk legend, inspiring popular songs and stories.
	Lyrical Ballads (1798) by Samuel Taylor Coleridge and William Wordsworth is popular reading fare in the new nation, as is a myth-making book called *The Life and Memorable Actions of George Washington* by Mason Locke Weems, who started the story—later found to be false—about the cherry tree.
1814	Lawyer Francis Scott Key writes "The Star Spangled Banner" after watching British ships fire on Baltimore's Fort McHenry during the War of 1812. The song becomes the nation's official anthem in 1931.
1835	Americans can read a piercing analysis of their national psyche in Alexis de Tocqueville's riveting *Democracy in America*, published in English this year.
1840s	The polka, a Bohemian dance catapulted from Prague to the capitals of Europe, is a major dance craze. Waltzes have also been popular.
1843	The Virginia Minstrels give the first public performance of a minstrel show, which will become a popular form of theatrical entertainment. White actors in blackface sitting on an unadorned stage tell anecdotes, jokes, and stories about black life and relations between blacks and whites. Later songs, skits, and dances are added. It is the only form of entertainment based solely on American culture, but it is also the origin of one of the more painful and false stereotypes of African Americans.
1847	Henry Wadsworth Longfellow publishes the book-length poem *Evangeline*, the first of several highly romanticized American legends that are much loved by the American reading public.
1849	Francis Parkman's *The California and Oregon Trail* catches the popular imagination, as does Edgar Allan Poe's new poem "Annabel Lee." Popular songs include "Nelly Was a Lady," by Stephen Foster, one of the most beloved songwriters of the pre–Civil War era. His songs remain popular well into the 20th century.
1850	"It Came upon the Midnight Clear," a Christmas hymn, is sung at holiday time.
1860	The first "dime novel," *Malaeska: The Indian Wife of the White Hunter*, by Ann Sophea Stephens, is published.
1862	Julia Ward Howe's "Battle Hymn of the Republic" is published. Other popular songs are marches and sentimental songs of loss.
1865	The juvenile book *Hans Brinker* by Mary Mapes Dodge is a best-seller.
	"Marching Through Georgia" is a popular song in the North.
	Americans attend burlesque, variety shows featuring coarse humor. (Only later will *burlesque* refer to strip shows.)
1866	John Greenleaf Whittier's *Snow-bound* is published. His nostalgic and patriotic poems ("Maud Muller" and "The Barefoot Boy") make him the most popular poet of the era.
1867	Horatio Alger publishes the first of the Ragged Dick series, the primary inspiration for the American "rags to riches" myth.
1868	Louisa May Alcott wins the hearts of the first generation of Americans (soon to be followed by others) with the publication of her book *Little Women*.

1869   *Josh Billings—His Sayings*, by Henry Shaw, is a collection of humorous sketches and rural wisdom, much of it in dialect.

1870s   Esther Howland's elaborate lace Valentines cost $5 to $10.

1873   Author Mark Twain names an era when he writes a novel called *The Gilded Age*, which describes the extravagance and corruption of post–Civil War life.

1876   Mark Twain's *The Adventures of Tom Sawyer* is published.

People are singing "I'll Take You Home Again, Kathleen" by Thomas Westendorf and the hymn "What a Friend We Have in Jesus" by Ira Sankey.

1877   The beloved juvenile book *Black Beauty*, written by Anna Sewell, is published.

1881   Tony Pastor presents the first "big time" vaudeville show in New York City. Vaudeville flourishes, making stars of such performers as Harry Houdini, George M. Cohan, and Eddie Cantor.

1883   James Whitcomb Riley's *The Old Swimmin' Hole and 'Leven More Poems* is a best-seller. His humor and sentimentality appeal to many.

Buffalo Bill's Wild West Show is organized and begins touring. This outdoor theatrical spectacle features shooting, riding, and other stylized activities of the American frontier. The show makes stars of persons such as Annie Oakley and Sitting Bull.

1886   Americans read *The Strange Case of Dr. Jekyll and Mr. Hyde* by Robert Louis Stevenson.

The first Nick Carter detective serial runs in *The New York Weekly*.

1888   The first public rodeo, an outgrowth of the Wild West Show, is held in Prescott, Arizona. It becomes an enduring form of popular entertainment.

1895   In New York City a demonstration of the Eidoloscope is probably the first projected movie show in America.

Paul Laurence Dunbar, the son of slaves, publishes a popular book of poems called *Majors and Minors*.

Popular songs are "The Band Played On" by John Palmer and Charles Ward and "America the Beautiful" by Katharine Lee Bates.

1899   Scott Joplin introduces a new genre, called ragtime, with "Maple Leaf Rag." It is an instant success.

The Gibson girl, the first (but hardly the last) media-generated ideal American woman, is the creation of illustrator Charles Dana Gibson. She is tall, with a pompadour hairstyle, and wears a modest shirtwaist.

1904   The Louisiana Purchase Exposition, which commemorates the Louisiana Purchase, opens a year late in Saint Louis.

Cy Young pitches the first perfect major-league baseball game—no hits, no runs.

1906   With his book *The Jungle*, muckraking writer Upton Sinclair produces a best-selling exposé of the meat-packing industry.

1907   Florenz Ziegfeld produces the first Ziegfeld Follies. For the next 24 years it will be famous for its elaborate staging and chorus of beautiful women. In the 1920s, the Follies make an enormous star of Fanny Brice, who brings down the house with such songs as "My Man" and "Second-Hand Rose."

1909   Al Jolson first sings "Mammy."

1912   Vernon and Irene Castle introduce the Texas Tommy and Grizzly, dances they invented, which make them famous.

W. C. Handy's *Memphis Blues* is about to make him—and the blues—famous.

1915   Edgar Lee Masters's *Spoon River Anthology* becomes an enduring favorite.

1920   F. Scott Fitzgerald's *This Side of Paradise* is an instant success. So is Sinclair Lewis's *Main Street*.

1923   The Charleston is performed on Broadway. It is soon the decade's most popular dance.

1924   Ring Lardner establishes his reputation with *How to Write Short Stories (with Samples)*.

1925   Innovations introduced in bridge make it enormously popular.

1927   The varsity drag, a dance, is all the rage on college campuses.

1930   Blondie, a flapper, and her playboy husband, Dagwood Bumstead, are an instant hit. The next year Dick Tracy makes his debut in the comics.

1932   Cole Porter writes "Night and Day."

The first of Laura Ingalls Wilder's *Little House* books is published.

Jack Benny and Fred Allen host popular radio shows. Allen's most famous show starts broadcasting in 1939.

1933   "The Lone Ranger," one of radio's most enduring and best-loved shows, begins local broadcast. By 1937, it goes national.

1934   Benny Goodman organizes his own orchestra and makes swing popular.

The comic strip *Li'l Abner*, created by Al Capp, becomes an American classic.

Americans read William Saroyan's book of short stories, *The Daring Young Man on the Flying Trapeze*.

John O'Hara's *Butterfield 8* is published.

Your Hit Parade debuts on radio.

1936   A book about Negro folk songs, sung by Huddie "Leadbelly" Ledbetter, makes this former chain-gang member who sings African-American folk and chain-gang music a popular performer.

1938   Orson Welles's "The War of the Worlds," a radio version of the 1898 H. G. Wells novel, creates a panic among its listeners, who believe its authentic sounding news reports that Martians have landed.

1939   Pocket Books begins a revolution in publishing by introducing cheap paperback editions of books, which sell for 25 cents.

Early 1940s   Frank Sinatra croons and makes bobby-soxers shriek and swoon with "This Love of Mine."

1943   In the midst of World War II, Americans listen to Glenn Miller's "Chattanooga Choo Choo" (1941).

Bill Mauldin gains fame for his Willie and Joe cartoons. Originally published in *Stars and Stripes*, they give those at home a funny yet heartbreaking perspective on life for enlisted men.

1944   Americans make *Forever Amber* by Kathleen Winsor a best-seller.

1945   Americans listen to popular songs like "Till The End of Time." The next year the big hit is "Let It Snow! Let It Snow! Let It Snow."

1948   Ed Sullivan's variety show begins its long run and becomes everyone's favorite Sunday-night entertainment. *Hopalong Cassidy* becomes television's first western.

People read General Dwight Eisenhower's best-selling war memoir, *Crusade in Europe*.

1950   The comic strip *Peanuts* makes its first appearance and becomes an immediate success, spawning a play, television shows, and many books about the much-beloved characters Charlie Brown, Lucy, and Snoopy.

Spiritual singer Mahalia Jackson debuts at Carnegie Hall. She has won nationwide acclaim for performing "I Believe" and "I Can Put My Trust in Jesus."

1951   Lucille Ball captivates Americans' hearts in her long-running show *I Love Lucy* and becomes the first woman to earn a million dollars in television.

Dave Brubeck forms the quartet bearing his name, and soon it becomes the most famous jazz group in the world.

J. D. Salinger, a reclusive author, writes the youth-cult novel *The Catcher in the Rye*.

Americans are captivated by TV's *Dragnet*.

1952   *Mad* comic strip, which will evolve into *Mad Magazine*, presents an unusual satirical take on life that appeals primarily to adolescents and introduces the expression "What, Me Worry?" into American culture.

The classic juvenile tale *Charlotte's Web* by E. B. White is published.

Americans are reading *The Power of Positive Thinking* by Norman Vincent Peale, one of the first major self-help best-sellers.

American Bandstand debuts in Philadelphia on television. It goes to network TV in 1957 and will remain a popular show with youth for decades.

1954   The television series *Davy Crockett* is a hit, as is the theme song and the coonskin hat, which soon adorns the heads of millions of boys.

1955   Author-actress Kay Thompson writes a charming story about a little girl who lives at the Plaza Hotel in New York, and the cult of Eloise is begun.

1956   Elvis Presley skyrockets to fame with songs like "Hound Dog," "Love Me Tender," and "Heartbreak Hotel." He will dominate rock music for much of the next decade.

1957   Beat author Jack Kerouac publishes *On the Road*.

1959   Little girls are introduced to Barbie, a busty, grown-up doll.

1961   *Catch-22*, Joseph Heller's black-humor novel about World War II, catches the attention of the reading public.

People are listening to "Moon River" by Henry Mancini and "Running Scared" and "Crying" by Roy Orbison.

Popular television shows are *Perry Mason*, *The Twilight Zone*, *Gunsmoke*, *Dr. Kildare*, and *The Dick Van Dyke Show*.

1962   Ken Kesey writes *One Flew Over the Cuckoo's Nest*.

Johnny Carson begins his three-decade reign as king of late-night talk television with *The Tonight Show*, which features interviews, sketches, and his famous opening monologue.

1964   American youth falls in love with the Beatles and their hit song, "I Want to Hold Your Hand."

Mary McCarthy writes *The Group*, a best-selling novel about college women.

1965   The Rolling Stones score a hit song with "(I Can't Get No) Satisfaction."

Late 1960s   Fashion reflects the rebellious times as young Americans deck themselves out in granny dresses (and glasses), jeans, love beads, and tie-died garments, and men and women sport long hair—much to the chagrin of their elders. After decades of mostly assimilative dressing, black youth wear Afros, an elegant hairstyle that many whites find frightening, and Afrocentric clothing, such as dashikis and kente cloth. Women abandon hats and gloves as fashion accessories. The bikini, first introduced in France in 1946, arrives on U.S. beaches.

1967   The Monterey Pop Festival is the first major rock festival. Jimi Hendrix and Janis Joplin are featured performers.

1969   *Sesame Street*, an educational but highly entertaining children's television show, breaks new ground.

Elvis Presley

1970s   In rock music, antiheroes such as Jimi Hendrix, Janis Joplin, and Jim Morrison dominate the early part of the decade but by the end of the seventies, the far more mainstream Bruce Springsteen will be the most popular singer.

1970   Musicians Paul Simon and Art Garfunkel continue to please with the ballad "Bridge Over Troubled Water."

1971   *All in the Family*, a frank television show about working-class life and America's social and racial prejudices, becomes a big hit.

Disney World, near Orlando, Florida, opens.

1973   Author Erica Jong has a runaway best-seller with *Fear of Flying* and its description of women's sexuality.

1980s	Michael Jackson and Madonna are the pop music icons of the decade. Americans read *The Executioner's Song* by Norman Mailer and *The Soul of a New Machine* by Tracy Kidder. Favorite television shows are *Sixty Minutes* and *Charlie's Angels*, and talk television produces such huge hit shows as *The Phil Donahue Show* and *The Oprah Winfrey Show*.
1990s	Americans read *A Thousand Acres* by Jane Smiley, *The Joy Luck Club* by Amy Tan, and *The Firm* by John Grisham. *Silence of the Lambs* is also a best-selling book, as well as one of the decades most popular movies. Well-received television shows include *Golden Girls*, *Cheers*, and the perennially popular cult series *Star Trek*.

An Affair to Remember: Americans and the Movies

For decades Americans have had a wonderful love affair with the movies, and Hollywood, the heart of the movie industry, has reigned supreme in the 20th century.

1903	Americans attend Edwin S. Porter's silent film *The Great Train Robbery*, at 12 minutes the longest film to date. It introduces the western genre, a staple of American film.
1905	The first nickelodeon opens in Pittsburgh; they spread like wildfire. For a nickel, viewers watch several 6- to-15-minute films and an occasional vaudeville act.
1908	D. W. Griffith, one of America's first great filmmakers, releases his first film, *The Adventures of Dollie*.
1912	The Keystone Kops debut.
1913	The first fan magazine, *Photoplay*, is started.
	Fatty Arbuckle receives the first "pie in the face" as a Keystone Kop in *A Noise from the Deep*.
1914	Americans watch Pearl White in *The Perils of Pauline*.
1915	D. W. Griffith makes *The Birth of a Nation*, a three-hour epic about the Civil War, and overnight feature-length films replace the shorts.
	Theda Bara plays "the vamp" in *A Fool There Was*.
1916	Mary Pickford is the top box-office star.
1918	Charlie Chaplin stars in *Shoulder Arms*. He is on his way to being world famous.
1920s	The era of the silent film is at its apex: Charlie Chaplin makes *The Kid* in 1921 and *The Gold Rush* in 1925. Genres also begin to take recognizable shapes. Buster Keaton provides humor in *Sherlock Jr.* Ernst Lubitsch makes sophisticated comedies of manners. Among westerns, the decade produces *The Covered Wagon* and *The Iron Horse*. Finally, epics such as Cecil B. DeMille's *The Ten Commandments* and *King of Kings* become popular.
1921	Rudolph Valentino becomes the first movie idol in such films as *The Sheik* and *Blood and Sand*, made in 1922.
1927	Clara Bow stars in *Wings*, the only silent film to win an Academy Award for Best Picture.
	Sound is introduced in *The Jazz Singer*, starring Al Jolson, who becomes an overnight sensation.
1928	Walt Disney's Mickey Mouse appears in his first cartoon, called *Steamboat Willie*. Characters such as Minnie Mouse, Donald Duck, and Pluto soon rival Mickey's popularity.
1930s	This is the golden era of the studio film when stars are the driving force behind the movies. Among the better known are Greta Garbo, Marlene Dietrich, Jean Harlow, Mae West, Katharine Hepburn, Bette Davis, Cary Grant, Clark Gable, James Stewart, Gary Cooper, Spencer Tracy, Jimmy Cagney, and Fred Astaire and Ginger Rogers. Americans relish their on- and off-screen antics.

Rudolph Valentino

1934 Frank Capra makes *It Happened One Night* and the movie wins all four top Oscars. The first movie of the *Thin Man* series is produced.

1935 The movies feature the classic *Top Hat*, with Fred Astaire and Ginger Rogers.

1937 Walt Disney makes his first feature-length animated film, *Snow White*.

1939 Margaret Mitchell's best-selling novel *Gone With the Wind* becomes a wildly successful movie. It is the first Technicolor film.

1939 Judy Garland captures the nation's hearts when she stars and sings in *The Wizard of Oz*.

1940s The industry is dominated by a handful of male directors: Frank Capra (*It's a Wonderful Life* and *Mr. Deeds Goes to Town*), John Huston (*The Maltese Falcon* and *Treasure of the Sierra Madre*), and William Wyler (*Mrs. Miniver*).

1940 *Fantasia* is Walt Disney's second feature-length film.

  Bob Hope and Bing Crosby entertain Americans with *Road to Utopia*.

1941 Orson Welles makes *Citizen Kane*, a landmark film.

1942- American movies become a propaganda tool during World War II, producing such films as
1945 those in Frank Capra's "Why We Fight" series.

1943 In the midst of World War II Americans go to the movies to see *Casablanca* with Humphrey Bogart and Ingrid Bergman.

1944 *National Velvet* premieres and makes Elizabeth Taylor a star.

  Judy Garland, the nation's favorite chanteuse, stars in *Meet Me in St. Louis*.

1945 At the movies, people watch *Spellbound* and *A Tree Grows in Brooklyn*. They adore stars such as Ingrid Bergman, Humphrey Bogart, Joan Crawford, and Barbara Stanwyck.

1947 Americans' love affair with the movies begins to draw to a close as attendance starts a long, steady decline. Some blame it on television, but others have suggested that the migration to the suburbs, where there were, at least initially, no movie theaters, ended movies' heyday as an American pastime.

1952   *Singin' in the Rain*, with Gene Kelly and Debbie Reynolds, is a lavish color musical.

1954   Hollywood produces the socially conscious *On the Waterfront*, which makes Marlon Brando a star.

1961   Everyone goes to see *West Side Story*.

1968   Barbra Streisand, whose popularity will match that of Fanny Brice and Judy Garland, stars in *Funny Girl*, the story of Fanny Brice.

1969   *Easy Rider* seems to embody 1960s values.

1970s   American films take a hard look at American culture in such cult films as *Five Easy Pieces* and *American Graffiti* but Americans also go to see the sentimental movies *Love Story* and *Rocky*, which makes a star of Sylvester Stallone.

1980s   Popular movies are *E. T.: The Extra-Terrestrial*, and *Raiders of the Lost Ark*, which makes Harrison Ford a star. Both are directed by Steven Spielberg.

1990s   Memorable movies include *Dances with Wolves* and *Pretty Woman*.

TEN FAVORITE AMERICAN MOVIES AND WHAT THEY GROSSED AS OF 1995

Movie	Gross (in millions, rentals to distributors)	Year
E.T.: The Extra-Terrestrial	399.8	1982
Star Wars	356.8	1977
Jaws	260.0	1975
Raiders of the Lost Ark	242.4	1981
Gone With the Wind	191.7	1939
Tootsie	177.2	1982
The Exorcist	165.0	1973
The Sound of Music	160.5	1965
The Sting	156.0	1973
Animal House	141.6	1978

SUPREME COURT DECISIONS AND CONGRESSIONAL LEGISLATION AFFECTING THE ARTS

1789   The Constitution gives Congress the power "to promote the Progress of Science and the useful Arts, by securing for limited Times to Authors and Inventors the exclusive Right to their respective Writings and Discoveries." In its first session (1790), Congress passes a patent law.

1832   *Wheaton v. Peters*. The Court establishes that the primary aim of copyright protection is to benefit the public, not the creator of the work.

1836   Fifty-six British authors petition Congress for copyright protection, but Congress does not intervene to stop piracy.

1846   Congress states that one copy of every copyrighted book should be sent to the Library of Congress.

1887   Bern Convention. For signatories, literary material copyrighted in one country enjoys protection in others. The United States does not sign.

1891   An international copyright law prevents pirating the works of foreign authors.

1909   Copyright Act. The basic U.S. copyright law, this bill grants authors, publishers, and composers control over their work and, under a somewhat vague "fair use" clause, offers some protection from use of their material. Over time this law will be extended to cover prints, music, photographs, drawings, paintings, movies, sound recordings, and computer programs.

1957   *Roth v. United States.* In this first important obscenity decision, the Court rules that some materials are obscene, by virtue of lacking any redeeming social value and appealing exclusively to prurient interest, but fails to hammer out a precise definition of what constitutes obscenity.

1964   *New York Times Co. v. Sullivan.* The Court protects the freedom of the press to publish information about public officials even if it is false. It only becomes libelous if published with malicious intent.

1965   Federal Aid to the Arts Act. Provides $63 million to fund a National Endowment for the Arts and the Humanities.

1973   *Miller v. California.* The Court attempts to refine the definition of obscenity, saying that a work may be banned if the average person, applying contemporary standards of the community, finds it prurient. The decision gives individual communities the power to regulate books, magazines, and movies.

1975   Copyright Act. The first major revision of the copyright law since 1909, the new act covers new technologies, changes the length of copyright protection, and tightens the fair use clause, among other objectives.

1988   Copyright Act. A further revision of previous acts brings U.S. copyright law in line with the Bern Convention. American artists now have the same international copyright protection afforded artists from other countries.

ADDITIONAL SOURCES OF INFORMATION

Abraham, Gerald. *The Concise Oxford History of Music.* Oxford University Press, 1979.

Allison, Alex W., ed. *Norton Anthology of Poetry.* 3rd ed. Norton, 1983.

Anderson, J. *The American Dance Festival.* Duke University Press, 1987.

Bercovitch, Sacvan, ed. *Cambridge History of American Literature.* 5 vols. Cambridge University Press, 1991.

Brustein, Robert. *Reimagining the American Theater.* Hill & Wang, 1991.

Connor, Janis C., and Joel Rosencranz. *Rediscoveries in American Sculpture.* University of Texas Press, 1989.

de Mille, Agnes. *The Book of the Dance.* Golden, 1963.

Elliott, Emory, ed. *Columbia Literary History of the United States.* Columbia University Press, 1988.

Green, Jonathan. *American Photography: A Critical History, 1945 to Present.* Abrams, 1985.

Hart, James D. *The Concise Oxford Companion to American Literature.* Oxford University Press, 1986.

Hartnoll, Phyllis, and Peter Founds, eds. *The Concise Oxford Companion to the Theater.* Rev. ed. Oxford University Press, 1993.

Janson, H. W., and Anthony F. *History of Art*. 3rd ed. Prentice Hall, 1986.

Kasson, Joy S. *Marble Queens and Captives: Women in 19th Century American Sculpture*. Yale University Press, 1990.

Kirstein, Lincoln. *Dance*. 1935, repr. Greenwood, 1970.

Magill, Frank N. *Masterpieces of African-American Literature*. HarperCollins, 1992.

Mumford, Lewis. *Roots of Contemporary American Architecture*. Dover, 1972.

Musgrove, John, ed. *A History of Architecture: Sir Banister-Fletcher's*. 19th ed. Butterworth, 1987.

Sadie, Stanley, ed. *The New Grove Dictionary of Music and Musicians*. 30 vols. Groves Dictionaries, 1980.

Scharf, Aaron. *Pioneers of Photography*. Abrams, 1976.

Scully, Vincent. *American Architecture and Urbanism*. Rev. ed. Holt, 1988.

Stebbins, Theodore E., Jr., et al. *A New World—Masterpieces of American Painting*. Museum of Fine Arts, 1983.

Terry, Walter. *The Dance in America*. Rev. ed. Da Capo, 1981.

Venturi, Robert. *Complexity and Contradiction in Modern Architecture*. Museum of Modern Art, 1977.

Index

F